NAVAL OCCURRENCES OF THE WAR OF 1812

Acknowledgements

The introduction to this volume began life as part of a study of three British pioneers of naval history, for the 1999 Symposium at the United States Naval Academy, Annapolis. With the panel short of time I restricted my presentation to a discussion of William James, the one name that was guaranteed some degree of recognition in an American audience. I was astonished by the degree of warmth James's comments elicited from the naval/academic audience, although they were mostly attacks on his honesty. This persuaded me that this most misunderstood of naval historians was due for a re-appraisal. In 2001 I presented a version of this introduction to the Anglo-American Historians Conference at the Institute of Historical Research in London. I am indebted to the organisers of both events for the opportunity to present my findings, to the convenors, fellow contributors and audience at the two papers for their advice, argument and ideas. Finally, I must record my thanks to all at Conway Maritime Press for believing that old historians deserve another hearing. The success of the reprint edition of James's *The Naval History of Great Britain* of 2002 helped to secure the publication of this, the bedrock of James's oeuvre.

Andrew Lambert, Kew, July 2004

This edition first published in Great Britain by Conway Maritime Press
An imprint of Chrysalis Books Group plc
The Chrysalis Building,
Bramley Road
London W10 6SP
www.conwaymaritime.com

ISBN 0 85177 987 5

British Library Cataloguing in Publication Data
A CIP catalogue record for this book is available from the British Library

Printed and bound in Great Britain by CPD.

NAVAL OCCURRENCES OF THE WAR OF 1812

A FULL AND CORRECT ACCOUNT OF THE NAVAL WAR BETWEEN GREAT BRITAIN AND THE UNITED STATES OF AMERICA, 1812–1815

W. JAMES

NEW INTRODUCTION BY
ANDREW LAMBERT

CONWAY MARITIME PRESS

CONTENTS

Introduction

By Professor Andrew Lambert

Laughton Professor of Naval History, King's College, London

This book was first published in June 1817, in a private edition of 1,500 copies. It was an immediate success, being adopted by the Royal Navy and lauded by British officers who had served in the war. While it may at first appear to be a simple catalogue of events, the book is neither simple, nor a catalogue. William James, a lawyer turned historian, was a man with powerful agendas, both personal and national. Although written shortly after the events it records, and by modern standards an 'instant' history, his book remains a fundamental text on this conflict.

William James became a naval historian by chance.[1] A combination of personal adversity, national pride and profound shock transformed his life. After a legal career in Jamaica he was passing through Philadelphia heading for Kingston, Ontario just as the War of 1812 broke out. Detained as an enemy alien James was astounded by the defeat of a British frigate in single combat by an American ship of the same nominal rate.[2] His experience at Jamaica, and personal acquaintance with Captain Dacres of HMS *Guerriere*, led him to suspect the American accounts were untrue. Despite his status James went on board American warships, and talked to their crew. He quickly collected enough evidence to determine that the USS *Constitution* was far larger, more heavily manned and armed than HMS *Guerriere*.[3] Further inaccurate claims that single ship actions had been between ships of equal force followed. The object of these claims was to show that American ships, and by extension the American cause, were superior to the British. James recognised that American accounts were written to boost public morale and create a national mythology. They were not intended to be accurate or true. When such American propaganda was repeated in Britain 'the press of this country unsuspectingly lent its aid in degrading the character of its own navy, and in exalting that of the United States'.[4]

James escaped from Philadelphia in late October 1813, reaching Halifax, Nova Scotia in November. Here he wrote for the local press and sent several articles to the *Naval Chronicle*. In March 1816 he published the pamphlet, *An Inquiry into the Merits of the Principal Naval Actions between Great Britain and the United States*. After examining every engagement in which a ship had been taken he concluded 'no British ship has been captured by an American one, of equal force'. He also noted how few of the ships captured by the Americans, naval or mercantile, actually reached United States' ports.[5]

Most of these ships were recaptured by Royal navy vessels before they could reach friendly ports. Some 2,430 copies were produced.

James's pamphlet differed from the other contemporary literature because he refused to accept the 'official' publications of either side as true or accurate. This reflected his legal training and courtroom experience. He had also interviewed several officers, but did not rely on oral testimony to settle controversial points, always seeking more concrete evidence. After the war James travelled to London for more information to compare with the extensive American publications. Arriving in June 1816 he quickly sold the remaining 500 copies of the pamphlet, which was generally well received and persuaded several officers to provide information. Ignoring the advice of his family to return to his legal career, James began work on a revised pamphlet. He approached the Admiralty for assistance, trusting that his laudable aim, 'to defend the character of British seamen', and the evident success of the pamphlet would support his case.[6] Despite being refused official support the revised edition quickly grew into a very long book, running to well over 700 pages in the original edition.

James opened his book by identifying the main American accounts of the war, which he subjected to a searching textual analysis, along with the underlying American version of the war. To correct this literature James developed a distinctive critical method, which was consciously contrasted with American hyperbole. The new work was more comprehensive, but it was still not a full 'history' of the naval war, coverage was still restricted to actions, partial engagements, sightings and the wider context in which they occurred. Although he used new evidence he also re-used large chunks, even whole paragraphs from the pamphlet. The volume concluded with over one hundred official documents. His purpose was still to free the war from 'American dross' and show how 'no events recorded in the naval annals of our country reflect a brighter lustre upon the character of British seamen'. His conclusion was essentially unaltered; 'no American ship of war has, after all, captured a British ship of the same force; but the reverse has occurred, and might have occurred, again and again, had the Americans been as willing to fight as they still are to boast'.[7] It hardly needs saying that James remained an advocate.[8] However, he also criticised British officers with uncommon freedom if he considered they had failed to do their duty.

While writing this book James's methods developed. Initially he had tried to balance the conflicting sources in the search for accuracy, but by 1817 he had developed an objective standard to apply to all actions between ships, to ensure that the real merit of those involved could be established.[9] This new methodology was based on the accurate measurement of force and a critical comparison of all available accounts to establish a factual truth. He deliberately did not attempt to counter the American national myth-making with similarly misleading work. Instead he strove for a solid factual explanation of events. This reliance on evidence was an entirely predictable response from a lawyer: it reflected his educational and professional background. It was also a significant step forward in historical methodology.

The Admiralty commended the accuracy and the importance of the new book, combining the compliment with an order for 40 copies. This official recognition was significant. It demonstrated that James had met his key objective, reversing the American version. He had done so without Admiralty support, allowing him to boast of his independence, and his objectivity.

While examining the British defeats at Lake Erie and Lake Champlain James realised that they had been caused by the failure, or worse, of the command ashore.[10] From this insight, and the growth of the American literature, he developed his 1818 study *A Full and Correct Account of the Military Occurrences of the late War between Great Britain and the United States of America.* This volume also included some naval material, which had come to hand after the 1817 work went to press. He excused the overlap by stressing that the two aspects of the war could not be separated. Once again he subjected American accounts to a cutting combination of well-directed mockery and robust criticism, concluding: 'He who shall succeed in teaching American writers to venerate truth, as much as their readers idolise vain-glory, will have achieved for the republic of America, a ten fold service, than the whole pantheon of demigods . . . that are presented to the world under the specious garb of "FAITHFUL HISTORY"'.[11]

He also condemned General Sir George Prevost, the cautious Governor General and Commander in Chief in the Canadas, who was blamed for the debacle at Lake Champlain and Plattsburg. Here the small British naval squadron had been captured, while the most powerful army yet assembled on the American continent retreated from weakly held American positions.[12] Prevost had formally requested Captain Downie to co-operate in a combined attack on the American position, and then delayed his own operation until after the naval attack had failed, a period of some two hours. Had he acted as he had promised Downie he would, the American positions on the River Saranac would have been taken, and the American squadron would have been no further trouble. Instead Prevost sent his men to breakfast. What annoyed James was that the British commander had, by ineptitude or cowardice, deprived Britain of the victory that the size and quality of the forces in place gave her the right to expect, with dire consequences for the outcome of the war, both in politics and the popular consciousness.[13]

The reviews were excellent. *The Times* considered the two books used accurate information on the war to provide a corrective to the public impression generated by American propaganda.[14] The *Quarterly Review* considered the Military book:

> a laudable effort to oppose a plain and unvarnished narrative of facts to the exaggerations and misstatements of the American Press. It is but justice to the author to declare, that he has evinced much zeal for the national honor and unimpeachable integrity. He has collected the evidence of our own accounts and those of the enemy with great accuracy, and compared the details with the utmost care and minuteness: his book is therefore highly valuable as a storehouse of materials for the future historian of the war.[15]

That the reviewer, Captain George Procter, did not see these works as history might surprise the modern reader, accustomed to 'instant' and 'contemporary' history, but cultured readers in the 1820s would have laughed at such usage. For them history, properly defined, was only concerned with a past that had long passed from living memory. Procter was seeking practical lessons for the future defence of Canada. In a similar vein Captain Samuel Warren, lately of HMS *Bulwark,* declared:

> I have read your work on the naval occurrences of the late American war: nothing could be better conceived than it was to put a stop to the vapouring of the American prints, and show things in their true light.

Captain Sir Thomas Hardy, another War of 1812 veteran, stressed: 'Both professions, particularly that to which I belong, must feel very much indebted to you for the pains you have taken'. Rear-Admiral Sir Pulteney Malcolm, Captain of the Fleet in 1814, agreed:

> I have read with attention both your works on the late American War. As far as events fall within my knowledge, your statements are correct, and your conclusions just, and I consider your labours as beneficial to the community, in as much as they tend to counteract erroneous opinions that were too common on the subject of the War.[16]

These men understood the purpose James had set himself, and were in no doubt that he had succeeded. Nor were they alone in this opinion.

It was, perhaps, the measure of James's effectiveness that he was universally vilified by the American press. The most outrageous lies were published about his background and character, in an attempt to discredit his work. No attempt was made to rebut his conclusions, or dispute his evidence, only to impugn his character. As he told Lord Liverpool, the Prime Minister:

> It is now nearly six years since I devoted my sole attention towards promoting the honor and glory of my country; and it is a heartfelt satisfaction to me to believe that I have in part succeeded. In doing so, my Lord, I have stirred a whole nation against me. By way of throwing discredit upon statements which they cannot disprove, they revile and slander me in every newspaper and periodical miscellany throughout the republic. More than a hundred newspapers announce the author of the 'Naval Occurrences' to be <u>a reprieved convict on a charge of forgery!</u> Thus, my Lord, should my fortunes not prosper here I am effectually disbarred from seeking to better them in the United States.[17]

The invective had an important purpose. American literature on the war was growing rapidly, war-time instant histories being refined and developed both as part of the policy debate on the future of the United States Navy[18] and to support American diplomacy. Little wonder James was vilified.

In late 1818 or early 1819 James began work on a detailed narrative of the French wars since 1793. The subject was attractive, as many of the leading figures of the period were still active. The Prime Minister immediately subscribed, the Admiralty ordered twenty copies.[19] Introducing his new book James reported that while working on the War of 1812 he had realised that existing accounts of the European wars were equally faulty. There were, he characteristically observed, 'gross mistakes' that a legally trained professional had the skills to correct through a thorough analysis of the evidence. The object was to produce something better than the usual run of naval histories, mere lists of ships, men and events.[20]

In *The Naval History of Great Britain* James reduced his coverage of the War of 1812, both to save space and because the 1817 text was still available. As he later observed: 'My analysis of the American accounts has already . . . sufficiently shown that, in the art of boasting and misrepresenting, the French could never compete with the Americans'.[21] As Captain Sir Philip Broke, hero of the *Shannon-Chesapeake* battle declared: 'Your work will remain in my opinion, the best naval history that has ever been written, . . . a standard national work . . . a useful national instruction on that naval power which is so important to our country'.

When James died, in May 1827, it was widely acknowledged that he had single-handedly corrected the American version of the War of 1812.[22]

James' work remained without a competitor for sixty years. Finally in 1882 Theodore Roosevelt began his literary career with *The Naval War of 1812,* in large part a critique of James.[23] The book was a great success, combining passion, a scientific approach and literary merit.[24] Roosevelt's book was adopted by the United States Naval Academy, and the Naval War College where he lectured while a copy was placed in the library of every American warship. Roosevelt ignored the torrent of bombastic American literature that had prompted James, and the contemporary objects behind the genre, while implying that James was no more credible than the American authors.[25] Relying almost entirely on the American official record, which he treated as inherently more reliable than James's work, Roosevelt adopted and developed James's original method of comparing force in terms of ships, men and guns. However, his agenda was different, stressing the close links between the two peoples, rather than preparing his countrymen for another war.[26] While well written and based on extensive research, Roosevelt's book was no more objective than James's. More significantly Roosevelt did not refer to James's two books on the War of 1812, only addressing the truncated account given in the *Naval History.* Because he ignored the arguments and the evidence deployed in 1817 and 1818, Roosevelt could not replace James.

William James's careful collection and skilful examination of the evidence produced a landmark in the development of naval history. His book deserves to reach a new audience, and return to the shelves of all who wish to understand the War of 1812. While the most enduring legacies of that conflict may be the independence of Canada, the American National Anthem and the colour scheme of the Presidential Mansion, this book offers a priceless opportunity to see the war through the eyes of a well-educated, and patriotic Englishman. The man and his book remain fundamental to any understanding of the origins of naval history, and the events of the War of 1812.

NOTES

1 See Lambert, A. D., 'Introduction', in William James, *The Naval History of Great Britain* (Conway Maritime Press, 2002, 6 vols), vols 1–3 for details of James and his career.
2 For an overview of the war see Lambert, A. D., 'Introduction' in R. Gardiner (ed.), *The Naval War of 1812* (Chatham Publishing, 1998), pp.9–17.
3 Martin, T. G., *A Most Fortunate Ship: the USS Constitution*, 2nd edn. (Annapolis, 1997), pp.155–60.
4 James, *The Naval History of Great Britain* (London, 1826) [henceforth 1826], Preface, p.ii.
5 James, *An Inquiry into the Merits of the Principal Naval Actions between Great Britain and the United States* (Halifax, N.S., 1816), p.102.
6 James to Admiralty, 26.11.1816: (The National Archives, Kew, Admiralty Papers (henceforth ADM) 1/4784.
7 James, *A Full and Correct Account of the Chief Naval Occurrences of the late War between Great Britain and the United States of America* (London, 1817), p.528.
8 James to Lord Liverpool (Prime Minister, 1812–1827), 1.9.1818: British Library Additional Manuscripts, Add. MSS 38,273, f.107.
9 This approach was clearly set out in the Preface to his 1826 *Naval History* at p.vii.
10 James, *Inquiry* (1816), p.102.
11 James, *A Full and Correct Account of the Military Occurrences of the late War between Great Britain and the United States of America.* (London, 1818, 2 vols) [henceforth 1818], Preface pp.xxxi–xxxii.
12 Hitsman, J. M., *The Incredible War of 1812: A Military History* (Toronto, 1965), pp.215–38. Hitsman generally takes a more positive view of Prevost, but the Plattsburg fiasco is beyond revision.
13 James, 1818, II, pp.205–228.
14 *The Times*, 1.6.1818, p.3. Also cited in W. James, *Warden Refuted* (London, 1819), p.48.
15 *The Quarterly Review*, XXVII, pp.405–449, at p.406. Cited in James, *The Naval History*, III (London, 1824), p.xii. Procter (1796–1842) was a War of 1812 veteran. His review took the form of an account of the war on the Canadian frontier, in which he frequently cited James's evidence and analysis in a devastating attack on Sir George Prevost, already the target of James's book.
16 James to Lord Melville (First Lord of the Admiralty 1812–27), 9.4.1827: Add. MSS 38,276, ff.186–9.
17 James to Lord Liverpool, 1.9.1818: Add. MSS 38,273, ff.107–9.
18 Symonds, C. L., *Navalists and Anti-Navalists: The Naval Policy debate in the United States, 1785–1827* (Delaware, 1980), p.191.
19 James to Lord Liverpool, 14.7.1820: Add. MSS 38,273, ff.202–3 & endorsements.
James, 1818: List of Subscribers.
James to Admiralty, 11.7.1820 & endorsement: ADM 1/4787.

20 James, *The Naval History of Great Britain, from the Declaration of War by France in 1793 to the Accession of George IV* (London, 1822–24, 5 vols) I, pp.xii–xxiii.

21 James, 1826, Preface pp.xii–xiii.

22 *The Naval and Military Magazine Vol.II* (London, 1827), p.205.

23 Roosevelt, T. *The Naval War of 1812* (New York, 1882).

24 I am indebted to the analysis of Roosevelt's book delivered by Michael Crawford at the Anglo-American Historians' Conference in London in July 2001.

25 Roosevelt, Appendix E, p.515.

26 *Ibid.* p.448.

Mr. WILLIAM JAMES.

ENGRAVED BY W. READ, FROM A PAINTING BY W. Mc. CALL.

A

FULL AND CORRECT ACCOUNT

OF THE CHIEF

NAVAL OCCURRENCES

OF

THE LATE WAR

BETWEEN

GREAT BRITAIN

AND

THE UNITED STATES OF AMERICA;

PRECEDED BY

A CURSORY EXAMINATION

OF THE

AMERICAN ACCOUNTS OF THEIR NAVAL ACTIONS FOUGHT PREVIOUS TO THAT PERIOD:

TO WHICH IS ADDED

AN APPENDIX;

WITH PLATES.

By WILLIAM JAMES.

"Truth is always brought to light by time and reflection; while the lie of the day lives by bustle, noise, and precipitation."

MURPHY'S TACITUS, B. ii. 39.

London:

PRINTED FOR T. EGERTON, WHITEHALL.

1817.

TO

SIR PHILIP BOWES VERE BROKE,

BARONET, KNIGHT-COMMANDER OF THE MOST HONORABLE ORDER OF THE BATH, AND CAPTAIN IN THE ROYAL NAVY;

WHO,

ON THE FIRST OF JUNE, 1813,

IN

HIS MAJESTY'S FRIGATE SHANNON,

CAPTURED,

AFTER A CLOSE ACTION OF

FIFTEEN MINUTES,

FOUGHT OFF BOSTON LIGHT-HOUSE,

(HIMSELF LEADING THE BOARDERS,)

THE

UNITED STATES FRIGATE CHESAPEAKE,

OF THE SAME FORCE;

THIS WORK

IS

MOST RESPECTFULLY DEDICATED,

BY

THE AUTHOR.

PREFACE

THE account that an American 44, had captured a British 49, gun frigate, reached the author, when a prisoner in the United States. An Englishman, early accustomed to regard the navy as the bulwark of his country, and not aware of any difference between the nominal or *rated*, and the real force of a ship, might well feel a degree of humiliation in the Guerriere's loss. The event naturally excited a spirit of inquiry; truth and fiction separated by degrees; and, before the author effected his escape from the United States, he had learned duly to appreciate the tales of American victories, both by sea and land.

Convinced that, the moment the actions between British and American ships could be submitted to arithmetical calculation, the popular delusion respecting them would cease, the author, upon his arrival at Halifax, Nova Scotia, commenced transmitting to the editor of the Naval Chronicle, under the signature of "Boxer," a series of letters on the subject. As these were written soon after the accounts had transpired, it was hardly possible to avoid some mistatements; nor would a literary correspondence admit of very minute details. Subsequently, the author published at Halifax, a pamphlet, entituled, – "An Inquiry into the merits of the principal Naval Actions between Great Britain and the United States, &c." – This was a decided improvement upon the letters; but, as nearly all the British ships had left the station, and the dearth of materials been encreased by the non-appearance in print of the British official accounts, in as many as twelve of the actions, much still remained to be done. The colonial public, however, gave the work a most flattering reception: in the short space of two months, nearly 2000 copies went off; and the remainder, about 500 in number, the author brought with him to England.

A second edition, or, rather, an entirely new work, is now offered to the public. Not only have the details of each action been more fully and correctly stated, and the comparative force of the parties, more clearly exhibited; but many naval occurrences of the late war, not noticed in the Halifax edition, have been added: and, as the American historians have commenced attacking the British naval character, from the war of 1776, it was incumbent upon the author to bestow a slight retrospect upon the events of that early period.

To obviate the charge of partiality, so often alleged against histories of war-events, the published official accounts, American as well as British, are inserted in an Appendix. The plates are intended to illustrate the subject, not to ornament the work. Plate 1 shows the description of shot used by the Americans, during the whole of the late war; at first, attempted to be concealed under the words "round and grape." Plates 2 and 3 explain themselves. The author had intended to represent, in a fourth plate, the profile-views of the British and American frigates, but wanted interest to procure copies of the sheer-draughts: indeed, it becomes him to state that, his own assiduity alone, enabled him to give any plates at all. He might, it is true, have procured a drawing of the action between the Shannon and Chesapeake, or Pelican and Argus; but here he must have trusted to the pencil of another; and so little is generally thought due to the relative size and force of the ships, provided the piece, as a whole, produces a striking effect, that he has preferred being a plate deficient, to introducing one, calculated to please the fancy, at the risk of entrapping the judgment, of his readers.

With respect to the general credit of his work, the author has spared no pains or expense, to render it worthy the subject upon which it treats. For the chief of his facts, not extracted from the official accounts and American naval histories, he is indebted to the ready communications of many distinguished naval officers: the remaining facts are the result of his own observation and inquiries, as well while a prisoner, as since his escape.

Before the reader pronounces upon any harsh expression he may observe in the work, let him study, attentively, the grounds upon which it is uttered. National character is a sensitive thing; and, surely, the existing peace between the two countries does not oblige us to let pass, unrefuted, the foulest aspersions, or wholly to suppress the feelings of a just indignation. How little the Americans consult any punctilio of the kind, may be seen in a collection of libels upon both British navy and army, published as late as September last; and dedicated to the "Honorable James Munro," on the eve of his becoming president of the United states. The high tone assumed by the American author, when speaking of the *intentions* of his government, coupled with the dedication of his work, is a convincing proof, that he was sanctioned in the performance of it; and that, had he thought the deck-plans, or sheer-draughts, of any of the American ships of war, would further his object, the American navy-board, when applied to on the subject, would not have thought it expedient to withhold them from his sight.

In the separate details of each action, particularly those of the late war, the author has endeavoured at a methodical arrangement, something like the following:

Meeting of the ships.		
Details of the action.	British and American accounts compared together.	
British / American } ship's damages,—loss.	do.	do.
British / American } ship's guns, and complement of men and boys.	do.	do.
Dimensions of the ships.	do.	do.

Comparative force of the ships computed, and exhibited in a statement.
Remarks arising out of that statement; illustrations, &c.

The merits of the different actions might have been detailed in less than half the space they occupy in the present work, had not the American editors, by heaping falsehood upon falsehood, so often compelled the author, – not unfrequently by a tedious operation to both the reader and himself, – to remove the obstruction ere he could proceed. Yet he does not pledge himself to have remarked upon all the contradictions and inconsistencies to be found in the American official accounts: much remains for the reader's discernment. Had the suppressed British letters duly appeared in the Gazette, there would have been something to counteract, in the public mind, the baneful effects of the American accounts, so freely circulated, without a word of comment, by British journalists; and the author would not now have to eradicate one impression, before he can hope to succeed with another.

There were a few boat-attacks and other spirited enterprises, performed upon the coast of the United States, that are not recorded in these pages. The chief reason for omitting them was, the impossibility of getting at the relative force of the parties; without which, the details would comprise no more than what had been seen by the public. The same motives, added to the work's having already exceeded, by upwards of 130 pages, the limits originally assigned to it, induced the author to leave out of his plan, the numerous gallant actions fought by British packets and merchant-ships, with American privateers. It is the actions between the public cruizers on each side, – the higher classes especially, – that stand as conspicuous national events; and which ought, therefore, to be handed down to posterity in characters of truth.

An earlier appearance of the present work, might have rendered it more acceptable; but the author had only to choose between, waiting till he had obtained the required information from officers dispersed all over the United Kingdom, and rashly committing to print, a mass of crude facts and imperfect details, upon so highly interesting a subject. Indeed, it was only in February last, that the full particulars of the wanton attack made by the U.S. ship Peacock upon the honorable East India company's cruizer Nautilus, appeared in an authenticated form; and yet more recently, that the last American work on the occurrences of the late war, arrived in this country. Without the latter, the advantage of the reply, after an adversary has exhausted his eloquence in embellishing his own, and blackening our cause, would have been lost: without the former, an important event of the late war, would only have reached the public, disfigured by American misrepresentation.

The question may be asked, – Have we not already, in the Annual Registers and other periodical works, faithful accounts of the naval events of the late American war? – In not one of them, are the actions between British and American ships correctly stated. Nor is it surprising, when we consider, that the editors, in the numerous cases in which the British official letters were not published, had hastily to glean their materials from the rumours of the day, or the official and other accounts of the Americans. Even here, had the authorities been cited, the antidote, in most cases, would have accompanied the poison; but, very often, the latter was rendered more potent by the editor's remarks; and more so still, when the judgment that dictated them, had become warped by the spirit of party.

The present work differs from others upon the same subject, in one material point; the attempt to exhibit the comparative force in naval actions, by placing in confrontation, first, the amount, in pounds-weight, or calibres, of the shot thrown by each ship or fleet, in a broadside, or discharge from all their guns upon one side, distinguishing the long guns from the carronades; then, the complement or complements of men and boys, and lastly, the size in tons, of each opposing ship or fleet. The reasons for adopting this method, have been fully set forth in the first or introductory chapter. Another point of difference consists, in submitting to the reader's view, the enemy's official account of each action. It is seldom we see a French official account; and then, the aid of a translator is required, to give it general currency: whereas an American official account no sooner meets the eye of an Englishman, than it finds its way to both his head and his heart.

In a work like the present, the reader may expect some political discussions, upon the origin of the late American war, the manner in which it was conducted by each party, and the merits of the treaty by which it terminated. If so, he will be disappointed: the author has confined his attention to naval subjects; and, should he have succeeded in exposing to ridicule, American bombast, and in vindicating the character of British seamen, from that pertinacious system of falsehood and detraction, upon which the Americans have founded their novel pretensions to excel us in deeds of arms on the ocean, – he has accomplished his object.

London, June 1st, 1817.

ERRATA.

Page 2 line 29, *dele* Neptune her charioteer.
— — 30, *for* his *read* a.
35 — 14, *for* 28 *read* 26.
— — 17, *for* four *read* two.
— — 19, *for* 6 *read* 2.
62 — 8, *for* 1780 *read* 1800.
141 — 10, *for* fore *read* main.
322 — 5, *for* squadron *read* squadrons.
332 — 12, *dele* men.
419 — 19, *for* larger than, *read* nearly as large as.
522 — 29, *for* four *read* three.
xviii — 13, *for* 29 *read* 20.

N.B. *The author has in preparation, a work, intended to be in uniformity to the present, upon the* military *occurrences of the late war between Great Britain and the United States of America.*

to face p. 1.

PLATE I

Dismantling, or American "round and grape" shot. see App. p. XVI. XXXIX.

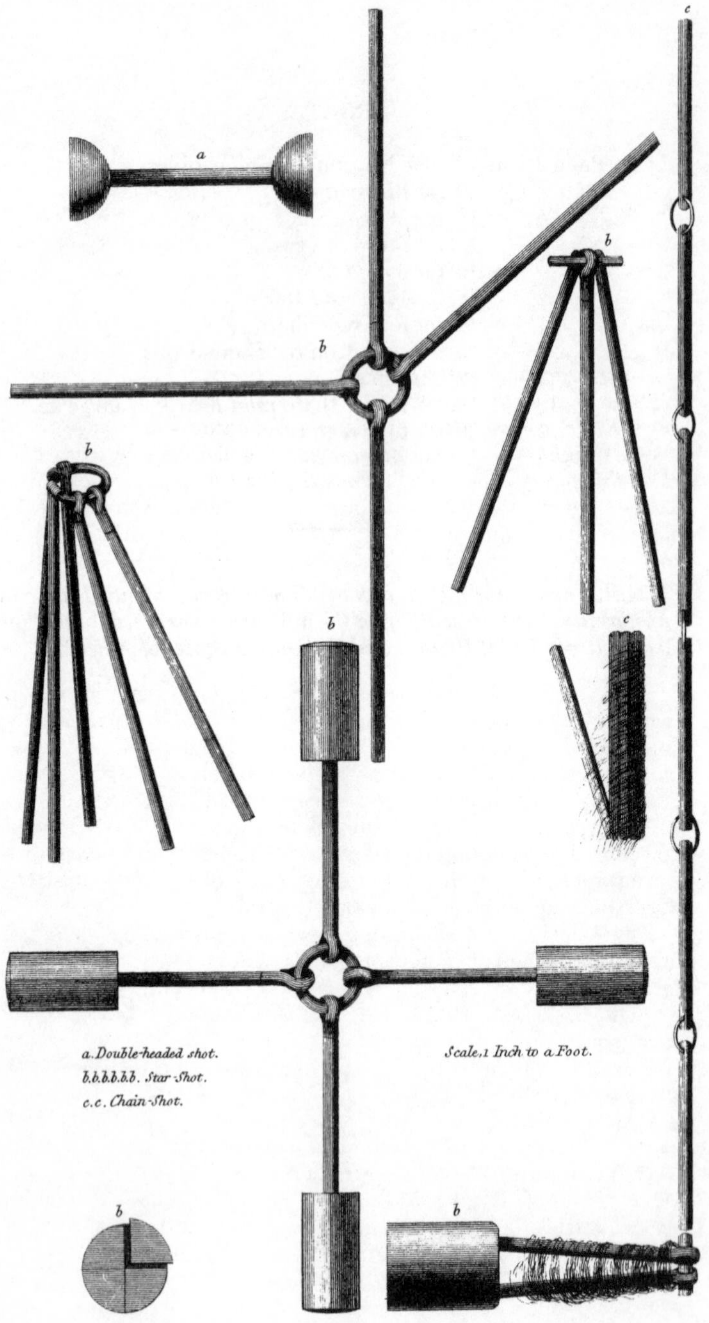

W. James del.

Mutlow sc.

Published as the Act directs May 20th 1817 by T. Egerton Whitehall.

CHAPTER I.

American naval histories—Their partiality—List of several—Nature of a ship's armament—Different kinds of cannon in use—Their comparative qualities—Advantages of large-sized shot—Weight of less consequence than diameter—Americans of a contrary opinion—Its fallacy exposed—British and American shot in use—Advantage of shifting guns—Definition of a ship's broad-side-weight of metal—Necessity of estimating the complement—Also the size in tons—British and American ships' rates—Deception upon the public—New order in council—Difference in ships of war, as to number of decks—Not a true criterion of force—Nor difference in rig, of size—Injunction to the reader on the foregoing heads.

IN a work professing to exhibit correct accounts of the naval occurrences of a war, it would be an insult to the reader's understanding, to call for his decision upon *exparte* statements. Yet, not one of the naval histories published in the United States, pays any respect to the statements of an enemy. American official accounts, however improbable or contradictory, are held too sacred to be doubted; and even idle rumour, and newspaper paragraphs, are often made the grounds of the most positive assertions, upon the most important points.

The American details of their naval actions, will be extracted from four of their principal works on that subject. It may be as well to give, at once, a summary of their respective title-pages:

"The NAVAL HISTORY of the UNITED STATES, from the commencement of the REVOLUTIONARY WAR to the present time; by THOMAS CLARK; second edition; published at PHILADELPHIA, January 3, 1814."

"An IMPARTIAL and CORRECT HISTORY of the War, &c.: carefully compiled from official documents: by JOHN LOW, at NEW YORK, in 1815."

"NAVAL MONUMENT, containing official and other accounts of the battles fought between the navies of the UNITED STATES and GREAT BRITAIN, during the late war, &c.: by A. BOWEN, at BOSTON, in 1816."

"HISTORICAL SKETCHES of the late war between the UNITED STATES and GREAT BRITAIN, &c.; by JOHN LEWIS THOMPSON, at PHILADELPHIA; third edition; 1816."

One of these works, the "Naval Monument," has a remarkably modest frontispiece. It represents America riding triumphant on the waves, and Neptune, her charioteer, pointing, with his trident, to a cluster of American worthies, fantastically stuck upon a tall monument; whose foundation, by the bye, is not clearly discernible. Addison has described the design in a very few words.—"One kind of burlesque," says he, "represents mean persons in the accoutrements of heroes."

The "Naval History of the United States" partakes rather of an official character; and Mr. Clark, in his first edition, did style himself,—"U. States topographical engineer." He has, evidently, been allowed access to all the public records. Both democrats and federalists lavishly praised his first edition; and the author has, very judiciously, placed in front of his second, under the imposing head of "Criticism," several complimentary scraps. Among them, is the following from the American "Portefolio:"

"This is a very interesting collection of facts and documents, no where else to be found in so convenient a form, on the most important subject which now engrosses the attention of the American people. The naval history of a country is a theme on which we all dwell with peculiar pleasure; since our national pride cannot fail to receive its highest gratification from a series of brilliant and daring achievements. The author of the present work has, therefore, rendered a useful service, by enabling the public at large to become more familiar with our naval annals."

A third edition, and a dedication to the late American secretary of state, Mr. Munro, confer some authority upon the "Sketches of the war." That, and the "Naval History," may be considered as speaking the sentiments of the American people, upon the great national subject that fills the pages of both.

The indulgence of the naval reader is now requested, while a few observations, chiefly calculated for such as are unacquainted with the subject, are submitted, upon the nature of a ship's armament, and upon what really constitutes her *force,—or* power to do and resist injury, when contending with an enemy.

That ships constructed for the purposes of war, mount guns or cannon, is well known. Guns have their cylinders of various diameters or calibers, from 2½ to 8 inches; and each gun is named from the weight of the shot, which its cylinder will admit to pass freely. Thus, a gun of a 2½ inch caliber, being capable of receiving and discharging an iron shot that weighs half a pound, is called a half-pounder, or more commonly, a *swivel,* from the way in which it is usually mounted; and a gun of an 8-inch caliber, discharging a shot weighing sixty eight pounds, is called a 68-pounder. Between these extremes, are several gradations, each distinguished in a similar manner.

The gun which throws a shot of sixty eight pounds weight, was invented in 1779, at Carron in Scotland; and thence called a carronade. This gun is shorter and lighter, in proportion to its caliber, than any of the common kind. The carronade admits of variety in caliber, but not to so great an extent as the long gun; the cylinders of few of the former being below four inches in diameter; the caliber of a 9-pounder.

No long gun at present in our service throws a heavier shot than of thirty two pounds. There is, however, a kind of gun, still shorter than the carronade, the diameter of whose bore extends to thirteen inches. These guns are named mortars and howitzers; and are designated according to the diameter of their bores, thus: "A 13-inch mortar;"—"An 8-inch howitzer." They are chiefly employed to throw shells; and, for that purpose, mounted on board peculiar vessels, called bomb-ships.

Within these few years, a sort of medium-gun has been invented, for sea-service, called by us, *Gover*'s, or *Congreve*'s gun. The Americans call their's a *Columbiad;* probably from its having been cast at the cannon-foundery situate in the district of Columbia, in the United States.

The English short long-gun weighs about two-fifths less than a gun of the same caliber, of the common construction; but a 68-pound-carronade weighs only one-sixth more than the lightest 24-pound gun, and a 42-pound carronade weighs considerably less than the lightest 18-pound gun.

Owing to this circumstance, the carronade requires fewer hands to work it, and can be loaded and pointed with more quickness and facility, than the long gun. The benefit to be derived from employing a species of cannon capable of throwing shot of so extraordinary a size, appears in the following extract from a celebrated treatise on gunnery:

"The most important advantage of heavy bullets is this, that with the same velocity, they break out holes in all solid bodies, in a greater proportion than their weight: that is, for instance, a 24-pound shot will, with the same velocity, break out a hole in any wall, rampart or solid beam, in which it lodges, above eight times larger than will be made by a 3-pound shot; for, its diameter being double, it will make a superficial fracture above four times as great as the 3-pounder, (more of a smaller hole being closed up by the springing of the solid body than of a great one,) and it will penetrate to more than twice the depth. By this means, the firmest walls of masonry are easily cut through their whole substance by heavy shot, which could never be effected by those of a smaller caliber; and in ships, the strongest beams and masts are hereby fractured, which a great number of smaller bullets would scarcely injure." (Robins, p. 285.)

In Rees's Encyclopedia, title, *Cannon,* are the following additional remarks upon large-sized shot.—"The 68-pound carronade is superior to the long 24 and 32-pounders, particularly in close combats, by the size of the holes which its shot makes in the side of a ship, and from its likewise passing through the same with less velocity. For a shot, especially if its diameter be but small, that passes very quickly through a ship's side, makes only a clean hole; whereas one of a large diameter that penetrates it with less celerity, makes a rough and ragged hole, by tearing and splintering the planks and timbers."

It may be necessary to offer a few words on the comparative distances to which cannon of the different calibers and descriptions will project a shot. Robins, who wrote upwards of thirty years before the invention of carronades; and therefore had reference to long guns only, says:—"The larger bullets being less resisted in proportion to their weight than the smaller, the distance to which these larger bullets fly with the same proportion of powder, exceeds the flight of the smaller ones, almost in the proportion of their diameters; so that a 32-pound shot, for instance, being somewhat more than six inches in diameter, and a 9-pound shot but four inches, the 32-pound shot will fly near half as far again, as that of 9-pound, if both pieces are so elevated as to range to the furthest distance possible." (P. 284.) In another place he says, "a 24-pounder, loaded in the customary manner, and elevated to 8°, ranges its bullet, at a medium, to about a mile and a half; whereas, a 3-pounder, which is of half the diameter, will, in the same circumstances, range but little more than a mile." (P. 256.)

Some information relating to the range of carronades, is here extracted from a little work entitled the "Naval Pocket Gunner."

"*Range with carronades,* 1-12*th the weight of the shot, with one wad; the line of fire from six to nine feet above the water's level.*"

Nature.	68-pndr.	42-pndr.	32-pndr.	24-pndr.	18-pndr.	12-pndr.
Point-blank	450 yds.	400 yds.	330 yds.	300 yds.	270 yds.	230 yds.
Five degrees	1280 . .	1170 . .	1087 . .	1050 . .	1000 . .	870 . .

Therefore, a ship, armed with carronades only, however large in caliber, would be quite at the mercy of an adversary, armed with long 12 or 18-pounders; provided the latter ship, by possessing the weather-gage, or a decided superiority in sailing, could choose her distance. Let the two ships once close, and the larger balls would soon establish their destructive superiority,

There is another advantage attending large cannon, which Mr. Robins justly calls "a capital one;"—"that of carrying the weight of their bullet in grape or lead-shot, and thereby annoying the enemy more effectually, than could be done by ten times the number of small pieces." (P. 285.)

On referring again to the "Naval Pocket Gunner," it appears, that the difference in the relative weights of grape-shot, when made up, is, in some cases, much greater than exists between the relative weights of round shot. For instance, a single grape-shot for a 24-pounder weighs two pounds; and, for an 18-pounder, one pound eight ounces: but while the grape, when made up, weighs for a 24-pounder, twenty four pounds four ounces, it weighs for an 18-pounder only sixteen pounds eight ounces.

It is commonly thought, that a shot fired at a very long range, should it even strike a ship, would do far less injury, than a shot fired from a short distance. The extract from Rees's Encyclopedia, already given, disproves this; and, to the same effect, are the words of Mr. Robins:—"It is a matter of experiment, that a bullet, which can but just pass through a piece of timber, and loses almost all its motion thereby, has a much better chance of rending and fracturing it, than if it passed through it with a much greater velocity." (P. 291.) And, in another place:—"In penetrating solid bodies, that bullet which has but just force enough to go through, will produce much greater effect, than a bullet which has a considerable velocity left, after it has got through." (P. 307.)

The Americans, it appears, have "accurately weighed together" their shot and ours, of the same caliber; and one naval commander officially states, that a British 32-pound shot weighs one pound three-quarters more than an American one. This alleged difference in weight (rather less than one-eighteenth) the Americans ascribe, not to the diameter of their shot being smaller than ours of the same nominal weight, but to the texture being looser, arising from some difference in the two methods of casting. Whenever the Americans *do* venture upon a calculation of comparative weight of metal, they take care to profit by this discovery.

It is not worth enquiring, whether or not this alleged trifling variation in weight between American and British shot, does exist; or whether it may not arise from a new shot having been picked out on one side, and an old one, dented in the casting, or abraded by rust, on the other. Under the article already quoted from Rees's Encyclopedia, it is stated, that "a hollow shot equal in diameter to a 68-pound shot, but weighing only forty pounds, fired from a suitable distance, penetrated a bulk-head, as thick as the sides of a first-rate; and afterwards striking against an oak post or stud, nine inches square, tore, shattered, and splintered it almost to pieces."

It has just appeared, that one advantage of a large shot, is the size of the hole it makes in a ship's side; and that the less the celerity of the shot in its passage through, the greater will be the damage. Were the exact weight, and not the diameter, of a shot to be taken, in proof of its destructive power, the above hollow shot, of eight inches diameter, filled with combustible matter till it weighed forty eight pounds, must be considered as less effective than a solid iron shot of the same diameter, weighing sixty eight pounds; and that, precisely as 48 is to 68. Either the Americans mean this, or they mean nothing. It is to be hoped, they will not again broach a principle so truly ridiculous.

The only kinds of shot used in the British navy, are, round, grape, and case or canister, a smaller species of grape. But the Americans, both in their public, and private-armed vessels, employ, under the denomination of "round and grape," chain, bar, star, and double-headed shot; which, in close combat especially, enables them to unrig a ship, much more quickly than could be accomplished by the shot in general use. An accurate representation of these dismantling shot may be seen in Plate I.

The editor of the "Naval History" says that,—"in an engagement between ship and ship, the effect produced is, by the broadside, or the *number* of guns placed in battery on one side of a ship." Mr. Clark should have said—"number *and description* of guns;" his present statement implying, that a 3 and a 32-pounder are productive of equal effect.

The armed schooners of the United States often appear with their guns fitted in a manner, that, one would think, requires only to be known, to be generally adopted. For instance, a schooner of 80 or 90 tons, upon which we should place six 12-pound carronades at least, would, as an American privateer, carry three long 12-pounders, upon pivot-carriages; so as to be used upon either broadside. Thus, while numerically of only half her former force, she throws the same weight of metal in broadside; and possesses the immense advantage of long guns over carronades of the same caliber.

All the American public ships derive a partial benefit from using shifting guns upon their upper decks; for which they are provided with spare ports, exclusive of those at the bow and stern. These guns, as well as those placed on pivot-carriages, belong to the broadside-force; and should be estimated accordingly. Mr. Clark, by including, in his statement of the force of our frigates, the shifting or boat-carronade which they usually carry, admits the correctness of this principle.

Standing bow or stern-chasers, or any other guns in the ship, for which no broadside-ports (in contra-distinction to the bow or bridle-port) are provided; or which, from the construction of their carriages, cannot be fought, otherwise than through ports, will not be estimated. By a ship's broadside-weight of metal, is therefore to be understood, the united calibers, in pounds, of all the long guns and carronades, which she can "place in battery on one side of her;" whether those guns are stationed upon her decks, or in her tops.

The guns of a ship are useless lumps of iron, without men to handle them. A ship that has not men enough for all her guns upon the broadside, must either allot to each gun fewer hands than can properly work it, or fully man a part only of her guns, and leave the remainder unsupplied. In either case, that ship's whole force or power is not brought into action.

Suppose two ships, equal in guns, to engage; one to have full crews for every gun upon her broadside, marines for her gangways and tops, seamen in abundance to trim sails, repair running-rigging, clear away wrecks of spars, stop shot-holes; in short, men for every possible service in the ship. Let the other ship have men enough to work two-third of her guns only, scarcely any to employ as marines, and so few for trimming sails and manœuvering the ship, or for hastily repairing slight accidents in the rigging, that she can neither take a position to rake her opponent, nor prevent being raked herself; her disability encreasing, by every shot that is fired. Will any one pronounce this to be an equal match? Yet, were a ship's force to be estimated from her guns only, the affirmative would be the answer, whatever absurdity it might involve.

Strictly speaking, every gun that cannot be manned, should be thrown out of the estimate. None would be by this such sufferers in fame, as the commanders of American privateers. One of their schooners, of ten heavy guns, might have captured, in quick succession, six merchant-ships, of twelve guns each; every one of which would, of course, be pronounced "superior" to herself. Yet the whole six British crews, would not, perhaps, outnumber the single American crew.

Again; when two ships grapple, of what consequence is an equality in cannon? She that has most men, with arms in their bands, will inevitably carry her opponent, unless, indeed, the advantage is rendered of no avail by a deficiency in valor. This fact has been established repeatedly, in the engagements with our packets, armed transports, and even merchant-ships, as many a disappointed privateersman can testify.

American editors, in their statements of actions, conceal, not only the weight of metal, but, invariably, the complements, on each side; aware that, as "successful contributors to national character," they dare not make the disclosure.

In the present work, a ship's complement will be added to her broadside-weight of metal; and, as a British ship's complement always consists of a great proportion of boys; (and of very young ones, too;) while scarcely any are to be seen on board an American ship, it would be to consider men and boys as equal in effectiveness, not to enumerate them separately. The same distinction must be observed, when non-combatant-passengers are on board.

Hitherto, estimates of the comparative force of ships have been usually considered as complete, when the force in guns and men was accurately stated; but, it is submitted, a disparity in size, especially if it amounts to any thing beyond a fifth or a fourth, ought also to be included. For instance, the larger ship remains steadier in a rough sea; by which her guns are pointed with more effect, as, from the roominess of her decks, they are worked with more ease. Her additional length necessarily places the men further apart; thereby diminishing the havoc made by the enemy's shot. The men have another security, in the additional thickness of her sides, through which the shot have to pass; and the ship herself is, from the same cause, enabled to withstand a longer and more furious cannonade. Then, the encreased diameter of the masts, yards, and rigging, adds to the difficulty of destroying or disabling them; and the stability of a ship's masts, after those of her adversary have fallen, generally decides the contest.

The advantage of thick sides has not escaped the discernment of the Americans; and, the discussion being confined to American ships, there could be no object in withholding it from the public, or in rendering it confused. Mr. Paul Hamilton, the American secretary of the navy, in his official letter, transmitting a "very valuable communication" from Captain Charles Stewart of the United States' navy, explicitly says:—"Besides, a 76" (a ship then proposed to be so rated) "is built of heavier timber, is intrinsically much stronger, than a frigate in all her works; and can sustain battering much longer, and with less injury. A shot which would sink a frigate, might be received by a 76 with but little injury. It might pass between wind and water through a frigate, when it would stick in the frame of a 76."—(N. Chron. vol. xxix. p. 466.)

This argument requires some explanation. If the accounts of the Americans are to be credited, we have no ship in the British navy, not even the Caledonia and her class, "built of heavier timber" than the American 76s, or 74s, as they are now rated. Consequently, one of the latter *may* have been "built of heavier timber, and be intrinsically much stronger in all her works," than an American frigate; as is notoriously the case between a British 74 and a British frigate. The possession of the President, however, has decidedly proved, that the difference, if any, in the size of scantling, between a British 74 and an American frigate, is in favor of the latter. Yet, in answer to a charge in the British journals, that the large American frigates were 74s in disguise, Mr. Clark declaims a great deal about a British 74-gun ship's superiority in "compactness and strength of sides."

Between two British ships of war, the tonnage bears some proportion to the thickness of sides: and so it may between two American ships of war; but, between a British, and an American, ship of war, that rule generally fails. The following table, the several items of which are the result of actual measurement, will sufficiently illustrate this:

Built.	Present rates.	Names.		Tons.	Thickness of topsides, including outside plank, timber, and inside plank, at mid-ship main-deck port-sill.		foremost quart-deck port-sill.	
					Ft.	in.	Ft.	in.
1797	54	President,—Am.		1533	1	8	1	5
1809 1816	74	San Domingo, Hero,	British	1819 1741	1	7	1	1
1813	60	Leander,	British	1571	1	5	1	0½
1813	46	Eurotas,	British	1084	1	3	—	11

The San Domingo was Admiral Warren's flagship on the American station; and the Hero, recently built at Deptford, is esteemed one of the finest second-class 74s in the service. The Leander was constructed purposely to match the President, and her class; and the Eurotas considered strong enough to carry Congreve's 24-pounders upon the main-deck. The latter's top-sides will answer for those of British 46-gun frigates, in general.

It would appear, then, that British and American builders differ in their ideas as to what is the due proportion between the thickness of a ship of war's top-sides, and her length, breadth, and tonnage. Derrick says:—"In the year 1744 or 1745, a general complaint was made of the ships in his majesty's navy, that their scantlings were not so large and strong as they should be."* Mr. Sepping's solid plan of building rises no higher than the level of the gun-deck. It may save the ship from sinking, but it will afford no additional shelter to the men at the guns.—True, no ship's side can resist a well-directed 18 or 24-pound shot, fired from a short distance; but may not a shot that is nearly spent, pass through a side fifteen inches thick, when it would lodge in a side twenty inches thick?

Some persons may imagine, that a stout, compact side would act as an impediment to sailing; a point so essential in a ship of war. On the contrary, the American ships are, proverbially, swift sailers; and the President, with such uncommon topsides, one of the swiftest among them. The quality of sailing depends chiefly upon the form of a ship's bottom, aided by her length. The Americans had, according to Charnock, discovered this, early in the war of 1776;† and they have now proved, clearly, that swift-sailing is not incompatible with the strongest construction.

* Derrick's Mem. of the R. Navy, p. 136.

† Charnock, M. Arch., vol. iii. p. 18.

A ship's masts and yards are generally in proportion to her size; but the lower-masts of American ships, are invariably stouter in proportion to their length, than the lower-masts of British ships. A comparison of the main-masts of different ships will explain this:

Main masts.	Br. 64.	Am. 44	Br. 46.*	Am. 36	Br. 32*	Am. 18	Br. 26*	Am. 14
	Ft. in.	Ft. in.	Ft. in.	Ft. in.	Ft. in.	Ft. in.	Ft. in.	Ft. in.
Length, ...	100 0	101 6	92 0	93 4	75 0	75 0	66 0	62 0
Diameter	2 9½	2 11	2 3½	2 6	2 0	2 1½	1 7¼	1 10½

It is easy to conceive, that the smaller the mast, the less will be the difficulty of destroying it by shot; but there are few persons who can form an adequate idea of the state of a ship, with her masts all gone; engaged with another, whose masts are all standing.

The masts, in their fall, crush men, and disable guns. If the wreck hangs over the side engaged, resistance is suspended; or, if a few guns can still be used, the flash from them sets the wreck in flames, and adds to the confusion. Having no locomotive power, no sail to counteract the motion of the sea, the ship becomes an ungovernable hulk, reeling from side to side, and dipping her guns at every roll. These, or a part of them, she may discharge at the enemy; but, under such circumstances, how many shot will take effect? The other ship, benefiting by the pressure of the wind upon her sails, rides steady amidst the waves; and advances, turns, and retreats, at pleasure. Her guns, she fires with precision; and either sinks her opponent, or compels her to surrender.

It remains to say a few words on the difference observable between British and American tonnage. According to an official paper laid before the American government, the President measured 1444 tons,—fractions not given;* whereas she measures, by our method, 1533-²⁵⁄₉₄ths of a ton.

The President's "keel for tonnage," as it appears in an American publication, is 145 feet; we make it 146 feet, 7¾ inches.—In both cases, it is a mere calculation, intended to allow for the rake or inclination of the ship's stem, and stern.

In casting the tonnage, the first multiplicator of the Americans, is the breadth across the frame, or *moulded breadth;* (by them usually called "breadth of beam;") of the British, the same, encreased by the thickness of the plank at the ship's bottom, or the *extreme breadth.* The second multiplicator of each, is the respective half-breadths. The American divisor is 95; the British 94. Thus:

* Present rates.
† Nav. Chron. vol. xxix. p. 458.

	Ft in.	Ft in.		Ft in.		Tons
Am. method .	145 0	× 43 6	= 6308	× 21 9	= 1371999 ÷ 5	= 1444 19/95ths.
Brits. ditto . .	146 7¾	× 44 4	= 6502	× 22 2	= 143044 ÷ 94	= 1533 25/94ths.

The President's "moulded breadth," as here stated, is as the Americans have made it; but, by actual measurement, it is two inches more. It is very common for ships, by *falling out* at the sides, to exceed, by a trifle, the builder's estimate.

This difference in tonnage, from not being generally known, occasions mistakes, in pronouncing upon the relative size of British and American vessels; and, in discussions of that nature, is, evidently, an advantage to the latter. All ships, therefore, American as well as British, whose tonnage may appear in the present work, will have been measured according to the British method.

The application of the *size in tons,* as part of a ship's force, cannot be reasonably objected to by the Americans; because, as has appeared already, British ships of greater tonnage than the American 44s, are exceeded by them, in thickness of topsides; and equalled, at least, in stoutness of spars.

To convey a better idea of a ship's size, than the tonnage alone may afford, the length on deck, and extreme breadth, of most, if not all, of the ships engaged, will be given; and, as the masts are such important auxiliaries in action, and the squareness of the yards may contribute to shew the size of the ship, the length and diameter of the main-mast and main-yard, will also, when obtainable, be added.

Having endeavoured to explain the nature of a ship's armament; as well as to point out, that an accurate statement of a ship's force, ought to comprise, her *broadside metal in pounds,* both in *long guns* and *carronades;* her *complement of men and boys;* and her *size in tons*—a clear view of the subject demands a few observations, upon the popular notion about the rate, the class or form, and the mode of rig, of armed vessels in general.

Previous to the invention of carronades, a ship of war was designated, or *rated,* according to the number of guns she actually mounted. At first, carronades, by two or four at a time, were introduced on board the frigates and higher classes: to receive which carronades, additional ports were cut through the sides of the quarter-deck; the ports for long guns not answering for carronades, without considerable alteration. These carronades became, then, an addition to the ship's armament, not expressed or understood by her *rate.* As new ships were added to the navy, carronade-ports were constructed by the builder, upon the forecastle, and all along the quarter-deck; except where the interference of the main rigging required a long gun. Thus, a ship was made to mount as many as eight or ten pieces of cannon, more than were expressed as her actual armament.

This addition to a ship's rated armament might be illustrated by the re-equipment of most of his majesty's ships, built earlier than the year 1790. There was, however, in existence until very lately, a ship built as long ago as 1757; which may best serve to establish the point. The Southampton frigate, in every list of the British navy from 1757 to 1792, is stated to have carried the following guns: twenty six 12-pounders upon the main-deck; four 6-pounders upon the quarter-deck; and two 6-pounders upon the forecastle; total 32 guns: precisely what she rated, in every list up to that announcing her loss, by shipwreck, in November 1812. But, at that period, the Southampton mounted, upon the quarter-deck and forecastle, ten carronades, 24-pounders, a 12-pound boat-carronade, and four long 6s; making, with her twenty six long 12s upon the main-deck, 41, instead of 32 guns, the number she rated.

The first British-built frigate, of "38 guns," was, according to Charnock's lists, the Minerva, of 940 tons, built in 1780; and, up to the year 1792, the establishment of guns for that class was,—twenty eight 18-pounders upon the main-deck; eight 9-pounders upon the quarter-deck; and two 12-pounders upon the forecastle; total, 38 guns. At present, the frigates of this class, encreased in size to 1080 tons, mount upon the quarter-deck and forecastle, fourteen carronades, 32-pounders, and two long 9s; making, with their main-deck battery, and boat-gun, 47, instead of 38 guns, the rated number.

Previous to the Prince Regent's order in council, recently promulgated, it would have puzzled any one out of the naval department, to enumerate the guns of a ship, from seeing her *rate* in the list. By people in general, the rate and actual armament, were considered as synonimous terms; and, therefore, in proportion as the two terms differed, was the deception upon the public. We read in Steel:—"La Traave, 44, taken by the Andromache, 38." The same list designates the former, as a *British* ship, thus: Traave, 36." And what did the Andromache mount?—According to the present admiralty-lists, 46 guns. We read, also, of the capture of "La Renommée, 44;" but, when that ship, with an altered name, and three more guns placed upon her, is captured from us, Mr. Steel calls her "Java, 38." The very same list contains the following statement: "La Furieuse, 50, taken July 6, by the Bonne Citoyenne, 18;" when a reference to Captain Mounsey's official letter* would have shewn the editor, that La Furieuse, although manned with a frigate's complement, and pierced for 48, mounted only 20 guns. The thing, in all its parts, was gallant enough, without the aid of exaggeration.

It was not the least inconvenience attending the rating system, that it had a partial application, even in our own service. For instance, one of Steel's "18-gun" sloops, if a brig, or a corvette-ship, mounted (without reckoning the boat-carronade) no more guns than her rate expressed; but, if a deep-waisted ship, 26 or 28 guns.

* Nav. Chron. vol. xxii, p. 346.

To what may we, in a great measure, impute the national surprise at the capture of a British frigate of "49 guns," by an American one of "44 guns," but the delusion created by the repeated victories of a British frigate of "38 guns" over a French frigate of "44 guns"?—Was the public to know, that the first British frigate was stated at the guns she mounted, the second at the guns she rated and that the reverse of this occurred in the case of the American, and the French frigate; thus: British frigate, 49 guns, American frigate, 44 (instead of 56) guns; British frigate, 38 (instead of 46) guns, French frigate, 44 guns?

Foreigners, with almost pardonable acrimony, will often speak of this habit of contrasting the rate of our ships with the mounting of theirs; and how can an Englishman reply? With what face can we blame the Americans, for having acted in the same manner towards us?

It is due to the gallantry of British seamen, and to the honorable character of British officers, to state, that most of the French ships of "44 guns" were larger, and far more numerously manned, than the "38 gun frigates" that captured them and, partly on account of the difference between French and English measures, usually mounted heavier metal; upon the main-deck, especially. Were an officer, in his public letter, to state how many guns his own ship mounted, it would be informing the lords of the admiralty, of what they are already supposed to know. He has only to describe the force of the enemy's ship; being well aware that a reference to the navy-office books, will procure, for any one who may desire to publish an account of the action, the true force of his ship. Nor does a British officer, if properly applied to, ever refuse to give the fullest information on the subject. It is the editors and publishers of such accounts, and not the British officers, who deserve censure for imposing upon the public.

The variation between the rate, and mounting, of the ships of the British navy, was, as we have seen, a gradual process; attributable rather to accident than design. Was that the case with the ships in the American navy?

An act of congress, dated the 27th of March, 1794, authorised the building of "four ships of 44 guns, and two of 36 guns;" and, in 1813, the following appeared in a Philadelphia newspaper:

Extract from a Report of the secretary at war,
April 1st, 1798.

"It appears that the first estimate rendered to congress, was for frigates of the common size and dimensions, rated at 36 and 44 guns; and that the first appropriations for the armament, were founded upon this estimate. It also appears that, when their size and dimensions came to be more maturely considered, due reference being had to the ships they might have to contend with, it was deemed proper, so to *alter their dimensions, without changing their rates,* as to extend their sphere of utility as much as possible.

"It was expected, from this alteration, that they would possess, in an eminent degree, the advantage of sailing; that, separately, they would be *superior to any single European frigate of the usual dimensions;* that, if assailed by numbers, they would be always able to lead a-head; that they could never be obliged to go into action but on their own terms, except in a calm; and that, in heavy weather, they would be *capable of engaging double-deck ships.*

"These are the principal advantages contemplated from the change made in their dimensions. Should they be realized, they will more than compensate for having materially swelled the body of expenditures."

Here is an official document, pointing out the "advantages" of sending forth ships, of greater size and force than their rate implies; evidently, to operate as a cheat or delusion upon the rest of the world. There was no "European frigate of the usual dimensions," but was known to be a third smaller, and a third weaker, than an American frigate "of 44 guns." But why to rate "of 44 guns"? Because the largest "European frigates" then *mounted* that number; consequently, a frigate "*of* 44 guns" was apparently equal to a frigate "*of* 44 guns." The difference between the *rate* and *mounting* was supposed to be a secret; the above "*Report of the secretary at war*" not being suffered to see the light, till of late years, when some of the "advantages" of the deception, had become, indeed, "realized"!

Happily, it was reserved for Britain to pluck the veil of deception from the rating system. Her gallant tars require not the aid of fiction, to give a colour to their claims. The order in council expresses, "that all the vessels in the navy shall in future be distinguished by the number of guns and carronades they actually mount, and not according to the erroneous denominations which had long since grown into use."—America, surely, will not now have the face to continue her rating system. In verification of the old proverb, she will find it her interest to be honest; but it will not be forgotten—who set her the example.

The *rate*, as we have seen, is an arbitrary distinction, liable to continual fluctuation. There is, between ships of war, another distinction, general and permanent. Thus we have, the three-decker, or ship with three whole battery-decks; the two-decker, or ship with two whole battery-decks; the one-decker, or frigate, and its variety, the corvette or cutter, with one whole battery-deck.

The corvette has simply one deck or battery, with sometimes two small spaces elevated from four to six feet above the level of the deck; one situate aft, called the poop or round-house, the other forward, called the top-gallant-forecastle. Upon one or both of these short decks, two or three small guns are sometimes employed in action; but, there being no ramparts to protect the men, the station is always a dangerous one, especially within the range of musketry.

The top-gallant-forecastle, extended aft from the stern to the belfry, (a little abaft the fore-mast,) and the poop or round-house, from the stern to nearly the centre of the ship, become the forecastle and quarter-deck. These are joined by a narrow platform, or range of planks, laid horizontally along the upper part of the ship's side, called the gangway; a vacancy being left in the middle, which opens to the upper or main-deck, and forms the waist. Ships of this construction are called deep-waisted; and, if armed for war, and with but one whole deck, frigates.

Vessels not deep-waisted, whether corvettes, or such as have two whole decks reaching from the stem to the stern, with or without a poop and top-gallant-forecastle, have also a quarter-deck and forecastle, of the same extent as if separated in the middle by the waist. But a ship of war's upper-deck, when of this fabric, is usually called, the spar-deck. Of this description, are the upper-decks of the Majestic, and Saturn, *razees;* of the Leander, Newcastle, and new Java; and of the President, and the large American frigates of her class. None of these vessels are therefore deep-waisted, or frigate-built ships; although courtesy has gained for them the appellation of frigates.

The frigate-class formerly descended very low. It was only in the year 1760, that deep-waisted ships, rating 18 guns and under, began to be classed as sloops; and not until very lately, that ships rating 24 guns, were removed to the same station. Yet neither the French nor the Spaniards admit any intermediate class between a frigate-built ship, however small, and a single-decked flush-ship; both calling the one a frigate, and the other a corvette. The Americans called the Cyane, rating 24 guns, a frigate; and most of our frigate-built 18 or 20-gun sloops, of the old rate, if they happened to fire a few shot at an American privateer, were similarly designated.

The quarter-deck and forecastle, with the deep-waist, are common to both regular two, and three-decked ships; and all the latter, and most of the former, have also a poop or round-house; but which, unlike that upon corvettes, is constructed with ramparts and ports, similar to the quarter-deck.

Without enquiring which ship's deck is the longer of the two, or has placed upon it the greater number and weight of guns, the world calls for proof, that ships of one denomination are not of equal force. Upon the same principle, persons imagine, that the ship of three decks, or batteries, must necessarily be superior in force to the ship of two; and so, in succession, down to the corvette.

Whether, on the contrary, a disparity, in some cases four-fold, may not exist between ships of war, having the same number of decks, a few examples will shew.

The class of three-deckers is limited, but even they are not equal in force. A comparison between ships of this class is not necessary.

For one of the two-deckers, let us take the Malta, with the force she mounted in 1812. To heighten the contrast, a two-decked "44" might be produced; but, as that useless class is now dismissed the service, the two-decked 50, or present 58, gun ship (not much better) will be opposed to the Malta.

	Malta		Old 50-gun ship.	
Lower-deck	2 Carron.	68-pndrs.	22 Long	24 pndrs.
	30 long	32 —		
Upper-deck	32 —	24 —	22 —	12 —
Quarter-deck and forecastle	20 Govers. L.	24 —	6 —	9 —
	2 carr.	68 —	8 carr.	24 —
	1 —	24 —	1 —	18 —
	1 —	18 —		
Poop	6 —	24 —		
	—		—	
Total	94 guns		59 guns	

Comparative force of two TWO-DECKERS:

		Malta		Old 50-gun ship.	
Broadside-metal in pounds	l. guns	1152		427	
	carr.	178		114	
		——	1330	——	541
Complement of men and boys			689		343
Size in tons			2255		1044

That a contest between two such ships, is not merely an ideal case, was proved on the 18th of August, 1798, when a British 50, the old Leander, under the command of the present Vice-admiral Sir Thomas Boulden Thompson, Bart, engaged, at close action, for six hours and a half, le Genereux, a ship very little inferior in weight of metal, and actually superior in number of men, to the Malta.

For the one-decked, or frigate-class, a ship as much a frigate as the new Leander, Newcastle, and new Java, will be produced. The Majestic, it is true, had been a 74; and the Anson and Indefatigable, 64s; yet they all classed as frigates. If the Majestic had not been intended to represent a frigate, why was her construction altered? The Americans called the Cyane, when they captured her, a frigate, and the same class of ship is often similarly designated by us. Most of these ships formerly mounted long guns upon the main-deck. One of the latter will be preferred; as the ship to which she is to be opposed, mounted on that deck long guns also. The Majestic, and the old 24-gun ship, respectively mounted as follows:

	Majestic		Old 24-gun ship.	
Main-deck	28 long	32-pndrs.	22 long	9 pndrs.
Quarter-deck and forecastle	1 —— brass	12 ——	2 ——	9 ——
	28 carr.	42 ——	8 carr.	18 ——
	1 ——	18 ——	1 ——	12 ——
	—		—	
Total	58 guns		33 guns	

Comparative force of two FRIGATES:

		Majestic		Old 24-gun ship.	
Broadside-metal in pounds	l. guns	460		108	
	carr.	606		84	
			——1066	——	192
Complement of men and boys			500	——	175
Size in tons			1642	——	538

Formidable as is the Majestic's, for a frigate's, broadside, some of the new American "44s" mount two 32-pounders upon their main-decks, more than she does. There would be some propriety in rating such ships, as the Majestic was rated, at "58 guns;" but, is it not a burlesque upon the rating-system to rate them at "44 guns"?

The American Commodore Macdonough, absolutely called two British armed sloops of 110, and 102 tons "sloops of war." (See App. No. 91.) Without contrasting vessels of the sloop-of-war class, it will be sufficient to shew the dimensions of an American *corvette,* as well as what armament she was calculated to carry. The late Andromeda in our service, (now sold out,) was formerly the American ship Hannibal. Her dimensions were these:

	Ft.	In.	
Length on deck from rabbit to rabbit	129	7	Tons 812
Breadth extreme	37	5⅝	

The Andromeda's masts and yards were those of a 42-gun frigate. She was pierced for 28 guns; and, although she carried 32-pound carronades, might have been armed with twenty four 42s, and two long 18-pounders. She would then have thrown as heavy a broadside as a British 46-gun frigate, of the new rate. The Americans, during the late war, employed two corvettes, about the size of the Andromeda; one named the Adams; the other, the John Adams. They were both reduced from frigates; and the latter, it is believed, carried 42-pound carronades.

It has already been shewn, how totally inadequate the number of decks, as well as the rate, of a ship is, to determine her force and size. Difference in the mode of rigging vessels, constitutes a third distinction; and is one that, as respects size particularly, may also lead to very erroneous conclusions.

Most people imagine, that a ship must be larger than a brig;

and a brig than a schooner. The American brigs Jones and Jefferson, on Lake Ontario, are each 530 tons; and the Mammoth, privateer-schooner, was 406 (376 Am.) tons. His majesty's ship-packets are 180 tons; the brig of war Hunter, on Lake Erie, was 74 tons; and the schooner Chippeway, at the same place, 32 tons.

In action, a three-masted, has certainly an advantage over a two-masted vessel. If a brig's main-gaff is shot away, or her boom-main-sail otherwise rendered useless, she directly falls off from the wind, and exposes herself to a raking fire: whereas, if a similar accident befals a ship's spanker, the mizen-top-sail, or mizenstay-sail, keeps her broadside to the enemy. In the engagements between our brig-sloops and the American ship-sloops, presently to be detailed, the truth of this will be manifest.

If, then, the reader wishes to understand thoroughly the merits of the several disputed cases, the elucidation of which is the sole object of the present work, he must not be biassed by ship's rates, number of decks, or other such equivocal distinctions, but must give his whole attention to each ship's *broadside-weight of metal, complement of men and boys,* and *size in tons.*

CHAPTER II.

War of 1776—*H. M. S. Glasgow and an American squadron—Nimrod and an American armed ship—Beaver and Oliver Cromwell—Yarmouth and Randolph—Cruel treatment of British prisoners of war—Ariadne and Ceres with the Raleigh and Alfred—Levant and General Hancock—Diligent and Providence—Serapis and Scarborough with squadron under Paul Jones—Savage and Congress—South Carolina American frigate—Anecdote of Captain Manly—Atalante and Trepassy with the Alliance—Sybil and Alliance—Gross amount of British and American captures.*

THE early pages of Mr. Clark's work, are devoted to the naval operations of the "revolutionary war." Almost every action in which a British armed ship was a party, is detailed with some circumstances to her disadvantage. As far as respects private-armed ships, it is hardly possible, at this day, to come at the truth; but, the proceedings of our public-armed ships being on record, from the earliest periods, the details of actions in which they have been concerned, will not be so difficult to procure,

At page 26 of his first volume, Mr. Clark informs us, that an American fleet, consisting of, "the Alfred, of 30 guns and 300 men; Columbus, of 28 guns and 300 men; Andrew Doria, of 16 guns and 200 men; Sebastian Cabot, of 14 guns and 200 men; and Providence, of 12 guns and 150 men," on their return from a successful expedition against the island of New Providence, fell in with H. M. S. Glasgow, of 20 guns, Captain Tyringham Howe, in company with a tender.—"The Cabot," says Mr. Clark, being foremost of the squadron, bore down upon her. After exchanging broadsides, the Cabot was so much damaged in her hull and rigging, by the superior weight of the enemy's metal, as to be obliged to abandon the contest, and refit. The Alfred came next alongside, and continued a close engagement for an hour and a half. During the action, the Alfred had her tiller and main-braces shot away. At day-break, the Glasgow, making all the sail she could crowd, stood in for Newport. The Cabot had four men killed, and seven wounded; the Alfred six killed, and six wounded; the Columbus one wounded. After this engagement the American fleet got safe into port. The escape of the Glasgow excited much displeasure against the commodore."

Captain *Schomberg** states this affair to have happened on the 6th of April 1776; and that, so far from the Glasgow effecting her *escape*, she compelled this mighty squadron of American ships, to "sheer off." She was much crippled in her masts and rigging; and had one man killed, and three wounded.

The Glasgow was 451 tons, and carried twenty long 9-pounders. The tender does not appear to have been armed. The Alfred and Columbus must have had either 9 or 12-pounders: the other three American vessels, 6-pounders.—What means Mr. Clark, then, by "the superior weight of the enemy's metal"?—A candid writer would have said—"the extraordinary precision of the enemy's fire." Some idea of what the Glasgow had to contend with, will appear by the numbers on each side: British force, 20 guns, 150 men; American force, 100 guns, 1150 men.

At page 39 of the same volume, Mr. Clark says—"In the month of September (1776) Captain Baird, commander of a Massachusett's armed ship, engaged the Nimrod, a British sloop of war, of 18 guns. After a severe action, the Nimrod struck her colours;"—and refers, for his authority, to two American miscellanies, the Remembrancer, and Pennsylvania Packet.

Passing over the circumstance of the armed ship's force being left to inference, it is sufficient to state, that neither this "severe action," nor the Nimrod's capture, can be found in *Shomberg*;—a work Mr. Clark admits of authority, by referring to it so often. But, in the navy-list for 1777, (the year *succeeding* the alleged capture,) the Nimrod's name appears, for the first time; and she is there stated to mount 14, instead of 18 guns.

At p. 51, we read,—"On the 11th of May (1777) the British sloop of war Beaver, of 14 guns and 125 men, fell in with an American privateer of superior force. After a smart action of three quarters of an hour, the privateer struck to the English vessel."—"*Schomberg's Naval Chronology,* vol. i, p. 436."—The passage quoted runs thus: "On the 18th of May, the Beaver sloop of war, of 14 guns and 125 men, commanded by Captain Jones, being on a cruize off St. Lucia, fell in with, and after a smart action of three quarters of an hour, captured the Oliver Cromwell, American privateer, of 24 guns, 10 swivels, and 10 cohorns, and 150 men, commanded by Captain Harman; 20 of whom were killed, and as many wounded. The Beaver had three men wounded. She was taken into the service, and named the Beaver's prize."

At p. 78, Mr. Clark recounts the blowing up of the American 32-gun frigate, the Randolph, while engaging the Yarmouth 64,

* *Schomberg's Nav. Chronol.* vol. i. p. 427

at night; having mistaken her for a "large sloop with only a square-sail set."—"The British ship," says the account, "was the Yarmouth of 64 guns, commanded by Captain Vincent. She was very much disabled by the action. Her sails were all torn to pieces in a most surprising manner. She had five men killed, and twelve wounded. All the other vessels escaped from the Yarmouth; which continued a chase of several days after them."—For this, *Schomberg* is not cited, but an American miscellany of note, the "*Porte-folio.*"

Captain *Schomberg* relates the same disastrous event thus:—"On the 7th of March, Captain Vincent, in the Yarmouth, of 64 guns, being on a cruize off the island of Antigua, about five o'clock in the evening, discovered and chased six sail. At nine, Captain Vincent came up with the largest, which, upon being hailed, hoisted American colours, and fired her broadside into the Yarmouth: she continued to engage for about twenty minutes, when on a sudden she blew up. Being very near to the Yarmouth, a great part of the wreck fell on board her, which cut her rigging and sails to pieces, killed five men, and wounded twelve others. On the 12th, Captain Vincent being in chase, saw a large piece of a wreck with four men on it; upon which he gave up the chase, and bore down to pick them up. They proved to be the only remaining part of the unfortunate crew of the ship which had blown up, while engaging the Yarmouth. These poor wretches had subsisted on nothing but rain-water, which they had caught in a piece of an old blanket. Captain Vincent learnt from them, that the ship was the Randolph, American privateer, of 36 guns, and 305 men."

The American account, in the very next paragraph to that stating the Yarmouth's loss in sails and men, "*by the action,*" says—"There were 315 persons on board the Randolph. When she blew up, it was fortunate for the Yarmouth that she was to-windward of her. Notwithstanding, she was covered with parts of the wreck. A large piece of timber, six feet long, fell on the poop. Another large piece struck her fore-top-gallant-sail." But, strange to say, not a word is there of a single man on the Yarmouth's decks having been hurt by this shower of spars, "six feet long."

To commemorate the "glorious event," a splendid oil-painting is still exhibited, shewing the Yarmouth, in size a three-decker, engaging the Randolph. The latter's consorts, (although one of them, the Moultrie of 20 guns, is admitted to have been closely engaged,) *may* be seen far off in the back-ground; the sails of the 64 are pierced with shot-holes; a top-gallant-yard is breaking in two; and a top-gallant-mast falling upon the deck. In short, the Yarmouth appears to have, by far, the worst of the action. So much for representing that as having preceded, which actually followed, and was the consequence of, the Randolph's destruction.

According to a paragraph respecting the fitting out of this Randolph, it would appear that "British sailors" were among the sufferers on this melancholy occasion. Mr. Clark says:—"The difficulty of procuring American seamen, when the frigate was fitting out, obliged Captain Biddle to comply with the request of a number of British sailors, then prisoners, to be allowed to enter on board his vessel. While bearing away for Charleston, the English sailors, in conjunction with others of the crew, formed the design of taking the ship. When prepared, three cheers were given by them on the gun-deck. But, by the firm and determined conduct of the captain and his officers, the ringleaders were seized and punished. The rest submitted without opposition."

This brings to recollection, a circumstance related by an American loyalist, who is now a commissioned officer in his majesty's land-service. He stated, that he was confined, as a prisoner of war, in the jail of Philadelphia, during the first American war; and there frequently witnessed the taking by force of British prisoners to man the U. States' vessels, then lying in the Delaware. That, on one occasion, thirty or forty sailors, selected as the most effective, were dragged forth; and that, on their comrades, within-side joining in their loud execrations against the authors of such cruelty, the soldiers appointed to guard the men, in their march to the ships, fired into the prison-windows!

The fact of the "British sailors" on board the Randolph trying to regain their liberty, proves, pretty clearly, that, instead of their having "requested to enter," the American commander and his officers had, like the authorities on shore, employed coercive means.

At p. 85, vol. I. of the "Naval History," we read that,—"on the 9th of March (1778) the Alfred of 20 guns, was captured by the British vessels, Ariadne of 20 guns, and Ceres of 14."—"*Schomberg's Naval Chronology,* vol. i. p. 451."—Upon consulting the authority, the passage is found to run thus:—"On the 9th of March, the Ariadne of 20 guns, and the Ceres sloop of war, of 14 guns, commanded by Captains Pringle and Dacres, being on a cruize off Barbadoes, chased two American frigates. At noon they came up with one of them, which struck, after a short resistance. She proved to be the Alfred, of 20 guns, and 180 men. Her consort was the Raleigh, of 32 guns, which escaped."

The ship that escaped was afterwards captured by the Experiment, of 50 guns, and Unicorn, of 20 guns; and taken into the service as a 32-gun frigate. No wonder Mr. Clark preferred being guilty of a false quotation, to disgracing his pages with the fact of the Raleigh having deserted her consort, when chased by two British ships; the largest of which was barely equal in force to the smallest of the American ships.

We next read (p. 87) of "the Levant, an English frigate, of 32 guns, commanded by Captain John Martin," being, on the 19th of September 1778, blown up in action with "the private-armed ship General Hancock, of Boston." The latter's force not mentioned. This loss does not appear in *Schomberg*. On the contrary, in his lists of the British navy, for 1777, 1778, and 1779, may be seen—"Levant, 28 guns, Captain Hon. G. Murray;" but the name "John Martin" no where appears among the post-captains, or commanders, in his majesty's navy. One of the last paragraphs in the American article, states, that the boatswain and seventeen men were saved; and that the crew "consisted of ninety seven seamen, exclusive of landsmen and boys."—The ship, therefore, was probably a British letter of marque; but evidently not, as alleged by Mr. Clark, "an English frigate of 32 guns."

At p. 96 is the following:—"In the month of May (1779) as the U. States' sloop of war Providence, of 10 guns, Captain Hoisted Hacker, was cruizing off Sandy Hook, she fell in with the British sloop of war Diligent, of 12 guns. A severe action ensued, and lasted an hour and a half; when the British vessel struck to the American. The Providence had four men killed, and ten wounded."

According to *Schomberg*'s and *Charnock*'s lists, the Diligent mounted 10 guns, 3-pounders, was allowed 45 men, and measured 89 tons. Mr. Clark, in another part of his book, states the force of the Providence at twelve 4-pounders, and 90 men; and captured American vessels of 12 guns, at that time, were from 198 to 220 tons. This, therefore, was no capture of a superior British force, as the statement implies.

At p. 105 is given a highly exaggerated account of the loss of H. M. ships, the Serapis, of 44, and Scarborough, of 20 guns. These two ships, with 294, and 135 men, were captured, according to the official accounts, after a sanguinary action of nearly four hours, by that notorious renegado, Paul Jones, in Le Bon Homme Richard, of 40 guns, and 375 men; the Alliance, of 36 guns, and 300 men; le Pallas, of 32 guns, and 275 men; and the Vengeance brig, of 12 guns, and 70 men: altogether, 120 guns, and 1020 men, opposed to 64 guns, and 420 men.

At p. 125 is the following:—"In September, the British sloop of war Savage, of 20 guns, and about 150 men, cruized along the southern coast of the United States. She had proceeded up the Potowmac, and plundered General Washington's estate. On the 6th of September, she was met off Charleston, by the privateer Congress, of the same force with herself. The Congress was commanded by Captain Geddes. Major M'Lane, a very distinguished partizan-officer of the American army, had, with a part of his command, volunteered to serve as marines on board her. As the crew of the Savage were all seamen, she had considerably the advantage of the Congress, the greater part of whose crew were landsmen. At half past ten, the Congress commenced firing her bow-chasers. At eleven, the action commenced with musketry; which, after much execution, was followed by a severe cannonade on both sides. The Savage, at the commencement of the engagement, had the advantage. She then lay on the Congress' bows, and raked her. But the latter succeeded in getting alongside the Savage, and soon disabled her so effectually that she could not manœuvre. An hour after the commencement of the action, all the braces and bow-lines of the Savage were shot away. Not a rope was left to trim the sails with. Her decks were cleared by the musketry of the Americans. The Congress continued alongside until accident obliged her to drop a-stern. The Savage was then almost a wreck; her sails, rigging, and yards, were so much injured, that it was with the utmost difficulty she could change her position time enough to avoid being raked. The cannonading soon recommenced, with greater vigour than ever. The quarter-deck and forecastle of the Savage were, in a short time, again nearly cleared; almost every man stationed in these places being either killed or wounded. Three guns on the main-deck of the Savage were rendered useless. The fire from the guns of each ship, scorched the men opposed to them in the other. The mizen-mast of the Savage was shot away, and got entangled in the after-rigging of the Congress. The colours of both vessels were shot away, when the boatswain of the Savage appeared forward with his hat off, calling for quarters. As all the boats of the Congress had been destroyed by shot, it was half an hour before any of her crew could board the Savage. She was found to be a complete wreck. Her decks were covered with blood, and killed and wounded men. The victory was, in a great measure, due to the exertion and activity of Major M'Lane and his brave soldiers."

This very circumstantial account, to make it complete, wanted only, what the Americans are generally unwilling to communicate—the force of their own ship. Fortunately, that appears in *Schomberg,* vol. ii. p. 57. He there says,—"On the 6th of September, Captain Charles Sterling, in the Savage sloop of war, of 14 guns, and 125 men, being on a cruize off Charlestown, fell in with, and was captured, after a furious and bloody conflict, by the Congress privateer, mounting 20 12-pounders, and four 6-pounders, with a complement of 215 men, commanded by Captain Geddes. Captain Sterling did not surrender the king's ship, until his mizen-mast was shot away, the main-mast in imminent danger of falling overboard, several of the guns rendered useless, 8 men killed, and 26 wounded. Among the former was the master, and among the latter were Captain Sterling, Lieutenant Shields, and 3 midshipmen."

Although the Congress was more than doubly superior to the Savage; (whose 14 guns were only 6-pounders;) yet, says the above candid historian, "the British sloop of war was captured by an American ship of the same force with herself."

At p. 138, is stated the capture, in the month of December, 1782, of the American frigate South Carolina, of 40 guns. *Schomberg,* the author cited, adds, "twenty-eight of which were 42-pounders on the main-deck, and twelve 12-pounders on the quarter-deck and forecastle, with a complement of 450 men, commanded by Captain Joiner. This frigate was built in Holland for the Americans: her length of keel was 160 feet."—It is not then in modern times only, that the Americans have employed frigates exceeding in force and size, the frigates of any other nation.

To cap the climax of American heroism during the "revolutionary war," Mr. Clark, in the same page of his book, gives the following anecdote:—"In the month of September, Captain Manly*, who in the commencement of the war commanded the Hancock frigate, was appointed to the command of the U. States' frigate Hague, before called the Deane. Cruizing in the West Indies, he was chased by an English 74, and grounded on a sand-bank near Guadaloupe. Three ships of the line having joined the 74, they came to anchor within point-blank shot of the Hague. With springs on their cables, they opened a most tremendous fire. The American frigate supported this cannonade for three days. On the fourth she was got off, when, hoisting continental colours, at the main-top-gallant mast, she fired 13 guns as a farewell defiance. She arrived safe in Boston." The reader will recover himself a little when he finds that, for this wonderful escape from three days' "tremendous cannonade," by four ships of the line, within "point-blank shot," an "*American* Biographical Dictionary" is Mr. Clark's sole authority.

The "Naval History" contains, also, the accounts of the capture of two of our sloops of war by the American frigate Alliance, "of 32 guns," and of that ship's action with a British frigate of "equal force;" but as these actions are more circumstantially given in the "life *of* Commodore Barry," vol. ii. p. 1. of the American *Portefolio,* the latter will be consulted in preference.

The European reader will find it difficult to comprehend, how Mr. Barry, admitted to have been "born in Ireland," could be "an American hero;" or how an acknowledged traitor to his country, could be "the first of patriots and best of men." In American language, these terms are synonimous; unless, indeed, a native of the United States becomes a traitor. In that case, the words revert to their original meaning, and no crime is so heinous.

The Alliance, "of 36 guns," says the commodore's biographist, "sailed from L'Orient early in 1781, on a cruize; and, having taken many valuable prizes, on the 29th of May an event occurred that deserves notice. On the preceding day two sail were discovered on the weather-bow standing for the Alliance. The strange sails were discovered to be a ship and a brig; the British flag was displayed, and having, by means of their sweeps, got within hailing distance, they respectively hailed, when it appeared that the ship was his Britannic majesty's ship of war

* An Englishman, born in Torbay. Naval Chron. vol. xxxii, p. 274.

Atalante, Captain Edwards, carrying *between* 20 and 30 guns, and her consort, the brig Trepasa, Captain Smith."—Then, the action is detailed and that "at three P.M. they both struck their colours." The time at which the firing commenced is not stated; but, "about two o'clock, the commodore (Barry) was wounded in the shoulder by a grape-shot."

"Soon after the commodore was wounded and left the deck, one of his lieutenants went to him while in the cockpit, and, representing the shattered state of the sails and rigging, the number of killed and wounded, and the disadvantages under which they laboured, from the want of wind, desired to know if the colours should be struck. ' No,' said he, ' and if the ship can't be fought without, I will be carried on deck.' When the lieutenant made known to the crew the determination of their brave commander, fresh spirit was infused into them, and they, one and all, resolved to stick by him.

"The Alliance had 11 killed and 21 wounded; among the latter, several of her officers; her rigging and spars much shattered, and severely wounded in her hull. The enemy had the same number killed, and 30 wounded. We have been led into the detail of this victory, as it was considered at the time of its achievement, a most brilliant exploit, and as an unequivocal evidence of the unconquerable firmness and intrepidity of the victor."

Here, then, the "unconquerable intrepidity" of an Irishman prevented the colours of an American ship from being struck. What renown, it may be asked, did the Americans gain by this? Suppose, even, the American lieutenant and his men had, without requiring to be stimulated by their Irish commander, effected the conquest, was the capture, or the defence, of these two sloops the most "brilliant exploit"?

Schomberg records the event thus:—"On the 28th of May, the Atalante sloop of war, of 14 guns, and 125 men, commanded by Captain Edwards, and the Trepassey, of 14 guns, and 80 men, Captain Smith, being on a cruize on the banks of Newfoundland, at noon on that day, were attacked by the Alliance, American frigate, of 40 guns, and 250 men. The sloops made a most determined and resolute defence; at one o'clock, Captain Smith, of the Trepassey, was killed. Lieutenant King, on whom the command devolved, continued the action with great gallantry for two hours longer. At this time, the Trepassey was a complete wreck, with 5 men killed, and 10 wounded, and the ship ungovernable; he was compelled to strike. Captain Edwards, in the Atalante, still maintained the action with uncommon bravery; but his antagonist having no longer any other to contend with, compelled him also to surrender, with the loss of many men, and the ship dreadfully cut to pieces. Mr. Samuel Arden, her lieutenant, behaved with unexampled bravery, having lost his right arm in the action; the instant it was dressed, he resumed his station upon deck, and animated the men to fight gallantly, where he continued till the ship struck."*

Among the frigates captured from the Americans during the war of 1776, were two of 32 guns each, carrying long 18s and 12s; and one, the Bricole, sunk at Charleston in 1780, was pierced for 60, and mounted 44 guns, 24 and 18 pounders. The Alliance mounted 40 guns; consisting, it is believed, of twenty-eight long 18-pounders upon the main-deck, and twelve long 12-pounders upon the quarter-deck and forecastle. The American frigate, Confederacy, of 36 guns, and 300 men, captured in 1801, measured 959 tons; which may therefore be stated as the size of the Alliance.

The Atalante mounted 16 guns, 6-pounders, and measured 300 tons; the Trepassey 14 guns, 4-pounders, and measured 187 tons. The following, then, will shew the relative force of the two captured sloops and the American frigate; and decide which party in this contest was entitled to honors:

	Atalante and Trepassey.	Alliance.
Broadside-metal in pounds (all long guns)	76	396
Complement of men and boys	205	250†
Size in tons	487	959

The next "brilliant exploit" of the same American frigate; is noted thus:—"The Alliance left L'Orient in February, 1782, from which time she continued cruizing with great success, till March of the following year; when, shortly after leaving Havannah, whither she had been ordered to bring to the United States a large quantity of specie, having in company the continental ship Luzerne, of 20 guns, Captain Green, three frigates were discovered right ahead, two leagues distant. The American vessels were hove about; the enemy gave chase. The Luzerne not sailing so fast as the Alliance, the commodore ordered the captain to throw her guns overboard. A sail was then discovered on her weather-bow, bearing down upon them. The Alliance hove out a signal, which was answered: she proved to be a French ship of 50 guns. Relying upon her assistance, the commodore concluded to bring the headmost of the enemy's ships to action; after inspiriting his crew by an address, and going from gun to gun, cautioning his men against too much haste, and not to fire till ordered, he prepared for action. The enemy's ship was of equal size with the Alliance: a severe engagement followed. It was very soon perceptible that the Alliance was gaining the advantage. Most of the enemy's guns were silenced; and after an action of fifty minutes, his ship was so severely damaged, that she hoisted a signal of distress, when her consorts joined her. The loss on board the Alliance was very

* Schomb. N. Chronol. vol. ii. p. 59.

† Short of her proper complement by 70 men, at least.

trifling; 3 killed, and 11 wounded. The enemy's loss was severe; 37 killed, and 50 wounded. The other English frigates were watching the movements of the French ship; the captain of which, upon coming up with the Alliance, assigned as a reason for keeping aloof from the action, that he was apprehensive the Alliance had been taken, and that the engagement was only a decoy. Chase was made, but the French ship being unable to keep up with the American, it was given over.—A gentleman of distinguished naval reputation, when in the Mediterranean with the American squadron, was introduced to Captain James Vashon, esquire, now vice-admiral of the red, the commander of the British frigate engaged with the Alliance. In the course of conversation he made particular enquiry after Captain Barry, related the circumstance of the action, and, with the frankness of a generous enemy, confessed that he had never seen a ship so ably fought as the Alliance; that he had never before, to use his own words, 'received such a drubbing,' and that he was indebted to the assistance of his consorts."*

Neither *Schomberg,* nor any other British naval historian, mentions this engagement. By a little industry, however, the following facts have been obtained; and may be relied on. The "three frigates" consisted of the Alarm of twenty-six long 12, and six long 6 pounders, commanded by the late Sir Charles Cotton; the Sybil of twenty-four long 9, and four long 6 pounders, commanded by the present Admiral Vashon; and the Tobago of sixteen long 4-pounders, commanded by the present Vice-admiral Martin. It was to extricate the Luzerne, of twenty long 9-pounders, that the Alliance bore down upon, and engaged, the Sybil; which ship was, in a manner, detached from her consorts. The action was fought within half-musket shot distance; and continued about seventeen minutes, when the Alliance hauled on board her fore and main-tacks, and stood from her antagonist; whose great inferiority of sailing rendered pursuit useless. The Alarm and Tobago were still at a considerable distance; and, so far from the Sybil being "severely damaged," and losing "37 killed and 50 wounded," she received very little injury in hull, spars, or rigging, and lost but 2 men killed, and 7 or 8 wounded. If, therefore, Captain Vashon made any signal, it must have been to acquaint his commanding officer, that the Sybil, alone, could manage the Alliance; thereby leaving the Alarm and Tobago at liberty to devote their attention to the French 50, and the American 20, gun ship, the friend and consort of the fugitive American frigate. It is almost needless to add, that the statement of this engagement, as given by Commodore Barry's biographist, including the alleged conversation between "Captain James Vashon, *esquire,"* and the American gentleman of distinguished naval reputation," is an entire fabrication.

* American Portefolio, vol. ii. p. 7.

To enable the reader fully to appreciate the gallant performance of the officers and crew of the Sybil, here follows the

Comparative force of the two ships:

	Sybil.	Alliance.
Broadside-metal in pounds (all long guns)	120	396
Complement of men and boys	200	320
Size in tons	594	959

A superiority, in weight of metal, of more than three to one, and in complement, of more than three to two, failed to give success; yet the American statement of the Alliance's two actions, concludes thus:—"We wish it to be understood, that the gallantry of our seamen is not of recent date, but is coeval with our national existence."

It is not simply by partial and fabricated accounts of actions, that the Americans have reared from comparative insignificance, the "Naval History of the revolutionary war;" Mr. Clark devotes twenty pages of his book to a mere list of British captured vessels; while he compels the reader to wade through the whole, in search of the few captured American vessels, with the names of which his industry had supplied him. The writer's motives appear in the following comparative statement of the gross numbers of American and British armed vessels, captured or destroyed during the first American war; as extracted from *Schomberg,* vol. v. p. 11 and 52:

American armed vessels.	British armed vessels.
No. 85; guns, 1755	No. 29; guns, 470

CHAPTER III.

The United States and France—Constellation engages and captures l'Insurgent—A statement of the comparative force of the ships—Constellation engages la Vengeance—Is beaten off—La Vengeance refitted—Encounters the Seine—Is captured—Statement of the comparative force of the ships—Americans claim a victory for Commodore Truxton—Description of his medal presented in consequence—French account of the engagement with the American frigate—Remarks thereon—Leopard and Chesapeake—American accounts of it—Statement of the comparative force of the vessels—Little Belt and President—Americans at Tripoli—British deserters.

THE only naval occurrences that strictly come within the plan of the present work, are those that have taken place between the United States and Great Britain; but, as the Americans still attach considerable importance to the two "memorable naval victories," they pretend to have gained over the French, a cursory examination of the American accounts of those actions, may not be an unprofitable digression. It will then be seen, whether America has displayed more moderation in recording her victories over France, to whose treasure and fleets she owed her independence, than she has in triumphing over us; to whom, it is admitted, she owes no extraordinary obligations.

The "Naval History" states that, on the 9th of February, 1799, the U. States' frigate Constellation, "of 36 guns," fell in with "a large ship" under French colours; that an action ensued, which lasted "one hour and a quarter," when the enemy struck, and proved to be l'Insurgent, "of 40 guns, and 417 men." Another American account fixes her complement at 340; but neither account mentions the nature of her armament.

This "brilliant victory" was echoed from one end of the union to the other; and a late American newspaper-puff, headed "Record of glory," recalls it to the public attention. It is of little consequence, whether the Constellation rated of "36 guns;" or, as Mr. Clark has made her, in his list of the American navy for the very year of the action, "of 44 guns:" the question is—what was her real force, as well as that of the frigate she captured?

A lieutenant of the Constellation, while, during the late war, she was lying in Norfolk, Virginia, blockaded by the British squadron, gave the following as her armament, at that period:—twenty-eight long 18-pounders upon the main-deck, twenty carronades, 32-pounders, and two (English) long 24-pounders, bored to carry a 32-pound shot, upon the quarter-deck and forecastle; total 50 guns: exclusive of boat-carronade, and top-guns, if any.

But a gentleman who was frequently on board the Constellation, while she was in the West Indies, in the years 1799 and 1780, declares, that her main-deck battery then consisted, not of 18, but of 24 pounders. In confirmation of this, a New-York paper, of the end of 1800, or beginning of 1801, (the precise date not recollected,) announced the arrival there from a southern port, of the U. States' frigate Constellation, for the purpose of "*exchanging her* 24s *for* 18s." Therefore, long subsequently to both her "victories," the Constellation mounted 24-pounders upon the main-deck. It is believed, that the chief part of her spar-deck battery then consisted of long 12s, and that they were afterwards exchanged for carronades. To make allowance for that, ten of her twenty-two spar-deck guns will be considered as long 12s, and the remainder as 32-pound carronades.

The complement of the Constellation was 440 at least; and her size is described as about equal to that of the Endymion. At all events, she could not well have been less than 1250 tons.

The nature of l'lnsurgent's guns no where appears. For some years subsequent to 1799, when a French frigate was captured, with 18-pounders upon the main-deck, it was invariably so expressed in the official account. The generality of the French 40-gun frigates, carried 12-pounders; and were from 850 to 950 tons. To give every advantage to the Americans, let us suppose that l'Insurgent mounted twenty-six long 18-pounders upon the main-deck, and fourteen long 9-pounders upon the quarter-deck and forecastle; total "40 guns." The difference between an English and a French 18-pound shot, in diameter, is as 5,040 to 5,277; (inches and decimal parts;) and, in weight, as 18 to 20½. pounds. So that, by adding one eighth to the nominal calibers of French guns, we have the weight of metal expressed in English pounds. The mean of the two American, accounts of l'Insurgent's complement is 379. Her tonnage may be stated at 950.

Comparative force of two FRIGATES:

		Constellation.		l'Insurgent.	
Broadside-metal in pounds	l. guns	396		263	
	carr.	192		71	
		——	588	——	334
Complement of men and boys			440	——	379
Size in tons			1250	——	950

Had the Constellation captured, in one action, two such ships as l'Insurgent, the Americans could not have boasted more than they did upon this occasion. A disclosure of the real strength of the parties, now shews, that the defence of the French frigate was highly creditable to her officers and crew.

The merchants of London, misled by the American statements, most of which were copied into the British journals, viewed the capture of l'Insurgent as a victory gained by an American, over a French frigate, greatly superior; and, acting with their accustomed liberality, subscribed for a piece of plate to be presented to Commodore Truxton. Had the rate of, and actual number of guns mounted by, a ship, meant the same thing, this "memorable victory" would have passed off without notice.

On the 1st of February, 1800, the Constellation fell in with, and engaged for upwards of three hours, the French frigate la Vengeance. Each party, as is usual in undecided cases, accused the other of "sheering off." At all events, the Constellation had her main-mast shot away; and was otherwise so greatly injured as to be compelled to bear up for Jamaica, to undergo the necessary repairs. Her loss in killed and wounded amounted to 39. La Vengeance was also much shattered, and lost a great many men. She afterwards put into Curaçoa, to get herself refitted. Commodore Truxton's account of this engagement, being deemed a *unique* piece of composition, will be found in the Appendix. (Nos. 1 and 2.)

On the 20th of August following, H.M.S. Seine, Captain (now Rear-admiral Sir) David Milne, fell in with, and after a long and sanguinary action, captured, this same la Vengeance; just from Curaçoa, where she had been completely refitted. The Seine was much cut up; and sustained a loss of 13 killed, and 29 wounded. La Vengeance was shattered almost to pieces; and, when carried into Jamaica, was thought not worth repairing. Her loss in the action, though not exactly ascertained, was known to have been very severe.

The Seine (captured from the French, June 29, 1798) mounted 42 guns: twenty-eight long 18-pounders upon the main-deck, and fourteen long 9-pounders upon the quarter-deck and forecastle. Her established complement consisted of 284 men and boys; and she measured 1146 tons.

La Vengeance mounted 52 guns: twenty-eight long 18-pounders upon the main-deck; sixteen long 12-pounders, and eight carronades, 42-pounders, upon the quarter deck and forecastle. Her complement was believed to be 453; but, as 291 men only were found on board, 390 will be an ample allowance. Captain Milne describes la Vengeance as "exactly of the dimensions of the Fisgard," taken from the French in 1797; and that ship was 1182 tons.

Comparative force of the two ships.

		Seine.		La Vengeance.	
Broadside-metal in pounds,	l. guns	315		391	
	carr.	00		189	
			315		580
Complement of men and boys			284		390
Size in tons			1146		1182

Here, evidently, a British frigate, of inferior force, captured a ship, which an American frigate, of at least equal force, was unable to capture; demonstrating that British, was, in this instance, more potent than American "thunder."—"Aye," say the Americans, "but la Vengeance struck her flag to the Constellation, only our commodore did not happen to know it."—Accordingly, it was so voted; and the honors of a conqueror,—a conqueror, too, over a "far superior force,"—were conferred upon the astonished Commodore Truxton. Nay, to silence all doubts, and perpetuate the "memorable victory," a medal was struck; of which an engraving may be seen in the first volume of the American Portefolio. Two ships are there represented, dismasted and much cut up; one, a complete two-decker, similar to the Majestic or Saturn, razees; the other, a small frigate. The reader may conjecture which ship is intended for the American.

As if to place this mock triumph in a still more ridiculous point of view, the French first lieutenant assured a distinguished British naval officer, that la Vengeance, when she encountered the Constellation, was laden with sugar, and had casks stowed between her main-deck guns; a few only of which could be cleared for action in time; that the American frigate kept hanging upon the quarter of la Vengeance, and never came fairly alongside; that the latter lost all three masts; and, from having an inexperienced crew, was compelled to remain stationary for the best part of three days; during which time the American frigate, with her fore and mizen-masts standing, lay in sight, *to-windward,* but made no attempt to renew the action.

If such is the behaviour of the Americans to their friends the French, we cannot complain of being unjustly dealt with. In the utmost display of their exaggerating talents, the Americans, perhaps, seek less to disparage others, than to exalt themselves; and it ought to be some consolation to us, that "the language of truth is uniform and consistent;" and that "to depart from it safely, requires memory and discretion."

The editor of the "Naval History" cannot describe even the affair of the Leopard and Chesapeake, without his accustomed misrepresentation. After nearly a page of preliminary observations, he says:—"The Chesapeake was altogether in an unprepared state; her guns and decks were lumbered with sails, cables, &c. and her men were not at quarters till the commencement of the attack. No opposition was made. The British commander continued pouring his broadsides into the undefended ship for about thirty minutes; when the Chesapeake having received considerable damage in her hull, rigging, and spars, she struck. She had 3 men killed, and 18 wounded."

Commodore Barron's letter is not noticed by Mr. Clark; although, on other occasions, American official letters are deemed unquestionable authority. It bears date, June 23d, 1807; states the Chesapeake's departure from Hampton roads; and then proceeds, as follows:—"Some time afterwards, we observed one of the two *line-of-battle* ships that lay off Cape Henry, to get under weigh, and stand to sea."—After mentioning the coming up of the Leopard, "one of the two *line-of-battle ships,"* and the interchange of correspondence, the commodore says:—"About this time I observed some appearances of a hostile nature, and said to Captain Gordon, that it was possible they were serious, and requested him to have his men sent to their quarters." Then, after a few excuses about the lumbered state of his ship, he adds: "Consequently, our resistance *was* but feeble. In about twenty minutes, I ordered the colours to be struck."

Here, we see the reason why Mr. Clark rejected this letter. First, the men *were* sent to quarters before the commencement of the attack; secondly, resistance was made; and thirdly, the action *did not* continue "thirty minutes."

Now for the veracity of the commodore himself. Captain Humphreys of the Leopard, in his letter, says,—"At the expiration of *ten* minutes from the first shot being fired," (between which and the second, there was an interval of two or three minutes,) "the pendant and ensign of the Chesapeake were lowered." In another part, he says,—"a few shot were returned, but none struck this ship;"—and, by a letter from one of the Leopard's officers, it appears,—"three broadsides only were fired."

These three broadsides, according to the items in the numerous "surveys" held upon the Chesapeake, lodged twenty two round shot in her hull; irreparably injured the fore and main-masts; badly wounded the mizen-mast; cut away thirteen lower shrouds and stays; shattered the fore-sail, main-sail, main-top-sail, and fore-top-mast stay-sail; injured and rendered unfit for service a spare fore-top-mast, and another spare spar; and damaged two boats.—What a pity the Americans never gave such surveys during the late war!—In addition, as appears by her log-minutes, the Chesapeake had three feet and a half water in the hold.—Three more such broadsides would have sunk her. And yet, the "Naval Monument" jeers us for having done so little injury to the ship.

Although sixty years are now elapsed since British 50-gun ships have been excluded from the line of battle, Commodore Barron found it convenient to make a "line-of-battle ship" of the Leopard, as the French captain, *Lejoielle,* had a 74 of the

Leander; which ship happened (odd enough) to be the other "line-of-battle ship" mentioned in the commodore's letter.

The Leopard's armament, upon the lower and upper-decks, was precisely the same as mounted by other ships of her class; for which see p. 16. Upon her quarter-deck and forecastle, she mounted six carronades, 24-pounders, an 18-pound launch-carronade, and two long 9-pounders; total 53 guns: being six short of her established number. The Leopard had her full complement on board; consisting of 318 men, and 25 boys: she had also on board, as passengers, 10 artillery-men, and 3 midshipmen belonging to some of the ships on the coast.

The Chesapeake mounted, at this time, twenty eight long 18-pounders upon the main-deck, fourteen carronades, 32-pounders, (leaving a vacant port on each side,) upon the quarter-deck; two carronades, 32-pounders, and two long 12-pounders, (leaving three vacant ports on each side,) upon the forecastle; total 46 guns. This was her peace-establishment. Her books bore the names of 440; but, among those, were 25 runnings and discharges: consequently, her actual complement consisted of 415; including 10 boys or lads. There were also several passengers on board, going to the Mediterranean. That the Chesapeake had, at least, five lieutenants, appears by the signature of her "5th lieutenant" to several of the official documents relating to the action. Nine men to every gun in the ship, would be considered as an extraordinary large complement, even in times of war.

Comparative force of the two ships.

		Leopard.		Chesapeake.	
Broadside-metal in pounds,	l. guns	405		264	
	carr.	90		256	
		——	495	——	520
Complement	men,	331		405	
	boys,	25		10	
		——	356	——	415
Size in tons			1044		1135

Many ships may meet at sea, and not be so equally matched as the Leopard and Chesapeake; although the latter *was* a "36-gun frigate," and the former a "50-gun ship:" which again shews the fallacy of the old rating system.

About four years subsequent to this event, the Americans thought fit to retaliate upon us. If a "line-of-battle ship" could attack a frigate, why not a frigate attack a sloop of war? The President therefore engaged the Little Belt; and the Little Belt engaged the President; and manfully too: which, added to a real and a very great disparity of force, constitutes the distinguishing feature between the action of the Little Belt and President, and that of the Leopard and Chesapeake.

A proof of the accuracy and fairness with which the Americans record transactions between themselves and other nations, will be seen in the following extract from a Boston chronological work:—"October 11, 1811, offer of reparation made by the British government, and accepted, respecting the affair between the Little Belt and President."

The "Naval History" details, very fully, the operations before Tripoli, from 1801, to the peace concluded in June, 1805, between the bashaw and the president of the United States. Great credit is due to the officers and seamen belonging to the American ships, for the gallantry displayed on several occasions.

It is fresh in the recollection of many officers of the British navy, how difficult it was, at this period, to keep the seamen from deserting to the Americans. The short peace of 1803 occasioned many of our ships to be paid off; and the nature of the service upon which the Americans were engaged, held forth a strong inducement to the manly feelings of the British tar. It was not to raise his arm against his own countrymen; but against barbarians, whose foul deeds excited indignation in every generous breast.

The Americans cannot deny, that the complements of their ships in the Tripolitan war, consisted chiefly of British seamen; supplied by a Scotch renegado at New York, and by numerous other crimps in the different sea-port towns of the United States: and that those complements were afterwards filled up, by similar means, at Cadiz and other ports of the Mediterranean.—Was not Commodore Preble, on account of being detected in some transaction of this sort, obliged to shorten his stay at Gibraltar, and to fix Syracuse, instead of Malta, for his next rendezvous?

To such as know the facility with which, either in the ships, or on the shores, of the United States, a deserter, or an emigrant, can obtain his naturalization, the term "American" requires an epithet to render it intelligible. In recording the exploits of "Americans," it is but to lop off the qualifying adjunct—"adopted," and every *native* reader feels a hero's blood flowing in his veins. On the other hand, should disgrace be attached to the deed, Mr. Clark, and his brother-writers, anticipating the reader's wishes, seldom fail to state, that the parties were not *American,* but *British* sailors.

CHAPTER IV.

United States of America declare war against Great Britain—Send a squadron in pursuit of the Jamaica-fleet—It falls in with, and chases, the Belvidera—Engagement between that ship and the President—Belvidera escapes—Squadron resumes its course after the convoy—Fails in overtaking it, and returns to Boston—Surprise of the Whiting in Hampton roads—Constitution is chased, and escapes—Capture of the Nautilus—Emulous and Gossamer—Alert attacks the Essex—Is captured—Force of the two vessels—Tar and feathering of a British seaman—Reported challenge from Sir James Lucas Yeo to Captain Porter—Essex and a "British frigate"—Essex and Shannon.

ON the 18th of June, 1812, the United States of America declared war against Great Britain; and orders were immediately dispatched from Washington, for the squadron that had been previously assembled at New York, to put to sea, for the capture or destruction of British vessels; and particularly, in search of a homeward-bound Jamaica-fleet, of eighty five sail, then known to be weakly convoyed, and not far from the American coast.

On the 21st, which was as early as an express could arrive with the orders, sailed this American squadron; consisting of the President, Commodore Rodgers, United States, Commodore Decatur, Congress, Captain Smith, Essex, Captain Porter, Hornet, Lieutenant-commandant Lawrence, and Argus, Lieutenant-commandant Sinclair; mounting, altogether, upwards of 250 guns, and manned with 2000 choice seamen.

The same American brig that gave Commodore Rodgers intelligence (App. No. 6) of the Jamaica-fleet's being so near, had just been boarded by the British frigate Belvidera; whose exact position, therefore, was also pointed out. Chase was instantly made, in full hopes to effect these two important objects; and, on the morning of the 23d, a "large sail" was seen in the N. E. standing to the S. W. This was H. M. S. Belvidera, of 947 tons, mounting 42 guns; namely, twenty six long 18s, fourteen carronades, 32s, and two long 9s; and manned with 230 men and boys; her established number then being 274.

Captain Byron, at first, stood towards the American squadron; but, observing the ships suddenly to take in their studding-sails, and haul up in chase of him, frequently wetting their sails to profit by the lightness of the wind, a suspicion of their hostile intentions caused him to tack, and stand off. By way of assuring the stranger, that they were the ships of a *friendly* power, the Americans hoisted their colours; but their evident anxiety to close had betrayed them, and the Belvidera continued her course.

As the leading ship of the squadron was fast approaching, Captain Byron, to prevent any question about who fired the first shot, ordered the priming to be wiped from every gun in the ship. Soon afterwards, the President fired those three well-directed shot, which occasioned the only loss the Belvidera sustained. (App. No. 5.) The Belvidera's guns were reprimed in an instant; and the fire returned from her four stern-chasers, two long 18s, and two 32-pound carronades; the only guns that would bear, or were fired at all: although the commodore's journal mentions, that the Belvidera fired her "four after main-deck guns on the starboard side." The full details of this interesting chase may be seen in the British and American accounts (Nos. 5. 6. and 7.) in the Appendix.

The fact of "the long bolts, breeching-hooks, and breechings, of guns and carronades, frequently breaking" on board the Belvidera, proves that there was some defect in the mode of securing them. This was not the fault of the officers and men: they every time repaired the accident as quickly as possible. Had the whole of the broadside-guns come into use, a repetition of such an accident would have been a serious evil; as it was, the Belvidera's captain got severely wounded.

The guns of the Belvidera were mostly pointed by her officers; with what precision appears in the commodore's account of the damages which the President sustained. Her loss, exclusive of the 22 by the bursting of the gun, was 6 killed and wounded; making 28 in all. For three days, the ships were employed in repairing the President's damages; a delay that, no doubt, saved the Jamaica-fleet; the loss of which would have been a severe national blow.

The Belvidera's officers insist, that the President could have got alongside several times; but that, just as they were about to fire their broadside, she yawed across their stern, and fired her broadside. This occasioned her to lose way, until she resumed her course; when she gradually advanced to the same spot, and then repeated the same extraordinary manoeuvre.

Comparing the force of the Belvidera, with that of the President, (for which see her name in App. No. 120.) even alone, it is hard to conjecture which party Captain Hull intended to compliment, when, in his letter (App. No. 4.) transmitting the log-extract, he said: I am confident, could the commodore have got alongside the Belvidera, she would have been his in less than *one hour.*"

After quitting the chase of the Belvidera, and repairing the damages sustained by her fire, the American squadron proceeded in search of the convoy. On the 1st of July, a little to the east-ward of Newfoundland-bank, the squadron fell in with a fleet of "cocoa-nut-shells, shaddock-rinds, orange-peels, &c." and the commodore and his officers promised themselves a West-India dessert to their next day's dinner. They longed in vain; and, after being thus tantalized from the 1st to the 13th, they steered for Madeira; thence for the Azores; and finally arrived at Boston on the 29th of August. What encreased the misfortune of the cruize, the scurvy broke out among the men; and conferred additional value upon the limes that were known to be in such profusion on board the Jamaica ships.

To the discretion and promptitude of Captain Byron, on his first falling in with the American squadron; to the skill of the Belvidera's officers and crew in pointing their guns, and working the ship; and to their bravery and perseverance in defending her, during a long and arduous chase, while engaged with a force so greatly superior, is the nation indebted for the little mischief done to British commerce, by a formidable American squadron; possessing the singular advantage of its hostile intentions being wholly unknown.

On the 8th of July, H. M. schooner Whiting, Lieutenant Maxey, from Plymouth, with dispatches for the American government, arrived in Hampton roads, ignorant of the war. As Lieutenant Maxey was proceeding on shore in his boat, the Dash privateer, Captain Garroway, bound on a cruize, got possession of him; and then ran alongside the Whiting; and, having upwards of 80 men in crew, captured her, without opposition. The dispatches had been sunk.

The Whiting was only 75 tons, mounting four carronades, 12-pounders; with a complement of 18 men and boys. Of these, a third were absent in the boat; and those in the schooner had not the least suspicion of being in an enemy's waters.

The Dash mounted one heavy long gun upon a pivot-carriage. This, and a suppression of the principal circumstances, enabled the American editors to state, with some degree of exultation:—"The British schooner mounts four guns, the Dash only one."—The Whiting was afterwards restored.

On the 12th of July, the U. S. ship Constitution, Captain Isaac Hull, sailed from Chesapeake-bay. On the 17th, in a calm, she fell in with H. M. ships, Africa 64, Shannon and Guerriere 46, Belvidera 42, and Æolus 38,* under the orders of Captain Broke, of the Shannon. Two of the frigates, (one the Belvidera,) assisted

* All according to the new rates; which will be observed throughout the work.

by the boats of the squadron, got, for a short time, within gun-shot; but the Constitution, by kedging, and other skilful manoeuvres, effected her escape, after an anxious chase of sixty four hours. The Belvidera's situation, when chased, was far more critical; owing to Captain Byron's ignorance of the war, and his having to sustain the fire of a ship of nearly double his own force.

On the 16th of July, the U. S. brig Nautilus, Lieutenant Crane, of 14 guns, and 106 men, was captured by H. M. S. Shannon, and others. She was afterwards fitted with sixteen 24-pound carronades, and commissioned as a cruizer.

On the 30th of July, the American privateer-brig Gossamer, of 14 guns, and 100 men, surrendered to H. M. brig Emulous, Captain Mulcaster, without firing a shot. This is introduced by way of illustrating the following remark of an American editor:—"Instances of the bold and daring intrepidity of the crews of the private-armed vessels of the United States, are so numerous, that the recital of them would swell the work, &c."

On the 13th of August, 1812, H. M. S. Alert, Captain T. L. P. Laugharne, bore down upon the U. S. frigate Essex, Captain David Porter; mistaking her for a vessel of less force. An action ensued, which continued, the American account says, eight minutes; when the Alert, having seven feet water in the hold, and three men wounded, surrendered. Captain Porter says the Essex sustained no loss. The British official account not having been published, these facts rest wholly on the American statements.

The Alert mounted, according to the American papers announcing her capture, twenty carronades, 18-pounders; and, according to the number paroled out of her, had a complement of 86 men and boys.

Mr. Clark first gives the Alert "20 guns;" but, in a subsequent page, she appears as—"ship Alert, guns mounted 26." And as to her complement, the "Naval Monument," and the "Sketches of the War," have both made it 130. Although Captain Porter could not find room in his letter, to give the force of his prize, either in guns or men, he could, to make the false assertion, that "the Alert was out for the purpose of taking the Hornet."

The Essex, when subsequently captured, mounted twenty four carronades, 32-pounders and two long 12-pounders, upon the main-deck; sixteen carronades, 32-pounders, and four long 12-pounders, upon the quarter-deck and forecastle; total 46 guns: a tolerable armament for a "32-gun frigate."

Captain Porter, in his "Journal of a Cruize," says the Essex had, when lying in the Delaware, in October, 1812, a complement of 328 men; of whom eleven only rated as landsmen.

The Alert was originally a *collier,* named the Oxford, purchased by government in 1804. Whether her original employment were not that for which she was best calculated, may appear from the following fact. The first time the "U. S. ship of war Alert" was trusted at sea, was, after the peace; when, as a store ship, she accompanied the frigate United States to the Mediterranean. The American papers jocosely remarked, that the Alert required every stitch of canvass set, to enable her to keep way with the United States, under her three top-sails. During the war, she remained as *a block-ship* at New York; yet Mr . Clark, to give importance to her capture, says:—"The Alert, upon her return to the United States," from Newfoundland, whither she had been sent by Captain Porter, as a cartel, "was fitted out as a government-vessel."

Along with the dimensions of the Alert and Essex, will be given the Southampton's, because Captain Porter's friends have contrived to connect her, in some degree, with the transactions of the Essex.

Dimensions of the three ships.

	Alert.		Essex.		Southampton.	
	Ft.	In.	Ft.	In.	Ft.	In.
Length of lower-deck from rabbit to rabbit,	105	0	138	7	124	4
Breadth, extreme,	29	4	37	3½	35	0

The Southampton's armament has been fully described at page 12. Her force, for the reasons just given, will appear in the same statement with that of the Essex and Alert.

Dimensions of the three ships.

		Alert.		Essex.		Southampton.	
Broadside-metal in pounds,	l. guns,	0		36		168	
	carr.	180		640		132	
		—	180	—	676	—	300
Complement,	men,	77		325		200	
	boys,	9		3		21	
		—	86	—	328	—	221
Size in tons,			393		867		671

Here is seen the value of the exploit which Captain Porter did perform, as well as of that which he would have performed, had the Essex met, and captured, the Southampton.

Shortly after the declaration of war, Captain Porter ill-used a British subject, for refusing to fight against his country. A New York paper, of June 27, 1812, gives the following account of the transaction:—

"The deposition states, that John Erving was born in Newcastle-upon-Tyne, England; that he has resided within the United States since 1800, and has never been naturalized; that on the 14th of October, 1811, he entered on board the Essex, and joined her at Norfolk; that Captain Porter, on the 25th of June, 1812, caused all hands to be piped on deck, to take the oath of allegiance to the United States, and gave them to understand, that any man who did not choose to do so should be discharged; that when deponent heard his name called, he told the captain, that being a British subject he must refuse taking the oath; on which the captain spoke to the petty officers, and told them they must pass sentence upon him; that they then put him into the petty launch, which lay alongside the frigate, and there poured a bucket of tar over him, and then laid on a quantity of feathers, having first stripped him naked from the waist; that they then rowed him ashore, stern foremost, and landed him. That he wandered about, from street to street, in this condition, until Mr. Ford took him into his shop, to save him from the crowd then beginning to gather; that he staid there until the police-magistrate took him away, and put him in the city-prison for protection, where he was cleansed and clothed. None of the citizens molested or insulted him. He says he had a protection, which he bought of a man in Salem, of the same name and description with himself, for four shillings and sixpence, which he got renewed at the custom-house, Norfolk. He says he gave, as an additional reason to the captain, why he did not choose to fight against his country, that, if he should be taken prisoner, he would certainly be hung."

This, having been copied into other papers, met the eye of Sir James Lucas Yeo, commanding the Southampton, then attached to the Jamaica-station. Persons acquainted with that officer, can judge of his feelings upon reading an account of the ill-treatment of a British sailor. Some expressions, marking his abhorrence of the act, and his contempt for the author, did very likely escape Sir James; and that, in the hearing of some of the American prisoners then on board the Southampton.—Through this channel, which was none of the purest, the words probably became what they appeared in the "Democratic Press," (a Philadelphia paper,) of the 18th of September, 1812. Thus:—"A passenger of the brig Lion, from Havannah to New York, captured by the frigate Southampton, Sir James Yeo, is requested to present his compliments to Captain Porter, commander of the American frigate Essex, would be glad to have *a tête à tête,* any where between the capes Delaware and the Havannah, where he would have the pleasure to break his own sword over his damned head, and put him down forward in irons."

"Captain Porter, of the U. S. frigate Essex, presents his compliments to Sir James Yeo, commanding his B. M. frigate Southampton, and accepts with pleasure his polite invitation. If agreeable to Sir James, Captain Porter would prefer meeting near the Delaware, where Captain P. pledges his honor to Sir James, that no American vessel shall interrupt their *tête à tête*. The Essex may be known by a flag, bearing the motto, "*Free trade and sailors' rights;*" and when this is struck to the Southampton, Captain Porter will deserve the treatment promised by Sir James."

Leaving Captain Porter's *deserts* out of the question, the whole of this farrago has been ascribed to some of the war-party, who wished to give the "gallant captain" an opportunity of publicly testifying his readiness to engage "an equal force." Although no such message was sent by Sir James Yeo, he cruized, for several weeks, along the southern coast of the United States, in hopes of falling in with the Essex, the nature of whose armament was fully known to him. The Southampton was well manned, and all that her officers and crew wanted, was the weather-gage, or an opportunity of getting on board the American, early in the action.

Captain Porter being a great favorite at Washington, Mr. Clark could do no less than give insertion to any little tale he might wish to see recorded in the "Naval History" of his country. One of them is as follows:—

"On the 30th of August, the Essex being in lat. 36° N. long. 62° W. a British frigate was discovered standing towards her, under a press of sail. Porter stood for her under easy sail, with his ship prepared for action; and, apprehensive that she might not find the Essex during the night, he hoisted a light. At 9, the British vessel made a signal: it consisted of two flashes, and a blue light. She was then, apparently, about four miles distant. Porter stood for the point where she was seen until midnight, when, perceiving nothing of her, he concluded it would be best to heave-to for her until morning, concluding she had done the same; but, to his great surprise, and the mortification of his officers and crew, she was no longer in sight. Captain Porter thought it to be not unlikely that this vessel was the Acasta, of 50 guns, sent out, accompanied by the Ringdove, of 22, to cruize for the Essex."

It did not, perhaps, occur to Mr. Clark, that ships usually carry log-books, in which are entered every day's proceedings, with the latitude, longitude, &c.; and that these can, at any time, be referred to, in case the false assertions of any historian, or paragraph-writer, may be worth the trouble of disproving.

Considering what a formidable man Captain Porter was, nothing less than the "Acasta, of 50 guns," and "Ringdove, of 22," could be "sent out to cruize for the Essex." Unfortunately for her commander's fame, on the 30th of August, 1812, the day mentioned, the Acasta was cruizing in lat. 43° N. long. 65° 16′ W.; and the Ringdove lying at single anchor in St. Thomas's. Was not the "British frigate," the Rattler, of 16 guns?

The next occasion upon which Captain Porter was baulked of a battle, is recorded thus:—

"On the 4th of September, the Essex being off the tail of St. George's bank, two ships of war were discovered to the southward, and a brig to the northward. The brig was in chase of an American merchant-ship. Porter immediately chased the brig, which attempted to pass, and join the rest of the squadron.

This he prevented, and compelled her to stand to the northward. He continued in chase of her, until a-breast of the American ship; when, the wind becoming light, she escaped by means of her sweeps. On shewing American colours, several signal-guns were fired by the ships to the southward. All sail was made by them in chase. At 4 P.M. they had gained the wake of the Essex, and were coming up with her very fast. Calculating on making his escape by some manœuvre, during the night, he fired a gun to-windward. The two ships still continued to gain on the Essex. The largest was considerably to-windward of the other, and about five miles a-stern of the Essex. Captain Porter determined to heave about, as soon as it grew dark; and, in case he should not be able to pass her, he determined to fire a broadside into her, and lay her on board. Every preparation was made for this purpose. The crew, as soon as the plan was proposed to them, gave three cheers, and were in high spirits. At 20 minutes after 7, the Essex hove about, and stood S. E. by S. until 30 minutes after 8, when she bore away S.W. without seeing any thing more of them. This was the more extraordinary, as a pistol was fired on board the Essex when nearest to them. The Essex arrived safe in the Delaware a few days afterwards." (Nav. Hist. vol. i, p. 180.)

The same event finds a place in the "Sketches of the War." There the port, from which Captain Porter was "cut off by the two large ships of war," is mentioned to have been New York. The intention to lay one of the British ships on board is deservedly noticed; and, it is added, that the Essex effected her escape into the bay of Delaware, "without the loss of a man."

One of the above "two ships of war" was the Shannon, Captain Broke; the other the Planter, a re-captured West Indiaman, her prize, and by no means a vessel to be mistaken for a "ship of war." But the best way to expose the Essex, and her *gallant* commander, will be, to detail the occurrence in the very words of one of the Shannon's officers.

"At noon, on the 4th of September, 1812, in lat. 39° 11′ N. long. 70° 22′ W. the Shannon had in company the re-captured ship Planter, when we saw a warlike-looking ship to the eastward, and chased towards her under all sail before the wind; but it headed us flat a-back. We observed a merchant-ship close to the chase, as if in the act of speaking. The two ships then, having a fresh breeze aft, came down upon us, the merchantman close a-stern of the ship of war; which, at 4. 30. P.M. then about 10 or 12 miles distant, hauled up, and made private signals; too far to be comprehended, had she been a friend. The strange ship then made every exertion to escape, leaving her merchant-ship behind, as we did our's; and having found, by keeping her wind some time, that she sailed nearly equal to us, she slanted off free, a point or two, so as to bring us into her wake, without allowing us to gain upon her in distance, or but very slightly. Her object appeared to be, to get in between us and the land. On our losing sight of her at dark, she was still above 10 miles off. Being well aware that she would alter her course in the dark, and seeing her good sailing, there appeared no chance of getting hold of her; and her merchant-ship being now near us, we tacked and seized her, intending to burn her directly, that the fugitive ship might see the flames; but it became so dark and squally, that Captain Broke would not risk the boats in getting out her people; consequently the ship was not burnt till next morning. She was a light American ship, from Cadiz, named the Minerva; and her people informed us, that the ship we had been chasing was the U. S. frigate Essex, Captain Porter, whom they had spoken the same day. During the night the ships lay-to; and, to prevent separation, each kept bright lights up, and several blue-lights were burnt."

One of Mr. Clark's good-natured critics describes the object of such a work as his to be to—"commemorate the glories of the American age and nation; to place some of its most illustrious heroes out of the reach of oblivion; and to consecrate their actions to imperishable fame." (N. Hist. vol. i. p. 1.)!!!

CHAPTER V.

Inactive state of the British navy since the battle of Trafalgar—Its effects upon the officers and men—Polishing system reprobated—Scarcity of oak-timber and seamen—Contract-ships—Impressed crews—Foreigners and ineffective hands—American navy considered—Their ships easily manned—Practical gunnery—American marines—Opposite feelings of British and American officers towards each other—Guerriere falls in with, and engages the Constitution—Details of the action—Guerriere surrenders—her damage—Final destruction—Loss of men—Constitution's damage—Loss—Force of each ship particularized—Statement of comparative force—Remarks thereon—British and American frigates—Their comparative dimensions and force—The latter compared in force with other classes of British ships—French frigates—Concluding remarks.

FROM the battle of Trafalgar to the peace of 1815, three-fourths of the British navy, at sea, were constantly employed in blockading the fleets of their enemies. Of the remainder, such as escaped the dull business of convoying, cruized about; but the only hostile ships that in general crossed their tracks, were disguised neutrals; from whom no hard knocks could be expected. Once a year or so, the capture of a French frigate by a British one, gave a momentary fillip to the service.

A succession of insipid cruizes necessarily begat, among both officers and men, habits of inattention. The situation of gunner on board our ships, became almost a sinecure. A twenty years' war, of itself, was sufficient to wear out the strength of our seamen; but a laxity of discipline, in all the essentials of a man-of-war's-man, produced a much more sensible effect.

Instead of the sturdy occupation of handling the ship's guns, now seldom used but on salutes, the men were taught to polish the traversing-bars, elevating-screws, copper on the bits, &c. by way of ornament to the quarter-deck. Such of the crew as escaped this menial office, (from the unnecessary wear it occasions, lately forbidden by an order of the board of admiralty,) were set to reeving and unreeving the top-sails, against time, preparatory to a match with any other of his majesty's ships that might happen to fall in company.

Many were the noble exceptions to this, and many were the commanders who, despising what was either finical or useless, and still hoping to signalize themselves by some gallant exploit, spared no pains, consistent with their limited means, and the restraints of the service, to have their ships, at all times, as men of war should be, in *boxing trim*.

As Napoleon extended his sway over the European continent, the British navy, that perpetual blight upon his hopes, required to be extended also. British oak, and British seamen, alike scarce, contract-ships were hastily built up, with soft wood and light frames; and then, manned with an impressed crew, chiefly of raw hands and small boys, sent forth to assert the rights, and maintain the character of Britons, upon the ocean. In June, 1812, when the war with America commenced, the British navy consisted of 746 ships, in commission. Had these been cleared of all the foreigners and ineffective hands, how many ships would the remainder have properly manned?

To the long duration of the war, and the rapid encrease of the navy, may be added a third cause of the scarcity of seamen: the enormous encrease of the army. In December, 1812, we had, in regulars alone, 229,149 men. How many frigates could have been manned, and well manned too, by draughts from the light dragoons, and the light infantry regiments? Nor is there a question,—so inviting were the bounties,—that *prime seamen* have enlisted in both.

The crews of our ships experienced a fourth reduction in strength, by the establishment, about six years ago, of the battalion-marines: a corps embodied for the purpose of acting on shore, in conjunction with the seamen and marines of the ships. The battalion-marines, about 2000 in number, consisted of the *pick* of the royal marines; which accordingly became reduced to weak, under-sized men, and very young recruits. Marines ought to be among the stoutest men in the ship; because, until engaged in close action, their station is at the guns; where great physical strength is required. Except on a few occasions in Canada, and the Chesapeake, the battalion-marines, although as fine a body of men as any in the two services, have remained comparatively idle.

The canker-worm that, in the shape of neglect, had so long been preying upon the vitals of the British navy, could not exist among the few ships composing the navy of the United States. America's half a dozen frigates claimed the whole of her attention. These she had constructed upon the most approved principles, both for sailing, and for war. Considering that the ramparts of a battery should have, for one object, the shelter of the men stationed at it, she had built up the sides of her ships in the most compact manner; and the utmost ingenuity had been exerted, and expense bestowed, in their final equipment.

With respect to seamen, America had, for many years previous to the war, been decoying the men from our ships, by every artful stratagem. The best of these were rated as petty-officers. Many British seamen had entered on board American merchant-vessels; and the numerous non-intercourse and embargo bills, in existence at different periods, during the four years preceding the war, threw many merchant-sailors out of employment. So that the U. S. ships of war, in their preparations for active warfare, had to pick their complements from a numerous body of seamen.

Highly to the credit of the naval administration of the United States the men were taught the practical rules of gunnery; and ten shot, with the necessary powder, were allowed to be expended in play, to make one hit in earnest.

Very distinct from the American seamen, so called, are the American marines. They are chiefly made up of natives of the country; and a deserter from the British would here be no acquisition. In the United States, every man may hunt or shoot among the wild animals of the forest. The young peasant, or *back-woodman,* carries a rifled-barrel gun, the moment he can lift one to his shoulder; and woe to the duck or deer that attempts to pass him, within fair range of his piece. To collect these expert marksmen, when of a proper age, officers are sent into the western parts of the Union; and to embody and finish drilling them, a marine-barrack is established near the city of Washington: from which depôt, the ships are regularly supplied.

No one act of the little navy of the United States, had been at all calculated to gain the respect of the British. First, was seen the Chesapeake allowing herself to be beaten, with impunity, by a British ship, only nominally superior to her. Then, the huge frigate President attacks, and fights for nearly three quarters of an hour, the British sloop Little Belt. And, even since the war, the same President, at the head of a squadron, makes a bungling business of chasing the Belvidera.

While, therefore, a feeling towards America, bordering on contempt, had unhappily possessed the mind of the British naval officer, rendering him more than usually careless and opiniative, the American naval officer, having been taught to regard his new foe with a portion of dread, sailed forth to meet him, with the whole of his energies roused. A moment's reflection assured him, that his country's honour was now in his hands; and what, in the breast of man, could be a stronger incitement to extraordinary exertions?

Thus situated were the navies of the two countries, when H. M. S. Guerriere, with damaged masts, a reduced complement, and in absolute need of that thorough refit, for which she was then, after a very long cruize, speeding to Halifax, encountered the U. S. ship Constitution, seventeen days only from port, manned with a full complement; and, in all respects, fitted for war.

An action ensued, the full details of which are given in the different official papers to be found in the Appendix. (Nos. 8. 9. 10. 11. and 12.) Captain Dacres says, the Constitution commenced returning his fire "at twenty minutes past four;" the American "Particulars" say, "at twenty minutes past five;" and that the Constitution from that time "continued to fire occasionally," until she closed the Guerriere "at five minutes past six." Captain Hull says:—"At five minutes before six P. M. being alongside, within pistol-shot, we *commenced* a heavy fire from all our guns;"—and he has had art enough to compute the duration of the action from that time. Were his long 24-pounders, which, during the preceding thirty five minutes, he "continued to fire occasionally at the Guerriere," loaded with blank-cartridge? Why, if the American commander had no desire to keep at long shot until he had disabled his opponet, did he not bear down sooner; he had the weather-gage?

The early fall of the Guerriere's mizen-mast brought the ship up in the wind, and exposed her to a dreadful raking fire, as well as to the riflemen in the Constitution's tops, who levelled their pieces, with full effect, at the Guerriere's officers and men.—It may be necessary to explain how the loss of the mizen-mast could bring the ship up in the wind. The wreck of the mast hung over the weather-side; the top, from its position, acting as a complete backwater, so as to bring the ship's head up to the wind, in spite of every effort of the helmsman. By those acquainted with the peculiar construction of French-built ships, about the *fore-foot* especially, this will be readily understood.

Upon the Guerriere's bowsprit getting foul of the Constitution's larboard quarter, the Americans attempted to board, but were driven back; and it was not till after the two ships had got clear, and some of the Guerriere's bow-guns were brought to bear, that the fore and main-masts fell over the side. Yet the "Particulars," rather than state what might shew, that the Constitution's men were afraid to board the Guerriere, say thus:—"We prepared to board, but immediately after, his fore and main-masts went by the board, and it was deemed unnecessary." The "Sketches of the War" explains this by stating, that the American lieutenant of marines who headed the party, was killed by a musket-shot. Captain Hull is silent about the boarding; but, in stating that the Constitution "ceased firing" upon the falling of the Guerriere's fore and main-masts, tacitly admits, that the two ships were, at that moment, clear of each other; and consequently, that the boarding-opportunity had already passed. The American crew therefore, were not restrained from boarding, because,—owing to the falling of the Guerriere's fore and main-masts, "it was deemed unnecessary."—They made the attempt, and were repulsed, with the loss of their boarding-officer.

Several of the Guerriere's guns and carronades broke loose, owing to rotten breechings, as well as the rotten state of the timbers, through which the long-bolts passed. The Guerriere had suffered so much from bad weather, and cruized so long without renewing her stores, that there was no rope left, wherewith to repair the loss of breechings. Those of the guns and carronades that escaped breaking loose, were completely disabled by the fall of the fore and main-masts. The Guerriere, now a complete wreck, was rolling her main-deck guns in the water, when, "at 6. 45." by the British account, the jack was lowered from the stump of the mizen-mast; and, at seven o'clock, the Constitution took possession of her prize.

Taking the mean of the two accounts, as to the time when the Guerriere commenced firing, the duration of the action was two hours and twelve minutes. Yet Mr. Clark, putting his own construction upon the obscure paragraph in Captain Hull's letter,—"so that, in thirty minutes after we got fairly alongside the enemy, she surrendered,"—informs his readers, that the Guerriere was captured "after a very short action."

Among other passages in Captain's Hull's letter, which are not very clear, may be noticed the following: "But, on our coming within gun-shot, she gave us a broadside, and filled away, and wore, giving us a broadside on the other tack, but without effect, her shot falling short."—This can only be explained by the circumstance of the Guerriere's powder being much deteriorated by damp and long-keeping. Robins says the action of damp powder is diminished, "according to the degree of moisture with which it is impregnated;" and that powder, to produce its proper effect, must be "in good condition at the time of using." Some very late experiments have also shewn, that the powder used by our ships in general will not project a shot, by any means so far as powder taken out of Walker's patent-barrels. That the Constitution's powder was of the very best sort, and in the most perfect state, the pains taken in her equipment, and her recent departure from a home-port, place beyond a doubt. Having also 24-pounders opposed to 18s, "within gun-shot" to her, might have been a trifle "out of gunshot" to the Guerriere.

The Guerriere was greatly shattered in her hull; so much so, that, in spite of all the efforts of the Americans, she, at day-light on the morning succeeding the action, was in a sinking condition. The people were removed from her, as quickly as possible; and, at a quarter past three in the afternoon, the Guerriere blew up: an irrefragable proof, that Captain Dacres, his officers and crew, had defended her to the last extremity.

The Guerriere's fore-mast fell from the Constitution's shot; aided perhaps by the absence of most of the shrouds on one side. It was not, altogether, Captain Hull's "round and grape," that led to its fall; but a brass swivel, fired from one of the Constitution's forecastle guns. The main-mast had been struck by lightning some months previous to the action; and fell by the mere weight of the fore-mast. It was comparatively uninjured by shot; but, as seen by the crews of both ships, was perfectly rotten in the centre. When it is added, that the bow-sprit had long been sprung, it will not be too much to say, that the Guerriere, at the time she engaged the Constitution, was, if not crippled, defective at least, in her masts and rigging.

The Guerriere's loss in the action was severe. One lieutenant out of two, and 14 men, were killed; 17 men, dangerously, her commander, master, two mates, and 15 men, severely, and the first lieutenant, a midshipman, 15 men and one boy, slightly wounded; total, killed and wounded, 78. About six died of their wounds. Mr. Clark has made no scruple of placing opposite to the Guerriere's name, British loss, 105;" including, perhaps, the "missing" at the end of Captain Hull's letter. As if to put the matter beyond a doubt, he has also taken care to have represented, in the brilliant view of the action forming the frontispiece to his work, several men struggling upon the Guerriere's spars, as they float in the water; although not a man was on either of her masts, when they fell, or was lost in any other way than by the fire of the Constitution.

Captain Hull mentions, in his letter, having sent a "report of the damages" sustained by the Constitution; but his government has not thought fit to publish it. The "Particulars" admit that the cabin had taken fire from the Guerriere's shot; and the "Sketches of the War," that the Constitution "had some spars shot away." Captain Dacres states, that the Constitution's stern was much shattered, and her lower-masts badly wounded. At all events, the moment the Guerriere blew up, Captain Hull, instead of continuing his cruize, bent his course for Boston; where the Constitution arrived on the 30th of August.

The Americans acknowledge a loss of only 7 killed, and 7 wounded; yet several of the Guerriere's officers counted 13 wounded; of whom 3 died after amputation. Captain Dacres computes the Constitution's killed and wounded at about 20. An equal number of killed and wounded, as expressed in Captain Hull's list, scarcely ever occurs; except in cases of explosion. In our service, every wounded man, although merely scratched, reports himself to the surgeon, that he may get his *smart-money*, a pecuniary allowance so named. No such regulation exists in the American service; consequently, their returns of loss in action, are made subservient to the views of the commander and his government.

The Guerriere's established armament consisted of twenty-eight long 18-pounders upon the main-deck; sixteen carronades, 32-pounders, a 12-pound launch-carronade, and two long 9-pounders, upon the quarter-deck and fore-castle; total 47 guns. The Guerriere, like most French ships, sailed very much by the head; and, to assist in giving her that trim, as well as to obviate the inconvenience of a round-house which intervened between the foremost and bridle ports on each side, and prevented the gun stationed at the former port from being shifted to the latter, when required to be used in chase, two additional 18-pounders, as standing-bow-chase guns, were taken on board at Halifax. These guns, not acting upon the broadside, will not be estimated as part of the broadside-force; nor will the launch-carronade, because, owing to its own defects, or the want of some of its appendages, no use whatever was made of it. When Captain Skene had the Guerriere, he had ports fitted upon her quarter-deck for two brass 12-pounders, given to him by the Duke of Manchester. Upon quitting the Guerriere, Captain Skene, of course, took with him his brass guns. The vacant ports led some of the Constitution's officers to suspect, that the Guerriere's people had, between the time of surrender and of taking possession, thrown two of her guns overboard.

It is singular that Captain Hull's letter does not mention the force of the Guerriere. The "Particulars" state, plainly enough,—"mounting 49 carriage-guns;"—but that was not in the official letter. The people, therefore, had a right to indulge their imaginations on the subject; bearing in mind, no doubt, that the commander of their frigate Constitution, whose size and force they well knew, had spoken of—"so fine a ship as the Guerriere." Had the citizens, in general, given the Guerriere 60 guns, little surprise would have been created; but what shall we say to "the senate and house of representatives of the United States of America, in congress assembled," passing a resolution, expressing, that the Constitution of "44 guns," had succeeded "in attacking, vanquishing, and capturing, the British frigate Guerriere, mounting 54 carriage-guns"?—The honorable mover of this flaming resolution prefaces it with,—"Far, very far, be it from me to boast";—and then gravely assures the house, that the facts stated in the resolution have been ascertained at the proper department, and the proofs are on the table"!!

Of men and boys, the Guerriere had, originally belonging to her, 302. The purser's steward (whose business it is to serve out the rations of the ship) declares, that Lieutenant Pullman, a lieutenant of marines, three midshipmen, and 33 seamen and marines, were absent from the ship in prizes; that the Guerriere victualled, on the morning of the action, exclusive of four or five women, and some prisoners, 264; that seven of these were Americans who had been in the ship some years; that Captain Dacres (highly to his credit) gave orders that they should go below; that they all did so, except one, stationed forward, who, not having heard the word pass, remained at his quarters; that 19 of the crew were boys; most of them very young.

This account allows the Guerriere to have had at quarters, 239 officers and men, and 19 boys; but, as Captain Dacres has stated the absent men at 24, and the number of men at quarters at 244, his account will be deemed the most correct. Captain Hull prefers the number on the "quarter-bill"; and the "Particulars," without any ceremony, state,—"manned with 302 men."

The Constitution's officers used every art to inveigle the Guerriere's men into their service. Sixteen or eighteen, Americans and other foreigners, and about eight British, who had been pressed in their way out to the United States, remained at Boston, when the cartel sailed. Most of the former, and two of the latter, had previously entered on board the Constitution. With the above exception, the Guerriere's surviving crew, and a fine set of men they were, returned to Halifax N. S. Several of them passed into the Shannon; where they found ample relief for their wounded pride, in the subsequent achievement of that ship.

Captain Dacres, in his official letter, says: "I feel it my duty to state, that the conduct of Captain Hull and his officers to our men, has been that of a brave enemy; the greatest care being taken to prevent our men losing the smallest trifle."—Unfortunately, Captain Dacres had made this declaration before he discovered the insidious attempts of the American officers upon his men; or that, when the latter, on removing from the Constitution, called for their bags, they were delivered up, nearly emptied of their contents.

The armament of the Constitution consisted of thirty long 24-pounders upon the main-deck, twenty four carronades, 32-pounders, and two long English 18s, bored to carry a 24-pound shot, (and therefore considered as 24s,) upon the quarter-deck and forecastle; total 56 guns. Except as to the improvement in the 18-pounders, this account of the Constitution's force is confirmed by the editor of the "Naval History," as will be seen presently. The Constitution had eight ports of a side upon her quarter-deck, a gangway-port, fitted to receive a shifting long gun or carronade, and five ports of a side upon her forecastle. Between the quarter-deck and forecastle, were breeching-rings and bolts, calculated for four guns of a side; if necessary to mount them: which guns, by the accounts of her officers, she mounted, when employed in the Mediterranean.

Although the Constitution did not, like the President and United States, carry guns in her tops, a deliberate contrivance for destruction was resorted to, of which many were the victims on board the Guerriere. Seven men were stationed in each top; six of whom were employed in loading for him that was the best marksman. Captain Dacres was wounded in the back by one of these riflemen; and, had the ball passed half an inch more in front, he, too, would have been numbered among the dead.

The employment of rifled-barrel pieces in naval warfare, is certainly a great improvement. We use them in the army, but not in the navy. Robins, speaking of rifles, says:—"The exactness to which those who are dexterous in the use of these pieces, attain, is indeed wonderful; and that, at such distances, that if the bullets were fired from the common pieces, in which the customary aberration takes place, not one in twenty of them could ever be traced."

The Constitution's complement, when she sailed from Boston on the 2d of August, was about 476. On the 17th, Captain Hull re-captured, from the Avenger sloop of war, the American brig Adeline; on board of which he placed a prize-master, and, it is understood, seven men. This leaves 468; the number stated by her own purser's steward to have been victualled, exclusive of a few prisoners, on the morning of the action. Among them, scarcely one was to be seen that would rate as a boy in the British service; yet three boys will be allowed. A great many of the Constitution's crew were recognized by Captain Dacres as British seamen, principally Irishmen. The Guerriere's people found among them several old acquaintances and shipmates. One fellow, who, after the action, was sitting under the half-deck, busily employed in making buck-shot cartridges to mangle his honorable countrymen, had served under the first lieutenant. He now went by a new name; but, on seeing his old commanding officer standing before him, a glow of shame overspread his countenance. Were it possible that the Constitution's ship's company could, at this time, have been inspected by the officers of the British navy, generally, how many, besides the commissioned officers and the riflemen, would have proved to be *native* Americans?

The Guerriere was captured from the French on the 19th of July, 1806, by the Blanche, Captain Lavie. The following was the force of the two ships:—Guerriere, twenty-eight long 18-pounders, and two 68-pound carronades (in the bridle-ports, and therefore of no use in the broadside,) upon the main-deck, ten long 9-pounders, and ten carronades, 32-pounders, upon the quarter-deck and forecastle; total 50 guns. Broadside-weight of metal, (allowing for difference between French and English caliber,) 514 lbs.; complement of men and boys, in action, 317; size in tons, 1084.—Blanche, twenty-eight long 18-pounders upon the main-deck, ten long 9-pounders, and eight carronades, 32-pounders, upon the quarter-deck and forecastle; total, 46 guns. Broadside-weight of metal 425 lbs.; complement of men and boys, in action, 244; size in tons, 1036.—This is introduced, merely in answer to several statements of the Americans, to the effect, that the Guerriere, when captured from the French, was of much greater force than we admitted her to be, when she was captured by the Constitution.

The Constitution was built at Boston, and launched on the 21st of October, 1797. She cost 302,718 dollars, 84 cents; or, 68,111*l.* 14*s.* sterling. Her full dimensions, in hull, spars, and sails, were found in a small M.S. memorandum-book, taken out of the Chesapeake frigate. In proof of its correctness, the dimensions of the President and Chesapeake, as there also given, agree exactly with the measurements since taken of those ships. The only apparent difference, except a trifle in the height of decks, between the dimensions of the Constitution, and of the President, appears in the "length of gun-deck;" which, in the former, is stated at "175 feet," in the latter "174 feet, 10½ inches:" a difference, in fact, not worth noticing. Mr. Clarke states the "gun-deck" of the three "American 44-gun ships," to be "about 176 feet;" and, it is understood, they are all as nearly of one size, though differing somewhat in model, as their builders could make them. The Constitution having the same "keel for tonnage," and breadth of beam" as the President, (see p. 10,) her tonnage, both American and English, must be the same.

Dimensions of the two ships.

		Guerriere.		Constitution.	
		Ft.	In.	Ft.	In.
Length of lower-deck, from aft-part of rabbit of stem to fore part of rabbit of stern-post		155	9	173	3
Breadth, extreme,		39	9	44	4
Main-mast,	length,	92	0	104	0
	diameter,	2	3½	3	5
Main-yard,	length,	81	6	95	0
	diameter,	1	7½	1	9

The Guerriere's spars are taken from those served out to the largest frigates of her class: the Constitution's, partly from the assertions of her own, and partly from the observations of British officers. Her main-mast was 2 feet 10 or 11 inches, in diameter, at the partners; but it had four quarter-fishes, each 3½ inches thick, reaching from a little above the main-deck to the top; hooped on after the mast was made: of course, adding to its strength, as well as bulk. The reader, therefore, may well conceive what impression the Guerriere's shot could make upon her opponent's masts.

Between French ships built in the Mediterranean, and in the ports of the Channel, there is nearly as much difference as between our oak and fir-built ships. The Guerriere was built at l'Orient, upon a sudden emergency; and therefore hastily run up, with half-seasoned wood. Her timbers were, at last, in so decayed a state, that, had the Constitution succeeded in towing her into Boston, she would not have been worth the cost of repairing.

By "a fine ship" is meant, a ship possessing some extraordinary qualification, either of size or force, or of both. "Fine" is not an absolute, but a relative term. How, then, are we to judge of the officer who, sitting in the cabin of, truly, so fine a ship as the Constitution, writes home to his government, that, with that ship under his command, he has captured—"*so fine a ship* as the Guerriere?"—Had the Guerriere captured the Constitution, then, indeed, the expression would have been correct; nor could Captain Dacres well have said more.

Comparative force of the two ships.

		Guerriere.		Constitution.	
Broadside-metal in pounds	l. guns,	261		384	
	carr.	256		384	
		—	517	—	768
Complement,	men,	244		465	
	boys,	19		3	
		—	263	—	468
Size in tons,			1084		1533

Three to *two* in weight of metal and size, and nearly double in men! A reasonable man would, at least, have divided his praises between the stronger party, which had conquered, and the weaker party, which had so bravely resisted. Not so the Americans; yet, from the excuses they make, when *their* ships are captured, it is evident they do not deny the principle.

"When we say to an American,—"Our frigates and your's are not a match."—He, very properly replies,—"You did not think so once." But what does this amount to?—Admitting we knew the force of the American 44-gun frigates, before the Guerriere's action, (which was only partially the case,) and yet considered that our 38-gun frigates were able to fight them, all that can be said is,—we are now convinced, that an American and a British ship, in relative force as *three* to *two,* are not equally matched. The facts are the same: it is the opinion only that has changed. Man the Constitution with 470 Turks, or Algerines; and even then, she would hardly be pronounced, now that her force is known, a match for the Guerriere. The truth is, the name *frigate* had imposed upon the public; and to that, and that only, must be attributed, the angry repinings of many of the British journalists, at the capture of the Guerriere. They, sitting safe at their desks, would have sent her, and every soul on board, to the bottom, with colours flying; because her antagonist was—"a frigate": whereas, had the Constitution been called "a 50-gun ship," a defence only half as honorable as the Guerriere's was, would have gained for her officers and crew universal applause.

Captain Hull, and the officers and crew of the Constitution, deserve much credit for what they *did* do; first, for attacking a British frigate at all; and next, for conquering one, a third inferior in force. It was not for them to reject the reward presented by the "senate and house of representatives," because it expressed to be, for capturing a ship, "mounting 54 carriage-guns"; when, in reality, she only mounted, at most, 49. They, no doubt, smiled at the credulity of the donors; and, without disputing the terms, pocketted the dollars. But are we to sit still, and hear our gallant seamen libelled, because it may suit the Americans to invent any falsehoods, no matter how flagrant, to force a valiant character upon themselves?—Let him, who thinks so, pack himself off to the United States, and there join in defaming his countrymen.

The editor of the "Naval History," who, seemingly, delights in mysterious language, says thus of the Guerriere's capture:—"It has manifested the genuine worth of the American tar; and that the vigorous co-operation of the country is all he requires, to enable him to meet, even under disadvantageous circumstances, and to derive glory from the encounter with, the naval heroes of a nation which has so long ruled the waves." In the midst of all this flummery, how came Mr. Clark to stumble upon "disadvantageous circumstances"? On which side were they?

The Americans had reason, indeed, to exult at the capture of a British frigate. When, too, it is known that, at the time of the Little Belt's affair, that ship and the Guerriere belonged to one station, and were actually seeking each other; and that the Guerriere's officers, by language of defiance, and otherwise, subsequently made themselves extremely obnoxious to the Americans, the reader will readily conceive, that no frigate in the navy could have been so desirable a trophy as the one they did take.

There is no question, that our vanity received a wound in the loss of the Guerriere. But, poignant as were the national feelings, reflecting men hailed the 19th of August, 1812, as the commencement of an era of renovation to the navy of England. Through such a mass of ships, however, the progress of amendment would necessarily be slow. A real scarcity of seamen retarded the operation; and, unfortunately, the class of ships, the least interested in preparations to meet the Americans, had the first pick of the men. So that, even at the conclusion of peace with the United States, not more than half our frigates had improved, in men, gunnery, or appointments; and as to our 18-gun brigs, it would have taken another three years' war, to render them as effective, as their implied force, the character of the officers, and the lives of the men, imperiously demanded.

An author, whose book, says one of his critics, "owes nothing to fiction, nothing to artful disposition of drapery, to affected attitude, or to gaudy, over-heightened colouring, but is all matter of authentic history,"—has subjoined to his account of the Guerriere's action, a dissertation upon the comparative force of the old British 38, (now 46,), and the American 44-gun ships. As it may be no less amusing than instructive to learn, by what species of logic the Americans have persuaded themselves, and would persuade the world, that the force of "the American 44-gun frigates and of the British 38s, is very nearly equal," Mr. Clark's highly-applauded arguments upon the subject are here given in his own words:

"Much having been said on the disparity of force between the American 44-gun frigates and the British 38, the rates of the Constitution and Guerriere, it will, perhaps, not be out of place here, to give a comparative view of the force of each. Both the American 44-gun ships and the British 38-gun ships are constructed on the same principles, and their guns are placed in the same relative position, forming batteries of a similar nature. The guns in each ship are placed on the main or gun-deck, the quarter-deck, and the forecastle. The gun-deck, which may be considered as the line of defence, is about 176 feet long in the American 44-gun ships, and about 160 feet in the English 38-gun ships. The line of defence, therefore, in the American 44-gun ships, exceeds the English by about 16 feet. But, it is to be observed, that the length of the line of defence by no means implies strength. This essentially consists in the number of guns that can be placed in battery, with advantage in a given line, and the strength of the ramparts and parapets, in which light the sides of the ship may be considered. A line of defence of 200 feet, mounting 30 guns in battery, would be about one-fourth weaker, and produce an effect one-fourth less, than a line of defence of 150 feet long, mounting the same number of guns, The American 44-gun ships mount thirty 24-pounders on the gun-deck, twenty four 32-pounder carronades, and two 18-pounders, on their quarter-deck and fore-castle, or upper decks. The British 38-gun ships mount twenty eight 18-pounders on their gun-deck, eighteen 32-pound carronades, and two 18-pounders, on their quarter-deck and forecastle, besides a 24-pounder shifting gun. In an engagement between ship and ship, the effect produced is by the broadside, or the number of guns placed in battery on one side of the ship; so that only half the number of guns in a ship can be considered as placed in battery, in its length or line of defence. The number of guns, therefore, of the American 44-gun ships, placed in battery in its line of defence, of 176 feet, will be 28. The number of guns in the English 38-gun ships, placed in battery in its line of defence, of 160 feet, will be 24; but, as they carry a shifting gun, which may be placed in battery on either side, the number will actually be 25; so that the number of guns in battery in the American 44-gun ships, will exceed those in the English 38-gun ships only one-tenth. But the American line of defence is one-tenth longer, and consequently would be one-tenth weaker than the English, if it had only the same number of guns in battery; consequently, the force of each, when the line of defence, and number of guns placed in battery are considered, is very nearly equal.

"The American 44-gun ships carry 24-pounders on their gun-decks; the English, 18-pounders. But, are not 18-pounders of sufficient weight of metal for the service of large frigates, and fully calculated to produce every effect that may be required in an engagement between frigates?—It has, moreover, been asserted by the officers of the Constitution, that the shot of the Java's 18-pounders were only three pounds lighter than those of the American 24-pounders, after accurately weighing them both;

so that, consequently, the difference in weight of metal was only one-eighth.

"It has been asserted in the British newspapers, that the American frigates were 74s in disguise. It has also been asserted by an English naval commander, in his official letter, that the American 44-gun ships were built with the scantling of a 74. If, by this assertion, he meant to insinuate that the American 44-gun ships were of the same nature with a 74, or ships of the line, he has manifested an extreme want of candor, or want of professional knowledge. 74-gun ships are all of the line; that is, they have guns mounted on two gun-decks, extending the whole length of the ship, or its line of defence, besides those on the quarter-deck and forecastle; and, in addition to these, there are guns on the poop. The length of the line of a 74 is about the same as that of the American 44-gun ship. A 74-gun ship mounts about 88 guns; consequently, the number of guns placed in battery in her line of defence, will be 44 guns; and, in the American frigate of 44 guns, only 28 in the same line of defence; consequently, the strength of the line of defence of a 74, is not very far from double that of an American 44-gun ship, considered in respect of the number of guns, without taking into consideration the difference in weight of metal, and the compactness and strength of sides.

"This, we believe, sufficiently demonstrates the illiberality and absurdity of comparing the American 44-gun frigates to British 74s, with a view to disparage the rising glory of the American navy, and to depreciate the noble exploits of her gallant tars."

Although this elaborate performance purports to have been drawn up by no less a man than the "United States' topographical engineer," it shall not escape such an examination, at least, as will serve to expose its most important fallacies.

That "the American 44-gun ships and the British 38-gun ships, are constructed on the same principles," is an assertion that might be easily disproved; the latter having a wide waist, that leaves no room for the use of guns along the gangways; and the former, an entire upper deck, reaching from stem to stern. (See plate 2.) But, as the British have built ships of a similar construction, and called them frigates; and, as the reader has already been put on his guard, against drawing any conclusions as to relative force, merely because two ships are classed under one denomination, (see pp. 17-18,) the above statement of Mr. Clark's may be allowed to pass.

Mr. Clark's 44-gun frigate being "one tenth longer" than the 38-gun frigate, has occasioned him to say a great deal in depreciation of a long "line of defence." Among *salt-water* engineers, or navy-men, a long ship is considered to have an advantage over a short one, as well from the additional room upon her decks, as from her ability to bring one or more guns, at either extreme of her "line of defence," to bear diagonally across her opponent. Of course, it is not meant to carry this principle *ad infinitum*, but to confine it to ships, or floating batteries in general. Agreeably to Mr. Clark's doctrine, our old first-rates, of 165 feet gun-deck, were preferable ships to our present first-rates, of 205 feet gun-deck; and the old three-decked 80s, of 156 feet, to a two-decked 80, of 197 feet.

In moderate weather, the ship with most decks, or "lines of defence," is certainly enabled to throw her shot more in a mass; and therefore with more destructive effect. On the other hand, blowing weather and a heavy sea, may compel her to shut her lower-deck ports; and at a time, too, when a large frigate, from the additional height of her ports, could fight every gun she mounted. So that, taking all circumstances into consideration, the question of comparative force still resolves itself into—the relative broadside-weight of metal.—Does the editor of the "Naval History" pretend to say, that American ships do not carry "shifting guns"?

After Mr. Clark has *proved* that the force of the American 44 and the British 38, is "very nearly equal," he asks:—"Are not 18-pounders of sufficient weight of metal for the service of large frigates; and fully calculated to produce every effect that may be required in an engagement between frigates?" If, by "large frigates," Mr. Clark means the American 44s, the answer to the first question is—*no*; because the deck-beams, sides, and timbers, of the 44, are calculated to bear 24-pounders. If, by "large frigates," he means the present British 46s, (old 38s,) the answer is,—*yes*; because the deck-beams, sides, and timbers of the latter, are calculated to bear only 18-pounders. This will appear clearer by stating, that, while the 30 long 24-pounders, with their carriages complete, placed upon the 44's main-deck, weigh 88 tons, 2 cwt, the 28 long 18-pounders, with their carriages complete, placed upon the 38's or 46's main-deck, weigh but 67 tons, 18 cwt.

As to the second question, that is already answered; unless Mr. Clarke means to say, that the effect produced by an 18-pounder, is equal to the effect produced by a 24-pounder; or that the "effect required to be produced in an engagement between frigates" does not consist of destruction at all, but of something else; which something he has not ventured to explain.

With respect to the Java's shot weighing more, or the Constitution's less, than the nominal weights, that has been fully answered in a preceding page. (p. 5.) Whenever Mr. Clark can prove, that British 18, and American 24, pound shot, approach nearer, in diameter, than 5.040 to 5.547, (inches and decimal parts,) his arguments will merit attention. A French 18-pound shot weighs 20¼ pounds, English; which is only a trifle beyond "three pounds lighter" than a shot weighing 24 pounds English; and the Java, from which the shot in question was taken, had been a French ship, and then recently fitted out for the first time.

Might not some of the French shot have been left on board? In that case, the reason for selecting, to be "accurately weighed," one of them, in preference to one of the English 18s, is obvious. As to the American shot selected to be placed in the opposite scale, who knows but that the American commanders order to be set apart, for this important service, one particular shot,—the smallest in the ship.

Instead of proceeding to disprove Captain Carden's assertion that "the American 44-gun ships were built with the scantling of a 74," Mr. Clark shifts his ground to the "nature" of a 74; and gives his readers a happy definition of "a ship of the line."

The force of the American 44-gun frigates, will now be fairly compared with that of several classes of British ships; and, if to shame the Americans, be a hopeless task, it may yet be possible to convince the unprejudiced part of mankind, that our three frigates were captured by American ships, equal in force to British 64s.

Because the Constitution carried lighter carronades than either the United States or President, Mr. Clark has selected her as his standard of an American 44-gun frigate. But the Constitution is as able as they are, to carry 42-pounders; and the new American 44-gun frigates, Guerriere and Java, are stated to carry long 32-pounders upon their main-decks. On the other hand, neither of our three captured frigates, the Guerriere in particular, was as effective as a well-manned, fully-equipped frigate of their class. As a mean in force, of the five American 44s, the United States will be preferred; and the full dimensions of an American 44-gun frigate can be given, with accuracy, by our fortunate possession of the President.

The British 38-gun frigate, selected as the standard of size, will be the Macedonian; first, because she was one of the finest in the British navy; and next, because she is now in the possession of the Americans: who will therefore have an opportunity of submitting the following statement of her dimensions, to the test of actual measurement.

In the diameter of the 44's main-mast, the quarter-fishes are included; inasmuch as they contribute to the security of the mast in action. The fore and main-masts of our ships have only a small fish, or *paunch,* in front, to admit the yard, in its descent, to pass clear of the mast-hoops.

The difference between these ships in the quantity and stoutness of rigging, is an important consideration. Were the American ship to lose from her shrouds, a quantity of cordage equal to the whole over the mast-heads of the British ship, she would still have enough left to support her masts.

The relative stoutness of top-sides cannot be fully expressed by feet and inches; for, while the timbers of the American 44 are placed as close together as they well can be, there is a considerable space between each timber of the British 38. About three inches

Comparative dimensions of the British 38, (or new-rated 46,) and the American 44-gun frigate.

			38. Ft.	38. In.	44. Ft.	44. In.
Length	*over all*, being from fore-part of figure-head, to aft-part of fife-rail,		180	3	204	0
	of spar-deck, being from aft part of apron to fore-part of stern-timber at the middle line,		163	6	182	9
	extreme, being from fore-part of stem at height of main-deck, to aft-part of stern-post, at height of wing-transom,		158	4	179	7
	of lower-deck, being from aft-part of rabbit of stem, to fore-part of rabbit of stern-post,		154	6	173	3
	of actual keel, being from fore part of fore-foot, to aft part of stern-post,		140	4	156	6
Breadth	*over all*, or to outside of main-wails,		40	2	45	0
	extreme, or of frame, including the plank at the bottom,		39	6	44	4
	moulded, or of frame only,		38	10	43	8
Depth in hold, being from under-side of lower-deck plank to limber streak,			13	6	13	11
Height	of lower-deck,	aft,	6	5	6	6½
		midships,			6	7½
		forward,			6	8
	between main and	quarter-deck,	6	7	7	2
		gangways,			7	0
		forecastle,	6	6	6	11
	from under side of false keel, to upper part of figure-head,		34	4	39	1
	from ditto, to upper-part of fife-rail,		38	8	42	4
	from upper side of 'midship main-deck port-sill, to water's edge at load-water mark,		7	6	8	8
Load-draught of water,		afore,	17	9	19	4
		abaft,	19	0	20	6
Main-deck beams,		broad, or *sided*,	1	0	1	4½
		deep, or *moulded*,	0	11	1	3½
Ditto ports,		width of,	3	0	3	5
		distance between,	7	3	7	5½
Topsides, thickness of, at		main-deck port-sills,	1	3	1	8
		quarter deck do.	0	11¼	1	5
Main-mast,		length,	92	0	101	6
		diameter,	2	3½	3	5 *
Main-yard,		length,	81	6	92	0
		diameter,	1	7½	1	8½
Main-shrouds,	Brit. frig. 7 pairs, Am. do. 9 pairs,	each in circumference	0	8	0	11

* Including the quarter-fishes, see p. 55.

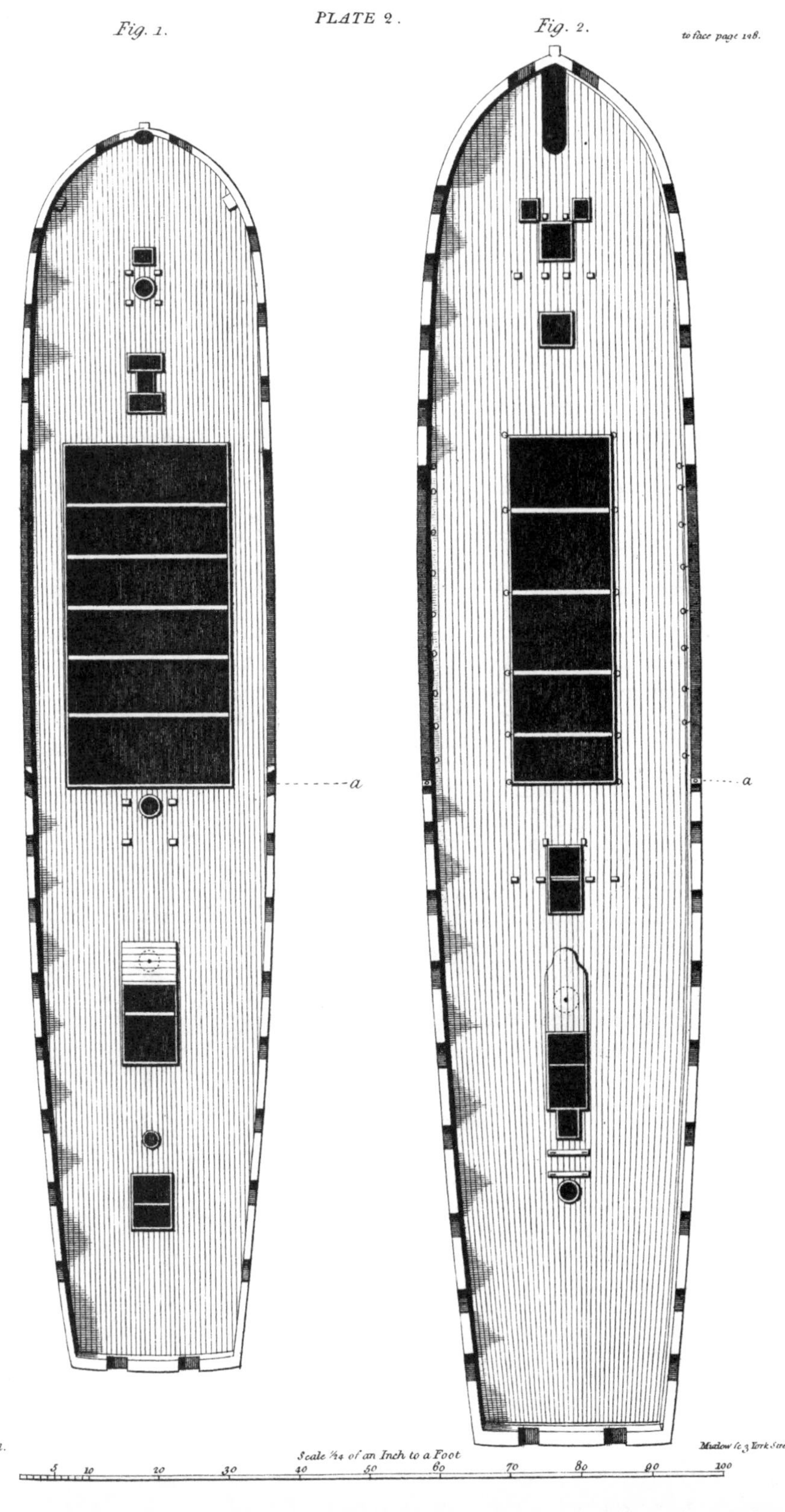
PLATE 2.
Fig. 1.
Fig. 2.
to face page 148.
a
a
ames del.
Mutlow sc 3 York Street
Scale 1/24 of an Inch to a Foot
5
10
20
30
40
50
60
70
80
90
100

below the main-deck port-sills, the President's sides are twenty-two inches through. In fact, an American ship of war is almost a bed of timber.

Plate 2 represents the plans, accurately taken, of the quarter-deck and forecastle of the President frigate, and a frigate built from the same draught as the Macedonian; and which, consequently agrees in dimensions with the 38-gun frigate in the above comparative statement. The difference between a narrow path or gang-way, for the convenience of walking to and from the quarter-deck, and a broad space, calculated for carrying four guns, is readily seen: as may be, in fig. 2. the ring-bolts for the breechings of those guns. The reason that rings are placed there, and not at the regular ports, is, that the breeching passes round each port-timber at the latter; while, at the former, there are no port-timbers, the hammock-staunchions forming the sides of the ports. There is, also, at the gangway, or entrance on board the ship (*a*. fig. 2.) a regular port; having an iron plate fitted to receive the bolt of a carronade-carriage. At *a* fig. 1. is seen the quarter-deck chace-port, with the forward inclination of its sides, and the want of room for the gun to recoil, otherwise than in an oblique direction. No gun is allowed for this port; the foremost quarter deck gun (usually a long gun) being intended to be shifted there, when necessary. The reason of the upper decks of the two ships differing so little in width, is, that fig. 1. is, what is called, *wall-sided,* while fig. 2.'s sides fall in as they rise. Upon the main-decks, the due breadth of each ship is preserved.

The regular armament of a 38 or 46-gun frigate, is that of the Java. The armaments of the Macedonian and Guerriere (except as to having a 12, instead of an 18-pound boat carronade) were the same as the Java's, till altered by their respective commanders. A 46-gun frigate's complement may be stated at 294 men, and 21 boys; total 315.

The President's armament may be seen at a subsequent page; also the number of men which she had on board, at the commencement of the action that placed her in our possession.

What have the Americans to urge against this? Is it not clear, that the relative efficiency or force of a British (old rate) 38, and

Comparative force of the British 38, (old rate,) and the American 44.

		British, (old rate,) 38.		American 44.	
Broadside-metal in pounds,	long guns,	261		408	
	carronades,	274		462	
			535		900
Complement,	men,	294		472	
	boys,	21		5	
			315		477
Size in tons,		1081		1533	

an American 44 gun frigate, instead of being, as Mr. Clark says, "very nearly equal," is in the proportion (taking no advantage of fractions) of *two* to *three?*

When the Guerriere was captured from the French, she was pronounced, in reference to ships like the Blanche, "of the largest class of frigates." Take the Guerriere, as she then was, for a standard of the *French* "44-gun frigate": her force was barely equal to that of the British frigate in the above comparative statement. What then becomes of the mass of groans and lamentations to be found in British newspapers, magazines, and registers, about the difference in the result of actions between British and French frigates, and British and American frigates? It now appears, clearly, that, in the one case, the ships were about equally matched; in the other, not so by a full third.

The relative force of the American 44-gun frigate and the higher classes of his majesty's ships, comes next to be considered.

In the year in which the American 44s were built, (1797,) we had in commission, four or five two-decked ships, rating also of "44 guns"; which, if the rate were any criterion, would be about equal in force to the American 44-gun frigates. But they were much inferior to the old 50-gun ship; whose force, as we have seen, (p.. 55,) did not equal even that of an American 36-gun frigate.

The guns of the British 64, and the 74 and 76, of the present rates, are here given together.

If the "admiralty-office navy-list" is correct, such of his majesty's ships as mount guns upon the poop, are still under-

	British.					
	64.		74.		76.	
Lower-deck,	26 long	24-prs.	28 long	32-prs.	28 long	32-prs.
Upper-deck,	26 —	18 —	28 —	18 —	30 —	24 —
Qr.-deck and forecastle,	2 —	9 —	8 —	12 —	6 —	12 —
					2 carr.	68 —
	12 carr.	32 —	12 carr.	32 —	12 —	32 —
Poop,	5 —	18 —	7 —	18 —	7 —	18 —
Total,	71 guns.		83 guns.		85 guns.	

rated. The force of the above 74 is precisely that of the San Domingo and Valiant, when on the American coast; and the force of the 76 is that of the Bulwark, when on the same station. Deducting from the latter, the two 68-pound carronades, which were the captain's guns; and, from each ship one of the 18-pound carronades, as being a boat-gun, both the Valiant and Bulwark, to correspond with the order in council, should rate as 82s. The San Domingo, although built in 1810, is not in the list, having been broken up this twelvemonth.

In the spring of 1814, the new Leander, built of pitch-pine, and intended to match the large American frigates, arrived on the

Halifax station. She then mounted thirty long 24-pounders upon the main-deck; and twenty-four carronades, 42-pounders, and four long 24-pounders, upon the spar-deck; total 58 guns; besides an 18-pound boat-carronade. There was here no disguise whatever: the ship had two complete batteries of a side, reaching from stem to stern. The Leander was not the sort of *frigate* to entice the American 44s within gun-shot. The Americans proclaimed both her and the Newcastle to be *two-deckers;* and who could say otherwise? With the reduction of two of her 24s, and two of her 42s; and using the remaining two upper-deck 24s as shifting guns, one on the forecastle, the other through the gangway-port, the Leander might have been constructed as a regular 54-gun frigate; and yet fought the same number of guns upon the broadside, within one, that she does at present. The Leander still mounts no more than 58 guns, and a boat-carronade; yet, in the "admiralty-office navy list" for March last, the Leander, Newcastle, Java, and ships of that class now building, rate of 60 guns; while, in the same list, the Saturn, *razee,* of much greater physical force, rates two guns fewer.

What created the greatest surprise at Halifax, when the Leander first arrived there, was the appearance of her ship's company. People naturally expected to see a picked crew of British seamen. Instead of which, they saw tall and short, old and young; and soon learnt that there were very few seamen in the ship. Nominally, the Leander was well manned, for her books contained the names of 485; but 44 of them appeared as—boys. During her first cruize, she captured the U. S. brig Rattlesnake; whose officers could not help smiling at the idea of such a crew being sent out to oppose the Constitution's; a sample of whose men, in the late crew of the Rattlesnake, 131 in number, was then on board the Leander. The flimsiness of that ship's topsides, and the smallness of her scantling, generally, also took the attention of the American officers; most of whom had served on board the Constitution.

Thin sides, however, have their advocates. It is said that, when a ship is closely engaged, the thinner her sides, provided they can resist grape, the less destructive will be the shot in its passage through. The case of this very same Leander, when so gallantly engaged at Algiers, is brought forward. There, most of the shot that struck her, passed through both sides, without splintering; leaving a hole no larger than the shot itself. But, had the Leander come to action with one of the American 44s; she having the weather-gage, and being determined to preserve, for the first half-hour at least, that distance, at which her skill in gunnery could best display itself, the latter's 24-pound shot would have found their way through the Leander's sides, quite slow enough to splinter; while her 24-pound shot, or the greater part of them, would have lodged in the sides of the American ship.—Had the Algerines commenced firing when they ought, the Leander would have had splinters enough.

Two other classes of newly-constructed frigates were also sent out upon the American station. The Severn, Liverpool, and Forth, differed from the 38s, in carrying 24s upon the main-deck, and four additional 32-pound carronades upon the quarter-deck and forecastle. They had about 350 men and boys; and measured a little under 1260 tons. It is difficult to say, for what description of American frigate, these ships were intended. For a comparative statement of their force, the Endymion's action may be consulted. The other class alluded to, consisted of the Majestic, Saturn, and Goliah, *razees,* or cut-down 74s. The force of the first-named of these newly-invented frigates has been already given. (See pp. 16-17.) In broadside-weight of metal, they were far too formidable to be esteemed a match for any of the American frigates, except the new Guerriere and Java. Their crews were tolerable: the Saturn's, indeed, was a remarkably fine one.

Comparative force of the American 44, *with the British* 60, —64, —74, —*and* 76.

		American 44.	British. 60.	British. 64.	British. 74.	British. 76.
Br. met. in pds.	l. guns,	408	408	555	748	844
	carr.	462	504	246	264	332
		— 900	— 912	— 801	—1012	—1176
Comple-ment,	men,	472	441	462	553	603
	boys,	5	44	29	37	37
		— 477	— 485	— 491	— 590	— 640
Size in tons,		1533	1571	1415	1718	1925

Upon the face of this statement, the American 44-gun-ship is inferior in force to the British 60. Nor, had the former met and engaged the Leander, should we have been allowed to say one word upon the quality of the men, and the disproportion of boys, in the two complements, nor upon the difference in stoutness of scantling; of which the relative size in tons is here a most fallacious criterion.

The President and the Africa were, at the first of the war, cruizing at no great distance apart. Had they met and engaged, here would have been a fair match. In broadside-weight of metal, the 64 is a trifle inferior; and, in bad weather, might, like the two-decked 44 or 50, be compelled to shut her lower-deck ports. In men, the 64 is also inferior, but has the advantage in boys. In size, no great disparity exists. It may therefore safely be affirmed that, except the new 60s, the only class of ship in the British navy, to which an American 44-gun frigate is equal in force, is the 64.

The 74 in the above comparative statement, if the boys are dismissed from the two complements, does not appear to be so decidedly superior to the American 44-gun ship, as to warrant the author of the "Naval History" in exclaiming against the "illiberality and absurdity of comparing the American 44-gun frigates to British 74s."

It is believed that the American government, in publishing Captain Stewart's paper, (see p. 8,) wherein he states, that a 74-gun ship is a match for "three large frigates," had for one object, to check the further progress of an opinion, then becoming prevalent throughout the United States, that an American 44-gun frigate was, in truth, not very unequal in force to a British 74. But Captain Stewart's 74 throws a broadside of 1612, instead of 1176 pounds, the force of the British 76, (with two 68-pound carronades added to her established armament,) and his "large frigate," 680, instead of 900 pounds. So that the American estimate relates to ships differing widely in force from those, between which the present comparison is made. It may serve to illustrate the remarks made at a preceding page (pp. 8-9) upon Captain Stewart's argument about the difference in scantling between 74s and frigates, to mention, that the top-sides of the Independence 74, at the lower-deck port-sills, are stated to be thirty one inches thick; while no British-built 74 measures, at that place, more than twenty six inches.

To complete the exposure of the Americans, for having gasconaded so much at the capture of our 38, by their 44 gun frigates, it remains only to suppose a case, wherein an American 44 is captured by a British ship, as much superior in force to her, as she was to the 38.

The set of figures that would give that proportion are—broadside-weight of metal, 1514;—complement, 722;—size in tons, 2173. As, however, no ship in the British navy, except the Caledonia or Nelson, throws a broadside equal to 1514 pounds, the above-mentioned 76 will, for argument's sake, be considered as possessing the required superiority in force.

Chance might have brought the President and Bulwark within sight of each other. But, where is the credulity to be persuaded, that the former would have staid to fight; much more, have fought on, till her masts were all shot away, her hull shattered to pieces, and a third of her crew killed and wounded?—Rather than miss the comparison, probability must be violated, and such a case be supposed to have happened.

To finish the comparison, we must also suppose, that the British, lost to all sense of shame,—bereft of reason, in fact,—do actually publish this capture of the American 44-gun ship by, their 76, as a "glorious victory,"—knight the conqueror,—make him free of cities,—escort him on his journeys with a body of troops,— cheer him as he passes,—erect triumphal arches to him,—weigh down his sideboard with plate,—strike off medals, adorned with emblematical devices,—set sculptors, painters, and poets to work, to immortalize the "brilliant exploit;"—and, finally, hang up, by way of sign, at every tenth public-house, a view of the action, reversing the size of the ships.—What would the other nations of Europe say?—What would America say?

CHAPTER VI.

Frolic leaves Jamaica for Honduras—Sails thence with convoy—Hears of the American war—Encounters, and is disabled by, a severe gale of wind—Falls in with the Wasp—Sends convoy a-head—Details of the action—Frolic surrenders—Re-capture of her, and capture of the Wasp—Frolic's and Wasp's damages, loss, and force—Statement of comparative force—Remarks thereon—Macedonian sails from England—Parts company with her convoy—Falls in with the United States—Sustains an irreparable accident at the onset—Details of the engagement—Damage, loss, and force, of each ship—Their relative size considered—Commodore Chauncey's opinion of the frigate United States—Statement of comparative force—Remarks thereon—Macedonian and French captured frigates.

H.M. brig Frolic arrived in the West Indies in 1807, and continued cruizing there till the middle of 1812; when she left Port Royal, Jamaica, to collect the homeward-bound trade at Honduras, and convoy them to England. She was, at this time, very short of complement; and the majority of her crew in a debilitated state, owing to the length of time they had been on the station. Upwards of 40 would have been invalided, had the war with America been known, or even suspected.

The Frolic left the bay of Honduras on the 12th of September, with about 14 sail under convoy; and, when off the Havannah, Captain Whinyates was informed by a Guernsey ship, of the war with America, and the loss of the Guerriere. On the night of Friday, the 16th of October, the Frolic and her convoy encountered a violent gale of wind, in which they separated, and she had her main-yard broken in two places, and her main-top-mast badly sprung; besides much other damage. Her fore-top-mast also had been previously sprung.

Six sail of the convoy had joined before dark the next evening; and, on the following morning, at daylight, while the Frolic's men were at work upon the main-yard, a sail hove in sight, which, at first, was taken for one of the missing convoy. Upon her nearing the Frolic, and not answering the signals, the main-yard was got off the casks, and lashed to the deck; and the Frolic hauled to the wind, under her close-reeved fore-top-sail, and boom-main-sail, to let the convoy get sufficiently a-head, to be out of danger.

Captain Whinyates, having, two days before, passed a Spanish convoy protected by a brig, hoisted Spanish colours, by way of decoy. As soon as the stranger, which proved to be the U. S. sloop of war Wasp, Captain Jones, discovered that the ships of the convoy were nine miles right to-leeward, under all sail before the wind, she bore down upon the Frolic.

The Frolic fired the first broadside, and continued to fire with such rapidity and precision, that, in about four minutes, the Wasp's fore-top-mast came down, and she received other considerable damage; but, at that instant, the Frolic's gaff-head braces being shot away, and having no sail upon the main-mast, she became unmanageable. The Wasp accordingly took a raking position, while the Frolic could not bring a gun to bear. After the Frolic had sustained considerable loss by the Wasp's fire, she fell on board the enemy; who, for upwards of 20 minutes, continued pouring in his unreturned broadsides, and did still more execution by his musketry. When resistance was quite at an end, the Americans boarded, and struck the Frolic's colours.

Mr. Clark gives a more circumstantial account of the action, than is contained in either official letter. (App. Nos. 13 and 14.) He begins by stating, that the merchant-ships were well manned, and that four of them mounted from 16 to 18 guns each; but that, "notwithstanding, Captain Jones resolved to attack them. The convoy made their escape under a press of sail. About 11 o'clock, the Frolic shewed Spanish colours. The Wasp immediately displayed the American ensign and pendant. At 32 minutes past 11, the Wasp came down to-windward on the larboard side of the Frolic. When within about 60 yards she hailed. The Frolic then hauled down Spanish colours, hoisted the British ensign, and opened a fire of cannon and musketry. This was instantly returned by the Wasp; and, nearing the enemy, the action became close and spirited. About four or five minutes after the commencement of the action, the main-top-mast of the Wasp was shot away, and having fallen, with the main-top-sail-yard, across the larboard fore and fore-top-sail braces, rendered her head-yards unmanageable during the remainder of the engagement. In two or three minutes more, her gaff and mizen-top-gallant-sail were shot away. She, however, kept up a close and constant fire. The sea was so rough, that the muzzles of the Wasp's guns were frequently under water. The Americans fired as the side of their ship was going down; their shot, of course, either struck the Frolic's deck, or below it. The English fired as their vessel rose; their balls, consequently, only struck the rigging, or were ineffectual. The Wasp, having now shot a-head of the Frolic, poured a broadside into her, which completely raked her. She then took a position on the Frolic's larboard-bow. A most spirited fire was now kept up from the Wasp: it produced great effect. The fire of the Frolic had slackened so much, that Captain Jones gave up his intention of boarding her, lest both vessels might be endangered by the roughness of the sea; but, in the course of a few minutes more, not a brace of the Wasp was left: all had been shot away. Her rigging was so much torn to pieces, that Captain Jones was afraid that her masts, being unsupported, would go by the board, and the Frolic thereby be enabled to escape; he therefore resolved to board, and at once decide the contest. With this intention he wore ship, and ran down upon the enemy; the vessels struck each other; the Wasp's side rubbed along the Frolic's bow; the jib-boom of the latter entered between the main and mizen rigging of the Wasp, directly over the heads of Captain Jones and his first lieutenant, Biddle, who were then standing together, near the capstan. The Frolic now lay in so good a position for being raked, that it was resolved not to board until another broadside had been poured into her. So near were the two vessels, that while the men were loading the guns, the rammers of the Wasp were pushed against the Frolic's sides; and two of her guns went through the bow-ports of the Frolic, and swept the whole length of her deck, About this time Jack Lang, a brave and intrepid seaman of the Wasp, and who had once been impressed by a British man-of-war, jumped on a gun with his cutlass, and was springing on board the Frolic, when Captain Jones, desiring to fire again before boarding, called him down; but, probably, urged on by his impetuosity, he did not hear the command of his captain, and was immediately on the bowsprit of the Frolic. Lieutenant Biddle, perceiving the ardor and enthusiasm of the Wasp's crew, mounted on the hammock-cloth to board; the crew immediately followed; but the lieutenant's feet being entangled in the rigging of the Frolic's bowsprit, and Midshipman Baker, in his ardor to board, laying hold of his coat, he fell back on the Wasp's deck; he directly sprang up, and, as the next swell of the sea brought the Frolic nearer, he got on her bowsprit, where Lang and another seaman were already. He passed them on the forecastle; and was much surprised at not seeing a single man alive upon the Frolic's deck, except the seaman at the wheel, and three officers. The deck was slippery with blood, and strewed with dead bodies. As he went forward, the captain of the Frolic, and two other officers, who were standing on the quarter-deck, threw down their swords, and made an inclination of their bodies as a sign of submission. The colours of the Frolic were still flying; none of her seamen, probably, dared to go into the rigging to strike them, for fear of the musketry of the Wasp. Lieutenant Biddle, himself, immediately jumped into the rigging, and hauled down the British ensign. Possession was taken of the Frolic 43 minutes after the commencement of the action. She presented a most shocking spectacle: her berth-deck was crowded with dead, wounded, and dying. Not above 20 of her crew escaped unhurt."

It was very good of Mr. Clark to suggest, that Captain Jones resolved to attack the "four well-manned ships, armed with 16 or 18 guns each." Captain Jones had no such intention; or he would not have waited till they were hull-down to-leeward, before he closed upon the Frolic. The mercantile knowledge of an American commander was sufficient to inform him, that those ships would have forfeited their insurances, had they not obeyed the Frolic's signal to make the best of their way. There can be little doubt that a disabled American sloop of war would have called them to her protection, instead of engaging single-handed, under circumstances so disadvantageous.

The argument about the two methods of firing is ingenious; but the disabled state of the Frolic before a shot was fired, and her totally unmanageable state almost immediately afterwards, accounts for the little execution she did. Previous to the loss of her boom-main-sail, her fire was very far from being "ineffectual:" it was such as, could it have been continued, would have captured the Wasp, in a quarter of an hour more. Owing to the Frolic's very light state, (she having scarcely any stores on board,) and her inability to carry sail, the heavy sea going, caused her motion to be much more quick and violent than that of the Wasp. Under such circumstances, it was difficult to point the guns with precision; but, highly to the credit of her officers, the Frolic's men had been exercised.

Mr. Biddle's family resides in Philadelphia, within a door or two of Mr. Clark's publisher who therefore could do no less than insert his neighbour's account of the action. But, in justice to a gallant young man, it is but fair to state, that Lieutenant Rodgers, of the Wasp, was the first American officer on board the Frolic.

Neither Captain Jones nor Lieutenant Biddle mentions a word about the crippled state of the Frolic, previous to the engagement. That, among honorable men, it is customary, in official accounts, to do justice to an enemy, the Americans themselves have had an instance, in Captain Hillyar's letter, detailing the capture of the Essex. He there particularly notices "the very discouraging circumstance of her having lost her main-top-mast." (App. No. 71.) And Captain Tobin, of the Andromache, in his letter, detailing the capture of la Traave, magnanimously excuses her feeble resistance thus:—"Indeed, such was the disabled state of her masts previously to our meeting, that any further opposition would have been the extreme of rashness." (Nav. Chron. vol. xxx. p. 443.)

The Frolic was much shattered in her hull; and both her masts fell over the side, in a few minutes after she surrendered. She lost 15 men killed; her first lieutenant and master, mortally, and her commander and second lieutenant, severely, wounded; also 43 of her men wounded severely and slightly: some of whom died afterwards. Not above 20 men remained on the Frolic's deck, unhurt: the remainder were below, attending the wounded, and performing other duties there. The only officer not badly wounded was the purser. It was the musketry of the Americans that so augmented the loss, particularly among the wounded. The second lieutenant, Frederick B. Wintle, had two balls in him, besides being wounded by three others.

The Wasp had a few shot in her hull, and one passed near the magazine; yet, according to Mr. Clark, or Lieutenant Biddle rather, the Frolic fired too high. The Wasp's main-top-mast was shot away, and her three lower-masts were wounded; but, owing to the goodness of the sticks, they remained standing. Captain Jones says, he had "five killed and five wounded;" (App. No. 14;) but some time after the Wasp and Frolic had been taken possession of by the Poictiers 74, two men were found dead in the Wasp's mizen-top, and one in the main-top-mast-stay-sail netting. When questioned as to their loss, the Americans gave different accounts; and it is not likely that Captain Jones could speak positively on the subject, considering that both his own vessel and his prize were taken from him, in less than two hours after the action terminated.

It is fortunate, that Captain Jones and Lieutenant Biddle did not apprize each other, how they meant to arm the Frolic, in their letters home; as the essential difference in their statements made even Americans waver. The real force of the Frolic was sixteen carronades, 32-pounders, two long 6-pounders, and a 12-pound boat-carronade, mounted upon the top-gallant-forecastle; total 19 guns. Her people had, somewhere in the West Indies, weighed up, out of shoal water, a 12-pound carronade; which, during the action, remained lashed to the deck, under the top-gallant forecastle. Captain Jones converted the Frolic's two 6s, and this dismounted carronade, into "four 12-pounders upon the main-deck," and the single carronade upon the top-gallant forecastle, into "two 12 pounders, carronades;" making the Frolic's total force amount to "22 guns." Lieutenant Biddle correctly enumerated the whole of the guns, but made "two long 9s" of the 6s; and, what must have been a wilful mistake, represented the mounted and dismounted 12-pound carronades, as "32-pound carronades," by giving the Frolic 18, instead of 16, of the latter.

The Frolic's complement, on going into action, consisted of 91 men, and 18 boys; (most of them very young;) together with one passenger, an invalided soldier; total 110. Captain Jones knew his interest too well, to touch upon the Frolic's complement. Her men, as stated before, had been for some years in a West India climate; and upwards of 40 of them ought to have been invalided: none, in short, were in robust health. They, however, behaved extremely well; and continued cheering during the whole of the action. One of them, when desired by Lieutenant Biddle to strike the Frolic's colours, then lashed to the main-rigging, very properly replied,—"As you have possession of the brig, you may do it yourself."

The Wasp mounted sixteen carronades, 32-pounders, and two brass long 12-pounders. She had also on board, two brass 4 or 6-pounders, which she usually carried in her tops; but which had been brought on deck in the gale of the 15th. They were mounted on small carriages; but not, it is believed, used in the action. Although Captain Jones could enumerate more guns than were any where to be found in the Frolic, he takes care that his own number shall not include these 4 or 6-pounders, by stating, that the Frolic, with her "22 guns," was superior to the Wasp by "four 12-pounders."

The muster-book of the Wasp contained 148 names; but only 130 prisoners were received by the agent at Bermuda. Captain Jones mentions the loss of two men, along with the jib-boom, on the 15th; and "Niles' prize-list" mentions a re-captured brig, as sent into Boston by the Wasp. The date of the re-capture does not appear; but, it is probable, it occurred on the Wasp's passage from France, whence she arrived in the Delaware some time in July. There could not have been more than eight men sent in the re-captured brig; which men, we will suppose, had not joined their ship previous to her sailing in October. Thus, fixing the number killed at eight, we have 138 for the complement of the Wasp on going into action. The cause of truth would have benefitted greatly, had the American commanders taken half as much pains to fix the complements of British ships. Never was a finer crew seen, than was on board the Wasp. She had four lieutenants; and, while the Frolic had only one midshipman, and he a boy, the Wasp had 12 or 13 midshipmen, chiefly masters and mates of merchantmen: stout able men, each of whom could take charge of a ship. Their chief employment in the action, was as captains of the guns. Among the crew, was one lad of 18; the remainder were from 20 to 35 years of age: all stout, athletic fellows, in full health and vigor. A great proportion of them were Irishmen; and several, deserters from British ships.

It is now that the reader can appreciate Mr. Biddle's vivid description, of "the ardor and enthusiasm of the Wasp's crew" in boarding the Frolic; whose originally debilitated crew had then become reduced in number to scarcely a third of the assailants, and were without an officer in a situation to head them. Captain Jones's statement, that "no loss was sustained on either side after boarding," was calculated to cast a slur upon the British. A view of the relative numbers at the boarding moment, is all that is required to dispel any such impression. If wounding an already wounded man is to be accounted a "loss," Captain Jones is incorrect in saying, "no loss was sustained on *either* side," for Mr. Biddle's friend, Jack Lang, on his mounting the Frolic's forecastle, actually lodged a musket-ball in Lieutenant Wintle's right thigh; and this, while he was preventing one of the Frolic's men from firing at Lieutenant Rodgers. Some one else of the boarding-party, at the same moment, fired at and wounded Captain Whinyates; who, like his brave second lieutenant, could scarcely keep the deck, from the severity of the wounds he had previously received.

The Frolic was built in 1806; the Wasp in 1801. The principal dimensions of the two vessels here follow:—

	Frolic, brig.		Wasp, ship.	
	Ft.	In.	Ft.	In.
Length on deck, from rabbit to rabbit,	100	0	105	10½
Breadth, extreme,	30	7	30	10

The Wasp's scantling was as stout as a British 28-gun frigate's; especially at her top-sides. She was taken into the service; but, unfortunately, foundered at sea, as is supposed, in the spring of 1814.

Comparative force of the two vessels.

		Frolic.		Wasp.	
Broadside-metal in pounds	l. guns,	6		12	
	carr.	268		256	
		—	274	—	268
Complement,	men,	92		137	
	boys,	18		1	
		—	110	—	138
Size in tons,			384		434

With Captain Jones' official letter before it, the American court of inquiry (App. No. 16) could not say less than—"the brilliant and successful action with his Britannic M. S. Frolic, of *superior force to the Wasp;* and even the most moderate American, while he may be brought to doubt the equality of force in some of the naval actions, will exultingly remind you that, "in the action of the Wasp and Frolic,"—using the words of Mr. Clark,—"the superiority of force, certainly, was on the side of the British."

Truly, there does appear to have been, in broadside-weight of metal, a "superiority" of—one *forty-sixth* part.—But have we not seen that, while the British brig went into action crippled by a gale, the American ship had her masts and yards all perfect; that, while the former began the attack with 92 men, and 18 boys, chiefly debilitated by sickness, the latter had 137 men, and one *nominal* boy, all lusty and healthful?—Let, then, the reader form his own judgment of the comparative force of the Frolic and Wasp.

However disagreeable to the Americans, it is but fair to mention, that, not many months previous to the capture of the Frolic by the Wasp, the Alacrity, a sister-brig to the former, and mounting the same number and description of guns, but without having been crippled by a gale, was captured off Bastia, in the island of Corsica, after a close action of half an hour, by the French brig of war Abeille, of 20 guns; asserted by the French (and not denied by the British) account to have been 24-pound carronades: complement not mentioned. The Alacrity's loss is stated to have been 15 killed, and 20 wounded; the Abeille's, 7 killed, and 12 wounded. In the Naval Chron. vol. xxxi. p. 486, will be found the sentence of the court-martial upon the Alacrity's surviving officers and crew. They were all acquitted; as, it need hardly be added, were those of the Frolic, with deserved encomiums upon the bravery displayed in her defence.

H.M.S. Macedonian sailed from England on or about the 29th of September, with an Indianman under convoy to a certain distance. Having parted with her, and while proceeding to the North American station, the Macedonian, on the 25th of October, fell in with the U.S. ship United States, seven days from Boston; which port she had left along with the squadron under Commodore Rodgers. An action ensued; of which the British and American details are given in the official letters to be found in the Appendix. (Nos. 18. and 19.)

In bearing down to attack the American ship, the whole of the Macedonian's carronades on the engaging side, had their chocks, which, in this frigate, were fitted outside, cut away by the raking fire of the United States. Thus was disabled the entire upper-deck battery of the Macedonian, before she had well begun the action. Subsequently, all the other carronades but two, were disabled by the same means. The "Sentence of the court-martial" does not fail to notice that, "previous to the commencement of the action, from an over-anxiety to keep the weather-gage, an opportunity was lost of closing with the enemy; and that, owing to this circumstance, the Macedonian was unable to bring the United States to close action, until she had received material damage;" but very justly acquits Captain Carden, his officers and crew, of "the most distant wish to keep back from the engagement."

Commodore Decatur's assertion, that the Macedonian was "at no time within the complete effect of his musketry and grape," is untrue: for, long before the action ended, Mr. O'Brien, the Macedonian's surgeon, extracted from the right arm-pit of a midshipman, an iron shot, weighing twelve ounces; which was either a canister or "grape," beyond dispute. Although, "for the first half-hour," the United States "did not use her carronades," the disabled state of the Macedonian, before that half-hour had elapsed, proves that she was within fair range of the American 24s, and it is at long shot, chiefly, that the "obvious superiority of gunnery"; shews itself. At such a safe distance, the "steady conduct" of the United States' crew, might, as the commander says, well equal the precision of their fire."

Admitting that Captain Carden erred in the distance at which he chose to engage the United States, and the way in which he approached her,* the disabled masts, shattered hull, and slaughtered crew, of the Macedonian, afford ample proofs that she was not surrendered, till all hopes were at an end. Captain Carden states the action to have lasted "two hours and ten minutes;" Commodore Decatur, "an hour and a half." Captain Hull has taught us how to explain this. Commodore Decatur dated the commencement of the action from the time his opponent was within carronade-range: so that, by adding to his account, "the first half-hour," in which, as he says, he did not use his carronnades, we have two hours as the duration of the action; only ten minutes short of the time stated by Captain Carden.

The damages of the Macedonian are very fully detailed in the British official account. For rendering her sea-worthy, and for afterwards conducting her home in safety, much credit is due to the American officers and crew. It is singular, no doubt, that the two ships, during a six week's passage across a wide extent of sea, should not have met one out of the many British cruizers a-float.

The Macedonian lost in the action, 1 master's mate, the schoolmaster, boatswain, 31 petty-officers, seamen and marines, and 2 boys, killed; 2 seamen mortally, 5 petty-officers and seamen dangerously, her first lieutenant, 1 midshipman, 23 petty-officers, seamen and marines, and 4 boys, severely; and her third lieutenant, 1 master's mate, and 30 petty-officers, seamen and marines, slightly wounded: total, killed 36; wounded 68.

The two accounts differ greatly as to the damage sustained by the United States. While Captain Carden says: "The enemy has suffered much in masts, rigging, and hull, both above and below water;" Commodore Decatur says: "The damage sustained by this ship was not such as to render her return into port necessary." The manner in which the action was fought, and the Macedonian's disabled state at the early part of it, afford no reasonable ground for supposing, that the damages of the United States were very important.—One of the officers writes as follows:—"It is remarkable that, during an action of one hour and a half, and a fire which I believe was never equalled by any single deck, not an accident occurred, nor a rope-yarn of our gun-tackle strained.—All the guns on the quarter-deck and forecastle of the Macedonian were dismounted, or rendered unserviceable."

The loss of the United States is stated by Commodore Decatur at no more than 5 killed, and 7 wounded. Among the latter is included, "Lieutenant Funk, who died four hours after the action." Mr. Clark, also, notices one of the seamen as having been mortally wounded; which coincides with Captain Carden's statement, that a lieutenant and six men had been thrown overboard. According to the proportions between the killed and

* See Clerk's "Essay on Naval Tactics," p. 24.

wounded, the American slightly wounded cannot have been enumerated; a circumstance that receives confirmation from the fact, that the American officers, when questioned on the subject of their loss, told each a different story.

The Macedonian's established armament was the same as the Guerriere's; but, owing to some alterations made at the instance of her commander, she also mounted 49 guns: twenty eight long 18-pounders upon the main-deck, eighteen (instead of the customary sixteen) carronades, 32-pounders, a 12-pound launch-carronade, and two French brass 9-pounders, upon the quarter-deck and forecastle. The launch-carronade, being usually mounted upon an elevating carriage, to fire over all, becomes part of the broadside-force.

So long as an enemy has a right to enumerate the guns of his adversary as a part of her force, it becomes of national importance that commanders should be restrained from mounting on board their ships, any more guns than the establishment allows; without, at least, furnishing and maintaining, at their own expense, the requisite number of additional hands.

The Macedonian victualled, on the morning of the action, 300 souls; consisting of 270 men, 22 boys, and a band of eight foreigners, then lately received out of the prisonship at Lisbon. The latter refused to fight; and were therefore put in the hold during the action. Of course, they will be excluded from the estimate. No complement is given to the Macedonian, in Commodore Decatur's letter.

The band, as may be supposed, instantly deserted to the enemy: whose triumph now became a fit subject for the display of their musical talents. Some of the Macedonian's foreigners, not of the band, also entered the American service. Nor is it surprising, that many of the British deserted; considering what powerful inducements were held out to them. They were given sums of money; promised grants of land; and kept continually drunk, until carried into the country, beyond the control of their officers. The law of honor is binding between nations, as well as individuals; and, surely, there cannot be a grosser infraction of it, than insidious attempts to withdraw from their allegiance the subjects of an honorable enemy.

The United States mounted thirty long 24-pounders, described as English ship-guns, upon the main-deck; sixteen carronades, 42-pounders, upon the quarter-deck; a 12 or 18-pound carronade, at her gangway-port on either side; (see plate 2. fig. 2, *a.*) six carronades, 42-pounders, and two long 24-pounders, upon the forecastle; making, with three howitzers, 6-pounders, one in each top, 58 guns. It is probable, owing to the commodore's complaint, that he could not reach the Macedonian with his carronades, that one of the forecastle 24s, instead of the shifting carronade, was fought through the gangway-port, and the latter placed upon an elevating carriage, so as to fire over all, in the usual manner; thus presenting a broadside of 32 guns. The force of the United States has been so estimated at a preceding page; (p. 64;) but, as the British officers, when brought on board, found both the 24s stationed upon the forecastle, (a reference to the plate, will shew the facility of transporting them from one end of the deck to the other,) the number of broadside-guns will, in the present instance, not be encreased beyond 31.

The top-guns, being considered as a masked or concealed battery, and the shifting carronade as a "boat-gun," are necessarily excluded from the American accounts. With those exceptions, a New York paper of May, 1813, mentions the recent reduction of the frigate United States' armament "from 54, to 48 guns:" which confirms Captain Carden's statement, as to the number of his opponent's guns; and as to their caliber, the correspondence, and other proceedings, relative to the New-London challenge, have since placed that beyond a doubt.

The complement of the United States was, as admitted by her officers, 478. Only four boys were seen in the ship; and the Macedonian's officers, it will be recollected, were upwards of six weeks on board.

The crew consisted of picked seamen, all young and vigorous. A great proportion were known to be British sailors: which accounted for many of the guns being named after British ships, and some of our celebrated naval victories. The Macedonian's men recognized several old shipmates; and an officer's servant, a young lad from London, named William Hearne, actually found among the hostile crew—his own brother!—This hardened traitor, after reviling the British, and applauding the American, service, used the influence of seniority, in trying to persuade his brother to enter the latter. The honorable youth, with tears in his eyes, replied:—

"If you are a d—d rascal, that's no reason I should be one."

The Macedonian was built at Woolwich in 1810. Her full dimensions have appeared already. The United States was built at Philadelphia; and launched on the 10th of May, 1797. She cost 299,336 dollars, or 67,350*l.* 14*s.* 7*d.* sterling. Her dimensions are similar to those of the President and Constitution; although her model may be somewhat different.

Two statements of the comparative size of the Macedonian and United States, have appeared in the American prints. Both make the Macedonian's "length on deck, 166 feet;" that of the United States "176 feet." One statement makes the Macedonian's "breadth of beam 42 feet 8 inches;" and that of the United States "42 feet:" the other statement makes the Macedonian's "breadth of beam 48 feet 8 inches, tonnage 1325;* "that of the United States" "48 feet, tonnage 1405." Admitting the "48" to be a typographical error, there are few Americans who will not still insist, that the two ships do not differ in length by more than 10 feet;

* The Macedonian's true American tonnage is 1031.

and that their extreme breadth is about the same. One could almost imagine, that the Macedonian had suddenly acquired the *stretching* qualities of her new masters.

If, during her stay at New York, that was the case, she had, when subsequently seen at New-London, shrunk to her original size. In October, 1813, the Macedonian, United States, and Hornet, each painted black, were, by an Englishman, seen at anchor about five miles above New London. Owing to the three ships lying close together, and their being painted alike, a spectator, standing on the banks of the river, was enabled to form a tolerable idea of their relative size. It required, truly, no very steady gaze to discover, which was the late British, which the American frigate. Upon the same person afterwards seeing H. M. ships Nymphe and Newcastle, also painted alike, anchored, head and stern, in Halifax harbour, he was forcibly struck with the same appearance of disparity, in hull, spars, and rigging.

How are we to understand Commodore Decatur, when he says: "She (the Macedonian) is a frigate of the largest class"?—Suppose the Newcastle, a frigate about the same size as the United States, had captured the Congress, a frigate about 50 tons larger than the Macedonian. Would Lord Stuart, in his official letter, have said:—"She (the Congress) is a frigate of the largest class"?—Perhaps Commodore Decatur had some scruples about considering his ship as *a frigate;* and meant only to compare the Macedonian with some of the old British 38-gun class; such as the Arethusa, Seahorse, and several others. He certainly has not, in any part of his letter, styled the United States a "frigate"; as Captains Hull, Bainbridge, and Stewart, in all their's, have not failed to style the Constitution.

As a proof how much the Americans, in expressing their opinions, are governed by circumstances, Commodore Chauncey, in a conversation respecting the capture of the President, held with some British naval officers, since the peace, declared, that he would much rather fight a battle in the frigate United States, because her sides were stouter than the President's, and she would, he thought, stand a longer battering. Captain Carden therefore deserves credit for his moderation, when speaking of his opponent's scantling; and the attempts of the Americans to equalize the two ships, in size, can now be better understood.

Comparative force of the two ships.

		Macedonian.		U. States.	
Broadside-metal in pounds	l. guns,	261		384	
	carr.	300		492	
		—	561	—	876
Complement,	men,	270		474	
	boys,	22		4	
		—	292	—	478
Size in tons,			1081		1533

Here, another case of "very nearly equal force," turns out to be a superiority on the American side, of full one third.—Nay, a special committee determined, that the Macedonian was *quite* equal to the United States; and, an act of congress of the 28th of June, 1798, having provided that,—"if a vessel of superior, or equal force, shall be captured by a public-armed vessel of the United States, the forfeiture shall accrue wholly to the captors,"—the amount of the Macedonian's valuation, 200,000 dollars, was paid over to Commodore Decatur, his officers, and crew.

The disparity in execution was, in this action, about the same as in the Guerriere's. Where ships are equal in force and gunnery, an accidental shot may disable one ship; so that she cannot manœuvre, nor bring more than a few guns to bear; while her fortunate adversary plays round her; sweeping her decks at every broadside. The relative execution, after that period, depends not more on the prowess of one party, than on the fortitude of the other. Should the disabled ship have been, from the first, instead of equally matched, the weaker of the two, her loss, both previous, and subsequent, to her disability, will be proportionably greater. If, not in force only, but in gunnery and equipment for war, she is decidedly inferior, is it extraordinary that, after a two hour's contest, the disparity in execution should be as great, as it certainly was, in both this and the preceding frigate-action?

The Americans have admitted, that "all the guns on the quarter-deck and forecastle of the Macedonian, were dismounted," while "not an accident occurred" on board the United States. This forms the prominent feature of this action; and is of itself sufficient to account for the inequality of loss.

The "Naval Monument," upon the authority of one of the officers of the frigate United States, says of the Macedonian,—"She is just such a ship as the English have achieved all their single-ship victories in. It was in such a ship that Sir Robert Barlow took the Africaine, that Sir Michael Seymour took the Brune, and afterwards the Niemen, that Captain Milne took the Vengeance, Captain Cooke *the* la Forte, Captain Lavie the Guerriere, Captain Rowley the Venus; and God knows how many others. She is in tonnage, men, and guns, just such a ship as the English prefer to all others; and have, till the Guerriere's loss, always thought a match for any single-decked ship afloat." (Nav. Mon. p. 24.)

The fact is, none of the ships here named, carried 24-pounders upon the main-deck; nor, except the Brune, Forte, and Guerriere, mounted more than 44 guns. If we deduct the "troops and artificers" from l'Africaine, and the "lascars" from la Forte, none of the ships had a greater complement than 320. In point of size, none, except la Vengeance (see pp. 32-33) and la Venus, exceeded the Chesapeake; and that by a trifle only.

Had not the Americans, (and they were the only nation,) in dread of "just such a ship, in tonnage, men, and guns," as the

Macedonian, constructed a class of ships, which they called frigates, each, by their own account, "superior to any European frigate of the usual dimensions,"—"just such a ship" as the Macedonian would still be "a match for any single-decked ship afloat."—Let the Americans, for the future, send to sea, frigates no larger and heavier than the strongest we ever, "in single-ship victories," took from the French, or from any other power; and we pledge ourselves, in case of war, to serve those frigates, twice out of three times, as we did the Africaine, Brune, Niemen, Vengeance, Forte, Guerriere, Venus, and "God knows how many others," not forgetting the U. S. frigate Chesapeake.

CHAPTER VII.

Java commissioned, and fitted for an East India Voyage—Departs from Spithead—Captures an American, merchant-man—Falls in with the Constitution and Hornet—Chases and engages the former—Full details of the action—American dismantling shot—Java's damages and loss—Final destruction—Constitution's damages and loss—Force of the Java in guns, men, and size—Recapture of the Java's prize by the Hornet—American subterfuge exposed—Force of the Constitution in guns, men, and size—Dimensions of the two ships—Statement of comparative force—Remarks thereon—Amelia and l'Arethuse French frigate.

ABOUT the middle of August, the French prize-frigate, la Renommée, lying in Portsmouth harbour, was commissioned as H. M. S. Java; and the command of her given to Captain Henry Lambert, a distinguished officer. The Java was fitted for the East Indies; and sailed from Spithead for that destination on the 12th of November; having on board a great quantity of naval stores, together with the following passengers: Lieutenant-general Hyslop, as governor of Bombay, two military officers of his staff, seven persons (including servants) in civil situations; also one master and commander, two lieutenants, one marine-officer, four midshipmen, one clergyman, one assistant surgeon, and 76 petty-officers and seamen, chiefly marine-society boys, for ships on the East India station. Two outward-bound Indiamen took advantage of her convoy.

On the 12th of December, the Java captured the American ship William; and a master's mate and 19 men were placed on board, with directions to keep company. On the 24th, being in want of water, Captain Lambert stood in for St. Salvador; and the two Indiamen, rather than go so far out of their way, proceeded alone on their passage.

On the 29th of December, when about ten leagues from the Brazil-coast, the Java, having her prize in tow, fell in with the U. S. ships Constitution, Commodore Bainbridge, and Hornet, Captain Lawrence; the latter having just left St. Salvador in search of the Constitution, which was away in the offing. Having cast off the prize, and ordered her to proceed to St. Salvador, the Java went in chase of the large ship to-leeward. The details of the action cannot be so well given, as in the very words of the Java's late first-lieutenant, when addressing the court-martial upon his trial for her loss. Lieutenant Chads' journal, was verified on oath by every witness examined upon the occasion. He proceeds, as follows:

"My public letter is before this honorable court; (App. No. 22.;) but, being written immediately after the action, and on board the enemy, it does not, nor indeed could the compass of a letter, contain the whole detail of so long an action; and which detail, therefore, I now submit to this honorable court.

"At 8 A. M. close in with the land, with wind at N. E. discovered a sail to the S. S. W. and another off the entrance of St. Salvador, cast off the prize in tow, and made all sail in chase of the vessel to leeward. At 10 made the private signal, which was not answered. At 11 hauled up, bringing the wind on our larboard quarter, took in all studding-sails, prepared for action, the stranger standing towards us under easy sail, and apparently a large frigate. At a little after noon, when about four miles distant, she made a signal, which was kept flying about ten minutes, when she tacked, and made sail from us, under all plain sail, running just good full; hauled up the same as the chase, but the breeze freshening, could not carry our royals; we were going at least ten knots, and gaining very fast on the chase. At 1. 30. she hoisted American colours. At 1. 50. having closed with the enemy to about two miles, he shortened sail to his top-gallant-sails, jib, and spanker, and luffed up to the wind; hoisted our colours, and put ourselves under the same sail, and bore down on him, he being at this time about three points on our lee-bow. At 2. 10. when half a mile distant, he opened his fire from the larboard-side, and gave us about two broadsides before we returned it, which was not done till within pistol-shot, on his weather-bow, with our starboard guns. On the smoke clearing away, found him under all sail before the wind; made sail after him. At 2. 25. engaged him with our larboard guns, received his starboard; at 2. 35. wore, and raked him close under his stern, giving him the weather-gage, which he did not take advantage of, but made sail free on the larboard tack; luffed up, and gave him our starboard guns, raking, but rather distant; made sail after him. At 2. 40. enemy shortened sail; did the same, and engaged him close to-windward. At 2. 50. he wore in the smoke, and was not perceived till nearly round, having just lost the head of our bowsprit, jib-boom, &c.; hove in stays, in the hopes of getting round quick and preventing our being raked, but the ship hung a long time, and we received a heavy raking broadside into our stern at about two cables' length distant; gave him our larboard guns on falling off; the enemy wore immediately; did the same.

"At 2. 55. brought him to close action within pistol-shot, (at this time the master was wounded, and carried below,) till 3. 5.; when, finding the day evidently gone, from all our rigging being cut to pieces, with our fore and main-masts badly wounded, Captain Lambert determined on boarding, as our only hope; bore up, and should have succeeded in laying him a-breast of his main-chains, but from the unfortunate fall of our foremast, the remains of our bow-sprit passing over his stern, and catching his mizen-rigging, which was a great misfortune, as it brought us up to the wind, and prevented our raking him. Whilst under the enemy's stern, attempting to board, there was not a soul to be seen on his decks; from which circumstance, I am induced to believe there was a good prospect of success. This manoeuvre failing, we were left at the mercy of the enemy; which he availed himself of, wearing across our bows, raking us, when our main-top-mast went, and wearing again, at 3. 2. under our stern. At 3. 30. our gallant captain was mortally wounded, and carried below. From this time, till our mizen-mast went, at 4. 15. he laid on our starboard-quarter, pouring in a tremendous galling fire; whilst, on our side, we could never get more than two or three guns to bear, and frequently none at all. After this we fell off, and the enemy shot a-head, which again gave us the chance of renewing the action, which was done with good spirits, broadside and broadside, Java very frequently on fire from firing through the wreck, which lay on the side engaged, till 4.35. when the Constitution made sail, and got out of gun-shot, leaving us a perfect wreck, with our main-mast only standing, and main-yard gone in the slings; cleared the wreck, and endeavoured to get before the wind, by setting a sail from the stump of the fore-mast and bow-sprit; got the main tack forward, the weather yard-arm remaining aloft; cleared away the booms, and got a top-gallant-mast out, and commenced rigging it for a jury fore-mast, and a lower-steering-sail as a fore-sail; but, before we could get this accomplished, we were obliged to cut away the main-mast, to prevent its falling in-board, from the heavy rolling of the ship. The enemy bore up to renew the action; made every preparation to receive him; re-loaded the guns with round and grape; mustered at quarters, and found 110 men missing, six quarter-deck guns, four forecastle, disabled, and many of the main-deckers, with the wreck lying over them, the hull knocked to pieces; and the fore-mast, in falling, had passed through the fore-castle and main-decks; all our masts and bow-sprit gone, the ship making water, with one pump shot away, consulted now with lieutenants Nerringham and Buchanan, when it was determined to engage him again, should he give us an opportunity of so doing with a probability of disabling him, which was now our sole object; but that it would be wasting lives resisting longer, should he resume a raking position, which unfortunately was the case; and when close to us, and getting his broadside to bear, I struck, and hailed him, to say we had done so, at 5. 50. At 6, she took possession of us, and proved to be the American frigate Constitution. The next day I found our loss was 22 killed, and 102 wounded: two of whom are since dead. The Americans allowed they had 10 killed; but differed very much about their wounded, which I found to be 44 severely, and four mortally; the slight wounds I could not ascertain.

"Having in the detail stated the number of killed and wounded on both sides, and as my account differs from the one in the public papers, and said to be the official report of Commodore Bainbridge, I beg leave to state to the court the manner in which I obtained this knowledge. Being, of course, anxious to discover the loss sustained by the enemy, I directed Mr. Capponi, assistant-surgeon, to lend his assistance in dressing their wounded; this he did, and reported to me the statement I have made. It having also been stated in the papers, that the Constitution was in a short time in a condition to commence a second action, I must beg to observe, that I do not think such a statement could have been authorised by Commodore Bainbridge, for her rigging was much cut, and her masts severely wounded; so much so, as to oblige her to return to America, which she certainly otherwise would not have done, for she was waiting only to be joined by the Essex on the coast of Brazil, when the further destination of this squadron, I was given to understand was India.

I will trouble the court with but one more remark. When the prisoners were removed from the Java, she was set fire to, although but 12 leagues distant from St. Salvador, with moderate weather the cause of which was, her shattered state, and not from any fear of taking her to a neutral port, as stated in Commodore Bainbridge's letter; for he repaired to the same port with his own ship, carrying in a valuable prize, the Eleanor schooner, from London."

Plate 1, displays a variety of the American "round and grape." (App. No. 25.) We all recollect what imprecations were hurled against us by the American journalists, when they received an account, that "combustible materials had been thrown from the Shannon upon the Chesapeake's decks." Upon that occasion, a celebrated paper, the "United States Gazette," used the following language: "Against such modes of assault, no skill, no courage, no foresight, can be found to avail; and it is no more dishonor thus to be overpowered, than it is to be beaten down by a thunderbolt. We speak with entire confidence and certainty on this point, that, if the Bonne Citoyenne had accepted the challenge of Captain Lawrence, and he had obtained a victory by the use of such means, we should have sickened at the sight of his laurels."—And yet, at the very time of uttering this rhapsody, the Americans, by the aid of their star, chain, and bar shot, had crippled, and captured, three British frigates, and two sloops of war;—nay, the very ship whose capture they were thus trying to excuse, had on board, and actually used, the very shot represented in the plate.—Confronting a man with his own words, is an admirable method; for, if he is not past blushing, it shames, as well as convicts him.

When ships engage at a short distance, less depends on the precision, than on the rapidity of firing; therefore, the ship, whose men are practised in gunnery, finds it to her interest to keep at long shot. Yet, as continually yawing away in the smoke, and avoiding close action, in the stronger ship especially, does not look well on paper, the commodore did right to complain of the enemy keeping at a much greater distance than he wished."—So far, however, from that having been the case, all the witnesses examined at the court-martial concur in stating, that the Constitution avoided close action, till the Java was disabled: then she approached; and, by successive raking fires, and the riflemen in her tops, committed nearly all the slaughter that occurred. (App. No. 22. and 26.)

If any could have saved the Java, it was boarding; and that was frustrated by the bow-sprit getting foul of the enemy's mizen rigging; and by the immediate fall of the fore-mast. The men were ready: so was the heroic boatswain, with his one arm mutilated, the other bearing his pipe, to cheer up his gallant comrades, that they might "make a clean spring" upon the enemy's decks.

In the falling of the Java's fore-mast upon the main-deck, and disabling the guns there, we see, at once, the advantage possessed by a ship having a sufficient space along the gangway, to cover the men stationed at the main-deck guns, over a ship having a waist, or large open space, extending nearly from side to side. (See Pl. 2.)

Both the British and American accounts agree, exactly, as to the time when the action commenced; but Commodore Bainbridge fixes its termination at the moment when the Constitution hauled out of gun-shot to repair damages: who else would not have fixed it, at the striking of the Java's colours?—The whole continuance of the action was three hours and 40 minutes.

The damage done to the Java has been fully detailed in Lieutenant Chads' address to the court. Her loss in the action, amounting to 22 killed; 2 mortally, 5 dangerously, 52 severely, and 43 slightly, wounded, appears at the end of the official letter. (App. No. 22.)

Captain Lambert fell by a rifle-ball fired from the Constitution's main-top. The bullet entered his left side, and lodged in the spine. He languished till the night of the 4th of January; and, on the next day, was buried at St. Salvador, with military honors. A midshipman, named Edward Keele, only 16 years of age, who was badly wounded, and had his leg amputated, enquired, soon after the action was over, if the ship had struck; and, seeing a ship's colour spread over him, grew uneasy, until he was convinced it was an English flag. This gallant youth died on the following day. The circumstance of the boatswain, with a tournaquet on his arm, (which he knew must be amputated, as soon as the surgeon was ready,) returning to his quarters, as if nothing had happened, is a strong trait of heroism and devotion.

Commodore Bainbridge, in his letter, says:—"The enemy had 60 killed, and 101 wounded, certainly; but, by the enclosed letter, written on board this ship, (by one of the officers of the Java,) and accidentally found, it is evident that the enemy's wounded must have been much greater than as above stated, and who must have died of their wounds previously to their being removed. The letter states 60 killed, and 170 wounded."

The surviving officers of the Java consider this letter, as the forgery of some one belonging to the Constitution. Let us submit its merits to the test of probability. It bears date on board the Constitution; and therefore was written after the prisoners had been removed. Is it likely, then, that the writer would have included among the "wounded," the men who had "died previously to their being removed."?—would he not have included those among the "killed"?—Commodore Bainbridge's number of the Java's wounded, agrees exactly with the British return of wounded, signed by the Java's surviving commanding-officer, and surgeon; why not then have relied upon the veracity of those officers, as to the number killed? Were there no persons among the Java's crew, not even those that entered on board the Constitution, to whom the commodore could refer as corroborating this extraordinary letter?—Admitting, for a moment, a British return of loss in action to be a fictitious instrument, it would, surely, in a case where it was necessary to shew that the ship had been defended to the last extremity, be an over, not an under estimate. But a British return of killed and wounded, cannot be otherwise than correct; the wounded, and the widows of the killed, having no other evidence to appeal to, in support of their title to relief.

Commodore Bainbridge's letter contains not one word about any damage sustained by the Constitution; not even that the sails and rigging were cut; as usually inserted, if only to jeer us for bad firing. There can be no doubt that the American government has suppressed the entire paragraph relating to the Constitution's injuries by the Java's shot: and that, perhaps, because the commodore was obliged to assign those injuries as an excuse (and, of course, he would describe them all) for breaking up his intended cruize to the South Seas; which, at that time, it was not expedient to make public. All the glory reaped from the Java's capture, was, in the opinion of the Constitution's officers, a poor compensation for the rich harvest they had long been anticipating from their intended cruize. Reluctantly, they quitted St. Salvador, on the 6th of January, upon their return to Boston; where, immediately upon her arrival, the Constitution underwent a thorough repair. Then the citizens, and several Englishmen also, saw clearly what she had suffered in the Java's action. Lieutenant Chads mentions the damage done to her spars and rigging; and, in direct proof of the advantage of stout masts, the Java's 18-pound shot had passed through two of the Constitution's lower-masts; yet they were deemed sufficiently secure, without being fished.

Commodore Bainbridge states the loss of the Constitution to have been "9 killed, and 25 wounded." That this is incorrect, appears as well from what Lieutenant Chads has stated, as from the following extract of a letter from Mr. Thomas Cooke Jones, late surgeon of the Java:—

"The Americans seemed very desirous not to allow any of our officers to witness the nature of their wounded, or compute their number. I ordered one of my assistants, Mr. Capponi, to attend when their assistant went round; and he enumerated 46, who were unable to stir from their cots, independent of the men who had received, what they called, "*slight hurts.*" Commodore Bainbridge was severely wounded in the right thigh; and four of their amputations perished under my own inspection. I have noticed these facts, that your readers may be convinced of the falsity of their official dispatches; and to authorise their being received with some degree of scepticism." (Naval Chron. vol. xxix. p. 415.)

The American newspapers informed us that lieutenant Aylwin, of the Constitution, died of his wounds on the 28th of January; and it was reported in Philadelphia, that two or three of the men had also died in the passage home. It cannot escape the reader, that it is as much the interest of the Americans, in actions in which they have been successful, to under-rate their own, as to over-rate the British loss. This it was that suggested to Mr. Clark the propriety of shewing, in appropriate columns, the "comparative loss in killed and wounded." Thus we have, in the Java's action:—"American loss, 34,"—"British loss, 171;"—when, if truth had been consulted, we should have had, (excluding the British "slightly wounded," because the Americans, with "slight hurts," cannot be enumerated,)—"American loss, 55;"—"British loss, 81;" a proportion about equal, as will be presently seen, to the comparative force of the two vessels. But the Java's second lieutenant says, that the greatest loss was sustained, "not in the early part of the action," but "after the ship became unmanageable, and the Constitution took a raking position;" (App. No. 26;) and the "Journal" admits, that the Constitution's wheel "was shot entirely away," within 20 minutes from the commencement of the action; when, also, as appears by the evidence of Lieutenant Saunders, four out of the nine men were killed. It is clear, therefore, that, had the Java not been so soon, and so completely disabled, there would have been a much less disparity in point of execution, than, under all the Java's disadvantages, did really exist between the two ships: and, when it is known that the men, owing to their awkwardness, inexperience, or some other cause, allowed two or three raking opportunities to pass, without firing more than half a dozen shot at the Constitution, the only surprise will be, that there was not a still greater disparity in the slaughter on board the two ships.

When the Java was fitted, she received on board, twenty-eight long 18-pounders upon the main-deck; sixteen carronades, 32-pounders, one launch-carronade, 18-pounder, and two long 9-pounders, upon the quarter-deck and forecastle; total, 47 guns. Not another gun of any description had the Java, when captured; and the launch-carronade, owing to some accident, was not even used. For that reason, probably, it was omitted in the statement of force, subjoined to Lieutenant Chads' letter. Determined not to be out-done by Captain Hull, Commodore Bainbridge made his prize-frigate of "49 guns" also; and the editors of the "Naval History," "Naval Monument," and "Sketches of the War," have not scrupled to particularize those "49 guns." The two first agree in adding two to the sixteen 32-pound carronades, and in substituting "one shifting gun, a 24-pounder," for the launch-carronade; but the two 9s, Mr. Clark (see p. 58) makes "two 18-pounders," Mr. Bowen "two large 12s." So little, however, is consistency studied by American historians, that Mr. Clark, in another page of his work, says,—"Java, guns mounted, 48."—But the most extraordinary statement of the Java's force, appears in the "Sketches of the War."—"The Java carried twenty eight 24-pounders on her gun-deck."—And this, too, in a third edition!—Was there no American honest enough to set the editor right?

The Java's complement, on leaving Spithead, was 277 officers, seamen and marines, and 23 boys; making, with the 97 passengers, a total of 397. The mate and 19 men, placed on board the William, reduced this number to 377; which agrees exactly with Lieutenant Chads' account of "ship's company and supernumeraries" present in the action.

The whole number of prisoners received out of the Java amounted to 356; subsequently reduced, by the death of the captain, one midshipman, Keele, (who, having died previous to the date of the surgeon's return, was included, among the "killed,") and one able seaman, to 353. Yet Commodore Bainbridge, after having "liberated and given up to the governor of St. Salvador, nine Portuguese seamen," and allowed "to land, without any restraint, three passengers, private characters," actually paroled "38 officers, and 323 petty-officers, seamen, marines, and boys;" total 361, instead of 341, the number of prisoners left, after deducting the 12 not paroled. How is this?

Commodore Bainbridge, apparently, was here guilty of as gross a fraud as any to be found upon the records of the admiralty-courts, wherein his countrymen, during a long reign of *neutrality,* had so often shocked honest men by their hardihood. The only difference is, that the national officer expects as much to be implied from his honor, as the merchant-captain or supercargo did from his oath.

Now for the fact. The William prize-ship was re-captured by the Hornet, on the afternoon of the action; arrived at St. Salvador on the same day that the Java did; and the prize-crew were landed from the Hornet, at the same time that the prisoners out of the Java were landed from the Constitution. The reader sees, then, how it was. The Java's mate and 19 men were added to the above-mentioned 341; and the *knowing* commodore paroled, as he said, 361 of the Java's crew. Not a word is there, in his letter, of any prisoners arriving from the Hornet, or of the Java's prize having been re-captured at all; although the William, at the date of the commodore's letter, was lying at anchor in St. Salvador, in company with the Constitution and Hornet. Aware that Captain Lawrence, in his official letter announcing the capture of the Peacock, would mention the re-capture of an American ship of 600 tons, and therefore expose the trick, it was contrived that his letter should comprise, only what occurred subsequently to the 6th of January, the day on which, as stated before, the Constitution left St. Salvador for the United States. (App. No. 29.) So that, after the commodore had, by his "60 killed," his 361 paroled, and 12 not paroled, *proved* that the Java had 433 men, his forbearing to state, in the official letter, that she had more than "upwards of 400." added to his scrupulous exception of the "three passengers, private characters," established, beyond power of contradiction, the *modesty* of the American officer!

But, in truth, who were these "three passengers, private characters," so generously exempted from parole?—No other, it would appear, than three of the Java's seamen, who had been fools enough to enter the American service. To have deducted them from the amount of prisoners received, would be making the Java's complement appear three men short of what it could, otherwise, be *proved* to have been. To have confessed the fact, would never do. Therefore, all the Java's passengers, naval, military, and civil, were paroled as officers, petty-officers, seamen, marines and boys," and the hiatus made by the three traitors, was cleverly filled up three *nominal* "passengers, private-characters, whom the commodore" (generous man!) "did not consider prisoners of war, and permitted to land without any restraint;" and of whom, of course, no further account was taken.

Without searching the Java's crew for Danes, Swedes, Italians, Spaniards, or any other foreigners; or even regarding the "nine Portuguese seamen" so politically "given up to the governor at St. Salvador," it is still fair not to include, as part of the Java's complement on going into action, the seven passengers in civil situations. That will reduce the number to 370; comprising 280 of her proper crew, the three military officers, and all the supernumerary naval officers and seamen on board.

To shew that the estimate is correct, the following recapitulation may be necessary:—

Java's proper crew, including boys,	300	
Deduct men sent on board prize,	20	
	——	280
Add passengers of every description,		97
		——
Total number on board, during action,		377
Deduct killed, (see p. 91,)		24
		——
Total number landed from Java,		353
Add prize-crew,		20
		——
Total No. alive of the 397 originally on board,		373
Deduct the "9 Portugeuse and 3 private persons,"		12
		——
Total No. paroled by Commodore Bainbridge,		361

The manner in which the Java's men were treated by the American officers, reflects upon the latter the highest disgrace. The moment the poor fellows were brought on board the Constitution, they were hand-cuffed, (a thing unknown in our service, except upon urgent necessity,) and pillaged of almost every thing. True, Lieutenant-general Hyslop got back his valuable service of plate, and the other officers were treated civilly. Who would not rather that the governor's plate was, at this very time, spread out upon Commodore Bainbridge's sideboard, than that British seamen, fighting bravely in their country's cause, should be put in fetters, and robbed of their little all?—What is all this mighty generosity but a political juggle,—a tub thrown to the whale?—Mr. Madison says to his officers: "Never mind making an ostentatious display of your generosity, where you know it will be proclaimed to the world. If you lose any thing by it, I'll take care congress shall recompense you, two-fold. Such conduct on the part of an American officer of rank, will greatly tend to discredit the British statements as to any other acts of your's not so proper to be made public; and will serve, besides, as an imperishable record of the national magnanimity and honor."—One object the Constitution's officers missed by their cruelty. Three only of the Java's men would enter with them: the remainder treated with contempt their re-iterated promises of high pay, rich land, and liberty.

Courage is an inherent principle in Britons; but courage alone will not make a seaman. If to know the duties of one, for the mere purpose of navigating a ship, requires some experience, how much more is required when a ship has an enemy to contend with. That she may manœuvre with success, (a most important operation,) the sails must be trimmed with the utmost nicety; and not a moment lost in looking for a rope, or considering what to do. Great judgment and presence of mind is often necessary, to repair a temporary damage by shot, or delay the fall of a tottering mast. A proficiency in all this constitutes the able seaman. Others of the crew are required at the guns. There stand men who, every one knowing exactly what he has to do, load and fire their gun with quickness and precision. Here stand men who, except a few, mere novices at the business, are looking upon each other for instruction; and, when they have succeeded in loading their gun, nine times out of ten, discharge it at random.

About forty or fifty of the Java's men had seen service; and, no doubt, were tolerable seamen. At the head of these, was the gallant-boatswain; and among them, were many who cheered, while having their wounds dressed in the cockpit. But the remainder consisted of newly-pressed landsmen, or of ill-disposed, weakly hands; the refuse of other ships. As to her supernumeraries, they, as stated before, were chiefly marine-society lads; rather an incumbrance, than a use, on board a ship of war. During the few weeks that intervened between the manning, and the capture, of the Java, disciplining the crew at the guns was, in a manner, prevented, by the lumbered state of the ship.

The marines of the Java were not much employed at the early part of the action, owing to the distance maintained by her opponent; and towards the last, the ship's dismasted state confined them to her decks. Of the 34 marines there stationed, "18," says the officer commanding them, "were very young recruits; the rest had been to sea before." Of what use are marines, acting as such, unless good marksmen? A musket-bullet will not perforate a ship's side. To reach the enemy, (from the level of the deck, at least,) it must catch him at the fleeting moment of exposure; as he hastily ascends the rigging, or incautiously shews his head above the bulwarks.—Can "very young recruits" hope to succeed at this?

The Java's gallant commander, previous to his leaving Spithead, made several applications for a more effective and better disposed crew; foreseeing, as he did, the probability of falling in with one of the large American frigates. He was reminded of the difficulty of procuring men; and told, that an East India voyage would make seamen!

The Java, thus manned, left England on the 12th of November and the official account of the Guerriere's capture had reached the admiralty since early in October. Let him who may think there was, at this time, in the British navy, a scarcity of frigates of the Java's class, turn to the list for November, 1812; where he will perhaps be surprised to see, among the ships in ordinary, the fine 24-pounder frigate Endymion; a ship as nearly equal in force to the American frigate Constitution, as any Briton could wish. True, the Endymion, according to the papers laid before parliament, in February, 1815, was ordered to be fitted in "July,

1812;" but she was not got ready till the "18th of May, 1813."

Doubtless, a voyage to the East Indies and back, with occasional drilling at the guns, *would* have greatly altered the character of the Java's men; and, had the Constitution then met that ship, even without her ninety seven passengers, the disparity in force would not have been so great.

With the change of the Constitution's commander, a slight change occurred in her armament; a single shifting 18-pound carronade having been substituted for two of her 32s. This shifting carronade she fought on either side, through the gangway-port, the same as the United States. (See pp. 79-80.) As a proof that the American commanders had the privilege of altering, in some degree, the armaments of their respective ships, the "Report of a committee" on the American naval establishment, dated in January, 1814, contains the following, as one of the "causes of the abuses complained of:"—"The great latitude allowed commanders, in altering, repairing, and furnishing their ships." With the exception of the 18-pound carronade, considered probably as a boat-gun, the "Sketches of the War" gives a similar account of the Constitution's force to that contained in Captain Chads' statement. But, most unaccountably, accuses that officer of "largely overrating" the Constitution's force. "He reported," says the editor, "her force to be—forty two long 24-pounders, sixteen carronades, 32-pounders, and one carronade, 18-pounder; being in all 59 guns."—Whence did the editor extract this account? Not an American newspaper that copied the letter, but gives the lie to his assertion.

The Constitution, having none of her men absent in prizes, had on board her full complement; which, according to the statement of her first lieutenant, consisted of 485. Admitting the regular establishment of the American 44-gun frigates to be no more than 475, "the great latitude allowed the commanders in furnishing their ships," enabled them to take on board supernumeraries; and the Guerriere's capture, and Commodore Bainbridge's interest at Boston, gave the Constitution, among the seamen, a decided preference. Only one boy was seen on board of her, and he was 17 years old; older, no doubt, than half the Java's marines. However, to avoid as much as possible an over-estimate, the Constitution's complement, on commencing action with the Java, will be considered as 477 men, and 3 boys. Some of the former had belonged to the Iphigenia; others to the Guerriere; and 40 or 50 were recognised as English. It need hardly be added, that the men, generally, were prime seamen; and the crew, altogether, a remarkably fine one.

The Java, as stated before, was originally a French ship. She measured as follows:—

	Ft.	In.
Length of lower-deck, from rabbit to rabbit,	152	5½
Breadth, extreme	39	11⅜

So trifling is the difference in size, between the Java and the other two captured frigates, that a reference to what has already appeared on the subject of comparative dimensions, will fully suffice. The circumstance related about the slight effect produced upon the Constitution's masts by the Java's shot, can be better understood, now that the relative stoutness of the two main-masts has been shewn. (See p. 55.)

Comparative force of the two ships.

		Java.		Constitution.	
Broadside-metal in pounds,	l. guns,	261		384	
	carr.	274		370	
		—	535	—	754
Complement,	men,	347		477	
	boys,	23		3	
		—	370	—	480
Size in tons,			1073		1533

The only material difference observable between the comparative force in this action, and the Constitution and Guerriere's, is, in the *complement;* but, when we consider that the Guerriere's was an old, the Java's a new ship's company, with a much greater proportion of boys than appears in the above statement, that difference becomes merely nominal.

Taking into view the loss and damage sustained by the Constitution, and the obstinate defence of the Java, against so superior a force, such as may have been disappointed at the result of the other two frigate-actions with the Americans, will not deny, surely, that, in this of the Java and Constitution, the honor of the British flag was nobly maintained.

Before quitting the Java entirely, it will tend to illustrate the subject, to bestow a few observations upon the action between H.M.S. Amelia, Captain Irby, and the French frigate l'Arethuse. This action was fought on the night of the 7th of February, 1813, off *l'Isles de Los,* on the African coast. Captain Bouvet's official account has been received in England, and a translation of it has appeared in print. (Nav. Chron. vol. xxix. p. 293.) The British and French accounts agree as to the time when the action commenced, but differ a trifle as to the period of its duration: the mean of the two accounts fixes this at 3 hours and 26 minutes; very little short of the Java's. As to the manner in which the action terminated, the two commanders differ materially. Captain Irby says:—"She (l'Arethuse) bore up, having the advantage of being able to do so, leaving us in an ungovernable state."—Captain Bouvet says:—"We were no longer in good condition, and the enemy, crouding all sail, abandoned the field of battle to us."—It may be considered, then, as *a drawn battle*. Whichever ship had lost her masts, must have struck her flag. The Amelia's killed amounted to 51; her wounded to 95. The two cartels having on board the surviving officers and crew of the Java, fell in with l'Arethuse, after her action with the Amelia. Lieutenant Chads, having, while a prisoner at the isle of France, known Captain Bouvet, who then commanded there, and bore a very high character, went on board l'Arethuse; and was shewn a list of 31 killed, and 74 wounded, in her action with the Amelia. It is probable, that most of the slightly wounded had, by this time, recovered; and were therefore not noticed.

It is due to the veracity of a British officer to state, that "Captain Irby, in his dispatch to the admiralty," does *not* mention l'Arethuse's consort, le Rubis, "as being in sight just before the commencement of the action." (Naval Chron. vol. xxix. p. 383.) On the contrary, after detailing the proceedings of the 6th, he says:—"And the next morning, one of the frigates (I believe l'Arethuse) was just visible from the deck."

The Amelia's armament was the same as the Java's. The British officers who were on board l'Arethuse, state that her main-deck guns were French 18s, not "24-pounders," as Captain Irby had been informed. The caliber of her carronades was not known. The carronades of la Traave, a fine 44-gun frigate, captured in October, 1813, consisted of sixteen 18-pounders.—Admit l'Arethuse to have had the same; and, adding one-eighth for the difference between French and English caliber, her broadside-weight of metal would amount to 445 pounds; but, as l'Arethuse's carronades may have been 24s or 32s, it is fair to consider the two ships as equal in guns, or broadside-weight of metal.

The Amelia, like the Java, had a number of supernumeraries on board; but, owing to the general sickness of the men, Captain Irby says:—"We had barely our complement fit for duty, and they much enervated." A sickly old, and a healthy new ship's company, are about equal in effectiveness. Captain Bouvet admits that he had in the action, an officer and boat's crew of le Rubis: say, in all, 340 men. Three days after the action, he took out of a Portuguese prize, in which the captain and crew of le Rubis had embarked after she became wrecked on the 6th, half that ship's complement; and the officers of the Java have stated, that l'Arethuse had, when they fell in with her, about 400 as fine seamen as ever sailed out of France. L'Arethuse, therefore, was not filled with conscripts and raw hands, in number crowding each other; but had a fair complement of experienced seamen, and good artillerists. Captain Bouvet particularly designates one of her officers as—"corporal of marine-artillery."

Referring to the relative numbers of killed on board the Amelia, and even the Macedonian instead of the Java; and taking into consideration the decided superiority of the Macedonian's antagonist, and the equality in force between the Amelia and l'Arethuse, we cannot but see how greatly the French crew excelled the American, in the precision of their fire." (App. No.

19.) Nor did Captain Irby's men perform badly; as the killed of l'Arethuse sufficiently testify.

The Amelia, like the Java, had been a French ship, (la Proserpine,) and measured within a few tons of the Java; and, as if still to continue the similitude, Captain Bouvet stated l'Arethuse to be a sister-ship to la Renommée, taken in 1811; which ship, unknown to him, was the identical Java.

It is clear that the French captain, when he engaged the Amelia, had heard nothing of the Java's loss. Previous to his leaving France, he very probably had of the Guerriere's. Without considering these things, the British journals were declaiming, at a fine rate, about the new spirit infused into the French marine, by the success of the Americans.

The action of the Amelia and l'Arethuse should have taught the Americans, not to over-rate their abilities; not to deal so much in the bombastic, when recounting their "brilliant exploits upon the water." They might have seen that, had Captain Bouvet kept off at first, and tried to fall his adversary's masts; or even been provided with some of those curious shot that fell out of the Java's foremast, the Amelia would, in all probability, have been his. But l'Arethuse approached boldly, within pistol-shot; slaughtered more, but disabled less, than the Constitution. There was no manoeuvring to avoid close action; no yawing away in the smoke; no unusual shot employed; no riflemen picking off the British officers:—"all," says Captain Irby, "fell by fair fighting."

CHAPTER VIII.

British official account of the Peacock and Hornet's action not published—American details of it—Captain Lawrence's time corrected—Peacock sinks—l'Espeigle not in sight—American print of the action—Peacock's loss—Hornet's damages and loss—Peacock's force in guns and men—Hornet's force in guns—Complement fixed—Relative size of the Peacock and Hornet fully considered—Statement of comparative force—Hornet's challenge to the Bonne Citoyenne—Captain Greene's reply—Unhandsome behaviour of the commanders of the Constitution and Hornet upon the occasion.

OF the action between H. M. late brig Peacock, and the U. S. ship Hornet, no British official account has been published. Fortunately, a gross misstatement which appeared on the subject, in the New York "Commercial Advertiser," of the 16th of April, 1813, called forth a reply, in the same public manner, from the Peacock's late first lieutenant. (App. No. 30.) This counter-statement must serve, in lieu of a British official account, to contrast with the official letter of Captain Lawrence. (App. No. 29.)

The action was fought on the 24th of February, 1813, close to the entrance of the Demarara river; and continued, according to Captain Lawrence, "less than 15 minutes;" but, "by Peacock's time, for 25 minutes;" when the British vessel, being totally cut to pieces, and in danger of sinking, hoisted a signal of distress at her fore-rigging. Shortly afterwards, the brig's main-mast went by the board.

As a proof that the Peacock could do no more, however well disposed her officers and crew may have been, she sank, in a few minutes after the action; carrying down, according to Captain Lawrence, thirteen of her own, and three of the Hornet's crew; but, of the former, four were afterwards saved by the enemy's boats. Another four of the Peacock's crew took to her stern-boat, just as the action ended; and arrived in safety at Demarara.

Captain Lawrence states that H. M. brig l'Espiegle was "about six miles in shore of him; and could plainly see the whole of the action." But Lieutenant Wright's letter is equally positive, "that H. B. M. brig l'Espeigle was not visible from the look-outs stationed at the Peacock's mast-heads, for some time previous to the action." (App. No. 30.) A court-martial has since been holden upon Captain John Taylor, of l'Espeigle, at the instance of the admiralty; and one of the charges was, for "failing in his duty, when in pursuit of the Hornet American sloop, after the capture of the Peacock." Of this charge he was acquitted.

In the engraving of this action, given in the "Naval Monument," l'Espeigle appears scarcely two miles from the spot; and, although the Peacock is represented with part of her hull under water, the remainder shews as many ports as she had upon her whole side!

Captain Peake, the gallant commander of the Peacock, was killed at the early, not "the latter part" of the action. She lost, also, four seamen killed; her master, a midshipman, the carpenter, and captain's clerk, and 29 seamen and marines, wounded; of whom three died, soon after being removed to the Hornet; total 38.

The damages of the Hornet are represented as trifling. One shot went through the fore-mast, and the bowsprit was slightly injured; but her hull suffered little or no injury. The Americans acknowledge a loss of only two men killed, and three wounded.

The Peacock was originally armed with 32-pound carronades; but Captain Peake, considering her scantling as too slight to bear them, got 24s in exchange. She had two long sixes instead of "nines"; and, admitting she had "a 12-pound carronade on her top-gallant-forecastle," and a swivel or two, it is denied that she had "one four or six-pounder."

The Peacock had long been the admiration of her numerous visitors, for the tasteful arrangement of her deck; and had obtained, in consequence, the name of the *yacht*. The breechings of the carronades were lined with white canvass; the shot-lockers shifted from their usual places; and nothing could exceed, in brilliancy, the polish upon the traversing-bars and elevating screws. If carronades, in general, as mounted in the British service, are liable to turn in-board or upset, what must have been the state of the Peacock's carronades after the first broadside?—The captain of l'Espeigle, attached to the same station, was, at his court-martial, found guilty of "neglecting to exercise the ship's company at the great guns."—A single discharge from the Peacock's carronades, in exercise, would have betrayed the very defective state of their fastenings; and our feelings might then have found some relief in the skill, as well as gallantry, evinced in her defence.

Captain Lawrence says:—"I find, by her quarter-bill, that her crew consisted of 134 men, four of whom were absent in a prize." The Peacock's officers declare that she had, "at the time she engaged the Hornet, a complement of 122 men and boys;" which, without the four men that were absent, was one above her established number. Of these, seventeen were boys. When we consider that the Peacock had been long on a West India station, it cannot be surprising, that the chief part of the crew were convalescents; although it is so, that she should have had her full complement on board.

According to the British lieutenant's letter, the Hornet mounted eighteen carronades, 32-pounders, and two long 9-pounders; but several American papers have stated her long guns as twelves.

In fixing the Hornet's complement of men in the action, there will not be much difficulty. Lieutenant Wright says she had 170 men; and that is now known to have been the establishment, exclusive of supernumeraries, of United States' vessels rating, like the Hornet, of "18 guns." Captain Lawrence states, that his master and seven men were absent in a prize; and that he mustered, on the day after the action, 270 souls, including the crew of the American brig Hunter, of Portland, taken a few days before by the Peacock."

It was very kind of Captain Lawrence to give the number of souls mustered. Relying upon that, the following statement will shew, clearly, that the Hornet must have had, in her action with the Peacock, 165 men; making, with the eight absent, a complement of 173; supernumeraries included.

Peacock's complement of men and boys,			122
Killed in action, and died after removing,		8	
Drowned,		9	
Escaped in the boat,		4	
			21
Peacock's surviving crew,			101
Brig Hunter's ship's company, exclusive of master and mate,			9
Hornet's original complement,		173	
Absent in a prize,		8	
Present in action,		165	
Killed and died of wounds,	2		
Drowned,	3		
		5	
Hornet's surviving crew,			160
Number of souls mustered,			270

The Hornet had three lieutenants, a lieutenant of marines, and a great shew of midshipmen. Her crew were all picked men; many of whom had belonged to her from the time she was commissioned. No boys were seen on board, yet two will be allowed, The exclusion of all men "on the sick list," in both crews, would be much more in favour of the Peacock than the Hornet.

The Peacock was built in 1807; upon the same model as the Frolic, and all the other British 18-gun brigs. Captain Lawrence, sensible that the Peacock would not rise up from the deep to confront him, says:—"I should judge her to be about the tonnage of the Hornet. Her beam was greater by five inches, but her extreme length not so great by four feet."

The first question that arises is;—if the Peacock sank so soon after the action, that several men were drowned in her, what time had the Hornet's people to measure her *length* and *breadth?*—The dimensions which the Peacock's carpenter, if asked for them, could have furnished the Hornet's commander, would have been precisely the same as those which will be presently given.

By dint of a little scrutiny into American statements, the dimensions of the Hornet can be obtained with tolerable accuracy. Captain Biddle, who commanded her when, at a subsequent day, she captured the Penguin, the Peacock's sister-brig, stated his prize to be "two feet shorter upon deck," and to have "greater breadth," than the Hornet. Fortunately, the American officers, anxious to shew what an extraordinary large brig they had captured, published in a New York paper, the Penguin's "length on deck," and "breadth of beam;" making the former "110 feet," the latter "31 feet 6 inches."—The absurdity of this will be shewn, when we arrive at the Penguin's action: at present, the figures are all we want.—The Hornet's "length on deck," then, is admitted to be 112 feet. Let us take Captain Lawrence's "five inches" as the difference between the Hornet's breadth, and the "31 feet 6 inches," stated to have been the Penguin's breadth; although the expression "greater breadth" would almost imply, that the excess was so trifling, as to be not worth computing. This would give for the Hornet's breadth, 31 feet 1 inch; only 3 inches more than that of the Wasp; a ship six, instead of "two, feet shorter upon deck than the Hornet."

These dimensions will make the Hornet 450 tons only; whereas, one of the lieutenants of the late U. S. ship Frolic, who had served in the same capacity on board the Hornet, described her as very little inferior in size to the Frolic; and she is 539 tons.

Dimensions of the two vessels.

	Peacock, brig.		Hornet, ship.	
	Ft.	In.	Ft.	In.
Length on deck, from rabbit to rabbit,	100	3	112	0
Breadth, extreme,	30	7	31	1

Some opinion may be formed of the stoutness of the Hornet's scantling by that of the Wasp; (see p. 76;) and the former's masts and yards are described as very little inferior in size to those of the late American ship Frolic; now the Florida in our service.

Comparative force of the two vessels.

		Peacock.		Hornet.	
Broadside-metal in pounds	l. guns,	6		9	
	carr.	192		288	
		—	198	—	297
Complement,	men,	105		163	
	boys,	17		2	
		—	122	—	165
Size in tons,			386		450

The Americans, now, for the first time declared, "that 24-pounders were as good as 32s"; and that, therefore, the two sloops, (although in relative broadside-metal, exactly as 3 to 2,) were "equally matched." Improving upon this, the editor of the "Naval Monument" says, plumply, "the Hornet shivered her *superior* antagonist to atoms."

Previous to his action with the Peacock, Captain Lawrence took advantage of another fortunate event that occurred to the Hornet. H. M. S. Bonne Citoyenne, Captain Pitt B. Greene, with half a million sterling on board, which she had brought from Rio de la Plata, was lying in St. Salvador, at the time the U. S. ships Constitution and Hornet were cruizing off the port. A king's packet, bound to England, was also detained there, by the presence of those ships.

The Constitution and Hornet anchored in the harbour; and their respective commanders were frequently at the house of Mr. Hill, the American consul; a man of notorious Anti-british feelings. The nature of the Bonne Citoyenne's cargo was well understood by all the merchants (of which the consul was one) at St. Salvador; and both Commodore Bainbridge and Captain Lawrence, as professional men, knew that the British commander dared not engage in a different service, from that upon which he had been ordered.

The consul, and the two American commanders, laid their heads together, to contrive something that, without any personal risk to either, should contribute to the renown of their common country. What so likely as a challenge to Captain Greene?—It could not be accepted; and then the refusal would be as good as a victory to Captain Lawrence. Accordingly, a challenge for the Hornet to meet the Bonne Citoyenne, was offered by Captain Lawrence, through the American to the British consul, Mr. Frederick Landeman. (App. Nos. 32. and 33.)

Without making the unpleasant avowal, that his government had, upon this occasion, reduced the vessel he commanded from a king's cruizer to a merchant-ship, Captain Greene transmitted, through the consular channel, an animated reply; refusing a meeting "upon terms so manifestly disadvantageous as those proposed by Commodore Bainbridge." (App. Nos. 34. and 35.) Indeed, it would appear, as if the commodore had purposely inserted the words, "or not interfering," lest Captain Greene should, contrary to expectation, have accepted the challenge. For, had the two ships met by agreement, engaged, the Constitution looked on "without interfering," and the British ship been the conqueror, the pledge of "honor" on the part of both American commanders, would have been fulfilled: and can any one, for a moment imagine, that Commodore Bainbridge would have seen the Bonne Citoyenne carry off a United States ship of war, without attempting her rescue?—It was more than his head was worth.—Where was the guarantee against re-capture, which always accompanies *serious* proposals of this sort, when a stronger force, belonging to either party, is to preserve a temporary neutrality?—Let the commander of the Montague 74, have made the same proposal to the Hornet, pledging his "honor not to interfere;" and see how deservedly he would have been ridiculed, not by Americans only, but by the whole of his countrymen.

Commodore Bainbridge, in his public letter, says: "The Bonne Citoyenne is a larger vessel, and of greater force in guns and men than the Hornet."—She is, certainly, a trifle larger; but, it is believed, mounted the same number and description of guns, with the addition of a boat carronade. Her complement was twenty five men less than the Hornet's; but her crew *had* been exercised at the guns, were well disposed, and commanded by a gallant officer.

Captain Lawrence's boast of his having blockaded the Bonne Citoyenne, and a packet, until the Montague chased the Hornet off, was well calculated to exalt him in the opinion of his friends; but what assurance had Captain Greene, that Commodore Bainbridge, as well apprized of the Bonne Citoyenne's destination, as of the nature of her cargo, was not cruizing in the offing. The British ship would have been a rich prize, indeed; and her commander most justly laughed at, had he become the dupe of so shallow an artifice. The blockade of the Bonne Citoyenne and packet by the Hornet, was a fine subject for the painter. Accordingly, the "Naval Monument" contains a clumsy wood-cut, representing the transaction in all its brilliancy.

That the American consul at St. Salvador should have been ungenerous enough to reduce a British officer to the necessity of refusing, under any circumstances, to meet a ship of his own class, creates no surprise whatever. But who could expect that two national officers, aware of the delicate situation in which a brother-officer, though apolitical enemy, was placed, would have urged the unhandsome request; much more, have triumphed over the answer, which they knew it was his duty to give?

CHAPTER IX.

Shannon and Tenedos reconnoitre Boston—Chesapeake gets in unperceived—President and Congress avoid the blockading ships, and escape to sea—Captain Broke detaches the Tenedos—Receives on board twenty two Irish labourers—Challenges the Chesapeake, and stands close in to Boston light-house—Chesapeake sails out, without receiving the challenge—The two ships engage—Details of the action—American spectators—Lieutenant Budd's official letter—Shannon's damages and loss—Chesapeake's also—Shannon's force, in guns and men—American method of computing a ship's complement—Chesapeake's force in guns—Names of her guns—Dismantling shot—Effects of her langridge on the Shannon's wounded—Cask of lime—a curious case on the subject—Chesapeake's complement—Difficulty of ascertaining it—The number fixed—Quality of the crew—American remarks thereon—Dimensions of the two ships, in hull and spars—Statement of comparative force—Remarks thereon.

ON the 2d of April, 1813, H. M. S. Shannon, 46, Captain Broke, accompanied by the Tenedos, 46, Captain Parker, reconnoitered the harbour of Boston, and discovered lying there, the U. S. frigate Congress ready for sea, President nearly so, and Constitution under repair.

On the 13th, the U. S. frigate Chesapeake, Captain Evans, got into Boston, through the eastern passage, unperceived by either of the British frigates; and, on the 1st of May, foggy weather, and a sudden favourable shift of wind, enabled the President, Commodore Rodgers, and Congress, Captain Smith, to avoid the Shannon and Tenedos, and escape to sea. The American accounts say, with a very grave air, that the British frigates sailed from the coast, purposely to avoid the commodore.

Having ascertained that the Chesapeake would soon be ready for sea again, Captain Broke, on the 25th of May, took a supply of provisions and water from the Tenedos; and detached her, with orders to Captain Parker, not to rejoin him before the 14th of June; the earliest date, at which, it was considered, the

Constitution could be got ready to accompany the Chesapeake, should the latter wait in port for that purpose.

On the 26th of May, the Shannon recaptured the brig Lucy, and on the 29th, the brig William; both belonging to Halifax. A meeting with the Chesapeake being now Captain Broke's sole purpose, nothing but the circumstance of those vessels belonging to the port of Halifax, could induce him to weaken the Shannon's crew, by sending them in. The master of the Lucy, and five recaptured men-of-war's-men, took her in charge; and a midshipman and four of the Shannon's men, the William.

On the afternoon of the 30th, the Shannon fell in with the British privateer-brig, Sir John Sherbrooke. This vessel had on board fifty two Irish labourers, taken three days previous out of the captured American privateer, Governor Plumer; which vessel had captured the ship Duck, from Waterford to Burin, Newfoundland; having on board these men as passengers. The commander of the Sir John Sherbrooke had persuaded thirty of the latter to join his vessel; and the remaining twenty-two were now pressed into the Shannon.

Early on Monday morning, Captain Broke addressed to the commanding-officer of the Chesapeake, a letter of challenge; which, for candour, spirit, and gentlemanly style, has rarely been equalled. (App. No. 36.) This letter was confided to a Captain Slocum, a discharged prisoner; who immediately departed in his boat for Marblehead, a port a few miles north of Boston. At the same time, the Shannon, with colours flying, stood in close to the light-house; and there lay-to. She had been as near to Boston during several of the preceding days; but thick rainy weather had obstructed the view of the harbour. The Chesapeake was now seen at anchor in President Roads, with royal yards across; and apparently ready for sea. She presently loosed her fore-top-sail; and, shortly afterwards, all her top-sails, and sheeted them home. But, from the wind being perfectly fair, and the ship not getting under way, the Shannon's people began to fear that she was not inclined to come out.

Between twelve and one, while the men were at dinner, Captain Broke went himself to the mast-head; and there observed the Chesapeake fire a gun, and loose and set top-gallant-sails. She was soon under way; and made more sail as she came down; having a light breeze in her favor. While aloft, Captain Broke saw that Captain Slocum's boat had not reached the shore in time for the delivery of his letter of challenge to the commander of the Chesapeake.

The Shannon now filled, and stood out from the land under easy sail, till 4 o'clock; when, the Chesapeake having hauled up, and fired a gun, as if in defiance, the Shannon hauled up also, and reeved top-sails. Both ships, now about seven miles distant, again bore away; the Shannon with her fore-sail brailed up, and her main-top-sail braced flat, and shivering, that the Chesapeake might overtake her. At a few minutes past 5, Boston light-house bearing west, distant about six leagues, the Shannon again hauled up, with her head to the southward and eastward; and lay-to, under topsails, top-gallant-sails, jib, and spanker; having barely steerage-way.

The Chesapeake came down upon the Shannon's starboard-quarter, with three ensigns flying: one at the mizen-royal-mast-head, one at the peak, and one in the starboard-main-rigging. She had, also, flying at the fore, a large white flag, inscribed with the words:—"FREE TRADE AND SAILORS' RIGHTS;"—upon a supposition, perhaps, that that favorite American motto would paralize the efforts, or damp the energy, of the Shannon's men.—The Shannon had only an old rusty blue ensign at the peak; nor was her outside appearance at all calculated to inspire a belief, of the order and discipline that reigned within. Captain Broke thought, at one time, that the Chesapeake would pass under his stern, and engage him upon the larboard-side; he therefore ordered his men, as she passed, to lay down flat so as to avoid, in some degree, the raking fire. But Captain Lawrence, either overlooking or waving this advantage, at 30 minutes past 5, gallantly luffed up, within half-pistol-shot, upon the Shannon's starboard quarter.

The Shannon's men had received orders, to fire as their guns would bear; and to aim principally at the enemy's ports. The first and second shot were discharged from the aftermost main-deck gun, and quarter-deck carronade; just as the Chesapeake, while rounding-to, brought her fore-mast in a line with the Shannon's mizzenmast. These two shot were distinctly heard before the Chesapeake commenced firing; and, by the American account, both shot took effect; killing and wounding several officers and men, The Chesapeake discharged her whole broadside in return; which was replied to by the Shannon's guns, as fast as the men could level them with precision.

In about seven minutes from the commencement of the action, the Chesapeake, having her jib-sheet and fore-top-sail-tie shot away, fell on board the Shannon; the fluke of the latter's waist anchor, (which, to assist in trimming the ship, had been stowed in the main-chains,) entering the former's quarter-gallery window. The shot from the Shannon's aftermost guns, now had a fair range along the Chesapeake's decks; beating in the stern-ports, and sweeping the men from their quarters. The shot from the foremost guns, at the same time entering the ports from the main-mast aft, did considerable execution.

When about 10 minutes had elapsed, an open cask of musket-cartridges, standing upon the Chesapeake's cabin-sky-light for the use of the marines, caught fire and blew up; but did no injury whatever. Even the spanker-boom, directly in the way of the explosion, was barely singed. The Chesapeake's head had, by this time, fallen off; so that she lay close along-side the Shannon; the latter's main-mast being nearly in a line with her opponent's taffrail.

Captain Broke now saw that the Chesapeake's quarter-deck division were deserting their guns. He instantly called out—"Board!" and, accompanied by the first lieutenant and 20 men, sprang upon the Chesapeake's quarter-deck. Here not an officer or man was to be seen. Upon her gangways, about 20 Americans made a slight resistance. These were instantly driven towards the forecastle; where a few endeavoured to get down the fore-hatchway, but in their eagerness prevented each other; a few fled over the bows, and reached the main-deck through the bridle-ports; and the remainder laid down their arms, and submitted.

Between 30 and 40 of the Shannon's marines quickly followed the first boarding party. These kept down the men who were ascending the main-hatchway; and answered a spirited fire, still continued from the main and mizen tops. The Chesapeake's fore-top was, in the mean time, stormed by Midshipman Smith and his top-men, about five in number; who either destroyed or drove on deck, all the Americans there stationed. This gallant young man had deliberately passed along the Shannon's fore-yard, which was braced up, to the Chesapeake's, also braced up; and thence into her top.

After those upon the forecastle had submitted, Captain Broke ordered one of his men to stand sentry over them; and sent most of the others aft, where the conflict was still going on. He was in the act of giving them orders to answer the fire from the Chesapeake's main-top, when the sentry called lustily out to him. On turning round, the captain found himself opposed by three of the Americans; who, seeing they were superior to the British then near them, had armed themselves a-fresh. Captain Broke parried the middle fellow's pike, and wounded him in the face; but instantly received from the man on the pikeman's right, a blow with the butt-end of a musket, which bared his scull, and nearly stunned him. Determined to finish the British commander, the third man cut him down with his broad-sword; and, at that very instant, was himself cut down by one of the Shannon's seamen. Captain Broke and his treacherous foe now lay side by side; each, although nearly powerless, struggling to regain his sword; when a marine dispatched the American with his bayonet. Captain Broke was not the only sufferer upon this occasion; one of his men was killed, and two or three were wounded. Can it be wondered, if all that were concerned in this breach of faith, fell victims to the indignation of the Shannon's men? It was as much as their commander could do, to save from their fury a young midshipman, who, having slid down a rope from the Chesapeake's fore-top, begged his protection. Mr. Smith, who had also descended from the fore-top, and a seaman, were at this time helping the captain on his legs. The seaman, while tying a handkerchief round his commander's head, called out, (pointing aft,)—"There, sir, there goes up the old ensign over the Yankee colours." The captain saw it hoisting; and was instantly led to the quarter-deck; where he seated himself upon one of the carronade-slides.

The gallant first lieutenant of the Shannon was struck on the head with a grape-shot from one of that ship's fore-mast guns, while in the act of hoisting the British colours over the American. Another gun was discharged, unfortunately, before the officer commanding that division, knew of the Chesapeake's surrender; and three or four of the Shannon's men shared the lamented fate of Mr. Watt, besides several being wounded.

Even after the British colours were flying on board the Chesapeake, some of her men kept firing up the main-hatchway, and killed a British marine. It was then, and not till then, that Lieutenant Falkiner, who was sitting on the booms, very properly directed three or four muskets that were ready, to be fired down. Captain Broke, from his seat upon the carronade-slide, told him to summon them to surrender, if they desired quarter. He did so: they replied—"We surrender;" and all hostility ceased. Soon after this, Captain Broke's senses failed him from loss of blood; and, the Shannon's jolly-boat arriving with a supply of men, (the two ships having separated, owing to the Chesapeake's quarter-gallery giving way,) he was carried on board his own ship.

Between the discharge of the first gun, and the period of Captain Broke's boarding, 11 minutes only elapsed; and, in 4 minutes more, the Chesapeake was completely his. Hundreds of spectators from Boston, and the surrounding neighbourhood, holding their watches in their hands, were astonished at the speedy termination of the firing; and the fact of the Shannon's first lieutenant having been killed by a cannon-shot, as he was hoisting the colours on board the Chesapeake, clearly proves, that the firing did not cease till the very moment of victory.

What a happy circumstance it was that, during the whole of this doubly auspicious day, no British cruizer, public or private, came in sight. If we except a very numerous assemblage of American pleasure-yachts, and a few gun-boats, the two frigates had the offing to themselves. At about 8 o'clock in the evening, the prisoners being divided, and properly secured, the British ship, and her fine prize, bent their course for Halifax; where they arrived in perfect safety on the Sunday following; being the fifth day after the action.

The "Report of the court of inquiry on the loss of the Chesapeake" (App. No. 40) grounds a string of suppositions upon "the cautious manner in which the enemy came on board."—Had the court tried to invest its proceedings with an air of ridicule, could it possibly have succeeded better, than by making such an assertion?

Let us see how the editor of the "Naval History" describes the boarding attempt. He says:—"The bugleman, who should have called the boarders, as ordered by Captain Lawrence, did not do his duty. The Shannon had sustained so much injury, that her commander, Commodore Brooke, was preparing to repel any attempt of boarding from the Chesapeake; but, at this moment, Brooke, perceiving the havoc his fire had occasioned on the deck of the Chesapeake, jumped on board her with about 20 men. They would soon have been driven back, but all the officers on deck were either killed or wounded. The second lieutenant, Budd, who commanded the first division below, led up the boarders; but only 15 or 20 men followed him. With these he defended the ship until disabled by a wound. Lieutenant Ludlow, though wounded, hurried on deck, where he soon received a mortal sabre-wound; 60 additional men being thrown on board from the Shannon, the crew of the Chesapeake, who had no officer to direct and rally them, were overpowered. The Chesapeake, however, was not surrendered by an act of submission, but was taken possession of by a force that overwhelmed all opposition." (N. Hist. vol. i. p. 205.)

"Jumped on board her with about 20 men."—This is a specimen of the "cautious manner" in which the British boarded. After confessing that "the crew of the Chesapeake," then consisting of, at least, 340 men, quite unhurt, "were overpowered" by 80 British, Mr. Clark gravely adds:—"The Chesapeake, however, was not surrendered by an act of submission, but was taken possession of by a force that overwhelmed all opposition"!

Aware of this inconsistency in Mr. Clark's statement, the "Sketches of the War" makes the 80 British "200." The same work assures its readers, that Captain Broke boarded, because he was "apprehensive of the Shannon's sinking"; and ascribes the Chesapeake's not capturing her "superior enemy" to the blowing up of the arm-chest.

Mr. Budd, the Chesapeake's second lieutenant, has made his official letter nearly as short as the action. (App. No. 39.) He gives both "A. Ms." and "P. Ms." before the combat began; but, afterwards, finds it his interest to be less precise. His assertion that the arm-chest "was blown up by a hand-grenade thrown from the enemy's ship," is utterly false. No hand-grenade whatever was thrown from the Shannon; although she had on board about a dozen in all. Mr. Budd wrote his letter fifteen days after the action; and must have made the assertion, knowing it to be false. It is probable, he took the hint from the paragraphs about the "infernal machine," &c. contained in the Boston papers describing the action; which papers had reached Halifax about two days before the date of his letter.

The "court of inquiry" makes a fine story of the firing down the hatchway. Not a word is there of the "magnanimous conquered foe" having fired from below, in the first instance, and killed a British marine. Captain Broke will long have cause to remember the treatment he experienced from this "magnanimous conquered foe." So far, indeed, from the conduct of the British being "a most unwarrantable abuse of power after success," Lieutenant Cox of the Chesapeake, in the hearing of several English gentlemen, has since admitted, that he owed his life to the forbearance of one of the Shannon's marines. When the American officer arrived on board the Shannon, and some of them were finding out reasons for being "taken so unaccountably," their first lieutenant, Ludlow, a gallant officer, and who fought hard in repelling the boarders, readily acknowledged, that the Shannon had beaten them *heartily* and *fairly*.

Five shot passed through the Shannon; one only below the main-deck: several struck, and most of them lodged in the starboard side, ranged in a line just above the copper. A long iron bar was seen sticking out of her copper. Until her shot-holes were stopped, the Shannon made a good deal of water, upon the larboard tack; but, upon the other, not more than usual. The "Report" actually states, that the Shannon "was reduced almost to a sinking condition."

The Shannon's fore and main-masts were slightly injured by shot; her bowsprit, previously sprung, and mizen-mast were badly wounded. No other spar was damaged. The Shannon carried a pole mizen top-mast; which, from its shortness, may have given rise to the assertion, among the boat-spectators, that her "mizen-royal-mast was shot away." The Shannon's rigging was very slightly injured. Notwithstanding these facts, the "Report" states the Shannon to have been "much cut in her spars and rigging."

The Shannon, besides her first lieutenant, lost the purser, captain's clerk, 20 seamen, marines, and supernumeraries, and 1 boy, killed; her commander, boatswain, a midshipman, and 56 seamen, marines, and supernumeraries, wounded; of whom 24, including the captain and boatswain, (the latter since dead,) were severely wounded; total killed and wounded 83. Three of the Irish supernumeraries fell in the action. To say that these rough sons of Erin, amidst the new and awful scene they were exposed to, behaved gallantly, would be superfluous, considering the land they came from. Perhaps their native valor received a slight stimulus, from the harsh treatment they had experienced, while on board the American privateer.

The Chesapeake was severely battered in her hull, on the starboard quarter particularly. A shot passed through one of her transoms; (equal in stoutness to a 64-gun ship's;) and several shot entered the stern-windows. She had two main-deck guns, and one carronade, entirely disabled. One 32-pound carronade was dismounted; and several carriages and slides were broken. Yet, says the "Report,"—"the Chesapeake was comparatively uninjured."

Her three lower-masts, especially the main and mizen-masts, were badly wounded. The bowsprit received no injury; nor was a spar of any kind shot away. Her lower-rigging and stays were a good deal cut; but neither masts nor rigging were so damaged, that they could not have been repaired, if necessary, without going into port.

Dreadful was the slaughter on board the Chesapeake. She lost her master, a lieutenant of marines, 3 midshipmen, and at least 56 petty-officers, seamen, and marines, killed; her gallant commander and first lieutenant, also her second, third, and fourth lieutenants, 4 midshipmen, and 106 petty-officers, seamen and marines, wounded; of whom, Captain Lawrence, Lieutenants Ludlow and Brome, one or two midshipmen, and several of the men, died of their wounds: total killed 61; wounded, (some of them very slightly,) 115; which comprises every one that reported himself to the Shannon's surgeon, three days after the action. This makes the gross number of killed and wounded amount to 176. The Chesapeake's surgeon, without, of course, noticing the very slightly wounded, writes from Halifax: "The whole number killed and wounded is estimated at about 160 to 170." Lieutenant Budd (without, it would appear, having any muster-roll in his possession,) gives the *names* of 47 killed, and 99 wounded. As the Americans talked much of an "explosion," the Shannon's surgeon was directed to examine their wounded: when he could find only one man at all burnt; and that was by the bursting of one of their powder-horns at a forecastle gun;—far enough from the explosion upon the quarter-deck.

After Mr. Clarke has told us of the Shannon's "destructive broadsides," and of three men being successively shot from the Chesapeake's wheel, he adds:—"The Chesapeake had evidently the advantage.—The greater part of the Americans were killed and wounded by the British boarders. The loss of the Shannon was principally occasioned by the cannon of the Chesapeake."—And the "court of inquiry" has decreed, "that the fire of the Chesapeake was much superior to that of the Shannon"!

The Shannon mounted twenty eight long 18-pounders upon the main-deck; upon the quarter-deck, twelve carronades, 32-pounders, two long 9-pounders, a 12-pound launch carronade through the fore-most starboard port, and a long brass 6-pounder through the opposite one; also two additional 12-pound carronades through the stern-ports; and, upon the forecastle, four carronades, 32-pounders, and two long 9-pounders; total, as the "Report" says,—"52 carriage guns:" besides a small swivel in the fore, and another in the main-top. The two stern-chase carronades had been frequently placed in the hold; where, as they were utterly useless in the broadside, and yet encreased the ship's nominal force, they had much better have remained. The Shannon, although she had, in all, 52 guns, (and those of five different calibers,) mounted, therefore, no more than 25 guns upon her broadside, including her boat-gun.

Captain Broke, in his letter of challenge, says, "The Shannon mounts twenty-four guns upon her broadside, and one light boat-gun; 18-pounders on her main-deck, and 32-pounder carronades on her quarter-deck and forecastle." If there is here any variation from the fact, it is that, instead of having, without her boat-gun, an upper broadside-battery of all "32-pounders," as the statement implies, the Shannon had, among them, two 9-pounders. Yet the editor of the American "'Portefolio," has had the assurance to complain of Captain Broke, for having "under-rated his ship's force."

The Shannon went into action with 276 officers, seamen and marines, of her proper complement, 8 recaptured seamen, 22 Irish labourers, who had been but forty eight hours in the ship, and 24 boys; of whom about 13 were under twelve years of age. The Irish supernumeraries had never been at sea, till they took passage in the Duck; and only four of them could speak English. We must, however, add them to the Shannon's complement; which they therefore swelled up to 330.

The Shannon's complement having been originally made up of draughts from different ships, the men were, at first, very quarrelsome among themselves; but Captain Broke's judicious plan of discipline, aided by his fatherly conduct, soon reconciled all parties, and made them, what in truth they were, a fine ship's company.

The first Halifax account of the action estimated the Shannon's full complement at 335; including, by mistake, the midshipman and four men sent away in the brig William; and who had rejoined their ship, upon her arrival in Halifax. Now that fact is explained, we have another instance of correctness in Captain Broke's letter of challenge. He stated the Shannon's complement to consist of "330 men and boys:"—yet, say the Americans, "he "under-rated his ship's force."

Lieutenant Budd, in his letter, says:—"The Shannon had, in addition to her full complement, an officer and sixteen men belonging to the Belle Poule, and a part of the crew belonging to the Tenedos." (App. No. 39.)—It appears that Mr. Budd, while on board the Shannon, observed three or four of the seamen's hats with "Tenedos" written in front. This is easily accounted for, when it is known, that the two ships had been cruizing together for three months; and had, of course, kept up a constant intercourse by boats. Suppose the U. S. frigate Congress, of the same force as the Chesapeake, had, at a subsequent day, sailed out from Portsmouth, N. Hampshire, to fight the Tenedos, (which ship, singly, blockaded her for some weeks,) such another acute observer as Mr. Budd would, upon seeing some of the Shannon's hats on the seamen's heads, have declared that the Tenedos had, in addition to her full complement, a part of the crew belonging to the Shannon."—Admitting, also, that seven, not "sixteen," of the Shannon's men, originally came from the Belle-Poule, what had that to do with the Shannon's complement in an action fought seven years afterwards? So that, all the draughted men a ship may receive on board, when manning for sea, are—"in addition to her full complement."—The Americans have another curious way of computing the complements of British ships; best illustrated by an anecdote. An American prisoner on parole near Halifax N. S. had the following conversation with an Englishman of the neighbourhood:—"Pray, what may be that frigate's complement?" pointing to one that had just anchored.— "About 302."—"What number of officers has she?"—"In all, about 63."—"Marines?"—"About 50." The American, then, after a short pause, turning to one of his countrymen present, says,—"They tell us the British don't half-man their ships, but I guess, our government would not think of giving to a ship like that, a greater complement than 415."—May not some calculation of this sort have been submitted to the "court of inquiry on the loss of the Chesapeake"?—The addition of the "63 officers," without the "marines," to the Shannon's "330 men and boys," amounts to very little short of "396;" the number appearing in the "Report," as the Shannon's complement.

After a writer in a Boston newspaper has insisted, that the "native Americans" on board the Chesapeake fought like heroes, and that the British part of the crew behaved treacherously, he very naturally asks—"Can any of your correspondents inform us, whether any Americans were on board the Shannon?"—Yes; there were some,—in her hold; though not so many, by several scores, as were in the Chesapeake's hold, in a very few seconds after the Shannon's 20 boarders sprang upon her quarter-deck.

The Chesapeake mounted twenty-eight long 18-pounders upon the main-deck; sixteen carronades, 32-pounders, upon the quarter-deck; four carronades, 32-pounders, and a long 18-pounder, shifting gun, upon the forecastle. Such an upper battery is possessed by no 18-pounder frigate in the British navy. The Chesapeake had, also, a 12-pound carronade; but it is doubtful whether or not it was mounted in the action. A very simple, and well contrived elevating carriage, and another for boat-service, belonged to it; but the carronade itself, quite perfect, was found dismounted; and will not be estimated. The Chesapeake's proper armament, therefore, consisted of 50 guns; although, in the action, she had only 49 mounted. Of these, she fought 25 upon the broadside; the same as the Shannon. The Chesapeake had a spare port on each side of her forecastle, between the bow-port, and that through which she fought her shifting 18-pounder.

The Chesapeake's guns had all names, engraven on small squares of copper-plate. To give some idea of American taste in these matters, here follow the names of her guns upon one broadside: Main-deck; "*Brother Jonathan, True Blue, Yankee Protection, Putnam, Raging Eagle, Viper, General Warren, Mad Anthony, America, Washington, Liberty for Ever, Dreadnought, Defiance, Liberty or Death.*"—Forecastle; "*United Tars,*" shifting 18-pounder, "*Jumping Billy, Ratler,*" carronades. Quarter-deck; "*Bull-dog, Spitfire, Nancy Dawson, Revenge, Bunker's Hill, Pocohantas, Towser, Wilful Murder,*" carronades; total 25.

An immense quantity of the dismantling shot represented in the plate; as well of single iron bolts, crow-bars, broken marline-spikes, old iron, &c. were taken out of the Chesapeake. The whole mass, weighing nearly half a ton, was sold at auction in Halifax; and the greater part has long since been converted into horse-shoes, plough-shares, and other articles of innocent utility.

A desire to torment, as well as to destroy, must have influenced the Americans; or why were the Chesapeake's canister-shot made up with angular and jagged pieces of iron, broken gun-locks, copper nails, &c.? Many of the Shannon's men suffered extremely by being so wounded; especially, during the tedious operation of extracting such abominable stuff from different parts of their bodies. Among the Chesapeake's small-arms, were found several rifle-guns; an additional proof that the Americans use them in their sea-fights.

A large cask of lime, with the head open, had been standing upon the Chesapeake's forecastle, but was knocked to pieces by one of the Shannon's shot. A bag of the same was found in the fore-top. Long after the Chesapeake arrived in Halifax, the remains of the lime were to be seen about the forecastle. For what precise use this lime was intended, has never been fully explained. The following relation of a circumstance, which took place before the use of gunpowder was known, may perhaps assist the reader in his conjectures.

"The French having invaded England, (Henry 3d, 1217,) Hubert de Burgh, governor of Dover Castle, discovering a fleet of 80 stout ships standing over to the coast of Kent, put to sea with 40 ships, and having gained the wind of them, ran down several of the smaller ships, and closing with the others, *three on board a quantity of quick-lime; which, blowing in their faces, blinded them so effectually*, that they found themselves obliged to bear away; but, being instantly boarded by the English, they were all either taken or sunk."—(*Scomberg's* Nav. Chronol. vol. i, p. 9.) That the Chesapeake's men made no such wicked use of the lime, is true; because that on the forecastle, being scattered by the shot, could not well injure any others than those standing round it; and Midshipman Smith, and his gallant followers, came too unexpectedly into the fore-top, to admit of the lime there placed, being used at all.

Now for the most difficult part in the estimate of an American ship's force: her complement of men on going into action.

Lieutenant George Budd, the surviving commanding officer of the Chesapeake, deposed, on the 19th of June, at the admiralty-office in Halifax, as follows:—"He does not know the number of hands on board at the time of capture, but will procure a copy of the muster-roll. He supposes there might have been about 340 hands on board at the time of capture."

This gentleman's official letter bears date four days previous to his deposition. In that letter, he gives the names of "47 killed;" and this, before, as it would appear above, he had "procured a copy of the muster-roll." How happened Mr. Budd not to know, that the "number of hands" late belonging to the Chesapeake, mustered after the action, amounted to 333? Even the number upon the books of the agent for prisoners, at Halifax, after most of the mortally wounded had died, amounted to 326. To suppose him acquainted with these facts, at the time that he made his deposition, would be accusing him of, at least, a wilful absurdity; for, his "47 killed," added to the 333 prisoners, would make 380, instead of "about 340." It is thought that, by "hands," Mr. Budd meant, "exclusive of officers;" which amounted to 70, at least. In that case, we should have 410 for the Chesapeake's complement, on going into action. Two muster-rolls were found: one contained, after deducting the runnings and discharges, the names of 389; the other, written up to the morning of the action, of 391. Some of the discharges bore date on the very day before the action. There can be no doubt, therefore, that on the *morning* of the action, the Chesapeake had a complement of 391.

It was currently reported at Boston, that several volunteers joined the Chesapeake, as she was getting under way. Some of the petty-officers, after their arrival at Melville-island prison, confessed that 30 or 40 hands, principally from the Constitution, came on board; but whose names, in the hurry and confusion, were not entered in the purser's books.

In corroboration of several men having joined the ship, a very short time before the action, a number of bags and hammocks were found lying in the boats, stowed over the booms; and, in direct proof that some of the Constitution's men were on board the Chesapeake, three or four of the Guerriere's Americans, who, after that ship's capture, enlisted on board the Constitution, (see pp. 52-53,) were among the prisoners taken out of the Chesapeake; and were immediately recognised by their former shipmates, now, as stated before, serving on board the Shannon.

Even 440, the number given as the complement of the Chesapeake in Captain Broke's letter, was not founded on mere surmise. That number was known to have been her complement on a former occasion; (see p. 35;) and, after the Chesapeake had been several weeks in Halifax, a letter was found in one of her lockers, dated in 1811, from Robert Smith, Esq. the secretary of state at that time, to Captain Samuel Evans, at Boston; directing him to open houses of rendezvous for manning the Chesapeake;

and enumerating the different classes, to the amount of 443. This, too, was in times of profound peace; when no Shannon was cruising, in defiance, off the harbour.

Again, the Congress, of the same force as the Chesapeake, arrived at Portsmouth, N. Hampshire, with (according to a published letter from one of her officers) 410 men of her crew on board; besides having lost four by death, and manned a prize with some others.

At the time the Chesapeake sailed out, the Constitution was lying in Boston, fully manned. So were several gun-boats, and one or two large privateers; and seamen were swarming in the town. Can it then, for a moment, be believed, that Captain Lawrence, knowing an enemy's frigate was waiting outside for him, would not take advantage of all this, and place on board his own ship an ample and effective crew? However, let the real number of the Chesapeake's crew have been what it may, the number upon the last-found muster-roll, is all that can, with propriety, appear in the statement of comparative force; and which number is thus accounted for:—

Killed in the action,	61	
Died in the passage.	4	
	—	65
Prisoners received by the agent,		326
		—
Number upon the last-found muster-roll,		391

Among the prisoners, there were but ten distinguished by the American officers as boys and only three that would come under that denomination on board a British ship of war. Seven, however, will be allowed.

The Chesapeake's gunner, Matthew Rogers, was an Irishman; the carpenter, George Miller, a native of Nova Scotia; and there were 34 others of the crew, recognized as British subjects. One man was hanged at Spithead; and several were pardoned. By some mismanagement, the first-named notorious traitor, Matthew Rogers, instead of being sent home for trial, was allowed to return, laughing in his sleeve, to his *adopted* country. A Boston journal, among other excuses for the Chesapeake's loss, contains some very amusing remarks about "the cowardice of some of the crew who were not Americans."—"There are no better sailors in the world," says the American editor, "than our own; and it seems hard that the war should be carried on for nothing but British sailors' rights, (!!) and that those same sailors should desert us in the moment of conflict. Cowardice is a species of treason. If renegado Englishmen are permitted to fight under our flag, it becomes prudent not to mix our own people with them to be destroyed;—for, at the critical moment when the boarders were called for, the foreigners all ran below, while not a native

American shrank from the conflict." Yet the name of the poor panic-struck bugleman, "William Brown," does not appear in the agent's "list of British subjects, late belonging to the Chesapeake." As, then, William Brown, unless he had misnamed himself, was certainly not a Portuguese, Dane, or Swede, the inference is pretty clear, that he was a "native American."

Another Boston editor attributes the success of the boarding-assault to "the bugleman's being killed early in the action:" when, a full twelvemonth afterwards, a court-martial, held at New London, "on certain persons, officers on board the U. S. frigate Chesapeake, at the time of her capture by the Shannon," finds—"William Brown, bugleman, guilty of cowardice; and sentences him to receive 300 lashes." (Nav. Chron. vol. xxxiii. p. 70.)

The Chesapeake's crew were remarkably stout, healthy young men; especially when contrasted with the Shannon's; most of whom were rather below the middle stature, and a great proportion old or elderly men. As one proof of stoutness in the Chesapeake's men, the hand-cuffs that had been placed upon her deck, ready to secure the British crew, as soon as the Shannon was captured, caused, when applied to the wrists of the Americans, many of them to wince with pain.

It requires a stout heart as well as a stout body, to bear the brunt of a boarding-assault. Men may, as the "Report" says, "behave well at their quarters, and fire on the enemy with great rapidity and precision;" but it is the personal conflict, the glittering broadsword, brandished aloft, that tries a seaman's valor.

The effect this had upon the Chesapeake's crew, is made one of the "causes of complaint" in the said "Report." Thus: "Against the crew generally; that they deserted their quarters, and ran below, after the ships were foul, and the enemy boarded." Mr. Clark, feeling it to be his province to rebut this serious charge, says:—"Her (the Chesapeake's) commander was but very slightly acquainted with his crew; the greater part of whom were new recruits." "She, as has been already observed, was but an indifferent vessel, and at the moment the Shannon appeared, was not in complete order for an engagement. But Lawrence had himself challenged a British vessel; the sight of one riding in defiance before him, was too much for his pride to bear. He, in consequence, put to sea on the 1st of June, having hoisted a white flag with '*Free trade and sailors' rights.*'—He (Captain Lawrence) addressed his men in a short discourse, but it was received with no marks of approbation. Discontent was apparent among a part of the crew, and complaints were muttered of not having received their prize-money. The boatswain, a Portuguese, was the principal instigator of this dissatisfaction. Lawrence, unacquainted with his crew, resolved to remove the cause of their complaint. He ordered the purser to give prize-checks to those who had received none." (Nav. Hist. vol. i. p. 205.)

It is evident, that Mr. Clark attributes Captain Lawrence's "being but very slightly acquainted with his crew," to the greater part of them being "new recruits."—In the American naval service, men enlist for two years, and sign articles, the same as in the merchant-service. We have seen that, in 1811, the Chesapeake recruited for, and no doubt obtained, a complement of 443. The men's terms of service would have about expired in April, 1813, when the Chesapeake arrived from a cruize. An intelligent English gentleman was at that time a resident of Boston; and the nature of his pursuits gave him a full opportunity of witnessing the manning and equipment of the United States' vessels then in port. He declares that the greater part of the Chesapeake's crew, as was very customary in the service, re-entered; that, to fill up her complement, four houses of rendezvous were opened; that the moment a man declared himself a candidate, he received a dollar, and accompanied an officer to the ship; where he was examined as to his knowledge of seamanship, age, muscular strength, &c. by a board of officers, consisting of the master, surgeon, and others; that, if approved, he signed the articles, and remained where he was; if rejected, returned home with a dollar in his pocket; that frequently, out of five boat-loads of men that would go off to the ship, in the course of the day, *three* would come back, not eligible. So much for Mr. Clark's "new recruits."—The features of the American war would have borne a very different aspect, could British ships have been manned in a similar way.

During her last cruize the Chesapeake sent in one prize, the Volunteer, "said to be worth 150,000*l.* sterling."—It could, therefore, be only among the men who belonged to her in that fortunate cruize, that "complaints were muttered of not having received their prize-money." And how could Captain Lawrence better "remove the cause of their complaint," than by ordering "the purser to give prize-checks to those who had received none"? All this clearly shews, that the majority of the Chesapeake's crew were the same she had been manned with since 1811; and, from the fastidiousness of her officers in filling up the deficiencies, and the fine appearance of the captured men, it is highly probable that the Chesapeake, under Captain Lawrence, had full as good a crew as she ever sailed with.

Not a word is there in the "Report" about "new recruits;" but the same object is attempted by a statement, that "most of the officers had recently joined the ship, some only a few days preceding the engagement."—Captain Lawrence arrived in the Hornet, from a cruize, on the 29th of March; and Mr. Clarke says he was, "shortly after his arrival at New York, appointed to the Chesapeake." That ship, we have seen, arrived at Boston about a fortnight afterwards; and, therefore, Captain Lawrence must have taken the command of her, within a day or two of that period. He probably brought with him some favorite officers. The Chesapeake's regular first lieutenant, Mr. Page, was left on shore sick; but still she had one lieutenant more than the Shannon; and where was there a braver man, or better officer, than her first lieutenant in the action, Ludlow? He, poor fellow, died a few days after he was brought to Halifax: previous to which it was hoped that his valuable life would be saved.

Has Mr. Clarke the effrontery to call the boatswain a Portuguese?—The Chesapeake's boatswain was brought in, mortally wounded; and his name in the agent's book, is, "Peter Adams." He was boatswain of the Constitution, when she took the Guerriere; and so far from being a "Portuguese," or even a British subject, was a native American.

Mr. Clarke says the Chesapeake "was but an indifferent vessel."—Would his government, had that been the case, have expended 150,000 dollars, only a few months before she was captured, in thoroughly repairing her?—Captain Evans, in a letter to the secretary of the navy, gave the Chesapeake a very high character; and the capture of the Volunteer, was considered to have wiped off the "unlucky" from her name. Her men, therefore, would naturally be stimulated to make more "prize-money;" and (what glee they must all have been in!) the very object of their wishes, "the finest ship of her rate in the British navy," was beckoning to them to come and take her.

According to Lieutenant Budd's letter, the Chesapeake "proceeded on a cruize, a ship of war in sight, believed to be the British frigate Shannon."—Is Mr. Clarke aware of the responsibility he attaches to Commodore Bainbridge, the naval commanding-officer at Boston, by declaring, that the Chesapeake was not in complete order for an engagement"?—Fortunately for the commodore, it is too well known that, however different may be the case with British, American ships of war never "proceed on a cruize," in ordinary cases even, till perfectly ready. It is known, also, that their men are drilled at the guns, in harbour as well as at sea: consequently, they cannot be out of practice.

The Shannon was built at Chatham in 1806. Two Shannons had previously been lost. One, a 32-gun frigate, was built in 1796; and lost by shipwreck, in 1800. The other, of 36 guns, was built in 1803; and, in the same year, struck the ground in a gale, and was wrecked under the batteries of Cape la Hogue. The seamen, in consequence, applied the term "unlucky" to the present Shannon; and she was not manned without the greatest difficulty; and then only, by draughts from other ships. The fact of the Chesapeake, also, having been denominated "an unlucky ship," is a strange coincidence.

The Chesapeake was built in Norfolk, Virginia, in 1797; and cost 220,677 dollars, 80 cents, or 61,299*l.* 8s. sterling. The American papers, announcing her launch, highly commended her model, strength, and workmanship.

Dimensions of the two ships.

		Shannon. Ft.	In.	Chesapeake. Ft.	In.
Length of lower-deck, from, rabbit to rabbit,		150	2	151	0
Breadth, extreme,		39	11⅜	40	11
Depth in hold,		12	11	13	9
Main-deck beams,	broad, or *sided*,	1	0	1	3½
	deep, or *moulded*,	0	11	1	0½
Main-mast,	length,	92	0	93	4
	diameter,	2	3½	2	6
Main-top-mast,	length,	55	2	58	10
	diameter,	1	4½	1	5¾
Main-yard,	length,	81	6	84	9
	diameter,	1	7⅛	1	7½
Main-top-sail-yard,	length,	60	9	63	8
	diameter,	1	0⅝	1	1¾

It appears, therefore, that whatever difference existed between the two ships, in point of size, was in favor of the Chesapeake; yet the Americans would have had us believe, that the Shannon was by far the larger ship. The Shannon is constructed somewhat differently from the Macedonian and her class, in having seven, instead of eight ports of a-side upon the quarter-deck; which occasioned Captain Broke to fit up the two gangways as ports, for the reception of his boat-guns. The Chesapeake has eight ports of a-side upon the quarter-deck, the same as the President; and a much larger forecastle, with an additional port on each side; which gives her, in all, the same number of broadside-ports as the President. This may account for the Chesapeake's having formerly rated of 44 guns.

Previous to her capture, the Chesapeake had undergone a very complete repair: since which she has returned from a long cruize off the Cape of Good Hope; and although, as Mr. Clarke says, "the worst ship in the navy of the United States," is now considered as one of the finest frigates of her class in the navy of Great Britain. Mr. Low, the editor of the "History of the War," was too well versed in figurative language, not to be ready with the very best *antithesis* to his friend's description of the Chesapeake. He therefore calls the Shannon —"the best frigate in the British navy."

Comparative force of the two vessels.

		Shannon.		Chesapeake.	
Broadside-metal in pounds	l. guns,	270		270	
	carr.	268		320	
		—	538	—	590
Complement,	men,	306		384	
	boys,	24		7	
		—	330	—	391
Size in tons,			1066		1135

Yet, says the "Report,"—"the capture of the U. S. frigate Chesapeake, by the *superior force* of the British frigate Shannon"!—But is not this language quite consistent with that used at the capture of our three frigates? If the Shannon and Chesapeake were admitted, by Americans, to have been equally matched, it would be giving the lie to all their former assertions; and hurling a host of "heroes" from the very pinnacle of fame, down to the level of ordinary men.

It was beneath the dignity of Americans, after having captured so many British vessels of "superior force," to attribute their defeat, in the present instance, to a "superiority of force". Therefore, the Shannon's "superiority" appears rather as a collateral circumstance; while the causes of the Chesapeake's capture are asserted to have been, "the almost unexampled early fall of Captain Lawrence, and all the principal officers; the bugleman's desertion of his quarters, and inability to sound his horn."

That "all the principal officers" fell early, is false. The first lieutenant received the wound that disabled him, while making an effort to repel the boarders; and neither the second, nor third lieutenant, was wounded, till the boarding took place. True, the Chesapeake's commander was mortally wounded. In how many of our naval combats with the Americans, has that happened to us? In using the word "unexampled," perhaps the court confined its view to what generally occurred on board American vessels: then, indeed, no one can dispute the correctness of the expression. The excuse about "the bugleman's desertion of his quarters, and inability to sound his horn," was a proper topic for Mr. Clarke and Mr. Low to expatiate upon, but cuts a very ridiculous figure in the solemn decree of a "court of inquiry."

The court first duly arranges some *ifs, probablys,* and *might haves,* and then designates the whole an "almost unexampled concurrence of disastrous circumstances." Were any of the Chesapeake's masts shot away? Did either of our three frigates surrender with their masts standing?—But, says the "Report,"—"if the Chesapeake had not accidentally fallen on board the Shannon, and the Shannon's anchor got foul in the after quarter-port of the Chesapeake, the Shannon must have very soon surrendered or sunk." Falling on board is then a "disastrous circumstance"? It may be so, in the opinion of Americans; but Britons always consider the event that enables them to grapple and man-fully oppose their enemy, as a fortunate, not a "disastrous" circumstance. Nor, had the ships kept clear, would the Shannon "have very soon surrendered or sunk."—It was in practical gunnery, wherein the Shannon's men so greatly excelled the common run of British crews. In bravery, all are alike. Had the Chesapeake hauled up sooner, and kept at long shot, she would also have found her match. Masts might have fallen; encreased slaughter ensued; and the action been protracted to the length of the Java's, still a succession of firing, such as the Shannon's was, must have given her the victory.

Had the two ships been dismasted, the conqueror might have been compelled to leave his trophy behind; nay, his own safety would have been hazarded. The action took place within easy signal-distance of Boston-light-house; and there were lying in Boston, besides the Constitution, several gun-boats, a brig, and some schooner privateers. The wind was fair. Even the Constitution, half rigged as she was, could have come out to the Chesapeake's rescue; and the gun-boats, already in the bay, might, with their long 32s and 24s, (the wind being light,) have considerably injured the Shannon, from the moment she became disabled. Or, suppose that, during the action, the wind had chopped round, and blown a gale from the seaward; one ship would have been in the very mouth of her own harbour; which, without a stick standing, she might have reached in safety: the other, embayed, and close on board an enemy's coast; upon which she could scarcely avoid being stranded. Even had the gale commenced after possession, the only difference is, that both ships must have shared the same fate.

These were, doubtless, some of the "favorable circumstances," which Mr. Clarke says, in addition to a "superiority of force," attended the Shannon; and the facility with which the Chesapeake could have procured the aid of her friends, was, upon the same principle, among the "particular disadvantages," under which she labored.

In most of our unsuccessful actions, the numerical superiority of the Americans has amounted, by the time the flag was struck, to two, three, four, and, in one instance, *seven* to one; and, in naval actions generally, the conquerors outnumber their prisoners. But, if we take the whole that were alive on each side, the reverse was the fact, when the Chesapeake surrendered to the Shannon; the former having 333, the latter but 307, hands on board, including a large proportion of boys. The truth is, the destructive fire of the Shannon came wholly unexpected. It appalled the majority of the Chesapeake's crew; caused the men, as the "Report" says, "almost universally to desert their quarters;" and then the sudden appearance of Captain Broke and the boarders, made the Chesapeake an easy conquest.

Although the Chesapeake's first lieutenant, at Halifax, two days before the appearance of unfavourable symptoms, when his wounds were perfectly easy, and he had no apprehension of danger, said, in the presence of several gentlemen:—"When I thought myself supported by at least twenty of the Chesapeake's crew, to resist the Shannon's boarders, I found they had all run below;"—although the "Report" has stated that even a midshipman "left his quarters;" and has charged "the crew generally, that they deserted their quarters;"—yet the court—

"cannot perceive, that the national flag has suffered any dishonor from the capture of the U. S. frigate Chesapeake"!

Whatever "superiority of force" existed, was clearly on the side of the Chesapeake. As Britons, that we scorn to estimate; and even the American star and chain-shot, and hogshead of lime, shall not be allowed to disturb the equality and fairness of the action. But Captain Broke did something more than capture a frigate of equal force: he sought and commenced the attack, close to an enemy's port, filled with armed vessels; and then, beat his ship in *eleven,* and captured her in *fifteen* minutes.

CHAPTER X.

Commodore Rodgers's account of his chase off the North Cape—The chasing ships identified as the Alexandria and Spitfire—Beneficial effects of Captain Cathcart's gallantry—Dominica falls in with and engages the Decatur—No British official account of the action—Enemy's details of it—Loss and force of each vessel—Statement of comparative force—Boxer encounters the Enterprize—Details of the action—No British official account—Damage and loss of each vessel—Their relative force, in guns, men, and size—American accounts— Statement of comparative force— Remarks thereon.

THE U. S. frigates President and Congress, left Boston upon a cruize on the 1st of May. The Congress parted company; and the President, towards the latter end of June, put into Bergen, in Norway; whence she departed on the 2d of July. Commodore Rodgers, having gained information, that thirty sail of whalers, under the protection of two brigs of war, would be at Archangel in the middle of July, bent his course for the North Cape, in the hopes of intercepting them. The commodore cruized about, till the 19th of July; when, just as he expected to fall in with the fleet, the President was chased from her cruizing ground by—"a line-of-battle ship and a frigate."—Here are the commodore's own words, extracted from his official letter, dated "Newport, September 27, 1813."

"In this object the enemy had the good fortune to disappoint me, by a line-of-battle ship and a frigate making their appearance off North Cape, on the 19th of July, just as I was in momentary expectation of meeting the enemy's convoy. On first discovering the enemy's two ships of war, not being able, owing to the haziness of the weather, to ascertain their character with precision, I stood towards them, until making out what they were, I hauled by the wind on the opposite tack to avoid them; but, owing to faint, variable winds, calms, and entire day-light, (the sun in that latitude, at that season, appearing at midnight several degrees above the horizon,) they were enabled to continue the chase upwards of 80 hours; during which time, owing to different changes of the wind in their favor, they were brought quite as near as was desirable. At the time of meeting with the enemy's two ships, the privateer Scourge, of New York, which I had fallen in with the day before, was in company; but their attention was so much engrossed by the President, that they permitted the Scourge to escape, without appearing to take any notice of her."

The above "line-of-battle ship and frigate" were no other than the Alexandria, an old fir frigate, of the same armament and size as the Southampton, (see p. 41,) and the Spitfire sloop, (formerly a fire-ship,) armed chiefly with 24-pound carronades.

It may, perhaps, afford some satisfaction to those of the President's officers, who differed in opinion from the commodore, as to the character of the two chasing ships, to see an extract from the Alexandria's log-book, commencing at noon, and ending at midnight, on the 19th of July.

Courses.	Dist.	Lat.	Long.	Bearings, &c. at noon.
S. 65 E.	144	71°46′	10°18′E.	N. Cape S. 72 E. 117 miles
1 3 4			Do. weather. At 2. saw a sail to	
2 3	S.E. by E.		windward; observed her to be a	
3 3			frigate, and a large schooner in	
4 2			company.	
5 2	S. by E.	Vble.	At 5. 40. wore.	
6 2 4			6. tacked.	
7 4 4				
8 2 4				
9 1 6	W. ½ N.		9. all sail in chase.	
10 1 6				
11 1 6				
12 1 6			12. sloop in company.	

Among the prisoners on board the President, at the time of the chase, were the master and mate of the snow Daphne, of Whitby. According to the Journal of these men, published in the newspapers, they, as well as many of the President's officers and men, were convinced that the chasing ships were a small frigate and a sloop of war. They describe, in a ludicrous manner, the preparations on board the President, to resist the attack of this formidable squadron. During each of the three days, a treble allowance of grog was served out to the crew; and an immense quantity of star, chain, and other kinds of dismantling shot, got upon deck in readiness for the action. It appears, also, that when the Eliza Swan, whaler, hove in sight, a few days afterwards, she was supposed to be a large ship of war; and the ceremony with the grog and dismantling shot was repeated. After a very cautious approach, the commodore most gladly discovered the chase to be a clump of a merchantman, and made prize of her accordingly.

It was then, indeed, the Alexandria and Spitfire, and not a "line-of-battle ship and frigate," that, for 80 hours, chased the U.S. ship President, Commodore Rodgers; and which were, at one time, "quite as near as was desirable"! The promptitude and gallantry of Captain Cathcart, saved a fleet of 30 ships; but, considering that the force of the Alexandria and Spitfire, united, scarcely amounted to half the force of the President, without reckoning the Scourge, with 10 guns, and at least 120 men, it must be pronounced a very fortunate circumstance, that the glasses on board the President possessed such extraordinary magnifying powers.

On the 5th of August, H. M. schooner Dominica, having under convoy the Princess Charlotte packet, from St. Thomas's, fell in with the privateer-schooner Decatur, off the southern coast of the United States. After a contest of three quarters of an hour, during which the boarders were twice repulsed, the Decatur's "whole crew" succeeded in getting upon the Dominica's deck. Here a desperate struggle ensued, and continued for several minutes: at last, the British crew were overpowered by double their number. No official account has appeared in the Gazette. The following details are extracted from a Charleston paper.

"A third attempt was made by the captain of the Decatur to board. The jib-boom of the Decatur was run into the main-sail of the enemy. The fire from the artillery and musketry was terrible, and well supported on both sides. The Dominica, not being able to disengage herself, dropped along-side; and it was in this position that Captain Diron ordered his whole crew to board, armed with pistols, sabres, &c. which order was executed with the promptness of lightning. Mr. Vincent Safith, first prize-master, and quarter-master T. Wasborn, were the two first on board the enemy: in doing which the prize-master received three wounds. The crew of the enemy fought with as much courage and bravery, as that of the Decatur did, with valor and intrepidity. Fire-arms now became useless, and the crews were fighting hand to hand with cutlasses, and throwing cold shot; when, the captain of the enemy and the principal officers being killed, the deck covered with dead and wounded, the English colours were hauled down by the conquerors. In consequence of the orders given by the captain of the Decatur, the vessels were then separated; the rigging and sails being in the worst state possible.

"During the combat, which lasted an hour, the king's packet, Princess Charlotte, remained a silent spectator of the scene; and, as soon as the vessels were disengaged from each other, she tacked, and stood to the southward.

"Killed and wounded on board the Decatur: killed 3; wounded 16; one of whom (the carpenter) since dead. On board the Dominica: killed 13; wounded 47; of whom 5 are since dead of their wounds: total, killed and wounded, 60. Among the killed are, G. W.

Barretté, commander; Mr. I. Sacker, master; Mr. D. Brown, purser; Mr. Archer and Mr. Parrey, midshipmen. Wounded, Mr. I. Nichols, midshipman. The surgeon and one midshipman were the only officers on board who were not killed or wounded. The lieutenant was left on shore sick.

"From the above statement," says the Charleston editor, it would appear, that this engagement has been the most bloody, and the loss in killed and wounded on the part of the enemy, in proportion to the number engaged, perhaps the greatest, of any action to be found in the records of naval warfare. The surviving officers of the Dominica attribute the loss of their vessel to the superior skill of the Decatur's crew in the use of musketry, and the masterly manœuvering of that vessel, by which their carriage-guns were rendered nearly useless. Captain Barretté was a young man of not more than twenty five years of age. He had been wounded early in the action by two musket-balls in the left arm; but he fought till the last moment, refusing to surrender his vessel, although he was urged by the few survivors of his crew to do so; declaring his determination not to survive her loss. One of the lieutenants of the Decatur received a severe sabre-wound in the hand from Captain Barretté, a few moments before he fell. Captain Diron is a Frenchman, and most of the officers and crew of his vessel are his countrymen. They have done themselves immortal honour by the humanity and attention displayed towards their prisoners after the victory; which is spoken of in high terms of approbation, by the surviving officers of the enemy's vessel."

"The crew of the Dominica, with the exception of eight or ten boys, were fine-looking young men; but, to see them in the mangled state in which they arrived, was enough to freeze the blood of one not accustomed to such sights, with horror. Among her crew is a small boy, not eleven years old, who was twice wounded, while contending for victory upon her deck."——Poor child! it would have suited thee better to be throwing *dumps* than "cold shot,"—to be gamboling in the nursery, than "contending for victory" upon a ship's deck.

The armament of the Dominica was, by the American account, twelve carronades, 12-pounders, two long 6-pounders, and a 32-pound carronades on a pivot; total 15 guns; together with a brass swivel. Her crew consisted of 67 men, and 10 boys. The Charleston paper gives 83 as her complement; but the sentence of the court-martial expressly states, that "there remained only 15 of the Dominica's crew that were not either killed or wounded"; which number, with the unwounded purser and midshipman, and the enemy's amount of killed and wounded, makes 77.

The Decatur mounted, according to the Charleston paper, six carronades, 12-pounders, and one long 18-pounder, on a pivot; "with 103 men." The sentence of the court-martial, relying upon the evidence adduced, declares she had on board "140 men." The

Americans are in the habit of excluding the *officers,* when computing the complements of their own vessels. Admitting the same plan to have been adopted in this case, the different prize-masters and other officers of the Decatur, might easily amount to 37. But, to be below, rather than above the estimate, the mean of the two numbers will be taken. Boys are seldom admitted on board privateers; and in this vessel, in particular, the crew consisted chiefly of desperate characters, who had been enured to their business, on board French West-India pickaroons. Two boys will be an ample allowance.

Both these schooners were captured by British cruizers, before the war terminated; and the Dominica was again taken into the service. The size of each vessel, therefore, is accurately obtained.

Comparative force of the two schooners.

		Dominica.		Decatur.	
Broadside-metal in pounds	l. guns,	6		18	
	carr.	104		36	
		—	110	—	54
Complement,	men,	67		120	
	boys,	10		2	
		—	77	—	122
Size in tons,			217		232

Here, in weight of metal, the British vessel was doubly superior; but the Decatur's long 18-pounder had caused considerable destruction, before the Dominica's shot could reach; and subsequently, the latter's guns were rendered nearly useless, by the privateer's excellent manoeuvres. Boarding immediately followed. Against such odds every human effort was unavailable: still the enemy, with difficulty, cut his way through the little band, to the colours lashed in the schooner's rigging.

The gallantry evinced on this occasion elicited praises from the enemy; but that enemy was a *Frenchman.* So careful is the *American* naval historian not to indulge in this weakness, that he has substituted,—"The resistance of the English was desperate," for all the commendatory expressions used in the French details. Mr. Clarke has also left out of his account, that the Dominica had boys in her crew, as well as that Captain Diron and most of his crew were Frenchmen. Indeed, so fearful is the editor, lest his readers should discover the first-published account to have been a translation, that he has substituted "cannon" for "artillery," and made other alterations, to place it beyond a doubt, that an American commander and crew effected the Dominica's capture.

But the editor of the "Sketches of the War" has proved himself the most able historian of any. He calls the action of the Dominica and Decatur—"a brilliant attack made by a privateer upon a—*large sloop of war*"!—"No event," says he, (p. 203,) "probably, in the naval annals, furnishes evidence of a more brilliant and decisive victory, gained by a vessel, so inferior in size, strength, and armament, to her antagonist."

Captain Diron, to flatter the sanity of the Americans, and suit his own convenience, named his vessel the Decatur, and commissioned her at the port of Charleston. It is for the latter reason only, that the action appears in these pages.

On the morning of the 5th of September, while H. M. brig Boxer, was lying at anchor near Penguin Point, a few miles to the eastward of Portland, in the United States, the American brig Enterprise made her appearance. Captain Blyth immediately got under weigh to engage her; leaving his surgeon, two midshipmen, and an army-officer, a passenger, on shore at a place called Manhegan, "shooting pigeons."

The action commenced about a quarter past 3 P.M. and in the very first broadside, an 18-pounder shot passed through Captain Blyth's body, and shattered his left arm. The same broadside killed a marine and a seaman; and wounded several others of the Boxer's crew. Almost immediately after the loss of her gallant commander, the Boxer's main-top-mast was shot away. This enabled the Enterprise to take a raking position, and to maintain it till the contest ended. No British official account of this action has been published.

The Boxer was much cut up in hull and spars; and lost, besides her commander, 3 men killed, and 17 men wounded, 4 of them mortally; total killed and wounded 21.

The Enterprise suffered but little injury in her hull and spars. Her rigging and sails were a good deal cut. She lost 1 man killed, her commander, a midshipman, and 11 men wounded, the 2 first, and 1 man, mortally; total killed and wounded 14. The American official letter describes no "slightly wounded." They may have amounted to a few more.

The Boxer arrived on the North American station, with the usual armament of her class; but her commander obtained, at Halifax, two additional carronades; making her force, in the action, twelve carronades, 18-pounders, and two long 6-pounders. Gun-brigs are not allowed boat-carronades; consequently, fourteen were all the guns the Boxer mounted. The American official account gives her no more; but Mr. Clarke, depending more upon "Niles' Weekly Register," quotes from that:—"His Majesty's *fine brig of war* Boxer, of 18 guns;" and again says:—"Boxer, guns mounted 18."

The Boxer had, on leaving St. John, N. Brunswick, a few days before the action, 71 men, 6 boys, and a passenger; total 78. Of these, 8 seamen were absent in a prize; and the passenger, surgeon, and 2 midshipmen, as stated before, on shore at Manhegan; leaving a residue of 60 men, and 6 boys.

The prisoners received from the Boxer, according to the American papers, amounted, including the mortally wounded, to 62; making, with the 4 killed in the action, 66. To put this beyond a doubt, some American gentlemen sought for the party that had been left at Manhegan. An Eastern paper gives the following as the substance of their information:—"They (the party on shore) gave precisely the same account of the force of the Boxer as the other officers, and without communication with them. The crew of the Boxer, at the time of the engagement, according to their statement, consisted only of 66."

The "Particulars of the action," furnished a newspaper-editor by one of the Enterprise's officers, stated that, out of "115 *picked men,*" the Boxer had, "when the action commenced, 104." The official letter declared, that she had "between 20 and 25 killed." (App. No. 45.) Captain Hull, next, wrote Commodore Bainbridge, that he, having "counted upwards of 90 hammocks," (two are generally allowed for each man,) had no doubt she "had 100 then on board;" but found it "impossible to get at the number killed." To convince the bulk of the Americans, that the Boxer had but 66 men and boys, was therefore a vain task. The few moderate men who attempted it, were scouted as traitors or *tories*; and even Mr. Clarke, the historian, takes the safe side. Although he would not acknowledge Lieutenant McCall's letter, as any authority for the number of guns mounted by the Boxer, he considers it unquestionable, as to the number of her killed.

The Enterprise mounted fourteen carronades, 18-pounders, and two long 9-pounders. One American journal, besides giving that as her force, states the guns, complement, and tonnage of the Boxer, with the utmost correctness. The complement of the Enterprise cannot be fixed with the same certainty as her guns. The commander of the British schooner Fly, captured by the Enterprise about the 26th of August, and carried into Portsmouth, N. Hampshire, says the latter sailed from that port in quest of the Boxer, Captain Burrows having received intelligence of her being on the coast, with part of her crew absent; that she (the Enterprise) then added several volunteers to her original complement, which consisted of 113 men, and 3 boys. Some American papers stated the Enterprise's complement as high as 125; others as low as 102. The latter probably meant, exclusive of officers. The U. S. brig Viper, of only 12 guns, had 93 men; Nautilus, of 14 guns, 106 men; Vixen, of the same force, 130 men; Rattlesnake and Syren, of 16 guns each, 131 and 137 men. The two last-named brigs had each 2 lieutenants, besides her commander; and so had the Enterprise. To avoid over-rating the latter's complement, let it be fixed at, including volunteers, 120 men, and 3 boys.

The Enterprise was originally a schooner; and her full dimensions, in hull, spars, and sails, as a schooner, appear in the M.S. memorandum-book, before referred to. (See p. 54.) Soon after the late war commenced, the Enterprise was cut in two, lengthened, (so as to have one more port of a-side,) and altered to a brig, at Washington. The Nautilus, captured by the Shannon, was also originally a schooner; and was altered to a brig without being lengthened. By adding, therefore, to the Enterprise's original length, the distance between the fore-side of one of the Nautilus's ports, to the aft side of the next port, which is 8 feet 6 inches, we have the present length of the Enterprise. This makes her 245 tons; but several British officers who have seen the Enterprise, state that she is about 260 tons. The Nautilus's top-sides are nearly as stout as those of our first-class brigs: while the Boxer had only one timber between each port; which made her top-sides pervious to every grape-shot that was fired. The spars of the Enterprise will be considered as no larger, than those which the Nautilus had, when captured.

Dimensions of the two brigs.

		Boxer.		Enterprise.	
		Ft.	In.	Ft.	In.
Length of lower-deck, from, rabbit to rabbit,		84	4	97	1
Breadth, extreme,		22	1¼	23	8
Main-mast,	length,	53	4	62	0
	diameter,	1	5½	1	10½
Main-yard,	length,	39	9	50	0
	diameter,	0	9⅛	0	10½

This is the proper place to give an extract from the American "Particulars:"—"At 3 P.M. tacked, and bore up for the enemy, taking him to be one of his majesty's brigs of the *largest size*"!

None of the praises lavished upon the "*fine brig of war* Boxer," could gain her a place among the national vessels of the United States. She was put up to auction, and sold as a merchant-brig; for which service only, (and that in peaceable times,) she was ever calculated.

Comparative force of the two brigs.

		Boxer.		Enterprise.	
Broadside-metal in pounds	l. guns,	6		9	
	carr.	108		126	
		—	114	—	135
Complement,	men,	60		120	
	boys,	6		3	
		—	66	—	123
Size in tons,			179		245

The superiority in weight of metal is trifling; that in number of men, *two-fold*. Gun-brigs are allowed but one lieutenant, one master's-mate, and two midshipmen. The absence of the two midshipmen, the shameful defection of the acting master's-mate, and three seamen, (App. No.46.) and the fall of her brave commander by the first broadside, rendered the Boxer's situation, at the very onset of the engagement, peculiarly unfortunate. On the other hand, the Enterprise, after her commander was wounded, had still two lieutenants, and four or five midshipmen, left, to carry on the action. These circumstances considered, the disparity between the two crews, was even greater than the numerical difference, already so great.

None but a novice in American history, will be surprised at the following paragraph in Mr. Low's book:—"The President of the United States, having considered the Boxer as equal in force to the Enterprise, has ordered her to be delivered up for the benefit of the captors."

CHAPTER XI.

Pelican arrives at, and suddenly departs from Cork, in quest of the Argus—Discovers, engages, and captures her—Damage and loss of each vessel—Pelican's force in guns and men—American accounts of both—Argus's force in guns—Dismantling and other curious shot—Argus compared in equipment with British gun-brigs and brig-sloops— Complement of Argus—Depositions of her officers—Size of each vessel considered—Argus's tonnage, by her officers' account—Corrected in their favor—Statement of comparative force—Remarks thereon.

AT about 6 o'clock on the morning of the 12th of August, H. M. brig Pelican arrived at Cork from a cruize. Before the sails were furled, Captain Maples received orders to put to sea again, in quest of an American sloop of war, which had been committing serious depredations in St. George's channel. By half-past 8, the Pelican was beating out of the harbour, against a very strong breeze, blowing right in; accompanied by a heavy sea: a proof of the earnestness of her officers and crew.

Fortunately, a fire of her own making discovered the U. S. brig Argus, at 4 o'clock on the morning of the 14th, in lat. 52° 15′ N. long. 5° 50′ W. She made no attempt to escape; her commander being confident, as it afterwards appeared, of taking any British brig of war, in "ten minutes."

At 6 A.M. the Argus fired her broadside which, with three cheers, was promptly returned by the Pelican; and the action commenced, within range of musketry. (App. Nos. 42 and 43.) The firing continued with great spirit, for 45 minutes; (the mean of the two statements;) when the Argus was boarded on the starboard-bow, and instantly carried, without even a shew of resistance; although the master's mate of the Pelican, who led the party, received his death from the fore-top, just as he stepped upon the enemy's gunwale. Of this no advantage was taken; but the colours of the American sloop of war were immediately hauled down, by the few of her own crew that had not run below.

After having read the "Report of the court of inquiry on the loss of the Chesapeake," (App. No. 40,) the reader may naturally expect, that the sentence upon the loss of the Argus, contains a severe animadversion upon the palpable misbehaviour of her crew: instead of which we are told, (App. No. 44,) that "every officer and man of the Argus, (with the exception of one man, and one boy,) made use of every practical exertion to capture the British sloop of war Pelican"; and that "every officer and man, with the exception before mentioned, displayed throughout the engagement, a zeal, activity, and spirit, in defence of the vessel and flag committed to their protection".

The American official account is remarkable for its precision. We have,—"6.—6. 4.—6. 8.—6. 12.—6. 14.—6. 18.—6. 25.—6. 30.—6. 38.—and 6. 47; and each of these trifling intervals is so crowded with circumstances, that the reader, unless he takes the trouble to sum up the figures, rises with a conviction that this "gallant defence against superior size and metal," lasted two hours, instead of 47 minutes.

The writer's precision did not extend to the manner of the Argus's surrender; nor to her force; nor to the Pelican's loss, or number of men, in the action; but the letter contains an excuse for the capture, as novel as it is ridiculous; no other than "the fatigue which the crew of the Argus underwent, from a very rapid succession of captures."—This "rapid" work consisted of twenty captures; all made on the same cruizing-ground, during a period of thirty-eight days. Nor was the labour of burning, an unprofitable one; for the American government allowed a compensation for every vessel destroyed.—The "court of inquiry," in its over anxiety to save the national honor, has made a sad blunder. Not satisfied with "fatigue" only, it must needs add, "exposure"; which was certainly very great, in the month of August. It was March when the court sat; which may be regarded as some apology.

Lieutenant Watson particularly dwells on the unmanageable state of the Argus, in consequence of her "having lost the use of her after-sails." The reader, if he has not already done it, is requested to apply this part of the American official account of the Argus's capture, to the case of the Frolic, at the commencement of her engagement with the Wasp; marking well the difference, between what was carried away by shot during the action, and what had been carried away by a gale two days previous. (See p. 71.)

On board the Pelican, two shot passed through the boatswain's and the carpenter's cabins. Her sides were filled with grape-shot; and her rigging and sails injured much. Her foremast, and main-top-mast, were slightly wounded, and so were her royals; but no spar was seriously hurt. Two of her carronades were dismounted. She lost one seaman killed, besides the master's mate, Mr. Young; and 5 seamen, slightly wounded; total

7: chiefly by the Argus's musketry and langridge; the latter to the torture of the wounded. Captain Maples had a narrow escape; a spent canister-shot striking, with some degree of force, one of his waistcoat-buttons, and then falling on the deck.

The Argus was tolerably cut up in her hull. Both her lower-masts were wounded, although not badly; and her fore-shrouds on one side nearly all destroyed: but, like the Chesapeake, the Argus had no spar shot away. Of her carronades, several were disabled. She lost in the action, 6 seamen, killed; her commander, two midshipmen, the carpenter, and 3 seamen, mortally, her first lieutenant, and 5 seamen, severely, and 8 others, slightly wounded; total 24: chiefly, if not wholly, by the cannon-shot of the Pelican.

Like all the other brigs of her class, the Pelican originally mounted 19 guns: sixteen carronades, 32-pounders, two long 6-pounders, and a 12-pound launch-carronade; but, when at Jamaica, Captain Maples procured two brass 6s, as standing chace-guns. In the action, these were pointed through the bow-ports; and therefore could not be used upon the broadside.

Although that "faithful record of events," the American "History of the War," was published three months after Lieutenant Watson's letter, giving the exact force of the Pelican in guns, had gone the round of the American journals; and although the title-page of the work assures its readers, that the contents have been "carefully compiled from official documents," Mr. Low states the Pelican's guns at—"twenty two 32-pound carronades, two long 9s, and two swivels."—Mr. Clarke had previously made the Pelican's shot in pounds 660;" but *he* had seen nothing American to contradict it.

The Pelican returned from Jamaica, in the spring of 1813, with 116 men and boys in complement. On the 20th of June, she received from the Salvador del Mundo, at Plymouth, a draught of twelve men and boys; but, departing suddenly the next day, left behind eight of her best men, absent on leave. In the course of July, while watering, and occasionally anchoring, on the north-coast of Ireland, she lost six more of her men by desertion; and the second lieutenant, who had gone on shore, had the misfortune to be absent, when the Pelican sailed from the coast. Her arrival at, and sudden departure from Cork, upon the service which, in less than 48 hours afterwards, she so gallantly performed, has already been mentioned. It was no proof of that "newly-acquired" caution on our part, which the Americans, at this time, fancied was due to their prowess, that Captain Maples, with a complement of 101 men, (including only 1 lieutenant,) and 12 boys, sailed out to engage an American sloop of war, whose number of men, as reported in all the public prints, was 150; and those picked seamen. On the day of leaving port, the Pelican pressed 2 men out of a brig; and at a quarter past 2 on the morning of the action, which was about four hours before the Argus was in her possession, she pressed a third man, from another brig. The Pelican, therefore, commenced action with 104 men, and 12 boys: the former of no extraordinary quality, and of rather diminutive size; and most of the latter under 13 years of age.

Mr. Low, determined to man the Pelican equal to the armament he had given her, states that she had "179 men, eleven of them volunteers for the occasion, from ships at Cork."—We here trace some confused account, of the draught which the Pelican received from the guard-ship at Plymouth.

The Argus mounted 20 guns: eighteen carronades, 24-pounders, and two long 12-pounders. This is confirmed by the depositions of the two lieutenants and master of the Argus, taken before the proper officer at Plymouth. Yet Mr. Low says:—"Argus, sixteen 24-pound carronades, and two long 9s;" and the editor of the "Naval History" calls "her shot in pounds 402"; which amounts to the same thing. Although, in the action of the Peacock and Hornet, the Americans advanced an opinion, that the facility with which 24-pound carronades could be worked and fired, rendered them about equal to 32s; yet the official letter adverts to the "superior metal" of the Pelican, and the "court of inquiry," finds, among other "facts," that, "in the number and caliber of her guns, the Pelician was *decidedly* superior to the Argus."

When taken possession of, the usual description of American shot was found among the Argus's stores; even bayonets lashed together with rope-yarn, to be discharged at the enemy!—The quantity of old iron (about 3 cwt.) and copper nails, shewed, at once, what had caused so much irritation in the wounds of the few British that suffered.

After the editor of the "Sketches of the War," could call the Dominica schooner a "large sloop of war," he may be allowed to contrast the American *gun-brig* Argus," with the "British *sloop of war* Pelican." This ingenious plan *has* suggested the idea of extracting from the "Naval Pocket Gunner," a work sanctioned by the office of ordnance, the proportions of some articles of gunner's stores served out to British gun-brigs, and brig-sloops of the Pelican's class, for "foreign service," in the way of comparison with the gunner's stores found on board the Argus, and sold at public auction.

	Br. gun-brig. No.	Br. brig-sloop. No.	Argus. No.
Muskets	25	40	84
Pistols	20	20	32
Swords	30	60	96
Strong pikes and Pole-axes	40	45	52

After a steady action of three quarters of an hour, the Argus had more powder left, than, by the above little work, was originally served out to the Pelican; and the former's round, grape, and canister, exclusive of bars of iron, old iron, &c. weighed, at the sale, 22 cwt.

The Argus's books contain the names, exclusive of runnings and discharges, of 157 persons; comprising 149 in "complement," and 8 "supernumeraries," 7 of them described as having entered, in April, from the U. S. frigate Chesapeake; the other a "deserter," at l'Orient. The Argus had carried thither from New York, (which port she left on the 21st of June,) Mr. Crawford, the minister to France, and his suite; but, as they all victualled themselves, their names do not appear on the brig's books. Besides the above 157 names, are those of 15 prisoners, taken out of a brig the day previous to the action. The Argus had captured twenty vessels; of which Captain Allen destroyed all but five. He gave up two to the prisoners; and manned in 3; of which two were recaptured, and the third got safe into France. The two lieutenants and master of the Argus agree in deposing, that, at the time of her "capture," she had on board "125 officers and mariners." The standing interrogatories of the court of admiralty, should be varied a little, to apply to cases of capture *after action*. Taking the officer's depositions in a literal sense, the Argus commenced action with 131 men; which admits 26 to have been distributed on board the three vessels (two brigs and a schooner) sent in, without reckoning the men stated by the British merchant-masters to have entered from their vessels; and which, after the unsuccessful issue of the action, would most likely be found, not among the crew, but among the prisoners. However, the number sworn to by the American officers, shall be considered as referring to the number on board at the commencement of the action.

Keeping pace with his other assertions on the relative force of the Argus and Pelican, Mr. Low describes the complement of the former thus: "94 men fit for duty, 5 sick, the rest absent in prizes."—It must have been upon some estimate of this sort, that the "court of inquiry" declared, "that the Pelican was decidedly superior to the Argus in the number of her crew."—No men were found "sick" in the Argus; but the whole 125 were at quarters in the action; and a finer set of men never was seen. Very few were less than six feet high; and not a boy, in our way of rating them, was on board; but 3 will be allowed. About 10 or 12 were believed to be British subjects: the American officers, in their depositions, swore the crew contained none, to their knowledge. This may be one reason of the tenderness evinced by the court of inquiry, as to the behaviour of the men at the moment of boarding. When the Argus's men were brought on board the Pelican, then was seen the contrast between the bodily strength and appearance of the two crews; to which party humiliating may be easily conceived.

After the prisoners had been divided, and a full third of the Pelican's crew placed on board the Argus, a strong breeze, and the unsupported state of the latter's fore-mast, induced the prize-master to bear up for Plymouth; while the Pelican proceeded to report her proceedings to the admiral at Cork. In her way thither, she fortunately fell in with the Leonidas 46; which ship relieved Captain Maples of about 30 of his sturdy prisoners.

The Pelican was built in 1812; the Argus, at Boston, in 1802 or 3, expressly for a government-vessel. The dimensions of the two brigs here follow:

		Pelican.		Argus.	
		Ft.	In.	Ft.	In.
Length of lower-deck, from, rabbit to rabbit,		100	0	95	6
Breadth, extreme,		30	9	27	7⅝
Main-mast,	length,	68	3	69	9
	diameter,	1	10	1	9½
Main-yard,	length,	54	7	55	2
	diameter,	0	11⅜	1	0¼
Main-top-mast,	length,	38	11	39	2
	diameter,	1	0	0	11
Main-top-sail-yard,	length,	42	0	44	0
	diameter,	0	8½	0	9½

So much for Lieutenant Watson's account of the "superior size" of the Argus. It is true, she was a trifle shorter, and full two feet narrower, than the Pelican; but the tauntness of her masts, and squareness of her yards, would make her appear on the water, if any thing, the larger vessel. As her tiller did not traverse on deck, as on board our brigs, she carried her ports further aft than the Pelican; which enabled her to fight, through them, one more gun of a side. The age of the Argus, and the number of vessels of her class in the service, prevented her being purchased by government; although her qualifications as a cruizer, called forth the following exordium from the editor of the "National Intelligencer":—"She is admitted to be one of the finest vessels in the service of her class; and the model of such a vessel, is certainly inestimable."—But this was previous to her capture.

After Messrs. Clarke and Low have shewn the Argus to have been but 298 tons, (her American measurement,) one makes the Pelican "485 tons," the other "584 tons." Mr. Lowe has certainly improved upon Captain *Lejoille*. (App. No. 3.) He thought of his opponent's guns only: the former has exerted his ingenuity upon guns, men, and size; and not of one vessel, but of both; gaining as well by under-rating on one side, as by over-rating on the other.

Captain Maples states the Argus at 360 tons. So he must have been informed by some one belonging to her; for, what is remarkable, her two lieutenants and master all swore, that she was "about 350 tons." Of this, no advantage shall be taken, whatever surprise it may create in America; but the actual tonnage of the Argus, as measured by the dock-yard surveyors, be compared with the Pelican's.

To every efficient purpose, the Argus was equal in size to the Pelican, and her top-sides were a trifle stouter; but the great additional breadth of the latter, swells her tonnage far beyond the Argus's. The reader must take this into his consideration, when he comes to the relative *size in tons*.

Comparative force of the two brigs.

		Pelican.		Argus.	
Broadside-metal in pounds	l. guns,	6		12	
	carr.	268		216	
		—	274	—	228
Complement,	men,	104		122	
	boys,	12		3	
		—	116	—	125
Size in tons,			385		316

Upon the face of this statement, the Argus, in broadside-weight of metal, was inferior to the Pelican by one sixth; but, in complement, had rather the advantage: an advantage that would be greatly encreased, could we estimate by weight, instead of number. How, then, are we to account for losing only one man killed, during a close and furious cannonade of three quarters of an hour? The compliment paid to the Argus's commander by Commodore Decatur, is a proof it could not have been for want of disciplining the crew. (App. No. 19.) It would appear, then, that the Americans perform best in gunnery, when they have high odds on their side.

How consolitary it is, to compare the condition of the least damaged of our captured sloops, with that of the U. S. sloop Argus.—She had, to the last, every spar standing; and, if we subtract the loss in killed and wounded, and the boys, from each side, there were, at the very moment when the Argus's colours were struck to the Pelican, 98 young, athletic Americans, opposed to 99 Britons, of various age and size. Nor was there, in this case, any frightened "bugleman" to make a scape-goat of; nor "British subjects" to accuse of treachery; nor could a deficiency of muskets, pistols, swords, or boarding-pikes, be alleged. Really, it would gratify us to be informed, in what consists that "moral and physical superiority" of the American, over the British sailor; the panegyrics upon which, for nearly these four years past, have so occupied the time, and so puzzled the brains, of the transatlantic philosophers.

CHAPTER XII.

Description of Lake Erie—Captain Barclay appointed to the command—List of his vessels—Building of the ship Detroit—Difficulty and expense of equipping British vessels on the lakes—Captain Barclay receives a small draught of seamen—Is forced to engage the American squadron—Details of the action—Lawrence surrenders—The American commander shifts his flag—Lawrence re-hoists her colours—British squadron surrenders—Damage and loss on each side—Force in guns, men, and size—Statement of comparative force—Effrontery of the Boston citizens and American editors— Commodore Perry and the engravers—Description of Lake Ontario—Sir James Yeo and Commodore Chauncey—Force of their respective squadrons—Sir James captures the Growler and Julia—American officer's account of that event—Statement of comparative force during each engagement—Commodore Chauncey convinced of his mistake.

LAKE Erie is a lake of North America, situated between 40° 50′ and 43° N. lat. and between 78° 50′ to 84° W. long. It is about 260 miles long from E. to W. and 40 to 60 miles broad. Its waters enter Lake Ontario by the river Niagara; but the immense cataract of that name completely obstructs the navigation. The boundary line between the Canadas and the States of America, runs through the centre of the lake.

In May, 1813, Captain Robert Heriot Barclay was appointed to the command of the British flotilla on this lake; an appointment which had been declined by Captain Mulcaster, on account of the exceedingly bad equipment of the vessels. With a lieutenant, and 19 rejected seamen of the Ontario squadron, Captain Barclay joined his command, towards the end of June; up to which date, the Lake Erie force consisted of the following vessels:—

		Guns.	Complement. Canadians.	Soldiers.	Total	Tons.
Queen Charlotte,		16	40	70	110	280
Lady Prevost,	Sc.	12	30	46	76	120
General Hunter,	B.	10	20	19	39	74
Erie,*	Sc.	3	6	9	15	55
Little Belt,	Slp.	3	6	9	15	54
Chippewa.	Sc.	1	6	7	13	32
Total,		45	108	160	268	615

This was the state of his majesty's squadron on Lake Erie, twelve months after the declaration of war: not a seaman among them; and, if we except the soldiers and provincial officers, (the latter included among the Canadians,) not one on board that could speak English! A single sloop of war of the Americans would have captured the whole.

All the before-mentioned vessels had been constructed to carry cargoes; one was now built solely for war. She was named the Detroit, pierced for 18 guns, and measured 305 tons. Although ship-rigged, as was also the Queen Charlotte, she was many tons smaller than some American privateer-schooners. (See pp. 17-18.)

The next difficulty was, to get guns for the new ship. For this, a neighbouring fort (Amhertsburg) was stripped; and 19, of four different calibers, obtained. It will convey some idea of the difficulty and expense of hastily fitting vessels at this distance from home, to mention, that every round shot cost one shilling a pound for the carriage from Quebec to Lake Erie; that powder was ten times as dear as at home; and that, for anchors, their weight in silver would be scarcely an over-estimate.

But, were the Americans on this lake any better off?—In five days an express reaches Washington. It would, under the most favorable circumstances as to weather and dispatch in office, take as many *months* to get an article ordered from England, or even permission to stir a peg out of the common routine of service. The American vessels were therefore completely at home; while the British vessels were upwards of 3,500 miles from home; penned up in a lake on the enemy's borders, inaccessible by water; and to which the land-carriage for heavy articles, ordnance and naval stores especially, was most difficult and tedious.

Early in September, Captain Barclay received a draught of seamen from the Dover troop-ship; and many of these would have scarcely rated as *ordinaries* on board our regular ships of war. He had now 50 British seamen to distribute among two ships, two schooners, a brig, and a sloop; armed, altogether, with 63 carriage-guns. It must have been the incredibility of this, that induced some of the British journals, in their accounts of the proceedings on this lake, to state "150," instead of 50 seamen. It

*Not afterwards heard of.

is asserted, on the express authority of Captain Barclay himself, that no more than 50 seamen were at any time on board the Lake Erie flotilla; the complements having been made up by Canadian peasants and soldiers,—without disparagement to either,—sorry substitutes for British seamen.

The ships of the Americans, as their newspapers informed us, were equipped in the most compleat manner; and, through the same channel, we learnt, that large draughts of seamen had repeatedly marched to Lake Erie from the sea-board. The best of riflemen were to be obtained on the spot. What else was required, to render the American ships in these waters quite as effective as the best appointed ships on the ocean?

On the 9th of September, Captain Barclay was lying, with his little squadron, in the port of Amherstburg, anxiously waiting the arrival of a promised supply of seamen. Almost surrounded by hostile shores; his people on half-allowance of food; not another day's flour in store; a large body of Indians, (whose friendship would cease, with the least abridgement in their accustomed supply,) close in his rear;—alike hopeless of succour and retreat,—what was Captain Barclay to do? Impelled by dread of famine, and, not improbable, of Indian treachery too, he sailed out in the evening, to risk a battle with an enemy's fleet, whose force he knew was nearly double his own.

At day-light next morning, the enemy was discovered to-leeward. The British commander bore up for him. The wind almost instantly changed, and brought the enemy to-windward. Thus had the American schooners, by a choice of distance, the full effect of their heavy long guns; while the British carronades dropped their high-priced shot uselessly in the water.

The Detroit, Captain Barclay's ship, was closely engaged, for two hours, with the Lawrence, Commodore Perry's flag-ship, supported by the schooners Ariel and Scorpion. The Lawrence then struck her colours; and the Detroit ceased firing; but, having only one boat, and that cut to pieces, she could not take possession.

A short time before the Lawrence surrendered, Commodore Perry abandoned her, and repaired on board the Niagara; which brig, from keeping out of range of the Queen Charlotte's carronades, had sustained but little damage. As soon as the Niagara advanced towards the Detroit, the Lawrence, which had now drifted out of reach of the latter's guns, re-hoisted her colours. Commodore Perry, in his letter, attempts to gloss this over; but his countrymen are the only persons who do not consider it as a shameful proceeding.

The Detroit, Queen Charlotte, and Lawrence, all suffered greatly, in hulls, masts, and rigging. The other vessels of the two squadrons were not materially injured.

Our loss was severe. "Every officers commanding vessels, and their seconds," says Captain Barclay, were either killed, or wounded so severely, as to be unable to keep the deck." Captain

Barclay had his remaining arm dreadfully shattered; and was otherwise severely wounded. The British loss in killed and wounded, amounted to 135.

Commodore Perry escaped without a scratch; and the only officers he lost, were a lieutenant of marines and a midshipman. His total loss amounted to 123. (App: No. 55.)

The guns of every vessel in the two fleets, are fully specified in the statement annexed to the British official account. It will there be seen, that we had 63 guns; of which 34, including those on pivots, were fought upon the broadside.

The Detroit and Hunter had each guns of four different calibers. These guns were to be supplied with proper shot, and levelled at the enemy, by Canadians and soldiers, "totally unacquainted with such service;" the few seamen dispersed among the vessels, having enough to do to attend to the navigation of them.

The complements of the six British vessels consisted of 50 seamen, (including officers and boys,) 85 Canadians of all sorts and sizes, and 210 soldiers of the Newfoundland and 41st regiments; total 345. How sensibly the loss of seamen was felt, will appear by a reference to the evidence of the officers examined at the court-martial. (App. No. 61.) There it also appears, that the matches and tubes supplied to the ships, were so defective, "that *pistols were obliged to be fired at the guns to set them off*."—Never before, surely, did any squadron go into action, so wretchedly fitted out as Captain Barclay's!

Commodore Perry, in his letter to General Harrison, says:—"From the best information, we have more prisoners than we have men on board our vessels." (App. No. 57.) If this "best information" had not turned out wholly false, why, in a letter written two days afterwards, and commencing, "I have caused the prisoners taken on the 10th instant to be landed at Sandusky," has he omitted to specify the number?—Not a word appears beyond the extorted admission, that there was "a number of Canadians among the prisoners, many of whom had families." (App. No. 59.)

The American vessels mounted 54 guns; of which 34, including those on pivots, were fought upon the broadside. The description of these guns, as given in Captain Barclay's statement, agrees with the American accounts published a few days previous to the action. Commodore Perry knew the advantage he should derive from merely enumerating the guns of the two squadrons; and, in his "statement of force," (App. No. 59.) failed not to specify, that three of our guns were on pivot-carriages; forgetting, apparently, that no fewer than fourteen of his own were similarly fitted. He had tried the relative weight of metal, and found it was two to one against him. The commodore, with his skill in figures, no doubt, can demonstrate that, although an *American* schooner, armed with twelve long *two*-pounders, would be, in number of guns, five times superior to a *French* schooner, armed, like the Porcupine, with one long 32-pounder and one 24-pound carronade, each on a pivot-carriage, the *French* vessel would, in reality, be double the force of the *American*. What have the British done, that a case of theirs, in principle the same, should be made an exception?

Commodore Perry, in his second letter to General Harrison, thanks him for the "timely re-enforcement" of the men he sent on board the squadron; and assures him that, "without those men, the victory could not have been achieved." (App. No. 60.) As the number of these men cannot be obtained, the complements of the American vessels must be estimated without them. The Lawrence and Niagara were each armed the same as the sloop of war Hornet; and still rate the same in the navy-lists. Allow each brig to have had 20 men fewer than the Hornet; and their respective complements would be 150. The Growler and Julia schooners, of two guns, taken from the Americans on Lake Ontario, had 40 men each. Allow the Caledonia brig, and the remaining six schooners of Com. Perry's fleet, to have had no more than 40 men each; and we have, for the united complements of the nine American vessels, without reckoning General Harrison's "timely reinforcement," 580 men, chiefly picked sailors and riflemen.

The size of each of the British vessels has already appeared. Some opinion may be formed of the size of American *brigs* of war, by Commodore Chauncey's letter respecting those built under his orders on Lake Ontario. (App. No. 65.) When the Lawrence and Niagara were launched, the American papers stated them to be of the same size as the Hornet. Allow them to have been a few tons smaller, and call them 450 each. Of two American Lake Erie schooners, subsequently captured by us, one measured 96, the other 86 tons. An average of 90 tons, for the Caledonia brig, and six schooners, will be a very moderate allowance.

The Detroit engaged her three opponents, the Lawrence, Ariel, and Scorpion, within pistol-shot distance; so that the brig's heavy carronades produced their full effect. By way of excuse for that fine vessel, supported as she was, surrendering to a force so inferior, the American commander says:—"Finding *their* fire very destructive, owing to *their* long guns, and its being mostly directed at the Lawrence, &c." (App. No. 58.) Who could infer from this, that *one* ship only had engaged the Lawrence; or that all the "long guns" in the British fleet, except two 12s, and a few of smaller caliber, were mounted on board that single ship?

It is not a little singular that, had the Somers made a fourth against the Detroit, and the Niagara, Caledonia, Porcupine, Tigress, and Trippe, been lying quietly at anchor in Put-in-bay, the broadside-weight of metal of the Lawrence, and her three assistants, would have equalled that of the whole of Captain Barclay's fleet; and, had the Lawrence and Niagara been the only American vessels on the lake, a superiority, in broadside-weight of metal, of nearly *one third,* would still have been on the American side.

Comparative force of the two squadrons.

		British.		American.	
Broadside-metal in pounds	l. guns,	195		256	
	carr.	264		672	
		—	459	—	928
Complements,	officers, seamen & boys	50		580	
	Canadians & soldiers,	295			
		—	345	—	580
Size in tons,			865		1530

Unabashed by this immense disparity, the hectoring of the Americans exceeded all bounds. Several years' experience had taught us, that Americans were not over-scrupulous in the way of commerce; that is, that, while they were, ostensibly, *fair neutrals,* the cargo they were carrying would be enemy's property, their real destination a prohibited one, and all their papers forgeries. But it was thought that a state of *open* war would improve their morals; that honor, or common honesty at least, would break out by starts among them; and that this work of reformation would begin with the eastern people; as they were notoriously of a grave and pious habit. That two years of war had produced not the slighest effect upon the "Boston citizens," they themselves took care to announce, by presenting to Commodore Perry, a "massy service of plate," engraven with the following words:—"*A very superior British force, on Lake Erie, was entirely subdued by Commodore O. H. Perry."!!*

After this, nothing said by the southern people, the government-editors, naval historians, &c. can create any surprise. The "Naval Monument" says;—"The victory of Commodore Perry was the result of skill, courage and enterprise, against superior force. Both the quality and amount of the force he had to contend with, ought to have given a triumph to the other side."—(Naval Mon. p. 89.) The "*Preface*" out-americans even this. It tells us of "the bold Nelsonian measure of breaking through the line;" and insists, that neither Cæsar in his famed letter, nor Nelson in his (by us thought) famed victories, are at all to be compared with the American Nelson, or the Nelson of all Nelsons,—Commodore Perry!

It would be an injustice to the "History of the war," not to give equal publicity to Mr. Low's eloquence on this same interesting occasion. He says, at p. 119,—"Hitherto we have seen the enemy beaten ship to ship, but now we were to witness them fleet to fleet; and a more decisive or splendid victory was never achieved. Compared with this all former naval victories lose their splendour; even the great Nelson, were he alive, must rank below Perry.—Nelson never captured an entire fleet; Perry has, and that with a fleet inferior in size, weight of metal, and number of men."—Does the facetious Mr. Low want a precedent for the capture of "an entire fleet"?—Let him turn to his friend Gulliver. Not one of *his* Lilliputian fleet escaped.

But Commodore Perry himself; how has he behaved in this business? He calls his victory a "signal" one. (App. No. 56.) Perhaps that word, similar to "clever," and some others, has a different meaning in the United States from what it has in England. Let that pass. Pass over also the concealment and equivocation observable in the commodore's details of the action. (App. No. 58.) We come, next, to his letter to "Messrs. Murray, Draper, Fairman, and Webster." (App. No. 64.) These engravers shewed him two views of the engagement, wherein the British, are represented much larger, and more fully armed, than the American vessels; yet he, Commodore Oliver Hazard Perry, of the United States' navy,—the man whose "modesty" has been as extravagantly praised as his "valor,"—has "no hesitation in pronouncing them a correct representation of the engagement." He does this, too, in a common newspaper-puff!!

Lake Ontario is also a lake of North America; about 600 miles in circumference. On its south side, it receives the waters of Lake Erie, by means of the river Niagara; the navigation of which is interrupted, as already stated. Near the S.E. it receives the river Oswego; and, on the N.E. its waters enter the river Iroquois: which river, at Montreal, takes the name of St. Lawrence, and flows into the gulf of that name. The navigation of this river is effectually interrupted by rapids and shoals, situate a few miles above Quebec. Our principal port on this lake is Kingston; that of the Americans Sackett's Harbour. The statements in Commodore Chauncey's long letters, respecting the operations on this lake, (App. Nos. 50. and 52.) have given rise, among the Americans, to very erroneous opinions as to the relative merits of that officer and Sir James Lucas Yeo, sent out to command against him, in the spring of 1813. Among Britons, Frenchmen, Spaniards, and Portuguese, gallantry and Sir James Lucas Yeo have long been associated terms. The fears of his friends were, not that he would decline fighting, but, lest his restrictive orders should not have been peremptory enough, to hinder him from attacking a force double his own. His ardor, like the gallant Barclay's, required to be checked, not stimulated.

The first enterprise in which Sir James engaged, is fully detailed in his letter to Mr. Croker. (App. No. 48.) At this time, Commodore Chauncey, with a superior force, was lying in Sackett's-harbour; waiting the equipment of the new ship General Pike. Towards the end of July, that fine ship being added to his squadron, the commodore left Sackett's-harbour; and, on the 8th of August, Sir James discovered him, at anchor off Niagara. The occurrences that attended this meeting, will be better understood, when the force of each squadron is known.

British squadron on Lake Ontario;
from the 8th of August to the end of 1813.

	Long guns.				Carrs.				Guns.	Compl[t.]	Tons.
	24s	18s	12s	9s	68s	32s	24s	18s			
Wolfe	*1	8			4	10			23	200	425
Royal George,		†3			2	16			21	175	340
Melville, B.		2				12			14	100	186
Moira, Sc.				2			12		14	92	175
Sidney Smith, Sc.			2			10			12	80	144
Beresford, Sc.	*1			*1				6	8	70	115
Total,	2	13	2	3	6	48	12	6	92	717	1385

Commodore Chauncey's letter informs us what vessels he had with him. Their force in guns, complements, and size, will be taken, partly from the American accounts, and partly from the information of British officers serving on the lakes, at the period of these operations. Sir James Yeo describes the enemy's squadron as "consisting of 13," he should have said "14 sail."

American squadron on Lake Ontario,
on the 8th of August, 1813.

	Long guns.					Carrs.			Guns.	Compl[t.]	Tons.
	32s	24s	18s	12s	9s	32s	24s	18s			
General Pike,		§28							28	400	820
Madison,			†5			20			25	210	590
Oueida, B.				2			16		18	115	287
Hamilton, Sc. } Scourge, Sc. }				*1	10			8	19	108	214
9 other schooners,	*7	*4	*3	*2	*4	*4			24	360	810
Total,	7	32	8	5	14	24	16	8	114	1193	2721

The Pike is described as a remarkably fine ship: the Americans themselves spoke of her, when she was launched, as equal in size to a British 36-gun frigate. She carried one of her 24s on the top-gallant forecastle, the other on the poop; both mounted upon circular carriages. One of the Madison's 18s was similarly mounted.

An attentive perusal of Commodore Chauncey's letter, (App. No. 50.) coupled with what Sir James says in his, (No. 49,) will shew which party was the most disposed to "avoid an action." At all events, Sir James's "long and cowardly manœuvring," as an

*On pivot-carriages. † One on ditto. § Two on ditto.

American historian calls it, enabled him to capture two schooners; having previously compelled two others to founder, in their over-strained efforts to avoid his fire.

The "United States' Gazette" of September 6, 1813, gave a letter from one of the General Pike's officers. The writer, having previously stated the American force at two ships, one brig, and eleven schooners, says:—"On the 10th, at midnight, we came within gun-shot, every one in high spirits. The schooners commenced the action with their long guns, which did great execution. At half past 12, the commodore fired his broadside, and gave three cheers, which was returned from the other ships,—*the enemy closing fast.* We lay by for our opponent, the orders having been given, not to fire until she came within pistol-shot, though the enemy kept up a constant fire. Every gun was pointed, every match ready in hand, and the red British ensign plainly to be descried by the light of the moon; when, to our utter astonishment, *the commodore wore, and stood S. E.* leaving Sir James Lucas Yeo to exult in the capture of two schooners, and in our retreat; which was certainly a very fortunate one for him."

No wonder, an order soon afterwards issued from Washington, that no officer should write with the intention of publication, accounts of the operations of the fleet and army. Sir James could not have had his assertions more ably supported, than they were by the Pike's officer. The latter was mistaken, however, as to any "execution" having been done by the American squadron. The Growler and Julia each mounted a long 32 and 12-pounder, on pivot-carriages, with a complement of 40 men; which was understood to be that of each of the other schooners; except the two which had upset. The captured schooners of course made no resistance; although the American editors trumped up a story about their desperate defence; how they tore and ripped up the enemy, &c.

The Pike's officer has described two other chases; differing chiefly from the last, in no loss having been suffered, or even shot fired. He says:—"We proceeded directly for Sackett's Harbour; where we victualled; and put to sea, the next day after our arrival, August 14.—On the 16th, we discovered the enemy again; again hurried to quarters; *again got clear of the enemy, by dint of carrying sail;* and returned to Sackett's harbour.—On the 18th we again fell in with the enemy steering for Kingston and we reached the harbour on the 19th. This is the result of two cruizes; the first of which, by proper guidance, might have decided in our favor, the superiority on the lake, and consequently in Canada."

This is what many of the American editors called,—"chasing the British commander, all round the lake."—Commodore Chauncey, although he had lost four of his fourteen vessels, appeared in September with eleven sail; having brought out with him, the schooner Elizabeth, of about the same force as the

Growler or Julia, and the new schooner Sylph; mounting, at that time, four long 32s upon pivot-carriages, and four long 6s. This schooner was described by the Americans as upwards of 400 tons. She was afterwards converted into a brig.

The details of the action of the 11th of September, will be found in Sir James's and Commodore Chauncey's letters. (App. Nos. 51 and 52.) The latter says: "I got several broadsides from this ship upon the enemy, which must have done him considerable injury, as many of the shot were seen to strike him, and people were observed over the sides plugging shotholes."—The only shot received by the British fleet that wanted a plug, struck the Melville; and that so far under water, that Captain Spilsbury had to run his guns in on one side, and out on the other, to enable him to stop it.

Another engagement took place on the 28th of September. Commodore Chauncey, having the weather-gage, kept his favourite distance; and one of his shot carried away the Wolfe's main-top-mast; which, in its fall, brought down the mizen-top-mast and cross-jack-yard. It was this, and not, as Mr. Clarke says, "a manoeuvre of the commodore's," that "threw the British in confusion." Even with this great advantage, Commodore Chauncey would not venture within carronade-range. Mr. Clarke, in describing this action, speaks of the "British *frigate* Wolfe"; upon which he had previously mounted "36 guns."—Only two shot from the Americans did any material damage; the one already mentioned, and another that struck the Royal George's fore-top-mast; which fell, upon her anchoring. Mr. Clarke says: "Prudence forbad any further pursuit on the part of the Americans;" and the editor of the "History of the War" adds: "The commodore was obliged to give up the chase; his ship was making water so fast, that it required all his pumps to keep her clear; and others of his vessels were much damaged. The General Pike suffered a considerable loss of men; among whom were 22 killed or wounded, by the bursting of a gun." Other American accounts stated the commodore's loss in men, at upwards of 60 killed and wounded.

It was therefore the damages and loss sustained by the American squadron; and not the "British batteries on Burlington heights,"—upon which not a musket was mounted,—that "obliged the commodore to give up the *chase.*" The effect produced by Sir James's few long guns, gave a specimen of what his carronades would have done, had his opponent allowed them to be used.

As Commodore Chauncey has asserted, that Sir James "was so much superior in point of force, both in guns and men, and *heaves* a greater weight of shot," the reader may desire to see a statement of the comparative force of the two squadrons, in each of the actions. The Growler and Julia had been converted into transports; (and were afterwards re-captured as such;) and their guns mounted upon Fort Henry at Kingston: they, therefore, became no accession to Sir James's force upon the lake. The Sylph and Elizabeth, in Commodore Chauncey's squadron, replaced the Growler, Julia, Hamilton, and Scourge. The force in guns of the two first-named vessels has already appeared: the Sylph's complement may be stated at 70; the Elizabeth's at the number found in each of the captured schooners.

Comparative force of the two squadrons.

		American. 1st action.	British. 1st, 2d, and 3d actions.	American. 2d and 3d actions.
Broadside-metal in pounds,	l. guns,	917	204	956
	carr.	712	1170	640
		—1629	—1374	—1596
Complements,		1193	717	1115
Size in tons,		2721	1385	2817

This is "heaving a greater weight, of shot" with a vengeance!—The immense disparity in long guns, accounts for Sir James's endeavouring to get the weather-gage; without which, his wary opponent would have hammered the British squadron to pieces; and remained himself comparatively uninjured.

An event that occurred long subsequent to these transactions, leaves it doubtful, whether it was Commodore Chauncey's wilful exaggeration, or the highly-magnifying powers of the American glasses, that occasioned him so far to over-rate the size and force of the vessels composing the British squadron.—As soon as the proclamation of peace reached Sackett's Harbour, the commodore, accompanied by some of his officers, went to Kingston on a visit to Sir James. The latter was ill in bed; but his first lieutenant, at the request of Commodore Chauncey, took him on board the several vessels of the squadron. When he came to the Montreal, and was assured that she was his old opponent the Wolfe, he and his officers testified their surprise, and appeared almost to doubt the lieutenant's word; the commodore himself declaring, that he took her for a vessel of twice the size and force. The Americans were next, to their equal surprise, shewn the brigs Melville and Moira; then named the Star and Charwell. Some one present, speaking of the events of 1813, observed, that the Pike alone, with the weather-gage, was a match for the whole of the British squadron:—it could not be denied.

CHAPTER XIII.

Phœbe leaves England—Is joined at Rio Janeiro by the sloops Cherub and Racoon—The ships arrive at Juan Fernandez—Captain Hillyar there hears of Captain Porter's depredations—Sends the Racoon to the river Columbia; and, with the Cherub, proceeds in search of the Essex and squadron—Phœbe and Cherub arrive at Valparaiso; where they discover, and blockade, the Essex and Essex Junior—Both American ships make a feint of attacking the Phœbe, when alone—Phœbe chases them to the anchorage—Essex sails out—Is attacked and captured—Details of the action—Damages and loss on both sides—Force of the respective vessels in guns, men, and size—Statement of comparative force—Remarks on Captain Porter's letter—His treatment of Captain Hillyar—Proceedings of the Cherub—Phœbe and Essex arrive at Plymouth—Captain Porter's prizes.

IN March, 1813, H. M. Ship Phœbe 42, accompanied by the Isaac Todd, letter of marque, left England, upon secret service; which service afterwards proved to be,—to destroy the United States' fur-establishment upon the river Columbia, N. W. coast of America. Towards the latter end of June, the two ships arrived at Rio Janeiro: whence, each taking on board six month's provisions, they sailed on the 9th of July, in company with the sloops of war, Cherub and Racoon; which had arrived there from England since February, and were now bound round Cape Horn, to protect the Southern whale-fishery. The Isaac Todd parted company before reaching the Falkland islands; and the three remaining ships arrived, in the middle of September, at the island of Juan Fernandez. It was here that Captain Hillyar first heard of the depredations of the Essex; as well as of Captain Porter's having armed three of the whale-ships, his prizes. This augmentation of force determined Captain Hillyar, not to allow the Cherub and Racoon to seek the Essex, as they had already been doing at the island of St. Catharine's: he therefore provisioned and stored the Racoon, for the service upon which the Phœbe had been ordered; and, with her and the Cherub, set sail from Juan Fernandez, about the 29th of September, in quest of the Essex and her three companions.

On the 2d of October, a short distance to-windward of Charles' Island, (one of the Galapagos,) the Racoon parted company for Columbia; and the Phœbe and Cherub, after exploring the gulph of Guyaquel, arrived at Lima for refreshments, in the middle of December.

It was not until the 7th of February, 1814, that Captain Hillyar was so fortunate as to gain a sight of the Essex. He found her, in company with the Essex Junior, of 20 guns and 60 men, and three of her prizes, at anchor in the port of Valparaiso, South America. Captain Porter arrived there, for the first time, in March, 1813; the very month in which the Phœbe left England:—a most satisfactory proof, that the latter was not "sent into the Pacific for the express purpose of seeking the Essex." (App. No. 73.)

At Valparaiso, Captain Hillyar took on board a supply of water and provisions; and commenced the blockade of the American ships. After he had lain off the port about a month; and at a time when the Cherub was between three and four miles to-leeward, the Essex, and Essex Junior, sailed out of the harbour together, and bore down upon the Phœbe's weather-quarter; the Essex *firing at her*. Captain Hillyar, resolving to engage the two ships, instantly stood for them; when they both put about, and ran for the anchorage: whither they were pursued by the Phœbe. This is an answer to all Captain Porter's hectoring about his having "endeavoured to provoke a challenge"; and explains why the American officers forfeited the good opinion of the inhabitants of Valparaiso; many of whom witnessed the whole transaction. There are documents in existence; proving, on the oath of many respectable residents of the place, that, when the Essex did so fire on the Phœbe, she was nearer the port than when she was captured.

On the 28th of March, the two American ships having appointed a rendesvouz at the Marqueses, and arranged every thing for escaping to sea the first opportunity, a fresh breeze from the southward drove the Essex out of the harbour. To the surprise of the British commanders, whose ships were both under close-reeved top-sails, the Essex approached with top gallant-sails set, over single-reeved top-sails. On rounding the outer-point of the bay, she braced close up, in hopes to weather the British ships, and escape; but, in the attempt, carried away her main-top-mast. Captain Porter now tried to regain the limits of the port: failing in that also, he dropped anchor, so near the shore, as to preclude the possibility of any ship passing a-head of him.

The wind blowing strongly from the direction in which the Essex lay, the British ships, instead of "having the choice of position," were obliged, the moment they passed her stern, to wear, to avoid going on shore. About this time, a shot from the Essex passed through several folds of the Phœbe's main-sail, as it was hauling up; which rendered it unfit to set, with the strong wind then blowing. The main-stay was also cut through by shot, and the jib-boom wounded. The Phœbe, having encreased her distance, by wearing, and lost the use of her jib and main-sail, did little or no injury to the Essex until she closed her at 35 minutes past 5. Then the action commenced, in earnest; and continued, without intermission, until 20 minutes past 6; when the Essex surrendered.

The Cherub, when the action commenced, was abaft the Phœbe's weather-beam; and afterwards used every exertion against the baffling winds and occasional calms, which followed the heavy firing, to close near the Essex: without which, her battery, consisting, except one six, of all carronades, could produce no effect.

As respects the duration of the action, Captain Hillyar, with true nobleness of mind, read to Captain Porter, nearly the whole of his official letter; referring him to the minutes taken by his clerk, with a watch in his hand, while the engagement was pending. Captain Porter, rather than avow this trait in his enemy, mentions the fact as a discovery of his own, thus: "Commodore Hillyar, as *I am informed,* has thought proper to state to his government, that the action lasted only 45 minutes; *should he* have done so, &c."

The assertion that the British fired for "about ten minutes" after the colours were struck, is the basest of all Capt. Porter's numerous falsehoods. The moment the flag of the Essex was seen moving from the mast-head, the Cherub ceased firing; and Captain Hillyar ordered the Phœbe's fire to cease; and ran to the main-deck to see his order enforced. Towards the head of the ship, where the captain's order, owing to the confusion of battle, and the deafning effect of continued firing, was not immediately heard, three or four guns might have been discharged. This happens in almost all actions; and Captain Porter, converting *ten seconds* into "ten minutes," has made it the foundation of his libellous attack.

The Phœbe's injuries were trifling. She had a few shot-holes between wind and water, which were got at without lightening. Her main and mizen-masts, and her sails and rigging, were rather seriously injured. Her first lieutenant and 3 seamen killed; 4 seamen and marines, severely, and 3, slightly wounded, comprised, the whole of her loss. The Cherub's larboard fore-top-sail sheet was shot away, and replaced in five minutes; several of her lower shrouds were cut through, also the main-top-mast stay, and most of the running rigging; and three or four shot struck her hull. No other damage did she sustain: although, in the engraving of the action, to be found both in Captain Porter's "Journal," and the "Naval Monument," the Cherub appears with her *fore-yard falling on deck!!*—One marine killed; her commander, severely, and 2 marines, slightly wounded; is all the loss which that ship sustained: making a total loss, upon the British side, of 5 killed, and 10 wounded.

When the Essex was boarded by the British officers, buckets of spirits were found in all parts of the main-deck; and most of the prisoners were in a state of intoxication. This second proof (see p. 126) that "American sailors want no grog," accounts for the Phœbe and Cherub: having sustained their principal injury during the three first broadsides. Afterwards, the firing of the Essex became very irregular; and nearly all her shot went over the British ships.

The upper works, masts and rigging of the Essex were much damaged; but Captain Hillyar considered, that she might perform a voyage to Europe, far distant as it was, with perfect safety. "My ship," says Captain Porter, "was cut up in a manner which was perhaps never before witnessed. The shattered state of the Essex will, I believe, prevent her ever reaching England." Yet his government was actually ashamed to publish, "the boatswain and carpenter's report of damages," which accompanied the letter.

The loss of the Essex, by Captain Porter's account, consisted of 58 killed and mortally wounded; 39 severely, and 27 slightly wounded; and 31 missing: total 154. When the Essex was taken possession of, only 23 killed, and 42 wounded, were found on her decks; a loss perfectly reconcileable with the injury her hull had sustained in the action, according to Captain Hillyar's, not Captain Porter's, description.

The Phœbe mounted twenty six long 18-pounders upon the main-deck; twelve carronades, 32-pounders, an 18 and a 12-pound launch-carronade, (one on each side,) upon the quarter deck; and two carronades, 32-pounders, and four long 9-pounders, upon the forecastle; total 46 guns. She had, also, one 3-pounder in the fore-top, two 3-pounders, (one on each side,) in the main, and one 2-pounder in the mizen-top.

The complement of the Phœbe, on leaving England, consisted of 295 men and boys. So far from these being "picked men," the Phœbe, after her severe losses in the action off Madagascar in 1811, and by the climate at the reduction of Java, was completed, principally, with landsmen. Including the volunteers from the Emily and Good Friends, lying at Valparaiso, the complement of the Phœbe, in the action with the Essex, consisted of 278 men, and 22 boys; making exactly 300.

The armament of the Cherub consisted of eighteen carronades, 32-pounders, upon the main-deck; six carronades, 18-pounders, and a 12-pound launch carronade, upon the quarter-deck; and two long 6-pounders upon the forecastle; total 27 guns. She had, on the day of the action, 102 men, and 19 boys; which was her full complement. Captain Porter has given her a complement of 180 "picked men."

The Essex's armament has already appeared: (see pp. 40-41:) it only remains to state, that a quantity of bar and chain-shot, and several rifles, were found on board of her. Her complement, as it was just previous to her leaving the Delaware in October, 1812, has also appeared. According to Captain Porter's "Journal," he left behind, 9 men sick; which reduced his crew to 319. Upon her arrival in the Pacific, the Essex re-captured the crews of some American whale-ships; and, during six months, captured ten other whalers, under the British flag; but partly owned, and chiefly manned, by Americans. The united crews of these Anglo-american ships, amounted to "302"; many of whom, as the "Journal" states, entered on board the Essex.

As soon as the near approach of the Phœbe was bringing the engagement to a conclusion, and "Lieutenant-commandant Downes" had taken away, in his boat, all the wounded *British subjects* of the crew, Captain Porter "directed those who could swim, to jump overboard, and endeavor to gain the shore:" the distance of which did not exceed three-quarters of a mile. He gave this precipitate order, because "the flames were bursting up each hatchway:" when not a trace of fire could be discovered by the captors; except some slight marks about the main-deck, supposed to have originated from the "explosion," not of "a large quantity of powder," but of some loose cartridges; the natural consequence of a drunken ship's company.

Captain Porter describes the fate of those that endeavoured to gain the shore, thus:—"Some reached it; some were taken; and some perished in the attempt; but most preferred sharing with me the fate of the ship." The number "taken," must mean the 16 saved by the Phœbe's people; those that "perished in the attempt," the "31 missing." The only difficulty is, about those that "reached the shore." Captain Hillyar believed that they amounted to 20 or 30; but, if the Essex's crew, in general, felt as great a dislike to fall into the hands of the British, as the crew of the Hornet, when she was in danger of being captured by the Cornwallis 74, there can be little doubt, that the majority of the unwounded men that remained in the Essex, were such as either could not swim, or were incapacitated by liquor.

Captain Porter, in his letter, written three months after the action, fixes the Essex's complement at 255; but he informed Captain Hillyar, within two days after his capture, that he had upwards of 260 victualled; and, at a subsequent day, that he went into action with 265. His clerk furnished a list of 261 names; but one of the Essex's officers observed to Captain Hillyar, that there were several men of the same name on board; yet, in the above list, none such appeared.

In that part of Captain Porter's letter, where he is describing his loss "*after* the colours were struck," he commits himself completely. He says: "*Seventy-five men, including officers,* were all that remained of my whole crew, after the action, capable of doing duty; and many of them severely wounded, some of whom have since died. The enemy still continued his fire, and my brave, though unfortunate companions, were *still falling* about me. I directed an opposite gun to be fired, to shew them we intended no further resistance; but they did not desist: *four men were killed* by my side, and *others* in different parts of the ship."

Without the means of enumerating those "still falling," or the "others killed in different parts of the ship," this account leaves 71, and "many of them severely wounded," as the number of "men, including officers," remaining in the ship, when possession was taken. But, what were the number of prisoners received?—Leaving out the 16, saved from drowning, and the 42, found on board wounded, 103 men, without a scratch about them, were taken from Captain Porter's ship!

It is of little consequence, whether the crew of the Essex consisted of 20 men more or less; but, as some number must be stated, her complement will be fixed at 265; including 3 boys, properly so called.

According to the representation of the three ships, in Captain Porter's drawing of the engagement, the Essex is about 400 tons less than the Phœbe, and about equal in size to the Cherub. Fortunately, having the Essex in our possession, we have something better to trust to, than the *disinterested* pencil, or pen, of Captain David Porter.

The dimensions of the Essex have appeared already. (See pp. 40-41.) Those of the Phœbe and Cherub are here given:—

	Phœbe.		Cherub.		
	Ft.	In.	Tons.	Ft.	In.
Length on deck, from rabbit to rabbit,	142	9		108	4
Breadth, extreme,	38	3	424	29	7½

The Phœbe having been pronounced, in America, "of superior force to the Essex," her force, singly, will be shewn; as well as that of herself and the Cherub, jointly.

Comparative force of the ships.

		Phœbe.		Essex.		Phœbe and Cherub.	
Broadside-metal in pounds,	l. guns,	263		36		266	
	carr.	242		640		596	
		—	502	—	676	—	862
Complement,	men,	278		262		380	
	boys	22		3		41	
		—	300	—	265	—	421
Size in tons,			926		867	(not necessary.)	

During the action, the Essex Junior lay at anchor, about four miles to-windward; in view of the whole. Had she ventured out, in the hopes to escape, and the Cherub been detached in pursuit, a second British and American frigate, tolerably matched, (the one with carronades having the weather-gage,) would have been left to themselves.

Captain Porter says:—"I must, in justification to myself, observe, that with our six 12-pounders only, we fought this action; our carronades being *almost* useless." And this, although he had previously told us, that he "ran down on both ships, with the intention of *laying the Phœbe on board;"* and was "enabled, for a short time, to *close with the enemy."*—He then again forgets himself, by stating, that the Cherub "kept up a distant firing, with her long guns;" when, by his own description of the Cherub's force, she had only one long gun in broadside.

In short, the American official account of this action is become the scoff of all reasonable men. Yet, Captain Porter's ends appear to have been fully answered. When he landed at New York, he "was welcomed by the cheering huzzas of the populace, and conveyed to his lodgings, in a coach drawn by his fellow-citizens;" and Mr. Madison, in his speech to congress, dated 20th September, 1814, utters the following rhapsody in his favour:—

"On the ocean, the pride of our naval arms has been amply supported. A second frigate has indeed fallen into the hands of the enemy; but the loss is hidden in the blaze of heroism with which she was defended. Captain Porter, who commanded her, and whose previous career had been distinguished by daring enterprise, and by fertility of genius, maintained a sanguinary contest against two ships, *one of them superior to his own,* and other severe disadvantages; till humanity tore down the colours, which valor had nailed to the mast. This officer and his comrades have added much to the rising glory of the American flag and have merited all the effusions of gratitude, which their country is ever ready to bestow, on the champions of its rights, and of its safety."

Every honest man must regret that this "champion of rights" did not meet a British officer who knew him, rather than the mild and gentlemanly Captain Hillyar. The latter believed, that an American naval officer was governed, like himself, by principles of honor; and therefore became, in most of the transactions that succeeded the capture, the dupe of the finished hypocrite, his prisoner.

The Cherub sailed from Valparaiso on the 16th of April, bound to the Gallipagos and Sandwich islands, in search of three of Captain Porter's prizes. To-windward of Owhyhee, (one of the Sandwich islands,) Captain Tucker retook the Sir Andrew Hammond; on board of which he found Lieutenant Gamble, of the United States marines, a midshipman, and six American seamen; also upwards of 100 natives of the islands of Wooho. After landing the latter, Captain Tucker cruized for American whalers; and, on the 20th of June, captured the Charon, a north-west trader. In the beginning of September, 1814, the Cherub again arrived at Valparaiso; and, on the 16th of October, was joined by the Racoon; which had completely destroyed the American fur-establishment upon the Columbia. On the 30th of November, the Cherub, with her two prizes, arrived at Rio Janeiro; and, on the 6th of May, 1815, at Spithead.

The Phœbe and Essex arrived at Rio early in September, and at Plymouth, on the 13th of November. The Essex proved a faster sailer than the Phœbe, especially in a strong breeze and heavy sea; and, in spite of Captain Porter's predictions, both ships performed the passage home, through much bad weather, without the slightest accident.

Let us now endeavor to trace what became of the 12 whale-ships captured by the Essex. On the 25th of July, 1813, Captain Porter dispatched home the Georgiana, armed with 16 guns; manned with a lieutenant and about 40 men; and laden with "a full cargo of spermaceti oil, which would be worth, in the United States, about 100,000 dollars." She was captured in the West Indies, by the Barrosa 42. The Policy, laden also with a full cargo of oil, was retaken by the Loire; and the New Zealander, having on board "all the oil of the other prizes," by the Belvidera. The Rose and Charlton were given up to the prisoners. The Montezuma, it is believed, was sold at Valparaiso. The Hector and Catharine, with their cargoes, were burnt at sea. The Atlantic, afterwards called the Essex Junior, was disarmed by the orders of Captain Hillyar, and sent to America as a cartel. The Sir Andrew Hammond was re-taken by the Cherub; the Greenwich burnt by the orders of the American officer in charge of her; and the Seringapatam taken possession of by her American crew. The mutineers carried her to New South Wales; whence she was brought to England, and delivered up to her owners, on payment of salvage.

Thus have we the end of all the "prizes taken by the Essex, in the Pacific, valued at 2.500,000 dollars;" and, as another item on the debit side of Captain Porter's account, the Essex herself now rates as a 42-gun frigate in the British navy.

CHAPTER XIV.

Gross libel upon the officers and crew of the Plantaganet—President and Loire—United States, Macedonian, and Hornet, chased into New-London by the Valiant and Acasta—The port blockaded—Challenge from the United States and Macedonian to the Endymion and Statira—Accepted as to the Macedonian and Statira—American finesse on the occasion—Boston account of the affair—Challenge between the Hornet and Loup Cervier—Ballahou captured by the Perry—Harlequin schooner—U. S. sloop Frolic falls in with the Orpheus and Shelburne—Surrenders without firing a shot—Shameful conduct of the Americans after surrender—Court of enquiry on the officers and crew of the Frolic—Americans blamed for excess of bravery—Their opinion of the French and Spaniards—Three cases quoted, where French sloops have acted differently from the U. S. sloop Frolic.

THE President sailed upon her third cruize, from Providence, Rhode island, on the 5th of December, 1813; and arrived at Sandy-hook, on the evening of the 18th of February: a period of 75 days. Commodore Rodgers dates his official letter on the 19th, and the following is its concluding paragraph:—"From the Delaware I saw nothing, until I made Sandy-hook, when I again fell in with another of the enemy's squadron; and, by some unaccountable cause, was permitted to enter the bay, although in the presence of a decidedly superior force, after having been obliged to remain outside, seven hours and a half, waiting for the tide."

This "unaccountable" story required something to back it. Accordingly, the following more circumstantial account appeared in the "Naval Monument":—

"A private letter from an officer on board the President states:—"Situations in which we have been placed this cruize, will add lustre to the well-established character of Commodore Rodgers."—"After passing the light saw several sail, one large sail to-windward; backed our main-top-sail, and cleared ship for action. The strange sail came down within gun-shot, and hauled her wind on the starboard-tack. We continued with our main-top-sail to the mast three hours; and, seeing no probability of the 74-gun ship's bearing down to engage the President, gave her a shot to-windward, and hoisted our colours; when she bore up for us, reluctantly. When within half gun-shot, backed his main-top-sail. At this moment, all hands were called to muster aft; and the commodore said a few, but impressive words, though it was unnecessary; for, what other stimulant could true Americans want, than fighting gloriously in the sight of their native shore, where hundreds were assembled to witness the engagement. Wore ship to engage; but, at this moment, the cutter being discovered coming back, backed again to take in the pilot; and the British 74 (strange as it must appear) making sail to the southward and eastward. Orders were given to haul a-board the fore and main tacks, to run in; there being then in sight, from our deck, a frigate and gun-brig. The commander of the 74 had it in his power, for five hours, to bring us, at any moment, to an engagement; our main-top-sail to the mast during that time."

"It was," says the editor of the Naval Monument, "afterwards ascertained, that the ship which declined the battle with the President, was the Plantaganet 74, Captain Lloyd. The reason given by Captain Lloyd for avoiding an engagement, was, that his crew were in a state of mutiny." (Nav. Mon. p. 232.)

This is a most atrocious libel upon the officers and crew of H. M. S. Plantaganet; which ship had left Sandy-hook about a fortnight previous to the arrival of Commodore Rodgers. Scarcely a ship in the service was so well manned as the Plantaganet. In proof of this, Captain Lloyd had a boat's crew, of 27 men, taken in the Chesapeake; and neither promises, threats, nor ill-usage, could induce one of them to desert. So sensible were the lords of the admiralty of the good behavior of these men, that they had all special leave granted; and the coxswain was promoted. This is the crew that the editor of the "Naval Monument" says, "were in a state of mutiny."—Nay, the editor of the "Sketches of the War" clinches the whole, by stating, that "Captain Lloyd, after returning to England, accounted for his counduct, by alleging a mutiny in his ship; and had several of his sailors tried and executed upon that charge"!!

Although the world at large, and the reflecting part of the American people, treat the thing as a gasconading puff, it still stands recorded among the archives at Washington, that a British 74-gun ship declined engaging an American frigate. What, then, was the British ship which was cruizing off the Hook, when the President arrived there?—The Loire, of 46 guns, Captain Brown. This ship chased the President, till she got close in; when Captain Brown, having an eye to the batteries at Sandy-hook, and the gun-boats which, he knew, were stationed withinside, hove-to. The Loire's crew, at this time, being reduced by manning prizes, to 130 men, and 20 boys,—40 of the former unable, from sickness, to attend their quarters,—none but a madman would have thought of fighting such a ship as the President. Fortunately for the Loire, Commodore Rodgers, with all his boasting, was less anxious to give battle, than to reach New York in safety.

On the 31st of May, 1813, the U. S. ships United States, Commodore Decatur, Macedonian, Captain Jones, and Hornet, Captain Biddle, all provisioned and stored for a cruize in the East Indies, left New York through Long Island Sound; the Sandy-hook passage being blockaded by a British force.

On the 1st of June, just as the three ships were clearing the sound, H. M. S. Valiant and Acasta hove in sight, and chased them back to New London: a little town situate on the river Thames, about three miles from the Sound, and containing from 5 to 6000 inhabitants. It had, at this time, one fort, and an excellent site for another; but, no means of successfully opposing the British 74 and frigate, could they have run in with safety. The United States and Hornet were compelled to start their water, and throw over-board a part of their provisions, to lighten them. A few shot were exchanged between the Acasta and United States. The British ships had no pilots on board, acquainted with the sound. Owing to this, they chased with much less effect; and were compelled to cast anchor off Gardner's island, 12 miles from New London.

For several weeks previous to this event, the New York and Boston papers had been filled with panegyrics on their "naval heroes;" whose valor, they had depicted as impetuous, amounting almost to rashness. Some of the papers, as if a little ashamed of what they had said, added "a razee" to the two British ships: and gave that as a reason why the commodore suffered his squadron to be chased into New London. But a letter, published in one American paper, and dated "Hartford, June 2," says:—"An express arrived this morning to the governor, stating, that Commodore Decatur, in the United States, with the Macedonian and Hornet, were yesterday chased into New London, by a British 74 and frigate."

After having blockaded the American squadron upwards of six months, the Valiant and Acasta were relieved by the Ramillies 74, Endymion 50, and Statira 46, under the command of Sir Thomas M. Hardy.

Tired out at length with his confinement, and the force now before New London happily excusing him, in the opinion of all, from venturing to cut his way out, Commodore Decatur resolved to put in practice a literary stratagem; one that, even in its failure, should redound to his advantage; by wiping off the impression of lukewarmness, which so many months of forbearance had, in some degree, attached to his character.

An excuse soon offered, for sending a "proposition for a contest" to the British commanding officer. (App. No. 67.) That it was beneath both Commodore Decatur's and Captain Jones's dignity, to challenge an *equal* force, is made to appear upon the face of the "proposition" itself. This "bold measure," in all its "rashness," was hawked about the Union for months afterwards; nor did it escape the American public, how scrupulous the commodore was, to notice his own "boat-gun," while he did not, seemingly, (although he did, in truth,) compute the "boat-gun" of the Endymion.

Persons, desirous to draw a parallel between the challenge which Captain Broke transmitted to Captain Lawrence, and that sent six months afterwards, by Commodore Decatur to Captain Hope, will ask:—"Where is the clear statement of broadside-force in guns, which is given in the former?—and why did Captain Broke enumerate, and Commodore Decatur wholly omit, the complement of his ship?"—The answer is obvious. Because it would then have appeared, that the United States was, in guns and men, nearly one-fourth superior to the Endymion; and no credit be gained by the challenging party.

Anxious as Captain Hope was to meet the United States, Sir Thomas Hardy would not consent to it; but had no hesitation whatever in permitting the Statira to meet the Macedonian; as they were sister-ships, carrying the same number of guns, and weight of metal.—(App. No. 68.)

Captain Stackpoole's letter is written in the true spirit of a British sailor. He corrects the commodore's mistake about the Statira mounting 50 guns; and adds: "In number of men, I am aware of having a superiority to oppose: all I request is, that both ships may quickly meet." (App. No. 67.)

The second paragraph of Commodore Decatur's reply to Sir Thomas Hardy, is as artfully, as it is ambiguously, expressed. (App. No. 69.) Why include the "Statira" and "Macedonian" as a part of "the proposition for a contest declined" by Sir Thomas?—And "declined in consequence of,"—not "the decided inferiority of the Endymion," but, "your entertaining a different opinion on this subject from my own."—Thus virtually saying: "I do not credit your statement of the Endymion's force; nor is that you have given of my ship's force, at all correct."

It is amusing to see, how warily the commodore proceeds in his letter. He had, he says, consented that the complements of the Endymion and Statira should be made up from the Ramillies and Borer; and "was induced to accord this indulgence, from a supposition that their crews might have been reduced by manning prizes, and a hope that, as the selected men would be divided between the two ships, the advantage would not be overwhelming."—What "indulgence" was there, in allowing the two British ships to have their "complements made up"? Were not the complements of the United States and Macedonian "made up"?—The Endymion's full complement, in men and boys, was 350; that of the Statira, 315; including 45 or 50 boys between them. The United States had a crew of 480; and the Macedonian 440, at least; including not 10 boys between them. Here then were 665 British, and 920 Americans; and yet Commodore Decatur only *hoped* "the advantage would not be overwhelming."

His excuse about the Statira, alone, availing herself of his "concession," can best be answered by the following question.—Was not the Constitution, with 475 men on board, lying in Boston, when Captain Broke challenged Captain Lawrence; and did the former make any stipulation to prevent the latter, if he chose, from taking on board the Chesapeake, in addition to her regular complement, the whole crew of the Constitution?

Commodore Decatur then cuts the matter short, by objecting to the guarantee; although two British officers had pledged their honors in support of it. (App. Nos. 67 and 70.) Perhaps the commodore wanted the Endymion to be sent into New London as a hostage. At all events, he flatly declined permitting the Macedonian to meet the Statira.

Thus ended this vaporing affair. It afforded materials for many swaggering paragraphs. Captain Jones, it is asserted, actually harangued his men upon the occasion; pretending to lament the loss of so fine a ship; which, he assured them, would have been their prize in a very short time. He had likewise the hardihood to tell them, that it was all owing to the refusal of the British, who were afraid to contend with Americans upon *equal terms!*

This was previous to the appearance in print of the whole correspondence. As soon as, by the contrivance of the British officers, (who were disgusted with the gross mistatements of the Americans,) the letters were published in a Boston paper, the New London "heroes" bit their lips with vexation. Notwithstanding the publication of the letters, however, a Boston work, entitled "The Massachuset's Manual; or, Political and Historical Register, for the Political Year from June, 1814, to June, 1815," contains, under the head of "Tablet of memory," the following account of this challenge:—

"January 17, 1814. The British frigates Statira and Endymion, off New London, were challenged by Commodore Decatur to fight the United States and Macedonian American frigates, but declined accepting it."

From the established gallantry of Captain Stackpoole, the high discipline of the Statira's men, and their exemplary behaviour at that ship's loss, on a subsequent day, there can be little doubt that, had she and the Macedonian met in single combat, that fine frigate would not now wear at her peak the stripes of America.

After this business was broken off, a verbal challenge passed between the commanders of the Hornet and Loup Cervier, late American Wasp. The latter vessel soon afterwards foundered at sea, and every soul on board perished: nothing respecting this challenge has therefore been made public on our side. The American "Portefolio," for November, 1815, in which the "Life of Captain James Biddle" is given, contains some account of it. It is there stated, that Captain Mends, of the Loup Cervier, said, that, if Captain Biddle would inform him of the number of souls he commanded, Captain Mends pledged his honor to limit his number to the same;" but that "Commodore Decatur would not permit Captain Biddle to acquaint Captain Mends with the number of his crew, and meet him on the terms stated; because, it was understood that, in that case, the Loup Cervier would have a picked crew from the British squadron." What do we gather from this?—Why, that the Americans, with all "picked men" on their side, were afraid to meet an *equal number of* British, because they *might have* "picked men" on their's.

Commodore Decatur's amended proposition was: "That the Hornet shall meet the Loup Cervier, under a mutual and satisfactory pledge, that neither ship shall receive any additional officers or men; but shall go into action with their original crews respectively." Was this fair, or not?—The Hornet's "original crew" was 170, including about 3 boys; the Loup Cervier's "original crew," 121 men, including 18 boys.—So that, deducting the boys, the numbers would stand:—Americans 167; British 103;—an "overwhelming" superiority in earnest!

To shew the world how little disposed Americans were, when contending with an enemy, to have a superior force, Captain Biddle offered to take away 2 of the Hornet's guns, to make her's equal in number to the Loup Cervier's. Captain Mends considered the 2 guns as an "advantage" not worth his notice: it was the immense superiority in men, that he wished to have reduced. The American account concludes with expressing a surprise that, after such "fair terms" had been offered, the British vessel should quit the station without fighting.

H. M. schooner Ballahou, Lieutenant Norfolk King, in the early part of 1814, fell in with the American privateer schooner Perry; and, the American account says, "after a chase of 60 minutes, 10 of which they closely engaged," was captured. No British official account of this action has appeared; nor is it known what loss was sustained on either side. The prize was carried into Wilmington, N. Carolina.

The Ballahou's original armament consisted of six carronades, 12-pounders; but, according to the American papers, only two of these were mounted; the remainder having been placed in the hold on account of bad weather. In a subsequent American prize-list, however, the Ballahou appears with "10 guns." Her complement consisted of 20 men and boys. The Perry mounted 5 guns, one, a long 18 or 24-pounder upon a pivot; and had a complement, as it is stated, of 80 men. The Ballahou was only 74 tons: the Perry said to be 180, American measurement.

What formidable vessels the Americans send to sea, rigged as schooners, may be seen from the force and dimensions of a schooner carried into Halifax N. S. towards the end of the war.

The Harlequin privateer-schooner, just after leaving Portsmouth N. Hampshire, upon her first cruize, mistook the Bulwark 74 for a merchant-man; and got too close to effect her escape. She mounted ten long 12-pounders, with double sights to every gun; and had a complement of 115 men. She was pierced for 18 guns and had bulwarks a trifle stouter, and 4 inches higher, than those of our first-class brigs.

Had the Harlequin been purchased into our service, and commissioned as a king's schooner, every one of her ports (except the bow-ports) would have been filled with guns; and her comeplement *reduced* from 115 men, to 65 or 70 men and boys. This forms the most essential difference in the regulations of the two navies.

Dimensions of the Harlequin, Am. schooner

		Ft.	In.	
Length of lower-deck, from, rabbit to rabbit,		105	8	323 tons.
Breadth, extreme,		26	10	
Depth in hold,		12	11½	
Main-mast,	length,	84	0	
	diameter,	2	0	
Fore-yard, length,		64	0	

There were, during the war, several American privateer-schooners, larger, and of greater force in men, than the Harlequin. Considering the facility with which a schooner can gain the wind of a square-rigged vessel, what gun-brig of the Boxer's class, could have hoped to capture such a vessel as the Harlequin; admitting that the latter had been enterprising enough to engage?

The U. S. ship Frolic, Captain Joseph Bainbridge, sailed from Portsmouth, N. Hampshire, on a cruize, early in February 1814. The following extract from the journal of an officer of H. M. schooner Shelburne, gives a detailed account of her capture.

"H. M. ship Orpheus and schooner Shelburne in company, in latitude 24° 12′ N. longitude 81° 25′ W.—At day-light on the morning of the 20th of April, 1814, being close-hauled on the larboard-tack, with a moderate breeze from the eastward, observed a strange sail on the weather-bow, standing towards us. The cut of her sails soon shewed her to be a man of war; and their whiteness, that she was American. Both vessels made all sail in chase. At 6.45. the chase took in her studding-sails; and hauled to the wind on the starboard-tack; she shortly afterwards tacked, crossed royal yards, and made signals, with which we were unacquainted. We immediately hoisted an American ensign and pendant; as did the chase, a short time afterwards. At 9. 30. saw the N. E. part of the island of Cuba, bearing about S. E. The chase continued standing by the wind, with the hope (as we afterwards understood) of gaining Matanza Bay; but, finding she was to-leeward of her port, the Orpheus well on her lee-quarter, and the Shelburne on the weather, at 12. 20. the chase again tacked; passing to-windward of the Orpheus, on opposite tacks, at a little more than gun-shot distance; as appeared by the latter, when the chase was on her weather-beam, firing two shot; neither of which quite reached her. As soon as the chase had tacked as above, the wind considerably freshened; and she now threw overboard her larboard guns; to enable her to carry more sail. After the chase had passed the Orpheus on the contrary tack, the Shelburne, having a decided advantage in sailing, kept away to cut her off; which the chase, discovering, kept away across the Orpheus's bows, and set studding-sails; hoping, by that means, to reach the Havannah before the chasing vessels could come up with her. But, finding that we had a much greater advantage free than by the wind, and the chase having considerably closed the Orpheus, she, at 1. 45. P. M. hauled down her colours, without firing a shot."

The prize proved to be the U. S. ship Frolic, commanded by Master-commandant, Joseph Bainbridge, (App. No. 75.) She mounted, when the-two shots were fired at her by the Orpheus, twenty carronades, 32-pounders, and two long 18s; but afterwards threw overboard ten carronades, and one long gun. She had a complement of 171 men; young, hale, and athletic. She had three lieutenants, and a lieutenant of marines; and is a sister-ship to the American Peacock, Wasp (2), Argus, (burnt at Washington,) Ontario, and Erie. Her full dimensions will be given at a subsequent page.

This gentle surrender was, according to the report of the British officers, attended with a circumstance fully as disgraceful to the Frolic's officers and crew. The locks of the great guns were broken, muskets, pistols, pikes, swords, bar and chain shot, &c. were thrown overboard; together with the pendant that was struck! A Nassau paper, of the 25th of April, adds: "The purser's store-room was next sacked; then the men got into the gun-room and the captain's cabin, and pillaged them. In short, the ship, we are told, bore the semblance of a town given up to the pillage of soldiery."

Perhaps these gentlemen were determined that, as their ship had not behaved like a man of war, they would destroy all appearance of her having been one. Certainly, such a surrender of a public vessel is unparalleled in the history of nations.

The American "Naval Monument" ascribes the Frolic's not firing, to "her armament having been thrown overboard in the chase;" and adds:—"By this event, we have lost a fine vessel, and a gallant crew, but we have lost no honor." (Nav. Mon. p.238.)—Of the same way of thinking, appeared the court of inquiry that sat upon the Frolic's loss; as her officers and crew were "honorably acquitted."—"Bravery of enterprise," says the above American work, (p. 9,) "certainly belongs, in common, to all our captains; the oldest at their head, who bearded the lion in his den. They have even been blamed for excess in this particular."!

A reference to the innumerable instances in our own naval records, where a much greater disparity of force than existed between the American ship Frolic and her captors, has not deterred a British commander and crew from doing their utmost to capture or cripple the enemy, might be deemed ostentatious. Suffice it, that no solitary instance can be found, where a British ship of war has behaved like the American ship of war Frolic.

In the height of their zeal to praise themselves, the Americans have treated, in a manner bordering on ridicule, the naval character of the French and Spaniards; thereby wishing to have inferred, that our victories at sea over the two latter powers, were, at all times, cheaply obtained. Captain *Schomberg*'s work contains many proofs to the contrary; and even, of French national vessels having resisted bravely, against double their force. As many as three cases, all, in some respects, similar to the present, will here be quoted:

1st case. "On the 20th (August, 1797,) Captain Thomas Woolley, in the Arethusa, of 38 (mounting 44) guns, on his passage from the West Indies, fell in with, and after an action of half an hour, captured la Gaieté, French corvette, of 20 guns, and 186 men; commanded by M. Guiene, enseigne de vaisseau. A French armed brig, l'Espoir of 14 guns, was in company with la Gaieté, but kept to-windward during the action; when, seeing the fate of her companion, she made off. The enemy had 2 men killed, and 8 wounded. The Arethusa, 1 seaman killed, and 3 wounded." *(Schomberg*'s Nav. Chronol. vol. iii. p. 39.)

2d case. "On the 23d (January, 1798,) Captain Graham Moore, in the Melampus of 36 (mounting 42) guns, being on a cruize to the westward, fell in with, and after a short, but close action, captured la Volage, French corvette, fitted out by the merchants of Nantz, mounting twenty 9-pounders, two 18-pounders, and 195 men; commanded by M. Desageneaux, captain of a frigate. She had 4 men killed, and 8 wounded. The Melampus, 2 mortally wounded, and 2 more, dangerously." *(Schomberg,* same vol. p. 96.)

3d case. "On the 5th of March, the Phœbe, of 36 (then of 42) guns, Captain Robert Barlow, being on a cruize off the coast of Ireland, observed, in the morning, a ship bearing down upon him; which, on her arriving within musket-shot, discovered her error, (having mistaken the Phœbe for an East-Indiaman,*) and hauled her wind; opening at the same time a well-directed and

*As the Frolic did the Orpheus for a West-indiaman.

spirited fire, in hopes to disable the Phœbe in her rigging, and by that means effect her escape. The enemy was, however, soon compelled to strike; paying dear for his temerity, having 18 men killed, and 25 wounded. She was the Heureux, mounted with twenty-two brass 12-pounders, and 220 men. The Phœbe had 1 man killed, and 5 wounded; 2 of them mortally." *(Schomberg,* same vol. p. 361.)

The last edition of the "Naval History" was out too early, to enable Mr. Clarke to handle the subject of the Frolic's capture; or, he would, no doubt, have made it appear, that the majority of her ship's company were British sailors, who had entered by choice, and yet felt disinclined to fight; and that the native Americans, with all their gallantry, were too few in number to manage the guns. Happily, no British sailor was discovered on board the Frolic. Her crew consisted of native Americans; and, in appearance, a finer set of men, than even the ships of war of the United States usually sail with. The editor of the "Sketches of the War" has shewn his wisdom, in taking no notice whatever of the Frolic's capture. We have, in the bloodless surrender of this fine American ship, another proof of the "moral and physical superiority of the American, over the British tar"!!

CHAPTER XV.

Epervier captures the Alfred—Mutinous state of her crew represented—Is ordered to the West Indies—Upon her return, falls in with and engages the Peacock—No British official account of the action—Epervier's carronades break loose—Her crew refuse to board—She surrenders—Her loss of men—Peacock's damage and loss—Epervier's force in guns—Her sorry ship's company described—Peacock's force in guns and men—Statement of comparative force—Full dimensions of Epervier and Peacock—Action of the Reindeer and Wasp—No British official account of it—Desperate resistance of the Reindeer's officers and men—She surrenders—Is destroyed—Her loss—Wasps damages and loss—Force of each vessel in guns and men—Statement of comparative force—Landrail and Syren—Wasp encounters, and sinks the Avon—Damage, loss, and force, of each vessel—Statement of comparative force—Plymouth account of the action.

HIS majesty's brig Epervier, Captain Wales, on the 23d of February, captured, without opposition, the American privateer-brig Alfred, of 16 guns, and 110 men: the Junon frigate in sight, about ten miles to-leeward. On the Epervier's arriving soon afterwards at Halifax, N. S. to which station she belonged, Captain Wales represented to the commanding officer there, the insufficiency of her crew for any service; as well as his doubts of the loyalty of part, owing to the discovery of a plan, concerted between them and the Alfred's late crew, to rise upon the British officers. On the very next morning, without a man of her crew being changed, the Epervier was ordered to the West Indies!

The Epervier was returning from Jamaica, with a quantity of specie on board; when, on the 29th of April, in lat 27° 47′ N. long. 80° 9′ W. she fell in with the U. S. ship Peacock, Captain Lewis Warrington. An action ensued; of which no British official account has been published.

The American official account (App. No. 76) details the action; and very fully describes the injuries which the Epervier sustained by the Peacock's fire: enough to shew, that the British vessel could not have floated much longer. But there were some important facts attending this action, which it was the interest of Captain Warrington and his officers to conceal. It must strike the reader as singular that, with so much damage done to the Epervier's hull, not a gun appears to have been disabled. An omission in Captain Warrington, it could not well have been; because of his accuracy in particularizing every rope that was injured, as well as in counting the shot-holes; distinguishing how many were "within a foot of the water-line." If, indeed, it had been an omission, his second letter would have noticed it: on the contrary, the Peacock's commander wrote five letters upon this action; and yet, in none of them is there a single word about the state of the Epervier's guns.

In the very first broadside which the Epervier fired, her three after-carronades were unshipped, and thrown nearly out of the ports. While tacking, they were replaced; and the larboard carronades brought to bear. These, the moment they got warm, drew out the breeching-bolts; and, in exchange for the Peacock's last broadside, the Epervier had actually but one carronade to fire. Captain Wales now endeavoured to get the brig round, to present a fresh broadside to the enemy; but her disabled state rendered that wholly impracticable. As a last resource, and one which British seamen are generally prompt to execute, Captain Wales called the crew aft, to follow him in boarding. These dastardly wretches replied,—"She is too heavy for us."—There was no alternative, but to strike the colours, to save the lives of the very few remaining good men in the vessel.

The sentence of the court-martial upon Captain Wales and his officers, attributes the loss of the Epervier "to the very great superiority of the enemy, the *insufficiency of the crew,* and the *drawing of the breeching-bolts."*—Of the fact, then, there can be no question; and the reader now sees, what were Captain Warrington's reasons for concealing the state of the Epervier's guns. Had he told the truth, it would have appeared, that he had been engaging an almost defenceless vessel; a vessel whose guns, for any use they were, might as well have been made of wood, as of iron.

If the Epervier's had been the best, instead of the worst ship's company in the service, their utterly defenceless state towards the end of the action, would almost have excused them for abandoning their treacherous guns. Had the Epervier's carronades been previously fired, in exercise, for any length of time together, the defect in the clinching of her breeching-bolts, would have been discovered; and perhaps remedied.

The Epervier lost 8 killed and mortally wounded; and 15 severely and slightly wounded. Among the former, her gallant first lieutenant, about the middle of the action. He had his left arm shattered, (since amputated,) and a severe splinter-wound in the hip; but he would hardly suffer himself to be carried below.

Considering the state of the Epervier's guns, it is by no means surprising that her opponent should escape with, the disabling of her fore-yard, a few top-mast and top-gallant backstays cut away, and a few shot through the sails. Her fore-yard was disabled, Captain Warrington says, from the Epervier's "first broadside"; which clearly points to the period at which the latter's guns produced their best effect. The Peacock's loss, as might be expected, was—only two men slightly wounded.

The Epervier was originally armed the same as the Frolic brig, and others of that class; but, when at Halifax, Captain Wales procured, in exchange for her two 6s and launch-carronade, two 18-pound carronades: so that the Epervier mounted, when captured, sixteen 32, and two 18, pound carronades; total 18 guns. Captain Warrington was so much engaged in counting the shot-holes, that he did not discover the difference between an 18, and a 32, pound carronade; although one weighs 10, the other 17 cwt. He therefore describes the Epervier as "rating, and mounting, eighteen 32-pound carronades." Lieutenant Nicholson, the prize-master, not wishing, in a public letter, to contradict what his superior officer had, no doubt, told him he should state, gives the Epervier the same force. But neither the captain, nor his lieutenant, knew how to *reckon,* according to the editor of the "Naval Monument"; for he makes the Epervier's guns, in number "22:" that is, he does so at the top of a page; (p. 131;) but, at the bottom, betrayed by a bad memory,—that potent friend to truth! —he unwittingly says: "She (the Epervier) mounts 18 guns."

The Epervier was commissioned towards the end of 1812; and her crew received on board at the Nore. By far the greater proportion consisted of landmen, and the waisters, after-guard, and other refuse, of the line-of-battle ships and frigates, sent on board the guard-ship for disposal. Of what quality those men were, may be easily conceived. The few seamen with which the Epervier left England, had deserted, previous to January, 1814. While the Epervier was at Halifax, repairing the damages sustained in the gale of the preceding November, so destructive to the shipping in that harbour, Captain Wales (then victualling 86 men, and 16 boys) received a draught of 14 men from one of his majesty's brigs, about proceeding to England; part of them landmen, and part *rated* A. B. or able.Why men should be rated as, and not be, able-bodied seamen, is thus explained. A captain receives an order to draught out of his crew into another ship, so many A. Bs. so many *ordinaries,* and so many *landmen.* Satisfied that his complement is already as economically fixed, as it well can be; and knowing that, if, in his way across the Atlantic, he should chance to meet his match, the quality of his men is to be his chief dependence, he directs the purser to rate so many *ordinaries* as A. Bs. and so many *landmen* as *ordinaries;* and probably, to complete the draught, a few of the oldest *boys* are, by the purser's magick power, converted into *men*. This is, literally, robbing Peter to pay Paul; but who can blame the captain?

The Epervier, at the time she engaged the Peacock, had but three men in a watch, exclusive of petty-officers, able to take helm or lead; and two of her men were each 70 years of age! She had some blacks, several other foreigners, lots of disaffected, and few even of ordinary stature: in short, a crew that was a disgrace to the deck of a British man of war. Her full number amounted, including one passenger from Jamaica, to 101 men, and 16 boys; although Captain Warrington, thinking the Epervier had not enough of such riff-raff on board, gives her "128 men."

Had the Epervier been manned with a crew of choice seamen, equal in personal appearance to those received out of the Chesapeake, and the Argus, after they had been respectively carried by boarding, we might have some faith in Captain Porter's assertion,—that British seamen were not so brave, as they had been represented.—But, shall we take the Epervier's crew as a sample of British seamen? As well might we judge of the moral character of a nation by the inmates of her jails; or take the first deformed object we meet, as the standard of the size and shape of her people.

The Peacock mounted twenty carronades, 32-pounders, and two long 18-pounders; total 22 guns. Of this there is no denial on the part of the Americans: indeed, one American paper stated that the Peacock mounted 24 guns; which was not the case. The Peacock had abundance of star and chain-shot on board; and employed them successfully against the Epervier's spars and rigging.

The conduct of the Frolic's men in throwing overboard her muskets, pistols, pikes, shot, &c. (see p. 167,) prevents us from giving, what would have been highly interesting, the quantity of gunner's stores served out to American ships of the Peacock's class.

The complement of the Peacock, including supernumeraries, amounted to 185; all picked seamen, without a boy among them; although two will be allowed. Several of her men were recognized as British seamen, and others as having served in the British navy. The Peacock's proper complement was, probably, no more than 171; the rest being supernumeraries. The employment of the latter, to a great extent, on board American ships, was proved by the muster-book of the Argus. (See p. 138.) The Peacock had 3 lieutenants, a lieutenant of marines, 10 midshipmen, and other officers in proportion; and was, in every respect, a well-equipped vessel.

The Epervier was built in 1812, by contract, as are nearly all the other vessels of her class: the Peacock, at New York in 1813. The full dimensions of both, in hull and spars, will appear presently.

Comparative force of the two vessels.

		Epervier, brig.		Peacock, ship.	
Broadside-metal in pounds	l. guns,	0		18	
	carr.	274		320	
		—	274	—	338
Complement,	men,	101		183	
	boys,	16		2	
		—	117	—	185
Size in tons,			382		539

This is one of the actions, in which, as Mr. Madison boasts, an American vessel captured a British vessel "of the same class." As an action, therefore, between "equal force," the 55,000 dollars, for which the Epervier sold, as well as the 118,000 found on board of her, became due to the fortunate captors, agreeably to the act of congress; (see p. 82;) and Captain Warrington and his officers, for their "most brilliant achievement," rank among the "naval heroes" of their country. No one will deny, that this is an easy way of acquiring a martial name!

As, by the capture of the President, we gained a knowledge of the American "44-gun frigates," so the capture of the corvette Frolic, has acquainted us, thoroughly, with the American "18-gun sloops." The American papers, at the time they announced the launching of the "U. S. ship Peacock, of 509 tons, pierced for 24 guns," stated that the Wasp and Frolic were precisely of the same dimensions. Since which, have been built, from the same model, the Erie and Ontario, at Baltimore, and the Argus (afterwards burnt) at Washington.

The Wasp, a sister-vessel to the Peacock and Frolic, having captured, successively, two brigs, similar to the Epervier, a statement, shewing the comparative dimensions of these British and American vessels, "of the same class," will at once discover, whether the implied equality of size is real or nominal.

Comparative dimensions.

		Epervier.		Peacock.	
		Ft.	In.	Ft.	In.
Length	*over-all*, being from fore-part of head, to aft-part of fife-rail,	115	4	132	2
	extreme, being from fore-part of stem at height of main-deck, to aft-part of stern, at height of wing-transom,	101	8	121	6
	of main-deck, being from aft-part of rabbit of stem, to fore-part of rabbit of stern-post,	100	3	119	5½
	of actual keel, being from fore part of fore-foot, to aft part of stern-post,	87	0	105	0

		Ft.	In.	Ft.	In.
Breadth	*over-all*, or to outside of main-wails,	31	0	32	6½
	extreme, or of frame, including plank at bottom,	30	6	32	0
	moulded, or of frame only,	30	0	31	5½
Depth in hold, from under-side of main-deck plank to limber streak,		12	9	14	2
Main-mast,	length,	68	3	75	0
	diameter,	1	10	2	1½
Main-yard,	length,	54	7	67	0
	diameter,	0	11⅜	1	4

Fig. 1, plate 3, is a profile-view of the late U. S. ship Frolic, (now the Florida in our service,) as is fig. 2, of a British 18-gun brig. The only variation between the latter, and any other of the largest class of brigs in the navy, except the Primrose, which is eight feet longer, is in the form of the *head;* that usually corresponding with the vessel's name. It is believed, that no variation whatever exists between fig. 1, and the American Peacock and her sister-ships. That the reader's attention may not be diverted from the main object of the representation, nothing but the naked hull of each vessel is given.

All the first-class 18-gun brigs in the British navy, except the Primrose before-named, were intended to be of the Epervier's dimensions. Some individual brigs are as much as three inches broader, owing to an accidental falling out of their sides; but the builder is not paid for a single ton beyond what is specified in the contract. A patriotic writer from Savannah, into which port the Epervier had been carried by the Peacock, furnished a newspaper-editor with her "dimensions." He makes her "length 107 feet," without stating what length. Upon applying the compasses to fig. 2, the reader will at once perceive, that this officious' *long-shore* gentleman (for he could not have been a seaman) ran his line from the upper and aft part of the Epervier's main-stem to the aft-part of the fife-rail; which measures just "107 feet." This he compares with the "length *on deck*" of the Peacock. He next proceeds to measure the Epervier's "breadth of beam;" and, in making that "32 feet," must have extended his line to nearly the outside of each main-chain. The brig's "depth of hold, 14 feet," he probably guessed at; as there was no possibility of measuring that, while the hold was full. Having thus prepared a set of figures, the tyro-surveyor sets about computing the tonnage. He takes up his old schoolbook, "Walsh's Mercantile Arithmetic;" and, from the directions there given, soon produces "467 75-95ths," as the Epervier's tonnage. This he immediately contrasts with the Peacock's tonnage, which, about a year before, was published in the newspapers as 509. But, had this subtle arithmetician been ignorant of the

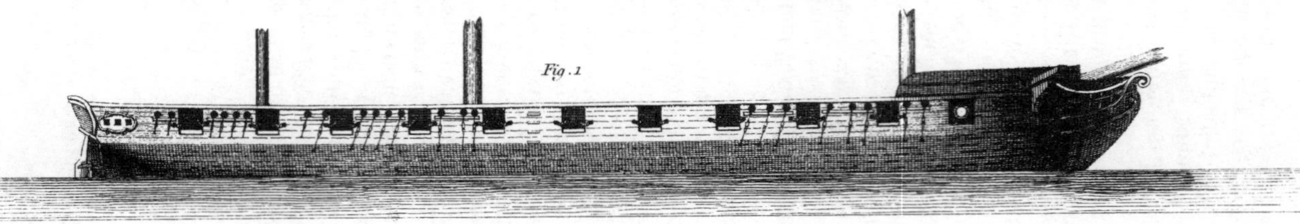

Fig. 1

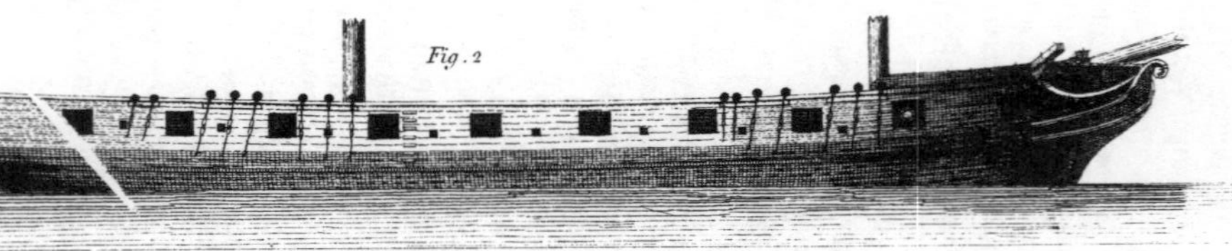

Fig. 2

Fig. 3

W. James del.

H. Mutlow sculp.

Published as the Act directs, May 20. 1817, by T. Egerton Whitehall.

Peacock's tonnage, and applied to her dimensions, as he had stated them, the same rule, by which he had computed the Epervier's tonnage, he would have made the Peacock measure 537 63-95ths of a ton; or, had he exaggerated the Peacock's "length" and "breadth of beam," as much as he had the Epervier's, and then made the calculation, he would have augmented the Peacock's tonnage to 631 88-95ths; which bears to 467 75-95ths, about the same proportion as 535 to 382, and not so great as 509 to 321 3-95ths; which was each vessel's true American tonnage, as Captain Warrington's carpenter could have informed him.

However, a correspondent who could demonstrate to a *fraction,* that, between the size of the two vessels, there existed only the trifling difference of about 40 tons, obtained a ready insertion for his paragraph; and soon had the additional satisfaction of seeing it spread, like wildfire, through every newspaper from Georgia to Maine. Even the "Naval Monument" has honored the writer, by finding room in its valuable pages for the flattering article.

Unfortunately, for at least 150 poor souls, the Epervier foundered at sea, ere she had completed her first cruize in the service of the United States. Any rational American, therefore, who may doubt that the Epervier's tonnage so greatly exceeded that of all other British brigs of the same class, has now lost the opportunity of ascertaining the fact; unless he has interest enough at Washington, to procure a sight of the original report of the builder, who valued her for the government.

No British official account of the action between H. M. brig Reindeer and the U. S. ship Wasp, having been published, the details are given, partly from the newspapers, but principally from Captain Blakeley's letter to his government, and his minutes of the action. (App. Nos. 78 and 79.)

The action was fought on the 28th of June, 1814, in the chops of the channel; and the vessels lay close alongside each other the whole time, except for a few minutes at the first, while the Reindeer was approaching her adversary. Several attempts were made to board the Wasp, but failed, owing to the riflemen in her tops, and the superior numbers upon her deck. In one of these efforts, Captain Manners fell, having received, according to a London newspaper, "14 wounds." The calves of his legs were shot away early in the action; yet did he keep the deck, encouraging his crew, and animating, by his example, the few officers remaining on board. A shot then passed through both his thighs. He fell on his knees; but quickly sprung up; and, though bleeding profusely, resolutely refused to quit the deck. Perceiving the dreadful slaughter which the musketry in the enemy's tops was causing, he called out to his men, "Follow me, my boys, we must board them."—While climbing into the rigging, two balls from the tops penetrated his skull, and came out beneath his chin. Placing one hand on his forehead, the other convulsively brandishing his sword, he exclaimed—"O God!" and dropped lifeless on his own deck.

One of the Reindeer's men was wounded in the head by a ramrod; which before it could be extracted, required to be sawed off close to the skull. The man, notwithstanding, recovered. After receiving this desperate wound, he, like his gallant chief, refused to go below; saying to those who begged him to leave his gun,—"If all the wounded of the Reindeer were as well able to fight as I am, we should soon make the American strike."

The loss on board the Reindeer, in officers, was very severe, owing chiefly to the close position of the vessels, which enabled the numerous riflemen in the Wasp's tops, to pick them off in every direction. Mr. Barton, the purser, fell early; and among the badly wounded, were the only lieutenant, the master, a master's-mate, a midshipman, and the boatswain. The total of killed and wounded was 67; and that out of 118. It is stated, that the Reindeer was surrendered by the captain's clerk, no higher officer being in a condition to execute the melancholy task. The shattered condition of the Reindeer's hull caused the enemy to set fire to her, on the afternoon of the day succeeding the capture.

The injuries which the Wasp sustained in the hull, sent her to l'Orient; where she remained, repairing, and making up her complement, from the 8th of July, until the 27th of August. Her loss is given at the end of Captain Blakeley's letter. To judge by the proportion between the killed and mortally wounded, 11, and the severely and slightly wounded; 15, all the latter have not been enumerated.

The Reindeer originally carried 32-pound carronades; but her great age as a fir-built vessel, and general weakness, in consequence, induced Captain Manners, rather than be put out of commission, to apply for 24s: which, with two 6s, and a boat-carronade, she mounted in the action. Captain Blakeley's letter stands a solitary instance of American correctness in this particular.

The Reindeer's complement had previously consisted of 123 men and boys; but, her second lieutenant, a midshipman, and 5 seamen, being absent, she had, in the action, only 98 men, and 20 boys. Here, again, the American commander deserves credit for his singularity. He states his opponent's complement at "118 men."

The Reindeer's crew had long served together; and were, at this time, under the command of an officer, who was "the idol and delight of his ship's company." Captain Blakeley says, "they were said to be the pride of Plymouth:"—no doubt, they were; and the few survivors of them still are, and ever will be, the pride of Britain.

The Wasp mounted the same as the Peacock. In Captain Blakeley's account of the Avon's action, he mentions a 12-pound carronade, as fitted upon the Wasp's top-gallant-forecastle. But this carronade not appearing in the British newspaper-account of the Wasp's force, when engaged with the Reindeer, it may have been subsequently added; or, perhaps, was the very 12-pound carronade, which, from the Reindeer's top-gallant-fore-castle, was so frequently fired at the Wasp in the early part of the action. (App. No. 79.) The usual kinds of extraordinary shot, in great abundance, were discharged from the Wasp's guns, and contributed greatly towards disabling the brig.

The complement of the Wasp was stated to consist of 175 men. The Frolic, we have seen, had 171, all men; and the Peacock, 183 men, and 2 boys. In confirmation of the Wasp's complement being 175, at least, one of her officers, subsequently to the Avon's action, writes home that she has, even then, a "complement of 173 men." (Nav. Mon. p. 141.) Captain Blakeley extols the "firmness" with which his men repelled the boarding-attempts of the Reindeer's crew. Considering the vast disparity in numbers, towards the end of the action especially, he should have transferred his praise to the gallantry of the assailants. Such acts of justice are seldom omitted in the official letters of British naval officers.

The Reindeer was built of fir, in 1804. The Wasp was built at Portsmouth, N. Hampshire, in 1813: and one of the late U. S. ship Frolic's officers declared, that it would puzzle any one to discover the slightest difference between her and the Wasp. The same dimensions as those given of the Epervier and Peacock, will suffice in this case; and the advantage possessed by the Wasp's riflemen, while firing from her tops, upon the enemy's decks, secure from being dislodged by boarders, on account of the Reindeer's tops being so many feet lower, will also be made evident by the relative length of the two main-masts. (See p. 175.)

Comparative force of the two vessels.

		Reindeer, brig.		Wasp, ship.	
Broadside-metal in pounds	l. guns,	6		18	
	carr.	192		320	
		—	198	—	338
Complement,	men,	98		173	
	boys,	20		2	
		—	118	—	175
Size in tons,			385		539

Here is a disparity of force! and the weaker party was the assailant. Still the British commander cannot be accused of rashness; because both vessels were—"sloops of war." The force employed by the Wasp, stationed upon a floating body, varying a trifle in construction; would have entitled the Reindeer to seek her safety in flight. But, had she run from the Wasp, Mr. Madison would have exulted as much in announcing, that a British ship had been chased, as captured, by an American ship "of-the same class;" and even Britons would have considered the act, as a stigma upon the national character.

When the Americans "promptly" boarded, and "all resistance ceased," the relative numbers of the unwounded, belonging to each vessel, were 149 and 51; including, among the latter, 16 or 17 boys. What the numbers were at the commencement, appears by the comparative statement.

Yet, it is immediately after giving a summary of this action, that the "New Annual Register for 1814" exclaims:—"It would seem, too, that when we were victorious over the Americans by sea, we were generally indebted for our success, to a greater superiority than even they had when they were successful."—Could an American editor, or Mr. Cobbett, have uttered a more unblushing falsehood, than is contained in this effusion of spleen? And that, too, from so respectable a work as the "Annual Register?"—a work, that is to hand down to posterity, a *true* account of historical events:—a work that will be considered as the highest authority, long after these pages are forgotten. The American historian will gladly catch at the passage; nay, it is perhaps already transcribed, to be cast in our teeth; and, 50 years hence, who shall gainsay or deny it?—Never was there a braver crew than the Reindeer's;—never a ship more ably fought, or more determinedly defended;—never an officer that better deserved a monument in Westminster-abbey, than the gallant, the heroic MANNERS!

On the 12th of July, H. M. cutter Landrail, Lieutenant Lancaster, in her way across the British channel, with despatches, was chased by the Syren American privateer; with which she maintained a running fight of an hour and 10 minutes, and a close action, within pistol-shot, of 40 minutes; in all, two hours.

The cutter lost, in this hard-fought action, 7 men wounded, but none killed. Her sails, when she arrived in Halifax, N. S. were riddled with shot-holes. The Syren lost 3 men killed, and 15 wounded, including some of her principal officers; total 18.

The Landrail mounted four 12-pound carronades; and had not even room for another gun. Still the American editors, in the first instance, gave her "10 guns;" and afterwards, by way of amending their statement, "8 guns;" at which the Landrail now stands in their prize-lists. Her complement consisted of 19 men and boys.

The Landrail was re-captured on her way to the United States, and carried into Halifax, N. S. The Syren's officer, who had been placed on board as prize-master, stated, that the schooner mounted one long 12 (believed to have been 18) pounder, upon a traversing-carriage, four long 6-pounders, and two carronades, 18-pounders: total 7 guns; that her complement was 75 men; and that she measured 180 tons, American; which is about 193, English.

Comparative force of the two vessels.

		Landrail.	Syren.
Broadside-metal in pounds	l. guns,	0	24
	carr.	24	18
		— 24	— 42
Complement, of men and boys		19	75
Size in tons,		78	193

This action decidedly proves how much execution may be done, by only two 12-pound carronades, if well-pointed; and reflects great honor upon Lieutenant Lancaster, and his little *boat's-crew.*

The U. S. ship Wasp, after remaining 18 days at l'Orient, sailed from that port, thoroughly refitted and manned, on the 27th of August; and, at about half past 8, on the night of the 1st of September, she fell in with H. M. brig Avon, Captain the Hon. J. Arbuthnot.

An action ensued; which continued, according to our newspaper-accounts, (the only British statement that has appeared,) two hours and 20 minutes; and, according to Captain Blakeley's letter, and minutes of the action, (App. Nos. 37 and 38) 43 minutes only: when the Avon, having lost her main-mast, and being actually in a sinking state, from the Wasp's fire, surrendered.

At this moment, the Castilian brig, of the same force as the Avon, hove in sight, and prevented the Wasp from taking possession. Captain Bremer passed within hail of the Avon, and stood for the American ship, then running before the wind. Just as the Castilian had got up, and fired a broadside into her, signals of distress were made from the Avon. Captain Bremer instantly hauled up for his sinking companion. He barely arrived in time to rescue the surviving crew from a watery grave; the Avon going down, just as the last boat reached the Castilian. Chase was again given by the Castilian, and continued, through the night, in the supposed direction of the Wasp; but she was not again seen.

Captain Blakeley, although he admits that he heard the enemy say, "he was sinking," places his own construction upon the Castilian's hasty return to the Avon. That the latter did sink, and that her crew would have perished, but for Captain Bremer's timely aid, are the best answers to so illiberal a charge.

The Wasp fought more warily in this action, than in the Reindeer's. She would not come fairly alongside, so as to give the Avon an opportunity of boarding. Her long 18s assisted her greatly; and, by her star and chain shot, she effected the complete destruction of the brig's rigging; the loss of which contributed to the fall of the main-mast at an early part of the action. Four of the Avon's carronades were disabled; chiefly by the usual defects in their fastenings.

The Avon lost her first lieutenant and 9 men, killed and mortally wounded; her commander, second lieutenant, a midshipman, and 29 seamen and marines, severely and slightly wounded; (principally the latter;) total 42.

According to Captain Blakeley, the Wasp received only four round shot in her hull; and had but two men killed, and one wounded. Some allowance is due, no doubt, for the usual concealment of part of the wounded.

The Avon mounted 18 guns: sixteen carronades, 32-pounders, and two long 6-pounders. Her complement, at the commencement of the action, consisted of 104 men, and 13 boys; total 117.

The Wasp on this occasion mounted an additional 12-pound carronade upon the top-gallant-forecastle; as appears by Captain Blakeley's letter and minutes of the action. Adding her 2 killed to the 173 *men,* stated, by one of her officers, to have been her complement, a few days after this action, we have that fixed beyond dispute.

The length of the Avon is exactly the same as that of all the other 18-gun brigs, with the exception already noticed; (see pp. 174-175;) but, being accidentally one inch broader, she measures 9 tons more, than the Epervier. Captain Blakeley speaks of her "great length"; and one of his officers saw so indistinctly through the moonlight, as to represent the Avon, as "longer and more lofty than the Wasp," and as having "eleven ports upon her side." The comparative "length" of the two vessels has been shewn already. (See p. 174-175, and Plate 3.) Like every other brig of her class in the service, the Avon has no more than 9 ports, and a bow or chase-port, of a side. Some commanders think it adds to the appearance of their vessel, to represent, by black paint, an additional port in the midst of the space between the aftermost port and the stern. Others again, have set the carpenter to fixing a *wooden* gun-muzzle there. (Jaseur in 1815.) To put the best construction upon the American officer's statement, we may suppose the Avon to have been similarly ornamented.

Captain Blakeley is the first American commander who has officially announced, that, on board the U. S. vessels, British and American shot are carefully weighed, and the difference, if any, noted down. The alleged trifling diminotion in weight of the American 32-pound shot, requires no additional observations. (See pp.2-3.)

Comparative force of the two vessels.

		Avon, brig.		Wasp, ship.	
Broadside-metal in pounds	l. guns,	6		18	
	carr.	256		332	
		—	262	—	350
Complement,	men,	104		173	
	boys,	13		2	
		—	117	—	175
Size in tons,			391		539

A Plymouth paper concludes its account of the Avon's capture, with: "This action will for ever rank among the most brilliant achievements recorded in the naval annals of this eventful war."—This is just the language of the "Boston Gazette," or "New-England Palladium," when recounting one of their naval victories.—Had the Plymouth editor already forgotten the Reindeer's action?—Did not that brig, with 24-pounders only, do five times as much execution as the Avon, with her 32-pounders?—The editor was fully justified in commending the bravery of the Avon's officers and crew; although their action with the Wasp was far from being, "one of the most brilliant achievements of the war."

The gunnery exhibited by the Wasp was admirable. On the other hand, the Castilian gave no proofs, that her men at all, excelled the Avon's, in that, with us, much neglected branch of naval tactics.

Although the American account makes out that three sail were in sight, when the Wasp abandoned the Avon, the British officers assert, positively, that no other vessel than the Castilian was in sight, or near the scene of action.

The same American officer who counted 11 ports upon the Avon's side, assured his friend, that, "with her present commander and crew, the Wasp could beat a 28-gun frigate." The writer might have reserved his boast, till the Wasp had beaten a ship of acknowledged equality.

CHAPTER XVI.

Gallant boat-attack at the mouth of the Rappahannock—Capture of four armed Schooners—Actual force engaged—American accounts of the affair—The Martin grounds on a shoal in the Delaware—Is attacked by a squadron of American gun-boats—Captures one of them—American accounts—Destruction of Commodore Barney's flotilla—Battle of Bladensburg—Americans retreat through Washington—British enter the capital of the United States—Destruction caused there—British squadron ascends the Potowmac—Defeats the batteries—Compels Alexandria to capitulate—Shameful behaviour of an American naval commander to a British midshipman—Squadron descends the Potowmac with 21 prizes—Engages and defeats the newly-erected batteries—Demonstration upon Baltimore—Attack and capture of the gun-boats at lake Pontchartrain.

ON the 3d of April, 1813, a detachment of boats, under the command of Lieutenant (now Captain) James Polkingthorne of the San Domingo, after rowing 15 miles, attacked four armed schooners drawn up in line, at the mouth of the Rappahannock river, in the Chesapeake bay. In his letter to Admiral Warren, Lieutenant Polkingthorne describes the issue of the enterprise, as follows:—"Arab, of 7 guns, and 45 men, run on shore and boarded by two boats of the Marlborough, under Lieutenants Urmston and Scott."—"Lynx, of 6 guns and 40 men, hauled her colours down on my going alongside in the San Domingo's pinnace."—"Racer, of 6 guns, and 36 men, boarded and carried, after a sharp resistance by the San Domingo's pinnace."—"Dolphin, of 12 guns, and 98 men. The guns of the Racer were turned upon her, and then gallantly boarded by Lieutenant Bishop, in the Statira's large cutter, and Lieutenant Liddon, in the Maidstone's launch."

The following is an accurate statement of the British force employed:

		Men.	
San Domingo's pinnace, including 2 officers,		23	each a 12-pound carronade
Maidstone's launch, do.		21	
Marlborough's,	barge, do.	21	
	cutter, do.	19	
Statira's cutter,	do.	21	
	Total,	105	men.

Thus were four American schooners, mounting together 31 guns, manned with 219 men; and whose united size exceeded 1000 tons; captured by five British boats, armed with two 12-pound carronades, and manned with only 105 men, officers included. Our loss was, 2 killed, and 11 wounded; the enemy's believed to be, 6 killed, and 10 wounded.—Mr. Clarke, with his usual address, leaves out the Arab, Lynx, and Racer schooners; and even conceals the force of the Dolphin. Thus:—"The privateer Dolphin of Baltimore, was captured after a long and gallant resistance, by a number of barges and launches, belonging to the blockading squadron. The British finally succeeded in capturing her, by boarding and overpowering her crew by superior numbers."

The editor of the "Sketches of the War" seems determined that his zeal shall not be questioned. He states the British barges at "17," containing "upwards of 40 men each"; or 680 in the whole. To make the enemy's loss proportionate, he states that at "nearly 50 in killed and wounded"!

In July, H. M. ships Junon and Martin, the former a 46-gun frigate, the latter mounting sixteen 24-pound carronades, and two long 9s, with 135 men and boys, were cruizing in Delaware-bay. On the 29th, about 8 in the morning, the Martin grounded on the outer ridge of Crow's shoal, within 2½ miles from the beach; and, it being a falling tide, could not be floated again, before the return of flood. The water ran so shoal, that it became necessary to shore the ship up; and the same cause prevented the Junon from afterwards anchoring nearer than 1¾ mile from the Martin. This afforded to the squadron of American gun-boats and block-vessels then in the Delaware, a fine opportunity to destroy the British sloop of war. They accordingly, ten in number, advanced, and deliberately took up their anchorage, about 1¼ mile distant, directly on her beam, on the opposite side to the Junon, and so as to bring that ship in a line with the Martin. Thus, by anchoring at the distance of 3 miles from the frigate, which, it was well known, could not approach nearer on account of the shoals, the American gun-boats had no force but the Martin's to contend with.

All this while, crowds of citizens, on foot, on horseback, and in carriages, were hastening to the beach, in the hopes to see verified, in the speedy destruction of the Martin, the wonderful accounts they had heard of American prowess on the ocean. Captain Senhouse had got his top-gallant-masts struck, and his sails furled; and, although he despaired of saving his ship from so formidable a force, determined to defend her to the last extremity. The gun-boats commenced the fire; and the Martin returned it, at first with her carronades; but, finding they could not reach, Captain Senhouse had the two 9-pounders transported from their ports, one to the top-gallant-forecastle, the other to the poop. With these two guns, and all the guns of the flotilla, was the fire kept up for nearly two hours, without the slightest injury to the Martin.

About 2 o'clock, the sternmost gun-boat in the line having separated a little from the rest, the Junon made a signal for the boats manned and armed. Accordingly, three boats were dispatched from the Martin, containing 40 officers and men, and four from the Junon, containing 100 officers and men, the whole under the orders of the Junon's gallant first-lieutenant Westphall. On the approach of the boats, the gun-vessels turned their fire from the Martin against them, but at too great a distance to be effective. The gun-boat which was the object of attack, kept up a spirited fire, but was quickly boarded and overpowered. The British boats lost, in this affair, 3 killed and mortally wounded, and 4 slightly wounded; the gun-boat 7 wounded. The last discharge from the gun mounted on board, broke its carriage. That prevented the British from returning the fire of the remaining gun-boats, which had dropped down in line, hoping to retake the prize; but which the captors towed off in triumph. As the gun-boats passed the Martin's bow, to attempt to save their companion, the Martin fired upon them with effect; and the Junon opened her fire, but her shot scarcely fell beyond the Martin.

Some of the gun-boats having grounded, the remainder anchored for their mutual protection. The tide had drifted the ships' boats, and the captured vessel, to a considerable distance. The gun-boats that had grounded, got off, and the whole anchored,—as if to renew the attack upon the change of tide,—within 2½ miles of the Martin, now weakened by the absence of 40 of her best hands. However, at 5 o'clock, to the surprise of the Martin's officers and crew; and, as it afterwards appeared, to the extreme mortification of the spectators on shore, this formidable flotilla weighed and beat up, between the Martin and the shore, without molesting her any further; and arrived, in safety, soon afterwards, at their station in the mouth of the river.

The force that attacked the Martin, consisted of 8 gun-boats, and two block-vessels; sloops of 100 tons each, which had been coasters. Their sides had been raised; heavy beams laid across; and the whole planked in, on the top, on each side, and at the ends; leaving only loop-holes for musketry, (through which pikes might be used in repelling boarders,) and three ports of a side. Here were mounted, six long 18-pounders. The covering extended the whole length of the vessel, and was large enough to contain 60 men; which was stated as the complement of each. The gun-boats were sloop-rigged; averaging about 80 tons; mounting each a long 32-pounder, and a 4-pounder, on traversing-carriages; and manned with 35 men each, as found on board the one captured. Each gun-boat was commanded by an experienced merchant-master; and the whole by "Master-commandant" Samuel Angus, of the United States' navy.—Here, then, was a force of 24 guns (one-third of them long 32s) and 400 men, opposed, for two hours, without success, to two guns, 9-pounders, and 135 men!

There could not have been a fairer account of the action, than was given by the eye-witnesses of it, upon their arrival in Philadelphia. They expressed their indignation at, what they termed, the cowardly behaviour of the gun-boats; and the government-editors, failing in their attempts to gloss the thing over, tried to hush it up. This accounts for Mr. Clarke's silence upon the subject. At the end of two years, however, the oral accounts of the spectators were forgotten, while the official account of the commanding-officer still shone in its pristine brilliancy. This determined the editor of the "Sketches of the War" to give it insertion, with such embellishments as he could collect. The account is far too long to be inserted at length: a brief extract will shew the spirit of it.

The attacking force is admitted to have been "eight gun-boats, and two block-ships."—"Between *both* the enemy's vessels, mounting in all 69 guns, and the gun-boat squadron, a cannonade followed, and continued about one hour and 45 minutes; in all which time, scarcely a shot struck either of the gun-boats, whilst at almost every fire, the latter told upon the hulls of the sloop and frigate. (!!) This difference of effect in the firing being discovered by the British, they manned their launches, barges, and cutters, *ten* in number, &c. &c."—"In this assault, (capture of gun-boat No. 121,) the British lost 7 killed, and 12 wounded."

But even this daring feat of the American gun-boats, was exceeded by one recorded in the same page; where the gallant Captain Angus, with "nine gun-boats, and two armed sloops, convoying three sloops laden with timber, engaged the British frigates Statira and Spartan, and compelled them to move from their anchorage to a situation out of reach of annoyance." In another page, the editor describes an action in the Chesapeake, between 15 gun-boats and three frigates, mounting "150 guns and upwards;" in which he makes one of the frigates to have been "so much shattered, that the vessels which came to her assistance, were obliged to employ all their hands to repair her."

These are the tales that contribute to swell out a work, whose publisher, by way of accounting to his readers for the early appearance of his third edition, informs them, "that all the copies of the second were engaged, long before they had escaped from the press."—How vitiated must be the taste of that public, whom such balderdash can please!

On the 22d of August, Rear-admiral Cockburn, with a detachment of boats, in which was a party of marines, under Captain Robyns, proceeded up the Patuxent river, at nearly the head of the Chesapeake-bay, in search of Commodore Barney's flotilla. (App. No. 81.) On opening the reach above Pig-point, the Rear-admiral discovered Commodore Barney's broad pendant in the headmost vessel, a large sloop, and the remainder of the flotilla extending in a long line a-stern of her. The boats now advanced towards them as rapidly as possible; but, on nearing them, the sloop bearing the broad pendant was observed to be on fire, and soon afterwards blew up; as did 15 out of the 16 remaining gun-boats. The one in which the fire had not taken, was captured. The Commodore's sloop was a large vessel, armed, as appears by the American papers, with 8 guns; the others were gun-boats, having, says the Rear-admiral, "a long gun in the bow, and a carronade in the stern. The caliber of the guns, and number of the crew of each, differed in proportion to the size of the boat, varying from 32-pounders, and 60 men, to 18-pounders, and 40 men."

A Boston paper of August 30, stated that "Commodore Barney's flotilla at Benedict, consisted of about 36 gun-boats; besides 10 or 15 barges." It seldom happens that the Americans over-rate their force; and it is probable, that this "formidable and so much vaunted flotilla," when it left Baltimore, in the preceding May, did consist of "36 gun-boats." Two, we know, were found by the boats of the Severn and Loire, drawn up and scuttled on the shores of the Patuxent; and others may have shared the same fate, during the many chases and narrow escapes which the flotilla had undergone, since the 1st of June, when two British boats, dispatched by Captain Barrie, burnt an American schooner in the very face of it. Rear Admiral Cockburn found 13 merchant-schooners, which had been under Commodore Barney's protection. Of these, such as were not worth bringing away, were destroyed; the remainder, moved to Pig-point, to receive on board the tobacco there found.

The destruction of this flotilla secured the right flank of the army under Major-general Ross, which had landed at Benedict on the 19th, and since advanced to Upper Marlborough: whither the Rear-admiral proceeded, over land, on the morning of the 23d; and, after a short conference, it was determined to make an immediate attempt upon the city of Washington; distant from Upper Marlborough about 16 miles. (App. No. 82.) In the afternoon of the 23d, the major-general, having left the marines of the ships under Captain Robyns, in possession of Upper Marlborough, and directed the marine-artillery and seamen to follow, moved on with the army, and bivouacked before dark about five miles nearer Washington.

At day-light on the morning of the 24th, the marine-artillery and seamen having joined in the night, the army was moved towards Bladensburg: on reaching which place, with the advanced brigade, the enemy was observed drawn up in force on a rising ground beyond the town, and well protected by artillery. Only a small proportion of the army had yet got up, and the men were almost exhausted with fatigue, and the sultriness of the weather. Without hesitation, however, they were led to the attack by their gallant general; and, in spite of the galling fire of the enemy, our troops advanced steadily on both his flanks, and in front. The moment they arrived on even ground with him, he fled in every direction, leaving behind him ten 18, 12, and 6 pounders, a quantity of ammunition, and 220 stand of arms, and a great number of killed and wounded; among the latter, Commodore Barney, and several other officers.

Many of the American papers stated their own force, on this occasion, to have been 8000 men: and these were stationed on ground highly advantageous; while the division of the British army that defeated them so quickly, amounted, says the Rear-admiral, to no more "than 1500 men;" and they fatigued with their long march. Our loss in this decisive affair, amounted to 64 killed, and 195 wounded. (App. No. 82.) Mr. Madison, the secretary of war, and the secretaries of state and of the navy, are said to have been present, at the commencement, at least, of the Bladensburg action. The American troops were commanded by General Winder. The village of Bladensburg is situated on the left bank of the eastern branch of the Potowmack, about five miles from Washington.

Immediately after the action, the remains of the American army retreated through Washington, and across the Potowmac, into Virginia; and the British army advanced upon Washington; which they reached about 8 o'clock at night. A fire was opened upon them from some of the houses at the entrance. These were stormed, and burnt; and immediate possession was taken of the capital of the United States.

The Americans, on their retreat through the town, had set fire to the dock-yard and arsenal, and the fort protecting them, to the frigate Essex the second, (a sister-ship to the Guerriere and Java,) just ready to be launched, the Argus corvette, (sister-vessel to the Wasp, Frolic, &c.) which had been launched since the 29th of January, and was then ready for sea, the old frigates, New York, rated a 36, and Boston, a 32; and also the entire frame, in pieces, of a 74-gun ship. They also had destroyed the two bridges leading from Washington, over the eastern branch of the Potowmac, and nearly 2000 stand of arms. The troops, on taking possession, set fire to the capital, including the senate-house, and house of representatives, the president's palace, the treasury, the war-office, and the great bridge across the Potowmac. A large quantity of ammunition and ordnance stores in the arsenal, were likewise destroyed; as were 194 pieces of cannon, (App. No. 83.) more than half of them long 32, 24, and 18 pounders; and two extensive rope-walks, filled with tar-rope, &c. situate at a distance from the yard. In short, public stores, to the amount, as the Americans have admitted, of upwards of seven millions of dollars, were destroyed at and near Washington.

At 9 o'clock on the night of the 25th, the British left Washington on their return. On the 26th, in the evening, they again reached Upper Marlborough, without a musket being fired; and, on the morning of the 27th, Nottingham; where they remained till the next day. Here Rear-admiral Cockburn found H.M. brig Manly, the tenders, and the boats. He hoisted his flag on board the former; and proceeded with the flotilla, to join Admiral Cochrane. On the evening of the 29th the troops reached Benedict; and re-embarked on the following day.

Much has been said, both in England and upon the European continent, about our "levelling with the dust the splendid palaces and sumptuous edifices, by which the city of Washington was so liberally embellished."—Passing over this ludicrous description of the American capital, it is only necessary to ask—whether the destruction of Washington was more than half a retaliation for the destruction of the British villages of Newark, Queenstown, and St. David's, in Canada?— "Splendid palaces and sumptuous edifices," there were none, in either of those villages. They consisted of lowly cottages, the poor inmates of which had no country-houses to retire to, after their humble dwellings had been "levelled with the dust." They had to quit their homes, not in a warm August evening, but in a bleak December night; exposed to a degree of cold, far exceeding that felt, at any period, by the inhabitants of Washington. Mr. Madison and his friends packed off their valuables, and themselves, before the enemy arrived. The poor inoffensive inhabitants of Newark had barely time to fly from the devouring flames, with the clothes upon their backs. What had the people of the Canadas done to provoke the ire of the American government?—Refused to listen to General Smythe's proclamation, and become traitors to their country.—After General M'Clure's candid confession, that the "proper" act he had committed "was by order of the secretary of war," (Hist. of the War, p. 156,) the "disavowal on the part of the American government" could have been tended only to amuse us.

Of the many expeditions up the bays and rivers of the United States, during the late war, none equalled in brilliancy of execution that up the Potowmac to Alexandria. This service was entrusted to that distinguished officer, Captain Sir James Alexander Gordon, of the Seahorse 46; taking with him, the Euryalus 42, Captain Charles Napier, Devastation, Ætna, and Meteor, bombs, Erebus, rocket-ship, and a small tender, or despatch-boat; and being afterwards joined by the Fairy brig, of

18 guns, Captain Henry L. Baker. (See App. No. 84.)

The squadron proceeded into the river on the 17th of August; but contrary winds, an intricate navigation, and the want of pilots, prevented the ships from reaching Fort Washington; the destruction of which was the main object of the expedition, till the 27th. After a slight bombardment, the principal fort, (the garrison of which had retreated after the bursting of the first shell,) and three minor batteries, mounting altogether 27 guns, were taken possession of. The guns had already been spiked; and their complete destruction, with their carriages, was effected by the seamen and marines of the squadron. These forts were intended for the defence of Alexandria; now compelled to surrender.

One hardly knows which to admire most, the prudence of Captain Gordon, in postponing giving an answer to the common council of Alexandria, till, says he, "I was enabled to place the shipping in such a position as would ensure assent to the terms I had decided to enforce," or the peremptory and humiliating conditions which he did enforce. It was in vain that they had sunk their vessels; they must get them up again; and put them in the state they were, when the squadron passed the Kettle Bottoms;—owners of vessels must send on board their furniture without delay; merchandize removed, must be brought back; and the merchants load their own vessels, which will be towed off by the captors! (App. Nos. 85. and 86.)

The last article of the capitulation provides, that British officers are to see the terms "strictly complied with."—One officer sent on this service was a midshipman of the Euryalus, a mere stripling. Having strayed alone to some distance from his boat, two American naval officers rode at, as if to run over him: one, a very powerful man, caught the youth by the shirt-collar and dragged him, almost suffocating, across the pummel of the saddle; galloping off with him. Fortunately, the shirt-collar gave way, and the lad fell to the ground. He was quickly upon his legs again, and ran towards a landing-place, where his boat was waiting; the American pursuing him. The boat and the men in it were hid under a steep bank or wall; and, on that account, could not level their carronade at the honorable gentleman, as he approached. The instant he saw the boat's crew, he turned pale with fright; and rode off in a contrary direction, as fast as his horse could carry him. The American editors thought this a good joke; and very readily informed us, that one of these worthies was the famed Captain David Porter, the other, and he that committed the atrocious and dastardly assault, "Master-commandant I. Orde Creighton." The first of these American officers had, for his "brilliant deeds" at Valparaiso, been appointed to the new frigate at Washington; whose name, to commemorate the exploits of Captain Porter's favorite ship, had been changed from the Columbia to the Essex; and his gallant brother-horseman had been appointed to the new corvette Argus: both of which ships were burnt, and their intended commanders, thrown out of employment, by the entry of the British into Washington, a few days previous. This is what infuriated the two "heroes," and determined them to sacrifice the first straggling Briton they could find. At the time this outrage was committed, a flag of truce was flying before Alexandria; whose inhabitants, in a body, disavowed the act, reprobating it as became them. Such conduct on their part, alone prevented Captain Gordon from enforcing the last article of the treaty.

After the British had retired from Washington, the Americans recovered a little from their panic; and took strong measures to oppose Captain Gordon's return down the Potowmac. Commodore Rodgers, with a chosen body of seamen from the Guerriere at Philadelphia, Captains Perry, Porter, and other "distinguished officers," a party of officers and men from the Constellation at Norfolk, the men that had belonged to Barney's flotilla, regular troops, rifle-men, artillerists, and militia, all flocked to the shores of the Potowmac, to "punish the base incendiaries."

Captain Gordon, with his little squadron, and 21 sail of prizes, left Alexandria on the 31st to run the gauntlet through this host of enraged foes. The Devastation which had grounded, was first attacked by some fire-vessels and row-boats under Commodore Rodgers. But a party of British boats quickly made the commodore face about; and fly, under as much alarm, *towards,* as he had once done *from,* an Alexandria. (See pp. 125-126.)

The full details of the retreat of the squadron down the river, the opposition it experienced from, and the complete dressing it gave to, the various newly-erected batteries on the shore, one of which had constructed a furnace for heating shot, will be found in Captain Gordon's interesting letter. (App. No. 84.) The toil and fatigue undergone by the officers and men, and the deprivations they so chearfully submitted to, were equalled only by their gallantry in defeating the batteries on shore, and their skill and perseverance in surmounting the difficulties of a most intricate and dangerous navigation. Happily, the loss in this daring enterprise, did not exceed, on board all the vessels, 7 killed, and 35 wounded.

The American newspaper-editors, for some days, feasted their readers with the anticipated destruction of the British squadron. "It is impossible the ships can pass such formidable batteries, commanded by our naval heroes, and manned by our invincible seamen"—"We'll teach them how to draw up terms of capitulation."—When news arrived that the ships had passed in safety, chagrin and disappointment were marked in every countenance. It was highly amusing to read the official letters of Commodores Rodgers, Porter, and Perry.—After an admission that they "did not succeed in the destruction of any of the enemy's vessels," they boldly recommend all their officers to the notice of the secretary, if not for what they *had* done, at least for what they *would* have done; and the three commodores omit not the usual compliments to one another, such as:—"my gallant friend,"—"that excellent officer,"—&c.

It being determined to make a demonstration upon the city of Baltimore, which might be converted into a real attack, should circumstances appear to justify it, the British squadron anchored off the mouth of the Petapsco, on the 11th of September; and, at day-light on the 12th, the troops under Major-general Ross were landed, near North Point. The water approach to Baltimore was threatened by a squadron of frigates and sloops, under Captain Nourse of the Severn. (App. No. 97.) Rear-admiral Cockburn, giving his usual preference to the post of danger, accompanied the major-general and the army. In the first skirmish, the gallant major-general was picked off by an American rifleman, and breathed his last on his way to the water-side for re-embarkation.

After the death of their brave general, the troops, accompanied by 600 seamen under Captain Edward Crofton, besides the marines of the squadron, and the 2d battalion of marines, pushed on with impetuosity; and obtained a victory over the Americans, 6 or 7000 strong, stationed on their own ground, and protected by field-pieces. They fled in every direction, leaving on the field of battle a considerable number of killed and wounded, and two pieces of cannon. The further particulars of this gallant affair will be found in Rear-admiral Cockburn's letter. "The brigade of sailors from his majesty's ships" are highly spoken of by Colonel Brooke. (App. No. 98.). Fortunately, the loss in the naval and marine departments, did not exceed 7 killed, 48 wounded, and 1 missing. The loss of the Americans was very great, but could not be correctly ascertained.

The troops and naval brigade remained on the field of battle all night; and, on the morning of the 13th moved on towards Baltimore; which was discovered to be defended by extremely strong works on every side, and immediately in front by an extensive hill, on which was an entrenched camp, and great quantities of artillery: it was supposed, also, that the Americans had from 15 to 20,000 men within their works. Vice-admiral Sir Alexander Cochrane did not consider it prudent to attack the city; and, on the morning of the 15th, the British arrived at their place of re-embarkation, "without," says the rear-admiral, "suffering the slightest molestation from the enemy; who, in spite of his superiority of number, did not even venture to look at us, during this slow and deliberate retreat."—The result of the demonstration was, the destruction by the Americans, of a quantity of shipping, the burning of an extensive rope-walk, and other public erections. It is to be regretted, however, that the water-attack could not have been persevered in, till, at least, the new frigate Java, and the sloops of war Erie and Ontario, had shared the fate of their sister-vessels at Washington. As the

British *did* retire, one cannot blame the Americans for claiming the victory. Nor was it at all extraordinary, that they should diminish their own, and augment our force, till they made that victory as brilliant as they could wish.

On the 13th of December, a most gallant attack was made, by a detachment of boats, under the orders of Captain Lockyer, upon a flotilla of American gun-boats, moored in line, with boarding-nettings triced up, and in every respect fully prepared for an obstinate resistance.—(App. No. 99.) The strength of the current, and the great distance the men had to row, occasioned a part of the boats to reach the enemy first; but nothing could withstand the attack of the British. Our loss was not so severe as might have been expected. A reference to Captain Lockyer's letter will fully shew, what a formidable American force he compelled to surrender.

CHAPTER XVII.

Lake Erie—British capture the Somers and Ohio—Also Scorpion and Tigress—Launching of British and American ships on Lake Ontario—British storm and carry Fort Oswego—Fail at Sandy Creek—Sir James blockades Sackett's harbour—Returns into port for provisions—Commodore Chauncey sails out—Comparative force of the two squadrons—St. Lawrence launched—Americans retire to Sackett's Harbour—An American editor's ludicrous charge against Sir James Yeo—Operations on Lake Champlain—Equipment of the Confiance—State on going into action—Promised co-operation not given—Action between the fleets—Captain Downie's extraordinary death—British fleet surrenders—Declaration of the American commander—Damage and loss on each side—Force of the respective squadrons—American painting of the action—Statement of comparative force—Remarks thereon—Charges against Sir George Prevost—His death before trial.

THE possession of Captain Barclay's fleet, had not only given to the Americans, the entire command of Lake Erie, and the large lakes, Huron and Superior, leading from it, but restored to them the immense territory of Michigan, and gained over on, their side, five nations of Indians,—our late allies. Had the spirit of the Americans, indeed, kept pace with the apathy and neglect, so conspicuous in another quarter, the province of Upper Canada could not have held out as it did.

On the 12th of August, the three U. S. schooners, Somers, Ohio, and Porcupine, being stationed close to Fort Erie, then in the possession of the Americans, for the purpose of flanking the British army in their approach against it, Captain Dobbs, with a detachment of about 70 seamen and marines from the Lake Ontario squadron, succeeded in getting his gig and five batteaux (magnified by the editor of the "Sketches of the War" into "9 large boats") across by land from the Niagara river, a distance of eight miles. Two of the schooners, the Somers and Ohio, were presently carried, sword in hand; "and the third," says Captain Dobbs, "would certainly have fallen, had the cables not been cut;

which made us drift to-leeward of her among the rapids." It is almost impossible, without having been on the spot, to form an adequate idea of the rapidity, and of course danger, of the Niagara-stream, as it approaches the cataract.

The British loss was Lieutenant Radcliffe of the Netley, (late Beresford,) and one seaman killed; and 4 seamen wounded. The enemy's loss was one seaman killed; 3 officers and 4 seamen wounded. The Somers mounted two long 12-pounders; the Ohio one long 12, all on pivots. Each schooner was commanded by a lieutenant; and had a complement of 35 men. The Somers had altered her armament, since the action of the last year; and, although the Ohio was not present in that action, her name appears in an American list of the preceding summer.

When we consider that, with the Porcupine, the Americans had a force of 92 pounds weight of metal, and 105 men, to oppose against not more than 75 men, without any artillery whatever, the exploit of Captain Dobbs and his brave followers, deserves every commendation. It proved that British seamen could find expedients, to capture two out of three fine American armed schooners, in waters, where the "gig and five batteaux" of the conquerors, were the only British vessels afloat.

Some time in August, the Americans dispatched the schooners Tigress and Scorpion, with troops, to attack Fort Mackinaw on Lake Huron. It is believed the schooner Ariel also accompanied the expedition; as she is mentioned to have foundered in some of the dangerous passages between those lakes. In their main object the Americans failed; but they compelled the British to destroy the small provincial schooner Nancy, of two 4s or 6s, and the trading schooner Mink, laden with furs. Lieutenant Worsely who had commanded the former, escaped with his few hands; and soon set about repairing his loss at the enemy's expense.

The Tigress had stationed herself at the Detour near St. Joseph's, for the purpose of cutting off all supplies from the garrison at Mackinaw. On the night of the 3d of September, Lieutenant Worsely, with a petty-officer and 17 seamen, and a detachment of the Royal Newfoundland regiment, amounting with their officers, and some Indian chiefs in company, to 70 men, embarked in four boats; and afterwards attacked, and carried, by boarding, the schooner Tigress. A body of Indians which had set out with the expedition from Mackinaw, was left three miles in the rear. Lieutenant Worsely sent the prisoners, under a guard, back to Mackinaw; manned the Tigress with part of the men he had remaining; and made sail in pursuit of the Scorpion. On the morning of the 5th, the latter returned from a cruize off French river. At day-dawn the next morning, she was attacked by the Tigress; and, after one broadside, also carried by boarding.

The British loss was, 2 seamen killed, Lieutenant Bulger, (the commanding officer of the detachment,) and 7 soldiers slightly wounded. The American loss was 3 seamen killed; all the officers of the Tigress, and 3 seamen, severely wounded.

The Scorpion mounted one long 24, and one long 12 pounder, both on pivots; and was commanded by Lieutenant Turner; with a complement of 34 men. The Tigress mounted one long 24-pounder, on a pivot; and was commanded by Sailing-master Champlin; with a complement of 28 men. They were both very fine vessels; the former measuring 68½, the latter 60½, feet on deck.

The "result of the court of inquiry" which sat upon the loss of these schooners, nearly fills a column of an American newspaper. It is there stated, that the Tigress' crew "was composed of men of the most ordinary class." This is a candid confession, and was very probably the case; yet *we* are never allowed to make the same excuse. The court of inquiry magnifies the British force that captured these schooners, into "about 300 sailors, soldiers, and Indians, conveyed in five large boats, armed with a 6 and 3 pounder, and 19 canoes"; and states that the British, besides mounting upon the Tigress their two guns, placed on board, a complement of "from 70 to 100 picked men."

On the 15th of April, 1814, were launched at Kingston, Lake Ontario, the British frigates Prince Regent and Princess Charlotte; the former of 1310, the latter of 815 tons. The armament of each ship here follows:

	Prince Regent.		Princess Charlotte.	
Main-deck	28 long	24 pndrs.	24 long	24 pndrs.
Spar-deck,	4 ——	24 ——	2 ——	24 ——
	4 carrs.	68 ——	2 carrs.	68 ——
	22 ——	32 ——	14 ——	32 ——
Total,	58 guns.		42 guns.	
	Complement, 485.		Complement, 315.	

The 68-pound carronades are the same that were mounted last year on board the Wolfe and Royal George. (See p. 148.) The latter, now named the Niagara, had replaced the two 68s with two long 18-pounders; the former, now the Montreal, her four, with the same number of 32-pound carronades. The schooners Moira and Sidney Smith were altered into brigs, and their names changed to the Charwell and Magnet; as were the names of the Melville and Beresford to the Star and Netley; but, it is believed, no alterations, beyond those already mentioned, were made in the armaments of any of the British vessels.

Before the end of March, Commodore Chauncey had succeeded in equipping two large brig-sloops, the Jones and Jefferson, of 530 (500 American, App. No. 65.) tons each. It has been stated, that they carried 42-pound carronades, and mounted 24 guns each; but they will be considered as having mounted the same as the U. S. ships Frolic and Peacock, (see pp. 174-175 and 177,) with the addition of a long 24-pounder upon a traversing carriage.

The Sylph, now a brig, (see p. 150,) mounted, in lieu of her former armament, fourteen carronades, 24-pounders, and two long 12s. On the 1st of May, was launched at Sackett's Harbour, the Superior, of about 1580 tons, pierced for 64 guns; (App. No. 65.) and, on the 11th of June, the Mohawk, of about 1220 tons. The following is stated as the armaments of these two ships:

	Superior.		Mohawk.	
Main-deck	30 long (Cols.*)	32 pndrs.	28 long	24 pndrs.
Spar-deck,	2 ——	24 ——	2 ——	24 ——
	30 carrs.	42 ——	18 carrs.	42 ——
Total,	62 guns.		48 guns.	
	Complement, 550.		Complement, 460.	

At the close of the operations of the last year, Commodore Chauncey had eight schooners, besides the Sylph. (See pp. 150-151.) He appears, this year, with only seven schooners; making, with his two frigates, a total of thirteen sail. The deficient schooner will be considered to have had the same armament as the Growler or Julia; whose force as well as that of all the other vessels of the last year's squadrons, both British and American, will be found at p. 148.

Intelligence having been received that, at Oswego, on this lake, the Americans had, by river-navigation, collected from the interior, several heavy guns, naval stores for their ships, and large depôts of provisions for their army, an attack upon the fort and town was determined upon; although the position was a very formidable one. On the 5th of May, the British fleet, consisting of seven sail, (the Netley, late Beresford, being absent,) appeared off the port; but, just as the men were on the point of landing, a heavy gale from the N.W. obliged the ships to gain an offing: in which attempt, some boats were necessarily cut adrift. The American editors, making a proper use of this, asserted, that the "shore-battery compelled the British to retire to their shipping." Early the next morning, every thing being ready, 140 troops, 200 seamen, armed with pikes, under Captain Mulcaster, and 400 marines, were put into the boats; and, under cover of the ships, the landing was effected; in spite of a heavy fire of round, grape, and musketry from the shore. The men, having to ascend a very steep and long hill, were greatly exposed, but their gallantry overcame every obstacle. They threw themselves into the fossé, and gained the ramparts; and Lieutenant John Hewitt, of the marines, climbed the flag-staff, under a heavy fire, and struck the American colours, which had been nailed to the mast.—The British lost in this affair 22 killed, and 73 wounded. The Americans acknowledge a loss of 69 in killed, wounded, and missing. Mr. Low declares our loss to have been 235; and that we landed "2000 men." The editor of the

*See p. 3.

"Sketches of the War" says, "3000 men;" and speaks of the British vessels, thus:—"Their principal ship, and the *other frigates*," &c.

The British carried away with them, seven long guns, 32s and 24s, a great quantity of ordnance stores, and large rope, 2400 barrels of provisions, and three schooners. They destroyed three long 24-pounder guns, one long 12, and two long 6s, a schooner, the barracks, and all the other public buildings. One of the schooners was the Growler, late Hamilton. Besides the above, a quantity of cordage, and other naval stores, and three long 32-pounders, were sunk in the river by the Americans themselves. Mr. Low, the war-historian, comprises all this loss in,—"Eight pieces of cannon, and some stores, worth about 100 dollars"!

The guns and stores for the new ship Superior, had, unknown to the British, been removed from Oswego, previous to the attack; and reached Sackett's-harbour, chiefly by land-conveyance. After departing from Oswego, Sir James anchored off Sackett's-harbour; which port he blockaded, till the early part of July; when it became necessary to return to Kingston for provisions. The American ship Superior had certainly been ready for several days; and the Mohawk was equipping with great expedition.

On the 30th of May, the daring spirit of the British officers and seamen, and their total unacquaintance with ambuscades, led to an unfortunate failure. Captains Popham and Spilsbury, with a detachment of seamen and marines, amounting to 181, pursued into Sandy-creek, (about 16 miles from Sackett's-harbour,) a flotilla of 18 boats, carrying a number of cannon, and other stores, for the new vessels. The British landed; and were unexpectedly assailed by 150 riflemen, 4 field-pieces, nearly 200 Indians, and a numerous body of militia and cavalry. The resistance of the British was noble. The winding of the creek, and the thickness of the wood on its borders, gave the enemy great advantages. After a loss of 18 killed, and 50 dangerously wounded, Captain Popham and his party surrendered.

On the 1st of August, the American commander, having his second frigate, the Mohawk, ready for the lake, again ventured out of port. Here the British were once more accused of unwillingness to fight "on equal terms." How far that was the case, at any time previous to the launching of the St. Lawrence, the following statement will shew:—

Comparative force of the two squadrons.

		British.	American. No. 1.	American. No. 2.	American. No. 3.
Broadside metal in pounds,	l.guns,	942	868	1372	1732
	carr.	1810	1448	2078	2456
		2752	2316	3450	4188
Complements,		1517	1311	1861	2321
Size in tons,		3510	3787	5367	6587

The British column, compared with No. 1, shews the relative force of the parties at the sacking of Oswego; with No. 2, the same, for some days before Sir James gave up the blockade of Sackett's-harbour; with No. 3, until the St. Lawrence appeared on the lake.

Admitting it was prudent not to be provoked by the roaring of Sir James's cannon at Oswego, (where he had one vessel short of the number comprised in the statement,) what reasonable excuse had Commodore Chauncey, for submitting to the indignity of being blockaded; and that, too, by an officer, whom he had boasted of having so often "chased round the lake"?— Was he determined not to risk a battle, unless he had three to two in his favor?

About the middle of October, when the season for cruizing on the lake was almost over, the British succeeded in getting ready their large ship St. Lawrence, of 2305 tons; and intended to mount 112 guns. A "peep into Kingston" by one of Commodore Chauncey's small vessels, gave him timely notice of this; and he retired to Sackett's-harbour, to stir out no more. All agreed in the propriety of this; but still the preponderance of force was not so great, on Sir James's side, as it had hitherto been (except at the Oswego-attack) on the side of Commodore Chauncey.

The Americans, however, declared the superiority would be "overwhelming;" and commenced building two 74s, (so to be *rated,)* each of whose broadsides would have about equalled that of the St. Lawrence. To meet this, on our part, a 74 was commenced upon; and a frigate, like the Princess Charlotte, constructed: but, before the lakes were open in the ensuing spring, peace came; otherwise, there is no saying whether the building mania would not have continued, while room remained on the lake for working the ships.

The editor of the "Naval Monument," justly apprehending greater difficulty in composing a Preface, than he had experienced in compiling his choice collection of newspaper-scraps, hired a scribbling zealot, or a "literary gentleman," as he styles him, of Boston, to do it for him. Sixteen close pages, where two would have sufficed, render it probable, that the writer engaged by the quantity, rather than the quality, of the matter he was to furnish; or, perhaps, he received so much a score for the hard names he could heap upon the British. He has honored Sir James Lucas Yeo, by referring to him in the following question:—"What perseverance was ever more indefatigable than Chauncey's in pursuit;—unless, indeed, that of his adversary in patience?—an adversary, not only beaten, but impossible to be made to fight; and he the sole British commander, on his return from the lakes, able to say even that."—It would be an affront to the reader, not to allow him to make his own comments upon this most ludicrous charge against Sir James Lucas Yeo!

Lake Champlain is a lake of North America; dividing the N.E. part of the state of New York from that of Vermont. It is 80 miles long, 18 where broadest, and the mean width about 6. This lake receives the waters of Lake George from the S. by South river; and sends its own waters a N. course, through Sorrel river, into the St. Lawrence; to which, however, there is no navigation.

As early as the year 1776, two formidable British and American flotillas appeared on this lake. Between them, they mounted upwards of 180 heavy guns; and we could then afford, "from the king's ships at Quebec, and transports, 8 officers, 19 petty-officers, and 670 men."—(*Schomberg*'s Nav. Chronol. vol. iv. p. 324.)

The first naval event of the late war, upon this lake, occurred on the 3d of June, 1813. Two American sloops appeared in sight of the British garrison at Isle au Noix. Three gun-boats immediately got under weigh to attack them; and the crews of two batteaux and two row-boats, were landed, to annoy the enemy in the rear; the channel being very narrow. After a contest of three hours and a half, the two sloops surrendered. They proved to be the Growler and Eagle, mounting 11 guns, and having a complement of 50 men, each; both under the command of Lieutenant Sidney Smith, of the United States' navy. We lost 3 men wounded: the Americans, 1 man killed; 8 severely wounded; and, including the latter, 99 prisoners. No British naval officer was present. The feat was performed by detachments of the 100th regiment, and royal artillery, under the direction of Major Taylor, of the former.

On the 1st of August, some officers and seamen having arrived from Quebec, Captain Everard, (late of the Wasp brig,) with the two prize-sloops, three gun-boats, and several batteaux, entered Plattsburgh; where he destroyed all the enemy's arsenals, block-houses, barracks, and stores of every description; together with the extensive barracks at Saranac.

Captain Everard, in his letter, says:—"Having captured and destroyed four vessels, without any attempt on the part of the enemy's armed vessels to prevent it; and seeing no prospect of inducing him to quit his position, where it was impossible for me to attack him, I am now returning to execute my original order."

This enterprising officer proceeded afterwards off Burlington and Shelburne; where he seized and destroyed several sloops laden with provisions; and did other considerable injury. At this time, according to Mr. Low, "the United States troops at Burlington, under command of Major-general Hampton, consisted of about 4000 men;" and Mr. Clarke informs us, that, on the 20th of August, "the American naval force on Lake Champlain consisted of—

	Guns.
" The President,	12
Commodore Preble,	11
Montgomery,	11
Frances,	6
Two gun-boats, one 18-pounder, each,	2
Six scows, one 12-pounder, each,	6
Guns,	48"

But, lest the American reader should enquire, why Commodore Macdonough, with such a force, did not attempt to capture or drive off the British "marauding party," Mr. Clarke describes the prize-sloops Growler and Eagle (without naming them) as "two large sloops of war"! (N. Hist. vol. i. p. 232.)

During the summer of 1814, each party strove to out-build the other, in time to commence operations on the lake before the season closed. The Americans, being quite at home, got a formidable force equipped, long before the principal vessel of the British was even off the stocks. This ship, named the Confiance, was launched on the 25th of August. On the 3d of September, Captain Downie arrived from Lake Ontario, accompanied by his late first-lieutenant in the Montreal, to take the command of the vessels upon this lake; consisting, besides the Confiance, of a brig, the two cutters or sloops before-named, and 10 gun-boats.

Between the 25th of August, and the 10th of September, a crew was got together for the Confiance; which vessel they had to mast and rig; and equip with guns and ordnance-stores. Captain Pring, in his official letter, says this crew was made up of draughts from different ships. That this was really the fact, will appear from the following list, comprising the names of the ships out of which they were draughted, &c.

Officers, including midshipmen,	20
Seamen, originally on the lake,	14
from H.M.S. Leopard,	57
Ceylon,	25
Ajax,	10
Warspite,	12
Vigo,	2
Indian,	6
Linnet,	1
Cornelia,	1
Royal Sovereign,	2
Montreal,	2
transports, (ent. for a limited time,)	25
Impressed men,	4
Volunteers,	2
Taken out of prison,	1
Marines, from battalion, and different ships,	65
Royal artillery,	3
Marine-artillery,	8
39th regiment of foot,	10
Total of Confiance's complement,	270

If this is not a motley collection, there surely never was one! Among the number, there were 19 foreigners, and 6 boys. The seamen were men of inferior quality and character; and who, as it is termed, *volunteered,* or rather, were forced from their respective ships; where they had been in disgrace. Some of them, indeed, had been liberated from irons, for the very purpose of proceeding to the lakes! None of the marines joined earlier than the 9th of September; and a part of the seamen, only the night before the action. Of course, time did not admit of the men becoming acquainted with their officers, or with each other. Captain Downie himself was acquainted with no officer on board his ship but his first-lieutenant; and the latter with none of the other officers!

On the 10th of September, his Excellency Sir George Prevost, the commander in chief, called for the instant co-operation of the naval force, in a meditated attack upon the American fleet and works at Plattsburg. It was solemnly agreed, that the attack by land and water should be simultaneous; and proposed, that Captain Downie, should give notice to the army of his approach towards the enemy, by scaling the guns of the Confiance.

Captain Downie's situation was one of peculiar delicacy. While he was fully aware of the unprepared state of his own ship, he knew that a powerful British army was anxiously waiting to co-operate; and that the season for active warfare was rapidly closing. The slightest backwardness on his part might injure the reputation of himself and those placed under his command; and,—had he not the most positive assurance, that the enemy's works should be stormed by the troops, at the very moment he was seen advancing to attack their fleet?

When the American people, in the summer of 1814, were blaming Commodore Chauncey for not leaving Sackett's harbour, in the new ships Superior and Mohawk, after the latter had been launched nearly two, and the former upwards of three months, that cautious commander, under date of the 10th of August, writes to the secretary of the American navy, thus—"I need not suggest to one of your experience, that a man of war may appear to the eye of a landsman, perfectly ready for sea, when she is deficient in many of the most essential points of her armament; nor how unworthy I should have proved myself of the high trust reposed in me, had I ventured to sea in the face of an enemy of equal force, without being able to meet him in one hour after my anchor was weighed."—How admirably this fits the case of the Confiance! And what Briton does not regret, that a very small portion of Commodore Chauncey's prudence, was not bestowed upon the framers of the expedition to Plattsburg?

On the morning of the 11th, with the carpenters still working at her, and half-fitted as she was, the Confiance, accompanied by the other British vessels, stood into the enemy's bay. Captain Downie then acquainted the crews of the different vessels, with the promised co-operation; and, just before the action commenced, Lieutenant Robertson went himself round the Confiance's quarters, and explained particularly to the crew, the nature of the co-operation, as he had understood it from Captain Downie. The guns of the Confiance were scaled several times, as was agreed upon; but the signal was not answered from the army. To the honor of the soldiers, and the officers in general, they all panted to rush forward; nay, they had advanced to the very picquets of the enemy; when it was thought advisable to check their glorious career. Two hours more would have given a victory to both army and navy, instead of a flight to one, and a defeat to the other!

Captain Downie now discovered, too late, the mistake his confidence had led him into. His squadron was already in the enemy's bay; where were lying, moored in line, a ship, brig, schooner, sloop, six row-gallies, and four gun-boats, anxiously awaiting the attack. (App. No. 90.) Several British officers who, since the conclusion of the war, have surveyed the Plattsburg bay and works, are fully of opinion that both squadrons were within reach of the American batteries on shore.

Unfortunately, as the British squadron advanced to the attack, a very light air, amounting almost to a calm, gave the American row-gallies and gun-boats an opportunity of commencing upon the Confiance, which was the leading ship, a heavy and galling fire. Having two anchors shot away from her bow, she was obliged to anchor, not so advantageously as had been intended. The Linnet brig, and Chubb cutter, took their allotted stations; but the latter presently had her main-boom shot away; and, drifting within the enemy's line, was compelled to surrender. The Finch had the misfortune, while proceeding to her station, to strike on a reef of rocks off Crabb-island; where there was an American battery of two guns, which fired at the Finch, and wounded two of her men; the only loss she sustained. Not a word of this appears in the American official account.

All the gun-boats, except the Murray, Beresford, and another, "abandoned the object assigned them;" (App. No. 90;) that is, ran away, almost as soon as the action commenced!—All surprise at this will cease, when it is known, that not one of the gun-boats had more than *three* seamen on board; their crews, with the exception of a few marines in some of them, being composed of a small detachment of the 89th regiment, and of Canadian militia, who spoke the French language only.

The American commander, Macdonough, aware that the British official account would forcibly dwell upon the hurried, half-finished state of the Confiance, and upon the accidental absence and defection of a part of the squadron, takes care to be before-hand, by stating thus:—"For *several days,* the enemy were on their way to Plattsburg by land and *water*. In this situation, the *whole force on both sides* became engaged." (App. No. 92.)

Within 15 minutes after the commencement of the action, fell the British commanding officer, the brave, the lamented Captain Downie. The way in which he met his death, is of too extraordinary a nature to be passed over. A shot from the enemy struck one of the Confiance's 24-pounders, and threw it completely off the carriage, against Captain Downie, who was standing close in the rear of it. He received the blow upon his right groin; and, although signs of life remained for a few minutes, never spoke afterwards. No part of his skin was broken: a black mark, about the circumference of a small plate, was the only visible injury. His watch was found flattened, with the hands pointing to the hour, minute, and second, at which the fatal blow was given!

The circumstance of the Confiance not being able, owing to the loss and damage she had sustained, to bring a fresh broadside to bear, as the Saratoga had succeeded in doing, was fatal to the former. She had every gun on the starboard side loaded with two shot, besides canister; also 17 of her guns disabled; and many of the others encumbered by wreck. The marines were of no use, as the action was fought out of the range of musketry. In this situation, Lieutenant Robertson, the Confiance's surviving commanding officer, very properly made the signal of submission.

The Linnet brig fought most gallantly; and actually drove her very superior antagonist, the Eagle, for shelter, between the Saratoga and Ticonderoga. Commodore Macdonough assigns a different reason for the Eagle's shifting her station,—her "not being able to bring her guns to bear." (App. No. 92.) It was not till 15 minutes after the surrender of the Confiance, and, when left alone in the combat, that the brave little Linnet hauled down her colours. The Americans admit that the action lasted, without intermission, two hours and 20 minutes.

Commodore Macdonough, taking Lieutenant Robertson, when presenting his sword, for the British commanding officer, spoke to him as follows:—"*You owe it, sir, to the shameful conduct of your gun-boats and cutters, that you are performing this office to me; for, had they done their duty, you must have perceived, from the situation of the Saratoga, that I could hold out no longer: and indeed, nothing induced me to keep up her colours, but seeing, from the united fire of all the rest of my squadron on the Confiance, and her unsupported situation, that she must ultimately surrender.*"—Here is an acknowledgment, candid and honorable in the extreme.—Can this be the "T. Macdonough" whose signature appears to the two American official accounts of the action?

The state of the two squadrons after the action, appears in the letters of Captain Pring, and Commodore Macdonough. And Captain Henley, of the Eagle, so long engaged with the Linnet, states that his vessel had thirty nine round shot in her hull, and four in her lower-masts. None of the British gun-boats were sunk, or even injured. Commodore Macdonough, discovering, with his glass, 10 gun-boats only, when he had been informed there were 13, wrote down at once:—"Three of their gallies are said to be sunk."

The Confiance's loss, as appears by Captain Pring's letter, could not at the time be accurately obtained. That ship had 83, instead of 40 wounded. This makes the total loss on the British side, 54 killed, and 116 wounded. The Chubb's loss amounted to half her complement. The gun-boats sustained no loss whatever.

The loss on the American side appears not to have been fully given. The "list of killed and wounded troops of the line, acting marines on board the squadron," forwarded by Captain Youngs of the "15th Infantry," (App. No. 93,). has been kept back. Besides, it is clear that "52 killed," and only "58 wounded" are out of all proportion. With nearly the same number of killed, our wounded were just double the American wounded. Consequently, exclusive of the "killed and wounded troops of the line," the *slightly wounded,* on board the American squadron have not been enumerated.

Commodore Macdonough says:—"The enemy's shot passed principally just over our heads."—The Saratoga's loss in the action proves, that either the Confiance's guns were fired low enough, or that 27 at least, of the Saratoga's men, were of an extraordinary height. Let it be recollected, that no musketry was employed on either side.—One tenth of the drilling which, as the commodore says, First-lieutenant Perry gave to the Saratoga's men, would perhaps have saved the Confiance's newly arrived ship's company from this intended reproach.

By admitting Commodore Macdonough's statement of the guns of the American, (App. No. 92.) we may be allowed to introduce Captain Pring's statement of the guns of the British squadron; (App. No. 90;) although the latter should differ, in some points, from that which the commodore has given to the public.

The Confiance mounted twenty-six long 24-pounders upon the main or flush-deck; also two carronades, 32-pounders, out of the bridle or bow ports, and the same out of the stern-ports. Upon the poop were mounted four carronades, 24-pounders; and upon the top-gallant-forecastle, two carronades, 24-pounders, together with a long 24-pounder, upon a traversing carriage. But, in consequence of there being only a ridge-rope or rail round either the poop or top-gallant-forecastle, the guns, there stationed, were disabled after the first discharge. They will, however, be estimated as part of the ship's force; but not the carronades out of the bridle and stern ports, because they could not be used in the broadside. Therefore, although the Confiance mounted, altogether, 37 guns, she fought 17 only upon the broadside. There were also in the hold, as part of the ballast, two long 18-pounders. These, Commodore Macdonough has shifted to the "berth-deck," and actually, in his statement of force, carried out, as part of the Confiance's "39 guns"!

Captain Downie, having no gun-locks on board, (they being in the Junon frigate, which had not arrived at Quebec in time,) attempted to substitute carronade-locks; which he contrived to fasten to the guns by means of copper hoops. But the plan was not found to answer; and matches were resorted to. Determined that we should derive no advantage from publishing this fact, an

American paper subjoins to an exaggerated account of the Confiance's force in guns;—"*with locks*" Any thing of this sort travels all through the United States, as fast as the mail can carry it.

Commodore Macdonough, in a second official letter, says,—"The Saratoga was twice set on fire by hot shot fired from the enemy's ship."—The latter part of this assertion is as gross a falsehood as ever was uttered; and, from the notorious fact, that neither the Confiance, nor any other of the British vessels, had a furnace on board, the writer must (shame to say!) have known it to be a falsehood. Had such a discovery been made, there would have been paragraph after paragraph, and column after column, of well-merited abuse! Lieutenant (now Captain) Robertson, of the Confiance, has declared, that the Saratoga certainly received some hot shot in the action, but that it must have been from the American batteries:—much more likely places to find furnaces for heating shot, than on board the just-launched, half-equipped Confiance.

The Linnet mounted sixteen long 12-pounders. Although Commodore Macdonough gives her no more, Sir George Prevost, in his official despatch, says:—"Linnet, 18 guns." The cutter Chubb mounted ten carronades, 18-pounders, and one long 6-pounder; the cutter Finch, six carronades, 18-pounders, and four long 6-pounders: the American account adds, "one columbiad 18-pounder;" which must be a mistake. These two cutters are named, in Sir George's letter, Broke and Shannon.

There were but ten gun-boats, instead of twelve, as stated by Sir George Prevost in his official despatch, and thirteen, as stated by Commodore Macdonough. Of the ten gun-boats, two mounted a long 24, and a 32 pound carronade, each; one a long 18, and a 32 pound carronade; four a long 18, each; and the remaining three, a 32-pound carronade, each; total 13 guns. Commodore Macdonough's statement differs much less from this than might be expected; considering that none of the gun-boats came into his possession.

The "Burlington Centinel," an American newspaper, says: "By the official accounts of the Champlain action, it appears, 37 officers, and 340 seamen, were taken prisoners." The "Naval Monument," instead of this list, has inserted one, containing the names of the paroled British officers, as low down as the carpenter; amounting in all to 26: therefore the newspaper-account of the number of officers, must be incorrect. The "Sketches of the War," states thus: The enemy's loss was, 84 men killed, 110 wounded, and 856 prisoners; who alone amounted to a greater number than those by whom they were taken." Typographical errors are much more frequent among figures than words; and no two *written* figures are so often confounded as the 3 and 8. Considering that the Americans estimated the total of the crews of the captured British vessels at no more than

500, it will be but charitable to suppose, that the typographical error of substituting an 8 for a 3, existed in the newspaper, pamphlet, or whatever it was, from which the paragraph had been copied. In that case, 356 would be the number of prisoners; not so many by 10, as the list of paroled officers, added to the "340 seamen" from the "Burlington Centinel," would give.

Perhaps, the best way to establish the point, will be to deduct from the actual complements of the captured vessels, the British return of killed; and then see what remains.

	Actual complement.
Confiance,	270
Linnet,	80
Chubb,	40
Finch,	30
	420
Deduct killed in action,	54
No. of prisoners, in all,	366

After this exposition, it is surely unnecessary to suppose a doubt can exist, as to the number of men and boys composing the united complements of the captured British vessels.

Two of the British gun-boats had 35 men and boys each; one 33; four, 29 each; and the remaining three, 25 each; total 294 men and boys: while the Americans gave the "13 gun-boats," 350 men.

The Linnet, and the two cutters, had their complements chiefly made up of detachments of the 39th regiment, and of Canadian militia who could speak little or no English; and the gun-boats, as stated before, had only *three* seamen to each. The number of boys is not exactly known; therefore, they will not be enumerated in the estimate of comparative force.

The armament of the American vessels appears in the statement subjoined to Commodore Macdonough's official letter. All the guns on board the row-gallies and gun-boats, the same as on the British side, will be brought into the broadside.

The following list comprizes the number of men, which the American officers assured Captain Pring, was the regular complement of each of their vessels.

	Men.
Saratoga,	250
Eagle,	142
Ticonderoga,	115
Preble,	45
Six lateen-rigged gun-boats, or row-gallies, 41 men each,	246
Four lugger-rigged ditto, 25 each,	100
Total,	898

But the detachments of the 6th, 15th, and 33d U. S. infantry, "acting marines on board the squadron," are not included in the above statement. Admitting the draughts from the three regiments, to have amounted to no more than a company, or captain's command, the united complements of the American vessels would be, at least, 950; which, therefore, will be the number fixed.

The American newspapers, of dates many weeks anterior to the action, announced that their squadron on Lake Champlain, was completely manned by seamen, drafted from the different ships on the sea-board. The gun-boats had on board most excellent artillerists; such as, from their station between the large vessels and the batteries, contrived to strike the British, between wind and water, almost every shot.

The public has heard much of the "frigate" Confiance. She is no more a frigate than the American ships General Pike and Madison on Lake Ontario. Is extraordinary size to constitute a "frigate"? The American corvettes; Adams and John Adams, were each larger than the Confiance; and yet not called frigates. H. M. late ship Andromeda (formerly the American Hannibal) was broader, though a trifle shorter, than the Confiance; and yet she was not called a frigate. The peculiar construction of a frigate has been already defined; and, without Commodore Macdouough can give the Confiance a regular quarter-deck and forecastle, fitted with ramparts and ports, neither his assertions, nor the wishes of the American people, can make that ship a "frigate."

Having magnified the Confiance into a "frigate," Commodore Macdonough could do no less than make "sloops of war" of the cutters Chubb and Finch. We have captured from the Americans, many gun-boats; none under 70, and one exceeding 112 tons; being two tons more than the largest of the commodore's "two sloops of war." Would not Commodore Macdonough himself be one of the first to ridicule us, had we announced, in a public despatch, the capture of the "U.S. *sloop of war* No. 23"?—Really such artifices to gain public applause, are pitiful in the extreme.

To shew that we have something beyond declamation to support us, when speaking of the size of the British vessels on Lake Champlain, here follow the principal dimensions of—as the American newspapers' denominated them—"four of the enemy's largest ships:"

		Length.				Breadth extreme.		Draught of water.		Tons.
		Gun-deck.		Actual Keel.						
		Ft.	In.	Ft.	in.	Ft.	In.	Ft.	In.	
Confiance,		146	3	138	0	36	1¼	7	10	831
Linnet,	B.	82	0½	75	0	26	6¼	7	6	260
Chubb,	Cut.	60	0	55	0	20	0	6	6	110
Finch,	Cut.	58	0	54	6	19	3	6	0	102

So that the gross tonnage of these "four large ships" scarcely exceeds the tonnage of a single American "36-gun frigate." (See p. 31.)—This will be the proper place to introduce, from the, "Burlington Centinel," an American paper published on the borders of Lake Champlain, the following paragraph:

"The British large ship taken by Commodore Macdonough is repaired, and painted. She is undoubtedly one of the finest ships of her class in the British navy, mounting twenty eight long double fortified 24s, with locks, and carrying in the whole, 39 guns: she is 460 feet in length, 40 feet in breadth; presenting a most formidable battery, and which, if it had been managed with the skill of a Macdonough, was sufficient of itself, to have captured or destroyed the whole of our fleet."—Here, the reader discovers a typographical error; making the Confiance more than double the length of the largest ship that ever was built!—This is from the same paper, that over-rated the number of British officers. The Americans are very happy in their mistakes of this sort; seldom erring, on the wrong side.

The British gun-boats were very inferior vessels of the kind; not two-thirds the size of the American ones, nor half so well equipped. An average of 45 tons, will be an over-estimate of their measurement.

The size of the American vessels comes, next, under consideration. As far as the British officers could judge, the Saratoga was of the same length and breadth as the Confiance; but her draught of water, 12 feet and upwards, in-stead of 7 feet 10 inches. The principal difference was, that the Saratoga had top-sides considerably stouter than those of the Confiance, and no useless poop or top-gallant forecastle. Admitting a trifling superiority of size in the Confiance, 800 tons will be a fair estimate for the Saratoga. We may judge through what a false medium the Americans have viewed the Confiance, by the following extorted confession of a Boston reviewer, while remarking upon Mr. Corney's painting of this "memorable contest:"—"The artist has made use of a stratagem to flatter the public, in representing the English *frigate,* which was commanded by Commodore Downie, of disproportionate size, particularly in the second painting."

The brig Eagle is about similar in size to the Lawrence or Niagara on Lake Erie, say 450 tons. As to the schooner Ticonderoga, the American papers, at the time of her launch, announced her as a fine vessel of about 400 tons; and the gallies or gun-boats, particularly the six new ones, were described as very superior vessels. These must have been, at least 85 tons each; while 70 tons may serve for the average of the remaining four. The Preble is stated to be a similar vessel to the Chubb and Finch.

The cutter Finch, having, while proceeding to her station, got fast aground; and then become engaged with the American battery on Crab island, no more took part in the action with

Commodore Macdonough's squadron, than the American sloops Montgomery and President, of 10 guns each, described by an American paper, the "*Watchman,*" as having also formed part of his force on that lake. As to the British gun-boats, only three out of the ten, engaged at all; and they, being unsupported, were soon compelled to retreat. Although the American batteries on shore, it is believed, did not fire, except at the Finch, (and yet, whence came the hot shot that struck the Saratoga?) they could completely cover the American gun-boats, in case any attempt had been made to carry them by boarding; and Mr. Corney's celebrated painting, according to the "Key" of it, represents, besides "Commodore Downie's big ship Confiance,"—"American militia ready to assist," in case any of the British vessels had got on shore. In this very painting, is also seen, the American sloops Montgomery, and President, at anchor, close to the scene of action. Under all these circumstances, neither the cutter Finch, nor more than half the united force of the British gun-boats will be considered as having had any share in the action. At the same time, no notice will be taken of the American sloops Montgomery and President, the batteries on shore, or the "militia ready to assist."

Comparative force of the two squadrons.

		British.		American.	
Broadside-metal in pounds	l. guns,	507		588	
	carr.	258		606	
		—	765	—	1194
Complement, of men and boys,			537		950
Size in tons,			1426		2540

Here, then, are the "*fearful odds,*" to which, say the Americans,—"our squadron was opposed."—Had not the British the better reason to exclaim against "fearful odds"?—and this, without computing the unfitted state of the Confiance, or the motley crews with which she and the other British vessels were manned?

Having seen a whole year's adulation bestowed upon one "illustrious hero," for making free with Nelson's language, Commodore Macdonough resolved to begin his official letter in the same strain. He knew that nothing would stamp a falsehood with currency, equal to a pious expression.—He, too, must proclaim his fleet-victory "a signal" one. Then, the Confiance, he calls a "frigate," and the two cutters, "sloops of war"; his falsehoods equalling, in number, the lines of his letter!

"After the battle ceased," says an American paper, "some citizens went on board, to compliment the commodore, who very seriously replied, that no praise was due to him, but to the Almighty, who had decided the contest, contrary to his expectation, and—*all human probability.*" What consummate hypocrisy!

The sentence of the court-martial upon Captain Pring and his officers, while it honorably acquits them, points, clearly, to the source whence the disaster originated. (App. Nos. 94. and 95.) Charges were preferred by Sir James Lucas Yeo against his late excellency, Sir George Prevost; but the latter departed this life previous to the day of trial. The following is a list of the charges:

"1.—For having, on or about the 11th of September, 1814, by holding out the expectation of a co-operation of the army under his command, induced Captain Downie, late of his majesty's ship Confiance, to attack the American squadron on Lake Champlain, when it was highly imprudent to make such attack without the co-operation of the land forces, and for not having afforded that co-operation."

"2.—For not having stormed the American work on shore, at nearly the same time that the said naval action commenced, as he had given Captain Downie reason to expect."

"3.—For having disregarded the signal for co-operation, which had been previously agreed upon."

"4.—For not having attacked the enemy on shore, either during the said naval action, or after it was ended; whereby his majesty's naval squadron; under the command of Captain Downie, might have been saved."

CHAPTER XVIII.

President, accompanied by a store-ship, leaves New York for the bay of Bengal—Strikes on a mudbank—Gets of, and pursues her course—Falls in with a British squadron—Is engaged by the Endymion, singly—Cuts away the latter's sails, and tries to escape—Endymion bends fresh sails, and resumes the chase—Pomone and Tenedos come up with the President—Pomone fires—President shews a light, and surrenders without returning the fire—Tenedos takes possession—American accounts of the affair—Endymion's damages—Fore-sail stripped from the yard by a chain-shot—Endymion's loss—President's damages and loss—No one hurt by the Pomone's fire—Endymion's force in guns and men—President's also—Commodore Decatur and the editor of the Bermuda Gazette—Dimensions of the two vessels—Statement of comparative force—Remarks thereon.

ON the afternoon of the 14th of January, 1815, the U. S. frigate President, Commodore Decatur, left New York upon a cruize in the bay of Bengal; the Peacock and Hornet to join her at the island of Tristran d'Acunha. The President was accompanied by the armed brig Macedonian, laden with naval stores and supplies. On going out, the President struck on a mud-bank; and, whatever the commodore, or the court of inquiry, (App. Nos. 103 and 105,) may have found it convenient to say, got off without any material damage. The two vessels pursued their course; and, about an hour before day-light on the morning of the 15th, were discovered by the British squadron that was cruizing off New York.

Fortunately, an extract from the Endymion's log-book has appeared in print. This document contains a circumstantial account of the day's proceedings; and bears upon the face of it the clearest evidence of authenticity.

"At day-light in the morning," says the extract, "all sail set in chase of a strange ship and brig in the east; wind N.W. and by N. Majestic, Tenedos, and Pomone, in company. Passed a-head of our squadron fast. At 1 P.M. all hands at quarters, gaining fast on the chase, and leaving the squadron. At 1. 18. observed the chase to throw over-board spars, casks, &c.

"At 2. the chase commenced firing from her stern-guns. At 2. 30. returned the enemy's fire from our bow-guns. At 2. 39. a shot from the enemy came through the head of the larboard fore-lower-studding-sail, foot of the main-sail, through the stern of the barge on the booms, and going through the quarter-deck, lodged on the main, without doing any other damage. The chase keeping up a quick fire from her stern-guns, returned it as our bow-guns could be brought to bear.

"At 4.10. shot away the enemy's jib-halyards. At 4.20. shot away the enemy's fore-top-gallant-sheet the enemy luffing occasionally, to bring his stern-guns to bear. Gaining fast on the chase; observed that our shot did considerable execution, the enemy's shot passing over us. At 5.10. gained the enemy's starboard-quarter, and preserved the position; evidently galling him much.

"At 5. 30. the enemy brailed up his spanker and bore away, shewing a disposition to cross our bow and rake us. Put the helm hard a-weather, to meet this manoeuvre; and brought the enemy to close action in a parallel line of sailing. At 6. 4. the enemy commenced firing musketry from his tops; returned it with the marine-party. Hauled up occasionally, to close the enemy, without losing the bearing of our broadside; enemy now distant, half musket-shot. Our sails and rigging much cut; the enemy's fire slackening considerably.

"At 6. 40. the enemy hauled up, apparently to avoid our fire. Succeeded in giving him two raking broadsides, and then hauled up also; again placing ourselves on his starboard-quarter. At 7.15. the enemy shot away our boat from the larboard-quarter, and lower, and main-top-gallant, studding-sails.

"At 7.18. the enemy not returning our fire. At 7. 25. the enemy kept more away, and re-commenced firing. At 7.30 the enemy shot away the larboard main-top-mast-studding-sail, and main-brace. At 7.32. the enemy hauled suddenly to the wind. Trimmed sails, and again obtained the advantage of giving him a raking fire; which he returned with one shot from his stern-gun. The enemy much shattered. At 7. 40. the enemy kept more away, firing at intervals.

"At 7. 58. the enemy ceased firing. Observed him to shew a light; called all hands to bend new sails; &c. Conceiving that the enemy had struck, ceased firing. At 8. 10. observed two of our squadron coming up. At 8. 52. new courses, main-top-sail, jib, fore-top-mast-staysail, and spanker, bent, and sails trimmed, ranging up with the chase.

"At 9. 5. observed one of our squadron run up on the larboard-beam of the enemy, and fire into her; which was not returned, but the light hoisted higher in the rigging. The ship of our squadron ceased firing, and shot a-head. At 9. 45. hailed by the Tenedos;

acquainted her of our not having a boat that could be hoisted out. Tenedos took possession of the chase."

The motionless state of the Endymion, while bending six new sails, reeving fresh rigging, &c. enabled the Pomone and Tenedos to pass a-head of her: the latter within hail. When these ships approached the President, she was standing to the eastward under a press of sail. The Pomone fired a broadside; which hurt no one, and was not returned. The President shortened sail, and luffed close up, shewing a light in her mizen-rigging; at the same time, hailing to say, she had surrendered. The Pomone, not hearing this, and mistaking the object of the light, fired a second broadside; which, similar to the first, neither hurt any one, nor was returned. The President, after again hailing, that she had surrendered, hauled down the light; and the Pomone did not fire again. The Tenedos had a fine raking position a-stern of the President; but Captain Parker, believing she had struck to the Endymion, did not fire a shot: he merely sent a boat to take possession; and his officer was the first on board.

This was at 11 o'clock at night. At three-quarters past 12, the Endymion, nearly as fresh as when she began the combat, got up to the President; but the Majestic, although the ships were laying-to for her, did not join until 3 in the morning.

The first American account of the President's loss, published, was an extract of a letter from Commodore Decatur to his wife. After detailing his action with the Endymion, he says:— "In three hours the Pomone and Tenedos were alongside, and the Majestic and Endymion *close to us*. All that was now left for me to do was, to receive the fire of the nearest *ships,* and surrender; for it was in vain to contend with the whole squadron."— Commodore Decatur had, no doubt, the same reason for using the word "ships" instead of "ship," that Commodore Perry had, for substituting "their" for "her;" when, in his letter, he was describing the effect of the Detroit's fire, upon the Lawrence. (See p. 145.)

Another published letter is from "an officer, whose situation on board the President, gave him an opportunity of witnessing every event that occurred during the action." He, alone, has had the hardihood to say,—"when, after receiving and *returning* a broadside, our flag was struck." Another officer says, "after receiving *four* or *five* broadsides from the Pomone, &c."

At last, comes Commodore Decatur's official letter, which is to clear up all disputed points. (App. No. 103.)—"We (the President and Endymion) continued engaged," says the commodore, "steering south, two hours and a half, when we completely succeeded in dismantling her. Previously to her dropping entirely out of the action, there were intervals of minutes, when the ships were broadside, in which she did not fire a gun."—We have here an admission; that the President and Endymion engaged for "two hours and a half."—"Dismantling" a ship, is far too extensive a term, for destroying a few sails; and which were all renewed in less than an hour. When finding fault with the Endymion's slow firing, had the commodore seen the reports of the President's carpenter and surgeon?—Where was his boasted "head of intelligence," at the moment he penned this paragraph?

He next tells us, that he was compelled to "abandon" the Endymion. And Captain *Lejoille* told us, that he was prevented, at the battle of the Nile, from taking possession of the Bellerophon. (App. No. 3.) Which is the most impudent assertion?—The commodore then says:—"In resuming our former course for the purpose of avoiding the squadron, we were compelled to present our stern to our antagonist; but such was his state, though we were thus exposed, and within range of his guns, for half an hour, that he did not avail himself of this favorable opportunity of raking us."

Here is a charge against the British ship! Although the Endymion, by her loss of sails, was fixed to one spot for nearly an hour; during which time the President, with every stitch of canvass set, and a fine breeze, had "resumed her course," and was running away, still the latter was within range of the former's guns for "half an hour." Preposterous as this assertion is, it forms one of the "proofs," upon which the American court of inquiry has decreed, that "the Endymion was subdued." (App. No. 105.) The reason why the Endymion did not fire at the President, at the moment the latter's stern was first presented to her, appears in the log-extract, thus:—"At 7. 58. the enemy ceased firing. Observed him to shew a light; called all hands to bend new sails, &c. Conceiving that the enemy *had struck, ceased firing."*

We shall see presently, that the Cyane shewed a light, as a signal of surrender to the Constitution. The same has been done by other British ships. (Nav. Chron. vol. xxv. p. 163.)—According to the testimony of Mr. Bowie, the President's late school-master, taken upon oath before the surrogate at Bermuda, Commodore Decatur himself hoisted a light, as a *signal of surrender*. "When the two ships were coming up," says Mr. Bowie, "a light was hoisted in the mizen-rigging of the President, as this deponent conceived, at the time, as an ensign or flag; but, as he afterwards had reason to believe,: as a sign that they had surrendered; for this deponent observed to the commodore, that, as long as that light was hoisted, the ships would fire; upon which Commodore Decatur ordered it to be taken down."—The account of the President's capture, published by the Pomone's "gun-room officers," states: "A few minutes previous to our closing her, she hoisted a light a-baft; which, in night-actions, substitutes the ensign." It can only be said, then, that, by the Pomone's officers and the President's school-master, a light was considered as the substitute of an ensign, and by Captain Hope and Commodore Decatur, as a signal of submission. That a light *was* shewn to the Endymion, has not been denied. For, although Commodore Decatur, full seven weeks after the action, published a supplementary letter, (App. No. 104,) wherein he refers to some immaterial statements contained in the "Bermuda Gazette," he passes over, in silence, the editor's assertion, that "at 8 o'clock the President ceased firing, and *shewed a light.*"

The strongest evidence of the President's not having struck to the Endymion, appears in Mr. Bowie's deposition:—"The President, he did not consider as having surrendered exclusively to the Endymion, for from her they might have escaped; and with her, had she been alone, they should have engaged again."

Admitting, therefore, that the Endymion dropped a-stern, on account of her principal sails being cut away; and that the President, having her sails entire, took that opportunity to quit her opponent; to what ship or ships, did the President surrender? The Pomone's gun-room officers say thus: "At 11, being within gun-shot of the President, who was still steering to the eastward under a press of sail, with royal, top-gallant, top-mast, and lower studding-sails set; finding how much we sail her, our studding-sails were taken in; and, immediately afterwards, we luffed-to port, and fired our starboard-broadside. The enemy, then, also luffed to-port, bringing his larboard-broadside to bear, which was momentarily expected, as a few minutes previous to our closing her, she hoisted a light a-baft; which, in night actions, substitutes the ensign. Our second broadside was fired, and the President still luffing up as if intent to lay us on board, we hauled close to-port, bracing the yards up, and setting the main-sail. The broadside was again ready to fire into his bows, raking, when she hauled down the light; and we hailed, demanding, if she had surrendered. The reply was in the affirmative; and the firing instantly ceased."

This is confirmed by the President's school-master. He says:—"When the Endymion dropped a-stern, we were confident of escaping. Shortly after, discovered two ships coming up, Pomone and Tenedos; when Commodore Decatur ordered all hands below to take care of their bags. One of the ships commenced firing; and Commodore Decatur called out, '*We have surrendered;*' and gave this deponent the trumpet to hail, and say, they had surrendered. The Pomone's fire did damage to the rigging; but *neither killed nor wounded any person.* The President did not return the Pomone's fire; but hoisted a flag in the mizen-rigging, as a sign of submission."

The Pomone's account states, that "the Tenedos, who was not more than three miles off, soon afterwards came up, and assisted the Pomone in securing the prize, and removing the prisoners." But the American officer, who transmitted the Pomone's hand-bill to the United States, says: "When the President struck, the Tenedos was on our stern, and the Pomone on our bow both within musket-shot. *The ship was first boarded by the boats of the*

Tenedos."—"With these exceptions,"—the American officer adds,—"the Pomone's account is essentially correct."

Commodore Decatur, in his deposition, says: "I fought the Endymion 2½ hours. After which she dropped a-stern, and I surrendered only to the Tenedos and Pomone." And, in another part of the same deposition, he says: "Resistance was made against the Endymion for 2½ hours, after which the Endymion dropped out of the fight. The next ships coming up, 24 hours after the action with the Endymion, were the Pomone and Tenedos; and to those two ships the President was surrendered. The Pomone had commenced her fire within musket-shot. The Tenedos did not fire at the time of such surrender. The Majestic was in sight also; the Endymion was then out of sight. No other ships besides those named, were then seen from the President."

Lieutenant John Gallagher, of the President, swears, that "the President surrendered to Majestic, Pomone, Tenedos, and Endymion. It was only because Commodore Decatur supposed the Pomone to be the Majestic, that he surrendered, when he did."—And Lieutenant Levi Twiggs, in his deposition, says: "We fought the Endymion from 3½ to 4½ hours; and surrendered to Pomone, supposing her Majestic."

Commodore Decatur, in the letter to his wife, places the Majestic and Endymion, at the moment of his surrender, *close* to him. In his official letter, he describes the former as within, and the latter as out of, gun-shot. In his deposition before the surrogate, he removes the Endymion "out of sight;" and speaks of the Majestic, as merely "in sight." And, while he here swears, that "no other ships" than the Pomone, Tenedos, and Majestic, "were then seen from the President," he, in his official letter, includes the "Despatch brig," as part of the "squadron" to which he surrendered: Here is vaccillation!

The Majestic's distance from the President, when the latter surrendered, may be conceived, from the fact (asserted in the Pomone's "handbill account," and confirmed by the American officer who enclosed it to his friend) of her not joining the squadron till "three in the morning;" and this, although the other ships were waiting for her to come up. Commodore Decatur himself truly presaged a "dark night:" of which the Endymion's being "out of sight" was the natural consequence. According to the before-mentioned confirmed account, that ship's absence from the squadron was not delayed beyond "three-quarters past 12;" although the commodore has extended it to "three hours after the surrender of the President"; which would be 2 in the morning. And the sentence of the court of inquiry, even assumes as a fact, "that the Endymion did not join the squadron, till *many* hours after the President had been *surrounded* by the *four* other ships, and had surrendered to *them*."

After all that has been said about the President's capture, it is confirmed, that the only two ships, between which any firing was exchanged, were the Endymion and President. Every captured merchant-ship, over whom a shot is fired to bring her to,—even the U. S. ship Frolic, captured by the Orpheus,—has a right to call her surrender—"a conflict,"—"contest"—"engagement,"—if Commodore Decatur, and his court, are correct in calling so,—the two harmless, unreturned broadsides fired at him by the Pomone. It is indifferent, whether or not the President struck, in the first instance, to the Endymion. It is not denied, that the two ships, uninterrupted by any others, fought, "broadside to broadside," for two hours and a half; and the plain tale of Mr. Bowie, the President's school-master, proves clearly, that, when the American ship hauled up from the Endymion, at 8 o'clock, her men—to use a familiar phrase—had *had enough;* and that the commodore was determined to surrender, without further resistance, to the first ship of the squadron that should come within gun-shot.

In the commodore's waiting to deliver his sword to "the senior officer of the squadron," we recognize an old trick, frequently practised, when a second British cruizer has come up, after the enemy had received as hearty a drubbing as the President got from the Endymion. The commodore's subsequent conduct, in trying to rob Captain Hope of the merit of his gallant performance, proves, that his sword's being "with politeness returned," only adds another to the many instances of misapplication of British magnanimity.

Is not the commodore sufficiently well acquainted with the British prize-act, to know, that every one of his majesty's ships, in sight at the commencement of the chase, or the final surrender, of a prize, is, whether she co-operates or not, entitled to share? For that reason, and not to prove that the President fought more than one ship, the word "squadron" was inserted in that insignificant "document," the commodore's "parole."

The Endymion's damages in the action were confined to the destruction of the only two boats she had on board, and considerable injury to her spars; sails, and rigging. An American chain-shot cut away twelve or fourteen cloths of her fore-sail; stripping it almost from the yard. The commodore's first letter, although written on board the Endymion, mentions nothing of that ship's damages from his fire, beyond his having "dismantled" her. His second, or supplementary letter, states only that, after the action, "she bent new sails, rove new rigging, and fished her spars." Yet the sentence of the court of inquiry tells us of the "shattered condition" of the Endymion.—Surely, "tattered" must have been the word used, but miscopied by the printer.

The Endymion lost 11 seamen and marines killed, and 14 seamen and marines wounded; total 25. No officer was hurt. How easy it was for Commodore Decatur, when desirous to mention the Endymion's loss, to say: "Her officers assert, that she lost eleven killed, and fourteen wounded";—and then, if he discredited the statement,—"but I think her loss was greater." Instead of which, he set his countrymen to calculating, how many dead men could be thrown overboard in the course of "36 hours;" how many cubic feet there were in the space "between the cabin-bulk-head and the main-mast" of a large frigate; and how many "badly wounded" could be there stowed. Captain Hope, much to his honor, chose to give his late gallant shipmates, Christian burial; and the season of the year justified him in deferring the ceremony, till the crew were at leisure.

The damages which the President sustained in her hull, are fully set forth in No. 107. in the Appendix. This is what the court of inquiry calls "little injury." A ship, riddled as the President was, both above and below water, might well have had "six feet water in the hold." Five or six of her guns were completely disabled; and, although her spars were all standing, her lower-masts were badly crippled.—These the President lost, on the 17th, in a violent gale of wind, from the eastward. Several of her guns were then thrown overboard; and, considering the battered state of her hull, it was a mercy she did not founder. The Endymion suffered by the same, gale, losing her fore and main-masts, and bowsprit; the two former, owing chiefly to the rigging, where it had been knotted after the action, giving way. She also threw several of her guns overboard.

The President's loss in the action, by the acknowledgement of her officers when at Bermuda, consisted of 3 lieutenants, and 32 seamen and marines, killed; her commander, (very slightly,) master, 2 midshipmen, and 66 seamen and marines, wounded; total 105.—Commodore Decatur, writing his official letter on board the Endymion, was unable, as he states, (App. No. 103,) to give a correct return of his loss.

In his first letter, there is not a word of a single man having been hurt by the Pomone's fire. But, when the commodore returns to New York, and meets with rather a cooler reception than he experienced on his arrival there, about two years previous, with the Macedonian, British frigate, he finds it necessary, to give the thing, if possible, a tinge of the brilliant. He recollects that Mr. Henry Robinson, the President's chaplain, and a "volunteer" on her quarter-deck, deposed before the surrogate at Bermuda, that "the Pomone's fire, which continued about *fifteen* minutes, did kill *some* men." The commodore therefore commences his supplementary letter with,—"In my official letter of the 18th of January, I omitted to state, that a *considerable number* of my killed and wounded was from the fire of the Pomone."

Let us endeavour to investigate this after-thought of the commodore's. That a "chaplain" should swear, or even speak, falsely, is difficult of belief; but that the chaplain of an American ship of war is not quite so sacred a character as he ought to be, was made evident in the case of the chaplain of the Essex frigate.

(Quarterly Review, vol. xiii. p. 358.) And was it not the President's chaplain, who wrote to his friends, that that ship *returned* the broadside fired at her just before she surrendered?—So it was stated in the American prints. On the other hand, in flat contradiction to the chaplain the schoolmaster swears, that the Pomone's fire "neither killed nor wounded any person, nor was returned by the President." Mr. Bowie, too, was on the quarter-deck, as well as the "volunteer." The fact of only one shot having entered the President's larboard side, (App. No. 107.) which was that opposed to the Pomone, corroborates Mr. Bowie's statement, of no man having been hurt. But, it may be asked,—where is the "correct return" of the President's loss, which was to be made out by Commodore Decatur upon his arrival in port?—And why is the term "considerable" preferred, to the actual number of men, if any, killed and wounded by the Pomone?—The interval between 8 and 11 o'clock, was too long for any difficulty or confusion to arise, in separating the loss that had been sustained by the Endymion's, from that said to have been sustained by the Pomone's fire; and that Commodore Decatur, before he wrote his official letter, had received his surgeon's return, whether correct or not, is evident, from his noticing the return, in that very letter. Under all these circumstances, the President's severe loss, in killed and wounded, will be considered as having been wholly effected by the Endymion's fire.

The Endymion mounted twenty six long 24 pounders upon the main-deck; twenty two carronades, 32-pounders, one 12-pound boat-carronade, and a long brass 18-pounder, upon the quarter-deck and forecastle; total, 50 guns. The boat-carronade was mounted upon an elevating carriage; and could therefore be fought upon the broadside. Not so the long 18. That was run out at either of the bow-ports, as a chase-gun; for which purpose only, it could be used, the ship having no vacant broadside-port.

On the 21st of September, a few days before she left Halifax N. S. the Endymion victualled 239 of ship's company, (officers included,) 60 marines, and 27 boys. She had 6 men absent in a prize, and one man, sick at the hospital; making, when they joined a complement of 333; about 17 short of her establishment. The number killed in action with the Prince of Neufchatel American-privateer, in October, and the wounded afterwards sent on board the Saturn, amounted to 60; and those lent by the Saturn, in return, (being one lieutenant, 4 midshipmen; 3 able seamen, 25 ordinary seamen and landmen, and 5 marines,) to 58. Consequently, to make the Endymion's complement what her officers state it to have been, when she commenced action with the President; Captain Hope must have pressed 15 men. She then would have 319 men, and 27 boys; total 346.

Commodore Decatur was on board the Endymion upwards of a fortnight; and, in his intercourse with her officers, must have heard of the affair with the privateer, and the severe loss it occasioned, as well as of the Endymion's wounded having been sent away in the Saturn, and of that ship having sent a draught of men in lieu of them. But, determined to act consistently, he conceals all his information, except that respecting the Saturn's men; and then, in his supplementary letter, tells the public, that "the Endymion had on board, in *addition to* her own crew, one lieutenant, one master's mate, and 50 men, belonging to the Saturn."

The President mounted thirty long 24-pounders upon the main-deck, fourteen carronades, 42-pounders, one long 24-pounder, as a shifting gun, and a brass 8-inch howitzer, fitted on a traversing carriage, upon the quarter-deck; and six carronades, 42-pounders, and one long 24-pounder, shifting gun, upon the forecastle; two brass 4-pounders in her fore, the same in her main, and one in her mizen, top, all on pivots: making a total of 58 guns; of which 33 were fought upon the broadside.

Lieutenant Gallagher of the President, swore that she mounted "52 guns"; and Commodore Decatur, the same, "besides a boat-gun."—A pretty "boat-gun" truly!—The same, no doubt, the commodore would have called the great Turkish bomb in St. James's Park, had it been on board the President.—Howitzers and mortars are not described by the weight of the shot they can throw, but by their diameters in inches. (See p. 3.) The bore of a 68-pound carronade is 8 inches in diameter, so was the bore of the President's howitzer. And, if an iron round shot, weighing 68 pounds, were deemed more destructive than a shell, filled with combustibles, weighing 49 pounds, the former would be discharged from an 8-inch howitzer. That it is the diameter, rather than the weight of a shot, that ought to guide us in appreciating its effects, has already been shewn. (See pp. 6-7.) The President's 8-inch howitzer, therefore, will be estimated as a 68-pounder. The American officers appear to exclude from the armament of their own ship, not only the "boat-gun," but the guns stationed in the tops. Why so?—Are cannon less destructive, pointed directly upon the enemy's deck from that eminence, than if fought through ports in the usual way? In every case, British as well as American, where a ship's top-guns exceed, in caliber, a *swivel*, or half-pounder, they will he estimated as part of her broadside-force.

The prisoners received from the President by the agent at Bermuda, amounted to 434; including 3 or 4 boys. Some of the badly wounded had died in the passage, and others were not fit to be removed. It was reported, that a midshipman had poisoned himself; and that 12 seamen had jumped overboard; in both cases, on account of their being British subjects, probably deserters. Without computing them at all; but, taking the 35 killed in action, 8 for such as had died since, or were not removable, and the 434 prisoners received, we have 477 for the President's complement. This corresponds exactly with the only paper found on board the President, her "Watch-bill;" which contains the names of 477 persons, as doing the duty of the ship. The "New York Evening Post," of January 26, 1815, speaking of the President's loss, says: "She had a picked crew of 500 men." It is seldom that American editors *over*-rate the crews of their ships.

Commodore Decatur and Lieutenant Gallagher both deposed, that the President "had 450 men"; and the former affected to be surprised at the number of prisoners in the hands of Mr. Miller, the agent. Feeling how much it needed an explanation, the commodore made some excuse about persons having come on board, without his knowledge, as *passengers;* although he had just done swearing, that "there were no passenger's on board the President."—As to Lieutenant Gallagher, an error of 30 or 40 units does not appear to trouble him. He, in the same deposition, swore the President was 1400 tons; although Commodore Decatur had sworn to her being 1440; and she really was 1444, American.

The President's men were very tall and stout; and, in the opinion of several British officers whose ships were lying in Bermuda, there were among them many British seamen. Mistakes, however, may happen; and it is better for the guilty to escape, than the innocent to suffer. Besides, it was then known at Bermuda that peace had been signed; which prevented that scrutiny among the President's men, that otherwise would have taken place. Commodore Decatur, in his deposition, certainly swore, that there were "no British subjects" on board the President, when captured. No more there would have been, had her whole crew consisted of British deserters, provided each man could have produced a "protection." He is then ycleped "citizen of the United States of America"; and no American will refuse to swear, that such a man, although notoriously born in Great Britain, is not a British subject. As applied to the Americans, the registrar, or person putting the standing interrogatory, should have substituted "natives of the United Kingdom" for "British subjects"; and then, if at all scrupulous about an oath, the American officer would seldom answer by an unqualified negative.

Commodore Decatur, in his supplementary letter, after dwelling upon the expression in his "parole," as a proof that he "was captured by the squadron," alludes to a statement in the Bermuda Gazette,—"The fact" was, indeed, "stated differently" in that paper; which gave it similar account, in substance, to that contained in the extract from the Endymion's log; nor was the editor, either "compelled," or even asked, "to retract" what he had stated. But here was the galling "fact." The Bermuda Gazette, of the 1st of February, had asserted that "68 men were discovered stowed away" on board the President, Commodore Decatur gave his honor it was not so; and Mr. Ward was induced to apologize.

The Bermuda Gazette of the 16th of March, however, declared that the original statement was correct; and that the act had been authorised by Commodore Decatur himself. Upon this, the governor of the island desired the editor to retract what he had said in confirmation of his first assertion. But, relying more upon the word of a British lieutenant*, than the honor of an American commodore, Mr. Ward flatly refused; and was, in consequence, dismissed from his office of king's printer.—Upon receiving the American paper, containing Commodore Decatur's supplementary letter, the editor of the Gazette made the following observations:

"As to his reference to ourselves, we should treat it with the contempt it deserves, did he not, by uttering as base a falsehood as ever was imposed upon the world, endeavour to induce a belief, that our original statement of the capture of the President was incorrect.—It was in conseqence of some observations we had made, occasioned by the *concealment of sixty eight men*, and which contained some severe reflections upon the officers of the President, that we were requested to smooth it over; nor can Commodore Decatur be so unpardonably ignorant, as to suppose, that a British editor could be *compelled* to retract a statement founded on truth.—We are convinced it was never expected, that what was intended as a mere palliative for the irritated feelings of men who were prisoners, would have been produced as an argument in an official letter; and, if a misapplied delicacy of sentiment, impelled Captain Hope to urge the step we took, Commodore Decatur should have jusly appreciated the noble principle upon which he acted, and should have considered our compliance, as a well-meant endeavour to render his situation as comfortable as we could. But it appears to have been his misfortune, that he could not feel the delicate attentions which were paid him.—As for ourselves, we never possessed, and we now disclaim, the least degree of private animosity against Commodore Decatur, or his officers. In the discharge of our public duty, we obtained the best information relative to their capture; and if, in telling a few plain truths, we hurt their feelings, "*why let the stricken deer go weep.*"

The Endymion was built in 1797; and has always been a remarkably fine sailer. She is distinguished from all other frigates of her class, (except one or two 64-razees,) by having, upon the main-deck, 26 gun-ports only. She measures as follows:

	Ft.	In.
Length of lower-deck, from rabbit to rabbit,	159	3⅝
Breadth, extreme,	42	7¾

The President was built at New-York in 1797–8; and cost, says Mr. Clarke, "220,910 dollars, 8 cents," or 61,363*l.* 18s. sterling. She *is* finished in a very superior style, with diagonal knees, &c.

* Now Capt. the Hon. G. I. Perceval.

has stouter. scantling than a British 74-gun ship; (see p. 9;) and, if we except the American Guerriere and Java, may be considered, in spite of the "hogged and twisted appearance," given her by the sentence of the court of inquiry, as one of the finest frigates in the world. Her full dimensions have already appeared. (See, pp. 62-64.)

Comparative force of the two ships.

		Endymion.		President.	
Broadside-metal in pounds,	l. guns,	312		408	
	carr.	364		508	
			676		916
Complement,	men,	319		472	
	boys,	27		5	
			346		477
Size in tons,			1277		1533

The condition of the two ships after the action, has already exposed Commodore Decatur's assertion of "having beaten" the Endymion. A statement of the relative force of the two ships, now shews, whether or not the force of the Endymion was "equal" to that of the President. Nor has the commodore the excuse of ignorance to offer, because he was on board the Endymion for several days. His character for veracity might be pronounced upon this alone, had he left us no other proofs of his effrontery.

Seeing how superior the President was to the Endymion, in guns, men, and size; knowing, also, that the former was commanded by an experienced officer; manned with a choice, well-trained crew; and lavishly supplied with every requisite appointment, it is not to be supposed, that the Endymion's loss would have been so trifling, had she and the President met singly. In that case, the latter would have had no other object to divert her attention, or confine her manœuvres; nor would the spirits of her men have been damped by the conviction, that, if they did not escape, they must be captured.—That the Endymion, however, would, even then, have ultimately conquered; the dreadful precision of her fire, her quickness in working, and evident superiority in sailing, added to the established bravery of her officers and crew, are strong grounds of belief.

It is worthy of remark, that Commodore Decatur's letter, announcing the President's capture, was written on board the very ship, which he once expressed himself so anxious to meet, in the frigate United States; and it bears date precisely a year and a day after his "very rash" letter of challenge. (See pp. 162-163.) To complete this, as it may be termed, retributive act, the identical ships' companies which were parties to that challenge, met, and fought, upon the present occasion. No wonder, then, that the action of the Endymion and President, should have caused among the sticklers for "superior prowess" in the United

States, emotions so powerful; especially, after it became known, beyond disputes, that the British, was inferior in force to the American vessel; by nearly a fourth.

The action between the Endymion and President has thrown some light upon the actions between the sister-ships of the latter, and our 38, or present 46 gun frigates. The superiority of 24, over 18 pounders is made evident. But the Endymion, besides that advantage over the Guerriere, Macedonian, and Java, possessed an important one in the precision of her fire. Captain Hope, aware of the excellence of the Broke-system, had long trained his men to the use of both great guns and small-arms; and many had been the anxious look-out on board the Endymion, for one of the American 44-gun frigates.

It would be an injustice to Captain Hope, not to notice the peculiar modesty of his official letter. He speaks of the cool and determined bravery of his officers and ship's company on the "fortunate occasion"; says, truly, that, "where every individual has so conspicuously done his duty, it would be injustice to particularize;" and, in proof of his men's exertions and abilities, appeals to "the loss and damage sustained by the enemy's frigate." Captain Hayes, in his letter, does ample justice to the Endymion; Corroborates every statement in her log-extract; and emphatically adds: "When the effect produced by her well directed fire upon the President is witnessed, it cannot be doubted, but that Captain Hope would have succeeded either in capturing or sinking her, had none of the squadron been in sight."

Yet, that repository of American "honorables,"— "heroes,"— "heroics,"—"heroisms,"—"lustres,"—"stars," and "glories,"— the "result of the court of inquiry on the capture of the frigate President," commences with alleging, that "there has been a diversity of opinions prevailing among the British commanders concerned in her capture"! (App. Nos. 105. and 106.)—We cannot dismiss this tragi-comico-farcical performance, without almost laughing at the gravity with which it utters the exordium upon Commodore Decatur and his "heroic officers and crew," for their design of "boarding the Endymion:" the execution of which, it says, was frustrated, in the first instance, by her "shunning the approach" of the President; and afterwards, by her "disabled state."—This is Captain *Lejoille* all over!—Supposing, for a moment, that Commodore Decatur had intended to board, and that the President's men were willing to make the attempt;—was success so certain?—He must, indeed, judge meanly of a well-manned and *well-disciplined* British ship of war, who would not pronounce such an attempt, as the likeliest of any to have gained for the Endymion's tars, those laurels, of which the commodore, and his friends, have laboured so hard to deprive them.

Before quitting the subject of this interesting action, it may be fair to ask,—Has Commodore Decatur evinced "the most determined resolution and heroic courage"? Has he made a "brave defence of the ship and the flag of the United States"?— In short, was he justified, (admitting that he had not struck to the Endymion,) in surrendering to the Pomone and Tenedos, without firing a shot?

Prudence will say that, having lost "one-fifth of his crew, his ship being crippled," and his escape very problematical, the commodore was right, by surrendering as he did, to stop the further effusion of blood. Boldness, on the other hand, will say that, as the commodore had men enough left, to work and fight his ship, a well-directed broadside might have crippled the Pomone; then, with her "royal, top-gallant, top-mast, and lower studding-sails set," and the advantage of a very dark night, the President might have led off the Tenedos; and, with a force so superior to her's, would soon have "thrown her out of the combat;" and, most probably, effected her escape. But that, did her first fire fail in crippling the Pomone, the President should have engaged the two frigates, till the fall of her masts, and the loss of something more than a "fifth" of her crew, had made her defence as gallant, as her surrender would *then* have been honorable,

CHAPTER XIX.

Levant and Cyane sail from Gibraltar—Fall in with the Constitution—Determine to engage her—No British official account of the action—Details of the action—Levant bears up to repair damages—Cyane surrenders—Levant, singly, recommences the action—Tries to escape—Surrenders—Gross misstatement in the American official account—Levant and Cyane's damages and loss—Constitution's also—Force of the British ships in guns and men—Shameful treatment of the British prisoners—Constitution's force in guns—Extraordinary piece consisting of seven musket-barrels—Dismantling shot—Furnace for heating shot—Constitution's force in men—Dimensions of the ships—Remarks on their relative tonnage—Statement of comparative force—Remarks thereon—Constitution and her prizes arrive at St. Jago—Discovered and chased out by the Leander, Newcastle, and Acasta—Escape of the Cyane—Recapture of the Levant—Escape of the Constitution—Meeting between the Constitution and Pique—American falsehood detected—Exemplary behaviour of the Pique's ship's company.

On the 20th of February, 1815, H. M. ships Levant and Cyane were proceeding in company, a few days out from Gibraltar, bound to the Western islands. About 1 o'clock in the afternoon, a strange sail was seen by the Cyane, upon her weather-bow; her consort, the Levant, Captain Douglas, then hull-down to-leeward. The Cyane stood on until about 4 o'clock; when, having ascertained the character of the stranger, Captain Falcon bore up to speak the commodore. At about a quarter past 5, the two ships passed within hail of each other. Captain Douglas, the senior officer, resolved to engage the enemy's frigate; in the hopes, by disabling her, to prevent her intercepting two valuable convoys, that sailed from Gibraltar about the same time as the Levant and Cyane. Both commanders, at this time, fully believed that she was the American frigate Constitution; having received intelligence, before leaving port, of her being in their intended track.

The two ships now tried for the weather-gage; but, finding they could not obtain it, they bore up, in hopes to prolong the engagement until night; when, by manœuvring in the dark, they might effect their object. The superior sailing of the Constitution, however, defeated that plan also; and, at 45 minutes past 5, the Levant and Cyane hauled to the wind on the starboard-tack. No British official account of this action has been published; therefore the details are taken, partly from the American accounts, and partly from the information of the British officers engaged.

The Constitution had previously fired her bow-chasers at the Cyane, without effect, her shot falling short; and now, having the two British ships "under the command" of her main-deck battery, (they being at a distance from her of full three-quarters of a mile,) she commenced firing her broadsides. Both ships returned her fire; but, having only carronades, their shot all fell short, while the Constitution's 24-pound shot, were cutting to pieces their sails and rigging. As the British became gradually disabled, the Constitution shortened her distance; and, by her superiority in sailing and working, frequently raked both her opponents.

It is stated in the American "Minutes of the action," that, when the firing commenced, the contending ships were "about 300 yards distant." According to the positive testimony of the British officers, examined at the court-martial, the distance was, as stated before, nearly three-quarters of a mile. The object in framing this assertion is evident. It is to shew, that the British had the use of their carronades from the first; and that the Constitution did *not* keep out of range, until she had crippled both ships.

At about 35 minute past 6, the Cyane was without a brace or bow-line, except the larboard fore-brace. Yet, seeing her consort exposed to a heavy raking fire, owing to the Constitution having filled across her, she gallantly stood in between them, and received the broadside. The firing continued at interevals for a few minutes longer; when the Cyane turned the hands up to refit the rigging. Before that could be accomplished, the Constitution had taken a position on her larboard-quarter, within hail. Being now totally unmanageable; with most of her standing and running rigging gone; main and mizen masts tottering, and other principal spars, wounded; several shot in the hull, nine or ten of which were between wind and water; five carronades disabled, chiefly by the *drawing of the bolts and starting of the chocks;* and the Levant, having bore up to repair damages, since 6. 40. and being now two miles to-leeward, still bearing away; the Cyane fired a lee-gun, and hoisted a light, as a signal of submission; (see p. 216;) and, soon after 7, was taken possession of by the Constitution.

At 8. 15, which was as soon as the Levant had rove new braces, the gallant little ship again hauled her wind, to ascertain the fate of her companion, as well as to renew the desperate contest.

On approaching the two ships, Captain Douglas, with a boldness bordering on rashness, ranged close alongside the Constitution, to-leeward, being unable to weather her; and the two ships, on opposite tacks, exchanged broadsides.

This, by the American account, was at half-past 8. The Constitution immediately wore under the Levant's stern, and raked her with a second broadside, At 9. 30. Captain Douglas, finding that the Cyane had undoubtedly struck her colours, put again before the wind: in doing which, the Levant received several raking broadsides, had her wheel shot away, and her lower-masts badly wounded. To fire her stern-chase guns, and steer at the same time, was impossible, owing to a sad mistake in the construction this new class of vessels! Seeing the Constitution ranging up on the larboard-quarter, the Levant, at 10 P.M. by the American, and at 10. 40, by the British account, struck her colours to this "gigantic enemy."*

One could almost cry out, shame! shame! at the Constitution firing successive broadsides into such a ship as the Levant. It is surprising, that she did not sink her. Had the Levant, on first bearing away, continued her course; she might have escaped; but that would have appeared like deserting her consort; and personal consideration in battle, was never the characteristic of a Douglas.

The reader has, no doubt, already discovered the important variation between Capt. Stewart's official letter, (App. No. 108,) and the "Minutes, of the action," (No. 109,) by some unaccountable blunder of the Americans, published along with it. According to the latter, the two ships were captured at successive periods, three hours and ten minutes apart, and the action, from first to last, continued three hours and fifty-five minutes; yet, says the former, "both of which, after a spirited action of *forty minutes*, surrendered to the ship under my command"!!— After this, a compliment to British gallantry could not be expected; yet the advance of the Levant, at half-past 8, and her ranging close up, and exchanging broadsides, with such an adversary, would have elicited admiration from the breast of a Turk!

The Levant lost 6 seamen, and marines, killed, and an officer, and 14 seamen and marines, wounded. The Cyane had 6 killed, and 13 wounded; total, 12 killed, and 29 wounded. Captain Stewart, to make the complements of the ships appear greater than they were, states 23 as the killed of the former ship, and 12, the latter. This is now become a stale trick; and scarcely deserves notice. The smallness of the British loss in this action, shews clearly, that the Americans had already began to relax in their discipline. The Constitution's fire, considering the disparity of force, falls far beneath the very worst *of* our's.

*Captain Stewart's own words, in his reply to the address of the common-council of New York.

"Old Ironsides," as, from her strength and compactness, she is very properly called in the United States, was too successful in keeping out of carronade-range, to allow many shot to reach her. Some, however, lodged in her sides; and a few others, it may be presumed, found their way through; or we should not hear of 6 men, killed and mortally wounded, and 6 others wounded, severely and slightly. That both British commanders had drilled their men at the guns, is proved by the precision of their fire, during the short period that their carronades would reach.

The Levant mounted 21 guns: eighteen carronades, 32-pounders, two long 9-pounders, and a 12-pound launch-carronade. Her established complement was 135 men and boys; but she had in the action 115 men, and 16 boys; total 131. Her marines were young raw recruits, that scarcely knew how to handle their musket; and, although considered as *men,* would all have rated as *boys* in the American service.

The Cyane was a deep-waisted or frigate-built ship and mounted 33 guns: twenty two carronades, 32-pounders, upon the main-deck, eight carronades, 18-pounders, an 18-pound launch-carronade, and two long 9-pounders, upon the quarter-deck and forecastle. Not another gun did she mount; yet Captain Stewart has given her an additional 18-pound carronade, and two long 12s in lieu of 9s; and, in the "Sketches of the War," all her "thirty four guns" are described as "32-pound carronades"!

The established complement of the Cyane was 161 men, and 24 (including 10 super-numerary) boys; total 185. But, on the morning of the action, she was deficient, in petty-officers and able seamen, 16, and had a surplus of 2 boys; making her complement, in action, 145 men, and 26 boys; total 171. Of this number, 4 men were sick, and not at quarters. In computing his prisoners, Captain Stewart has committed a mistake; which, added to that respecting the killed of the two British ships; makes their united complements appear greater than they were by 34 men.

Three of the Cyane's men deserted to the Americans; but, generally, the two crews resisted the repeated offers made to them to enlist with the enemy. It was stated by the British officers, at the court-martial, that the crews of the two ships were, for three weeks, kept constantly in the Constitution's hold, with both hands and legs in irons; and there allowed but three pints of water during the 24 hours.—This, too, in a tropical climate!—It was further proved that, after the expiration of the three weeks, upon the application of Captain Douglas, one third of the men were allowed to be on deck, four hours out of the 24; but had not the means of walking, being still in irons; that, on mustering the crews when they were landed at Maranham, five of the Levant's boys were missing; that, upon application and search for them, two were found locked up in the American captain of marine's cabin; that a black man at Maranham was employed as a crimp, and enticed one of the Levant's boys to enter the American Service.—Upon these facts, let the reader employ his own thoughts: if he possesses a British heart, he will need no prompter.

With the second change of her commander, the Constitution appeared with two carronades fewer than she mounted in the Java's action; but one of her long 24s, as a shifting gun, was made to supply the place of those carronades. Two additional long 24-pounders, and some carronades, were seen in her hold. A similar discovery on board a British ship of war, would have been made a proper use of. No such advantage shall be taken. Upon her capstan, the Constitution mounted a piece, resembling seven musket-barrels, fixed together with iron bands. It was discharged by a lock; and each barrel threw 25 balls, within a few seconds of each other; making 145 shot from the piece within two minutes. The American officers said it was intended to act against boarders. Every species of dismantling shot was, this time, seen, in great abundance, on board the American ship: a confirmation of her having employed such artillery in her former actions. But, above all, the Constitution now had on board, *a furnace for heating shot!*—The American officers said it would heat balls to a white heat in 15 minutes; but that hot shot were "not to be used in action, unless the ship was assailed by a superior force."—What an American officer would call "superior force", may be partly imagined by the numerous American descriptions of "equal force" to be found in these pages. Nay, as the Levant and Cyane were pronounced, by Captain Stewart himself, to have possessed. "superiority in weight and number of guns," (App. No. 108,) what, but the certainty of capturing them, and the loss that would be sustained by their destruction, prevented the full employment of the hot shot?

On the morning of the action, the Constitution victualled, in crew, according to the report of her officers, 469 men, and 3 boys. An officer, and 7 or 8 men, were absent in a prize, which afterwards arrived at New York: the Constitution's original complement, therefore, was 480 at least. Her men were provided with leather caps, for boarding; fitted with narrow plates of iron, crossing at the top, and bending upward from the lower edge of the cap, to prevent a blow from striking the shoulder, after having glanced on the head.

The Levant was built of fir, in 1813; the Cyane, of oak, in 1804. Upon the latter's arrival at New York, the rottenness of her timbers was visible at every shot-hole. Indeed, it was that which occasioned her breeching-bolts to draw. The Cyane formerly mounted long guns upon the main-deck. (See p. 16.) When her ports were altered for the reception of carronades, fresh bolts were fitted, without the removal of the old ones; which, subsequently, were taken out, and shifted to a sounder part of the timber; but, in the action, such was the general rottenness of the timbers, all four breeching-bolts drew!

The dimensions of the Constitution have been given already. (See pp. 55-56.) After her action with the Java, she was in a manner rebuilt; and constructed with three quarter-deck stern-chase ports; for which, her two additional long 24s; along with the aftermost shifting one, were intended: giving her a force, from her stern, of five long 24-pounders. The dimensions of the two British ships here follow:

	Levant.			Cyane.			
	Tons.	Ft.	In.		Tons	Ft.	In.
Length of main-deck, from rabbit to rabbit,		116	0	of lower-deck,		118	2
Breadth, extreme,	462	29	10½		539	32	0½

The "Boston Gazette" contains the following paragraph, respecting the size and force of these two vessels:—"The Cyane is frigate-built; and is of the same tonnage, and capable of the same armament, as the late U.S. frigate Essex. The Levant is exactly equal in tonnage, and armament to the late" (meaning the *new,* now lost) "U.S. ship Wasp; both (independently of the advantage which two ships have over one) being decidedly superior to the Constitution."

The impudence of this *federal puff* is beyond anything. The Cyane's *American* tonnage is 520; that of the Essex, according to her very builder's statement, 850. The only material difference, as to dimensions, between the "late U.S. ship Wasp" and the Cyane is, that the latter was built up, so as to carry a quarter-deck and forecastle: reduce them, and the two ships would measure exactly the same. It is true; the Levant, and about a dozen of her sister-vessels, all run up in the same year, *ought* to have been equal in tonnage and armament to the late U.S. ship Wasp." But, although mounting 21 instead of 19 guns, they are far inferior vessels to the brigs; whose capture by the American sloops, they were constructed to avenge.

It having been shewn, that the two British ships mounted, in broadside, all carronades, except two 9s, and that the Constitution mounted, in broadside, seventeen long 24s, exclusive of her carronades, the reader will see the propriety of our deviating a little, from the usual way of exhibiting the comparative force in guns.

The united tonnage of the Levant and Cyane, would affect the superficial extent, not the thickness, of their sides: consequently, were the *size in tons* to be introduced at all, it should be the mean or average tonnage of the two British vessels, 500; which bears to 1533, a much smaller proportion, than existed, in point of strength and compactness, between the top-sides of the stoutest of the two British ships, and those of the Constitution. We have therefore thought it best, to exclude from the estimate, altogether, the *size in tons.*

Comparative force of the ships.

		Levant and Cyane.		Constitution.	
Broadside-metal in pounds,	l. guns,		18		408
	carr.		742		320
Complement,	men,	260		469	
	boys,	42		3	
		—	302	—	472

The "corporation of the city of New York" declared, that the victory over the Levant and Cyane, ought to be classed *"among the most brilliant feats recorded in naval history"!*—On anchoring at Boston, "this glorious yankee vessel," says a Boston paper, "was welcomed by federal salutes. Captain Stewart landed under a salute; and was escorted to the Exchange coffee-house, by troops, amidst the repeated cheers of citizens of both sexes, who filled the streets, wharves, and vessels, and occupied the houses. A band of music played national airs," &c. &c. It appears, also, by the same paper, that the manager of the play-house knew his interest too well, not to crave leave to announce, that "the gallant Captain Stewart, and the officers of the Constitution" (all, of course, "in full regimentals") would honor the theatre with their presence.—To recount all the extravagances which this event gave rise to, in different parts of the Union, among the *federalists*, especially, would exceed the limits of this work. Yet they had official authority, in some degree, to warrant their rejoicings. Does not Captain Stewart assert, that the enemy had a "superiority in the weight and number of gun's," besides the "advantages derived from a divided and more active force"?

The same motive that induced Commodore Perry to reject the weight of metal, in the Lake Erie action, (see p. 144,) induced Captain Stewart to adopt it, in the action with the Levant and Cyane. How "active" the British ships were, may be judged from the well-known fact, that, out of a fleet which the Cyane convoyed to Newfoundland, every vessel, but one, ran by her with ease; and her officers declare, that the Levant could but just outsail her.

Respecting the advantages to be derived from a "divided force," Captain Stewart, upon another occasion, expressed quite a different opinion from that contained in his letter. A "Report," signed by this gentleman, and aproved by Captains Hull and Morris, has already been noticed. (See p. 8.) An estimate is there given, of the comparative force of American "ships of the line, say 74s, and large frigates." "Ships of the line," says Captain Stewart, "are much stronger in scantling, thicker in the sides and bottom, less penetrable to shot; and, consequently, less liable to be torn or battered to pieces, or sunk. I am aware that some are of opinion, that a more divided force is better calculated for action, from the advantageous position that would be given to a part. Suppose three frigates, of 50 guns" (the "round of shot" of each, previously stated at "1360 pounds") "were to undertake to batter at 74-gun ship; (round of shot, "3224 pounds";) "and that two of them were to occupy the quarter and stern of the 74, (this is placing them in the most favorable position,) the other frigate engaged a-breast; every thing would then depend on the time the frigate a-breast could maintain that position, to enable the other two to act, with effect, on the stern and quarter. But, it must appear evident to all acquainted with the two classes of ships, that the frigate a-breast could not withstand the fire of so heavy and compact a body, many minutes; and, in all probability, would be dismasted or sunk, the first or second broadside. This would decide the fate of the other two." (Nav. Chron. vol. xxix, p. 460.)

From this we are to understand that, although "some are of opinion that a more divided force is better calculated for action," Captain Stewart, at the time he framed that "valuable communication," considered, that "three large frigates," placed "in the most favorable position," would be compelled to yield to a "74-gun ship;" owing to the latter being "stronger in scantling, and thicker in sides."

Why, then, should there be an exception, because *two*, instead of *three* ships, are engaged? The Constitution has "stronger scantling and thicker sides" than a British 74; (see pp. 62-63;) and what were the vessels opposed to her?—Two ships, averaging 500 tons!—If Captain Stewart, in his supposititious case, can excuse *three* ships, having a superiority "in point of metal," of a *thirteenth*, for yielding to one; why will he not, in his real case, excuse *two ships*, having a superiority in point of metal, (admitting, for argument sake, the equality of long guns and carronades,) of only *a twenty fourth*, for yielding to one?

Digressing for a moment; suppose the U.S. ships Peacock and Hornet, soon after leaving New York together, had fallen in with the Endymion, close to-windward of them; and (the only improbable part of the supposition) had staid to engage her till finally captured.

How would the American citizens have behaved on this occasion?—Why, they would have received Captains Warrington and Biddle, precisely as they did Captain Stewart;—published accounts in every paper of the "heroic defence against decidedly superior force:" not failing to point out, as they did in the Essex's action, the great disparity between carronades and long guns, when the latter have the choice of distance. Mr. Madison, too, in his next speech to congress, would have declared, that the two little sloops continued the unequal contest, till (as he said of the Essex) "humanity tore down the colours which valor had nailed to the mast."

How would Captain Hope have behaved? He would have told a plain tale of his good-fortune, applauding the American commanders, for having so long maintained a contest; in which, from the nature of their armament, and from their leeward position, they could not hope to succeed.

It need scarcely be added, that the surviving officers and ship's companies of the Levant and Cyane, were, at their several courts-martial, most honorably acquitted for the surrender of their ships, and justly applauded for the gallant defence they made, against an enemy's ship, so decidedly superior.

The Constitution carried the Levant and Cyane into Port Praya, in the island of St. Jago; where they all arrived on the 7th of March. In his way, thither, Captain Stewart planned a sort of *deceptio visús* upon his countrymen at New York, by painting the Cyane so as to make her resemble a 36-gun frigate. That corresponds with his behaviour all through this affair.

On the 8th of March, in a thick fog, H. M, ships Leander, Newcastle, and Acasta, arrived off the harbour, in quest of the U.S. ships President, Constitution, and Congress; the master of an American captured vessel having informed Sir George Collier, the British commanding officer, that those three ships had left port in company. The Constitution, and her two prizes, cut their cables, and stood to sea. In a little while, Captain Stewart made a signal for the Cyane to tack. She did so; and—*no ship followed her*. In two hours afterwards, the same signal was made to the Levant. She tacked also; and, in seven minutes afterwards, "the whole enemy's squadron," says the Constitution's log-extract, (App. No. 110,) "tacked in pursuit of the Levant, and gave up the pursuit of this ship"—The Cyane and Constitution were thus left to themselves; and the Levant, with so many ships in pursuit of her, was of course recaptured.

The feelings of the British officers on board the Constitution, at the moment the three ships tacked after the Levant, may be better conceived than described, Nor were the American officers slow in expressing their joyful surprises not unmingled with contempt, at the seeming forbearance of the British frigates. When the force of those ships, (each of two of which threw a heavier broadside than the Constitution,) and the distinguished character of the officers commanding them, come under consideration, it absolves the British from any thing like an unwillingness to fight: at the same time, we must all regret, that it should have been deemed expedient to withhold from the public eye, those "untoward circumstances" which led to the Constitution's,—as it now appears,—most unaccountable escape.

According to the "Sketches of the War," Captain Stewart had, on a previous cruize in the Constitution; done more than capture the "frigate Cyane" and her consort; more than effect his escape from a formidable British squadron; more, in short, than any French, Spanish, or American commander of a frigate, could boast of having done:—compelled a British frigate to fly before him!—Here are the words of the American editor, extracted, from p. 240, of his book:—"During her cruize, she captured the British public schooner Pique, and fell in with the frigate la Pique,

Captain Maitland, who fled on the approach of the Constitution. No effort was left untried by Captain Stewart, to overtake and bring her to action; but she escaped in the night, after a long chase; and Captain Maitland, on his arrival in England, was complimented by the admiralty, for his strict observance of his instructions, in flying from an American frigate."

The latter assertion may accompany that alleging the trial and execution of the Plantaganet's men for mutiny: (see p. 161:) our attention is better bestowed upon the merits of this extraordinary chase.—We shall first present the reader with an extract from the Pique's log-book:

H.	K	F.	Courses.	Wind.	Remarks, & c. H. M. S. Pique, Feb. 23, 1814
1 2 &c.					At noon observed several strangers, one apparently a man of war in chase.

Courses.	Dist.	Lat.	Long.	Bearings at noon.
N. 84 W.	142 M.	18.1 N	67. 22.	Mona Islds. N. 73W. 19 m.

H.	K	F.	Courses.	Wind.	Remarks
1	3		N.W. ½ W.		P. M. Light airs—braced the yards by, to allow the chase to come up.—At 4. light airs.—At 4.30. observed chase take in her main-stay-sail.—At 4.50. observed her take in royal, top-gallant, lower, and top-mast, studding-sails.—Hauled to the wind on larboard-tack, and made all sail to close her; hoisted an ensign. Stranger shortened sail, in 1st reef top-sails, hoisted American colours, and hauled her wind on opposite tack: appeared to be a large frigate, having 16 ports of a-side. Cleared for action; stranger S.E. by S. 3 miles.—At 5 Island of *Zachee* N. by E. 12 or 13 miles:—8 cloudy, lost sight of stranger :—10 in first reefs:—12 squally.
2	2	2		E.S.E.	
3	1	4			
4 5 6	ship's head from N.W. to N.				
7	9		N.W.	E.N.E.	
8	9	6			
9	9	4	N. ½ E.		
10			N.		
11	10	4			
12		2	N. ½ W.		

The first symptom of the Pique's "flying," was her bracing the yards by, "to allow the chase to come up;" the second, her hauling to the wind, and making all sail "to close her." On the other hand, the Constitution evinced a strong disposition "to overtake and bring her to action," when she took in all her sail, and hauled to the wind, at a distance from the Pique of full three miles. Had the Pique, in her efforts to close, hauled upon the same tack as the Constitution, the latter would have been upon her weather-bow; and, by putting her helm up, might have raked the Pique effectually, without a possibility of her bringing more than three guns to bear. The Constitution would have luffed-to again; and might have repeated this manœuvre, till she had completely crippled her adversary; only that the narrowness of the passage would have compelled her to tack, before she had stood on much further. About 1 o'clock in the morning, the Pique gained the wind of the Constitution, crossing her bow at about 1½ mile distance. The editor of the "Sketches of the War," no doubt, took his account of this affair from Captain Stewart's official letter. The latter could not be contented with exculpating himself; but, the odium he had such an easy way of getting rid of, must endeavour to cast upon the officers and crew of a British frigate.

A British merchant-master, who was a prisoner on board the Constitution when she fell in with the Pique, was as much surprised as any of us, when he afterwards read in the newspapers, that the Constitution had chased that ship, and could not bring her to action. He says, that the first-lieutenant saw, from the number of her main-deck ports, that the Pique was only a 42, or, as then rated, 36 gun frigate, and was desirous to bring her to action; but that the captain seemed averse to it. In the night, the Constitution bore up; rounded the Square-handkerchief shoal; and, in 48 hours afterwards, was off Charlestown; far enough from the Pique.

It is true, that Captain Maitland had received secret orders, not to engage one of the large class of American frigates. This was afterwards complained of in the house of commons; but, certainly, without the slightest grounds. Before the end of 1813, the American frigate Guerriere, carrying long, or columbiad 32-pounders, upon the main-deck, was fitting; and, but for the Majestic's appearance in the Delaware, would have got to sea. The Guerriere shews the same number of ports of a-side as the Constitution; and a reference to the Majestic's force, as given at p. 17, and to the Phœbe's, at p. 157, will shew, what would have been the disparity of force between the Guerriere and a frigate of the Pique's class. As soon as the American frigate appeared in sight, and discovered her "16 ports of a-side," Captain Maitland could do no less than read to his crew, the instructions he had received.—Ignorant how to set about "flying,"—the orders to do which, the Pique's men would have most reluctantly executed,—Captain Maitland hauled his wind, hoisted an ensign, and cleared for action. This order needed no repetition. At about half-past 4, the ship's company, as usual, were piped to supper; but, to a man, refused their grog, saying, they wanted none, while an enemy's frigate was in sight: they could do their duty without! When we reflect upon the relative numbers on board the two frigates, this admirable trait in the Pique's men, was certainly a very strong proof, how much British seamen had been *cowed,* by the naval successes of the Americans!

CHAPTER XX.

St. Lawrence schooner, bearing despatches relating to the peace, is attacked and captured by the Chasseur brig—No British official account of the action—Damages and loss of each vessel—Their respective force in guns, men, and size—Statement of comparative force—American accounts of actions between their privateers and British ships of war—Penguin falls in with, and engages, the Hornet—No British official account of the action published—Full details of it—Penguin surrenders—Her damages, destruction, and loss—Hornet's damages and loss—Force of each vessel in guns, men, and size—American method of measurement—Statement of comparative force—Remarks thereon—Peacock falls in with the E. I. C. brig Nautilus—Captain Warrington, after a knowledge of peace, wantonly attacks and captures her—Lieutenant Boyce's gallant behaviour, and dreadful wounds—Other loss sustained—Force of the two vessels—The transaction fully considered.

His Majesty's schooner St. Lawrence, Lieutenant Gordon, on the 26th of February, 1815, while proceeding with despatches from Rear-admiral Cockburn, relating to the peace between Great Britain and the United States, fell in with the American privateer-brig Chasseur.

The latter attacked the schooner, and an engagement ensued; which, the Americans state, lasted, at close quarters, only 15 minutes, when the St. Lawrence was carried by boarding. No British official account has been published; but unofficial accounts state, that the action continued much longer. Owing to the nature of the despatches, it is probable they were not sunk. At all events, a great many private letters from officers to their friends fell into the enemy's hands; and, shameful to say, were afterwards published in the American newspapers.

The St. Lawrence was a good deal cut up; and, according to a New Providence paper, lost 6 men killed, and 18 wounded. The Americans made the killed, as they generally do, much greater. The Chasseur was also injured in her hull and spars; and lost, by the American returns, 5 men killed, and 8 wounded.

The St. Lawrence mounted twelve carronades, 12-pounders, and one long 9-pounder. The Americans gave her two more carronades. Her complement, on going into action, was 42 officers and men, and 9 boys. She had also a few passengers. The Americans stated her complement to be 75, exclusive of passengers; but 51 comprised the number of her crew.

The American accounts differ as to the armament of the Chasseur. As far as can be collected from them, she mounted six long 9 pounders, and eight carronades, 18-pounders, total 14 guns; but had formerly mounted sixteen much heavier guns. The New Providence paper states her complement to have been 117 men. The American accounts do not admit so many.

The St. Lawrence was formerly the American letter of marque Atlas, of 240 tons, and mounting 10 guns; taken at Ocracock bar, on the 24th of July, 1813. She was comparatively a mere shell; with scarcely any bulwarks. The Chasseur was pronounced one of the finest privateers out of America; and in point of sailing, had no competitor. She was pierced for 18 guns; had regular bulwarks, stouter than those of our first-class brigs; and measured 275 tons, American, or 287, English.

Comparative force of the two vessels.

		St. Lawrence schooner.		Chasseur brig.	
Broadside-metal in pounds,	l. guns,	9		27	
	carr.	72		72	
		—	81	—	99
Complement,	men,	42		115	
	boys,	9		2	
		—	51	—	117
Size in tons,			240		287

The principal disparity in this action, was in number of men. The vessels being close to each other, so that musketry could be used, that superiority was greatly augmented; and the enemy, at last, boarded, with an overwhelming force. Men are not in the best trim for fighting, just upon receiving the news of peace. Sailors are then dwelling upon their discharge from servitude, the sight of long absent friends, and all the ties of their homes and families. Even that, though it perhaps contributed to weaken the efforts, could not impair the courage, of the crew of the St. Lawrence: they defended her, till nearly half their number were killed or wounded.

The Americans boasted, that the Chasseur, upon a former cruize, "fought" two sloops of war. According to an extract from her log, published in a New York paper, it appears, she did "exchange a few shots" with one of our brigs; and, on another occasion, was "fired at" by a brig; but, each time,—took to her heels. How many American privateers, besides the Chasseur, have "fought" British ships in a similar manner!

*

While on this subject, it may be as well to exhibit to the reader, without any order of date, a few instances of the "bold and daring intrepidity of the crews of the private-armed vessels of the United States."

The Warrior, according to the American accounts, was an extraordinary large brig, of between 4 and 500 tons, mounting 22 heavy guns, and having a complement of 150 men. She was therefore a match for any of our 18-gun sloops. "An extract from the Warrior's log-book," (alluding to a ship in chase) says:— "Thinking her to be a sloop of war, got all ready and clear for action."—"At 3. 30. luffed-to to let the enemy come up; when they took in all their light sails, and lulled-to also; then discovered her to be a frigate:—made all sail, &c."—Here appeared an intention to fight "a sloop of war;" but, upon another vessel heaving in sight, we read: "Shortly after, discovered her to be a man of war brig, which gave chase to us; *out-sailed her with ease*."—And again: "Was chased by a sloop of war."—Not another word about "getting clear for action," and "luffing-to to let the enemy come up."—What is to be inferred from all this, but that these hectoring paragraphs were invented, either by the captain of the privateer, to get him and his vessel a brilliant name, or by the newspaper editor, to make a column of dry detail go down with his readers. Another editor gives an extract from the log-book of the "private-armed schooner Roger, of 14 guns and 75 men," in which appears the following entry: "April 12th, lat. 27. long. 66. fell in with, and *chased*, a man of war brig"!

But "Captain Guy R. Champlin, of the private-armed schooner General Armstrong, of New York," performed a still greater exploit. In a letter, dated "Charleston, April 5, 1813," he states that, on the 11th of March, "about 5 leagues N. E. of Surinam," he engaged a "British frigate, mounting 28 guns on her gun-deck, 6 or 8 on her quarter-deck, and 4 on the forecastle."—He admits that the General Armstrong (mounting 18 guns) was severely cut up in hull; lost 7 men killed, and 16 (including himself) wounded; and with difficulty escaped. The loss of the "frigate" he describes thus: "We saw them throw over many of their killed."—"The Sketches of the War" gives much the same account, only preferring "a heavy frigate" to the particulars of the frigate's force, as stated in the captain's letter.—The reader will scarcely believe that this "heavy frigate" was no other than the Coquette, (now broken up,) a sister-vessel to the Cherub; whose force in guns, men, and size, has already appeared. (See p. 157.). A lie is seldom so well told, but some inconsistency betrays it. Where is there a British frigate "mounting 28 guns on her gun-deck," that mounts no more than "6 or 8 on her quarter-deck"?—Six is the precise number mounted by the Coquette and her class.—A reference to the Coquette's log-book, shews that she lost in the action, 4 men wounded, but none killed. It is true, 2 died of their wounds; but their bodies were not committed to the deep till late in the evening; when the privateer had been some hours out of sight: yet, say the Americans, "we saw them throw over many of their killed"!

The editor of the "Sketches of the War" has, however, left Captain Champlin, and all other American officers, far behind him. Mr. John Lewis Thomson was determined to have the course to himself. "The Charybdis," says he, at p. 94, "fell in with the privateer Blockade, of New York, of 8 guns; and, after an obstinate engagement of 1 hour and 20 minutes, in which the Charybdis lost 28 of her officers and men killed and wounded, and the Blockade 8 men only, the latter was carried, and taken into port";—when, in truth, the Blockade was captured by H. M. brig Charybdis, without a shot being fired, beyond, probably, one to bring her to: she had actually thrown overboard 9 out of her 10 guns, in her efforts to escape! A reference to Captain Clephan's official letter, (Nav. Chron. vol. xxix. p. 80,) is all that is required to substantiate the fact.

On the 23d of March, 1815, H. M. brig Penguin, Captain James Dickinson, fell in with the U. S. ship Hornet, Captain Biddle; and an action ensued. It may be proper to mention that, although the ratification of the peace had been signed by Mr. Madison since February, the second article rendered captures made at the greatest distance, legal till June. The American officer heard of the peace, on the 20th, from a neutral vessel; but the man of war in sight, on the 23d, was evidently a *brig;* whose force, therefore, was known to be inferior to the Hornet's.

No British official account of this action has been published; but a copy of the letter of the Penguin's surviving senior-officer, will be found in the Appendix. (No. 111.) The two accounts agree, within 5 minutes, as to the time when the action commenced; but, while the British account fixes the period of surrender at 2. 25. (40 minutes from the commencement,) the American account, without giving the date of surrender, declares that, "from the firing of the first gun to the *last time* the enemy cried out he had surrendered, was exactly 22 minutes by the watch."—In confirmation of the Penguin's time being the most correct, an old man, a Dane, who, along with three or four other men, lives on the island of Tristran d'Acunha, and is called the governor of it, held his watch in his hand during the action; (which was fought in full view of him;) and declared to the officers of both vessels, that, between the first and last cannon shot, 41 minutes and some seconds elapsed.

With respect to Captain Biddle's assertion, that, when the Penguin got foul of the Hornet, and lost her bowsprit and foremast, her first lieutenant hailed "that they had surrendered," the American commander certainly mistook Lieutenant M'Donald's words. They were, according to the testimony of the Penguin's late second lieutenant, "What ship is that?"—This is material;

because Captain Biddle charges the Penguin's people with firing at him after surrender. "An officer of the U.S. sloop of war Peacock," in a letter, published in the "New England Palladium," has not scrupled to apply the term "ruffians" to two of the Penguin's marines, who then fired; and one of whom hit Captain Biddle in the chin or neck; but the writer exultingly adds: "They were observed by two of Biddle's marines, who levelled, and laid them dead upon the deck, at the instant."

The same officer states, that, in a conversation which Captain Biddle had with Lieutenant M'Donald, the latter ascribed the failure of the boarding-attempt to the backwardness of his men. This is considered as the invention of some of the American officers. The Penguin's crew were chiefly landmen and boys; unskilled in gunnery; and, except a very small portion, had never before been in action; but there were, among them, many with British hearts; and who, when the boarders were called, were only prevented from springing on the Hornet's deck, by the fall of the Penguin's bowsprit and fore-mast, and the immediate hauling off of the American vessel. Captain Biddle, referring to the circumstance of his being wounded after the first hail, adds: "It was with difficulty I could restrain my crew from firing into him again"; and yet the Peacock's officer has divulged to us, that the "two fellows" who fired, were both shot dead.

The Penguin was much shattered in her hull; and, besides the loss of fore-mast and bowsprit, her main-mast was completely crippled. Her after-carronades on the side engaged, were "rendered useless by the *drawing of the breeching-bolts.*" (App. No. 111.) Previous to which, indeed, the carronades had frequently, in their recoil, turned half round; and much labour and loss of time ensued, before they could be replaced. No accident of this sort occurred on board the Hornet, owing to the superior manner in which American carronades are fitted. Such of the carronades upon the Penguin's larboard-side as remained fixed to the ports, were covered by the wreck of the fore-mast; and the want of masts and sails, rendered it impossible to bring the other broadside to bear. The Penguin was therefore perfectly defenceless; and further resistance would have been a waste of lives. Her shattered state alone, led to her final destruction early on the morning of the 25th.

Captain Dickinson was first lieutenant of the Amphion, in the action off Lissa; and was esteemed a very gallant officer. Besides her commander, the Penguin lost her boatswain, and 4 seamen and marines, killed; 4 others mortally wounded; and her second lieutenant, (very severely,) purser's clerk, 2 midshipmen, (each of whom lost a leg,) and 24 seamen and marines, wounded; most of them slightly; total 38. One of the wounded midshipmen died on his passage to St. Salvador, in the U.S. brigantine Tom Bowline.—Captain Biddle says: "They acknowledge a loss of 14 killed." The Penguin's first and second lieutenants, and master, all agree in stating, that except the midshipman, (whose death was not known to Lieutenant M'Donald at the date of his letter,) no more than 10 men were killed, or mortally wounded.

It is a very unpleasant task to be compelled to contradict statement after statement in the official correspondence of a national officer. Yet Captain Biddle's name is familiar to the reader, as the man who, though himself the prize-master, wrote home, on a former occasion, a false account of a British man of war's armament. (See p. 74.) He now ventures to say, that the Hornet "did not receive a single round shot in her hull." Why, several shot-holes along the Hornet's quarter, stared the Penguin's officers and men in the face as they stepped from the boat up her sides. Her round-house was completely shot away, and she received one shot under water, that kept the men constantly at the pumps. All this was known to every man belonging to the Penguin. How, indeed, could it be kept secret? Yet, says Mr. Biddle, "this ship did not receive a single round-shot in her hull"!

After such a statement, we cannot be surprised that the Hornet's loss should be made so trifling as 1 killed, and 11 wounded; of whom one died. Lieutenant M'Donald says, that the the Penguin was not taken possession of, till 35 minutes after she surrendered. Even some time then elapsed before the prisoners were removed. Just as Mr. Kirk, one of the Penguin's midshipmen, and the very first prisoner that reached the Hornet, was stepping upon her deck, the crew were in the act of throwing a man over-board; but a struggle, or convulsive twitch in the body, occasioned his being hauled in again. The poor wretch's lower jaw had been nearly all shot away; yet he lived, and was walking about the deck in the course of a few days. This shews in what a hurry the American officers were, to get their killed out of the way before the arrival of the prisoners; and the time necessary to remove every appearance of blood and carnage, contributed to the delay in sending for them. Even when the British did come on board, buckets of water were dashing about, and brooms at work, on all parts of the deck. The Penguin's second lieutenant, counted 16 of the Hornet's men lying in their cots; and several of her men told some of their former ship-mates, whom they discovered among the Penguin's crew, that the Hornet had 10 men killed by the first and second broadsides; and that several of the dangerously wounded were thrown overboard, because their surgeon was afraid to amputate, owing to his want of experience! (See p. 90.)

The Penguin mounted the usual armament of her class; sixteen carronades, 32-pounders, two long 6-pounders, and a 12-pound boat-carronade. She had one swivel only; and that was mounted upon the capstan, and shot away, the first broadside. Captain Biddle places "swivels in her tops;" and has converted her long 6s into "12s." To give these double effect, he adds: "She had a spare port forward, so as to fight both her long guns of a side." How happened it not to occur to Captain Biddle, that she might have fought one of her "swivels" through the *hawse-hole?* The fact is, the American captain was sick in his cabin, with the *creak* in his neck; and saw little or nothing of the Penguin, after she struck. But, had he only read that part of his letter to "Mr. Mayo, who had been in charge of the prize," that gentleman would have told him, that the Penguin's long guns were not stationed forward, but in two 'midsipports; whose carronades had been shifted to the foremost ones. Here was a blunder! Even had the Penguin's long guns been in their usual places, does so experienced a naval officer as Captain Biddle, venture to assert, that either of those guns could be used out of the bow-port, but as a chase-gun, pointed forwards. (See plate 3. fig. 2.) The Peacock's officer, in his letter in the "Palladium," says thus: "On examining her (the Penguin's) guns after the action, a 32-lb. carronade on the side engaged, was found, with its tompion, as nicely puttyed and stopped in, as it was the day she left Spithead."—The Penguin's late second lieutenant, Mr. Elwin, (who commanded the fore-mast guns,) and her late master, Mr. Atkinson, both declare, most solemnly, that the above paragraph is, in all its parts, a gross falsehood; and that the Penguin had not even a sham or wooden gun-muzzle, (see p. 182,) as a pretext for the assertion.

The Penguin was commissioned, for the first time, in November, 1813; and waited at Sheerness, for men, till June, 1814. Her complement was then made up; and consisted, with a full allowance of boys, of very young and very old men; the former, pressed men; the latter, discharged ineffectives. Of her 121 men and boys, 12 only had ever been in action. The Penguin was, in the September following, ordered to the Cape of Good Hope. There she lost a great many of her men by sickness; and, previous to her sailing on the cruize in which she was captured, received a loan of 12 supernumerary marines from the Medway 74. Her purser was left sick at the Cape. On going into action with the Hornet, she had, of her proper crew, 93 men, and 17 boys; making, with the 12 supernumerary marines, 105 men, and 17 boys; total 122. Captain Biddle says: "The enemy acknowledge a complement of 132." This gentleman has enough to answer for; let us, therefore, consider the error to have been the printer's, in the substitution of a 3 for a 2. But, there is still a mistake in the number of prisoners received. These amounted to 116,—instead of "118, including the 4 that died of their wounds,"—which, with the 6 killed in action, makes 122; the total of the Penguin's complement. The New York account of this "brilliant victory," published on the 4th of July, (the best day in the year for embellishments of this sort,) gave the Penguin "a crew of 158 men."

The Hornet, this time, mounted eighteen 32-pound carronades, and two long 18, instead of 9 pounders; which 18s, owing to their additional length and weight, were fought through two 'midship ports, similar to the Penguin's 6s. The Hornet mounted, in her tops, swivels or musquetoons, each throwing 50 buckshot at a discharge; and, upon her starboard-quarter, two large swivels, fitted on chocks. Chain and bar shot, old nails, &c. in abundance, were fired from her guns: the former contributed chiefly to the fall of the Penguin's fore-mast and bowsprit; the latter afflicted the wounded, in the usual manner. Captain Biddle says, that he was "8 men short of complement." In this solitary instance he appears to have been correct; for the British officers state, that the Hornet commenced action with 165 men; making, with the 8 absent, 173; the number proved as that ship's complement when she engaged the Peacock. (See p. 101.) Lieutenant M'Donald says, "not a boy was amongst them;" but Lieutenant Elwin saw one, so called, a servant in the officer's mess-room; and he was between 16 and 17 years old.—That some of the Hornet's men were natives of the United Kingdom, was well known to several of the Penguin's ship's company; and, if a still greater number were not of that description, how are we to account for the unmanly and frantic consternation, so general on board the Hornet, when that ship afterwards expected to be captured by the Cornwallis 74?—"Many of our men," says an extract from a private journal of one of the Hornet's officers, "had been impressed and imprisoned for years in that horrible service, and hated them and their nation with the most deadly animosity; while the rest of the crew, horror-struck by the relation of the sufferings of their shipmates, who had been in the power of the English, and now equally flushed with rage, joined heartily in execrating the present authors of our misfortune. Captain Biddle mustered the crew, and told them, he was pleased with their conduct during the chase, and hoped still to perceive the propriety of conduct which had always marked their character, and that of the American tar generally; that we might soon expect to be captured, &c. Not a dry eye was to be seen at the mention of capture." (Nav. Chron. vol. xxxiv. p. 379.) In another place, we are termed "a cruel and vindictive enemy." Mr. Biddle calls all this "propriety of conduct"!—Of whatever nation the Hornet's men were, they, in the first instance, were picked seamen; and, by constant drilling at the guns, during five or six years, might well acquire that skill in gunnery, which they evinced in their actions with the Peacock and the Penguin.

So much has appeared about the size of the British 18-gun brigs, that, to notice any thing more of what the Americans have said upon the subject, may be deemed superfluous. To set the question quite at rest, it will only be necessary to place opposite to the Penguin's actual dimensions, as taken by her builder, the dimensions given to her by Captain Biddle, and since published in a New York paper.

Dimensions of H. M. late brig Penguin.

When built.	Ft.	In.	*When captured.*	
Length of deck, from rabbit to rabbit	100	5	"Length on deck,	110 ft."
Breadth over both wails,	31	1½	"Breadth of beam,	31½ ft."
Ditto extreme, or for measurement,	30	7½		
Ditto moulded, or across the frame,	30	1½		
Thickness of top-sides, at 'midship port-sill,	0	11¼	"Thickness of bulwarks,	12 in."
Do. do. at upper port-timber,	0	9½	"Ditto at top of port,	10½ in."
Height from water's edge to top of hammocks a-mid-ships, when stowed,	11	7	"Height of bulwarks where hammocks are stowed,	13 ft."
Distance between carronade-slides,	7	2	"Distance between guns,	10 ft."
Ditto from centre-line or axis of one carronade, to centre-line or axis of the next,	8	1		

In the *Times* newspaper, of September 3, 1815, is the following paragraph:—"A Swiss paper observes, that there are in Switzerland, no fewer than eleven different foot-measures, and 50 different kinds of weight."—Who knows but this may be, in some degree, the case in the United States?—Either the foot-measure employed upon the Penguin, by Captain Biddle's officers, differs materially from the English foot-measure, or some error exists in the wording of the items. For instance, fig. 3. pl.3. will shew, that, according to *English* foot-measure, the Penguin was "110 feet" round the bottom and inside of her bulwarks, and not "on deck." The Hornet's "length on deck," measured in the same place, and by the same rule, would be at least 123, instead of 112 feet. It is doubtful, whether the "31½ feet" may not have been intended for 31 feet 1½, the breadth over both wails. Any difference in the remainder of the items is immaterial. The dimensions of the Hornet have already been compared with those of the brig Peacock; a vessel of the same size as the Penguin. (See pp. 102-103.)

As Britons, we should be ashamed to offer this trifling disparity of force, as an excuse for the Penguin's capture. The chief cause is to be sought in that which cannot be made apparent in figures,—the immense disparity between the two vessels in the fitting of their guns, and the effectiveness of their crews.

Comparative force of the two vessels.

		Penguin, brig.	Hornet, ship.
Broadside-metal in pounds,	l. guns,	6	18
	carr.	268	288
		—274	—306
Complement,	men,	105	163
	boys,	17	2
		—122	—165
Size in tons,		387	450

A ship's gun, cast adrift, not only becomes utterly useless as a weapon of offence or defence, but, in the very act of breaking loose, maims and disables the men stationed at it; and, if the sea is rough, (as Captain Biddle says it was in the present instance,) continues to cause destruction among the crew, generally, till again lashed to the ship's side. How much is the evil encreased, if, as in the Penguin's case, instead of one gun, several guns break loose. In the midst of all this delay and self-destruction, the enemy, uninterrupted in his operations, and animated by the feeble resistance he meets, quickens his fire; and, conquering at last, fails not to ascribe, solely to his skill and valor, that victory, which accident had partly gained for him.

On the 27th of April, the U. S. ships Peacock and Hornet were so closely pursued by the Cornwallis 74, that the first-named ship parted from her consort, and afterwards proceeded alone to the Indian seas; the intended cruizing ground of the American squadron, when joined by the President. (See p. 213.)

On the 30th of June, the Peacock, being off Anjier, in the Straits of Sunda, fell in with the honorable East India company's cruiser Nautilus, commanded by Lieutenant Charles Boyce. The British and American accounts of this rencontre, differ, materially, as to one fact;—the knowledge of Captain Warrington, at the time he approached the Nautilus with a hostile intention, that peace had been signed between Great Britain and the United States. We will, in the first instance, suppose the American officer to have been unacquainted with the circumstance, till, as he admits, (App. No. 118,) he was hailed, and *asked if he knew of it,* by the Nautilus's commander. After that, would not a humane man,—would not a brave officer, have deferred firing, till he had ascertained the fact?—But Captain Warrington says: "I considered the *assertion,* coupled with his arrangements for action, a finesse on his part, to amuse us, till he could place himself under the protection of the fort." It *was,* then, an "assertion," as Lieutenant Boyce states;—happy inconsistency!—and a most important assertion too, concluding with, "I have Mr. Madison's proclamation on board."—Had not the Nautilus "shortened sail," and "hove-to"?—Did that appear as if her commander wished to "place himself under the protection of the fort"? And that fort, instead of being at a short distance," was five miles off.—Was it not time for Lieutenant Boyce to make "arrangements for action," when he saw a ship like the Peacock bearing down upon him, with ports ready-opened?—It never occurred to that officer, that his vessel's being "in an unprepared state," (see p. 33,) would serve for an excuse. Let us suppose, for a moment, that, just as the American commander was listening to the hail from the Nautilus, she became suddenly transformed into H. M. ship Volage, a sister-vessel to the Cyane, (see p. 233,) and at that time cruizing in the East Indies:—Captain Warrington would then have promptly hailed in turn, with the best speaking-trumpet in the ship; thanked Captain Drury for his politeness; and been the first to urge the folly, not to say wickedness, of wounding and killing each other, while any doubt existed about peace having been signed. But it was a vessel he could almost hoist on board the Peacock; he therefore called out: "Haul down your colours instantly."—This "reasonable demand," (App. No. 117,) Lieutenant Boyce considered, very properly, as an imperious and insulting mandate; and, fully alive to the dignity of the British flag, and to the honor of the service of which he was so distinguished an ornament, prepared to cope with a ship, whose immense superiority, as she over-shadowed his little bark, gave him nothing to expect short of a speedy annihilation.—Then, says Captain Warrington, (App. No. 118,) "one of the forward guns was fired at her, which was immediately returned by a broadside from the brig: our broadside was then discharged, and his colours were struck, after having six lascars killed, and seven or eight wounded."—The Nautilus's master, Mr. Joseph Bartlett, was on board the Peacock, during the action, (App. No. 114,) and swears positively, that "two or three broadsides were fired;" and that the American continued his fire, even after the flag, and, as it appears, until the pendant, of the Nautilus was hauled down. Nineteen of the crew have deposed to the same effect. Captain Warrington's object in framing this falsehood, was evidently to shew, what execution had been done by his *one* broadside.

From the first gun fired, two of the Nautilus's men were killed; and Lieutenant Boyce was dangerously wounded: a grape-shot, measuring two inches and one-third, in diameter, entering at the outside of his hip, and passing out close under the back-bone. This severe wound did not, however, disable him. In a few minutes, a 32-pound shot struck obliquely on his right knee, shattering the joint, splintering the leg-bone downwards, and the thigh-bone a great way upwards!—This, as may be supposed, laid him prostrate on the deck. The first, and only lieutenant, received a mortal wound: the master, who would have been the next officer, was on board the Peacock. It was then, and not till then, that the gallant Boyce, lying bleeding on the deck, ordered the Nautilus's colours to be struck.

Of the "six *lascars* killed," two were European invalids, and one a seaman: of the "seven or eight (lascars) wounded," two were seamen;—and was Lieutenant Mayston a "lascar"?—was Lieutenant Boyce a "lascar"?—That Captain Warrington well knew he was uttering a falsehood, is clear; because the Peacock's surgeon had, at Lieutenant Boyce's request, attended the Nautilus's wounded; and his official return would certainly have noticed a distinction so evident, as that of native and European. Those who know in what low estimation persons of colour are held by the government and people of the United States, can readily understand, why Captain Warrington used the word "lascars." What is killing half a dozen "lascars," and depriving another of an arm, and two others of a leg each?—It was not so, when John Pierce, an "American citizen," was killed, or said to have been killed, by an accidental shot from the Leander. Captain Whitby was proclaimed as a murderer; and the American government was not satisfied till our's had tried him for the crime. (See Nav. Chron. vol. xxviii. p. 270.)

The Nautilus's first lieutenant, Mr. Mayston, languished till the 3d of December,—a period of five months!—when a mortification of his wound carried him off. About a fortnight after the action, Lieutenant Boyce suffered amputation, very near his hip, on account of the length and complication of the fracture. The pain and danger of the operation was augmented by the proximity of the grape-shot wound. His life was subsequently despaired of; but, after a long course of hopes and fears to his numerous friends, this brave and amiable young man (or what Captain Warrington has left of him) still survives.

The damage and loss of the Peacock, as stated in Lieutenant Boyce's letter, was as much as, from the shortness of the action, and the immense disparity between the two vessels, could reasonably be expected.

Of course, the American captain, who had himself escaped unhurt, the moment he was informed of the casualties on board his prize, either visited, or sent a condoling message to, her so dreadfully mangled commander?—Reader! he did neither.—Captain Warrington,—in the words of the poor sufferer, in his memorial to the court of directors,—"proved himself totally destitute of fellow-feeling and commiseration; for, during the time he retained possession of the Nautilus," (which was till 2 o'clock the next afternoon,) "he was not once moved to make a common-place inquiry after the memorialist, in his then deplorable condition."—In an American officer, we had perhaps no right to look for the politeness of a gentleman; but we did expect the feelings of a man.

The armament of the Nautilus consisted of ten carronades, 18-pounders, and four long 9-pounders; total 14 guns. Her complement, composed of European invalid-soldiers, natives of India, British seamen, and boys, amounted to about 100: equal, perhaps, to a regular man of war's complement of 60 or 70. She measured about 180 tons. Lieutenant Boyce's account (App. No. 118.) of the Peacock's force in guns, agrees with that given at a preceding page: (p. 174:) that her complement was now larger than there stated, is not improbable. Perhaps, it was to strike terror into the minds of the lascars on board the Nautilus, as the Peacock lay alongside, that Captain Warrington made his men wear their boarding-helmets or scull-caps; (see p. 232;) but it produced no such effect.

The reader is referred to the Boxer's force, as stated at p. 132, and to the Peacock's, at p. 174, as the best means of judging of the comparative force, in broadside-weight of metal, complement, and size in tons, between the Nautilus and Peacock. The disparity there shewn, and the gallantry so conspicuous in the officers and crew of the British vessel, will remind him of the Little Belt and President; (see p. 35;) nor will he fail to contrast Lieutenant Boyce's surrender of the Nautilus, with Master-commandant Joseph Bainbridge's surrender of the Frolic, the Peacock's sister-ship. (See p. 168.) We know not where to refer the reader, for a parallel to the behaviour of Captain Warrington!

It now becomes necessary to consider the facts attending this action, or more particularly the commencement of it by Captain Warrington, as they arise out of the statements of the British officers, who had gone on board the Peacock, and remained in her during, and long after, the engagement. Captain Warrington admits, that the master-attendant, an Anjier, came on board, "*a few minutes* before coming in contact with the brig." (App. No. 118.) Mr. Macgregor, upon his oath, says: "Rather more than a quarter of an hour."—The portion of credit due to any assertion of Captain Warrington, may be measured by the concealment and falsehood, so conspicuous in his account of the Epervier's action. (See pp. 170-172.) He was guilty of falsehood fully as gross and illiberal, when he subsequently charged the Epervier's officers, with assisting the crew in embezzling the specie that was on board; but the brig's first lieutenant, as soon as he recovered from his desperate wounds, compelled Captain Warrington to recall his words.—Nothing appears in Captain Warrington's letters, about the arrival on board the Peacock of the Nautilus's master, Mr. Bartlett; and who was the "officer of the army" that came in the second boat?—Cornet White, a passenger on board the Nautilus, who requested to accompany Mr. Bartlett, in the gig, to obtain information. Captain Warrington had his reasons, no doubt, for concealing, in his official despatch, that he had any of the Nautilus's officers or crew on board his vessel.—Scarcely had Mr. Bartlett stepped upon the deck, than, without being allowed to ask a question, he was hurried below. Happily, Mr. Macgregor met with rather better success. The instant he arrived on board, he communicated to the Peacock's first lieutenant, the most authentic information of peace having been concluded between Great Britain and America, grounded on no less authority than Mr. Madison's proclamation; which Mr. Macgregor had himself received from an American ship, passing the Straits on her way to China. What effect had this communication?—Captain Warrington, whom the single word "Peace!" ought to have made pause, before he proceeded to spill the blood of his fellow-creatures, ordered Mr. Macgregor "to be taken below."—Had the master-attendant no opportunity of communicating his important intelligence to any other of the Peacock's officers?—In his way below, Mr. Macgregor met the purser, who was in superintendance of the magazine, and repeated to him what he had told his first lieutenant. The purser jocosely said:—"*I do not know how we can avoid a little brush.*" Almost immediately afterwards, Mr. Macgregor (according to Lieutenant Boyce's memorial) heard orders given, to return the ammunition into the magazine; which shewed an evident relinquishment of the intention to attack the Nautilus. But, while the orders were executing, they were countermanded; and all hostile preparations resumed. It was then that Mr. Macgregor was desired to retire into one of the side cabins; and, very soon afterwards, the firing commenced.—Captain Warrington, in his letter, to Mr. Macgregor, says: "In consequence of the information received from you, and the several different sources from which I have heard that a peace had been concluded, &c."—Here it would appear, as if Captain Warrington had received information of the peace, from other parties than those in the two boats, which, he admits, came on board just previous to the action. But the official letter says: "The next day, after receiving such intelligence as they" (the "master-attendant" and "officer of the army") had to communicate on the subject, (part of which was official,) I gave up the vessel, &c." This proves, that the source of all Captain Warrington's information on the subject, arose out of the communication of those very persons, who, as he says, "were, with their men, passed below;" and that part of such communication consisted of a copy of Mr. Madison's proclamation, is pretty evident, from the words, "part of which was official."—But, says Captain Warrington, the master-attendant and "officer of the army," "very improperly, omitted mentioning that peace existed." In addition to the positive oath of Mr. Macgregor, as to his previous conversation with the Peacock's first lieutenant and purser, it may surely be asked,—Would two officers, who had voluntarily entered on board the ship of a nation, with whom they knew a peace had just been concluded, have acted so "very improperly" as to suffer themselves to be made prisoners, without some such words as—"Peace is signed"—bursting from their lips? Even the ceremony of gagging, however quickly performed, could not have stopped an exclamation, which their personal liberty, and every thing that was dear to them as men, would prompt them to utter. The same motives would have operated upon the two boats' crews; and there cannot be a doubt, that they all gave some sort of intimation, that peace had been signed. But Captain Warrington, as the purser said, wanted to have a *little brush* with the British brig. He saw, at once, what a diminutive vessel she was; and, accordingly, ordered his men to fire into her. They did so; and how much in earnest, has already appeared. Fearful that these facts would come to light, Captain Warrington had additional reasons for endeavouring to lessen the enormity of his offence, in stating that "lascars" were the only sufferers.—Poor wretches! and were they to be butchered with impunity, because their complexion and the American captain's were of different hues?—Whose heart was the blackest, the transaction in which they lost their lives, has already shewn to the world.—Had it been the Volage, as we said before, that was in sight to-leeward, every man in the Peacock, in less than three minutes after the master-attendant and the other officers came on board, would have been informed of the peace. Captain Warrington would have approached the stranger, if he approached at all, without opening his ports, or displaying his helmets. In short, he that hectored so much in one case, would have fawned as much in the other; and the commander of the U. S. sloop Peacock would have run no risk of being, by his government, "blamed for ceasing"—or rather, for not commencing—"hostilities, without more authentic evidence, that peace had been concluded." (App. No. 118.)

The governor-general of India, the lieutenant-governors of Batavia, and of Java, and the different heads of departments throughout the British dominions in the east, also the king's navy, and the king's army, serving there, have all been unanimous in bestowing the tribute of praise upon the noble behaviour of Lieutenant Boyce. Nor has less unanimity prevailed, as to the opinion entertained of Captain Warrington. The governor-general of India, sitting in council, says: "He contemplates Captain Warrington's proceeding, as destitude of any possible extenuation."—Captain John Hayes, master-attendant at Calcutta, in his public letter, describes Captain Warrington as "the ruffian who has alike dishonoured himself, and disgraced the Columbian eagle."—It was, indeed, a dastardly act; an act, in all its circumstances, surpassing the generality of those, which, when committed by an Algerine pirate; an acknowledged *barbarian,—have* so often made our blood boil with indignation. The name of WARRINGTON will be held in execration by every man, no matter of what country, upon whom the calls of humanity have been allowed to operate.—But the people of the United States boast of their civilization; and, as to their navy in particular, see what a celebrated Massachusett's orator, and a *federalist* too, Mr. Cyrus King,—whether in earnest or burlesque it is difficult to determine,—has said of it: "A navy identified with glory itself; the heroes of which, if I may be permitted the allusion, have fixed the stars of our flag in the heavens, as a new and brilliant constellation in this western hemisphere; a sign in which we conquer; our heavenly guide to victory."—Truly, Captain Warrington himself, (as the frontispiece to the "Naval Monument" shews,) is one of these fustian "heroes;" his slaughter of the Nautilus's crew, arose, no dobut, from a "heavenly" impulse; and his attack and capture of the little vessel,—his behaviour to his wounded prisoner,—his lies,—meanness, and proceedings altogether, have added considerable "glory" to the American navy!!!

To view the affair in a national light, let us reverse the case. A British, attacks and captures an American cruizer, under circumstances, as to force and otherwise, precisely similar to those already related:—that it can be only a supposititious case, is a Briton's consolation. The moment the news reaches America, the whole eighteen United States are up in arms; the lives of the British residents are put in jeopardy; the vocabulary of abuse is exhausted upon the British nation; and a demand of reparation, accompanied by a threat, is instantly forwarded to the British government. That government, with its known magnanimity, and more upon principle than policy, disavows the act; punishes its officer; and, as in the Chesapeake's case, offers to pension the wounded, and the families of the killed.—What either government *will* do, in the case of Lieutenant Boyce and Captain Warrington, is difficult to say:—what both governments *ought* to do, rises uppermost in the breast of every honorable man acquiainted with the transaction.

CHAPTER XXI.

American list of the naval triumphs and captures on each side—Gross errors in their prize-lists detected—No account given by Americans of their own captured privateers and merchantmen—True account of British and American vessels, of all sorts, captured or destroyed—Our loss in national vessels much exaggerated—American loss in the same grossly deficient—True account stated.—American and British triumphs submitted to arithmetical calculation—Remarks thereon—Reason given for our triumphs having been so few—Majestic and new Guerriere—Nymphe and Constitution—Tenedos and Congress—Captain Broke's system of discipline—Practises on board many of the frigates and other vessels on the North American station—Concluding remarks.

The editor of the American "Sketches of the War," winds up his account of the naval transactions between the two countries, in the following words:—"Thus terminated a war of two years and eight months, in which the naval arms of the United States were fifteen, and those of Great Britain, four times, triumphant: and during which, the former lost 3 frigates, 7 sloops, and 5 smaller vessels, of war; whilst the latter lost 5 frigates, 19 sloops of war, (one of which was blown up by a land-battery,) several gun-brigs and schooners, 2 brigs cut out from under the guns of a fort; and upwards of 1500 merchantmen, captured by private-armed vessels."—We thank Mr. Thomson for furnishing so good a *text* for the present chapter; and shall make use of it accordingly.

Inverting his order, let us commence with the "1500 merchantmen." Mr. Clarke, whose work was published on the 3d of January, 1814, gave, occupying 43 pages, a list of captured British vessels, amounting to 729; "extracted from Niles's Weekly Register."—As this miscellany was held in high esteem by the Americans, Mr. Thomson, most probably, took from it his number; which agrees with Mr. Clarke's, when we consider, that the one comprized the captures made during the whole, the other, during about half, of the "two years and eight months."—The general correctness of "Niles's Weekly Register," as a prize-list, may be tolerably appreciated by the following extracts, which a very slight glance has discovered:

"266. Brig Union, from Guernsey for Grenada, sent into Old Town" (close to New York) "by the General Armstrong, privateer, & c."

"295. Packet Townsend, from Falmouth for Barbadoes, heavily armed, captured by the Tom of Baltimore, & c."

"673. Schooner Fame, of Barbadoes, laden with Madeira wine, captured by the Saratoga, & c."

"270. Brig Union, from Guernsey for St. Christopher's, sent into New York by the General Armstrong."

335. "The British king's packet Townsend, 9 guns, and 28 men, taken by the Tom of Baltimore, & c."

715. "Schooner Fame, from Barbadoes for Berbice, & c. captured by the Saratoga."

There are several items which agree in every thing but a slight difference in the name, as: "Brig Two Friends;"—"Brig Friends;"—"Packet Ann;"—"Brig Ann;"—no doubt referring to the same vessel. Even *American* vessels are included in Mr. Niles's list, thus: "698. An *American* schooner from one of the eastern ports, &c. for Halifax."—We read also: "116. Brig General Blake, under *Spanish* colours, &c." None of the captured British ships of war are left out; not even, "630. His Britannic majesty's *gun-vessel* burnt on Lake Ontario." Of what description some of the merchant-prizes are, will appear by this:—"704, 705, 706, 707, 708, 709, 710. Seven *small-craft* captured on the St. Lawrence, &c."—As some allowance, therefore, for the double entries, and the vessels not British, we may safely deduct, from Mr. Thomson's list of "1500," one-fifth; which will reduce it to 1200; and that including, not only "merchantmen," but every description of vessel, from the frigate Guerriere down to "a Nova-Scotia shallop." Mr. Thomson has not thought it worth his while, to state how many American "merchantmen" were captured by the British, during the "two years and eight months."—According to a list laid before parliament, in February, 1815, previous to the returns from Ireland, the East Indies, and the Cape of Good Hope being received, and not including captures by privateers, there were, detained in ports of the United Kingdom, and captured or destroyed, 1407 American merchant-vessels. If to this we add, "228 American privateers;" and, as appears by list No. 120 in the Appendix, 64 American national cruizers; and consider the incompleteness of the parliamentary list, for want of the full returns, as sufficient to cover any inaccuracies to be found in it, we are thus enabled to shew, the relative numbers of British and American vessels, of every description, captured or destroyed during the late war:

	No.		No.
British vessels of every description	1200	American vessels of every description,	1699

Let those who consider the numbers as less unequal than they ought to be, reflect that, while the Americans had scarcely any unarmed merchant-ships afloat, we had them darkening every sea; and that, although the force of the Americans in national cruizers, was comparatively insignificant, their privateers amounted, in number, to a third of our navy in commission.

Now for the separate consideration of the national cruizers, captured or destroyed, during the "two years and eight months." —Our "5 frigates" include, of course, the Confiance and Cyane; but the remainder of Mr. Thomson's list is quite unintelligible. The whole number of British sloops and "gun-brigs" captured or destroyed by the Americans, as well on the lakes, as on the ocean, amounts, excluding the two "frigates" Confiance and Cyane, and including the two recaptured sloops Frolic and Levant, to 16. By adding Commodore Macdonough's "two sloops of war," (see pp. 208-209,) and Mr. Thomson's "large sloop of war," (see pp. 130-131,) we have certainly his number,—"19 sloops of war." But how has he scraped together his "several gun-brigs"? The "two brigs, cut out from under the guns of a fort," must mean, the provincial vessel, Detroit, captured from the Americans, when General Hull surrendered, and the Caledonia, a trading-vessel belonging to the north-west company; magnified into a cruizer by the American editors.

Mr. Thomson says, his countrymen lost but "3 frigates" during the late war; and yet, according to his own book, besides the President, Chesapeake, and Essex, "a new first-rate frigate at Washington," and the "U. S. frigate Adams, at Penobscot," were among the number. It is singular, too, that, in his description of the loss at Washington, he mentions not a word about the frame of the 74-gun-ship, or the two old frigates, New York and Boston. His "7 sloops" should have been 9; and his "5 smaller vessels," 48. (See App. No. 120.) With such lists before them, no wonder the people of the United States firmly believe, that they have had the best of the war. Here follow the aggregate numbers, in guns, men, and tons, of national cruizers, captured or destroyed on each side; according to the lists Nos. 119 and 120 in the Appendix.

	British.					American.			
	No.	Guns	Men.	Tons.		No.	Guns	Men.	Tons.
National cruizers,	30	530	2751	10273	National cruizers,	64	660	2994	14848

This differs a trifle from Mr. Thomson's statement. A full fourth of the loss on our side, consists of the fleets on Lakes Erie and Champlain. Had prudent, or promised arrangements, been adopted by the commander-in-chief in the Canadas, both fleets would have gained victories; and the proportion between the respective guns, men, and tons, in the above statement, would then have been, like that between the number of vessels, fully as two to one. What other advantages we should have gained by the undisturbed possession, during the war, of Lakes Erie and Champlain, it is painful to contemplate.

The capture of the gale-crippled Frolic, at the first of the war, gave the Americans full information of the force, in every particular, of the largest of our brig-rigged sloops. The masts of a vessel are the first part distinguishable; and it is notorious that, during the "two years and eight months," no American sloop of war ventured to attack a British *ship-rigged* sloop of war; although the latter, as may be seen by the Cherub's force, (pp. 157-159,) was far inferior, in complement and size, and, in broadside-weight of metal, superior, by a trifle only, to the Peacock and the other American corvettes. This affords a tolerable proof, that a difference of *rig* alone, in one class of our cruizers, would have caused a sensible reduction in the list of American "triumphs."

Owing to the gallant defences made by our ships, the Americans, out of 15 captured (exclusive of 1 sunk, and 2 re-captured) British cruizers, at sea, carried only 9 into port. If we except the Vixen, which was shipwrecked, the whole of the 23 captured American cruizers, at sea, were got safe into port by the British. (See App. No. 121.) The following statement shews the aggregate number, so carried in by each party:—

	British.					American.			
	No.	Guns	Men.	Tons.		No.	Guns	Men.	Tons.
National cruizers, at sea, got in,	9	171	919	3314	National cruizers, at sea, got in,	22	330	2430	6714

When we reflect upon the immense losses which our navy annually sustains, by ship-wreck, and by that most destructive enemy, the *dry-rot,* the loss of British national cruizers to the Americans, sinks into comparative insignificance. It is the question,—Which party was most "triumphant"?—that a Briton requires to have answered. Mr. Thomson boasts, that the "naval arms of the United States, were fifteen times, triumphant."—He must here include all our unsuccessful actions with American national vessels, and, no doubt, that in which "a large sloop of war" was captured by an American privateer; (see p. 129;) but, as the conquerors, in the latter instance, were Frenchmen, Americans can have no triumph to claim. How came Mr. Thomson to omit the cases of the Landrail and Syren, and St. Lawrence and Chasseur?—Those actions were not less "triumphant to the naval arms of the United States," than any of the fourteen he has recorded. Let us, now, submit each of these boasted "triumphs," to a simple arithmetical calculation. One action, however,—the Levant and Cyane's with the Constitution,—cannot well be tried by that test; because, there, carronades were opposed to long guns, together with the weather-gage. Taking from the comparative statement of force in each of the remaining fifteen actions, the sum-total of the broadside-metal, in pounds and complement, (size in tons omitted, because not so generally applicable,) on each side, and comparing them together, we obtain—giving up all fractions to the Americans—the following results:

Americans "triumphant" over the British,

once,	when *superior* in force, as 19 to	18.
once,		16.
three times,		14.
twice,		13.
five times,		12.
once,		10.
once,		7.
once,		5.

These are the "victories,"—these the "*unparalleled* exploits," that have turned the brains of the American people, and made "heroes" (prostituted word!) more plentiful in the United States, than in the oldest nation of Europe; and these are the "victories," too, which form the basis of that extraordinary discovery,—"the moral and physical superiority of the American, over the British tar"!!

It is admitted by the American editor, that the "naval arms of Great Britain have been four times triumphant." One of the instances alluded to,—that of the Endymion and President,—shall be excepted; because, although the action was fought exclusively between those ships, the final surrender was made to a squadron. Had the Americans on board the corvette Frolic, felt the same regard for the honor of the flag, as the British in the Reindeer, of similar inferiority of force we might still have been "four times triumphant." As it is, we must be contented; and, pursuing the same method of extracting the relative force, as done in the American "triumphs," here follow the results of our three successful actions.

British "triumphant" over the Americans,

once,	when *superior* in force as 19 to	17.
once,		14.
once,	when *inferior* in force as 17 to	19.

As respects arithmetical proportion, two of these cases are allied to some of the American "triumphs;" but, in the first, the British had an inferiority in complement; which was never the case on the part of the Americans. The two first cases in their list, approach nearest in point of proportion, to the first case in our's; but, when we reflect upon the brig Frolic's previous disabled state,—the Penguin's inefficient crew,—the gallant defences made by both vessels,—the numerical superiority of the Argus's crew,—her easy capture, and whole-masted state,—we have nothing to regret, but that these important circumstances cannot be expressed in figures.

The second case of proportions, in the British, has four numerical parallels in the American list; yet it was the capture of the Essex which the editor of the "New Annual Register" brought forward, to support his humiliating position, "that, when we were victorious over the Americans by sea, we were generally indebted for our success, to a greater superiority than even they had when they were successful." (See p. 180.)

The last case in the British list,—and that which, to the encreased shame of what has just been quoted, was the first in point of date,—ranks by itself.—Does any one believe, that the American government, than the whole fifteen triumphs, would not rather have had to record, one such triumph as the Shannon's over the Chesapeake?—Then, might Americans have boasted, with reason, of "the moral and physical superiority" of their seamen; and invented, if possible, new forms of language, to express the ecstacy of their feelings. So completely, however, has the American public been deluded, by the letters of the officers, the speeches of the public orators, and the stories of the naval-history and newspaper editors, that it is a question if any alteration in their list of "triumphs," except encrease of number, could give to the American people, a higher opinion of themselves than they now entertain.

Considering what a number of British ships, after the first six or eight months of the war, were sent upon the American coast, it is not unreasonable to ask,—How happened it, that we have so few victorious actions to record?—did we ever allow the Americans an opportunity of meeting us at sea, in fair single combat?—In answering this, we will omit some few cases that occurred (pp. 103, 164-165) between the smaller classes of cruizers, and pass to the frigates, of each nation.

One case, in which there was an equality of force, and another, in which a decided inequality was against us, have been already detailed. (See pp. 162-163, 126-127.) After Commodore Rodgers's boast of his having sought, an engagement with a 74, (see pp. 160-161,) those who could not persuade themselves, that he had previously run from a 32-gun frigate and sloop, were much surprised when, in the fine new frigate Guerriere, all ready for sea, he was prevented from leaving the Delaware, by the presence of the Majestic, *razee;* carrying the same weight of metal, though, perhaps, not so great a number of men.

After Captain Broke left Boston Bay, with the Chesapeake, for Halifax, the Nymphe, Captain Epworth, took his station, and cruized there alone, for several weeks; the Tenedos, which was to have joined the Shannon on the 14th of June, having proceeded to watch the harbour of Portsmouth N. Hampshire. The Nymphe was armed like any other 46-gun frigate, except as to having two long 18s, instead of 9s, upon the forecastle, and a shifting 68-pound carronade upon the quarter-deck. While the Nymphe was thus blockading Boston, the Constitution frigate, Captain Stewart, lay in President Roads, with royal yards across, ready for sea. The Boston papers all noticed the presence of the Nymphe; one of them adding:—"She intends, if opportunity offers, to meet the Constitution, as soon as she leaves port; in which case, the Nymphe will have a decided and important advantage, as the Shannon had over the Chesapeake."—If the disparity of force, in this case, made success improbable, more decidedly gallant was the Nymphe's behaviour.

For six weeks, during the autumn of 1813, did Captain Hyde Parker, in the Tenedos 46, exert his utmost to entice out of Portsmouth, the U. S. frigate Congress, Captain Smith, then lying there, perfectly ready for sea; but some "decided and important advantage" possessed by the former, kept the latter ship at her anchors; and the citizens of New Hampshire were not doomed to be spectators of a similar scene, to that so recently viewed from the hills of Massachusetts.—Lest the reader's confidence, as to the performances of a British frigate, should not yet have quite recovered from the shock it received at the first of the war, it may be right to inform him, that a British 46-gun frigate of 1813, was half as effective again as a British 46-gun frigate of 1812. Not that the whole of the latter had neglected discipline, or were poorly manned: there were several exceptions; and among them the Shannon. Captain Broke, when the Shannon was first fitted, in 1806, had her guns laid, (a most important operation,) under his own directions. He, next, had proper sights fitted to them: in short, as Captain S. G. Pechell, in his very useful little pamphlet, says,—"nothing seems to have escaped Captain Broke in rendering his guns effective."—By constant training, the men were taught to manage them properly and were frequently practised in firing at marks. The guns, with the rammers, sponges, &c. placed in readiness, were considered as the brightest ornaments of the Shannon's decks; and there, also, might be seen, shot and powder enough for several broadsides. That the officer's comforts were, by this, somewhat abridged, Captain Broke's cabin gave the strongest proof. The Statira, Tenedos, Nymphe, Menelaus, Lacedemonian, Niemen, Armide, Seahorse, and several other 46-gun frigates on the North American station, would each have shewn, had an opportunity offered, how well she could support the character of a British frigate. Many of the 42-gun class, on the same station, were behind the former in nothing but physical force. Foremost of the 74s, in gunnery, stood the St. Domingo, Captain S. G. Pechell. Highly disciplined, also, were the Ramilies, Hogue,

Dragon, Superb, and Bulwark. Each longed for a meeting with the Independence; but either of the three last-named only, was able to cope with her.

The chief credit due to the Americans in the naval conduct of the late war, is for the high state of preparation in which their few ships were, at its commencement; especially, when compared with the generality of our own, at the same period. Considering the opinion which the Americans then entertained of a British frigate, Captain Hull deserved credit for bearing down upon the Guerriere: so would Captain Jones for attacking the Frolic, as the first sloop, had the latter not been visibly disabled. But, upon the whole, there does not appear to be one American triumph detailed in these pages, in which the Americans would not have been chargeable with cowardice, had they declined to engage.

In which of those triumphs, were the British not the assailants?—in how many of them, had they, from the moment they could distinguish the force of their opponent, any reasonable hopes of success?—To attack, *then*, is the mark of true intrepidity.—Next, come the boarding-assault, and the repulse of boarders: when did Americans attempt the former, till, by repeated vollies of great guns and musketry, the number of their enemies had dwindled to a mere handful? How American seamen shine in repelling boarders, the respective surrenders of the Chesapeake and Argus, stand as lasting monuments.—How British seamen behave, as well in boarding, as in repelling boarders, let the fate of the two last-named vessels, and the blood-stained decks of the Reindeer and Dominica, tell: there, indeed, was bottom.—In proof of which party holds most sacred the honor of the flag, take the surrender of the American ship Frolic, as a prominent (though not the only) example, on one side; on the other,—the seven killed, and four wounded commanders,—the slaughtered crews, and the shattered hulls, of our captured ships.

To conclude: the naval actions between Great Britain and the United States, being now freed from American dross, and brought fairly to the light of day, no events recorded in the naval annals of our country, reflect a brighter lustre upon the character of British seamen: and, though our losses may have been severe, we have this consolation,—that no American ship of war has, after all, captured a British ship of war, of the same force; but that the reverse has occurred, and might have occurred, again, and again,—had Americans been as willing to fight, as they still are to boast.

THE END

APPENDIX.

No. 1.

From Commodore Truxton to the American secretary of the navy.

U.S. Ship Constellation, at sea, Feb. 3, 1800.

SIR,

On the 30th ult. I left St. Christopher's with the Constellation in excellent trim, and stood to-windward, in order to gain the station for myself before the road of Guadaloupe; and at half past seven A.M. of the day following, I discovered a sail to the S.E. to which I gave chase; and for the further particulars of that chase, and for the action after it, I must beg to refer to the extracts from my journal, herewith; as being the best mode of exhibiting a just and candid account of all our transactions in the late business, which has ended in the almost entire dismantlement of the Constellation; though, I trust, to the high reputation of the American flag.

I have the honour to be, &c.

THOMAS TRUXTON.

Benjamin Stoddart, Esq. Secretary of the navy.

No. 2.

Occurrences on board the United States' ship Constellation, of 38 guns, under my command, February 1st.

Throughout these twenty-four hours, very unsettled weather: kept on our tacks, beating up under Guadaloupe; and at half-past seven A.M. the road of Basseterre bearing E. five leagues distance, saw a sail in the S.E. standing to the S.W. which from her situation I at first took for a large ship from Martinique, and hoisted English colours on giving chase, by way of inducement for her to come down and speak me; which would have saved us a long chase to-leeward of my intended cruising-ground; but, finding she did not attempt to alter her course, I examined her more minutely as we approached her, and discovered that she was a heavy French frigate, mounting at least 54 guns. I immediately gave orders for the yards, &c. to be slung with chains, top-sail-sheets, &c. stoppered, and the ship cleared, and every thing prepared for action, and hauled down the English colours. At noon the wind became light, and I observed the chase, that we had before been gaining fast on, held way with us; but I was determined to continue the pursuit, though the running to leeward I was convinced would be attended with many serious disadvantages; especially if the objects of my wishes were not gratified.

Passed two schooners standing to the northward: one of them showed American colours, and was a merchant-vessel, and the other I supposed to be of the same description.

Feb. 2, at one P.M. the wind being somewhat fresher than at the noon preceding, and appearance of its continuance, our prospect of bringing the enemy to action began again to brighten, as I perceived we were coming up with the chase fast, and every inch of canvass being set that could be of service, except the bag-reefs, which I kept in the top-sails, in case the chase finding an escape from our thunder impracticable, should haul on a wind, and give us fair battle; but this did not prove to be her commander's intention. I however got within hail of him at eight P.M. hoisted our ensign, and had the candles in the battle-lanterns all lighted, and the large trumpet in the lee-gangway ready to speak to him, and to demand the surrender of his ship to the United States of America; but he, at that instant, commenced a fire from his stern and quarter guns, directed at our rigging and spars. No parley then being necessary, I sent my principal aid-de-camp. Mr. Vandyke, to the different officers commanding divisions on the main battery, to repeat strictly my orders, before given, not to throw away a single charge of powder, but to take good aim, and fire directly into the hull of the enemy; and load principally with two round shot, and now and then with a round shot and a stand of grape, &c.; to encourage the men at their quarters; to cause or suffer no noise or confusion whatever; but to load and fire as fast as possible, when it could be done with certain effect. These orders being given, in a few moments I gained a position on his weather-quarter, that enabled us to return effectually his salute; and thus a close and as sharp an action as ever was fought between two frigates commenced, and continued until within a few minutes of one A.M. when the enemy's fire was completely silenced, and he was again sheering off.

It was at this moment that I considered him as my prize, and was trimming in the best manner I could, my much shattered sails; when I found my main-mast was totally unsupported by rigging, every shroud being shot away, and some of them in several places, that even stoppers were useless, and could not be supplied with effect. I then gave orders to the officers to send the men up from the gun-deck to endeavour to secure it, in order that we might go along-side of the enemy again as soon as possible; but every effort was in vain, for the main-mast went over the side in a few minutes after, and carried with it the top-men, among whom was an amiable young gentleman, who commanded the main-top, Mr. James Jervis, son of James Jervis, Esq. of New York. It seems this young gentleman was apprised of the mast going, in a few minutes, by an old seaman; but he had already so much of the principle of an officer ingrafted on his mind, not to leave his quarters on any account, that, he told the man, if the mast went they must go with it, which was the case, and only one of them was saved.

I regret much his loss, as a promising young officer, and amiable young man, as well as on account of a long intimacy that has subsisted between his father and myself, but have great satisfaction in finding that I have lost no other, and only two or three slightly wounded, out of 39 killed and wounded: 14 of the former, and 25 of the latter.

As soon as the main-mast went, every effort was made to clear the wreck from the ship, as soon as possible; which was effected in about an hour. It being impossible to pursue the enemy, and as her security was then the great object, I immediately bore away for Jamaica, for repairs, &c. finding it impossible to reach a friendly port in any of the islands to-windward.

I should be wanting in common justice, was I to omit to journalize the steady attention to order, and the great exertion and bravery of all my officers, seamen, and marines, in this action; many of whom I had sufficiently tried before on a similar occasion, and all their names are recorded in the muster-roll I sent to the secretary of the navy, dated the 19th of December last, signed by myself.

All hands are employed in repairing the damages sustained in the action, so far as to get the ship into Jamaica as soon as possible.

THOMAS TRUXTON

No. 3.

The French captain's letter.

Corfu, September 8, 1798.

I have the pleasure to announce to you my arrival at Corfu. I have been here for some days past, having brought in the English ship Leander of 74 guns, which I met near the isles of Goza and Candia, about a league from the shore. This ship has been sent to carry despatches from *Bequiers** Road, where the English had attacked us on the 1st of August. We were at anchor, but in a position certainly not very secure for our squadron; of this bad situation they took advantage, and having placed us between two fires, a most dreadful slaughter took place, the ships not being at a greater distance than pistol shot, and at anchor. From the circumstance of the wind, with relation to the English ships, we should have been superior in the contest, if l'Orient, our admiral's ship, had not blown up in the air, which threw us all into disorder; as, to avoid the flames that had already reached le Tonnant, every vessel was obliged to shift its station. Having, however, placed my ship in a situation favourable to the direction of its cannon, I fought her until three in the morning of the following day to that in which, at ten in the evening, l'Orient blew up.

* *Aboukir.*

By a singular accident, I missed having a broadside at Captain Darby, who sailed with us in the last war from the Cape of Good Hope to Cadiz. His ship, the Bellerophon, of 74 guns, sailed past me about half-past ten in the evening, having lost her main-mast and mizen-mast. I fired three of our shots at her, which carried away the mast she was hoisting, and struck away one of the lanterns off the poop.

I immediately ordered one of my officers to go in pursuit of, and to bring on board of my ship the captain of this ship; but in half an hour afterwards, when I was about to send my boat on board her, the fire from several English ships being directed against me, compelled me rather to think of answering their guns, than of taking possession of the other ship; and the slow manner in which the officer whom I had despatched, proceeded to execute my orders, was the cause of my failing to take possession of this other ship.

As to the Leander, I was obliged to fight with her for nearly four hours and three-quarters. She carries 74 guns, 24 and 30-pounders on her lower deck, and 12-pounders on her upper. I should have made myself master of her in less than an hour, had we been at close fighting; during the engagement we boarded her, and I should have succeeded in making prize of her by boarding, if I had a more active crew.

LEJOILLE, jun.

No. 4.

From Captain Hull to the American secretary of the navy.

U.S. Frigate Constitution, August 28, 1812.

Sir,

The enclosed account of the affair between the President, Commodore Rodgers, and the British frigate Belvidera, was taken by an officer on board the Belvidera, and fell into my hands by accident. It clearly proves that she only escaped the commodore by superior sailing, after having lightened her, and the President being very deep.

As much has been said on this subject, if Commodore Rodgers has not arrived, to give you his statement of the affair, if it meet your approbation I should be pleased to have this account published to prevent people from making up their minds hastily, as I find them willing to do.

I am confident, could the commodore have got alongside the Belvidera, she would have been his in less than one hour.

I have the honor to be, &c.

ISAAC HULL.

The Hon. Paul Hamilton, &c.

No. 5.

An account of the proceedings of his majesty's ship Belvidera, Richard Byron, Esq. captain, 23d day of June, 1812.

A.M. at 4, 40, Nantucket shoal, saw several sail bearing S.W.; made sail towards them; at 6, 30, they bore S.W. by S.; made them out to be three frigates, one sloop, and one brig of war, standing to the S.E. under a press of sail. Observed them to make signals, and haul up in chase of us, hauling down their steering-sails, in a confused and irregular manner. Tacked ship, and made the private signal, which was not answered; made all sail possible, N.E. by E. At 8, moderate and fine weather, the headmost ship of the chase, S.S.W. ½ W. apparently gaining ground on us at times, and leaving her consorts. At 11, 30, hoisted our colours and pendant; the chase hoisted American colours; two of them hoisted commodore's broad pendants. At noon the commodore and the second headmost ship of the chase S.W. ¾ W. about 2¾ of a mile, Nantucket shoal N. 4° E. 48 miles, moderate and fine weather; cleared ship for action, commodore of chase gaining, the other ships dropping; observed the chase pointing her guns at us. At 3, 40, the commodore fired the three shot, one of which struck the rudder-coat, and came into the after-gun-room; the other two came into the upper or captain's cabin, one of which struck the muzzle of the larboard chase-gun, the other went through the beam under the skylight, killed William Gould, (seaman), wounded John Hill, (armourer,) mortally, Joseph Lee, (seaman,) severely, George Maclen, (ship's carpenter,) badly, Lieutenant Bruce, James Kelly, and James Larmont, (seamen,) slightly. At 3, 45, commenced firing with our stern-guns; shot away her larboard lower steering-sail; keeping our ship a steady course N.E. and by E. At 4, the chase bore up, and fired her larboard broadside, which cut our rigging and sails much, the long bolts, breeching-hooks, and breechings, of guns and carronades, frequently breaking; (by one of which Captain Byron was severely wounded in the left thigh;) all of which was instantly replaced. Kept up a constant fire, which was returned by our opponent with bow-chase-guns, and at times by her broadsides; which, by her superiority of sailing, she was enabled to do, till 6, 45, when we cut away our square sheet, and small bower anchors, barge, yawl, and jolly-boats, and started 14 tons of water. We then gained on him, when he bore up, and fired three broadsides, part of which fell short of us. At 7, opponent ceased firing, and the second frigate commenced, but finding her shot fall short, ceased also. Employed fishing our cross-jack-yard, and main-top-mast, (both badly wounded,) knotting and splicing our rigging, which was much cut and damaged. At 11, altered our course to E. by S. ½ S. and lost sight of our opponents.

No. 6.

Extract from the journal of Commodore Rodgers.

June 23d—Pleasant breezes from N.W. to W.N.W.; at 3 A.M. spoke an American brig from Madeira, bound to New York, the master of which informed me, that four days before, in lat. 36°, long. 67°, he passed a fleet of British merchantmen, under convoy of a frigate and a brig, steering to the eastward. I now perceived that this was the convoy of which I had received intelligence, prior to leaving New York, and shaped our course east in pursuit of them. At 6 A.M. Nantucket shoal, bearing N.E. distant 35 miles, saw a large sail in N.E. standing to S.W. which was soon discovered to be a frigate. The signal was made for a general chase, when the several vessels of the squadron took in their studding sails, and made all sail by the wind, on the starboard tack, in pursuit. At a quarter before 7, the chase tacked, made all sail, and stood from us, by the wind on the same tack. At half-past 8, he made signals, when, perceiving we were coming up with him, he edged away a point or thereabouts, and set his top-gallant studding-sails. At 11, cleared ship for action, in the expectation that we would soon be up with the chase; the breeze about this time, however, began to incline more to the westward, and became lighter, which I soon discovered was comparatively an advantage to our opponent. At a quarter past 1 P.M. the chase hoisted English colours. At 2, the wind veered to the W.S.W. and became lighter. At 20 minutes past 4, having got within gun-shot of the enemy, when, perceiving that he was training his chase-guns, and in the act, as I supposed, of firing, that the breeze was decreasing, and we now sailed so nearly alike, that to afford him an opportunity of doing the first injury to our spars and rigging, would be to enable him to effect his escape, I gave orders to commence a fire with the bow-chase guns at his spars and rigging, in the hope of crippling one or the other, so far as to enable us to get alongside. The fire from our bow-chase guns he instantly returned, with those of his stern, which was now kept up by both ships without intermission, until 30 minutes past 4 P.M. when one of the President's chase guns burst, and killed and wounded 16 persons, among the latter myself. This was not, however, the most serious injury; as, by the bursting of the gun, and the explosion of the passing-box, from which it was served with powder, both the main and forecastle decks, near the gun, were so much shattered, as to prevent the use of the chase gun, on that side, for some time. Our main-deck guns being single shotted, I now gave orders to put our helm to starboard, and fire the starboard broadside, in the expectation of disabling some of her spars, but did not succeed, although I could discover that his rigging had sustained considerable damage, and that he had received some injury in the stern.

I now endeavoured, by altering course half a point to port, and wetting our sails, to gain a more effectual position on his starboard quarter, but soon found myself losing ground. After this, a similar attempt was made at his larboard quarter, but without any better success, as the wind, at this time, being very light, and both sailing so nearly alike, that, by making an angle of only half a point from the course he steered, enabled him to augment his distance. No hope was now left of bringing him to close action, except that derived from being to-windward, and the expectation the breeze might favour us first. I accordingly gave orders to steer directly after him, and to keep our bow-chase guns playing on his spars and rigging, until our broadside would more effectually reach him. At 5, finding from the advantage his stern guns gave him, that he had done considerable injury to our sails and rigging, and being within point-blank shot, I gave orders to put the helm to starboard, and fire our main-deck guns. This broadside did some farther damage to his rigging, and I could perceive that his fore-top-sail-yard was wounded, but the sea was so very smooth, and the wind so light, that the injury done was not such as materially to affect his sailing. After this broadside, our course was instantly renewed in his wake, under a galling fire from his stern-chase guns, directed at our spars and rigging, and continued until half-past 6; at which time, being within reach of his grape, and finding our sails, rigging, and several spars, particularly the main-yard, which had little to support it except the lifts and braces, much disabled, I again gave orders to luff across his stern, and give him a couple of broadsides.

The enemy, at this time, finding himself so hardly pressed, and seeing, while in the act of firing, our head-sails to lift, and supposing the ship had, in a measure, lost the effect of her helm, gave a broad yaw, with the intention of bringing his broadside to bear; finding the President, however, answered her helm too quick for his purpose, he immediately resumed his course, and precipitately fired his four after main-deck guns, on the starboard side, although they did not bear upon us at the time by 25 or 30 degrees, and he now commenced lightening his ship, by throwing overboard all his boats, waste-anchors, &c. and by this means was enabled, by a quarter before 7, to get so far a-head, as to prevent our bow-chase guns doing execution, and I now perceived, with more mortification than words can express, that there was little or no chance left of getting within gun-shot of the enemy again. Under every disadvantage of disabled spars, sails, and rigging, I, however, continued the chase with all the sail we could set, until half-past 11 P.M. when perceiving he had gained upwards of three miles, and not the slightest prospect left of coming up with him, I gave up the pursuit, and made the signal to the other ships as they came up to do the same.

During the first of the chase, while the breeze was fresh, and sailing by the wind, I thought the whole of the squadron gained upon the enemy. It was soon discoverable, however, the advantage he acquired by sailing large, and this, I conceived, he must have derived in so great a degree by starting his water, as I could perceive, upwards of an hour before we came within gun-shot, water running out of his scuppers.

While in chase it was difficult to determine whether our own situation, or that of the other vessels of the squadron, was the most unpleasant. The superior sailing of the President was not such, off the wind, as to enable us to get upon the broadside of the enemy. The situation of the others was not less irksome, as not even the headmost, which was the Congress, was able, at any time, to get within less than two gun-shots' distant, and even at that but for a very little time.

No. 7.

From Captain Porter to the American secretary of the navy.

At sea, August 17, 1812.

SIR,

I have the honor to inform you, that on the 13th his Britannic majesty's sloop of war Alert, Captain T. L. P. Laugharne, ran down on our weather quarter, gave three cheers, and commenced an action, (if so trifling a skirmish deserves the name,) and after eight minutes firing struck her colours, with seven feet water in the hold, much cut to pieces, and three men wounded.

I need not inform you that the officers and crew of the Essex behaved as I trust all Americans will in such cases, and it is only to be regretted, that so much zeal and activity could not have been displayed on an occasion that would have done them more honor. The Essex has not received the slightest injury.

The Alert was out for the purpose of taking the Hornet!

I have the honor to be, &c.

D. PORTER.

Hon. Paul Hamilton, secretary of the navy.

No. 8.

From Captain Dacres to Vice-Admiral Sawyer.

Boston, September 7, 1812.

SIR,

I am sorry to inform you of the capture of H.M. late ship Guerriere, by the American frigate Constitution, after a severe action, on the 19th of August, in latitude 40° 20′ N. and longitude 55° W. At 2 P.M. being by the wind on the starboard tack, we saw a sail on our weather beam, bearing down on us. At 3, made her out to be a man of war; beat to quarters, and prepared for action. At 4, she closing fast, wore to prevent her raking us. At 10 minutes past 4, hoisted our colours, and fired several shot at her: at 20 minutes past 4, she hoisted her colours, and returned our fire; wore several times to avoid being raked, exchanging broadsides. At 5, she closed on our starboard beam, both keeping up a heavy fire, and steering free, his intention being evidently to cross our bow. At 20 minutes past 5, our mizen-mast went over the starboard quarter, and brought the ship up in the wind; the enemy then placed himself on our larboard bow, raking us, a few only of our bow-guns bearing, and his grape and riflemen sweeping our deck. At 40 minutes past 5, the ship not answering her helm, he attempted to lay us on board; at this time Mr. Grant, who commanded the forecastle, was carried below, badly wounded. I immediately ordered the marines and boarders from the main-deck; the master was at this time shot through the knee, and I received a severe wound in the back. Lieutenant Kent was leading on the boarders, when the ship coming to, we brought some of our bow-guns to bear on her, and had got clear of our opponent; when, at 20 minutes past 6, our fore and main-masts went over the side, leaving the ship a perfect unmanageable wreck. The frigate shooting a-head, I was in hopes to clear the wreck, and get the ship under command to renew the action; but just as we had cleared the wreck, our spritsail-yard went, and the enemy having rove new braces, &c. wore round within pistol-shot, to rake us, the ship laying in the trough of the sea, and rolling her main-deck guns under water, and all attempts to get her before the wind being fruitless: when, calling my few remaining officers together, they were all of opinion that any further resistance would only be a needless waste of lives, I ordered, though reluctantly, the colours to be struck.

The loss of the ship is to be ascribed to the early fall of the mizen-mast, which enabled our opponent to choose his position. I am sorry to say we suffered severely in killed and wounded; and mostly whilst she lay on our bow, from her grape and musketry; in all, 15 killed, and 63 wounded, many of them severely. None of the wounded officers quitted the deck till the firing ceased.

The frigate proved to be the United States' ship Constitution, of 30 24-pounders on her main-deck, and 24 32-pounders, and two 18-pounders on her upper deck, and 476 men. Her loss in comparison with our's is trifling, about 20; the first lieutenant of marines and 8 killed; and first lieutenant, and master of the ship, and 11 men wounded; her lower masts badly wounded, and stern much shattered; and very much cut up about her rigging.

The Guerriere was so cut up, that all attempts to get her in would have been useless. As soon as the wounded were got out of her, they set her on fire; and I feel it my duty to state, that the conduct of Captain Hull and his officers to our men, has been that of a brave enemy; the greatest care being taken to prevent our men losing the smallest trifle, and the greatest attention being paid to the wounded; who, through the attention and skill of Mr. Irvine, surgeon, I hope will do well.

I hope, though success has not crowned our efforts, you will not think it presumptuous in me to say, the greatest credit is due to the officers and ship's company for their exertions, particularly when exposed to the heavy raking fire of the enemy. I feel particularly obliged for the exertions of Lieutenant Kent, who, though wounded early by a splinter, continued to assist me. In the second lieutenant, the service has suffered a severe loss. Mr. Scott, the master, though wounded, was particularly attentive, and used every exertion in clearing the wreck, as did the warrant-officers. Lieutenant Nicholl, of the royal marines, and his party, supported the honorable character of their corps, and they suffered severely. I must recommend Mr. Snow, master's mate, who commanded the foremost main-deck guns, in the absence of Lieutenant Pullman, (and the whole after the fall of Lieutenant Ready,) to your protection, he having received a severe contusion from a splinter. I must point out Mr. Garley, acting purser, to your notice, who volunteered his services on deck, and commanded the after quarter-deck guns, and was particularly active, as well as Mr. Bannister, midshipman.

I hope, in considering the circumstances, you will think the ship entrusted to my charge, properly defended. The unfortunate loss of our masts; the absence of the third lieutenant, second lieutenant of marines, three midshipmen, and 24 men, considerably weakened our crew; and we only mustered at quarters 244 men and 19 boys, on coming into action; the enemy had such an advantage from his marines and riflemen, when close, and his superior sailing enabled him to choose his distance.

I enclose herewith a list of killed and wounded on board the Guerriere; and have the honour to be, &c.

Vice-admiral Sawyer. JAS. R. DACRES.

List of officers, seamen, and marines, killed and wounded on board H.M.S. Guerriere, &c. (of which the names are given, comprising,)

Killed—The second lieutenant, 7 petty-officers and able seamen, 3 ordinary seamen, 1 landman, 1 serjeant and 2 privates of marines:—total 15.

Wounded dangerously—7 petty-officers and able seamen, 5 ordinary seamen, and 5 private marines:—total 17.

Wounded severely—The captain, master, 2 master's mates, 5 petty-officers and able seamen, 4 ordinary seamen, 1 landman, and 5 private marines:—total 19.

Wounded slightly—The first lieutenant, 1 midshipman, 9 petty-officers and able seamen, 3 landmen, 1 boy, and 3 private marines:—total, 18.

15 killed, 63 wounded:—total 78.

JAMES R. DACRES,
JOHN IRVINE, surgeon of the navy.

No. 9.

From Commodore Hull, to the American secretary of the navy.

United States' frigate Constitution,
off Boston Light, Aug. 30, 1812.

Sir,

I have the honour to inform you, that, on the nineteenth instant, at two P.M. being in latitude 41° 42′, and longitude 55° 48′, with the Constitution under my command, a sail was discovered from the mast-head, bearing E. by S. or E.S.E. but at such a distance we could not tell what she was. All sail was instantly made in chase; and soon found we came up with her. At 3 P.M. could plainly see that she was a ship on the starboard-tack, under an easy sail, close on a wind; at half-past 3 P.M. made her out to be a frigate: continued the chase until we were within about three miles, when I ordered the light sails to be taken in, the courses hauled up, and the ship cleared for action. At this time the chase had backed his main-top-sail, waiting for us to come down. As soon as the Constitution was ready for action, I bore down with an intention to bring him to close action immediately; but on our coming within gun-shot, she gave us a broadside and filled away, and wore, giving us a broadside on the other tack, but without effect—her shot falling short. She continued wearing and manuvering for about three quarters of an hour, to get a raking position; but finding she could not, she bore up, and run under her top-sails and jib, with the wind on the quarter. I immediately made sail to bring the ship up with her; and 5 minutes before 6 P.M. being alongside within half pistol-shot, we commenced a heavy fire from all our guns, double-shotted with round and grape, and so well directed were they, and so warmly kept up, that in 15 minutes his mizen-mast went by the board, and his main-yard in the slings, and the hull, rigging, and sails, very much torn to pieces. The fire was kept up with equal warmth for 15 minutes longer, when his main-mast and fore-mast went, taking with them every spar excepting the bowsprit. On seeing this, we ceased firing; so that in 30 minutes after we got fairly alongside the enemy she surrendered, and had not a spar standing; and her hull, both below and above water, so shattered, that a few more broadsides must have carried her down.

After informing you that so fine a ship as the Guerriere, commanded by an able and experienced officer, had been totally dismasted, and otherwise cut to pieces, so as to make her not worth towing into port, in the short space of 30 minutes, you can have no doubt of the gallantry and good conduct of the officers and ship's company I have the honour to command. It only remains, therefore, for me to assure you, that they all fought with great bravery; and it gives me great pleasure to say, that, from the smallest boy in the ship to the oldest seaman, not a look of fear was seen. They all went into action giving three cheers, and requesting to be laid close alongside the enemy.

Enclosed, I have the honor to send you a list of killed and wounded on board the Constitution, and a report of the damages she has sustained; also a list of killed and wounded on board the enemy, with his quarter bill, &c.

I have the honor to be, &c.

The Hon. Paul Hamilton, Esq. &c. ISAAC HULL.

Return of killed and wounded on board the U.S. frigate Constitution, Isaac Hull, Esq. captain.

Killed—1 lieutenant of marines, and 6 seamen:—total, 7.
Wounded—2 officers, 4 seamen, and 1 marine:—total, 7.
Total killed and wounded, 14.

List of killed and wounded on board the Guerriere.
(Same as given in Captain Dacres' letter.)

Missing—Lieutenant John Pullman, Mr. Gaston, and 22 seamen and marines.

(Report of Constitution's "damages," and Guerriere's "quarter-bill," *not published.*)

No. 10.

"Particulars of the late action between the U.S. frigate Constitution, and the British frigate Guerriere; communicated by an officer on board the Constitution." *Am. Paper.*

Lat. 41° 42′ N. long. 55° 33′ W. Thursday, August 20, (*nautical time*,) fresh breeze from N.W. and cloudy; at 2 P.M. discovered a vessel to the southward, made all sail in chase; at 3, perceived the chase to be a ship on the starboard tack, close hauled to the wind; hauled S.S.W. At half-past 3, made out the chase to be a frigate; at 4, coming up with the chase very fast; at a quarter before 5, the chase laid her main-top-sail to the mast; took in our top-gallant-sails, stay-sails, and flying-jib; took a second reef in the top-sails; hauled the courses up; sent the royal-yards down, and got all clear for action; beat to quarters, on which the crew gave three cheers. At 5, the chase hoisted three English ensigns; at 5 minutes past 5, the enemy commenced firing; at 29 minutes past 5, set our colours, one at each mast-head, and one at the mizen-peak, and began firing on the enemy, and continued to fire occasionally, he wearing very often, and we manuvring to close with him, and avoid being raked. At 6, set the main-top-gallant-sail, the enemy having bore up; at five minutes past 6, brought the enemy to close action, standing before the wind; at fifteen minutes past 6, the enemy's mizen-mast fell over on the starboard-side; at twenty minutes past 6, finding we were drawing a-head of the enemy, luffed short round his bows to rake him; at twenty-five minutes past 6, the enemy fell on board of us, his bowsprit foul of our mizen-rigging. We prepared to board, but immediately after his fore and main-masts went by the board, and it was deemed unnecessary. Our cabin had taken fire from his guns; but was soon extinguished without material injury. At half-past 6, shot a-head of the enemy, when the firing ceased on both sides; he making the signal of submission by firing again to leeward. Set fore-sail and main-sail, and hauled to the eastward to repair damages; all our braces, and much of our standing and running rigging, and some of our spars, being shot away. At 7, wore ship, and stood under the lee of the prize; sent our boat on board, which returned at 8, with Captain Dacres, late of his Britannic majesty's ship Guerriere, mounting 49 carriage-gungs, and manned with 302 men. Got our boats out, and kept them employed in removing the prisoners and baggage from the prize to our ship. Sent a surgeon's-mate to assist in attending the wounded; wearing ship occasionally to keep in the best position to receive the boats. At 20 minutes before 2 A.M. discovered a sail off the larboard beam, standing to the S.; saw all clear for another action; at 3, the sail stood off again. At day-light was hailed by the lieutenant on board the prize, who informed he had four feet of water in the hold, and that she was in a sinking condition. All hands employed in removing the prisoners, and repairing our own damage, through the remainder of the day. Friday, the 21st, (*nautical time* as before,) commenced with light breezes from the northward, and pleasant; our boats and crew still employed as before. At 3, made the signal of recall for our boats, (having received all the prisoners,) they immediately left her on fire, and at past 3 she blew up. [*Here follows the loss on each side, as given already.*]

No. 11.

Captain Dacres' address to the court on his trial.

Mr. president, and gentlemen of the court,

By my letter to Admiral Sawyer, and the narrative of the principal officers, I trust that you will be satisfied that every exertion was used in defending the ship, as long as there was the smallest prospect of resistance being of any use. In my letter, where I mention the boarders being called, it was my intention, after having driven back the enemy, to have boarded in return; and in consequence, I ordered down the first lieutenant on the main-deck, to send every body up from the guns; but finding his deck filled with men, and every preparation made to receive us, it would have been almost impossible to succeed. I ordered the men down to their quarters, and desired Mr. Kent to direct part of his attention to the main-deck, the lieutenant being killed. The main-mast fell without being struck by a single shot—the heart of the mast being decayed, and it was carried away solely by the weight of the fore-mast; and, though every thing was done, we could not succeed in getting the ship under command; and on the enemy wearing round to rake us, without our being able to make any resistance, and after having used every exertion to the best of my abilities, I found myself obliged to order the colours to be struck, which, nothing but the unmanageable state of the ship, (she lying a perfect wreck,) could ever have induced me to do; conceiving it was my duty not to sacrifice uselessly the lives of the men, without any prospect of success, or of benefit to their country.

On the larboard side, about thirty shot had taken effect, about five sheets of copper down; and the mizen-mast had knocked a large hole under her starboard counter; and she was so completely shattered, that the enemy found it impossible to refit her sufficiently to attempt carrying her into port, and they set fire to her as soon as they got the wounded out. What considerably weakened my quarters was, permitting the Americans belonging to the ship to quit their quarters, on the enemy hoisting the colours of that nation; which, though it deprived me of the men, I thought was my duty.

I felt much shocked, when on board the Constitution, to find a large proportion of that ship's company British seamen; and many of whom I recognized as having been foremost in the attempt to board.

Notwithstanding the unlucky issue of this affair, such confidence have I in the exertions of the officers and men who belonged to the Guerriere; and I am so well aware that the success of my opponent was owing to fortune, that it is my earnest wish, and would be the happiest period of my life, to be once more opposed to the Constitution, with them under my command, in a frigate of similar force to the Guerriere.

I cannot help noticing, that the attachment of the ship's company, in general, to the service of their king and country, reflects on them the highest credit; for, although every art was used to encourage them to desert, and to inveigle them into the American service, by high bounties and great promises, by the American officers, in direct contradiction to the declaration to me that they did not wish such a thing, only eight Englishmen have remained behind, two only of which number have volunteered for their service.

Leaving the characters of my officers and ship's company, as well as my own, to the decision of this honorable court, the justice of whose sentence no person can presume to question, I close my narrative, craving indulgence for having taken up so much of their time.

No. 12.

Sentence.

Having attended to the whole of the evidence, and also to the defence of Captain Dacres, the court agreed,—that the surrender of the Guerriere was proper, in order to preserve the lives of her valuable remaining crew; and that her being in that lamentable situation was from the accident of her masts going, which was occasioned more by their defective state than from the fire of the enemy, though so greatly superior in guns and men. The court do, therefore, unanimously and honourably acquit the said Captain Dacres, the officers and crew, of his majesty's late ship the Guerriere, and they are hereby honourably acquitted according. The court, at the same time, feel themselves called upon to express the high sense they entertain of the conduct of the ship's company in general, when prisoners, but more particularly of those who withstood the attempts made to shake their loyalty, by offering them high bribes to enter into the land and sea service of the enemy, and they will represent their merit to the commander in chief.

No. 13.

From Captain Whinyates to Admiral Warren.

H.M.S. Poictiers, at sea,
Oct. 23, 1812.

Sir,

It is with the most bitter sorrow and distress I have to report to your excellency the capture of H.M. brig Frolic, by the ship Wasp, belonging to the United States of America, on the 18th instant.

Having under convoy the homeward-bound trade from the bay of Honduras, and being in latitude 36° N. and 64° W. on the night of the 17th, we were overtaken by a most violent gale of wind, in which the Frolic carried away her main-yard, lost her top-sails, and sprung the main-top-mast. On the morning of the 18th, as we were repairing the damages sustained in the storm, and re-assembling the scattered ships, a suspicious ship came in sight, and gave chase to the convoy.

The merchant ships continued their voyage before the wind under all sail; the Frolic dropped a-stern, and hoisted Spanish colours, in order to decoy the stranger under her guns, and to give time for the convoy to escape. About 10 o'clock, both vessels being within hail, we hauled to the wind, and the battle began. The superior fire of our guns gave every reason to expect its speedy termination in our favor; but the gaff-head-braces being shot away, and there being no sail on the main-mast, the brig became unmanageable, and the enemy succeeded in taking a position to rake her, while she was unable to bring a gun to bear.

After lying some time exposed to a most destructive fire, she fell with her bowsprit betwixt the enemy's main and mizen rigging, still unable to return his fire.

At length the enemy boarded, and made himself master of the brig, every individual officer being wounded, and the greater part of the men either killed or wounded, there not being 20 persons remaining unhurt.

Although I shall ever deplore the unhappy issue of this contest, it would be great injustice to the merits of the officers and crew, if I failed to report that their bravery and coolness are deserving of every praise; and I am convinced, if the Frolic had not been crippled in the gale, I should have had to make a very different report to your excellency. The Wasp was taken, and the Frolic re-captured the same afternoon, by H.M.S. the Poictiers. Being separated from them, I cannot transmit, at present, a list of killed and wounded. Mr. Charles M'Kay, the first lieutenant, and Mr. Stephens, the master, have died of their wounds.

I have the honor to be, &c.

T. WHINYATES.

To the Right Hon. Sir J. B. Warren, Bart, &c.

No. 14

From Captain Jones to the American secretary of the navy.

New York, Nov. 24, 1812.

SIR,

I here avail myself of the first opportunity of informing you of the occurrences of our cruize, which terminated in the capture of the Wasp on the 18th of October, by the Poictiers, of 74 guns, while a wreck, from damages received in an engagement with the British sloop of war Frolic, of 22 guns, 16 of them 32lb. carronades, and four 12-pounders on the main deck, and two 12-pounders, carronades, on the top-gallant-forecastle, making her superior in force to us by four 12-pounders. The Frolic had struck to us, and was taken possession of about two hours before our surrendering to the Poictiers.

We had left the Delaware on the 13th; the 15th, had a heavy gale, in which we lost our jib-boom and two men. Half-past 11, on the night of the 17th, in latitude 37° N. and longitude 65° W. we saw several sail, two of them apparently very large; we stood from them some time, then shortened sail, and steered the remainder of the night the course we had perceived them on. At day-light on Sunday the 18th, we saw them a-head; gave chase, and soon discovered them to be a convoy of six sail, under the protection of a sloop of war; four of them large ships, mounting from 16 to 18 guns. At 32 minutes past 11 A.M. we engaged the sloop of war, having first received her fire, at the distance of 50 or 60 yards, which space we gradually lessened, until we laid her on board, after a well supported fire of 43 minutes; and although so near while loading the last broadside, that our rammers were shoved against the sides of the enemy, our men exhibited the same alacrity which they had done during the whole of the action. They immediately surrendered upon our gaining their forecastle, so that no loss was sustained on either side after boarding.

Our main-top-mast was shot away between four and five minutes from the commencement of the firing, and falling together with the main-top-sail-yard, across the larboard fore and fore-top-sail-braces, rendered our head-yards unmanageable the remainder of the action. At 8 minutes the gaft and mizen-top-gallant-mast came down, and at 20 minutes from the beginning of the action, every brace, and most of the rigging was shot away. A few minutes after separating from the Frolic, both her masts fell upon deck; the main-mast going close by the deck, and the fore-mast 12 or 15 feet above it.

The courage and exertions of the officers and crew fully answered my expectations and wishes. Lieutenant Biddle's active conduct contributed much to our success, by the exact attention paid to every department during the engagement, and the animating example he afforded the crew by his intrepidity. Lieutenants Rodgers, Booth, and Mr. Rapp, shewed, by the incessant fire from their divisions, that they were not to be surpassed in resolution or skill. Mr. Knight, and every other officer, acted with a courage and promptitude highly honorable, and I trust have given assurances that they may be relied on whenever their services may be required.

I could not ascertain the exact loss of the enemy, as many of the dead lay buried under the masts and spars that had fallen upon deck, which two hours exertion had not sufficiently removed. Mr. Biddle, who had charge of the Frolic, states, that from what he saw, and from information from the officers, the number of killed must have been about 30, and that of the wounded about 40 or 50. Of her killed is her first lieutenant, and sailing-master; of the wounded, Captain Whinyates, and the second lieutenant.

We had five killed and five wounded, as per list: the wounded are recovering. Lieutenant Claxton, who was confined by sickness, left his bed a little previous to the engagement; and though too indisposed to be at his division, remained upon deck, and showed, by his composed manner of noticing its incidents, that we had lost by his illness the services of a brave officers.

I am respectfully your's,

JACOB JONES.

Hon. Paul Hamilton, secretary of the navy.

No. 15.

From Lieutenant J. Biddle, late of the Wasp.

H.B.M. ship Poictiers, 74, at sea, Oct. 21, 1812.

MY DEAR FATHER,

The fortune of war has placed us in the hands of the enemy. We have been captured by this ship, after having ourselves captured his Britannic majesty's brig Frolic.

The Frolic was superior in force to us; she mounted 18 32lb. carronades, and two long nines. The Wasp, you know, has only 16 carronades. The action lasted 43 minutes; we had 5 killed, and the slaughter on board the Frolic was dreadful. We are bound into Bermuda. I am quite unhurt.

In haste, &c.

J. BIDDLE.

No. 16.

Sentence of court of inquiry on the commander of the Wasp.

The court having heard the statement and evidence in this case, and having maturely considered the circumstances attending the surrender of the U.S. ship of war the Wasp, to his Britannic majesty's ship of the line the Poictiers, of 74 guns; particularly the crippled and disabled state of the Wasp from the brilliant and successful action with his Britannic majesty's ship the Frolic, of superior force to the Wasp, about two hours before the Poictiers hove in sight, and the force and condition of the Poictiers, which made it useless for them to contend, and rendered them unable to escape, are unanimously of opinion, that there was no impropriety of conduct on the part of the officers and crew of the said ship Wasp, during the chase by the Poictiers, or in the surrender; but that the conduct of the officers and crew of the Wasp on said occasion was eminently distinguished for firmness and gallantry, in making every preparation and exertion, of which their situation would admit.

No. 17.

Vote of congress.

Congress voted 25,000 dollars, and their thanks, to Captain Jacob Jones, officers, and crew of the Wasp; also a gold medal to Captain Jones, and silver medals to each of the officers, in testimony of their high sense of the gallantry displayed by them in the capture of the British sloop Frolic.

No. 18.

From Captain Carden to Mr. Croker.

U.S. ship United States, at sea, Oct. 28, 1812.

Sir,

It is with the deepest regret I have to acquaint you, for the information of my lords commissioners of the admiralty, that H.M. late ship Macedonian was captured on the 25th instant, by the U.S. ship United States, Commodore Decatur, commander. The detail is as follows: –

A short time after day-light, steering N.W. by W. with the wind from the southward, in latitude 29° N. and longitude 29° 30′ W. in the execution of their lordships' orders, a sail was seen on the lee-beam, which I immediately stood for, and made her out to be a large frigate, under American colours. At 9 o'clock I closed with her, and she commenced the action, which we returned; but, from the enemy keeping two points off the wind, I was not enabled to get as close to her as I could have wished. After an hour's action the enemy backed, and came to the wind, and I was then enabled to bring her to close battle. In this situation I soon found the enemy's force too superior to expect success, unless some very fortunate chance occurred in our favor, and with this hope I continued the battle to two hours and ten minutes; when, having the mizen-mast shot away by the board, top-masts shot away by the caps, main-yard shot in pieces, lower-masts badly wounded, lower-rigging all cut to pieces, a small proportion only of the fore-sail left to the fore-yard, all the guns on the quarter-deck and forecastle disabled but two, and filled with wreck, two also on the main-deck disabled, and several shot between wind and water, a very great proportion of the crew killed and wounded, and the enemy comparatively in good order, who had now shot a-head, and was about to place himself in a raking position, without our being enabled to return the fire, being a perfect wreck, and unmanageable log, I deemed it prudent, though a painful extremity, to surrender his majesty's ship; nor was this dreadful alternative resorted to till every hope of success was removed, even beyond the reach of chance, nor till, I trust their lordships will be aware, every effort had been made against the enemy by myself, my brave officers, and men; nor should she have been surrendered whilst a man lived on board, had she been manageable. I am sorry to say our loss is very severe; I find, by this day's muster, 36 killed, three of whom lingered on a short time after the battle; 36 severely wounded, many of whom cannot recover; and 32 slightly wounded, who may all do well:—total 104.

The truly noble and animating conduct of my officers, and the steady bravery of my crew to the last moment of the battle, must ever render them dear to their country.

My first lieutenant, David Hope, was severely wounded in the head, towards the close of the battle, and taken below, but was soon again on deck, displaying that greatness of mind and exertion, which, though it may be equalled, can never be excelled. The third lieutenant, John Bulford, was also wounded, but not obliged to quit his quarters; second lieutenant, Samuel Mottley, and he, deserve my highest acknowledgments. The cool and steady conduct of Mr.

Walker, the master, was very great during the battle; as also that of Lieutenants Wilson and Magill, of the marines.

On being taken on board the enemy's ship, I ceased to wonder at the result of the battle. The United States is built with the scantling of a 74-gun ship, mounting 30 long 24-pounders (English ship-guns) on her main-deck, and 22 42-pounder carronades, with two long 24-pounders, on her quarter-deck and forecastle, howitzer-guns in her tops, and a travelling carronade on her upper-deck, with a complement of 478 picked men.

The enemy has suffered much in masts, rigging, and hull, above and below water; her loss in killed and wounded I am not aware of, but I know a lieutenant and six men have been thrown overboard.

Enclosed you will be pleased to receive the names of the killed and wounded on board the Macedonian; and

I have the honor to be, &c.

J. S. CARDEN.

John W. Croker, Esq.

List of officers and men killed and wounded on board H.M.S. Macedonian, &c. (of which the names are given, comprising,)

Killed—1 master's-mate, the schoolmaster, boatswain, 23 petty-officers and seamen, 2 boys, 1 serjeant and 7 privates of marines:—total, 36.

Wounded dangerously—7 petty-officers and seamen; (2 since dead;) *severely*—1 lieutenant, 1 midshipman, 18 petty-officers and seamen, 4 boys, and 5 private marines:—total, *dangerously* and *severely*, 36.

Wounded slightly—1 lieutenant, 1 master's-mate, 26 petty-officers and seamen, and 4 private marines:—total, 32.

J. S. CARDEN, captain.

No. 19.

Commodore Decatur to the American secretary of the navy.

U.S. ship United states, at sea, Oct. 30, 1812.

Sir,

I have the honor to inform you, that on the 25th instant, being in latitude 29° N. longitude 29° 30′ W. we fell in with, and after an action of an hour and a half, captured H. B. M.'s ship Macedonian, commanded by Captain Carden, and mounting 49 carriage-guns. (The odd gun shifting.) She is a frigate of the largest class, two years old, four months out of dock, and reputed one of the best sailers in the British service. The enemy, being to-windward, had the advantage of engaging us at his own distance, which was so great, that for the first half hour we did not use our carronades, and at no time was he within the compleat effect of our musketry and grape; to this circumstance, and a heavy swell, which was on at the time, I ascribe the unusual length of the action.

The enthusiasm of every officer, seaman, and marine, on board this ship, on discovering the enemy, their steady conduct in battle, and precision of their fire, could not be surpassed. Where all met my fullest expectations, it would be unjust in me to discriminate. Permit me, however, to recommend to your particular notice my first lieutenant, William H. Allen. He has served with me upwards of five years, and to his unremitted exertions in disciplining the crew, is to be imputed the obvious superiority our gunnery exhibited in the result of this contest.

Subjoined is a list of the killed and wounded on both sides. Our loss, compared with that of the enemy, will appear small. Amongst our wounded, you will observe the name of Lieutenant Funk, who died a few hours after the action: he was an officer of great gallantry and promise, and the service has sustained a severe loss in his death.

The Macedonian lost her mizen-mast, fore and main-top-masts, and main-yard, and was much cut up in her hull. The damage sustained by this ship was not such as to render her return into port necessary; and, had I not deemed it important that we should see our prize in, should have continued our cruize.

With the highest consideration and respect,

I am, Sir, your's, &c.

Hon. Paul Hamilton. STEPHEN DECATUR.

[*Here follow the names of five killed, and seven wounded, on board the United States.*]

No. 20.

Vote of congress.

The national legislature voted their thanks to Commodore Decatur, officers, and crew, of the frigate United States; also a gold medal to Commodore Decatur, and silver medals to each of the officers, in honor of the brilliant victory gained by the frigate United States over the British frigate Macedonian.

No. 21.

Extract from the sentence of the court-martial upon Captain Carden, his officers and crew.

Having most strictly investigated every circumstance, and examined the different officers and ship's company; and having very deliberately and maturely weighed and considered the whole and every part thereof, the court is of opinion;—that previous to the commencement of the action, from an over-anxiety to keep the weather-gage, an opportunity was lost of closing with the enemy; and that owing to this circumstance the Macedonian was unable to bring the United States to close action until she had received material damage; but as it does not appear that this omission originated in the most distant wish to keep back from the engagement, the court is of opinion, that Captain J. S. Carden, his officers, and ship's company, in every instance throughout the action, behaved with the firmest and most determined courage, resolution, and coolness; and that the colours of the Macedonian were not struck, until she was unable to make further resistance. The court does therefore most honorably acquit Captain J. S. Carden, the officers, and company of H. M. late ship Macedonian, and Captain Carden, his officers, and company, are hereby most honourably acquitted accordingly.

The court cannot dismiss Captain Carden, without expressing their admiration of the uniform testimony which has been borne to his gallantry and good conduct throughout the action, nor Lieutenant David Hope, the senior lieutenant, the other officers and company, without expressing the highest approbation of the support given by him and them to the captain, and of their courage and steadiness during the contest with an enemy of very superior force; a circumstance that, whilst it reflects high honor on them, does no less credit and honor to the discipline of his majesty's late ship Macedonia.

The court also feels it a gratifying duty to express its admiration of the fidelity to their allegiance, and attachment to their king and country, which the remaining crew appear to have manifested, in resisting the various insidious and repeated temptations which the enemy held out to them, to seduce them from their duty; and which cannot fail to be duly appreciated.

No. 22.

From Lieutenant Chads, to Mr. Croker.

United States frigate Constitution, off St. Salvador, Dec. 31, 1812.

SIR,

It is with deep regret that I write to you, for the information of the lords commissioners of the Admiralty, that H.M.S. Java is no more, after sustaining an action on the 29th inst. for several hours, with the American frigate Constitution, which resulted in the capture and ultimate destruction of H.M.S. Captain Lambert being dangerously wounded in the height of the action, the melancholy task of writing the detail devolves on me. On the morning of the 29th instant, at 8 A.M. off St. Salvador, (coast of Brazil,) the wind at N.E. we perceived a strange sail; made all sail in chase, and soon made her out to be a large frigate. At noon, prepared for action, the chase not answering our private signals, and tacking towards us under easy sail: when about four miles distant she made a signal, and immediately tacked and made all sail away upon the wind. We soon found we had the advantage of her in sailing, and came up with her fast, when she hoisted American colours; she then bore about three points on our lee-bow, at 50 minutes past 1 P.M. the enemy shortened sail, upon which we bore down upon her; at 10 minutes past 2, when about half a mile distant, she opened her fire, giving us her larboard broadside, which was not returned till we were close on her weather-bow. Both ships now manuvred to obtain advantageous positions, our opponent evidently avoiding close action, and firing high to disable our masts; in which he succeeded too well, having shot away the head of our bowsprit, with the jib-boom, and our running rigging so much cut as to prevent our preserving the weather-gage.

At 5 minutes past 3, finding the enemy's raking fire extremely heavy, Captain Lambert ordered the ship to be laid on board, in which we should have succeeded, had not our fore-mast been shot away at this moment, the remains of our bowsprit passing over his taffrail; shortly after this the main-top-mast went, leaving the ship totally unmanageable, with most of our starboard guns rendered useless from the wreck lying over them.

At half-past 3, our gallant captain received a dangerous wound in the breast, and was carried below; from this time we could not fire more than two or three guns until a quarter past 4, when our mizen-mast was shot away. The ship then fell off a little, and brought many of our starboard guns to bear: the enemy's rigging was so much cut that he could not avoid shooting a-head, which brought us fairly broadside and broadside. Our main-yard now went in the slings; both ships continued engaged in this manner till 35 minutes past 4, we frequently on fire in consequence of the wreck lying on the side engaged. Our opponent now made sail a-head out of gun-shot, where he remained an hour repairing his damages, leaving us an unmanageable wreck, with only the main-mast left, and that tottering. Every exertion was made by us during this interval to place the ship in a state to renew the action. We succeeded in clearing the wreck of our masts from our guns; a sail was set on the stumps of the foremast and bowsprit; the weather-half of the main-yard remaining aloft, the main-tack was got forward in the hope of getting the ship before the wind, our helm being still perfect; the effort unfortunately proved ineffectual, from the main-mast falling over the side, and from the heavy rolling of the ship, which nearly covered the whole of our starboard guns. We still waited the attack of the enemy, he now standing towards us for that purpose. On his coming nearly within hail of us, and from his manuvres perceiving he intended a position a-head, where he could rake us without a possibility of our returning a shot; I then consulted the officers, who agreed with myself, that our having a great part of our crew killed and wounded, our bowsprit and three masts gone, several guns useless, we should not be justified in wasting the lives of more of those remaining; who, I hope their lordships and the country will think, have bravely defended his majesty's ship. Under these circumstances, however reluctantly, at 50 minute past 5, our colours were lowered from the stump of the mizen-mast, and we were taken possession of a little after 6, by the American frigate Constitution, commanded by Commodore Bainbridge, who, immediately after ascertaining the state of the ship, resolved on burning her, which we had the satisfaction of seeing done as soon as the wounded men were removed. Annexed I send you a return of the killed and wounded; and it is with pain I perceive it is numerous; also a statement of the comparative force of the two ships, when I hope their lordships will not think the British flag tarnished, although success has not attended us. It would be presumption in me to speak of Captain Lambert's merits; who, though still in danger from his wound, we still entertain the greatest hopes of his being restored to the service and his country.

It is most gratifying to my feelings, to notice the gallantry of every officer, seaman and marine on board. In justice to the officers, I beg leave to mention them individually. I can never speak too highly of the able exertions of Lieutenants Herringham and Buchanan, and also Mr. Robinson, master, who was severely wounded, and Lieutenants Mercer and Davis, of the royal marines, the latter of whom also was severely wounded. To Captain John Marshall, R.N. who was a passenger, I am particularly obliged, for his exertions and advice throughout the action. To Lieutenant Alpin, who was on the main-deck, and Lieutenant Saunders, who commanded the forecastle, I also return my thanks. I cannot but notice the good conduct of the mates and midshipmen, many of whom are killed, and the greater part wounded. To Mr. T. C. Jones, surgeon, and his assistants, every praise is due for their unwearied assiduity in the care of the wounded. Lieutenant-General Hislop, Major Walker, and Captain Wood, of his staff, the latter of whom was wounded, were solicitous to assist and remain on the quarter-deck.

I cannot conclude this letter, without expressing my grateful acknowledgments thus publicly, for the generous treatment Captain Lambert and his officers have experienced from our gallant enemy, Commodore Bainbridge and his officers.

I have the honor to be, &c.

HENRY D. CHADS.

P.S. The Constitution has also suffered severely, both in her rigging and men; having her fore and mizen-masts, main-top-masts, both main-top-sail-yards, spanker-boom, gaff, and trysail-mast, badly shot; and the greatest part of the standing rigging very much damaged; with ten men killed, the commander, fifth lieutenant, and 46 men wounded, 4 of whom are since dead.

Force of the two Ships.

JAVA.	CONSTITUTION.
28 long 18-pounders	32 long 24-pounders
16 carronades, 32-pounders	22 carronades, 32-pounders
2 long 9-pounders	1 carronade, 18-pounder
—	—
46 guns	55 guns
Ship's company and supernumeraries, 377.	Crew, 480.

A list of killed and wounded of H.M.S. Java, in action, &c. (of which the names are given, comprising,)

Killed—3 mates, 2 midshipmen, 1 supernumerary clerk, 7 petty officers and able seamen, 3 landmen, 4 marines, and 2 supernumeraries:—total, 22.

Wounded dangerously—Captain Lambert, (since dead,) the boatswain, 4 petty officers and able seamen, (1 since dead,) and 1 ordinary seamen:—total 7.

Wounded severely—1 master, 1 second lieutenant of marines, 3 midshipmen, 10 petty officers and able seamen, 8 ordinary seamen, 6 landmen, 1 boy, 1 serjeant of marines, 2 corporals of ditto, 12 privates of ditto, 1 passenger, (Captain Wood,) 1 supernumerary mate, and 5 ditto seamen:—total, 52.

Wounded slightly—Lieutenant Chads, 1 midshipman, 10 petty officers and able seamen, 8 ordinary seamen, 8 landmen, 3 boys, 1 serjeant and 5 private marines, 1 supernumerary commander, 1 ditto lieutenant, and 4 ditto seamen:—total 43.

T. C. JONES, surgeon.
2d January. H. D. CHADS, 1st lieut.

No. 23.

Extract of another letter from Lieutenant Chads.

St. Salvador, Brazil, Jan. 4, 1813.

I am sorry to find the Americans did not behave with the same liberality towards the crew that the officers experienced; on the contrary, they were pillaged of almost every thing, and kept in irons.

J. W. Croker, Esq. &c. &c.

No. 24.

From Commodore Bainbridge to the American secretary of the navy.

U.S. frigate Constitution, St. Salvador,
Sir, Jan. 3, 1813.

I have the honor to inform you, that on the 29th ultimo, at 2 P.M. in S. latitude 13° 6′, and W. longitude 30°, and about 10 leagues distance from the coast of Brazil, I fell in with and captured H.B.M.'s frigate Java, of 49 guns, and upwards of 400 men, commanded by Captain Lambert, a very distinguished officer. The action lasted one hour and 55 minutes, in which time the enemy was completely dismasted, not having a spar of any kind standing. The loss on board the Constitution was nine killed and 25 wounded, as per enclosed list. The enemy had 60 killed, and 101 wounded, certainly; (among the latter, Captain Lambert mortally;) but by the enclosed letter, written on board this ship, (by one of the officers of the Java,) and accidentally found, it is evident that the enemy's wounded must have been much greater than as above stated, and who must have died of their wounds previously to their being removed. The letter states 60 killed, and 170 wounded.

For further details of the action, I beg leave to refer you to the enclosed extracts from my journal. The Java had, in addition to her own crew, upwards of 100 supernumerary officers and seamen, to join the British ships of war in the East Indies; also Lieutenant-general Hislop, appointed to the command of Bombay, Major Walker, and Captain Wood, of his staff, and Captain Marshall, master and commander in the British navy, going to the East Indies, to take command of a sloop of war there.

Should I attempt to do justice, by representation, to the brave and good conduct of all my officers and crew during the action, I should fail in the attempt; therefore, suffice it to say, that the whole of their conduct was such as to merit my highest encomiums. I beg leave to recommend the officers, particularly, to the notice of government; as also the unfortunate seamen who were wounded, and the families of those brave men who fell in the action.

The great distance from our own coast, and the perfect wreck we made the enemy's frigate, forbade every idea of taking her to the United States; I had therefore no alternative but burning her, which I did on the 31st ultimo, after receiving all the prisoners and their baggage; which was very hard work, only having one boat left, out of eight, and not one left on board the Java.

On blowing up the frigate Java I proceeded to this place, where I have landed all the prisoners on their parole, to return to England, and there remain until regularly exchanged; and not to serve in their professional capacities, in any place, or in any manner whatsoever, against the United States of America, until their exchange shall be effected.

I have the honor to be, &c.

W. BAINBRIDGE.

To the secretary of the navy, &c.

No. 25.

Extract from Commodore Bainbridge's journal.

Tuesday, December 29, 1812.—At 9 A.M. discovered two strange sails on the weather bow; at 10 discovered the strange sails to be ships: one of them stood in for the land, and the other stood off shore, in a direction towards us; at 11 A.M. tacked to the southward and eastward, and took in the royals; at 30 minutes past 11 made the private signal for the day, which was not answered, and then set the main-sail and royals, to draw the strange sail off from the neutral coast, and separate her from the sail in company.

Wednesday, Dec. 30, (nautical time,) lat. 13° 6′, S. long. 31° W. 10 leagues from the coast of Brazil, commenced with clear weather, and moderate breezes from the E.N.E.; hoisted our ensign and pendant. At 15 minutes past meridian, the ship hoisted her colours, an English ensign, having a signal flying at the main.

At 26 minutes past 1 P.M. being sufficiently from the land, and finding the ship to be an English frigate, took in the main-sail and royals, tacked ship, and stood for the enemy. At 50 minutes past 1 P.M. the enemy bore down with an intention of raking us, which we avoided by wearing. At 2 P.M. the enemy being within half a mile of us, and to-windward, and having hauled down his colours, except the union-jack at the mizen-mast-head, induced me to give orders to the officer of the third division to fire a gun a-head of the enemy, to make him shew his colours; which being done, brought on a fire from us of the whole broadside, on which the enemy hoisted his colours, and immediately returned our fire. A general action, with round and grape, then commenced, the enemy keeping at a much greater distance than I wished, but could not bring him to a closer action without exposing ourselves to several rakes. Considerable manœuvres were made by both vessels to rake, and avoid being raked. The following minutes were taken during the action: –

At 10 minutes past 2 P.M. commenced the action within good grape and canister distance, the enemy to-windward; but much further than I wished. At 30 minutes past 2, our wheel was shot entirely away. At 40 minutes past 2 determined to close with the enemy, notwithstanding his raking. Set the fore and main-sails, and luffed up close to him. At 50 minutes past 2, the enemy's jib-boom got foul of our mizen-rigging. At 3, the head of the enemy's bowsprit and jib-boom shot away by us. At 5 minutes past 3, shot away the enemy's fore-mast by the board. At 15 minutes past 3, shot away his main-top-mast just above the cap. At 40 minutes past 3, shot away the gaft and spanker-boom. At 55 minutes past 3, shot away his mizen-mast nearly by the board. At 5 minutes past 4, having silenced the fire of the enemy completely, and his colours in the main-rigging being down, we supposed he had struck; we then hauled down courses, and shot a-head to repair our rigging, which was extremely cut, leaving the enemy a complete wreck. Soon after discovered that the enemy's flag was still flying; hove to, to repair some of our damage. At 20 minutes past 4, the enemy's main-mast went nearly by the board. At 50 minutes past 4, wore ship and stood for the enemy. At 25 minutes past 5, got very close to the enemy, in a very effectual raking position, athwart his bows, and was at the very instant of raking him, when he most prudently struck his flag; for had he suffered the broadside to have raked him, his additional loss must have been extremely great, as he laid as an unmanageable wreck upon the water.

No. 26.

Extract from minutes of a court-martial assembled on board H.M.S. Gladiator, at Portsmouth, 23d April, 1813, to try the surviving officers and crew of the Java, &c.

Lieutenant W. Allen Herringham, second lieutenant, sworn.

Q. Did you suffer much from the musketry of the Americans?

A. I believe there were a number of gun-shot wounds. Captain Lambert was killed by a musket-shot.

Q. At what part of the action did you sustain the greatest loss?

A. Not in the early part of the action. After the ship became unmanageable, and the Constitution took a raking position, our loss became considerable.

William Batty Robinson, the master, sworn.

Q. Do you remember if they annoyed you much by musketry, whilst you were on deck?

A. A good deal from the tops.

Lieutenant James Saunders, R.N. a passenger, sworn.

Q. Did you suffer much in the forecastle from the enemy's musketry?
A. Very much indeed.
Q. Were you stationed there?
A. Yes.
Q. At what period of the action did you suffer most?
A. When the bowsprit went.
Q. Did the Americans appear to avoid close action at the first part of it?
A. Yes.
Q. Did you understand that the American lost her wheel?
A. I afterwards found that she lost her wheel by the first broadside from the Java, and that four men were killed.

James Humble, boatswain, sworn.

Q. How long had the action lasted when you were wounded?
A. Better than an hour, I believe.
Q. Did you suffer much from the musketry on the forecastle?
A. Yes: and likewise from the round and grape.
Q. Did you come up again, after going below?
A. Yes: I was down about an hour, when I got my arm put a little to rights by a tournaquet being put on it—nothing else; my hand was carried away, and my arm wounded about the elbow. I put my arm in to the bosom of my shirt, and went up again, when I saw the enemy a-head of us, repairing his damages. I had my orders from Lieutenant Chads, before the action began, to cheer up the boarders with my pipe, that they might make a clean spring in boarding.
Q. Did the Java receive much damage from the enemy, before the Java returned any fire at all?
A. Yes: we received, beside what I have stated, much damage in the rigging.

James Macdonald, boatswain's-mate, sworn.

Q. Did the Americans appear to you to avoid close action, or not, in the early part of the action?
A. They kept at long balls: they kept edging away until the Java was disabled.
Q. Did you hear Captain Lambert order the Java to be laid on board the American?
A. Yes.
Q. What distance were you then from the enemy's stern?
A. Not quite a cable's length, upon our lee-beam; the helm was put a-weather.
Q. Do you remember the bowsprit touching the mizen-rigging?
A. Yes: it took the mizen-rigging, which appeared to me to prevent our boarding at the time.
Q. Were the men all ready?
A. Yes: they had all been called, and were all ready for jumping on board at the forecastle, marines and all.
Q. Did you see any of the enemy's men ready to receive the boarders?

A. No: I did not see any of them at the time.
Q. Did you hang some time by the mizen-rigging?
A. Not long.
Q. Did they get their chasers out, and rake you?
A. Yes.

Christopher Speedy, captain of the forecastle, sworn.

Q. Did they annoy you much on the forecastle by musketry?
A. More by round and grape, and double-headed; I picked up five bar-shot which fell out of the fore-mast in rolling: I put three of them in our guns, and fired them back again.
Q. Did the Americans appear to avoid close action?
A. He did always avoid close action—he kept away; whenever the smoke cleared away, we always found him yawing from us.
Q. Do you remember when the Java endeavoured to board her?
A. Yes: it was just as the fore-mast fell.
Q. Were you all ready for boarding?
A. They were called on the gangway and forecastle, and were all ready, boarders and marines.
Q. Did you see many of the enemy ready to oppose the boarders?
A. Not many on deck: I saw some men there, but there were a great many in the tops.

Lieutenant Robert Mercer, royal marines, sworn.

Q. Had you any of your men at small-arms?
A. I believe 34: upwards of 20 on the quarter-deck, and 10 on the forecastle.
Q. Did the enemy make use of their small-arms much?
A. Yes, from the decks, and from the tops.
Q. Were your decks exposed to their tops?
A. Yes, very much: they could see us to take aim.
Q. Do you remember when the Java attempted to lay the enemy on board?
A. Yes: Captain Lambert spoke to me about it; he said it was his intention to board, and desired me to prepare the marines on that occasion, which was done.
Q. Did the Americans appear to avoid close action?
A. Yes, they evidently did: they continually kept away.
Q. What sort of men were the marines?
A. Eighteen of them were very young recruits: the rest have been to sea before.

No. 27.

Sentence of the court-martial.

The court agreed, that the capture of his majesty's late ship Java was caused by her being totally dismasted in a very spirited action with the U.S. ship Constitution, of considerably superior force; in which the zeal, ability, and bravery of the late Captain Lambert, her commander, was highly conspicuous and honorable, being constantly the assailant, until the moment of his much-lamented fall; and that, subsequently thereto, the action was continued with equal zeal, ability, and bravery, by Lieutenant Henry Ducie Chads, the first lieutenant, and the other surviving officers and ship's company, and other officers and persons who were passengers on board her, until she became a perfect wreck, and the continuance of the action would have been a useless sacrifice of lives; and did adjudge the said Lieutenant Henry Ducie Chads, and the other surviving officers and ship's company, to be most honorably acquitted. Rear-admiral Graham Moore, president; who, in returning Lieutenant Chads his sword, addressed him nearly as follows:—"I have much satisfaction in returning you your sword; had you been an officer who had served in comparative obscurity all your life, and never before heard of, your conduct on the present occasion has been sufficient to establish your character as a brave, skilful, and attentive officer."

No. 28.

Vote of Congress.

The congress of the United States voted 50,000 dollars, and their thanks, to Commodore Bainbridge, officers and crew; also a gold medal to Commodore Bainbridge, and silver medals to each of the officers of the Constitution, with suitable devices.

No. 29.

From Captain Lawrence to the American secretary of the navy.

U.S. ship Hornet, Holmes' Hole,
March 29, 1813

Sir,

I have the honor to inform you of the arrival, at this port, of the U.S. ship Hornet, under my command, from a cruize of 145 days, and to state to you, that after Commodore Bainbridge left the coast of Brazils, (January 6,) I continued off the harbour of St. Salvador, blockading the Bonne Citoyenne, until the 24th, when the Montague, 74, hove in sight, and chased me into the harbour; but night coming on, I wore, and stood out to the southward. Knowing that she had left Rio Janeiro for the express purpose of relieving the Bonne Citoyenne, and the packet, (which I had also blockaded for 14 days, and obliged her to send her mail to Rio in a Portuguese smack,) I judged it most prudent to shift my cruising ground, and hauled by the wind to the westward, with the view of cruizing off Pernambuco; and, on the 14th of February, captured the English brig Resolution, of 10 guns, from Rio Janeiro, bound to Maranham, with coffee, &c. and about 23,000 dollars in specie. I took out the money, and set her on fire. I then ran down the coast for Maranham, and cruized there a short time; from thence run off Surinam. After cruizing off that coast, from the 15th until the 22d of February, without meeting a vessel, I stood for Demarara, with an intention, should I not be fortunate on that station, to run through the West Indies on my way to the United States; but on the 24th, in the morning, I discovered a brig to-leeward, to which I gave chase, run into a quarterless four, and, not having a pilot, was obliged to haul off; the fort at the entrance of Demarara river at this time bearing S.W. distant 2½ leagues. Previous to giving up the chase, I discovered a vessel at anchor, without the bar, with English colours flying, apparently a brig of war. In beating round Caroband bank, in order to get at her, at half-past 3 P.M. I discovered another sail on my weather-quarter, edging down for us. At 4. 20. she hoisted English colours, at which time we discovered her to be a large man-of-war-brig; beat to quarters, and cleared ship for action, and kept close by the wind, in order, if possible, to get the weather gage. At 5. 10. finding I could weather the enemy, I hoisted American colours, and tacked. At 5. 25. in passing each other, exchanged broadsides, within half pistol-shot. Observing the enemy in the act of wearing, I bore up, and received his starboard broadside, run him close on board on the starboard quarter, and kept up such a heavy and well-directed fire, that, in less than 15 minutes she surrendered, (being totally cut to pieces,) and hoisted an ensign, union down, from his fore-rigging, as a signal of distress. Shortly after, her main-mast went by the board. Despatched Lieutenant Shubrick on board, who soon returned with her first lieutenant, who reported her to be H.B.M. late brig Peacock, commanded by Captain William Peake, who fell in the latter part of the action; that a number of her crew were killed and wounded; and that she was sinking fast, she having then six feet water in her hold. Despatched the boats immediately for the wounded, and brought both vessels to anchor. Such shot-holes as could be got at were then plugged, guns thrown overboard, and every possible exertion used to keep her afloat, until the prisoners could be removed, by pumping and baling, but without effect, as she unfortunately sunk in 5½ fathoms water, carrying down 13 of her crew, and three of my brave fellows. Lieutenant Connor, and Midshipman Cooper, and the remainder of my men employed in removing the prisoners, with difficulty saved themselves, by jumping into a boat that was lying on the booms, as she went down. Four men of the 13 mentioned, were so fortunate as to gain the fore-top, and were afterwards taken off by our boats.

Previous to her going down, four of her men took to her stern-boat, that had been much damaged during the action, who, I sincerely hope, reached the shore. I have not been able to ascertain from her officers the exact number of killed. Captain Peake, and four men, were found dead on board. The master, one midshipman, carpenter, and captain's clerk, and 29 men wounded, most of them very severely, three of which died of their wounds after being removed, and nine drowned. Our loss was trifling in comparison: J. Place, killed; S. Coulson, and J. Dalrymple, slightly wounded; G. Coffin, and L. Todd, severely burnt by the explosion of a cartridge. Todd survived only a few days. Our rigging and sails were much cut. One shot through the fore-mast, and the bowsprit slightly injured. Our hull received little or no damage.

At the time I brought the Peacock to action, the Espiegle, (the brig mentioned as being at anchor,) mounting 16 32-pound carronades, and two long nines, lay about six miles in-shore of me, and could plainly see the whole of the action. Apprehensive she would beat out to the assistance of her consort, such exertions were used by my officers and crew, in repairing damages, &c. that by 9 o'clock our boats were stowed, a new set of sails bent, and the ship completely ready for action. At 2 A.M. got under weigh, and stood by the wind to the northward and westward, under easy sail. On mustering next morning, found we had 270 souls on board, including the crew of the American brig Hunter, of Portland, taken a few days before by the Peacock.

The Peacock was deservedly styled one of the finest vessels of her class in the British navy. I should judge her to be about the tonnage of the Hornet; her beam was greater by five inches, but her extreme length not so great by four feet. She mounted 16 24-pound carronades, two long nines, one 12-pound carronade on her top-gallant-forecastle, as a shifting gun, and one 4 or 6 pounder, and 2 swivels, mounted aft. I find, by her quarter-bill, that her crew consisted of 134 men, four of whom were absent in a prize.

The cool and determined conduct of my officers and crew during the action, and their almost unexampled exertions afterwards, entitle them to my warmest acknowledgments; and I beg leave most earnestly to recommend them to the notice of government–

JAMES LAWRENCE.

P.S. At the commencement of the action my sailing-master and seven men were absent in a prize, and Lieutenant Stewart and six men on the sick-list.

Hon. William Jones, secretary of the navy.

No. 30.

From Lieutenant Wright to the editor of the "Commercial Advertiser."

SIR,

I wish you to communicate, for the information of G.C.K. and those who may have read his paper, published in your last night's journal, that the force of H.B.M.'s late brig Peacock, at the time she engaged the U.S. sloop Hornet, was 16 24-pounder carronades, and two long 6-pounders, with a complement of 122 men and boys; and that the Hornet carried 18 32-pounder carronades, and two long 9-pounder guns, and 170 men. That the action continued, by Peacock's time, for 25 minutes; and that H.B.M.'s brig l'Espiegle was not visible from the look-outs, stationed at the Peacock's mast-heads, for some time previous to the action.

F. A. WRIGHT, senior lieutenant of
H.B.M.'s late sloop Peacock.

New York, April 17, 1813.

No. 31.

Vote of congress.

The congress of the United States passed a resolution, that the president be requested to present to the nearest male relative of Captain James Lawrence, a gold medal, and a silver medal to each of the commissioned officers who served him in the sloop of war Hornet, in her conflict with the British sloop of war Peacock, in testimony of the high sense entertained by congress of the gallantry and good conduct of the officers and crew in the capture of that vessel, &c.

No. 32.

From Captain Lawrence to the American consul at St. Salvador, Brazils.

(Extract.)

When I last saw you, I stated to you my wish to meet the Bonne Citoyenne, and authorized you to make my wishes known to Captain Greene. I now request you to state to him, that I will meet him whenever he may be pleased to come out, and pledge my honor that neither the Constitution, nor any other American vessel, shall interfere.

No. 33.

From the American, to the British Consul.

(Extract.)

Commodore Bainbridge, of the Constitution frigate, confirms to me the request of Captain Lawrence, in these words:—"If Captain Greene wishes to try equal force, I *pledge my honor* to give him an opportunity, by being out of the way, or not interfering."

No. 34.

From the British, to the American consul.

Fort de St. Pedro, December 20, 1812.

SIR,

I transmitted your letter to me of yesterday, to Captain P. B. Greene, to whom the substance is directed; and, having received his reply, I herewith insert it verbatim.

I am, &c.

FREDERICK LANDEMAN.

— Hill, Esq. &c. &c.

No. 35

From Captain Greene to the British consul.

I hasten to acknowledge the favor of your communication, made to me this morning from Mr. Hill, consul of the United States of America, on the subject of a challenge, stated to have been offered through Mr. Hill, by Captain Lawrence, of the U.S. sloop of war the Hornet, to myself, as commander of H.B.M.'s ship the Bonne Citoyenne, anchored in this port, pledging his honor, as well as that of Commodore Bainbridge, that no advantage shall be taken by the Constitution, or any other American vessel whatever, on the occasion. I am convinced, Sir, if such rencontre was to take place, the result could not be long dubious, and would terminate favorably to the ship which I have the honor to command; but I am equally convinced, that Commodore Bainbridge could not swerve so much from the paramount duty he owes to his country, as to become an inactive spectator, and see a ship belonging to the very squadron under his orders, fall into the hands of an enemy. This reason operates powerfully on my mind, for not exposing the Bonne Citoyenne to a risk, upon terms so manifestly disadvantageous, as those proposed by Commodore Bainbridge. Indeed, nothing could give me greater satisfaction than complying with the wishes of Captain Lawrence; and I earnestly hope, that chance will afford him an opportunity of meeting the Bonne Citoyenne under different circumstances, to enable him to distinguish himself in the manner he is now so desirous of doing. I further assure you, that my ship will, at all times, be prepared, wherever she may be, to repel any attacks made against her; and I shall also act offensively, whenever I judge it proper to do so.

I am, Sir, with great regard, &c.

P. B. GREENE.

No. 36.

From Captain Broke to Captain Lawrence.

H.B.M. ship Shannon, off Boston,
June, 1813.

Sir,

As the Chesapeake appears now ready for sea, I request you will do me the favor to meet the Shannon with her, ship to ship, to try the fortune of our respective flags. To an officer of your character it requires some apology for proceeding to further particulars. Be assured, Sir, that it is not from any doubt I can entertain of your wishing to close with my proposal, but merely to provide an answer to any objection which might be made, and very reasonably, upon the chance of our receiving unfair support.

After the diligent attention which we had paid to Commodore Rodgers; the pains I took to detach all force but the Shannon and Tenedos to such a distance, that they could not possibly join in any action fought in sight of the Capes, and the various verbal messages which had been sent into Boston to that effect, we were much disappointed to find the commodore had eluded us by sailing on the first change, after the prevailing easterly winds had obliged us to keep an offing from the coast. He, perhaps, wished for some *stronger* assurance of a fair meeting. I am therefore induced to address you more particularly, and to assure you, that what I write I pledge my honor to perform, to the utmost of my power.

The Shannon mounts 24 guns upon her broadside, and one light boat-gun; 18-pounders upon her main-deck, and 32-pound carronades on her quarter-deck and forecastle; and is manned with a complement of 300 men and boys, (a large proportion of the latter,) besides 30 seamen, boys, and passengers, who were taken out of recaptured vessels lately. I am thus minute, because a report has prevailed in some of the Boston papers, that we had 150 men, additional, lent us from la Hogue, which really was never the case. La Hogue is now gone to Halifax for provisions; and I will send all other ships beyond the power of interfering with us, and meet you wherever it is most agreeable to you, within the limits of the undermentioned rendezvous; viz. –

From 6 to 10 leagues east of Cape Cod light-house; from 8 to 10 leagues east of Cape Ann's light; on Cashe's ledge, in latitude 43 north; at any bearing and distance you please to fix off the south breakers of Nantucket, or the shoal on St. George's bank.

If you will favor me with any plan of signals or telegraph, I will warn you (if sailing under this promise) should any of my friends be too nigh, or any where in sight, until I can detach them out of my way; or I would sail with you under a flag of truce to any place you think safest from our cruizers, hauling it down when fair to begin hostilities.

You must, Sir, be aware that my proposals are highly advantageous to you, as you cannot proceed to sea singly in the Chesapeake, without imminent risk of being crushed by the superior force of the numerous British squadrons which are now abroad; where all your efforts, in case of a rencontre, would, however, gallant, be perfectly hopeless. I entreat you, Sir, not to imagine that I am urged by mere personal vanity to the wish of meeting the Chesapeake; or that I depend only upon your personal ambition for your acceding to this invitation: we have both nobler motives. You will feel it as a compliment if I say, that the result of our meeting may be the most grateful service I can render to my country; and I doubt not that you, equally confident of success, will feel convinced, that it is only by repeated triumphs in *even combats* that your little navy can now hope to console *your* country, for the loss of that trade it can no longer protect. Favor me with a speedy reply. We are short of provisions and water, and cannot stay long here.

I have the honor to be, Sir,
Your obedient humble servant,
P. B. V. BROKE, Captain of
H.B.M. ship Shannon.

N.B. For the general service of watching your coast, it is requisite for me to keep another ship in company, to support me with her guns and boats when employed near the land, and particularly to aid each other, if either ship in chase should get on shore. You must be aware that I cannot, consistently with my duty, wave so great an advantage for this *general* service, by detaching my consort, without an assurance on your part of meeting me directly; and that you will neither seek or admit aid from any other of *your* armed vessels, if I detach *mine* expressly for the sake of meeting you. Should any special order restrain you from thus answering a formal challenge, you may yet oblige me by keeping my proposal a secret, and appointing any place you like to meet us (within 300 miles of Boston) in a given number of days after you sail; as, unless you agree to an interview, I may be busied on other service, and, perhaps, be at a distance from Boston when you go to sea. Choose your terms, but let us meet.

To the commander of the U.S. frigate Chesapeake.

Endorsement on the envelope.

We have 13 American prisoners on board, which I will give you for as many British sailors, if you will send them out; otherwise, being privateersmen, they must be detained.

No. 37.

From Captain Capel to Mr. Croker.

Halifax, June 11, 1813.

Sir,

It is with the greatest pleasure I transmit you a letter I have just received from Captain Broke, of H.M.S. Shannon, detailing a most brilliant achievement in the capture of the U.S. frigate Chesapeake, in 15 minutes. Captain Broke relates so fully the particulars of this gallant affair, that I feel it unnecessary to add much to his narrative; but I cannot forbear expressing the pleasure I feel in bearing testimony to the indefatigable exertions and persevering zeal of Captain Broke, during the time he has been under my orders. Placing a firm reliance on the valor of his officers and crew, and a just confidence in his system of discipline, he sought every opportunity of meeting the enemy on fair terms; and I have to rejoice with his country and his friends at the glorious result of this contest. He gallantly headed his boarders in the assault, and carried all before him. His wounds are severe, but I trust his country will not be long deprived of his services.

I have the honor to be, &c.

THOMAS BLADEN CAPEL, captain
and senior officer at Halifax.

J. W. Croker, Esq. &c. &c.

No. 38

From Captain Broke to Captain Capel.

Shannon, Halifax, June 6, 1813.

Sir,

I have the honor to inform you, that being close in with Boston light-house, in H.M.'s ship under my command, on the 1st instant, I had the pleasure of seeing that the U.S. frigate Chesapeake (whom we had long been watching) was coming out of the harbour to engage the Shannon. I took a position between Cape Ann and Cape Cod, and then hove-to for him to join us. The enemy came down in a very handsome manner, having three American ensigns flying. When closing with us he sent down his royal yards; I kept the Shannon's up, expecting the breeze would die away. At half-past 5 P.M. the enemy hauled up within hail of us on the starboard side, and the battle began, both ships steering full under the top-sails. After exchanging between two and three broadsides, the enemy's ship fell on board of us, her mizen-channels locking in with our fore-rigging. I went forward to ascertain her position; and, observing that the enemy were flinching from their guns, I gave orders to prepare for boarding. Our gallant band, appointed to that service, immediately rushed in, under their respective officers, upon the enemy's decks, driving every thing before them with irresistible fury. The enemy made a desperate but disorderly resistance. The firing continued at all the gangways, and between the tops; but, in two minutes' time, the enemy were driven, sword in hand, from every post; the American flag was hauled down, and the proud old British union floated triumphant over it. In another minute they ceased firing from below, and called for quarter. The whole of this service was achieved in 15 minutes, from the commencement of the action.

I have to lament the loss of many of my gallant shipmates, but they fell exulting in their conquest.

My brave first lieutenant, Mr. Watt, was slain in the moment of victory, in the act of hoisting the British colours: his death is a severe loss to the service. Mr. Aldham, the purser, who had spiritedly volunteered the charge of a party of small-arm men, was killed on his post at the gang-way. My faithful old clerk Mr. Dunn, was shot by his side. Mr. Aldham has left a widow to lament his loss: I request the commander-in-chief will recommend her to the protection of my lords commissioners of the admiralty. My veteran boatswain, Mr. Stephens, has lost an arm: he fought under Lord Rodney, on the 12th of April. I trust his age and services will be duly rewarded.

I am happy to say that Mr. Samwell, a midshipman of much merit, is the only other officer wounded besides myself, and he not dangerously. Of my gallant seamen and marines, we had 23 slain, and 56 wounded. I subjoin the names of the former. No expressions I can make use of, can do justice to the merits of my valiant officers and crew. The calm courage they displayed during the carronade, and the tremendous precision of their fire, could be equalled only by the ardour with which they rushed to the assault. I recommend them all warmly to the protection of the commander-in-chief. Having received a severe sabre-wound at the first onset, whilst charging a part of the enemy who had rallied on their forecastle, I was only capable of giving command till assured our conquest was complete; and, then directing second lieutenant Wallis to take charge of the Shannon, and secure the prisoners, I left the third lieutenant, Mr. Falkiner (who had headed the main-deck boarders) in charge of the prize. I beg to recommend these officers most strongly to the commander-in-chief's patronage, for the gallantry they displayed during the action, and the skill and judgment they evinced in the anxious duties which afterwards devolved upon them.

To Mr. Etouch, the acting master, I am much indebted for the steadiness with which he conducted the ship into action. The lieutenants Johns and Law, of the marines, bravely boarded at the head of their respective divisions. It is impossible to particularize every brilliant deed performed by my officers and men; but I must mention, when the ships' yard-arms were locked together, that Mr. Cosnaghan, who commanded in our main-top, finding himself screened from the enemy by the foot of the top-sail, laid out at the main-yard-arm to fire upon them, and shot three men in that situation. Mr. Smith, who commanded our fore-top, stormed the enemy's fore-top from the fore-yard-arm, and destroyed all the Americans remaining in it. I particularly beg leave to recommend Mr. Etouch, the acting master, and Messrs. Smith, Leake, Clavering, Raymond, and Littlejohn, midshipmen. This latter officer is the son of Captain Littlejohn, who was slain in the Berwick. The loss of the enemy was about 70 killed, and 100 wounded. Among the former were the four lieutenants, a lieutenant of marines, the master, and many other officers. Captain Lawrence is since dead of his wounds.

The enemy came into action with a complement of 440 men; the Shannon, having picked up some re-captured seamen, had 330. The Chesapeake is a fine frigate, and mounts 49 guns; 18's on her main-deck, 32's on her quarter-deck and forecastle. Both ships came out of action in the most beautiful order, their rigging appearing as perfect as if they had been only exchanging a salute.

I have the honor to be, &c.

P. B. V. BROKE.

To Captain the Hon. T. Bladen Capel, &c. Halifax.

[*Then follows the names of the killed, 24 in all.*]

No. 39.

From Lieut. Budd to the American secretary of the navy.

Halifax, June 15, 1813.

Sir,

The unfortunate death of Captain James Lawrence and Lieutenant Augustus C. Ludlow, has rendered it my duty to inform you of the capture of the late U.S. frigate Chesapeake.

On Tuesday, June 1st, at 8 A.M. we unmoored ship, and at meridian got under way from President's Roads, with a light wind from the southward and westward, and proceeded on a cruize. A ship was then in sight in the offing, which had the appearance of a ship of war, and which, from information received from pilot-boats and craft, we believed to be the British frigate Shannon.

We made sail in chase, and cleared ship for action. At half-past 4 P.M. she hove to, with her head to the southward and eastward. At 5 P.M. took in the royals and top-gallant-sails; and at half-past 5 hauled the courses up. About 15 minutes before 6 P.M. the action commenced within pistol-shot. The first broadside did great execution on both sides; damaged our rigging; killed, among others, Mr. White, the sailing-master, and wounded Captain Lawrence.

In about 12 minutes after the commencement of the action, we fell on board of the enemy, and immediately after, one of our arm-chests on the quarter-deck was blown up, by a hand-grenade thrown from the enemy's ship. In a few minutes one of the captain's aids came on the gun-deck, to inform me that the boarders were called. I immediately called the boarders away, and proceeded to the spar-deck, where I found that the enemy had succeeded in boarding us, and had gained possession of our quarter-deck.

I immediately gave orders to haul on board the fore-tack, for the purpose of shooting the ship clear of the other, and then made an attempt to regain the quarter-deck, but was wounded and thrown down on the gun-deck. I again made an effort to collect the boarders; but in the meantime, the enemy had gained complete possession of the ship.

On my being carried down to the cockpit, I there found Captain Lawrence and Lieutenant Ludlow, both mortally wounded; the former had been carried below previously to the ship's being boarded; the latter was wounded in attempting to repel the boarders. Among those who fell early in the action, was Mr. Edward J. Ballard, the fourth lieutenant, and Lieutenant James Broom of marines.

I herein enclose to you a return of the killed and wounded; by which you will perceive that every officer upon whom the charge of the ship would devolve, was either killed or wounded previously to her capture. The enemy report the loss of Mr. Watt, their first lieutenant; the purser, the captain's clerk, and 23 seamen killed; and Captain Broke, a midshipman, and 56 seamen wounded.

The Shannon, had, in addition to her full complement, an officer and 16 men belonging to the Belle Poule, and a part of the crew belonging to the Tenedos.

I have the honor to be, &c.

GEORGE BUDD.

Hon. W. Jones, secretary to the navy, Washington.

[*Here follow the names of 47 killed, and 99 wounded.*]

No. 40.

Report of the court of inquiry on the loss of the Chesapeake.

The court are unanimously of opinion, that the Chesapeake was gallantly carried into action by her late brave commander; and no doubt rests with the court, from comparison of the injury respectively sustained by the frigates, that the fire of the Chesapeake was much superior to that of the Shannon.

The Shannon being much cut in her spars and rigging, and receiving many shot in and below the water-line, was reduced almost to a sinking condition, after only a few minutes cannonading from the Chesapeake, while the Chesapeake was comparatively uninjured. And the court have no doubt, if the Chesapeake had not accidentally fallen on board the Shannon, and the Shannon's anchor got foul in the after-quarter-port of the Chesapeake, the Shannon must have very soon surrendered or sunk.

It appears to the court, that as the ships were getting foul, Captain Lawrence ordered the boarders to be called; but the bugleman, W. Brown, stationed to call the boarders by sounding a bugle, had deserted his quarters, and when discovered and ordered to call, was unable, from fright to sound his horn; that a midshipman went below immediately to pass the word for the boarders; but not being called in the way they had been usually exercised, few came upon the upper deck; confusion prevailed; a greater part of the men deserted their quarters and ran below. It appears also to the court, that when the Shannon got foul of the Chesapeake, Captain Lawrence, his first lieutenant, the sailing-master, and lieutenant of marines were all killed or mortally wounded, and thereby the upper deck of the Chesapeake was left without any commanding officer, and with only one or two young midshipmen. It also appears to the court, that previously to the ships getting foul, many of the Chesapeake's spar-deck division had been killed and wounded, and the number stationed on that deck thereby considerably reduced; that these being left without a commissioned officer, or even a warrant-officer, except one or two inexperienced midshipmen, and not being supported by the boarders from the gun-deck, almost universally deserted their quarters. And the enemy availing himself of this defenceless state of the Chesapeake's upper deck, boarded and obtained possession of the ship with very little opposition.

From this view of the engagement, and careful examination of the evidence, the court are unanimously of opinion, that the capture of the late United States frigate Chesapeake, was occasioned by the following causes:—the almost unexampled early fall of Captain Lawrence, and all the principal officers; the bugleman's desertion of his quarters, and inability to sound his horn; for the court are of opinion, if the horn had been sounded when first ordered, the men being then at their quarters, the boarders would have promptly repaired to the spar-deck, probably have prevented the enemy from boarding—certainly have repelled them, and might have returned the boarding with success, and the failure of the boarders on both decks, to rally on the spar-deck, after the enemy had boarded, which might have been done successfully, it is believed, from the cautious manner in which the enemy came on board.

The court cannot, however, perceive in this almost unexampled concurrence of disastrous circumstances, that the national flag has suffered any dishonor from the capture of the United States frigate Chesapeake, by the superior force of the frigate Shannon, of 52 carriage-guns, and 396 men. Nor do this court apprehend that the result of this engagement, will in the least discourage our brave seamen from meeting the enemy hereafter on equal terms.

The court being also charged to enquire into the conduct of the officers and men during and after the engagement, and thereupon having strictly examined and maturely considered the evidence as recorded, do find the following causes of complaint.

First. Against Lieutenant Cox; that being stationed in command of the second division on the main-deck, he left his division during the action, while his men were at their quarters, and went upon the upper deck; that when there, and the enemy boarding, or on the point of boarding, he left the deck to assist Captain Lawrence below, went down with him from the spar-deck to the berth-deck; did not return to his division, but went forward on the gun-deck; that, while there, and the men were retreating below, he commanded them to go to their duty, without enforcing his commands. But as a court of inquiry allows an accused person no opportunity of vindicating his conduct, the members of this court trust that their opinion on the conduct of Lieutenant Cox may not be deemed conclusive against him, without trial by court-martial.

Second. Against Midshipman Forrest; that he left his quarters during the action, and did not return to them, and now assigns no reason for his conduct satisfactory to this court.

Third. Against Midshipman Freshman; that he behaved in an unofficer like manner at Halifax, assuming a false name at the office of the commissary of prisoners when obtaining his parole, and was paroled by the name of William Brown.

Fourth. Against the crew generally; that they deserted their quarters, and ran below after the ships were foul, and the enemy boarded. But it appearing that they behaved well at their quarters before, and fired on the enemy with great rapidity and precision; the court ascribe their misconduct to the confusion naturally incident to the early fall of their officers, and the omission of the call of boarders in the accustomed manner.

Yet this court is very far from exculpating those who are thus criminal. It is unable to designate by name all the individuals who thus abandoned their duty, because most of the officers had recently joined the ship, some only a few days preceding the engagement, and of course could not distinguish the men. The court, therefore, respectfully submit to higher authority, the expediency of withholding the wages of the crew. The persons whom the court are able to designate by name, as deserters from their stations, are William Brown, bugleman, Joseph Russell, captain of second gun, Peter Frost, and John Joyce, seamen.

The court further find, that the following persons entered the British service at Halifax; viz. Henry Ensign, Peter John, Andrew Simpson, Peter Langrun, Magness Sparring, Joseph Galla, Martin Anderson, Francis Paris, John White, boy, Thomas Arthur, Charles Reynolds, John Pierce, jun. Andrew Denham, Thomas Jones, Charles Goodman, Joseph Antonio, Christopher Stephens, Charles Bowden, Charles Westerbury, Joseph Smith, George Williams, and George Cordell.

The court further find and report, that William Wainwright, William Worthington, and James Parker, the last of whom was born at Salem, Massachussets, were claimed by the enemy as British subjects, and sent on board of the enemy's ships of war.

This court respectfully beg leave to superadd, that unbiassed by any illiberal feelings toward the enemy, they feel it their duty to state, that the conduct of the enemy after boarding and carrying the Chesapeake, was a most unwarrantable abuse of power after success.

The court is aware that, in carrying a ship by boarding, the full extent of the command of an officer cannot be readily exercised; and that improper violence may unavoidably ensue. When this happens in the moment of contention, a magnanimous conquered foe will not complain. But the fact has been clearly established before this court, that the enemy met with little opposition on the upper deck, and none on the gun-deck. Yet after they had carried the ship, they fired from the gun-deck down the hatchway upon the berth-deck, and killed and wounded several of the Chesapeake's crew, who had retreated there, were unarmed and incapable of making any opposition: that some balls were fired even into the cock-pit; and what excites the utmost abhorrence, this outrage was committed in the presence of a British officer standing on the hatchway.

W. BAINBRIDGE, President.

No. 41.

From Mr. Croker to Admiral Warren.

Admiralty-office, 9th July, 1813.

SIR,

I have had the pleasure of receiving and communicating to my lords commissioners of the admiralty, a letter from Captain the Hon. B. Capel, of H.M.S. la Hogue, enclosing a copy of his letter to you, and of that of Captain Broke to him, announcing the capture, in 15 minutes, of the U.S. frigate Chesapeake, of 49 guns, and 440 men, by H.M.S. Shannon.

My lords have before had occasion to observe, with great approbation, the zeal, judgment, and activity, which have characterized Captain Broke's proceedings since the commencement of the war; and they now receive, with the highest satisfaction, a proof of professional skill and gallantry in battle, which has seldom been equalled, and certainly never surpassed; and the decision, celerity, and effect, with which the force of H.M.S. was directed against the enemy, mark no less the personal bravery of the officers, seamen, and marines, than the high discipline and practice in arms, to which the ship's company must have been sedulously and successfully trained.

My lords, to mark their sense of this action, have been pleased to direct a medal to be presented to Captain Broke; Lieutenants Wallis and Falkiner, who, in consequence of the wound of Captain Broke, and the death of the gallant first lieutenant, Watt, succeeded to the command of the Shannon and the prize, to be promoted to the rank of commanders; and Messrs. Etough and Smith to that of lieutenants; and my lords will be glad to attend to the recommendation of Captain Broke, in favor of the petty-officers and men who may have particularly distinguished themselves.

You will convey to Captain Broke, his officers and ship's company, these sentiments of their lordships, with an expression of their satisfaction at hearing that the captain's wound is not likely long to deprive his country of his valuable services.

I am, Sir,
Your most obedient humble servant,
J. W. CROKER.

To Admiral Warren.

No. 42

From Captain Maples to Admiral Thornborough.

H.M.B. Pelican, St. David's Head, E. 5 leagues,
August 14, 1813.

Sir,

I have the honor to inform you, that in obedience to your orders to me of the 12th instant, to cruize in St. George's Channel, for the protection of the trade, and to obtain information of the American sloop of war, I had the good fortune to board a brig, the master of which informed me that he had seen a vessel, apparently of a man of war, steering to the N.E. At 4 this morning I saw a vessel on fire, and a brig standing from her, which I soon made out to be a cruizer; made all sail in chase, and at half-past 5 came alongside of her, (she having shortened sail, and made herself clear for an obstinate resistance,) when, after giving her three cheers, our action commenced, which was kept up with great spirit on both sides 43 minutes, when we lay her alongside, and were in the act of boarding, when she struck her colours. She proves to be the U.S. sloop of war Argus, of 360 tons, 18 24-pound carronades, and two long 12-pounders; had on board, when she sailed from America, (two months since,) a complement of 149 men, but in the action 127; commanded by Lieutenant-commandant W.H. Allen, who, I regret to say, was wounded early in the action, and has since suffered amputation of his left thigh.

No eulogium I could use would do sufficient justice to the merits of my gallant officers and crew, which consisted of 116; the cool courage they displayed, and the precision of their fire, could only be equalled by their zeal to distinguish themselves; but I must beg leave to call your attention to the conduct of my first lieutenant, Thomas Welsh; of Mr. W. Glanville, acting master; Mr. W. Ingram, the purser, who volunteered his services on deck; and Mr. Richard Scott, the boatswain.

Our loss, I am happy to say, is small: one master's mate, Mr. William Young, slain in the moment of victory, while animating by his courage and example all around him; and one able seaman, John Kitery; besides five seamen wounded, who are doing well. That of the enemy I have not been able to ascertain, but it is considerable; her officers say, about 40 killed and wounded.

I have the honor to be, &c.

J. F. MAPLES, Commander.

Admiral Thornborough, &c. &c.

No. 43.

From Lieutenant Watson to the American secretary of the navy.

Norfolk, March 2, 1815.

SIR,

Circumstances, during my residence in England, having heretofore prevented my attention to the painful duty which devolved on me by the death of my gallant commander, Captain W. H. Allen, of the late U.S. brig Argus, I have now the honor to state for your information, that, having landed the minister plenipotentiary (Mr. Crawford) and suite at l'Orient, we proceeded on the cruize which has been directed by the department, and after capturing 20 vessels, (a list of the names, and other particulars, of which, I have the honor to enclose,) being in latitude 52° 15′ N. longitude 5° 50′ W. on the 14th of August, 1813, we discovered, at 4 o'clock A.M. a large brig of war, standing down under a press of sail upon our weather-quarter, the wind being at south, and the Argus close-hauled on the starboard-tack. We immediately prepared to receive her, and at 4. 30. being unable to get the weather-gage, we shortened sail, and gave her an opportunity of closing. At 6, the brig having displayed English colours, we hoisted our flag, wore round, and gave her the larboard broadside, (being at this time within grape-distance,) which was returned, and the action commenced within the range of musketry. At 6. 4. Captain Allen was wounded, and the enemy shot away our main-braces, main-spring-stay, gaff and try-sail mast. At 6. 8. Captain Allen, being much exhausted by the loss of blood, was taken below. At 6. 12. lost our sprit-sail-yard, and the principal part of the standing-rigging on the larboard-side of the fore-mast. At this time I received a wound on the head from a grape-shot, which, for a time, rendered me incapable of attending to duty, and was carried below. I had, however, the satisfaction of recollecting, on my recovery, that nothing which the most gallant exertions could effect would be left undone by Lieutenant W. H. Allen, junior, who succeeded to the command of the deck.

Lieutenant Allen reports, at 6. 14. the enemy, being on our weather-quarter, edged off for the purpose of getting under our stern, but the Argus luffed close to with the main-top-sail a-back; and, giving him a raking broadside, frustrated his attempt. At 6. 18. the enemy shot away our preventer main-braces and main-top-sail-tye; and the Argus, having lost the use of her after-sails, fell off before the wind, when the enemy succeeded in passing our stern, and ranged up on the starboard side. At 6. 25. the wheel-ropes and running-rigging of every description being shot away, the Argus became unmanageable; and the enemy, not having sustained any apparent damaged, had it completely in his power to choose a position, and continued to play upon our starboard-quarter, occasionally shifting his situation, until 6. 30. when I returned to the deck, the enemy being under our stern, within pistol-shot, where he continued to rake us until 6. 38. when we prepared to board, but, in consequence of our shattered condition, were unable to effect it. The enemy then passed our broadside, and took a position on our starboard-bow. From this time until 6. 47. we were exposed to a cross or raking fire, without being able to oppose but little more than musketry to the broadside of the enemy, our guns being much disabled, and seldom brought to bear.

The Argus having now suffered much in hull and rigging, as also in killed and wounded, among the former of whom, (exclusive of our gallant captain,) we have to lament the loss of two meritorious young officers, in Midshipmen Delphy and Edwards; and being exposed to a galling fire, which, from the enemy's ability to manage his vessel, we could not avoid, I deemed it necessary to surrender, and was taken possession of by H.B.M. sloop Pelican, of 21 carriage-guns; viz.—16 32-pound carronades, four long 6s, and one 12-pound carronade. I hope this measure will meet your approbation, and that the result of this action, when the superior size and metal of our opponent, and the fatigue which the crew, &c. of the Argus underwent, from a very rapid succession of captures is considered, will not be thought unworthy of the flag under which we serve.

I have the honor to inclose a list of killed and wounded, and feel great satisfaction in reporting the general good conduct of the men and officers engaged on this occasion, and particularly the zeal and activity displayed by Lieutenant Allen, who, you will observe, for a time commanded on deck.

I have the honor to be, &c.

W. H. WATSON, late first lieutenant
U.S. Brig Argus.

Hon. B. Crowninshield, secretary of the navy.

[*Here follows the names of 6 killed; 5 mortally, and 12 severely and slightly wounded.*]

No. 44.

Court of inquiry on the loss of the Argus.

The court, in pursuance of the authority by which they were convened, having carefully examined into the causes of the loss by capture of the U.S. sloop of war Argus, under the command of the late W. H. Allen, master-commandant in the navy of the U.S.; and also into the conduct of the officers and crew of the said sloop of war, before and after her surrender to the enemy's ship Pelican, and having maturely deliberated upon all the testimony, they find the following facts: –

First: it is proved that in the number of her crew, and in the number and calibre of her guns, the Pelican was decidedly superior to the Argus.

Secondly: they find that the crew of the Argus was very much exhausted by the continued and extraordinary fatigue and exposure to which they had been subjected for several weeks, and particularly for 24 hours immediately preceding the action.

Thirdly: they find that every officer and man of the Argus, (with the exception of one man, Jacob Allister, and one boy, Henderick,) made use of every practicable exertion to capture the British sloop of war Pelican.

They are therefore of opinion, that every officer and man, with the exception before-mentioned, displayed throughout the engagement a zeal, activity, and spirit, in defence of the vessel and flag committed to their protection, which entitles them to the undiminished confidence and respect of their government and fellow-citizens, and do therefore honourably acquit them.

No. 45.

From Lieutenant M'Call to Commodore Hull.

U.S. brig Enterprise, Portland,
September 7, 1813.

Sir,

In consequence of the unfortunate death of Lieutenant William Burrows, late commander of this vessel, it devolves on me to acquaint you with the result of the cruize. After sailing from Portsmouth on the 1st instant, we steered to the eastward, and on the morning of the 3d, off Wood island, discovered a schooner, which we chased into this harbour, where we anchored. On the morning of the 4th weighed anchor, and swept out, and continued our course to the eastward. Having received information of several privateers being off Manhagan, we stood for that place, and on the following morning, in the bay near Penguin point, discovered a brig getting under way, which appeared to be a vessel of war, and to which we immediately gave chase. She fired several guns, and stood for us, having four ensigns hoisted. After reconnoitering and discovering her force, and the nation to which she belonged, we hauled upon a wind to stand out of the bay, and at 3 o'clock shortened sail, tacked to run down, with an intention to bring her to close action. At 20 minutes after 3 P.M. when within half pistol-shot, the firing commenced from both, and after being warmly kept up, and with some manuvering, the enemy hailed, and said they had surrendered, at 4 P.M.; *their colours, being nailed to the masts, could not be hauled down.* She proved to be H.B.M.'s brig Boxer, of 14 guns, Samuel Blythe, Esq. commander, who fell in the early part of the engagement, having received a cannon-shot through the body; and I am sorry to add that Lieutenant Burrows, who had gallantly led us into action, fell also about the same time by a musket-ball, which terminated his existence in eight hours.

The Enterprise suffered much in spars and rigging; and the Boxer in spars, rigging, and hull, having many shots between wind and water.

It would be doing injustice to the merit of Mr. Tillinghast, second lieutenant, were I not to mention the able assistance I received from him during the remainder of the engagement, by his strict attention to his own division, and other departments; and of the officers and crew generally, I am happy to add, their cool and determined conduct have my warmest approbation and applause.

As no muster-roll, that can be fully relied on, has come into my possession, I cannot exactly state the number of killed and wounded on board the Boxer; but from information received from the officers of that vessel, it appears there were between 20 and 25 killed, and 14 wounded. Enclosed is a list of the killed and wounded on board the Enterprise.

I have the honor to be, &c.

EDWARD R. M'CALL, senior officer.

Isaac Hull, Esq. commanding naval-officer
on the eastern station.

List of killed and wounded on board the U.S. brig Enterprise, &c.

Killed—1 ordinary seaman.

Wounded—William Burrows, Esq. commander, *since dead;* Kervin Waters, midshipman, *mortally;* 1 carpenter's mate, *since dead;* 2 quarter-masters, 1 boatswain's-mate, 5 seamen, and 1 marine.

No. 46.

Sentence of the court-martial on the surviving officers and crew of the Boxer.

The court proceeded to inquire into all the particulars attending the capture of H.M.'s brig Boxer by the enemy, and to try Lieutenant David M'Crery, her surviving officers and company, for the same; and having heard Lieutenant M'Crery's official letter and narrative of the action, and strictly examined the said lieutenant, and the surviving officers and company, produced to the court, and carefully investigated all the particulars attending the capture of H.M.'s brig Boxer, by the U.S. vessel of war Enterprise; and having very maturely and deliberately weighed and considered the whole and every part thereof, the court is of opinion that the capture of H.M. brig Boxer, by the U.S. vessel of war Enterprise, is to be attributed to a superiority in the enemy's force, principally in the number of men, as well as to a greater degree of skill in the direction of her fire, and the destructive effects of her first broadside.

The court is also of opinion, that the surviving officers and company (with the exception hereinafter made) appear to have done their utmost to capture the enemy's vessel, and to defend H.M. brig Boxer; and to have conducted themselves with courage, and a determination not to surrender while any prospect of success remained; and the court will therefore adjudge Lieutenant M'Crery, the surviving officers and company, to be acquitted, with the exception of Mr. Hugh James, quarter-master, doing duty as master's-mate, John Dod, James Jackson, and William Slattery, seamen; who have not appeared before the court, and have been stated to have deserted their quarters during the action; and through cowardice, negligence, or disaffection, to have withdrawn themselves from their duty in the engagement; and the said

Lieutenant M'Crery, the surviving officers and company, are hereby acquitted accordingly, with the exception of the said Mr. Hugh James, John Dodd, James Jackson, and William Slattery.

No. 47.

Vote of congress.

The congress of the United States presented to the nearest male relative of Lieutenant William Burrows, and to Lieutenant M'Call of the brig Enterprise, a gold medal, with suitable emblems and devices; and a silver medal to each of the commissioned officers, in honor of their gallantry and good conduct in the conflict with the Boxer.

No. 48.

From Sir James Yeo to Mr. Croker.

H.M.S. Wolfe, Kingston, Upper Canada,
29th June, 1813

Sir,

I have the honor to inform you, for the information of the lords commissioners of the admiralty, that on the 3d instant, I sailed with his majesty's squadron under my command from this port, to co-operate with our army at the head of the lake, and annoy the enemy by intercepting all supplies going to the enemy, and thereby oblige his squadron to come out for its protection.

At daylight on the 8th, the enemy's camp was discovered close to us at Forty-mile creek. It being calm, the large vessels could not get in, but the Beresford, Captain Spilsbury, the Sir Sidney Smith, Lieutenant Majoribanks, and the gun-boats under the orders of Lieutenant Anthony, (first of this ship,) succeeded in getting close under the enemy's batteries, and by a sharp and well-directed fire, soon obliged him to make a precipitate retreat, leaving all his camp equipage, provisions, stores, &c. behind, which fell into our hands. The Beresford also captured all his bateaux, laden with stores, &c. Our troops immediately occupied the post. I then proceeded along to the westward of the enemy's camp, leaving our army in front. On the 13th we captured two schooners and some boats, going to the enemy with supplies; by them I received information that there was a dépôt of provisions at Genessee river. I accordingly proceeded off that river, landed some seamen and marines of the squadron, and brought off all the provisions found in the government stores; as also a sloop laden with grain for the army. On the 19th I anchored off the Great Sodas, landed a party of the 1st regimental royal Scots, and took off 600 barrels of flour and pork, which had arrived there for their army.

I have the honor to be, &c.

J. L. YEO, commodore.

No. 49.

From Sir James Yeo to Admiral Warren.

H.M.S. Wolfe, on Lake Ontario,
August 10, 1813.

Sir,

I have the honor to inform you, that the enemy's squadron was discovered at anchor off Fort Niagara, on the morning of the 8th instant, consisting of 13 sail; that of his majesty 6. They immediately weighed, and stood out in a line of battle; but on our approaching nearly within gun-shot, they fired their broadsides, wore, and stood under their batteries. Light airs and calms prevented me from closing with them again, until this night, when having a fine breeze, we stood for them.

At 11, we came within gun-shot of their line of schooners, which opened a heavy fire, their ships keeping off the wind to prevent our closing. At half-past 12, this ship came within gun shot of the Pike and Madison, when they immediately bore up, fired their stern-chase guns, and made sail for Niagara, leaving two of their schooners astern, which we captured, the Growler and Julia, each mounting one long 32, and one long 12, and 40 men.

From information obtained from the prisoners, I hear that their new ship, the General Pike, mounts 28 long 24-pounders, and has 400 men; and that all their schooners mount from 2 to 4 long 32-pounders.

The enemy have disappeared; I therefore suppose they have gone to Sackett's harbour to refit.

I am happy to add that (except in the sails and rigging) his majesty's squadron have not sustained any injury, and have the honor to be, &c.

J. L. YEO, commodore.

The Right Hon. Sir J. B. Warren, Bart.
Halifax.

No. 50.

From Commodore Chauncey to the American secretary of the navy.

U.S. ship General Pike, at Sackett's harbour,
13th August, 1813.

Sir,

I arrived here this day with these ships, the Madison, Oneida, Governor Tomkins, Conquest, Ontario, Pert, and Lady of the Lake: the Fair American and Asp I left at Niagara. Since I had the honor of addressing you last, I have been much distressed and mortified; distressed at the loss of a part of the force entrussed to my command, and mortified at not having been able to bring the enemy to action. The following movements and transactions of the squadron since the 6th instant, will give you the best idea of the difficulties and mortifications that I have had to encounter.

On the 7th at day-light, the enemy's fleet, consisting of two ships, two brigs, and two large schooners, were discovered bearing W.N.W. distant about 5 or 6 miles, wind at west. At 5, weighed with the fleet, and manuvred to gain the wind. At 9, having passed to-leeward of the enemy's line and abreast of his van-ship, (the Wolfe,) hoisted our colours, and fired a few guns to ascertain whether we could reach him with our shot. Finally they fell short, I wore, and hauled upon a wind on the larboard-tack; the rear of our schooners then about 6 miles astern. The enemy wore in succession, and hauled upon a wind on the same tack: he tacked and made all sail to the northward. As soon as our rear vessels could fetch his wake, tacked and all sail in chase. In the afternoon the wind became very light, and, towards night, quite calm. The schooners used their sweeps all the afternoon in order to close with the enemy, but without success. Late in the afternoon I made the signal of recal, and formed in close order. Wind during the night from the westward, and, after midnight, squally. Kept all hands at quarters and beat to-windward, in hopes to gain the wind of the enemy. At 2 A.M. missed two of our schooners. At day-light, discovered the missing schooners to be the Hamilton and Scourge. Soon after, spoke the Governor Tomkins, who informed me, that the Hamilton and Scourge both overset and sunk, in a heavy squall about 2 o'clock; and, distressing to relate, every soul perished, except sixteen. This fatal accident deprived me at once of the services of two valuable officers, Lieutenant Winter, and Sailing-master Ogwood; and two of my best schooners, mounting together 19 guns. This accident giving to the enemy decidedly the superiority, I thought he would take advantage of it, particularly as, by a change of wind, he was again brought dead to-windward of me. Formed the line upon the larboard-tack, and hove to. Soon after 6 A.M. the enemy bore up, and set studding-sails, apparently with an intention to bring us to action. When he had approached us within about 4 miles, he brought to on the starboard-tack; I wore, and brought to on the same tack. Finding that the enemy had no intention of bringing us to action, I edged away to gain the land, in order to have the advantage of the land-breeze in the afternoon. It soon after fell calm, and I directed the schooner to sweep up and engage the enemy. About noon we got a light breeze from the eastward. I took the Oneida in tow, as she sails badly: our schooners was within 1½ or 2 miles of his rear; the wind shifted to the westward, which again brought him to windward. As soon as the breeze struck him he bore up for the schooners, in order to cut them off before they could rejoin me; but, with their sweeps, and the breeze soon reached them also, they were soon in their station. The enemy finding himself foiled in his attempt upon the schooners, hauled his wind and hove to. It soon after became very squally, and the appearance of its continuing so during the night; and as we had been at quarters for nearly 40 hours, and being apprehensive of separating from some of the heavy-sailing schooners in the squall, induced me to run in towards Niagara, and anchor outside the bar. General Boyd very handsomely offered any assistance in men that I might require. I received 150 soldiers, and distributed them in the different vessels, to assist in boarding, or repelling boarders, as circumstances might require. It blew very heavy in squalls during the night. Soon after day-light discovered the enemy's fleet bearing north; weighed and stood after him. The wind soon became light and variable, and before 12 o'clock quite calm. At 5, fresh breezes from north, the enemy's fleet bearing north, distant about 4 or 5 leagues. Wore the fleet in succession, and hauled upon a wind on the larboard-tack; at sundown, the enemy bore N.W. by N. on the starboard-tack. The wind hauling to the westward, I stood to the northward all night, in order to gain the north-shore; at daylight, tacked to the westward, the wind having changed to N.N.W. Soon after, discovered the enemy's fleet bearing S.W. I took the Asp, and the Madison the Fair American, in tow, and made all sail in chase. It was at this time we thought of realizing what we had been so long toiling for; but before 12 o'clock the wind changed to W.S.W. which brought the enemy to-windward: tacked to the northward. At 3, the wind inclining to the northward, wore to the southward and westward, and made the signal for the fleet to make all sail. At 4, the enemy bore S.S.W. bore up, and steered for him. At 5, observed the enemy becalmed under the land, nearing him very fast, with a fine breeze from N.N.W. At 6, formed the order of battle, within about 4 miles of the enemy. The wind at this time very light. At 7, the wind changed to S.W. and a fresh breeze, which again placed the enemy to-windward of me. Tacked and hauled upon the wind on the larboard-tack under easy sail, the enemy standing after us. At 9, when within about two gun-shot of our rear, he wore to the southward. I stood on to the northward under easy sail; the fleet formed in two lines, a part of the schooners forming the weather-line, with orders to commence the fire upon the enemy as soon as their shot would take effect; and as the enemy reached them to edge down upon the line to-leeward and pass through the intervals, and form to-leeward. At about half-past 10, the enemy tacked and stood after us. At 11, the rear of our line opened his fire upon the enemy. In about 15 minutes the fire became general from the weather-line, which was returned by the enemy. At half-past 11, the weather-line bore up and passed to-leeward, except the Growler and Julia, which soon after tacked to the southward, which brought the enemy between them and me. Filled the main-top-sail, and edged away two points, to lead the enemy down, not only to engage him to more advantage, but to lead him from Growler and Julia. He, however, kept his wind, until he completely separated those two vessels from the rest of the squadron; exchanged a few shot with this ship as he passed without injury to us, and made sail after our two schooners: tacked, and stood after him. At 12 (midnight) finding that I must either separate from the rest of the squadron, or relinquish the hope of saving the two which had separated, I reluctantly gave up the pursuit, rejoined the squadron then to leeward, and formed the line on the starboard-tack.

The firing was continued between our two schooners and the enemy's fleet until about 1 A.M. when, I presume, they were obliged to surrender to a force so much their superior. Saw nothing more of the enemy that night. Soon after daylight, discovered them close in with the north shore, with one of our schooners in tow, the other not to be seen. I presume she may have sunk. The enemy shewed no disposition to come down upon us, although to-windward, and blowing heavy from W. The schooners labouring very much, I ordered two of the dullest to run into Niagara, and anchor. The gale encreasing very much, and as I could not go into Niagara with this ship, I determined to run to Genessee bay, as a shelter for the small vessels, and with the expectation of being able to obtain provisions for the squadron, as we were all nearly out, the Madison and Oneida having not a single day's on board when we arrived opposite Genessee bay. I found there was every prospect of the gale's continuing, and if it did, I could run to this place, and provision the whole squadron with more certainty, and nearly in the same time that I could at Genessee, admitting that I could obtain provisions at that place. After bringing the breeze as far as Oswego, the wind became light, inclining to a calm, which had prolonged our passage to this bay. I shall provision the squadron for five weeks, and proceed up the lake this evening; and when I return again, I hope to be able to communicate more agreeable news than this communication contains. The loss of the Growler and Julia, in the manner in which they have been lost, is mortifying in the extreme; and, although their commanders disobeyed my positive orders, I am willing to believe that it arose from an error of judgment, and excess of zeal, to do more than was required of them; thinking, probably, that the enemy intended to bring us to a general action, they thought, by gaining the wind of him, they would have it more in their power to annoy and injure him, than they could by forming to-leeward of our line. From what I have been able to discover of the movements of the enemy, he has no intention of engaging us, except he can get decidedly the advantage of wind and weather, and as his vessels in squadron sail better than our squadron, he can always avoid an action; unless I can gain the wind, and have sufficient day-light to bring him to action before dark. His object is, evidently, to harass us by night-attacks, by which means he thinks to cut off our small dull-sailing schooners in detail. Fortune has evidently favored him thus far, and I hope that it will be my turn next; and, although inferior in point of force, I feel very confident of success.

I have the honor to be, &c.

ISAAC CHAUNCEY.

Hon. secretary of the navy.

No. 51.

From Sir James Yeo to Admiral Warren.

H.M.'s ship Wolfe, off the False Duck islands,
Sir, on Lake Ontario, Sept. 12, 1813.

I have the honor to acquaint you, that H.M.'s squadron under my command, being becalmed on Genessee river, on the 11th instant, the enemy's fleet of 11 sail, having a partial wind, succeeded in getting within range of their long 24 and 32-pounders; and from their having the wind of us, and the dull sailing of some of our squadron, I found it impossible to bring them to close action. We remained in this mortifying situation five hours, having only six guns in all the squadron that would reach the enemy; (not a carronade being fired;) at sun-set a breeze sprang up from the westward, when I steered for the False Duck islands, under which the enemy could not keep the weather gage, but be obliged to meet us on equal terms. This, however, he carefully avoided.

Although I have to regret the loss of Mr. William Ellery, midshipman, and three seamen killed, and seven wounded, I cannot but conceive it fortunate that none of the squadron have received any material damage, which must have been considerable, had the enemy acted with the least spirit, and taken advantage of the superiority of position they possessed.

Inclosed is a list of killed and wounded.

Killed 3; wounded 7. J. L. YEO.

No. 52.

From Commodore Chauncey to the American secretary of the navy.

U.S. ship General Pike, off Duck island,
September 13, 1813.

Sir,

On the 7th, at day-light, the enemy's fleet was discovered close in with Niagara river, wind from the southward. Made the signal, and weighed with the fleet, (prepared for action,) and stood out of the river after him: he immediately made all sail to the northward. We made sail in chase, with our heavy schooner in tow; and have continued the chase all round the lake, night and day, until yesterday morning, when he succeeded in getting into Amherst bay; which is so little known to our pilots, and said to be full of shoals, that they are not willing to take me in there. I shall, however, (unless driven from my station by a gale of wind,) endeavour to watch him so close, as to prevent his getting out upon the lake.

During our long chase, we frequently got within one or two miles of the enemy; but our heavy-sailing schooners prevented our closing with him until the 11th, off Gennessee river. We carried a breeze with us, while he lay becalmed, to within three-quarters of a mile of him, when he took the breeze, and we had a running fight 3½ hours, but by his superior sailing he escaped me, and run into Amherst bay yesterday morning.

In the course of our chase on the 11th, I got several broadsides from this ship upon the enemy, which must have done him considerable injury, as many of the shot were seen to strike him, and people were observed over the sides plugging shot-holes. A few shot struck our hull, and a little rigging was cut, but nothing of importance. Not a man was hurt.

I was much disappointed that Sir James refused to fight me, as he was so much superior in point of force, both in guns and men, having upwards of 20 guns more than we have, and heaves a greater weight of shot.

This ship, the Madison, and the Sylph, have each a schooner constantly in tow, yet the others cannot sail as fast as the enemy's squadron; which gives him decidedly the advantage, and puts it in his power to engage me when and how he chuses.

I have the honor to be, &c.

ISAAC CHAUNCEY.

Hon. William Jones, secretary of the navy.

No. 53.

From Sir James Yeo to Sir George Prevost.

H.M.'s ship Wolf, at Kingston,
SIR, November 15, 1813.

I yesterday received Captain Barclay's official statement of the ill-fated action on Lake Erie; and as your excellency must wish to be informed of every particular, I have the honor to enclose a copy of the same. It appears to me, that though his majesty's squadron were very deficient in seamen, weight of metal, and particularly long guns, yet the greater misfortune was the loss of every officer, particularly Captain Finnis, whose life, had it been spared, would, in my opinion, have saved the squadron.

I have the honor to be, &c.

JAMES L. YEO, Commodore.

His Excellency Sir George Prevost, Bart.
governor and general-in-chief.

No. 54.

From Captain Barclay to Sir James Yeo.

H.M.'s late ship Detroit, Put-in bay,
SIR, Lake Erie, Sept. 12, 1813.

The last letter I had the honor of writing to you, dated the 6th instant, I informed you, that unless certain intimation was received of more seamen being on their way to Amherstburg, I should be obliged to sail with the squadron, deplorably manned as it was, to fight the enemy, (who blockaded the port,) to enable us to get supplies of provisions and stores of every description. So perfectly destitute of provisions was the port, that there was not a day's flour in store, and the crews of the squadron under my command were on half allowance of many things, and when that was done there was no more. Such were the motives which induced Major-general Proctor, (whom by your instructions I was directed to consult, and whose wishes I was enjoined to execute, as far as related to the good of the county,) to concur in the necessity of a battle being risked, under the many disadvantages which I laboured; and it now remains to me, the most melancholy task, to relate to you the unfortunate issue of the battle, as well as the many untoward circumstances that led to that event.

No intelligence of seamen having arrived, I sailed on the 9th instant, fully expecting to meet the enemy next morning, as they had been seen among the islands; nor was I mistaken. Soon after day-light they were seen in motion in Put-in bay, the wind then south-west, and light, giving us the weather-gage. I bore up for them, in hopes of bringing them to action among the islands, but that intention was soon frustrated by the wind suddenly shifting to the south-west, which brought the enemy directly to-windward.

The line was forming according to a given plan, so that each ship might be supported against the superior force of the two brigs opposed to them. About 10, the enemy cleared the islands, and immediately bore up, under sail, in a line a-breast, each brig being also supported by the small vessels. At a quarter before 12, I commenced the action, by firing a few long guns; about a quarter past, the American commodore, also supported by two schooners, one carrying four long 12-pounders, the other a long 32 and 24-pounder, came to close action with the Detroit; the other brig of the enemy, apparently destined to engage the Queen Charlotte, supported in like manner by two schooners, kept so far to-windward as to render the Queen Charlotte's 24-pounder carronades useless, while she was, with the Lady Prevost, exposed to the heavy and destructive fire of the Caledonian, and four other schooners, armed with long and heavy guns, like those I have already described.

Too soon, alas! was I deprived of the service of the noble and intrepid Captain Finnis, who, soon after the commencement of the action, fell; and with him fell my greatest support. Soon after Lieutenant Stokes, of the Queen Charlotte, was struck senseless by a splinter, which deprived the country of his services at this very critical point.

As I perceived the Detroit had enough to contend with, without the prospect of a fresh brig, Provincial-lieutenant Irvine, who then had charge of the Queen Charlotte, behaved with great courage; but his experience was much too limited to supply the place of such an officer as Captain Finnis, hence she proved of far less assistance than I expected.

The action continued with great fury until half-past 2, when I perceived my opponent drop a-stern, and a boat passing from him to the Niagara; (which vessel was at this time perfectly fresh;) the American commodore, seeing that as yet the day was against him, (his vessel having struck soon after he left her,) and also the very defenceless state of the Detroit, which ship was now a perfect wreck, principally from the raking fire of the gun-boats, and also that the Queen Charlotte was in such a situation that I could receive very little assistance from her, and the Lady Prevost being at this time too far to-leeward, from her rudder being injured, made a noble, and, alas! too successful an effort to regain it, for he bore up, and, supported by his small vessels, passed within pistol-shot, and took a raking position on our bow; nor could I prevent it, as the unfortunate situation of the Queen Charlotte prevented us from wearing. In attempting it we fell on board her. My gallant First-lieutenant Garland was now mortally wounded, and myself severely, that I was obliged to quit the deck. Manned as the squadron was, with not more than 50 British seamen, the rest a mixed crew of Canadians and soldiers, and who were totally unacquainted with such service, rendered the loss of officers more sensibly felt, and never in any action was the loss more severe: every officer commanding vessels, and their seconds, were either killed, or wounded so severely, as to be unable to keep the deck.

Lieutenant Buchan, in the Lady Prevost, behaved most nobly, and did every thing that a brave and experienced officer could do, in a vessel armed with 12-pound carronades, against vessels carrying long guns. I regret to state that he was severely wounded. Lieutenant Bignal, of the Dover, commanding the Hunter, displayed the greatest intrepidity; but his guns being small, (2, 4, and 6-pounders,) he could be of much less service than he wished.

Every officer in the Detroit behaved in the most exemplary manner. Lieutenant Inglis shewed such calm intrepidity, that I was fully convinced that, on leaving the deck, I left the ship in excellent hands; and for an account of the battle after that, I refer you to his letter, which he wrote me for your information.

Mr. Hoffmeister, purser of the Detroit, nobly volunteered his services on deck, and behaved in a manner that reflects the highest honor on him. I regret to add, that he is very severely wounded in the knee.

Provincial-lieutenant Purvis, and the military officers, Lieutenants Gordon, of the Royal Newfoundland Rangers, and O'Keefe, of the 41st regiment, behaved in a manner which excited my warmest admiration. The few British seamen I had behaved with their usual intrepidity; and, as long as I was on deck, the troops behaved with a calmness and courage worthy of a more fortunate issue to their exertions.

The weather-gage gave the enemy a prodigious advantage, as it enabled them not only to choose their position, but their distance also, which they did in such a manner, as to prevent the carronades of the Queen Charlotte and Lady Prevost from having much effect; while their long guns did great execution, particularly against the Queen Charlotte.

Captain Perry has behaved in a most humane and attentive manner, not only to myself and officers, but to all the wounded.

I trust, that although unsuccessful, you will approve of the motives that induced me to sail under so many disadvantages, and that it may be hereafter proved that, under such circumstances, the honor of his majesty's flag has not been tarnished.

I enclose the list of killed and wounded.

I have the honor to be, &c.

R. H. BARCLAY, commander,
and late senior officer.

Sir James Lucas Yeo, &c. &c.

No. 55.

From Lieutenant Inglis to Captain Barclay.

H.M. late ship Detroit, Sept. 10, 1813.

Sir,

I have the honor to transmit you an account of the termination of the late unfortunate battle with the enemy's squadron.

On coming on the quarter-deck, after your being wounded, the enemy's second brig, at that time on our weather-beam, shortly afterwards took a position on our weather-bow, to rake up; to prevent which, in attempting to wear, to get our starboard-broadside to bear upon her, a number of the guns of the larboard-broadside being at this time disabled, fell on board the Queen Charlotte, at this time running up to-leeward of us. In this situation the two ships remained for some time.

As soon as we got clear of her, I ordered the Queen Charlotte to shoot a-head of us, if possible, and attempted to back our fore-top-sail, to get a-stern; but the ship lying completely unmanageable, every brace cut away, the mizzen-top-mast and gaff down, all the other masts badly wounded, not a stay left forward, hull shattered very much, a number of the guns disabled, and the enemy's squadron raking both ships, a-head and a-stern, none of our own in a situation to support us, I was under the painful necessity of answering the enemy, to say we had struck, the Queen Charlotte having previously done so.

I have the honor to be, &c.

To Captain Barclay. GEORGE INGLIS.

A statement of the force of his majesty's squadron on Lake Erie, and that of the United States.

His majesty's squadron.

Detroit.—Two long 24-pounders, one long 18-pounder on *pivot;* six long 12-pounders, eight long 9-pounders, one 24-pound carronade, one 18-pound carronade.

Queen Charlotte.—One long 12-pounder, on *pivot;* two long 9-pounders, fourteen 24-pound carronades.

Lady Prevost.—One long 9-pounder, on *pivot;* two long 6-pounders, ten 12-pound carronades.

Hunter.—Four long 6-pounders, two long 4-pounders, two long 2-pounders, two 12-pound carronades.

Little Belt.—One long 12-pounder, on *pivot;* two long 6-pounders.

Chippeway.—One long 9-pounder, on *pivot.*

United States' squadron.

Lawrence.—Two long 12-pounders, eighteen 32-pound carronades.

Niagara.—Two long 12-pounders, eighteen 32-pound carronades.

Caledonia.—Two long 24-pounders, one 32-pound carronade, all on *pivots.*

Ariel.—Four long 12-pounders, on *pivots.*

Somers.—One long 24-pounder, one 32-pound carronade, both on *pivots.*

Porcupine.—One long 32-pounder, on *pivot.*

Tigress.—One long 32-pounder, on *pivot.*

Scorpion.—One long 32-pounder, one 24-pound carronade, both on *pivots.*

Trippe.—One long 24-pounder, on *pivot.*

R. H. BARCLAY.

A list of killed and wounded on board his majesty's ships and vessels in an action with the American squadron on Lake Erie, &c.

Three officers, 38 men killed; nine officers, 85 men, wounded.

Names of officers killed and wounded.

S. J. Garden, Royal Newfoundland Regiment, killed.

Detroit.—Killed, First-lieutenant J. Garland.—Wounded, Captain R. H. Barclay, dangerous; J. M. Hoffmeister, purser, dangerously.

Queen Charlotte.—Killed, Captain R. Finnis.—Wounded, First-lieutenant James Stokoe, severely; James Foster, midshipman, slightly.

Lady Prevost.—Wounded, Lieutenant Edward Buchan, commanding, dangerously; First-lieutenant F. Roulette, severely.

Hunter.—Wounded, Lieutenant G. Bignell, commanding, severely; Henry Gateshill, master's-mate, slightly.

Chippeway.—Wounded, Master's-mate J. Campbell, commanding, slightly.

R. H. B. commander, and late senior officer.

No. 56.

From Commodore Perry to the American secretary of the navy.

U.S. brig Niagara, off the Western Sister,
Lake Erie, September 10, 1813.

SIR,

It has pleased the Almighty to give to the arms of the United States, a signal victory over their enemies on this lake. The British squadron, consisting of two ships, two brigs, one schooner, and one sloop, have this moment surrendered to the force under my command, after a sharp conflict.

I have the honor to be, &c.
O. H. PERRY.

Hon. W. Jones, secretary of the navy.

No. 57.

From Commodore Perry to General Harrison.

September 11, 1813.

DEAR SIR,

We have a great number of prisoners, which I wish to land: will you be so good as to order a guard to receive them, and inform me of the place? Considerable numbers have been killed and wounded on both sides. From the best information, we have more prisoners than we have men on board our vessels.

In great haste,
Your's very truly,
O. H. PERRY.

General Harrison.

No. 58.

From Commodore Perry to the American secretary of the navy.

U.S. schooner Ariel, Put-in bay,
SIR, September 13, 1813.

In my last I informed you that we had captured the enemy's fleet on this lake. I have now the honor to give you the most important particulars of the action. On the morning of the 10th instant, at sun-rise, they were discovered from Put-in bay, where I lay at anchor with the squadron under my command. We got under way, the wind light at S.W. and stood for them. At 10 A.M. the wind hauled to S.E. and brought us to windward; formed the line, and bore up. At 15 minutes before 12, the enemy commenced firing; at 5 minutes before 12 the action commenced on our part. Finding their fire very destructive, owing to their long guns, and its being mostly directed at the Lawrence, I made sail, and directed the other vessels to follow, for the purpose of closing with the enemy. Every brace and bow-line being shot away, she became unmanageable, notwithstanding the great exertions of the sailing-master. In this situation she sustained the action upwards of two hours, within canister-distance, until every gun was rendered useless, and the greater part of her crew either killed or wounded. Finding she could no longer annoy the enemy, I left her in charge of Lieutenant Yarnall, who, I was convinced, from the bravery already displayed by him, would do what would comport with the honor of the flag. At half-past 2, the wind springing up, Captain Elliott was enabled to bring his vessel, the Niagara, gallantly into close action. I immediately went on board of her, when he anticipated my wish by volunteering to bring the schooners, which had been kept a-stern by the lightness of the wind, into close action. It was unspeakable pain, that I saw, soon after I got on board the Niagara, the flag of the Lawrence come down, although I was perfectly sensible that she had been defended to the last, and that to have continued to make a shew of resistance, would have been a wanton sacrifice of her brave crew. But the enemy was not able to take possession of her, and circumstances soon permitted her flag again to be hoisted.

At 45 minutes past 2, the signal was made for "close action." The Niagara being very little injured, I determined to pass through the enemy's line; bore up and passed a-head of their two ships and a brig, giving a raking fire to them from the starboard-guns, and to a large schooner and sloop from the larboard-side at half-pistol-shot distance. The smaller vessels at this time having got within grape and canister-distance, under the direction of Captain Elliott, and keeping up a well-directed fire, the two ships, a brig and a schooner, surrendered, a schooner and sloop making a vain attempt to escape.

Those officers and men who were immediately under my observation evinced the greatest gallantry, and I have no doubt that all others conducted themselves as became American officers and seamen. Lieutenant Yarnall, first of the Lawrence, although several times wounded, refused to quit the deck. Midshipman Forrest, (doing duty as a lieutenant) and sailing-master Tailor, were of great assistance to me. I have great pain in stating to you the death of Lieutenant Brooks of the marines, and Midshipman Lamb, both of the Lawrence, and Midshipman John Clarke of the Scorpion: they were valuable and promising officers. Mr. Hambleton, purser, who volunteered his services on deck, was severely wounded late in the action. Midshipman Claxton and Swartevant of the Lawrence, were severely wounded. On board of the Niagara, Lieutenants Smith and Edwards, and Midshipman Webster, (doing duty as sailing-master,) behaved in a very handsome manner. Captain Breevoort, of the army, who acted as a volunteer in the capacity of a marine officer on board that vessel, is an excellent and brave officer, and with his musketry did great execution. Lieutenant Turner, commanding the Caledonia, brought that vessel into action in the most able manner, and is an officer that in all situations may be relied on. The Ariel, Lieutenant Packet, and Scorpion, Sailing-master Champlain, were enabled to get early into action, and were of great service.* Captain Elliott speaks in the highest terms of Mr. Magrath, purser, who had been dispatched in a boat on service previous to my getting on board the Niagara; and, being a seaman, since the action has rendered essential service, in taking charge of one of the prizes. Of Captain Elliott, already so well known to the government, it would be almost superfluous to speak. In this action he evinced his characteristic bravery and judgment, and, since the close of the action, has given me the most able and essential assistance.

I have the honor to enclose you a return of killed and wounded, together with a statement of the relative fore of the squadrons. The captain and first lieutenant of the Queen Charlotte, and the first lieutenant of the Detroit, were killed; Captain Barclay, senior officer, and the commander of the Lady Prevost, severely wounded; the commanders of the Hunter and Chippeway, slightly wounded. Their loss in killed and wounded I have not yet been able to ascertain; it must however have been very great.

Very respectfully, &c.

O. H. PERRY.

Hon. W. Jones, secretary of the navy.

No. 59.

Extract of a letter from Commodore Perry to the same.

U.S. schooner Ariel, Put-in bay,
September 13, 1813.

Sir,

I have caused the prisoners taken on the 10th instant to be landed at Sandusky, and have requested General Harrison to have them marched to Chilicothe, and there wait until your pleasure shall be known respecting them.

* Assisted the Lawrence in engaging the Detroit.

The Lawrence has been entirely cut up: it is absolutely necessary she should go into a safe harbour. I have therefore directed Lieutenant Yarnall to proceed to Erie in her, with the wounded of the fleet, and dismantle and get her over the bar as soon as possible.

The two ships in a heavy sea this day at anchor lost their masts, being much injured in the action. I shall haul them into the inner bay at this place, and moor them for the present. The Detroit is a remarkably fine ship, sails well, and is very strongly built. The Queen Charlotte is a much superior vessel to what has been represented. The Lady Prevost is a large fine schooner.

I also beg your instructions respecting the wounded. I am satisfied, Sir, that whatever steps I might take, governed by humanity, would meet your approbation. Under this impression I have taken upon myself to promise Captain Barclay, who is very dangerously wounded, that he shall be landed as near Lake Ontario as possible, and I had no doubt you would allow me to parole him. He is under the impression that nothing but leaving this part of the country will save his life.

There is also a number of Canadians among the prisoners, many of whom have families.

I have the honor to be, &c.
O. H. PERRY.

Hon. William Jones, secretary of the navy.

Statement of the force of the British squadron.

Ship	Detroit	19 guns—1 on pivot, and 2 howitzers
	Queen Charlotte . .	17 ditto—1 ditto
Schooner	Lady Prevost	13 ditto—1 ditto
Brig	Hunter	10 ditto
Sloop	Little Belt	3 ditto
Schooner	Chippeway	1 do. And 2 swivels: total 63 gs.

Note.—The Detroit is a new ship, very strongly built, and mounting long 24s, 18s, and 12s.

Statement of the force of the U.S. squadron.

Brig	Lawrence	20 guns
	Niagara	20 ditto
	Caledonia	3 ditto
Schooner	Ariel	4 ditto (one burst early in the action.)
	Scorpion	2 ditto
	Somers	2 ditto
Sloop	Trippe	1 ditto
Schooner	Tigress	1 ditto
	Porcupine	1 ditto—Total, 54 guns.

The exact number of the enemy's force has not been ascertained, but I have good reason to believe, that it exceeded ours by nearly one hundred men.

List of killed and wounded on board the U.S. squadron, &c.
(Here follow the names, then,)

Recapitulation

	Killed.	Wounded.	Total.
Lawrence	22	61	83
Niagara	2	25	27
Caledonia	0	3	3
Somers	0	2	2
Ariel	1	3	4
Trippe	0	2	2
Scorpion	2	0	2
	27	96	123

S. HAMBLETON, purser.
O. H. PERRY, captain and senior officer.

No. 60.

From Commodore Perry to General Harrison.

U.S. schooner Ariel, Sept. 15, 1813.

Sir,

The very great assistance in the action of the 10th instant derived from those men you were pleased to send on board the squadron, renders it a duty to return you my sincere thanks for so timely a reinforcement. In fact, Sir, I may say, without those men the victory could not have been achieved; and equally to assure you, that those officers and men behaved as became good soldiers and seamen. Those who were under my immediate observation evinced great ardour and bravery. Captain Prevort, of the 2d regiment of infantry, serving on board the Niagara, I beg leave to recommend particularly to your notice: he is a brave and gallant officer, and, as far as I am capable of judging, an excellent one. I am convinced you will present the merit of this officer to the view of the honorable secretary of war, as I shall to the honorable secretary of the navy.

Very respectfully, &c.
O. H. PERRY.

Major-General W. H. Harrison,
commander-in-chief of the N.W. army.

No. 61.

Extracts from the court-martial on Captain Barclay.

(Parliamentary papers.)

Provincial Lieutenant Francis Purvis of the Detroit, examined.

Q. How many experienced seamen had you on board the Detroit when the action commenced?

A. To the best of my knowledge, not more than *ten*, officers included.

Q. Can you recollect how many of those ten seamen were killed and wounded?

A. To the best of my recollection, seven or eight were killed or wounded.

Q. How near were the enemy to you at the early part of the engagement?

A. The Detroit, in engaging the Lawrence, was within pistol-shot, and within pistol-shot of the Niagara. The latter came down after the Lawrence had struck.

Captain Barclay asked: –

Were the matches and tubes so bad, that were supplied to me from Amherst bay, that I was obliged to prime without the latter, and fired pistols at the guns to set them off?

A. Yes; we fired pistols at the guns to set them off during the whole of the action.

Q. Why did you not take possession of the Lawrence when she struck?

A. We had only one boat, and that was cut to pieces; and the Niagara, another large brig, being to-windward, came down too quickly upon us.

Q. Did the enemy's gun-boats do much damage?

A. More than any of their vessels: they had long two and thirties.

Lieutenant Thomas Stokoe of the Queen Charlotte, examined.

Q. How many men had you on board the Queen Charlotte that you could call experienced seamen?

A. Not more than *ten*, with the petty officers. We had on board between 120 and 130 men, officers and all together.

Q. How many men had you on board that had been accustomed to work the great guns with a ship in motion?

A. Only the men that came up from the Dover three days before we sailed. We had *sixteen* of them, boys included, from the Dover: the rest we had learnt ourselves, since our arrival on the Lake.

Q. Do you know whether the other vessels that composed the squadron of Captain Barclay were equally deficient in seamen?

A. All the other vessels were equally deficient in point of seamen, except the Detroit might have a few more on account of being a larger vessel.

Q. At half an allowance, how many days' provisions had you on board the Queen Charlotte when you went out?

A. We might have had a week's, at half-allowance, of provisions, but not of spirits; they were preserved for the action, and all consumed on that day. We had none served out for several days before.

Q. Did you understand that the enemy's vessels were well manned?

A. Yes, they were remarkably well manned. I believe, from the information I received from the American officers, that the Lawrence had more able seamen on board, than we had in our whole squadron. I was on board the Lawrence about a quarter of an hour, and on board the Niagara two or three days: she appeared to be very well manned; they chiefly manned the prizes from her.

Captain Barclay asked: –

Was I obliged to take from the Queen Charlotte stores of various descriptions, even to sails, cables, and anchors, as well as a proportion of *pistols to fire the guns off with*, before I could make the Detroit at all fit for the lake?

A. Yes, you were.

No. 62

Sentence of the court-martial on Captain Barclay.

That the capture of his majesty's late squadron was caused by the very defective means Captain Barclay possessed to equip them on Lake Erie; the want of a sufficient number of able seamen, whom he had repeatedly and earnestly requested of Sir James Yeo to be sent to him; the very great superiority of the enemy to the British squadron; and the unfortunate early fall of the superior officers in the action. That it appeared that the greatest exertions had been made by Captain Barclay, in equipping and getting into order the vessels under his command; that he was fully justified, under the existing circumstances, in bringing the enemy to action; that the judgment and gallantry of Captain Barclay in taking his squadron into action, and during the contest, were highly conspicuous, and entitled him to the highest praise; and that the whole of the other officers and men of his Majesty's late squadron conducted themselves in the most gallant manner; and did adjudge the said Captain Robert Heriot Barclay, his surviving officers and men, to be most fully and honorably acquitted.—Rear-admiral Foote, president.

No. 63.

Vote of congress.

The congress of the United states voted their thanks to Commodore Perry, and through him to the officers, petty-officers, seamen, marines, and infantry serving as such, attached to the squadron under his command, for the decisive and glorious victory of Lake Erie; also gold medals, &c. and three months extra-pay to all the petty-officers, seamen, marines, and infantry, who were in the engagement.

No. 64.

From Commodore Perry to Messrs. Murray, Draper, and company.

Extracted from an American newspaper.

Newport, May 23, 1814.

Gentlemen,

I have examined two views of the action on Lake Erie, drawn by Mr. Sully, and Mr. Kearney, from information given them by the commanding officers of the American vessels on Erie. I have no hesitation in pronouncing them a correct representation of the engagement at those particular moments.

Wishing that your pecuniary success may equal your exertions in obtaining correct information of the battle.

I am, Gentlemen, your obedient servant,

O. H. PERRY.

Messrs. Murray, Draper, Fairman, and Webster.

No. 65.

From Commodore Chauncey to the American secretary of the navy.

Sackett's harbour, May 1, 1814.

Sir,

I am happy to have it in my power to inform you, that the United States ship Superior, was launched this morning without accident. The Superior is an uncommonly beautiful and well-built ship, something larger than the President, and could mount 64 guns, if it was thought advisable to put as many upon her. This ship has been built in the short space of 80 days; and when it is taken into view, that two brigs of 500 tons each have also been built, rigged, and completely fitted for service, since the first of February, it will be acknowledged that the mechanics employed on this station have done their duty.

I have the honor to be, &c.

ISAAC CHAUNCEY.

Hon. secretary of the navy, &c.

No. 66.

From Commodore Decatur to Sir Thomas M. Hardy.

U.S. ship United States, New London,
17th January, 1814.

Sir,

Having been informed by Nicholas Moran, the master of a sloop recently captured by his Britannic Majesty's ship Endymion, now lying before this port, that, whilst he was on board the Ramillies, and in your hearing, Captain Hope of the Endymion did ask you, whether the frigate United States would not avoid an action. He further states, that he heard you declare it to be your wish, that the U.S. ship

Macedonian, should have a meeting with H. B. S. Statira; that you would furnish men, and give room for such meeting; but that you would not permit the challenge to come from your side.

The Endymion, I am informed, carries 24-pounders; and mounts 50 guns in all. This ship also carries 24-pounders, and mounts 48 guns; besides a 12-pound carronade, a boat-gun.

The Statira mounts 50; the Macedonian, 47; metal the same. So that the force on both sides is as nearly equal as we could expect to find.

If Mr. Moran's statement be correct, it is evident Captains Hope and Stackpoole have the laudable desire of engaging with their ships, the United States and Macedonian: we sir, are ready, and equally desirous for such meeting forthwith.

The only difficulty that appears to be in the way, is from whom the formal invitation is to come. If, sir, you admit Moran's statement to be correct, the difficulty will be removed, and you will be pleased to consider this as an invitation. At the same time we beg you will assure Captains Hope and Stackpoole, that no personal feeling towards them, induces me to make this communication. They are solicitous to add to the renown of their country: we honor their motives.

Captain Biddle, who will have the honour to deliver you this, is authorised on our part, to make any arrangements which may be thought necessary.

I have the honour to be, &c.

S. DECATUR.

To Sir Thomas M. Hardy.

No. 67.

From Captain Stackpoole to Commodore Decatur.

H.M.S. Statira, off N. London,
January 17, 1814.

SIR,

Captain Sir Thomas M. Hardy, Bart. and commodore off New London, has this afternoon handed me a letter from you, expressing a desire that the U.S. ship Macedonian, commanded by Captain Jones, should meet H.M.S. Statira, under my command; and that the U.S. ship United States, bearing your broad pendant, would embrace the same opportunity of meeting the Endymion, commanded by Captain Hope. In the event of Sir Thomas Hardy's permitting our joint acceptation of this rendezvous, I, of course, must be the senior officer; but, in the interim, I shall confine my reply to your obliging letter, as to the future acts of H.M. ship I have the honor to command.

It will afford her captain, officers, and crew, the greatest pleasure, to meet Captain Jones in the Macedonian to-morrow, next day, or whenever such a meeting may suit his purpose: let him only be pleased to appoint the day and place. Say, six or ten leagues south of Montauk point, or further if he pleases; my only subject for selecting this distance from the shore is to avoid any interruption. Little, I think, can be apprehended, as all the captains commanding frigates, excepting one, in these seas, are junior to me; and, in the event of chance, or by accident meeting him, I will hoist a flag of truce, pledging the word and honour of a British officer, (further I cannot offer,) to keep the truce flying, till the Macedonian is out of sight; and, in the event of a junior officer appearing, the same guarantee shall be kept flying until I can detach him.

In accepting this invitation, sir, it is not to vaunt, or, in the most trifling degree, to enhance my own professional character, or take from what is so justly due to Captain Jones; although I have been twice mortified, in being obliged to retreat, in the 26th and 28th of August, 1812, by six American men of war; and, for 12 weeks together, cruizing alone, it has never fallen to the Statira's lot to meet one singly.

The honor of my king, defence of my country, engaged in a just and unprovoked war, added to the glory of the British flag, is all I have in view.

I perceive a statement in your letter, of the comparative force of the two ships; and, as I fear you have been led into error, shall take this opportunity to say, the Statira carries only 46 guns, instead of 50, with two little boat-guns, of more utility in exercising the men, than any effect they might have in the hour of battle; and, without any external finery to recommend her, is simply a British man of war, of her class: nevertheless, a more fair and equal match, in ship and guns, may not soon occur. In number of men, I am aware of having a superiority to oppose: all I request is, that both ships may quickly meet.

Having received your communication by the hand of Sir T. M. Hardy, Bart. I shall convey my reply through the same channel, requesting you will be so good as to hand it to the captain of the Macedonian.

I am, sir, with every consideration,
Your obedient humble servant,
HASSARD STACKPOOLE.

To Commodore Decatur, commanding the U.S.
ship United States, New London.

No. 68.

Sir T. M. Hardy to Commodore Decatur.

Ramillies, off New London,
January 18, 1812.

Sir,

I have the honor to acknowledge the receipt of your letter of yesterday's date, by Captain Biddle, signifying a desire on your part, and that of Captain Jones, as commanders of the ships United States and Macedonian, to meet H.B.M. ships Endymion and Statira, in consequence of a conversation reported to you by Mr. Moran, master of a sloop recently captured; and, in reply, I beg to inform you, I have no hesitation whatever to permit Captain Stackpoole, in the Statira, to meet the Macedonian, as they are sister-ships, carrying the same number of guns, and weight of metal; but, as it is my opinion, the Endymion is not equal to the United States, being 200 tons less, and carrying 26 guns on her main-deck, and only 32-

pound carronades on her quarter-deck and forecastle, when, I am informed, the United States has 30 guns on her main-deck, and 42-pound carronades on her quarter-deck and forecastle, I must consider it my duty, (though very contrary to the wishes of Captain Hope,) to decline the invitation on his part.

The captains of H.B.M. frigates under my orders, as well as myself, cannot too highly appreciate the gallant spirit that has led to the communication from you, sir; and are equally convinced, that no personal feeling towards each other can ever influence a laudable ambition to add to the naval renown of our respective countries.

I have the honor to enclose a letter from Captain Stackpoole, bearing your address; and I pledge my honor to facilitate, by every means in my power, the meeting on the rendezvous pointed out by him, and that none of the captains of H.M. ships, junior to me, shall interfere. Captain Stackpoole's proposal amply provides against that of a senior officer.

Should success attend the Macedonian, I guarantee her proceeding unmolested to any port to the eastward of this anchorage; and I propose the same from you, sir, for the Statira to proceed to Bermuda.

Captain Coote will have the honor to deliver this letter, and to make any arrangements that may be necessary.

I have the honor to be, &c.

T. M. HARDY.

Commodore S. Decatur, &c. &c. New London.

No. 69.

From Commodore Decatur to Sir T. M. Hardy.

U.S. ship United States, New London,
January 19, 1814.

SIR,

I have the honor to acknowledge the receipt of your favor of yesterday, with the enclosure from Captain Stackpoole, by the hands of Captain Coote.

The proposition for a contest between H.B.M. frigates Endymion and Statira, and this ship and the Madedonian, was made by me in the full belief that their force was equal; but it has been declined in consequence of your entertaining a different opinion on this subject from my own.

I do not think myself authorised to comply with the wishes of Captains Jones and Stackpoole, for a meeting in their ships.

This squadron is now under sailing-orders from the government; and I feel myself bound to put to sea the first favourable opportunity that may occur.

In my proposal for a meeting of the four ships, I consented, and I fear incautiously, that you should make up the complements of the Endymion and Statira from the crews of the Ramillies and Borer.

I was induced to accord this indulgence, from a supposition that their crews might have been reduced by manning prizes; and a hope that, as the selected men would be divided between the two ships, the advantage would not be overwhelming.

But, sir, if the Statira is to avail herself alone of this concession, it must be obvious to you, and every one, that I should be yielding to you an advantage I could not excuse to my government; and in making the crew of the Macedonian any degree equal to such a conflict, I should be compelled to break up the crews of this ship and the Hornet, and thus render a compliance with my orders to proceed at sea utterly impracticable. I beg leave also to state, that the guarantee against recapture, in case the Macedonian should prove successful, is very far from satisfactory.

You will have the goodness, sir, to inform Captain Stackpoole, that his letter was shewn to Captain Jones, according to his request; that Captain Jones is extremely desirous that a meeting should take place between the Statira and Macedonian, but is controuled by me for the reasons I have stated.

Whether the war we are engaged in be just and unprovoked on the part of Great Britain, as Captain Stackpoole has been pleased to suggest, is considered by us as a question exclusively with the civilians; and I am perfectly ready to admit, both my incompetence and unwillingness, to confront Captain Stackpoole in its discussion.

I am, Sir, &c.

S. DECATUR.

To Commodore Sir T. M. Hardy, Bart. &c.

No. 70.

From Sir T. M. Hardy to Commodore Decatur.

Ramillies, off New London, Jan. 20, 1814.

Sir,

I have the honor to acquaint you, that I will communicate to Captain Stackpoole your letter of the 19th instant, which I this evening had the honor of receiving by Captain Biddle; and I have nothing further to offer, in addition to my former letter, on the subject of the meeting between the ships of the United States, and those of his Britannic majesty, but that I will give every guarantee in my power, in case of the Macedonian's success, should the meeting ever take place.

I beg to assure you, sir, I shall hail with pleasure the return of an amicable adjustment of the differences between the two nations.

I have the honor to be, &c.

T. M. HARDY.

Commodore Stephan Decatur.

No. 71.

From Captain Hillyar to Mr. Croker.

Valparaiso bay, March 30, 1814.

SIR,

I have the honor to acquaint you, for the information of the lords commissioners of the admiralty, that a little past 3 o'clock in the afternoon of the 28th instant, after nearly five months anxious search, and six weeks still more anxious look-out, for the Essex and her companion, to quit the port of Valparaiso, we saw the former under weigh, and immediately, accompanied by the Cherub, made sail to close with her. On rounding the outer point of the bay, and hauling her wind for the purpose of endeavouring to weather us, and escape, she lost her main-top-mast, and afterwards, not succeeding in an effort to regain the limits of the port, bore up, and anchored so near the shore, (a few miles to the leeward of it,) as to preclude the possibility of passing a-head of her, without risk to his majesty's ships. As we drew near, my intention of going close under her stern was frustrated, by the ship breaking off; and, from the wind blowing extremely fresh, our first fire, commencing a little past 4, and continuing about 10 minutes, produced no visible effect. Our second, a few random shot only, from having increased our distance by wearing, was not, apparently, more successful; and having lost the use of our main-sail, jib, and main-stay, appearances were a little inauspicious. On standing again towards her, I signified my intention of anchoring, for which we were not ready before, with springs, to Captain Tucker, directing him to keep under weigh, and take a convenient station for annoying our opponent. On closing the Essex, at 35 minutes past 5, the firing re-commenced; and, before I gained my intended position, her cable was cut, and a serious conflict ensued; the guns of his majesty's ship gradually becoming more destructive, and her crew, if possible, more animated, which lasted until 20 minutes past 6; when it pleased the Almighty Disposer of events to bless the efforts of my gallant companions, and my personal, very humble ones, with victory. My friend, Captain Tucker, an officer worthy of their lordships' best attentions, was severely wounded at the commencement of the action, but remained on deck till it terminated, using every exertion against the baffling winds, and occasional calms which followed the heavy firing, to close near the enemy. He informs me that his officers and crew, of whose loyalty, zeal, and discipline, I entertain the highest opinion, conducted themselves to his satisfaction.

I have to lament the death of four of my brave companions, and one of his. With real sorrow, I add, that my first-lieutenant, Ingram, is among the number: he fell early, and is a great loss to his majesty's service. The many manly tears which I observed this morning, while performing the last momental duty at his funeral on shore, more fully evinced the respect and affection of his afflicted companions, than any eulogium my pen is equal to. Our lists of wounded are small, and there is only one for whom I am under anxiety. The conduct of my officers and crew, without an individual exception that has come to my knowledge, before, during, and after the battle, was such as became good and loyal subjects, zealous for the honor of their much-loved, though distant, king and country.

The defense of the Essex, taking into consideration our superiority of force, the very discouraging circumstance of her having lost her main-top-mast, and being twice on fire, did honor to her brave defenders, and most fully evinced the courage of Captain Porter, and those under his command. Her colours were not struck, until the loss in killed and wounded was so awfully great, and her shattered condition so seriously bad, as to render further resistance unavailing.

I was much hurt on hearing, that her men had been encouraged, when the result of the action was evidently decided, some to take to their boats, and others to swim on shore. Many were drowned in the attempt; 16 were saved by the exertions of my people, and others. I believe between 30 and 40 effected their landing. I informed Captain Porter that I considered the latter, in point of honor, as my prisoners; he said, the encouragement was given, when the ship was in danger from fire; and I have not pressed the point. The Essex is completely stored and provisioned for, at least six months, and, although much injured in her upper-works, masts, and rigging, is not in such a state as to give the slightest cause of alarm, respecting her being able to perform a voyage to Europe with perfect safety. Our main and mizen-masts, and main-yard, are rather seriously wounded. These, with a few shot-holes between wind and water, which we can get at without lightening, and a loss of canvas and cordage, which we can partly replace from our well-stored prize, are the extent of the injuries his majesty's ship has sustained.

I feel it a pleasant duty to recommend to their lordships' notice my now senior lieutenant, Pearson, and Messrs. Allan, Gardner, Portner, and Daw, midshipmen. I should do very great injustice to Mr. George O'Brien, the mate of the Emily, merchantman, who joined a boat's crew of mine in the harbour, and pushed for the ship, the moment he saw her likely to come to action, were I to omit recommending him to their lordships. His conduct, with that of Mr. N. Murphy, master of the English brig Good Friends, were such as to entitle them both to my lasting regard; and prove, that they were ever ready to hazard their lives in their country's honorable cause. They came on board when the attempt was attended with great risk, and both their boats were swamped. I have before informed their lordships, that Mr. O'Brien was once a lieutenant in his majesty's service; (may I now add, that youthful indiscretions appear to have given place to great correctness of conduct;) and as he has proved his laudable zeal for its honor, I think, if restored, he will be found one of its greatest ornaments. I enclose returns of killed and wounded; and, if conceived to have trespassed on their lordships' time by this very long letter, hope it will be kindly ascribed to the right cause—an earnest wish that merit may meet its due reward.

I have the honor to be, &c.

JAMES HILLYAR.

P.S. There has not been found a ship's book, or paper of any description, (charts excepted,) on board the Essex, or any document relative to the number serving in her previous to the action. Captain

Porter informs me, that he had upwards of 260 victualled. Our prisoners, including 42 wounded, amount to 161; 23 were found dead on her decks; 3 wounded were taken away by Captain Downes, of the Essex Junior, a few minutes before the colours were struck; and, I believe, 20 or 30 reached the shore: the remainder were killed or drowned.

[*Here follow the names of four killed and seven wounded on board the Phœbe; and one killed and three wounded on board the Cherub.*]

JAMES HILLYAR, captain.

J. W. Croker, Esq. &c. &c.

No. 72.

From Captain Hillyar to Captain Porter.

Phœbe, April 4, 1814.

MY DEAR SIR,

Neither in my conversations, nor the accompanying letter, have I mentioned your sword. Ascribe my remissness, in the first instance, to forgetfulness: I consider it only in my servant's possession, with my own, until the master may please to call for it; and, although I omitted, at the moment of presentation, from my mind being much engrossed in attending to professional duties, to offer its restoration, the hand that received it will be most gladly extended to put it in possession of him, who wore it so honorably in defending his country's cause.

Believe me, my dear sir,
Very faithfully your's,
JAMES HILLYAR.

Captain Porter.

No. 73.

From Captain Porter to the American secretary of the navy.

Essex Junior, at sea, July 3, 1814.

SIR,

I have done myself the honor to address you repeatedly since I left the Delaware, but have scarcely a hope that one of my letters has reached you; therefore consider it necessary to give a brief history of my proceeding since that period.

I sailed from the Delaware on the 27th of October, 1812, and repaired, with all diligence, (agreeably to instruction from Commodore Bainbridge,) to Port Praya, Fernando de Noronha, and Cape Frio, and arrived at each place on the day appointed to meet him. On my passage from Port Praya to Fernando de Noronha, I captured H.B.M. packet Norton, and after taking out 11,000*l.* sterling in specie, sent her, under command of Lieutenant Finch, for America. I cruized off Rio de Janeiro, and about Cape Frio, until the 12th of

January, 1813, hearing frequently of the commodore by vessels from Bahia. I here captured but one schooner, with hides and tallow. I sent her into Rio. The Montague, the admiral's ship, being in pursuit of me, my provisions now getting short, and finding it necessary to look out for a supply, to enable me to meet the commodore, by the 1st of April, off St. Helena, I proceeded to the island of St. Catherine's, (the last place of rendezvous on the coast of Brazil,) as the most likely to supply my wants, and at the same time afford me that secrecy, necessary to enable me to elude the British ships of war on the coast, and expected there. I here could procure only wood, water, rum, and a few bags of flour; and hearing of the commodore's action with the Java, the capture of the Hornet by the Montague, and a considerable augmentation of the British force on the coast, and of several being in pursuit of me, I found it necessary to get to sea as soon as possible. I now, agreeably to the commodore's plan, stretched to the southward, scouring the coast as far as Rio de la Plata. I heard that Buenos Ayres was in a state of starvation, and could not supply our wants, and that the government of Monteviedo was very inimical to us. The commodore's instructions now left it discretionary with me what course to pursue, and I determined on following that which had not only met his approbation, but the approbation of the then secretary of the navy. I accordingly shaped my course for the Pacific, and after suffering greatly from short allowance of provisions, and heavy gales off Cape Horn, (for which my ship and men were illy provided,) I arrived at Valparaiso on the 14th March, 1813. I here took in as much jerked beef, and other provisions, as my ship would conveniently stow, and run down the coast of Chili and Peru. In this track I fell in with a Peruvian corsair, which had on board 24 Americans, as prisoners, the crews of two whale-ships which she had taken on the coast of Chili. The captain informed me, that as the allies of Great Britain, they would capture all they should meet with, in expectation of a war between Spain and the United States. I consequently threw all his guns and ammunition into the sea, liberated the Americans, wrote a respectful letter to the vice-roy, explaining the cause of my proceedings, which I delivered to her captain. I then proceeded for Lima, and re-captured one of the vessels as she was entering the port. From thence I proceeded for the Gallapagos islands, where I cruized from the 17th of April, until the 3d of October, 1813; during which time I touched only once on the coast of America, which was for the purpose of procuring a supply of fresh water, as none is to be found among those islands, which are, perhaps, the most barren and desolate of any known.

While among this group, I captured the following British ships, employed chiefly in the spermaceti whale-fishery; viz. –

Letters of marque.

	Tons.	Men.	Guns.	Pierced for
Montezuma	270	21	2	—
Policy	175	26	10	18
Georgiana	280	25	6	18
Greenwich	338	25	10	20
Atlantic	353	24	8	20

Rose	220	21	8	20
Hector	270	25	11	20
Catherine	270	29	8	18
Seringapatam	357	31	14	26
Charlton	274	21	10	18
New Zealander	259	23	8	13
Sir A. Hammond	301	31	12	18
	3369	302	107	

As some of those ships were captured by boats, and others by prizes, my officers and men had several opportunities of shewing their gallantry.

The Rose and Charlton were given up to the prisoners; the Hector, Catherine, and Montezuma, I sent to Valparaiso, where they were laid up; the Policy, Georgiana, and New Zealander, I sent for America; the Greenwich I kept as a store-ship, to contain the stores of my other prizes, necessary for us; and the Atlantic, now called the Essex Junior, I equipped with 20 guns, and gave command of her to Lieutenant Downes.

Lieutenant Downes had convoyed the prizes to Valparaiso, and on his return brought me letters, informing me that a squadron, under the command of Commodore James Hillyar, consisting of the frigate Phœbe, of 36 guns, the Racoon and Cherub sloops of war, and a store-ship of 20 guns, had sailed on the 6th of July for this sea. The Racoon and Cherub had been seeking me for some time on the coast of Brazil, and on their return from their cruize, joined the squadron sent in search of me to the Pacific. My ship, as it may be supposed, after being near a year at sea, required some repairs to put her in a state to meet them, which I determined to do, and to bring them to action, if I could meet them on nearly equal terms. I proceeded now, in company with the remainder of my prizes, to the island of Noaheevah, or Madison island, lying in the Washington groupe, discovered by Captain Ingraham, of Boston. Here I caulked, and completely overhauled my ship, made for her a new set of water-casks, her old ones being entirely decayed, and took on board, from my prizes, provisions and stores for upwards of four months, and sailed for the coast of Chili on the 12th December, 1813. Previous to sailing, I secured the Seringapatam, Greenwich, and Sir Andrew Hammond, under the guns of a battery, which I erected for their protection. After taking possession of this fine island for the United states, and establishing the most friendly intercourse with the natives, I left them, under the charge of Lieutenant Gamble, of the marines, with 21 men, with orders to repair to Valparaiso after a certain period.

I arrived on the coast of Chili on the 12th January, 1814; looked into Conception and Valparaiso; found at both places only three English vessels; and learned that the squadron, which sailed from Rio de Janeiro for that sea, had not been heard of since their departure, and were supposed to be lost in endeavouring to double Cape Horn.

I had completely broken up the British navigation in the Pacific: the vessels which had not been captured by me were laid up, and dared not venture out. I had afforded the most ample protection to our own vessels, which were, on my arrival, very numerous, and unprotected. The valuable whale-fishery there is entirely destroyed, and the actual injury we have done them may be estimated at two and a half millions of dollars, independent of the expenses of the vessels in search of me. They have furnished me amply with sails, cordage, cables, anchor, provisions, medicines, and stores of every description; and the slops on board them have furnished clothing for the seamen. We have, in fact, lived on the enemy since I have been in that sea, every prize having proved a well-found store-ship for me. I had not yet been under the necessity of drawing bills on the department for any object, and had been enabled to make considerable advances to my officers and crew on account of pay.

For the unexampled time we had kept the sea, my crew had been remarkably healthy. I had but one case of the scurvy, and had lost only the following men by death; viz.—John S. Cowan, lieutenant; Robert Miller, surgeon; Levi Holmes, Edward Sweeney, ordinary seaman; Samual Groce, seaman; James Spafford, gunner's-mate; Benjamin Geers, John Rodgers, quarter-gunners; Andrew Mahan, corporal of marines; Lewis Price, private marine.

I had done all the injury that could be done the British commerce in the Pacific, and still hoped to signalize my cruize by something more splendid, before leaving that sea. I thought it not improbable that Commodore Hillyar might have kept his arrival secret; and, believing that he would seek me at Valparaiso, as the most likely place to find me, I therefore determined to cruize about that place; and, should I fail of meeting him, hoped to be compensated by the capture of some merchant-ships, said to be expected from England.

The Phœbe, agreeably to my expectations, came to seek me at Valparaiso, where I was anchored with the Essex; my armed prize, the Essex Junior, under the command of Lieutenant Downes, on the look-out off the harbour. But, contrary to the course I thought he would pursue, Commodore Hillyar brought with him the Cherub sloop of war, mounting twenty-eight guns, eighteen 32-pound carronades, eight 24s, and two long 9s on the quarter-deck and forecastle, and a complement of 180 men. The force of the Phœbe is as follows:—thirty long 18-pounders, sixteen 32-pound carronades, one howitzer, and six 3-pounders in the tops: in all, fifty-three guns, and a complement of 320 men; making a force of eighty-one guns, and 500 men. In addition to which, they took on board the crew of an English letter of marque, lying in port. Both ships have picked crews, and were sent in the Pacific, in company with the Racoon, of 22 guns, and a store-ship, of 20 guns, for the express purpose of seeking the Essex; and was prepared with flags, bearing the motto, "God and country; British sailors' best rights; traitors offend both." This was intended as a reply to my motto, "Free trade and sailors' rights," under the erroneous impression that my crew were chiefly Englishmen, or to counteract its effects on their own crews. The force of the Essex was 46 guns: forty 32-pound carronades, and six long 12s; and her crew, which had been much reduced by prizes, amounting only to 255 men. The Essex Junior, which was intended chiefly as a store-ship, mounted 20 guns: ten 18-pound carronades, and ten short 6s, with only 60 men on board. In reply to their motto, I wrote at my mizzen, "God, our country, and liberty: tyrants offend them."

On getting their provisions on board, they went off the port for the purpose of blockading me, where they cruized for near six weeks; during which time I endeavoured to provoke a challenge, and frequently, but ineffectually, to bring the Phœbe alone to action: first, with both my ships, and afterwards with my single ship, with both crews on board. I was several times under way, and ascertained that I had greatly the advantage in point of sailing; and once succeeded in closing within gun-shot of the Phœbe, and commenced a fire on her, when she ran down for the Cherub, which was 2½ miles to-leeward. This excited some surprize, and expressions of indignation, as, previous to my getting under way, she hove-to off the port, hoisted her motto-flag, and fired a gun to-windward. Commodore Hillyar seemed determined to avoid a contest with me on nearly equal terms; and from his extreme prudence in keeping both his ships ever after constantly within hail of each other, there were no hopes of any advantages to my country from a longer stay in port. I therefore determined to put to sea the first opportunity which should offer; and I was the more strongly induced to do so, as I had gained certain intelligence that the Tagus, rated 38, and two other frigates, had sailed for that sea in pursuit of me; and I had reason to expect the arrival of the Racoon, from the N.W. coast of America, where she had been sent for the purpose of destroying our fur-establishment on the Columbia. A rendezvous was appointed for the Essex Junior, and every arrangement made for sailing; and I intended to let them chase me off, to give the Essex Junior an opportunity of escaping. On the 28th of March, the day after this determination was formed, the wind came on to blow fresh from the southward, when I parted my larboard cable, and dragged my starboard anchor directly out to sea. Not a moment was to be lost in getting sail on the ship. The enemy were close in with the point forming the west-side of the bay; but, on opening them, I saw a prospect of passing to-windward, when I took in my top-gallant-sails, which were set over single-reefed top-sails, and braced up for this purpose; but, on rounding the point, a heavy squall struck the ship, and carried away her main-top-mast, precipitating the men who were aloft into the sea, who were drowned. Both ships now gave chase to me, and I endeavoured, in my disabled state, to regain the port; but finding I could not recover the common anchorage, I ran close into a small bay, about three-quarters of a mile to-leeward of the battery on the east-side of the harbour, and let go my anchor within pistol-shot of the shore, where I intended to repair my damages as soon as possible. The enemy continued to approach, and shewed an evident intention of attacking, regardless of the neutrality of the place where I was anchored; and the caution observed in their approach to the attack of the crippled Essex, was truly ridiculous, as was their display of their motto-flags, and the number of jacks at all their mast-heads. I, with as much expedition as circumstances would admit of, got my ship ready for action, and endeavoured to get a spring on my cable; but had not succeeded, when the enemy, at 54 minutes past 3 P.M. made his attack: the

Phœbe placing herself under my stern, and the Cherub on my starboard-bow; but the Cherub, soon finding her situation a hot one, bore up and ran under my stern also; where both ships kept up a hot raking fire. I had got three long 12-pounders out of the stern-ports; which were worked with so much bravery and skill, that in half an hour we so disabled both as to compel them to haul off to repair damages. In the course of this firing, I had, by the great exertions of Mr. Edward Barnewell, the acting sailing-master, assisted by Mr. Linscott, the boatswain, succeeded in getting springs on our cable three different times; but the fire of the enemy was so excessive, that, before we could get our broadside to bear, they were shot away, and thus rendered useless to us.

My ship had received many injuries, and several had been killed and wounded; but my brave officers and men, notwithstanding the unfavorable circumstances under which we were brought to action, and the powerful force opposed to us, were no ways discouraged. All appeared determined to defend their ship to the last extremity; and to die in preference to a shameful surrender. Our gaff, with the ensign, and the motto-flag at the mizen, had been shot away; but "Free trade and sailors' rights," continued to fly at the fore. Our ensign was replaced by another; and, to guard against a similar event, an ensign was made fast in the mizen-rigging; and several jacks were hoisted in different parts of the ship. The enemy soon repaired his damages for a fresh attack: he now placed himself, with both his ships, on my starboard-quarter, out of the reach of my carronades, and where my stern-guns could not be brought to bear. He there kept up a most galling fire, which it was out of my power to return; when I saw no prospect in injuring him without getting under way, and becoming the assailant.

My top-sail sheets and haliards were all shot away, as well as the jib, and fore-top-mast staysail haliards. The only rope not cut, was the flying-jib haliards; and that being the only sail I could set, I caused it to be hoisted, my cable to be cut, and ran down on both ships, with an intention of laying the Phœbe on board. The firing on both sides was now tremendous. I had let fall my fore-top-sail, and fore-sail, but the want of tacks and sheets rendered them almost useless to us; yet we were enabled, for a short time, to close with the enemy; and, although our decks were now strewed with dead, and our cockpit filled with wounded; although our ship had been several times on fire, and was rendered a perfect wreck, we were still encouraged to hope to save her, from the circumstances of the Cherub, from her crippled state, being compelled to haul off. She did not return to close action again, although she had apparently had it in her power to do so; but kept up a distant firing with her long guns. The Phœbe, from our disabled state, was enabled however, by edging off, to choose the distance which best suited her long-guns, and kept up a tremendous fire on us, which mowed down my brave companions by the dozen. Many of my guns had been rendered useless by the enemy's shot; and many of them had had whole crews destroyed. We manned them again from those which were disabled; and one gun, in particular, was three times manned; fifteen men were slain at it in the course of the action; but, strange as it may appear, the captain of it escaped with only a slight wound.

Finding that the enemy had it in his power to choose his distance, I now gave up all hopes of closing with him; and as the wind, for the moment, seemed to favor the design, I determined to endeavour to run her on shore, land my men, and destroy her. Every thing seemed to favor my wishes. We had approached the shore within musket-shot, and I had no doubt of succeeding, when, in an instant, the wind shifted from the land, (as is very common in this port in the latter part of the day,) and played our head down on the Phœbe; where we were again exposed to a dreadful raking fire. My ship was now totally unmanageable; yet, as her head was toward the enemy, and he to-leeward of me, I still hoped to be able to board him. At this moment, Lieutenant-commandant Downes came on board to receive my orders, under the impression that I should soon be a prisoner. He could be of no use to me in the wretched state of the Essex; and finding (from the enemy's putting his helm up) that my last attempt at boarding would not succeed, I directed him, after he had been about ten minutes on board, to return to his own ship, to be prepared for defending and destroying her in case of an attack. He took with him several of my wounded, leaving three of his boats' crew on board to make room for them. The Cherub had now an opportunity of distinguishing herself, by keeping up a hot fire on him during his return. The slaughter on board my ship had now become horrible; the enemy continuing to rake us, and we unable to bring a gun to bear. I therefore directed a hawser to be bent to the sheet-anchor, and the anchor to be cut from the bows, to bring her head round; this succeeded. We again got our broadside to bear; and as the enemy was much crippled, and unable to hold his own, I have no doubt he would soon have drifted out of gun-shot before he discovered we had anchored, had not the hawser unfortunately parted. My ship had taken fire several times during the action, but alarmingly so, forward and aft, at this moment. The flames were bursting up each hatchway, and no hopes were entertained of saving her. Our distance from the shore did not exceed three-quarters of a mile; and I hoped many of my brave crew would be able to save themselves, should the ship blow up, as I was informed the fire was near the magazine; and the explosion of a large quantity of powder below served to increase the horrors of our situation. Our boats were destroyed by the enemy's shot, I therefore directed those who could swim to jump overboard, and endeavour to gain the shore. Some reached it, some were taken by the enemy, and some perished in the attempt; but most preferred sharing with me the fate of the ship. We who remained, now turned our attention wholly to extinguishing the flames; and when we had succeeded, went again to our guns, where the firing was kept up for some minutes, but the crew had by this time become so weakened, that they all declared to me the impossibility of making further resistance; and entreated me to surrender my ship to save the wounded, as all further attempts at opposition must prove ineffectual, almost every gun being disabled by the destruction of their crews. I now sent for the officers of divisions to consult them; but what was my surprise to find only Acting-lieutenant, Stephen Decatur M'Knight, remaining; who confirmed the report respecting the condition of the guns on the gun-deck; those on the spar-deck were not in a better condition.

Lieutenant Wilmer, after fighting most gallantly throughout the action, had been knocked overboard by a splinter, while getting the sheet-anchor from the bows, and was drowned. Acting-lieutenant John G. Cowell had lost a leg; Mr. Edward Barnewell, acting sailing-master had been carried below, after receiving two severe wounds, one in the breast, and one in the face; and Acting-lieutenant Wm. H. Oldenheimer, had been knocked overboard from the quarter an instant before, and did not regain the ship until after the surrender. I was informed that the cockpit, the steerage, the wardroom, and the birth-deck could contain no more wounded; that the wounded were killed while the surgeons were dressing them; and that, unless something was speedily done to prevent it, the ship would soon sink from the number of shot-holes in her bottom. And on sending for the carpenter, he informed me, that all his crew had been killed or wounded; and that he had once been over the side to stop the leaks; when his slings had been shot away, and it was with difficulty he was saved from drowning. The enemy, from the smoothness of the water, and the impossibility of our reaching him with our carronades, and the little apprehension that was excited by our fire, which had now become much slackened, was enabled to take aim at us as at a target. His shot never missed our hull, and my ship was cut up in a manner, which was, perhaps, never before witnessed. In fine, I saw no hopes of saving her; and at twenty minutes past 6, P.M. gave the painful order to strike the colours. Seventy-five men, including officers, were all that remained of my whole crew, after the action, capable of doing duty; and many of them severely wounded, some of whom have since died. The enemy still continued his fire, and my brave though unfortunate companions were still falling about me. I directed an opposite gun to be fired, to shew them we intended no further resistance; but they did not desist; four men were killed at my side, and others in different parts of the ship. I now believe he intended to shew us no quarters, and that it would be as well to die with my flag flying, as struck; and was on the point of again hoisting it, when, about ten minutes after hauling the colours down, he ceased firing.

I cannot speak in sufficiently high terms of the conduct of those engaged for such an unparalleled length of time (under such circumstances) with me in the arduous and unequal conflict. Let it suffice to say, that more bravery, skill, patriotism, and zeal, were never displayed on any occasion. Every one seemed determined to die in defence of their much-loved country's cause, and nothing but views of humanity could ever have reconciled them to the surrender of the ship; they remembered their wounded and helpless shipmates below. To Acting-lieutenant M'Knight and Oldenheimer, I feel much indebted for their great exertions and bravery throughout the action, in fighting and encouraging the men at their divisions, for the dexterous management of the long guns, and for their promptness in re-manning their guns as their crews were slaughtered. The conduct of that brave and heroic officer, Acting-lieutenant John G. Cowell, who lost his leg in the latter part of the action, excited the admiration of every man in the ship, and after being wounded, would not consent to be taken below, until loss of blood rendered him insensible. Mr. Edward Barnewell, acting sailing-master, whose activity and courage were equally conspicuous, returned on deck after receiving his first wound, and remained after receiving his second, until fainting with loss of blood. Mr. Samuel B. Johnston, who had joined me the day before, and acted as marine-officer, conducted himself with great bravery, and exerted himself in assisting at the long-guns; the musketry after the first half hour being useless from our long distance.

Mr. M. W. Bostwick, whom I had appointed acting purser of the Essex Junior, and who was on board my ship, did the duties of aid in a manner which reflects on him the highest honour; and Midshipman Isaacs, Farragut, and Ogden, as well as Acting-midshipmen James Terry, James R. Lyman, and Samuel Duzenbury, and Master's-mate William Pierce, exerted themselves in the performance of their respective duties, and gave an earnest of their value to the service: the three first are too young to recommend for promotion; the latter I beg leave to recommend for confirmation, as well as the acting lieutenants, and Messrs, Bamewell, Johnston, and Bastwic.

We have been unfortunate but not disgraced. The defence of the Essex has not been less honorable to her officers and crew, than the capture of an equal force; and I now consider my situation less unpleasant than that of Commodore Hillyar, who, in violation of every principle of honor and generosity, and regardless of the rights of nations, attacked the Essex in her crippled state within pistol-shot of a neutral shore, when for six weeks I had daily offered him fair and honourable combat, on terms greatly to his advantage. The blood of the slain must rest on his head; and he has yet to reconcile his conduct to Heaven, to his conscience, and to the world. The annexed extract of a letter from Commodore Hillyar, which was written previous to his returning me my sword, will shew his opinion of our conduct.

My loss has been dreadfully severe, 58 killed, or have since died of their wounds, and among them Lieutenant Cowell; 39 were severely wounded, 27 slightly, and 31 are missing; making in all 154 killed, wounded, and missing, a list of whose names is annexed.

The professional knowledge of Dr. Richard Hoffman, acting surgeon, and Dr. Alexander Montgomery, acting surgeon's mate, added to their assiduity, and the benevolent attentions and assistance of Mr. D. P. Adams, the chaplain, saved the lives of many of the wounded. Those gentlemen have been indefatigable in their attentions to them; the first two I beg leave to recommend for confirmation, and the latter to the notice of the department.

I must in justification of myself, observe, that with our six 12-pounders only, we fought this action—our carronades being almost useless.

The loss in killed and wounded has been great with the enemy; among the former is the first lieutenant of the Phœbe, and of the latter, Captain Tucker of the Cherub, whose wounds are severe. Both the Essex and Phœbe were in a sinking state, and it was with difficulty they could be kept a-float until they anchored in Valparaiso next morning. The battered state of the Essex will, I believe, prevent her ever reaching England; and I also think it will be out of their power to repair the damages of the Phœbe, so as to enable her to double Cape Horn. All the masts and yards of the Phœbe and Cherub are badly crippled, and their hulls much cut up; the former had eighteen 12-pound shot through her, below her water-line, some three feet under water. Nothing but the smoothness of the water saved both the Phœbe and Essex.

I hope, sir, that our conduct may prove satisfactory to our country, and it will testify it by obtaining our speedy exchange, that we may again have it in our power to prove our zeal.

Commodore Hillyar, I am informed, has thought proper to state to his government, that the action lasted only 45 minutes. Should he have done so, the motive may be easily discovered; but the thousands of disinterested witnesses, who covered the surrounding hills, can testify that we fought his ships near two hours and a half. Upwards of 50 broadsides were fired by the enemy, agreeably to their own accounts, and upwards of 75 by ours. Except the few minutes they were repairing damages, the firing was incessant.

Soon after my capture I entered into an agreement with Commodore Hillyar to disarm my prize, the Essex Junior, and proceed with the survivors of my officers and crew in her to the United states, taking with me all her officers and crew. He consented to grant her a passport, to secure her from recapture. The ship was small, and we knew we had much to suffer; yet we hoped to reach our country in safety, that we might again have it in our power to serve it. This arrangement was attended with no additional expense, as she was abundantly supplied with provisions and stores for the voyage.

In justice to Commodore Hillyar I must observe, that although I can never be reconciled to the manner of his attack on the Essex, or his conduct before the action, he has, since our capture, shewn the greatest humanity to my wounded, whom he permitted me to land, on condition that the United States should bear their expenses; and has endeavoured, as much as lay in his power, to alleviate the distresses of war, by the most generous and delicate deportment towards myself, my officers, and crew. He gave orders that the property of every person should be respected. His orders, however, were not so strictly attended to as might have been expected; besides being deprived of books, charts, &c. &c. both myself and officers lost many articles of our clothing: some to a considerable amount. I should not have considered this last circumstance of sufficient importance to notice, did it not mark a striking difference between the navy of Great Britain and that of the United States, highly creditable to the latter.

By the arrival of the Tagus, a few days after my capture, I was informed that, besides the ships which had arrived in the Pacific in parsuit of me, and those still expected, others were sent to cruize for me in the China seas, off New Zealand, Timour, and New Holland; and that another frigate was sent to the river la Plata.

To possess the Essex, it has cost the British government near six millions of dollars, and yet, sir, her capture was owing entirely to accident; and if we consider the expedition with which naval contests are now decided, the action is a dishonor to them. Had they brought their ships boldly to action with a force so very superior, and having the choice of position, they should either have captured or destroyed us in one-fourth the time they were about it.

During the action our consul-general, Mr. Poinsett, called on the governor of Valparaiso, and requested that the batteries might protect the Essex. The request was refused; but he promised, that if she should succeed in fighting her way to the common anchorage, he would send an officer to the British commander, and request him to cease firing, but declined using force under any circumstances, and there is no doubt a perfect understanding existed between them. This conduct, added to the assistance given to the British, and their friendly reception after their action, and the strong bias of the faction which governs Chili in favor of the English, as well as their hostility to the Americans, induced Mr. Poinsett to leave that country. Under such circumstances, I did not conceive that it would be proper for me to claim the restoration of my ship, confident that the claim would be made by my government to more effect. Finding some difficulty in the sale of my prizes, I had taken the Hector and Catherine to sea, and burnt them, with their cargoes.

I exchanged Lieutenant M'Knight, Mr. Adams, and Mr. Lyman, and 11 seamen, for part of the crew of the Sir Andrew Hammond, and sailed from Valparaiso on the 27th of April; where the enemy were still patching up their ships, to put them in a state for proceeding to Rio de Janeiro, previous to going to England.

Annexed is a list of the remains of my crew to be exchanged, as also a copy of the correspondence between Commodore Hillyar and myself on that subject. I also send you a list of the prisoners I have taken during my cruize, amounting to 343.

I have the honor to be, &c.

D. PORTER.

Hon. secretary of the navy of the United
States, Washington.

P.S. To give you a correct idea of the state of the Essex at the time of her surrender, I send you the boatswain's and carpenter's report of damages; I also send you a report of the divisions.

[*Here follows a return of killed, as already numbered; but* no "report of damages" *sustained by the Essex; nor* "list of the remains of her crew."]

No. 74.

From Captain Porter to the American secretary of the navy.

New York, July 13, 1814.

SIR,

There are some facts relating to our enemy, and although not connected with the action, serve to shew his perfidy, and should be known.

On Commodore Hillyar's arrival at Valparaiso, he ran the Phœbe close alongside the Essex, and enquired politely after my health, observing that his ship was cleared for action, and his men prepared for boarding. I observed, "sir, if you, by any accident, get on board of me, I assure you that great confusion will take place: I am prepared to receive you, but shall only act on the defensive." He observed, coolly and indifferently, "Oh, sir, I have no such intention." At this instant his ship took a-back on my starboard-bow, her yards nearly locking with those of the Essex. I called all hands to board the enemy, and, in an instant, my crew were ready to spring on her decks. Commodore Hillyar exclaimed, with great agitation, "I had no intention of getting on-board of you—I had no intention of coming so near you—I am sorry I came so near you." His ship fell off, with her jib-boom over my decks, her bows exposed to my broadside, her stern to the fire of the Essex Junior, her crew in the greatest confusion, and in 15 minutes I could have taken or destroyed her. After he had brought his ship to anchor, Commodore Hillyar, and Captain Tucker, of the Cherub, visited me on shore; when I asked him if he intended to respect the neutrality of the port. "Sir," said he, "you have paid such respect to the neutrality of this port, that I feel myself bound in honor to do the same."

I have the honor to be, &c.

D. PORTER.

Hon. secretary of the navy, &c.

No. 75.

From Captain Pigot to Vice-admiral Cochrane.

H.M.S. Orpheus, New-Providence,
April 25, 1814.

Sir,

I have the pleasure to acquaint you, that on the 20th instant, after a chase of 60 miles, the point of Matanzas, in Cuba, bearing S.S.E. five leagues, we captured the U.S. ship Frolic, commanded by Master-commandant Joseph Bainbridge. She had mounted twenty 32-pound carronades, and two long 18s, with 171 men; but, a few minutes before striking her colours, threw all her lee-guns overboard, and continued throwing also her shot, small-arms, &c. until taken possession of. She is a remarkably fine ship, of 509 tons, and the first time of her going to sea. She has been out from Boston two months, and frequently chased by our cruisers. Their only capture was the Little Fox, a brig laden with fish, which they destroyed.

I have the honor to be, &c.

H. PIGOT, captain.

The Hon. Alexander Cochrane,
commander-in-chief, &c.

No. 76.

From Captain Warrington to the American secretary of the navy.

U.S. sloop Peacock, at sea, lat. 27° 47′,
Sir, Long. 80° 9′, April 29, 1814.

I have the honor to inform you, that we have this morning captured, after an action of 45 minutes, H.M. brig Epervier, rating and mounting eighteen 32-pound carronades, with 128 men, of whom eight were killed, and 15 wounded; (according to the best information we could obtain;) among the latter is her first lieutenant, who has lost an arm, and received a severe splinter-wound on the hip. Not a man in the Peacock was killed, and only two wounded, neither dangerously. The fate of the Epervier would have been determined in much less time, but for the circumstance of our fore-yard being totally disabled by two round-shot in the starboard-quarter, from her first broadside, which entirely deprived us of the use of our fore and fore-top-sails, and compelled us to keep the ship large throughout the remainder of the action.

This, with a few top-mast, and top-gallant back-stays, cut away, and a few shot through our sails, is the only injury the Peacock has sustained. Not a round-shot touched her hull: our masts and spars are as sound as ever. When the enemy struck, he had five feet water in his hold, his main-top-mast was over the side, his main-boom shot away, his fore-mast cut nearly in two, and tottering, his fore-rigging and stays shot away, his bowsprit badly wounded, and 45 shot-holes in his hull, 20 of which were within a foot of his water-line. By great exertion, we got her in sailing order just as dark came on.

In 15 minutes after the enemy struck, the Peacock was ready for another action, in every respect, but her fore-yard; which was sent down, fished, and had the fore-sail set again, in 45 minutes: such were the spirit and activity of our gallant crew. The Epervier had under convoy an English hermaphrodite brig, a Russian and a Spanish ship, which all hauled their wind, and stood to the E.N.E. I had determined upon pursuing the former, but found that it would not answer to leave our prize in her then crippled state, and the more particularly so, as we found she had 120,000 dollars in specie, which we soon transferred to this sloop. Every officer, seaman, and marine, did his duty, which is the highest compliment I can pay them.

I am, respectfully,

L. WARRINGTON.

P.S. From Lieutenant Nicholson's report, who was counting up the Epervier's crew, there were 11 killed, and 15 wounded.

L. W.

The secretary of the navy, &c.

No. 77

Vote of congress.

Congress voted their thanks to Captain Lewis Warrington, officers, and crew of the Peacock, for the skill and bravery displayed in the capture of the Epervier. They also gave to Captain Warrington a gold medal, with emblematic devices; to each of the commissioned officers a silver medal, with like devices; and to each of the midshipmen and sailing-masters a sword.

No. 78.

From Captain Blakeley to the American secretary of the navy.

U.S. sloop Wasp, l'Orient,
July 8, 1814.

Sir,

On Tuesday, the 28th ultimo, being then in lat. 48° 36′ N. and long. 11° 15′ W. we fell in with, engaged, and, after an action of 19 minutes, captured, his Britannic majesty's sloop of war the Reindeer, William Manners, Esq. Commander. Annexed are the minutes of our proceedings prior to, and during the continuance of the action.

Where all did their duty, and each appeared anxious to excel, it is very difficult to discriminate. It is, however, only rendering them their merited due, when it is declared of Lieutenants Reilly and Bury, first and third of this vessel, and whose names will be among those of the conquerors of the Guerriere and Java, and of Mr. Tillinghost, second lieutenant, who was greatly instrumental in the capture of the Boxer, that their conduct and courage on this occasion fulfilled the highest expectation, and gratified every wish. Sailing-master Carr is also entitled to great credit, for the zeal and ability with which he discharged his various duties.

The cool and patient conduct of every officer and man, while exposed to the fire of the shifting-gun of the enemy, and without an opportunity of returning it, could only be equalled by the animation and ardour exhibited, when actually engaged, or by the promptitude and firmness with which every attempt of the enemy to board was met, and successfully repelled. Such conduct may be seen, but cannot well be described.

The Reindeer mounted sixteen 24-pound carronades, two long 6 or 9-pounders, and a shifting 12-pound carronade, with a complement on board of 118 men. Her crew were said to be the pride of Plymouth.

Our loss in men has been severe, owing, in part, to the proximity of the two vessels, and the extreme smoothness of the sea, but chiefly in repelling boarders. That of the enemy, however, was infinitely more so, as will be seen by the list of killed and wounded on both sides.

Six round-shot struck our hull, and many grape, which did not penetrate far. The fore-mast received a 24-pound shot, which passed through its centre, and our rigging and sails were a good deal injured.

The Reindeer was literally cut to pieces in a line with her ports: her upper-works, boats, and spare spars, were one complete wreck. A breeze springing up next afternoon, her fore-mast went by the board.

Having received all the prisoners on board; which, from the number of wounded, occupied much time, together with their baggage, the Reindeer was, on the evening of the 29th, set on fire, and in a few hours blew up.

I have the honor to be, &c.

J. BLAKELEY.

Hon. William Jones, &c.

No. 79.

American minutes of the action between the U.S. sloop Wasp and H.B.M. sloop Reindeer, on the 28th of June, 1814, in latitude 48° 36′ N. and longitude 11° 14′ W.

At 4 A.M. light breezes and cloudy; at a quarter past 4, discovered two sail, two points before the lee-beam; kept away in chase; shortly after [afterwards] discovered one sail on the weather-beam; altered the course, and hauled-by, in chase of the sail to-windward; at 8, sail to-windward bore E.N.E. wind very light; at 10, the strange sail bearing E.N.E. hoisted an English ensign and pendant, and displayed a signal at the main. (blue and yellow diagonally.) Meridian, light airs and cloudy; at half-past 12, the enemy shewed a blue and white flag diagonally at the fore, and fired a gun; 15 minutes after 1, called all hands to quarters, and prepared for action; 22 minutes after 1, believing we could weather the enemy, tacked ship and stood for him; 50 minutes after 1, the enemy tacked ship and stood from us; 56 minutes after 1, hoisted our colours, and fired a gun to-windward, which was answered by the enemy with another to-windward; 20 minutes after 2, the enemy still standing from us, set the royals; 25 minutes after 2, set the flying-jib; 29 minutes after 2, set the upper stay-sails; 32 minutes after 2, the enemy having tacked for us, took in the stay-sails; 37 minutes after 2, furled the royals; 51 minutes after 2, seeing that the enemy would be able to weather us, tacked ship; 3 minutes after 3, the enemy hoisted his flying-jib; brailed up our mizen; 15 minutes after 3, the enemy on our weather-quarter, distant about 60 yards, fired his shifting-gun, a 12-pound carronade, at us, loaded with round and grape-shot, from his top-gallant-forecastle; 17 minutes after 3, fired the same gun a second time; 19 minutes after 3, fired it a third time; 21 minutes after 3, fired it a fourth time; 24 minutes after 3, a fifth shot, all from the same gun. Finding the enemy did not get sufficiently on the beam, to enable us to bring our guns to bear, put the helm a-lee; and, at 26 minutes after 3, commenced the action with the after-carronade on the starboard-side, and fired in succession; 34 minutes after 3, hauled up the main-sail; 40 minutes after 3, the enemy having his bow in contact with our larboard quarter, endeavoured to board us, but was repulsed in every attempt; at 44 minutes after 3, orders were given to board in turn, which were promptly executed, when all resistance immediately ceased; and, at 45 minutes after 3, the enemy hauled down his flag.

J. BLAKELEY.

List of killed and wounded on board the U.S. sloop of war Wasp, in the action with the Reindeer.

Killed, and since dead (including 2 midshipmen)		11
Wounded severely	5	
——— slightly	10—	15
Total		26

List of the killed and wounded on board H.B.M. sloop Reindeer.

Killed—William Manners, Esq. Commander; John Thomas Barton, purser; and 23 petty-officers and seamen.

Wounded—Thomas Chambers, first lieutenant; Richard Jones, master; and 40 petty-officers and seamen.

Recapitulation.

Killed		25
Wounded dangerously	10	
——— severely	17	
——— slightly	15—	42
Total		67

No. 80.

Vote of Congress.

The president of the United States, at the request of congress, presented to Captain Johnston Blakely, of the sloop of war Wasp, a gold medal, with suitable devices, and a silver medal, with like devices, to each of the commissioned officers; and also a sword to each of the midshipmen and sailing-masters of that vessel, in testimony of the high sense entertained by the legislature of the nation, of their gallantry and good conduct in the action with the British sloop of war Reindeer.

No. 81.

From Rear-admiral Cockburn to Vice-admiral Cochrane.

On board the Resolution tender, off Mount-calvert,
Monday night, August 22, 1814

Sir,

I have the honor to inform you, that after parting from you at Benedict, on the evening of the 20th instant, I proceeded up the Patuxent with the boats and tenders, the marines of the ships being embarked in them, under the command of Captain Robyns, (the senior officer of that corps in the fleet,) and the marine-artillery, under Captain Harrison, in their two tenders: the Severn and Hebrus frigates, and the Manly sloop, being directed to follow us up the river, as far as might prove practicable.

The boats and tenders I placed in three divisions: the first under the immediate command of Captains Sullivan (the senior commander employed on the occasion) and Badcock; the second, under Captains Money and Somerville; the third, under Captain Ramsay; the whole under the superintendence and immediate management of Captain Wainwright, of the Tonnant, Lieutenant James Scott (first of the Albion) attending as my aid-de-camp.

I endeavoured to keep, with the bots and tenders, as nearly as possible a-breast of the army under Major-general Ross, that I might communicate with him as occasion offered, according to the plan previously arranged; and, about mid-day yesterday, I accordingly anchored at the ferry-house, opposite Lower Marlborough, where I met the general, and where the army halted for some hours; after which he marched for Nottingham, and I proceeded on for the same place with the boats. On our approaching the town, a few shot were exchanged between the leading boats and some of the enemy's cavalry; but the appearance of our army advancing caused them to retire with precipitation. Captains Nourse and Palmer, the Severn and Hebrus, joined me this day with their boats, having found it impracticable to get their ships higher than Benedict.

The major-general remained with the army at Nottingham, and the boats and tenders continued anchored off it during the night, and, soon after day-light this morning, the whole again moved forward; but the wind blowing, during the morning, down the river, and the channel being excessively narrow, and the advance of our tenders consequently slow, I judged it advisable to push on with the boats only, leaving the tenders to follow as they could.

On approaching Pig-point, (where the enemy's flotilla was said to be,) I landed the marines under Captain Robyns, on the left bank of the river, and directed him to march round and attack, on the land-side, the town, situated on the point; to draw from us the attention of such troops as might be there for its defence, and the defence of the flotilla. I then proceeded on with the boats; and, as we opened the reach above Pig-point, I plainly discovered Commodore Barney's broad pendant in the headmost vessel, a large sloop, and the remainder of the flotilla extending in a long line a-stern of her. Our boats now advanced towards them as rapidly as possible; but, on nearing them, we observed the sloop, bearing the broad pendant, to be on fire, and she, very soon afterwards, blew up. I now saw clearly that they were all abandoned, and on fire, with trains to their magazines; and out of the 17 vessels, which composed this formidable, and so much vaunted flotilla, 16 were, in quick succession, blown to atoms; and the 17th (in which the fire had not taken) we captured. The commodore's sloop was a large armed vessel; the others were gunboats, all having a long gun in the bow, and a carronade in the stern. The calibre of the guns, and number of the crew of each, differed in proportion to the size of the boat, varying from 32-pounders, and 60 men, to 18-pounders, and 40 men. I found here, lying above the flotilla, under its protection, 13 merchant-schooners; some of which, not being worth bringing away, I ordered to be burnt: such as were in good condition, I directed to be moved to Pig-point. Whilst employed taking these vessels, a few shots were fired at us by some of the men of the flotilla, from the bushes on the shore near us; but Lieutenant Scott, whom I had landed for that purpose, soon got hold of them, and made them prisoners. Some horsemen likewise shewed themselves on the neighbouring heights, but a rocket or two dispersed them; and Captain Robyns, who had got possession of Pig-point without resistance, now spreading his men through the country, the enemy retreated to a distance, and left us in quiet possession of the town, the neighbourhood, and our prizes.

A large quantity of tobacco having been found in the town at Pig-point, I have left Captain Robyns, with the marines, and Captain Nourse, with two divisions of the boats, to hold the place, and ship the tobacco into the prizes; and I have moved back with the third division to this point, to enable me to confer on our future operations with the major-general, who has been good enough to send his aid-de-camp to inform me of his safe arrival, with the army under his command, at Upper Marlborough.

In congratulating you, sir, which I do most sincerely, on the complete destruction of this flotilla of the enemy, which has lately occupied so much of our attention, I must beg to be permitted to assure you, that the cheerful and indefatigable exertions, on this occasion, of Captains Wainwright, Nourse, and Palmer, and of Captain Sullivan, the other commanders, officers, and men, in the boats you have placed under my orders, most justly entitle them to my warmest acknowledgments, and my earnest recommendations to your favourable notice.

I have the honor to be, &c.

G. COCKBURN, rear-admiral.

Vice-admiral the Hon. Sir Alexander
Cochrane, K. B. &c.

No. 82.

From the same to the same.

H.M. sloop Manly, off Nottingham,
Patuxent, August 27, 1814.

SIR,

I have the honor to inform you, that agreeably to the intentions I notified to you in my letter of the 22nd instant, I proceeded by land, on the morning of the 23d, to Upper Marlborough, to meet and confer with Major-general Ross, as to our further operations against the enemy; and we were not long in agreeing on the propriety of making an immediate attempt on the city of Washington.

In conformity, therefore, with the wishes of the general, I instantly sent orders for our marine and naval forces, at Pig-point, to be forthwith moved over to Mount Calvert, and for the marine-artillery, and a proportion of the seamen, to be there landed, and with the utmost possible expedition to join the army, which I also most readily agreed to accompany.

The major-general then made his dispositions, and arranged that Captain Robyns, with the marines of the ships, should retain possession of Upper Marlborough, and that the marine-artillery and seamen should follow the army to the ground it was to occupy for the night. The army then moved on, and bivouacked before dark about five miles nearer Washton.

In the night, Captain Palmer of the Hebrus, and Captain Money of the Traave, joined us with the seamen and with the marine-artillery, under Captain Harrison. Captain Wainwright of the Tonnant, had accompanied me the day before, as had also Lieutenant James Scott, acting first lieutenant of the Albion.

At day-light, on the morning of the 24th, the major-general again put the army in motion, directing his march upon Bladensburg; on reaching which place, with the advanced brigade, the enemy was observed drawn up in force on a rising ground beyond the town; and by the fire he soon opened on us as we entered the place, gave us to understand he was well protected by artillery. General Ross, however, did not hesitate in immediately advancing to attack him; although our troops were almost exhausted with the fatigue of the march they had just made, and but a small proportion of our little army had yet got up. This dashing measure was, however, I am happy to add, crowned with the success it merited; for, in spite of the galling fire of the enemy, our troops advanced steadily on both his flanks, and in his front; and, as soon as they arrived on even ground with him, he fled in every direction, leaving behind him ten pieces of cannon, and a considerable number of killed and wounded; amongst the latter Commodore Barney, and several other officers. Some other prisoners were also taken, thought not many, owing to the swiftness with which the enemy went off, and the fatigues our army had previously undergone.

It would, sir, be deemed presumption in me to attempt to give you particular details respecting the nature of this battle; I shall, therefore, only remark generally, that the enemy 8000 strong, on ground he had chosen as best adapted for him to defend, where he had time to erect his batteries, and concert all his measures, was dislodged, as soon as reached, and a victory gained over him, by a division of the British army, not amounting to more than 1500 men, headed by our gallant general, whose brilliant achievements of this day it is beyond my power to do justice to, and indeed no possible comment could enhance.

The seaman, with the guns, were, to their great mortification, with the rear-division, during this short, but decisive action. Those, however, attached to the rocket-brigade, were in the battle; and I remarked, with much pleasure, the precision with which the rockets were thrown by them, under the direction of First-lieutenant Lawrence, of the marine-artillery. Mr. Jeremiah M'Daniel, master's-mate of the Tonnant, a very fine young man, who was attached to this party, being severely wounded, I beg permission to recommend him to your favourable consideration. The company of marines I have on so many occasions had cause to mention to you, commanded by First-lieutenant Stephens, was also in the action, as were the colonial marines, under the temporary command of Captain Reed, of the 6th West India regiment, (these companies being attached to the light brigade,) and they respectively behaved with their accustomed zeal and bravery. None other of the naval department were fortunate enough to arrive up in time to take their share in this battle, excepting Captain Palmer, of the Hebrus, with his aid-de-camp, Mr. Arthur Wakefield, midshipman of that ship, and Lieutenant James Scott, first of the Albion, who acted as my aid-de-camp, and remained with me during the whole time.

The contest being completely ended, and the enemy having retired from the field, the general gave the army about two hours rest, when he again moved forward on Washington. It was, however, dark before we reached that city; and, on the general, myself, and some officers advancing a short way past the first houses of the town, without being accompanied by the troops, the enemy opened upon us a heavy fire of musketry, from the capitol and two other houses; these were therefore almost immediately stormed by our people, taken possessions of, and set on fire; after which the town submitted without further resistance.

The enemy himself, on our entering the town, set fire to the navy-yard, (filled with naval stores,) a frigate of the largest class almost ready for launching, and a sloop of war lying off it; as he did also the fort which protected the sea-approach to Washington.

On taking possession of the city, we also set fire to the president's palace, the treasury, and the war-office; and, in the morning, Captain Wainwright went with a party to see that the destruction in the navy-yard was complete; when he destroyed whatever stores and buildings had escaped the flames of the preceding night. A large quantity of ammunition and ordnance stores were likewise destroyed by us in the arsenal; as were about 200 pieces of artillery of different calibres, as well as a vast quantity of small-arms. Two rope-walks of a very extensive nature, full of tar-rope, &c. situated at a considerable distance from the yard, were likewise set fire to and consumed. In short, sir, I do not believe a vestige of public property, or a store of any kind, which could be converted to the use of the government, escaped destruction: the bridges across the Eastern Branch and the Potowmac were likewise destroyed.

This general devastation being completed during the day of the 25th, we marched again, at nine that night, on our return, by Bladensburg, to Upper Marlborough.

We arrived yesterday evening at the latter, without molestation of any sort, indeed without a single musket having been fired; and, this morning we moved on to this place, where I have found his Majesty's sloop Manly, the tenders, and the boats, and I have hoisted my flag, *pro tempore*, in the former. The troops will probably march to-morrow, or the next day at farthest, to Benedict for re-embarkation, and this flotilla will of course join you at the same time.

In closing, sir, my statement to you, of the arduous and highly important operations of this last week, I have a most pleasing duty to perform, in assuring you of the good conduct of the officers and men who have been serving under me. I have been particularly indebted, whilst on this service, to Captain Wainwright of the Tonnant, for the assistance he has invariably afforded me; and to Captains Palmer and Money, for their exertions during the march to and from Washington. To Captain Nourse, who has commanded the flotilla during my absence, my acknowledgments are also most justly due, as well as to Captains Sullivan, Badcock, Somerville, Ramsay, and Bruce, who have acted in it under him.

Lieutenant James Scott, now first of the Albion, has, on this occasion, rendered me essential services; and as I have had reason so often of late to mention to you the gallant and meritorious conduct of this officer, I trust you will permit me to seize this opportunity of recommending him particularly to your favourable notice and consideration.

Captain Robins, (the senior officer of marines with the fleet,) who has had, during these operations, the marines of the ships united under his orders, has executed ably and zealously the several services with which he has been entrusted, and is entitled to my best acknowledgments accordingly; as is also Captain Harrison of the marine-artillery, who, with the officers and men attached to him, accompanied the army to and from Washington.

Mr. Dobie, surgeon of the Melpomene, volunteered his professional services on this occasion, and rendered much assistance to the wounded on the field of battle, as well as to many of the men taken ill on the line of march.

1 colonial marine killed, 1 master's mate, 2 serjeants, and 3 colonial marines wounded, are the casualties sustained by the naval department; a general list of the killed and wounded of the whole army will, of course, accompany the report of the major-general.

I have the honor to be, &c.

G. COCKBURN, rear-admiral.

Vice-admiral the Hon. Sir Alex. Cochrane, K. B. &c.

P.S. Two long 6-pounder guns, intended for a battery at Nottingham, were taken off and put on board the Brune, and one taken at Upper Marlborough was destroyed.

Return of the killed, wounded, and missing, of the troops under the command of Major-general Ross, in action with the enemy, on the 24th August, 1814, on the heights above Bladensburg.

Washington, August 25, 1814.

Total—1 captain, 2 lieutenants, 5 serjeants, 56 rank and file, 10 horses, killed; 2 lieutenant-colonels, 1 major, 1 captain, 14 lieutenants, 2 ensigns, 10 serjeants, 155 rank and file, 8 horses, wounded.

H. G. SMITH,
D. A. A. G.

No. 83.

Return of ordnance, ammunition, and ordnance-stores, taken from the enemy by the army under the command of Major-general Robert Ross, between the 19th and 25th August, 1814.

August 19.—One 24-pound carronade.

August 22.—One 6-pound field-gun, with carriage complete. 156 stand of arms, with cartouches, &c. &c.

August 24, at Bladensburg.—Two 18-pounders, five 12-pounders, three 6-pounders with field-carriages. A quantity of ammunition for the above. 220 stand of arms.

August 25, at Washington.—Brass: six 18-pounders, mounted on traversing platforms; five 12-pounders, four 4-pounders, one 5½ inch howitzer, one 5½ inch mortar. Iron: twenty-six 32-pounders, thirty-six 24-pounders, thirty-four 18-pounders, twenty-seven 12-pounders, two 18-pounders, mounted on traversing platforms; nineteen 12-pounders, on ship-carriages; three 13-inch mortars, two 8-inch howitzers, one 42 pound gun, five 32-pound carronades, five 18-pound carronades, thirteen 12-pound guns, two 9-pound guns, two 6-pound guns.

Total amount of cannon taken, 206. 500 barrels of powder, 100,000 rounds of musket-ball cartridges, 40 barrels of fine-grained powder, a large quantity of ammunition of different natures made up.

The navy-yard and arsenal having been set on fire by the enemy before they retired, an immense quantity of stores of every description was destroyed; of which no account could be taken. Seven or eight very heavy explosions during the night denoted that there had been large magazines of powder.

F. G. J. WILLIAMS,
Lieut. Royal Artillery, A.Q.M.
J. MICHELL,
Captain commanding artillery.

N.B. The remains of near 2000 stand of arms were discovered which had been destroyed by the enemy.

No. 84

From Captain Gordon to Vice-admiral Cochrane.

Seahorse, Chesapeake, Sept. 9, 1814.

SIR,

In obedience to your orders, I proceeded into the river Potowmac, with the ships named in the margin,* on the 17th of last month; but from being without pilots to assist us through that difficult part of the river called the Kettle-Bottoms, and from contrary winds, we were unable to reach Fort Washington until the evening of the 27th. Nor was this effected but by the severest labour. I believe each of the ships was not less than twenty different times a-ground, and each time we were obliged to haul off by main strength; and we were employed, warping, for five whole successive days, with the exception of a few hours, a distance of more than fifty miles.

The bomb-ships were placed on the evening of the 27th, and immediately began the bombardment of the fort; it being my intention to attack it with the frigates at day-light the following morning. On the bursting of the first shell, the garrison were observed to retreat; but,

* Seahorse, Euryalus, Devastation, Ætna, Meteor, Erebus, and Anua-Maria, dispatch boat.

supposing some concealed design, I directed the fire to be continued. At 8 o'clock, however, my doubts were removed, by the explosion of the powder-magazine, which destroyed the inner buildings; and, at day-light on the 28th, we took possession. Besides the principal fort, which contained two 32-pounders, (columbiads,) two 32-pounders, and eight 24-pounders, there was a battery on the beach of five 18-pounders, a martello-tower, with two 12-pounders and loop-holes for musketry, and a battery in the rear of two 12, and six 6 pound field-pieces. The whole of these guns were already spiked by the enemy; and their complete destruction, with their carriages also, was effected by the seamen and marines, sent on that service, in less than two hours. The populous city of Alexandria thus lost its only defence; and, having buoyed the channel, I deemed it better to postpone giving any answer to a proposal made to me for its capitulation, until the following morning, when I was enabled to place the shipping in such a position, as would ensure assent to the terms I had decided to enforce.

To this measure I attribute their ready acquiescence, as it removed that doubt of my determination to proceed, which had been raised in the minds of the inhabitants, by our army having retired from Washington. This part of our proceedings will be further explained by the accompanying documents.

The honorable Lieutenant Gordon, of this ship, was sent, on the evening of the 28th, to prevent the escape of any of the vessels comprised, in the capitulation; and the whole of those which were sea-worthy, amounting to 21 in number, were fitted and loaded by the 31st.

Captain Baker, of the Fairy, bringing your orders of the 27th, having fought his way up the river, past a battery of five guns, and a large military force, confirmed the rumours which had already reached me, of strong measures having been taken to oppose our return, and I therefore quitted Alexandria, without waiting to destroy those remaining stores, which we had not the means of bringing away.

Contrary winds again occasioned us the laborious task of warping the ships down the river, in which a day's delay took place, owing to the Devastation grounding. The enemy took advantage of this circumstance, to attempt her destruction by three fire-vessels, attended by five row-boats; but their object was defeated by the promptitude and gallantry of Captain Alexander, who pushed off with his own boats, and being followed by those of the other ships, chased the boats of the enemy up to the town of Alexandria. The cool and steady conduct of Mr. John Moore, midshipman of the Seahorses, in towing the nearest fire-vessel on shore, while the others were removed from the power of doing mischief by the smaller boats of the Devastation, entitles him to my highest commendation.

The Meteor and the Fairy, assisted by the Anna-Maria dispatch-boat, a prize gun-boat, and a boat belonging to the Euryalus, with a howitzer, had greatly impeded the progress of the enemy in their works; notwithstanding which, they were enabled to increase their battery to 11 guns, with a furnace for heating shot. On the 3d, the wind coming to the N.W. the Ætna and Erebus succeeded in getting down to their assistance; and the whole of us, with the prizes, were assembled there on the 4th, except the Devastation, which, in spite of our utmost exertions in warping her, still remained five miles higher up the river. This was the moment when the enemy made his greatest efforts to effect our destruction.

The Erebus, being judiciously placed by Captain Bartholomew, in an admirable position for harassing the workmen employed in the trenches, was attacked by three field-pieces, which did her considerable damage, before they were beaten off; and, another attempt being made to destroy the Devastation by fire-vessels, I sent the boats, under Captain Baker, to her assistance. Nothing could exceed the alacrity with which Captain Baker went on this service, to which I attribute the immediate retreat of the boats and fire-vessels. His loss, however, was considerable, owing to their having sought refuge under some guns in a narrow creek, thickly wooded, from which it was impossible for him to dislodge them.

On the 5th, at noon, the wind coming fair, and all my arrangements being made, the Seahorse and the Euryalus anchored within short musket-shot of the batteries, while the whole of the prizes past betwixt us and the shoal, the bombs, the Fairy and Erebus, firing as they passed, and afterwards anchoring in a favorable position for facilitating, by means of their force, the further removal of the frigates. At 3 P.M. having completely silenced the enemy's fire, the Seahorse and Euryalus cut their cables, and the whole of us proceeded to the next position taken up by the troops: where they had two batteries, mounting from 14 to 18 guns, on a range of cliffs of about a mile extent, under which we were, of necessity, obliged to pass very close. I did not intend to make the attack that evening; but, the Erebus grounding within range, we were necessarily called into action. On this occasion the fire of the Fairy had the most decisive effect, as well as that of the Erebus; while the bombs threw their shells with excellent precision, and the guns of the batteries were thereby completely silenced by about 8 o'clock.

At day-light on the 6th I made signal to weigh; and so satisfied were the whole of the parties opposed to us, of their opposition being in ineffectual, that they allowed us to pass without further molestation. I cannot close this detail of operations, comprising a period of 23 days, without begging leave to call your attention to the singular exertion of those whom I had the honor to command, by which our success was effected. Our hammocks were down only two nights during the whole time. The many laborious duties which we had to perform, were executed with cheerfulness, which I shall ever remember with pride; and which will ensure, I hope, to the whole of the detachments, your favorable estimation of their extraordinary zeal and abilities.

To Captain Napier I owe more obligations than I have words to express. The Euryalus lost her bowsprit, the head of her fore-mast, and the heads of all her top-masts, in a tornado which she encountered on the 25th, just as her sails were clued up, whilst we were passing the flats of Maryland point; and yet, after 12 hours work on her refittal, she was again under weigh, and advancing up the river. Captain Napier speaks highly of the conduct of Lieutenant T. Herbert on this, as well as on every other of the many trying occasions which have called his abilities into action. His exertions were also particularly conspicuous in the prizes; many of which, already sunk by the enemy, were weighed, masted, hove-down, caulked, rigged, and loaded, by our little squadron, during the three days we remained at Alexandria.

It is difficult to distinguish, amongst officers who had a greater share of duty than often falls to the lot of any, and which each performed with the greatest credit to his professional character. I cannot omit to recommend to your notice the meritorious conduct of Captains Alexander, Bartholomew, Baker, and Kenah: the latter of whom led us through many of the difficulties of the navigation; and particularly to Captain Roberts, of the Meteor, who, besides undergoing the fatigues of the day, employed the night in coming the distance of 10 miles, to communicate and consult with me upon our further operations, preparatory to our passing the batteries.

So universally good was the conduct of all the officers, seamen, and marines of the detachment, that I cannot particularize with justice to the rest; but I owe it to the long-tried experience I have had of Mr. Henry King, first lieutenant of the Seahorse, to point out to you, that such was his eagerness to take the part to which his abilities would have directed him on this occasion, he even came out of his sick bed to command at his quarters, while the ship was passing the batteries;* nor can I ever forget how materially the service is indebted to Mr. A. Louthain, the master, for both finding and buoying the channel of a navigation, which no ship of a similar draught of water had ever before passed, with their guns and stores on board; and which, according to the report of a seaman now in this ship, was not accomplished by the President, American frigate, even after taking her guns out, under a period of 42 days.

Enclosed is a list of killed and wounded, and also of the vessels captured.

I have the honor to be, &c.

JAMES A. GORDON, captain.

To Sir A. Cochrane, commander-in-chief, &c.

Return of killed and wounded on board H.M. ships employed in the Potowmac river, between September 1 and 5, 1814.

Total—7 killed; 35 wounded.

J. A. GORDON, captain.

Vessels captured.

A gun-boat, of two guns; 3 ships, 4 brigs, and 13 other vessels:—total 21.

---

* The first two guns pointed by Lieutenant King disabled each a gun of the enemy.

No. 85.

From Captain Gordon to the common-council of Alexandria.

H.M.S. Seahorse, off Alexandria,
GENTLEMEN, August 29.

In consequence of a deputation yesterday received from the city of Alexandria, requesting favorable terms for the safety of their city, the under-mentioned are the only conditions in my power to offer: –

The town of Alexandria (with the exception of the public works) shall not be destroyed, unless hostilities are commenced on the part of the Americans; nor shall their dwelling-houses be entered, or the inhabitants molested in any manner whatever, if the following articles are strictly complied with: –

Article I. All naval and ordnance stores (public or private) must be immediately given up.

Art. II. Possession will be immediately taken of all shipping; and their furniture must be sent on board by their owners without delay.

Art. III. The vessels that have been sunk must be delivered up in the state they were on the 19th of August, the day the squadron passed the Kettle-bottoms.

Art. IV. Merchandize of every description must be instantly delivered up; and, to prevent any irregularities that might be committed in its embarkation, the merchants have it in their option to load the vessels generally employed for that purpose, when they will be towed off by us.

Art. V. All merchandize that has been removed from Alexandria since the 19th instant, is to be included in the above articles.

Art. VI. Refreshments of every description to be supplied the ships, and paid for at the market price, by bills on the British government.

Art. VII. Officers will be appointed to see that articles, Nos. II. III. IV. and V. are strictly complied with; and every deviation, or non-compliance on the part of the inhabitants of Alexandria, will render this treaty null and void.

I have the honor to be, &c.

JAMES A. GORDON, commander of
H.M. ship Seahorse, and senior officer
of H.M. ships before Alexandria.

To the common-council of the town of Alexandria.

No. 86.

The common-council's answer.

At a meeting of the common-council of Alexandria, on the 29th of August, 1814:

The terms proposed to the common-council, by the commander of the squadron of British ships now off Alexandria, are acceded to.

THOMAS HERBERT, president.

No. 87.

From Captain Blakeley to the American secretary of the navy.

U.S. sloop of war Wasp, at sea, lat. 46° N.
Long. 16° W. Sept. 11, 1814.

SIR,

After a protracted and tedious stay at l'Orient, had at last the pleasure of leaving that place on Saturday, 27th of August. On the 30th, captured the British brig Lettice, Henry Cockbain, master; and, on the 31st of August, the British brig Bon Accord, Adam Durno, master. In the morning of the 1st of September, discovered a convoy of 10 sail to-leeward, in charge of the Armada, 74, and a bomb-ship; stood for them, and succeeded in cutting out the British brig Mary, John D. Allan, master, laden with brass cannon, taken from the Spaniards, iron cannon, and military stores, from Gibraltar to England; removed the prisoners, set her on fire, and endeavoured to capture another of the convoy, but was chased off by the Armada. On the evening of the same day, at half-past 6, while going free, discovered four vessels, nearly at the same time, two on the starboard, and two on the larboard-bow, being the farthest to-windward. At 7, the chase, a brig, commenced making signals, with flags, which could not be distinguished for want of light, and soon after made various ones, with lanterns, rockets, and guns. At 29 minutes after 9, having the chase under our lee-bow, the 12-pound carronade was directed to be fired into him, which he returned; ran under his lee-bow to prevent his escaping, and commenced the action. At 10 o'clock, believing the enemy to be silenced, orders were given to cease firing, when I hailed, and asked if he had surrendered. No answer being given to this, and his fire having recommenced, it was again returned. At 12 minutes after 10, the enemy having suffered greatly, and having made no return to our last two broadsides, I hailed him the second time, to know if he had surrendered, when he answered in the affirmative. The guns were then ordered to be secured, and the boats lowered to take possession. In the act of lowering the boat, a second brig was discovered, a little distance a-stern, and standing for us. Sent the crew to their quarters, prepared every thing for another action, and awaited his coming up. At 36 minutes after 10, discovered two more sails a-stern, standing towards us. I now felt myself compelled to forego the satisfaction of destroying the prize. Our braces having been cut away, we kept off the wind until others could be rove, and with the expectation of drawing the second brig from his companions; but in this last we were disappointed. The second brig continued to approach us, until she came close to our stern, when she hauled by the wind, fired her broadside, which cut our rigging and sails considerably, and shot away a lower main-cross-tree, and retraced her steps to join her consorts, when we were necessitated to abandon the prize. He appeared, in every respect, a total wreck. He continued for some time firing guns of distress, until, probably, delivered by the two last vessels who made their appearance. The second brig could have engaged us, if he thought proper, as he neared us fast; but contented himself with firing a broadside, and immediately returned to his companions.

It is with real satisfaction that I have again the pleasure of hearing testimony to the merits of Lieutenants Reilly, Tillinghast, Baury, and sailing-master Carr; and to the good conduct of every officer and man on board the Wasp. Their divisions and departments were attended and supplied with the utmost regularity and abundance, which, with the good order maintained, together with the vivacity and precision of their fire, reflects on them the greatest credit. Our loss is two killed, and one slightly wounded with a wad. The hull received four round-shot, and the fore-mast many grape-shot. Our rigging and sails suffered a great deal. Every damage has been repaired the day after, with the exception of our sails.

Of the vessel with whom we were engaged, nothing positive can be said with regard to her name or force. While hailing him, previous to his being fired into, it was blowing fresh, (then going 10 knots,) and the name was not distinctly understood. Of her force, the four shot that struck us are all 32-pounds in weight, being a pound and three-quarters heavier than any belonging to this vessel.* From this circumstance, the number of men in her tops, her general appearance, and great length, she is believed to be one of the largest brigs in the British navy.

I have the honor to be, &c.

J. BLAKELEY.

Hon. W. Jones, &c.

P.S. I am told the enemy, after his surrender, asked for assistance, and said he was sinking. The probability of this is confirmed by his firing single guns for some time after his capture.

No. 88.

American minutes of the action between the U.S. ship Wasp, J. Blakely, Esq. commander, and H.B.M. sloop of war, lat. 30°, long. 11°, on the 1st September, 1814.

At 7 o'clock, called all hands to quarters, and prepared for action; 7. 26. hoisted an American jack at the fore, and pendant at the main; 7. 30. set the main-sail; 7. 34. perceived the chase making signals with lights, &c.; 7. 45. set the mizen, and hoisted an American ensign at the peake; 7. 48. hoisted a light at the peake, and brailed up the mizen; 7. 54. set the mizen to come up with the chase; 8. 3. the chase hauled down his lights; 8. 7. burned a blue-light on the fore-castle; 8. 17. set the flying-jib; 8. 34. hauled down the light at the peake; 8. 38. the chase fired a gun from his stern-port; 8. 55. hauled up the main-sail; 9. 15. set the main-sail; 9. 18. the chase fired a gun to the leeward; 9. 20. being then on the weather-quarter of the chase, he hailed and enquired "What ship is that?" Not answered, but asked "What brig is that?" He replied, "His majesty's brig —." Blowing fresh, the name was not distinctly understood. He again hailed, and asked, "What ship is that?" when he was told to heave to, and he

* See p. 5.

would be informed. He repeated his question, and was answered to the same effect. Mr. Carr was then sent forward to order him to heave to, which he declined doing; at 9. 25. the enemy set his fore-top-mast studding-sail; at 9. 26. fired the 12-pound carronade, to make him heave-to, when the enemy commenced action by firing his larboard guns. We then kept away, ran under his lee, and at 9. 29. commenced the action. At 10 o'clock, ordered the men to cease firing, and hailed the enemy, to know if he had surrendered; no answer was returned to this, he resumed his fire, and we continued ours; 10. 10. manned our starboard-guns, and fired three or four of them, when orders were again given to cease firing; 10. 12 hailed the enemy, "Have you surrendered?" when they answered in the affirmative. We were on the eve of taking possession, when a sail was descried close on board of us: orders were then given to clear the ship for action, which were promptly executed. We were then on the point of wearing, to engage the second, which we perceived to be a brig of war, when, at 10. 26. discovered two more sails, one a-stern, the other one point on our lee-quarter, standing for us; orders were then given to stand from the strange sails. The first sail seen approached within pistol-shot, fired a broadside, and cut away our lower main-cross-trees, and did other damage, and immediately stood for the other two sails last discovered. Continued on our course.

List of killed and wounded on board the U.S. sloop of war the Wasp, Johnson Blakely, Esq. commander, in the action with H.B.M. sloop of war —, on the 1st of September, 1814.

Killed—Joseph Martin, boatswain; Henry Staples, quarter-gunner.

Wounded—James Snellings, seaman; clavicle, or collar-bone, fractured by a wad.

Recapitulation.

Killed	2
Wounded	1
Total	3

W. M. CLARKE, surgeon.

No. 89.

From Sir James Yeo to Mr. Croker.

H.M.S. St. Lawrence, Kingston,
September 24, 1814.

SIR,

I have the honor to transmit, for the information of the lords commissioners of the admiralty, a copy of a letter from Captain Pring, late commander of H.M. brig Linnet.

It appears to me, and I have good reason to believe, that Captain Downie was urged, and his ship hurried into action, before she was in a fit state to meet the enemy.

I am also of opinion, that there was not the least necessity for our squadron giving the enemy such decided advantages, by going into their bay to engage them. Even had they been successful, it would not, in the least, have assisted the troops in storming the batteries; whereas, had our troops taken their batteries first, it would have obliged the enemy's squadron to quit the bay, and given our's a fair chance.

I have the honor to be, &c.

JAMES LUCAS YEO, commodore,
and commander-in-chief.

J. W. Croker, Esq. &c. &c.

No. 90.

From Captain Pring to Sir James Yeo.

U.S. ship Saratoga, Plattsburgh bay,
Lake Champlain, Sept. 12, 1814.

SIR,

The painful task of making you acquainted with the circumstances attending the capture of H.M. squadron yesterday, by that of the Americans, under Commodore Macdonough, it grieves me to state, becomes my duty to perform, from the ever-to-be-lamented loss of that worthy and gallant officer, Captain Downie, who unfortunately fell early in the action.

In consequence of the earnest solicitation of his excellency Sir George Prevost, for the co-operation of the naval force on this lake to attack that of the enemy, who were placed for the support of their works at Plattsburg, which, it was proposed, should be stormed by the troops at the same moment that the naval action should commence in the bay, every possible exertion was used to accelerate the armament of the new ship, that the military movements might not be postponed, at such an advanced season of the year, longer than was absolutely necessary.

On the 3d instant, I was directed to proceed, in command of the flotilla of gun-boats, to protect the left-flank of our army advancing towards Plattsburg; and, on the day following, after taking possession of, and paroling the militia of isle de Motte, I caused a battery of three long 18-pounder guns to be constructed, for the support of our position abreast of Little Chazy, where the supplies for the army were ordered to be landed.

The fleet came up on the 8th instant, but, for want of stores for the equipment of the guns, could not move forward until the 11th. At day-light we weighed, and, at 7, were in full view of the enemy's fleet, consisting of a ship, brig, schooner, and one sloop, moored in line abreast of their encampment, with a division of five gun-boats on each flank. At 40 minutes past 7, after the officers commanding vessels, and the flotilla, had received their final instructions as to the plan of attack, we made sail in order of battle.

Captain Downie had determined on laying his ship athwart-hawse of the enemy's, directing Lieutenant M'Ghee, of the Chubb, to support me in the Linnet, in engaging the brig to the right; and

Lieutenant Hicks, of the Finch, with the flotilla of gun-boats, to attack the schooner and sloop on the left of the enemy's line.

At 8, the enemy's gun-boats and smaller vessels commenced a heavy and galling fire on our line. At 10 minutes after 8, the Confiance, having had two anchors shot away from her larboard-bow, and the wind baffling, was obliged to anchor, (though not in the situation proposed,) within two cables' length of her adversary. The Linnet and Chubb soon afterwards took their allotted stations, something short of that distance: when the crews on both sides cheered, and commenced a spirited and close action. A short time, however, deprived me of the valuable services of Lieutenant M'Ghee; who, from having his cables, bowsprit, and main-boom shot away, drifted within the enemy's line, and was obliged to surrender.

From the light airs, and smoothness of the water, the fire on both sides proved very destructive, from the commencement of the engagement; and, with the exception of the brig, that of the enemy appeared united against the Confiance.

After two hours' severe conflict with our opponent, she cut her cable, ran down, and took shelter between the ship and schooner, which enabled us to direct our fire against the division of the enemy's gun-boats, and ship, which had so long annoyed us, during our close engagement with the brig, without any return on our part. At this time the fire of the enemy's ship slackened considerably, having several of her guns dismounted; when she cut her cable, and winded her larboard-broadside to bear on the Confiance, who in vain endeavoured to effect the same operation. At 33 minutes after 10, I was much distressed to observe the Confiance had struck her colours.

The whole attention of the enemy's force then became directed towards the Linnet. The shattered and disabled state of the masts, sails, rigging, and yards, precluded the most distant hope of being able to effect an escape by cutting the cable: the result of doing so must, in a few minutes, have been, her drifting alongside the enemy's vessels, close under our lee; but, in hope that the flotilla of gun-boats, who had abandoned the object assigned them, would perceive our wants, and come to our assistance, which would afford a reasonable prospect of being towed clear, I determined to resist the then destructive cannonading of the whole of the enemy's fleet, and, at the same time, dispatched Lieutenant Drew to ascertain the state of the Confiance.

At 45 minutes after 10, was apprised of the irreparable loss she had sustained by the death of her brave commander, (whose merits it would be presumption in me to extol,) as well as the great slaughter which had taken place on board; and, observing from the manuvres of the flotilla, that I could enjoy no further expectation of relief, the situation of my gallant comrades, who had so nobly fought, and were even now fast falling by my side, demanded the surrender of H.M. brig entrusted to my command, to prevent a useless waste of valuable lives; and, at the request of the surviving officers and men, I gave the painful orders for the colours to be struck.

Lieutenant Hicks, of the Finch, had the mortification to strike on a reef of rocks to the eastward of Crab island, about the middle of the engagement, which prevented his rendering that assistance to the squadron, that might, from an officer of such ability, have been expected.

The misfortune which this day befel us, by capture, will, sir, I trust, apologize for the lengthened detail, which, in justice to the sufferers, I have deemed it necessary to give of the particulars which led to it; and, when it is taken into consideration, that the Confiance was 16 days before on the stocks, with an unorganized crew, composed of several drafts of men, who had recently arrived from different ships at Quebec, many of whom only joined the day before, and were totally unknown either to the officers or to each other, with the want of gun-locks, as well as other necessary appointments, not to be procured in this country, I trust you will feel satisfied of the decided advantage the enemy possessed, exclusive of their great superiority in point of force, a comparative statement of which I have the honor to annex.* It now becomes the most pleasing part of my present duty, to notice to you the determined skill and bravery of the officers and men in this unequal contest; but it grieves me to state, that the loss sustained in maintaining it has been so great. That of the enemy, I understand, amounts to something more than the same number.

The fine style in which Captain Downie conducted the squadron into action, amidst a tremendous fire, without returning a shot, until secured, reflects the greatest credit to his memory, for his judgment and coolness; as also for Lieutenants M'Ghee and Hicks, for so strictly attending to his example and instructions. Their own accounts of the capture of their respective vessels, as well as that of Lieutenant Robertson, who succeeded to the command of the Confiance, will, I feel assured, do ample justice to the merits of the officers and men serving under their immediate command; but I cannot omit noticing the individual conduct of Lieutenants Robertson, Creswick, and Hornby, and Mr. Bryden, master, for their particular exertion in endeavouring to bring the Confiance's starboardside to bear on the enemy, after most of their guns were dismounted on the other.

It is impossible for me to express to you my admiration of the officers and crew serving under my personal orders. Their coolness and steadiness, the effect of which was proved by their irresistible fire directed towards the brig opposed to us, claim my warmest acknowledgments; but more particularly or preserving the same, so long after the whole strength of the enemy had been directed against the Linnet alone. My first lieutenant, Mr. William Drew, whose merits I have before had the honor to report to you, behaved on this occasion in the most exemplary manner.

By the death of Mr. Paul, acting second lieutenant, the service has been deprived of a most valuable and brave officer: he fell early in the action. Great credit is due to Mr. Giles, purser, for volunteering his services on deck; to Mr. Mitchell, surgeon, for the skill he evinced in performing some amputations required at the moment, as well as his great attention to the wounded during the action; at the close of which the water was nearly a foot above the lower-deck,

* By some mistake, not forwarded with the despatches.

from the number of shot which struck her between wind and water. I have to regret the loss of the boatswain, Mr. Jackson, who was killed a few minutes before the action terminated. The assistance I received from Mr. Muckle, the gunner, and also from Mr. Clarke, master's-mate, Messrs. Towke and Sinclair, midshipmen, (the latter of whom was wounded in the head,) and Mr. Guy, my clerk, will, I hope, recommend them, as well as the whole of my gallant little crew, to your notice.

I have much satisfaction in making you acquainted with the humane treatment the wounded have received from Commodore Macdonough: they were immediately removed to his own hospital on Crab island, and were furnished with every requisite. His generous and polite attention also to myself, the officers and men, will ever hereafter be gratefully remembered. Inclosed I beg leave to transmit you the return of killed and wounded; and have the honor, &c.

DANIEL PRING, captain, late of
H.M. sloop Linnet.

Sir James Lucas Yeo &c. &c.

A statement of the enemy's squadron engaged with H.M. late squadron on lake Champlain, September 11, 1814.

Ship Saratoga, of eight long 24-pounders, twelve 32-pound carronades, six 42-pound carronades.

Brig Eagle, of eight long 18-pounders, twelve 32-pound carronades.

Schooner Ticonderago, of four long 18-pounders, ten 12-pounders, three 32-pound carronades.

Cutter Preble, of seven long 9-pounders.

Six gun-boats, of one long 24-pounder, one 18-pounder carronade.

Four gun-boats, of one long 12-pounder each.

Impossible to ascertain the number of men.

A return of the killed and wounded on board H.M. late squadron, &c.

Confiance—3 officers, 38 seamen and marines, killed; 1 officer, 39 seamen and marines, wounded.

Linnet—2 officers, 8 seamen, killed; 1 officer, 13 seamen and marines, wounded.

Chubb—6 seamen and marines, killed; 1 officer, 15 seamen and marines, wounded.

Finch—2 seamen and marines, wounded.—Total 129.

From the Confiance's crew having been landed immediately after the action, no opportunity has offered to muster. The number stated is the whole as yet ascertained to have been killed and wounded.

No. 91.

From Commodore Macdonough to the American secretary of the navy.

U.S. ship Saratoga, off Plattsburg,
SIR, September 11, 1814.

The Almighty has been pleased to grant us a signal victory on lake Champlain, in the capture of one frigate, one brig, and two sloops of war, of the enemy.

I have the honor to be, &c.

T. MACDONOUGH, commodore.

Hon. W. Jones, secretary of the navy, &c.

No. 92.

From the same to the same.

U.S. ship Saratoga, Plattsburg bay,
SIR, September 13, 1814.

I have the honor to give you the particulars of the action which took place on the 11th instant, on this lake.

For several days the enemy were on their way to Plattsburg, by land and water, and it being well understood that an attack would be made, at the same time, by their land and naval forces, I determined to wait at anchor the approach of the latter. At 8 A.M. the look-out boat announced the approach of the enemy. At 9, he anchored in a line a-head, at about 300 yards distance from my line; his ship opposed to the Saratoga; his brig to the Eagle, Captain R. Henley; his galleys, 13 in number, to the schooner, sloop, and a division of our galleys; one of his sloops assisting their ship and brig, the other, their galleys; our remaining galleys with the Saratoga and Eagle.

In this situation, the whole force on both sides became engaged, the Saratoga suffering much from the heavy fire of the Confiance. I could perceive at the same time, however, that our fire was very destructive to her. The Ticonderoga, Lt. Com. Cassin, gallantly sustained her full share of the action. At half-past 10 o'clock the Eagle, not being able to bring her guns to bear, cut her cable, and anchored in a more eligible situation, between my ship and the Ticonderoga, where she very much annoyed the enemy, but, unfortunately, leaving me exposed to a galling fire from the enemy's brig. Our guns on the starboard-side being nearly all dismounted, or not manageable, a stern-anchor was let go, the bower-cable cut, and the ship winded with a fresh broadside on the enemy's ship, which soon after surrendered. Our broadside was then sprung to bear on the brig, which surrendered in about 15 minutes after.

The sloop that was opposed to the Eagle had struck some time before, and drifted down the line, the sloop, which was with their galleys, having struck also. Three of their galleys are said to be sunk; the others pulled off. Our galleys were about obeying, with alacrity, the signal to follow them, when all the vessels were reported to me in a sinking state. It then became necessary to annul the signal to the galleys, and order their men to the pumps.

I could only look at the enemy's galleys going off in a shattered condition, for there was not a mast in either squadron that could stand to make sail on; the lower rigging being all shot away, hung down as though it had been just placed over the mast-heads.

The Saratoga had 55 round-shot in her hull; the Confiance 105. The enemy's shot passed principally just over our heads, as there were not 20 whole hammocks in the nettings at the close of the action; which lasted, without intermission, two hours and 20 minutes.

The absence and sickness of Lieutenant R. Perry, left me without the services of that excellent officer. Much ought fairly to be attributed to him, for his care and attention in disciplining the ship's crew, as her first lieutenant. His place was filled by a gallant young officer, Lieutenant P. Gamble, who, I regret to inform you, was killed early in the action. Acting-lieutenant Vallette worked the first and second divisions of guns with able effect. Sailing-master Brun's attention to the springs, and in the execution of the order to wind the ship, and occasionally at the guns, meets with my entire approbation; also Captain Young's commanding the acting marines, who took his men to the guns. Mr. Beale, purser, was of great service at the guns, and in carrying my orders throughout the ship, with Midshipman Montgomery. Master's-mate Joshua Justin had command of the third division: his conduct, during the action, was that of a brave and correct officer. Midshipmen Monteath, Graham, Williamson, Platt, Thwing, and Acting-midshipman Balwin, all behaved well, and gave evidence of their making valuable officers.

The Saratoga was twice set on fire by hot shot from the enemy's ship.

I close, sir, this communication, with feelings of gratitude, for the able support I received from every officer and man attached to the squadron which I have the honor to command.

I have the honor to be, &c.

T. MACDONOUGH.

Hon. W. Jones, secretary of the navy.

P.S. Accompanying this is a list of killed and wounded; a list of prisoners; (not published;) and a precise statement of both forces engaged. Also letters from Captain Henley, and Lieut. Com. Cassin.

Recapitulation of killed and wounded:
(the names having been first given;)

	Killed.	Wounded.
Saratoga	28	29
Eagle	13	20
Ticonderoga	6	6
Preble	2	0
Borer	3	1
Centipede	0	1
Wilmer	0	1
Total	52	58

Gun-boats—Nettle, Allen, Viper, Burrows, Ludlow, Alwyn, Ballard, none killed or wounded.

GEORGE BEALE, jun. purser.

Statement of the American force engaged on the 11th of September, 1814.

Ship Saratoga—eight long 24-pounders, six 42-pound carronades, and twelve 32-pound carronades	26
Brig Eagle—twelve 32-pound carronades, and 8 long 18-pounders	20
Schooner Ticonderoga—eight long 12-pounders, four long 18-pounders, and five 32-pound carronades	17
Six row-gallies—one long 24, and one short 18-pounder, each	12
Four row-gallies—one long 12-pounder	4
Sloop Preble—seven long 9-pounders	7
Total, guns	86

Statement of the enemy's force, &c.

Frigate Confiance—twenty-seven long 24-pounders, four 32-pound carronades, six 24-pound carronades, and two long 18-pounders on the berth-deck	39
Brig Linnet—sixteen long 12-pounders	16
Sloop Chubb—ten 18-pound carronades, one long 6-pounder	11
Sloop Finch—six 18-pound carronades, one 18-pounder, (columbiad,) and one long 6-pounder	11
Three galleys; viz.—Sir James Yeo, Sir George Prevost, Sir Sydney Beckwith, one long 24-pounder, and one 32-pound carronade, each	6
Broke—one 18-pounder, and one 32-pound carronade	2
Murray—one 18-pounder, and one 18-pound carronade	2
Wellington, Tecumseth, and one other, (name unknown,)—one 18-pounder, each	3
Drummond, Simcoe, and three others, (names unknown,) one 32-pound carronade, each	5
Total, guns	95

List of British officers captured, &c. and sent to Greenbush: consisting of

(Besides Captain Daniel Pring, on parole:) 8 lieutenants, 1 master, 2 surgeons, 1 assistant ditto, 2 master's mates, 4 midshipmen, 2 pursers, 1 captains clerk, 1 boatswain, 2 gunners, and 1 carpenter:—total 26.

No. 93.

From Captain Youngs to Commodore Macdonough.

U.S. ship Saratoga, Lake Champlain,
September 13, 1814.

Sir,

I have the honor of enclosing to you a list of killed and wounded troops of the line, (acting marines on board the squadron Lake Champlain,) in the action of the 11th instant.

In attempting to do justice to the brave officers and men I have had the honor to command, my feeble abilities fall far short of my wishes. First Lieutenant Morrison, 33d infantry, stationed on board the U.S. brig Eagle, was wounded, but remained on deck during the action, animating his men by his honorable conduct. Second Lieutenant James Young, 6th infantry, on board the U.S. schooner Ticonderoga merits my warmest thanks: I would particularly recommend him to your notice. Second Lieutenant Wm. B. Howell, 15th infantry, in the U.S. ship Saratoga, rendered me every assistance; notwithstanding his having been confined for ten days of a fever, yet, at the commencement of the action he was found on deck, and continued until the enemy had struck, when he was borne to his bed. I would also recommend him to your notice.

The conduct of the non-commissioned officers and privates was so highly honorable to their country and themselves, it would be superfluous to particularize them.

I have the honor to be, &c.

WHITE YOUNGS, captain 15th infantry,
commanding detachment of acting marines.

Commodore T. Macdonough, &c.

[*List referred to not made public.*]

No. 94.

Sentence of court-martial on Captain Pring, the surviving officers, &c.—28th August 1815.

The court having maturely weighed the evidence, is of opinion, that the capture of H.M.S. Confiance, and the remainder of the squadron, by the American squadron, was principally caused by the British squadron having been urged into battle previous to its being in a proper state to meet the enemy; by the promised co-operation of the land forces not being carried into effect, and by the pressing letters of their commander-in-chief, whereby it appears that he had on the 10th of September, 1814, only waited for the naval attack to storm the enemy's works: that the signal of the approach on the following day, was made by the scaling of the guns, as settled between Captain Downie and Major Coote; and the promised co-operation communicated to the other officers and crews of the British squadron before the commencement of the action. The court, however, is of opinion, that the attack would have been attended with more effect, if a part of the gun-boats had not withdrawn themselves from the action, and others of the vessels had not been prevented by baffling winds from getting into the stations assigned them: that Captain Pring of the Linnet, and Lieutenant Robertson, who succeeded to the command of the Confiance, after the lamented fate of Captain Downie, (whose conduct was marked by the greatest valor,) and Lieutenant C. Bell, commanding the Murray, and Mr. Robertson, commanding the Beresford, gun-boats, who appeared to take their trial at this court-martial, conducted themselves with great zeal, bravery, and ability, during the action: that Lieutenant

W. Hicks, commanding the Finch, also conducted himself with becoming bravery: that the other surviving officers and ships' crew, except Lieutenant M'Ghie of the Chubb, who has not appeared here to take his trial, also conducted themselves with bravery; and that Captain Pring, Lieutenant Robertson, Lieutenant Hicks, Lieutenant C. Bell, and Mr. J. Robertson, and the rest of the surviving officers and ships' company, except Lieutenant M'Ghie, ought to be most honorably acquitted; and they are hereby most honorably acquitted accordingly.

No. 95.

Sentence on Lieutenant M'Ghie, on the 18th of September, 1815.

The court having heard the circumstances, determined, that the Chubb was not properly carried into action, nor anchored so as to do the most effectual service; by which neglect, she drifted into the line of the enemy: that it did not appear, however, that there was any want of courage in Lieutenant M'Ghie; and therefore, the court did only adjudge him to be severely reprimanded.

No. 96.

Vote of congress.

The congress of the United States resolved, that their thanks be presented to Commodore Macdonough, and through him to the officers, petty-officers, seamen, marines, and infantry serving as marines, attached to the squadron under his command, for the decisive and splendid victory gained on Lake Champlain; that gold medals be struck, emblematical of the action between the two squadrons, and presented to Commodore Macdonough, Captain R. Henley, and Lieutenant Stephen Cassin; that silver medals, &c.

No. 97.

From Rear-admiral Cockburn to Vice-admiral Cochrane.

H.M.S. Severn, in the Patapsco, Sept. 15.

Sir,

In furtherance of the instructions I had the honor to receive from you on the 11th instant, I landed at day-light of the 12th, with Major-general Ross, and the force under his command, at a place the general and myself had previously fixed upon, near to North Point, at the entrance of the Patapsco, and in conformity with his wishes, I determined on remaining on shore, and accompanying the army to render him every assistance within my power during the contemplated movements and operations; therefore, so soon as our landing was completed, I directed Captain Nourse of this ship, to advance up the Patasco with the frigates, sloops, and bomb-ships, to bombard the fort, and threaten the water-approach to Baltimore; and I moved on the army, and seamen (under Captain E. Crofton) attached to it, on the direct road leading to the above-mentioned town. We had advanced about five miles without other occurrence than taking prisoners a few light-horse-men; when the general and myself being with the advanced guard, observed a division of the enemy posted at a turning of the road, extending into a wood on our left; a sharp fire was almost immediately opened upon us from it, and as quickly returned with considerable effect by our advanced guard, which pressing steadily forward, soon obliged the enemy to run off with the utmost precipitation, leaving behind him several men killed and wounded; but it is with the most heartfelt sorrow I have to add, that in this short and desultory skirmish, my gallant and highly valued friend the major-general received a musket ball through his arm into his breast, which proved fatal to him on his way to the water-side for re-embarkation.

Our country, sir, has lost in him one of its best and bravest soldiers, and those who knew him, as I did, a friend most honoured and beloved; and I trust, sir, I may be forgiven for considering it a sacred duty I owe to him to mention here, that whilst his wounds were binding up, and we were placing him on the bearer, which was to carry him off the field, he assured me, the wounds he had received in the performance of his duty to his country, caused him not a pang; but he felt alone, anxiety for a wife and family dearer to him than his life, whom in the event of the fatal termination he foresaw, he recommended to the protection and notice of his majesty's government and the country.

Colonel Brooke, on whom the command of the army now devolved, having come up, and the body of our troops having closed with the advance, the whole proceeded forward about two miles further, where we observed the enemy in force drawn up before us, apparently about six or seven thousand strong; on perceiving our army he filed off into a large and extensive wood on his right; from which he commenced a cannonade on us from his field-pieces, and drew up his men behind a thick paling, where he appeared determined to make his stand. Our field-guns answered his with evident advantage, and as soon as Colonel Brooke had made the necessary dispositions, the attack was ordered, and executed in the highest style possible. The enemy opened his musketry on us from his whole line, immediately that we approached within reach of it, and he kept up his fire till we reached and entered the wood, when he gave way in every direction, and was chased by us a considerable distance with great slaughter; abandoning his post of the Meeting House, situated in this wood, and leaving all his wounded and two of his field-guns in our possession.

An advance of this description against superior numbers of an enemy so posted, could not be effected without loss. I have the honor to enclose a return of what has been suffered by those of the naval department, acting with the army on this occasion; and it is, sir, with the greatest pride and pleasure, I report to you that the brigade of seamen with small arms commanded by Captain Edward Crofton, assisted by Captains Sullivan, Money, and Ramsey, (the three senior commanders in the fleet) who commanded divisions under him, behaved with a gallantry and steadiness which would have done honor to the oldest troops, and which attracted the admiration of the army. The seamen under Mr. Jackson, master's mate of the Tonnant, attached to the rocket-brigade, commanded by the first lieutenant, Lawrence, of the marines, behaved also with equal skill and bravery. The marines, landed from the ships under the command of Captain Robyn's, the senior officer of that corps, belonging to the fleet, behaved with their usual gallantry.

Although, sir, in making to you my report of this action, I know it is right I should confine myself to mentioning only the conduct of those belonging to the naval department, yet I may be excused for venturing further to state to you, generally, the high admiration with which I viewed the conduct the whole army, and the ability and gallantry with which it was managed and headed by its brave colonel, which ensured to it the success it met with.

The night being fast approaching, and the troops much fatigued, Colonel Brooke determined on remaining for the night on the field of battle, and on the morning of the 13th, leaving a small guard at the Meeting House to collect and protect the wounded, we again moved forwards towards Baltimore; on approaching which, it was found to be defended by extremely strong works on every side, and immediately in front of us by an extensive hill, on which was an entrenched camp, and great quantities of artillery; and the information we collected, added to what we observed, gave us reason to believe, there were at least, within their works, from 15 to 20,000 men. Colonel Brooke lost no time in reconnoitring these defenses, after which he made his arrangement for storming during the ensuing night, with his gallant little army, the entrenched camp in our front, notwithstanding all the difficulties which it presented. The subsequent communications which we opened with you, however, induced him to relinquish again the idea, and therefore yesterday morning the army retired leisurely to the Meeting House, where it halted for some hours, to make the necessary arrangements respecting the wounded, and the prisoners taken on the 12th, which being completed, it made a further short movement in the evening towards the place where it disembarked, and where it arrived this morning for re-embarkation, without suffering the slightest molestation from the enemy; who, in spite of his superiority of number, did not even venture to look at us during this slow and deliberate retreat.

As you, sir, were in person with the advanced frigates, sloops, and bomb-vessels, and as, from the road the army took, I did not see them after quitting the beach, it would be superfluous for me to make any report to you respecting them. I have now, therefore, only to assure you of my entire satisfaction and approbation of the conduct of every officer and man employed under me, during the operations above detailed, and to express to you how particularly I consider myself indebted to Captain Edward Crofton, (acting captain of the Royal Oak,) for the gallantry, ability, and zeal, with which he led on the brigade of seamen in the action of the 12th, and executed all the other services with which he has been entrusted since our landing;

to Captain White, acting captain of the Albion, who attended me as my aid-de-camp the whole time, and rendered me every possible assistance; to Captains Sullivan, Money, and Ramsay, who commanded divisions of the brigade of seamen; to Lieutenant James Scott, of the Albion, whom I have had such frequent cause to mention to you on former occasions, and who in the battle of the 12th, commanded a division of seamen, and behaved most gallantly, occasionally also acting as an extra aid-de-camp to myself. Captain Robyns, who commanded the marines of the fleet, and who was severely wounded during the engagement, I also beg to recommend to your favorable notice and consideration; as well as Lieutenant George C. Urmston, of the Albion, whom I placed in command of the smaller boats, to endeavour to keep up a communication between the army and navy, which he effected by great perseverance, and thereby rendered us most essential service. In short, sir, every individual seemed animated with equal anxiety to distinguish himself by good conduct on this occasion; and I trust, therefore, the whole will be deemed worthy of your approbation. Captain Nourse of the Severn, was good enough to receive my flag for this service: he rendered me great assistance in getting the ships to the different stations within the river; and when the storming of the fortified hill was contemplated, he hastened to my assistance with a reinforcement of seamen and marines; and I should consider myself wanting in candour and justice, did I not particularly point out, sir, to you, the high opinion I entertain of the enterprise and ability of this valuable officer, not only for his conduct on this occasion, but on the very many others on which I have employed him, since with me in the Chesapeake.

I have the honor to be, &c.

GEORGE COCKBURN.

Vice-admiral the Hon. Sir A. Cochrane, K. B.
commander-in-chief, &c. &c.

No. 98.

From Colonel Brooke, to Vice-admiral Cochrane.

DEAR SIR,

I beg leave to be allowed to state to you, how much I feel indebted to Captain Crofton, commanding the brigade of sailors from his majesty's ships under your command, as also to Captains Sullivan, Money, and Ramsay, for their very great exertions in performing every formation made by his majesty's troops; having seen myself those officers expose themselves in the hottest of the enemy's fire, to keep their men in line of march with the disciplined troops. The obedient and steady conduct of the sailors, believe me sir, excited the admiration of every individual of the army, as well as my greatest gratitude.

Believe me to be, dear sir, &c.

A. BROOKE.

Vice-admiral the Hon. Sir A. Cochrane, K. B.
commander-in-chief, &c. &c.

Return of killed, wounded and missing, of naval and marine brigades.

Killed, 7; wounded, 48; missing, 1:—total, 56.

No. 99.

From Captain Lockyer to Vice-admiral Cochrane.

H.M. sloop Sophie, Cat-island roads,
December 18, 1814

Sir,

I beg leave to inform you, that in pursuance of your orders, the boats of the squadron which you did me the honor to place under my command, were formed into three divisions, (the first, headed by myself; the second, by Captain Montresor, of the Manley; and the third, by Captain Roberts of the Meteor,) and proceeded, on the night of the 12th instant, from the frigate's anchorage, in quest of the enemy's flotilla.

After a very tedious row of 36 hours, during which the enemy attempted to escape from us, the wind fortunately obliged him to anchor off St. Joseph's island, and nearing him on the morning of the 14th, I discovered his force to consist of five gun-vessels, of the largest dimensions, which were moored in a line a-breast, with springs on their cables, and boarding-nettings triced up, evidently prepared for our reception.

Observing also, as we approached the flotilla, an armed sloop endeavouring to join them, Captain Roberts, who volunteered to take her, with part of his division, succeeded in cutting her off, and capturing her without much opposition. About 10 o'clock, having closed-to within long gun-shot, I directed the boats to come to a grapnel, and the people to get their breakfasts; and, as soon as they had finished, we again took to our oars, and pulling up to the enemy, against a strong current, running at the rate of nearly three miles an hour, exposed to a heavy and destructive fire of round and grape. About noon I had the satisfaction of closing with the commodore, in the Seahorse's barge. After several minutes' obstinate resistance, in which the greater part of the officers and crew of this boat were either killed or wounded, (myself amongst the latter, severely,) we succeeded in boarding, and being seconded by the Seahorse's first barge, commanded by Mr. White, midshipman, and aided by the boats of the Tonnant, commanded by Lieutenant Tatnell, we soon carried her, and turned her guns with good effect upon the remaining four.

During this time Captain Montresor's division was making every possible exertion to close with the enemy, and with the assistance of the other boats, then joined by Captain Roberts, in about five minutes we had possession of the whole of the flotilla.

I have to lament the loss of many of my brave and gallant companions, who gloriously fell in this attack; but considering the great strength of the enemy's vessels, (whose force is underneath described,) and their state of preparation, we have by no means suffered so severely as might have been expected.

I am under the greatest obligations to the officers, seamen, and marines, I had the honor to command on this occasion, to whose gallantry and exertions the service is indebted for the capture of these vessels: any comment of mine would fall short of the praise due to them. I am especially indebted to Captains Montresor and Roberts, for their advice and assistance: they are entitled to more than I can say of them, and have my best thanks for the admirable style in which they pushed on with their divisions to the capture of the remainder of the enemy's flotilla. In an expedition of this kind, where so many were concerned, and so much personal exertion and bravery was displayed, I find it impossible to particularize every individual who distinguished himself, and deserves to be well spoken of; but I feel it my duty to mention those, whose behaviour fell immediately under my own eye.

Lieutenant George Pratt, second of the Seahorse, who commanded that ship's boats, and was in the same boat with me, conducted himself to that admiration which I cannot sufficiently express. In his attempt to board the enemy he was several times severely wounded; and, at last, so dangerously, that I fear the service will be deprived of this gallant and promising young officer.

I cannot omit to mention also the conduct of Lieutenants Tatnell and Roberts, of the Tonnant, particularly the former, who, after having his boat sunk alongside, got into another, and gallantly pushed on to the attack of the remainder of the flotilla. Lieutenant Roberts was wounded in closing with the enemy.

I have the honor to be, &c.

NICHOLAS LOCKYER.

No. 1, gun-vessel—one long 24-pounder, four 12-pounder carronades, and four swivels, with a complement of 45 men; Captain Jones, commodore.

No. 2, gun-vessel—one long 32-pounder, six long 6-pounders, two 5-inch howitzers, and four swivels, with a complement of 45 men; Lieutenant M'Ives.

No. 3, gun-vessel—one long 24-pounder, four long 6-pounders, and four swivels, with a complement of 45 men.

No. 4, gun-vessel—one long 24-pounder, four 12-pounder carronades, with a complement of 45 men.

No. 5, gun-vessel—one long 24-pounder, four 12-pounder carronades, with a complement of 45 men.

No. 6, armed sloop—one long 6-pounder, two 12-pounder carronades, with a complement of 20 men.

NICHOLAS LOCKYER.

A list of the killed and wounded in the boats of H.M. ships, at the capture of the American gun-vessels near New Orleans.

Tonnant—1 able seaman, 2 ordinary seamen, killed; 1 lieutenant, 4 midshipmen, 4 able seamen, 4 ordinary, 2 landmen, 3 private marines, wounded.

Norge—1 quarter-master killed; 1 master's-mate, 4 able seamen, 3 ordinary seamen, 1 private marine, wounded.

Bedford—1 seaman killed; 2 lieutenants, 1 master's-mate, 2 seamen, wounded.

Royal Oak—1 seaman wounded.

Ramillies—4 seamen killed; 9 seamen wounded.

Armide—1 seaman killed.

Cydnus—1 midshipman, 1 seaman, 2 private marines, wounded.

Seahorse—1 midshipman, 1 volunteer of the first class, 1 able seaman, 1 ordinary seaman, 1 private marine, killed; 1 lieutenant, 2 midshipmen, 1 lieutenant of marines, 7 able seamen, 7 ordinary seamen, 1 landman, 4 private marines, wounded.

Trave—1 volunteer of the first class, 1 captain of the fore-top, killed; 1 private marine wounded.

Sophie—1 captain wounded.

Meteor—3 seamen wounded.

Belle Poule—2 seamen wounded.

Gorgon—1 master's-mate wounded.

Total—3 midshipmen, 13 seamen, 1 private marine, killed; 1 captain, 4 lieutenants, 1 lieutenant of marines, 3 master's-mates, 7 midshipmen, 50 seamen, 11 marines, wounded.

Grand total—17 killed, 77 wounded.

No. 100.

From Rear-admiral Hotham to Vice-admiral Cochrane.

Superb, at anchor, before New London,
January 23.

Sir,

I have the honor to acquaint you with the capture of the U.S. ship President, on the 15th instant, by the following force; viz.—the Majestic, Captain Hayes; Tenedos, Captain Hyde Parker; Endymion, Captain Hope; Pomone, Captain Lumley; which I had collected off the bar of New York, under the direction of Captain Hayes. She, and the Macedonian armed brig, of 420 tons, loaded with provisions, sailed on the preceding evening, under the command of Commodore Decatur; but the present season of the year, and the dark nights, of which he availed himself, have not enabled him to elude the vigilance of Captain Hayes, and the commanders of H.M. ships under his orders, who have well discharged the important duty I assigned to them; and I beg leave to offer you my congratulations on the design of the American government being defeated.

You will perceive by the reports Captain Hayes has delivered to me, (copies of which I do myself the honor to transmit to you herewith,) the ardour displayed by Captain Hope in the pursuit, the intrepidity with which he brought the enemy's ship to close action, and the undaunted spirit with which the Endymion's inferior force was singly employed, for the space of two hours and a half, leaving honorable evidence of judgment in the position she was placed in, and of the destructive precision of her fire, in the sinking state of her antagonist, the heavy loss sustained by him, and his inability to make further resistance when the Pomone arrived up with him; while the loss sustained by the Endymion was comparatively small:

and although the distinguished conduct of Captain Hope, his officers, and ship's company, can derive no additional lustre from my commendation, I cannot withhold my tribute of applause; nor can I refrain from assuring you, that the judicious conduct of Captain Hayes, in the direction of the force entrusted to his orders, and the exertions exhibited by him, and by Captains Parker, Hope, and Lumley, have justified the confidence I had placed in their zeal, and have rendered them worthy of your approbation.

I have the honor to be, &c.

H. HOTHAM, rear-admiral.

To the Hon. Sir A. Cochrane, K. B. vice-admiral of the red, commander-in-chief, &c. &c.

No. 101.

From Captain Hayes to Rear-admiral Hotham.

Majestic, at sea, January 17, 1815.

SIR,

I have the honor to acquaint you, that notwithstanding my utmost endeavours to keep the squadron committed to my charge close in with Sandy Hook, agreeably to your directions, for the purpose of preventing the escape of the U.S. ship President, and other vessels ready for sea at Staten island, we were repeatedly blown off by frequent gales; but the very great attention paid to my orders and instructions by the respective captains, in situations difficult to keep company, prevented separation; and, whenever the wind did force us from the coast, I invariably, on the gale moderating, placed the squadron on that point of bearing from the Hook I judged it likely, from existing circumstances, would be the enemy's track; and it is with great pleasure I have now to inform you of the success of the squadron in the capture of the U.S. ship President, Commodore Decatur, on Sunday night, after an anxious chase of 18 hours.

On Friday the Tenedos joined me, with your order to take Captain Parker, in that ship, under my command. We were then in company with the Endymion and Pomone, off the Hook, and in sight of the enemy's ships; but that night the squadron was blown off again in a severe snow-storm. On Saturday the wind and weather became favourable for the enemy, and I had no doubt but he would attempt his escape that night. It was impossible, from the direction of the wind, to get in with the Hook; and, as before stated, (in preference to closing the land to the southward,) we stood away to the northward and eastward, till the squadron reached the supposed track of the enemy; and, what is a little singular, at the very instant of arriving at that point, an hour before day-light, Sandy-hook bearing W.N.W. 15 leagues, we were made happy by the sight of a ship and brig standing to the southward and eastward, and not more than two miles on the Majestic's weather-bow; the night-signal for a general chase was made, and promptly obeyed by all the ships.

In the course of the day the chase became extremely interesting, by the endeavour of the enemy to escape, and the exertions (of the

British commanders) to get their respective ships alongside of him: the former, by cutting away his anchors, and throwing over-board every moveable article, with a great quantity of provisions; and the latter, by trimming their ships in every way possible to effect their purpose. As the day advanced, the wind declined, giving the Endymion an evident advantage in sailing; and Captain Hope's exertions enabled him to get his ship alongside of the enemy, and commence close action, at half an hour past 5 o'clock in the evening, which was continued with great gallantry and spirit on both sides for two hours and a half, when the Endymion's sails being cut from the yards, the enemy got a-head: Captain Hope taking this opportunity to bend new sails, to enable him to get his ship alongside again, the action ceased; till the Pomone, getting up at half-past 11 at night, and firing a few shots, them enemy hailed to say she had already surrendered.

This ship, on being taken possession of, proved to be the President, as above stated, commanded by Commodore Decatur.

The vessel in company with her was the Macedonian brig, a merchant-ship, laden with provisions, which made her escape by very superior sailing.

And now, sir, a very pleasing part of my duty is, the bearing testimony to the able and masterly manner in which the Endymion was conducted, and the gallantry with which she was fought; and when the effect produced by her well-directed fire upon the President is witnessed, it cannot be doubted but that Captain Hope would have succeeded either in capturing or sinking her, had none of the squadron been in sight.

For your further information, I have the honor to enclose Captain Hope's letter, with a return of killed and wounded on board the Endymion. I have not yet been able to ascertain the loss of the President, but I believe it to be much greater than the Endymion's, and she had six feet water in the hold when taken possession of. Both ships were very much cut in masts and rigging; and, had the present most severe gale commenced twelve hours sooner, the prize would undoubtedly have sunk. As soon as the weather will permit a communication, I shall procure further particulars, and then send the Endymion and Pomone, with the prize and prisoners, to Bermuda.

I have the honor to be, &c.

JOHN HAYES, captain.

Rear-admiral the Hon. Sir H. Hotham.

P.S. The ships having parted company in the gale, no further particulars have been obtained.

Number of persons of all descriptions on board the President, previous to the action, about 490.

Number and calibre of her guns.

Main-deck: thirty long 24-pounders. Quarter-deck: fourteen 42-pounder carronades, one long 24-pounder, one 24-pounder howitzer. Forecastle: six 42-pounder carronades, one long 24-pounder. Foretop: two brass 6-pounders. Main-top: two brass 6-pounders. Mizentop: two smaller guns:—Total 59.

No. 102.

From Captain Hope to Captain Hayes.

H.M.S. Endymion, at sea, January 15.

SIR,

I enclose a return of the killed and wounded, and I have great pleasure in bearing testimony of the very great assistance I received from the senior lieutenant, Morgan, during the whole day's proceedings: together with the cool and determined bravery of my officers and ship's company, on this fortunate occasion. Where every individual has so conspicuously done his duty, it would be injustice for me to particularize; but I trust the loss and damage sustained by the enemy's frigate, will shew the steady and well-directed fire kept up by H.M. ship under my command.

Although our loss has been severe, I am happy to state, that it is trifling when compared with that of the enemy.

I have the honor to be, &c.

H. HOPE.

To John Hayes, Esq. captain of H.M.S. Majestic, and senior officer off New York.

[*Here follow the names of 11 killed, and 14 wounded.*]

No. 103.

From Commodore Decatur to the American secretary of the navy.

H.B.M. ship Endymion, at sea, January 18, 1815.

SIR,

The painful duty of detailing to you the particular causes which preceded and led to the capture of the late U.S. frigate President, by a squadron of H.B.M. ships, (as per margin,) has devolved upon me. In my communication of the 14th, I made known to you my intention of proceeding to sea on that evening. Owing to some mistake of the pilots, the ship, in going out, grounded on the bar, where she continued to strike heavily for an hour and a half. Although she had broken several of her rudder-braces, and received such other material injury as to render her return into port desirable, I was unable to do so from the strong westerly wind which was then blowing. It being now high water, it became necessary to force her over the bar before the tide fell. In this we succeeded by ten o'clock, when we shaped our course along the shore of Long island for 50 miles, and then steered S.E. by S. At 5 o'clock three ships were discovered a-head; we immediately hauled up the ship, and passed two miles to the northward of them. At day-light we discovered four ships in chase: one on each quarter, and two a-stern, the leading ship of the enemy a razee; she commenced a fire upon us, but without effect. At meridian, the wind became light and baffling; we had increased our distance from the razee, but the next ship a-stern, which was also a large ship, had gained, and continued to gain upon us considerably. We immediately occupied all hands to lighten ship, by starting water, cutting away the anchors, throwing overboard provisions, cables, spare spars, boats, and every article that could be got at, keeping the sails wet, from the royals down. At 3, we had the wind quite light; the enemy, who had now been joined by a brig, had a strong breeze, and were coming up with us rapidly.

The Endymion (mounting 50 guns, 24 pounders on the main-deck) had now approached us within gun-shot, and had commenced a fire with her bow-guns, which we returned from our stern. At five o'clock she had obtained a position on our starboard-quarter, within half point-blank shot, on which neither our stern nor quarter-guns would bear; we were now steering E. by N. the wind N.W. I remained with her in this position for half an hour, in the hope that she would close with us on our broadside, in which case I had prepared my crew to board; but from his continuing to yaw his ship to maintain his position, it became evident, that to close was not his intention. Every fire now cut some of our sails or rigging. To have continued our course under these circumstances, would have been placing it in his power to cripple us, without being subject to injury himself; and to have hauled up more to the northward to bring our stern guns to bear, would have exposed us to his raking fire. It was now dusk, when I determined to alter my course south, for the purpose of bringing the enemy a-beam; and, although their ships a-stern were drawing up fast, I felt satisfied I should be enabled to throw him out of the combat before they could come up, and was not without hopes, if the night proved dark, (of which there was every appearance,) that I might still be enabled to effect my escape. Our opponent kept off at the same instant we did, and our fire commenced at the same time. We continued engaged, steering south, and steering-sails set, two hours and a half, when we completely succeeded in dismantling her. Previously to her dropping entirely out of the action, there were intervals of minutes, when the ships were broadside, in which she did not fire a gun. At this period, (half past 8 o'clock,) although dark, the other ships of the squadron were in sight, and almost within gun-shot. We were of course compelled to abandon her. In re-assuming our former course for the purpose of avoiding the squadron, we were compelled to present our stern to our antagonist; but such was his state, though we were thus exposed and within range of his guns for half an hour, that he did not avail himself of this favourable opportunity of raking us. We continued this course until eleven o'clock, when two fresh ships of the enemy (the Pomone and Tenedos) had come up. The Pomone had opened her fire on the larboard bow, within musket-shot; the other, about two cables' length a-stern, taken a raking position on our quarter; and the rest (with the exception of the Endymion) within gun-shot. Thus situated, with about one fifth of my crew killed and wounded, my ship crippled, and a more than four-fold force opposed to me, without a chance of escape left, I deemed it my duty to surrender.

It is with emotions of pride I bear testimony to the gallantry and steadiness of every officer and man I had the honor to command on this occasion; and I feel satisfied that the fact of their having beaten a force equal to themselves, in the presence, and almost under the guns, of so vastly a superior force, when, too, it was almost self-evident that, whatever their exertions might be, they must ultimately be captured, will be taken as evidence of what they would have performed, had the force opposed to them been in any degree equal.

It is with extreme pain I have to inform you, that Lieutenants Babbitt, Hamilton, and Howell fell in the action. They have left no officers of superior merit behind them.

If, sir, the issue of this affair had been fortunate, I should have felt it my duty to have recommended to your attention Lieutenants Shubrick and Gallagher. They maintained throughout the day the reputation they had acquired in former actions. Lieutenant Twiggs, of the marines, displayed great zeal; his men were well supplied, and their fire incomparable, so long as the enemy continued within musket range.

Midshipman Randolph, who had charge of the forecastle division, managed it to my entire satisfaction.

From Mr. Robinson, who was serving as a volunteer, I received essential aid; particularly after I was deprived of the services of the master, and severe loss I had sustained in my officers on my quarter-deck.

Of our loss in killed and wounded, I am unable, at present, to give you a correct statement; the attention of the surgeon being so entirely occupied with the wounded, that he was unable to make out a correct return when I left the President; nor shall I be able to make it until our arrival in port, we having parted company with the squadron yesterday. The enclosed list, with the exception, I fear, of its being short of the number, will be found correct.

For 24 hours after the action it was nearly calm, and the squadron were occupied in repairing the crippled ships. Such of the crew of the President as were not badly wounded, were put on board the different ships; myself and a part of my crew were put on board this ship. On the 17th we had a gale from the eastward, when this ship lost her bowsprit, fore and main-masts, and mizen-top-mast, all of which were badly wounded; and was, in consequence of her disabled condition, obliged to throw overboard all her upper-deck guns: her loss in killed and wounded must have been very great. I have not been able to ascertain the extent. Ten were buried after I came on board; (36 hours after the action;) the badly wounded, such as were obliged to keep their cots, occupy the starboard side of the gun-deck, from the cabin-bulk-head to the main-mast. From the crippled state of the President's spars, I feel satisfied she could not have saved her masts, and I feel serious apprehensions for the safety of our wounded left on board.

It is due to Captain Hope to state, that every attention has been paid by him to myself and officers that have been placed on board his ship, that delicacy and humanity could dictate.

I have the honor to be, &c.

STEPHEN DECATUR.

The Hon. Ben. W. Crowinshield,
secretary of the navy.

British squadron referred to in the letter.

Majestic razee, Endymion, Pomone, Tenedos, Despatch brig.

[*Here follow the names of 24 killed, and 55 wounded.*]

No. 104.

Extract of a letter from Commodore Decatur to the American secretary of the navy.

New York, March 6, 1815.

Sir,

In my official letter of the 18th January, I omitted to state, that a considerable number of my killed and wounded was from the fire of the Pomone, and that the Endymion had on board, in addition to her own crew, one lieutenant, one master's mate, and fifty men belonging to the Saturn, and when the action ceased, was left motionless and unmanageable, until she bent new sails, rove new rigging, and fished her spars; nor did she rejoin the squadron for six hours after the action, and three hours after the surrender of the President. My sword was delivered to Captain Hayes, of the Majestic, the senior officer of the squadron, on his quarter-deck; which he, with great politeness, immediately returned. I have the honor to enclose you my parole, by which you will perceive the British admit the President was captured by the squadron. I should have deemed it unnecessary to have drawn your attention to this document, had not the fact been stated differently in the Bermuda Gazette, on our arrival there; which statement, however, the editor was compelled to retract, through the interferences of the governor, and some of the British officers of the squadron.

No. 105.

From Commodore Murray, to the American secretary of the navy.

New York, April 17, 1815.

Sir,

I herewith transmit to you the result of the court of inquiry, respecting the capture of the frigate President, with the opinion of the court.

We have been more minute in our investigation than might, at first view, have been deemed necessary; but, as there has been a diversity of opinions prevailing among the British commanders concerned in her capture, it was desirable, in our view, to lay before the world, in the most correct manner, every circumstance which led to that event, which has afforded another high proof of American heroism, and so highly honorable to her commander, officers, and crew, that every American citizen must feel a pride in knowing that our flag has been so nobly defended.

The minutes of the court having been read and approved, the court was cleared, and, after due deliberation, resolved to express the sentiments and opinions of the members, on the matters submitted to them, as follows: –

In execution of the orders of the honorable the secretary of the navy, we have (with the exception of the two very young midshipmen) examined every officer belonging to the President, within the reach of the court, who survived the late glorious contest between the frigate President, and a squadron of his Britannic majesty.

We are of opinion, that the primary cause of the loss of the President was her running on the bar, as she was leaving this port. The violence and continuance of the shocks she received for an hour and a half, or more, considering she was laden with stores and provisions for a very long cruize, could not but have injured her greatly, and must have impeded her sailing. Her hogged and twisted appearance, after she arrived at Bermuda, must have been the effect of this unfortunate accident. We are convinced that it was owing to this, that the enemy were able to overtake her.

The striking of the President on the bar cannot be imputed to the fault of any officer who was attached to her; on the contrary, every possible precaution was taken, and the utmost exertions were used by her commander and officers, to ensure her safe passage over the bar, and to relieve her after she had struck. The accident was occasioned by some mistake in placing the boats, which were to serve as beacons for the President, through a channel always dangerous for a vessel of her draught, but particularly so at such a time as she was obliged to select for passing it, when the land-marks could not be distinguished.

From the time that the superiority of the enemy's force was ascertained, and it became the duty of the President to evade it, we are convinced that the most proper measures were pursued, and that she made every possible effort to escape. No means, in our opinion, were so likely of success, as those which were adopted by Commodore Decatur. Any suggestions, that different measures would have been more proper, or more likely to accomplish the object, we think, are without foundation, and may be the result of ignorance, or the dictates of a culpable ambition, or of envy.

We consider the management of the President, from the time the chase commenced till her surrender, as the highest evidence of the experience, skill, and resources of her commander, and the ability and seamanship of her officers and crew. We fear that we cannot express, in a manner that will do justice to our feelings, our admiration of the conduct of Commodore Decatur, and his officers and crew, while engaged with the enemy, threatened with a force so superior, possessed of advantages which must have appeared to render all opposition unavailing, otherwise than it might affect the honor of our navy, and the character of our seamen. They fought with a spirit which no prospect of success could have heightened; and, if victory had met its common reward, the Endymion's name would have been added to our list of naval conquests. In this unequal conflict the enemy gained a ship, but the victory was our's. When the President was obliged to leave the Endymion, to avoid the other ships, which were fast coming up, the Endymion was subdued; and if her friends had not been at hand to rescue her, she was so entirely disabled, that she soon must have struck her flag. A proof of this is, that she made no attempt to pursue the President, or to annoy her by a single shot, while the President was within reach; when, with the hope to escape from the overwhelming force which was nearly upon her, the President presented her stern to the Endymion's broadside. A proof that the Endymion was conquered is, the shattered condition in which she appeared, while the President in the contest with her had sustained but little injury; and the fact, that the Endymion did not join the squadron till many hours after the

President had been surrounded by the other four ships, and had surrendered to them, is a strong corroborative evidence of the disabled state in which the President left the Endymion.

We think it due to Commodore Decatur, and his heroic officers and crew, to notice the proposition he made to board the Endymion, when he found she was coming up, and the manner in which this proposition was received by his gallant crew. Such a design, at such a time, could only have been conceived by a soul without fear, and approved with enthusiastic cheerings by men regardless of danger. Had not the enemy perceived the attempt, and availed himself of the power he had, in the early part of the action, to shun the approach of the President, the American stars might now be shining on the Endymion. In the subsequent part of the engagement, the enemy's squadron was too near to permit the execution of this design; and the disabled state of the Endymion would have frustrated the principal object which Commodore Decatur had in making so bold an attempt, which was, to avail himself of the Endymion's superior sailing, to escape with his crew from his pursuers.

We conclude by expressing our opinion, that Commodore Decatur, as well during the chase, as through his contest with the enemy, evinced great judgment and skill, perfect coolness, the most determined resolution, and heroic courage. That his conduct, and the conduct of his officers and crew, is highly honorable to them, and to the American navy, and deserves the warmest gratitude of their country; that they did not give up their ship till she was surrounded and overpowered by a force so superior, that further resistance would have been unjustifiable, and a useless sacrifice of the lives of brave men.

The order of the secretary of the navy requires us to express an opinion as to the conduct of the officers and crew of the President, after the capture. The testimony of all the witnesses concurs in enabling us to give it our decided approbation.

By the court,

ALEXANDER MURRAY, president,

True copy from the original,

CADWALADER D. COLDEN, judge-advocate.

Navy department, April 20, 1815.

Approved, W. B. CROWNINSHIELD.

No. 106.

From the American secretary of the navy to Commodore Decatur.

Navy department, April 20, 1815.

SIR,

In the course of official duty, it is my highest satisfaction to render justice to the gallantry and good conduct of the brave officers and seamen of the U.S. navy.

In giving an official sanction to the recent proceedings of the court of enquiry, instituted at my request, to investigate the causes of the loss, by capture, of the frigate President, late of the navy of the U.S.

while under your command; and to enquire into the conduct of the commander, officers, and crew, of the said frigate, before and after surrender to the enemy, it would be equally unjust to your merit, as well as to my sentiments and feelings, to pass over this investigation with a mere formal approbation. I have therefore, sir, to express to you, in the fullest manner, the high sense of approbation which the president of the U.S. and this department, entertain for your professional character as an officer, who, in every instance, has added lustre to the stars of the union: and whose brilliant actions have raised the national honor and fame, even in the moment of surrendering your ship to an enemy's squadron of vastly superior force, over whose attack, singly, you were decidedly triumphant; and you will be pleased to present to each of your gallant officers and crew, the thanks of your government, for their brave defense of the ship, and the flag of the United States.

The proceedings and opinion of the court of enquiry, of which Commodore Alexander Murray is president, are approved.

I am, very respectfully, &c.

B. W. CROWNINSHIELD.

Commodore Stephen Decatur, U.S. navy, New York.

No. 107.

Defects of the President, by shot received in action with the Endymion.

(Not before published.)

Quarter-deck, starboard-side.—After-port-sill, string, and water-ways, shot to pieces. *Second* port from after, timber shot through; and between the *second* and *third* ports, timbers and quick-work torn to pieces; shot went through the other side. The after-port-timber shot through at the *fourth* port. One shot through, between the *fourth* and *fifth* ports. At the *sixth* port, plank-sheer shot away, and two shots through, between the *sixth* and *seventh* ports; and part of the quarter-deck and beams, ripped up by shot.

Between the *quarter-deck and forecastle*.—The water-ways, plank-sheer, with two streaks of the gang-way, shot away.

Main-deck, starboard-side.—*Second* port from forward, the spirketting and water-ways shot. One shot between the *second* and *third* ports, in wake of deck, which has injured the water-ways. *Fourth* port, the after-port-timber shot through. *Fifth* port, fore-mast port-timber cut through. *Sixth* port, the sheer-streak and clamp shot through. Between the *tenth* and *eleventh* ports, the clamp and diagonal knees shot. *Twelfth* port, the foremast port-timber and quick-work shot. *Thirteenth* port, the upper sill and clamp shot away. *Fifteenth* port, the upper sill and clamp shot. Three shots in the buttock, one of which went into the after-magazine. Several shot went through both sides, between the main and quarter-deck, waist, &c. Several shot through between wind and water, and some under water, which cut the timbers and knees much.

One shot through from larboard-side at the *tenth* port, which carried away the upper cill, clamp, and diagonal knees.

No. 108

From Captain Stewart to the American secretary of the navy.

U.S. frigate Constitution, May, 1815.

Sir,

On the 20th of February last, the island of Madeira bearing about W.S.W. distant 60 leagues, we fell in with H.B.M. two ships of war, the Cyane and Levant, and brought them to action about 6 o'clock in the evening; both of which, after a spirited engagement of 40 minutes, surrendered to the ship under my command.

Considering the advantages derived by the enemy, from a divided and more active force, as also their superiority in the weight and number of guns, I deem the speedy and decisive result of this action the strongest assurance which can be given the government, that all under my command did their duty, and gallantly supported the reputation of American seamen.

Inclosed you will receive the minutes of the action, and a list of the killed and wounded on board this ship. Also inclosed you will receive, for your information, a statement of the actual force of the enemy, and the number killed and wounded on board their ships, as near as could be ascertained.

I have the honor to be, &c.

CHARLES STEWART.

Hon. B. W. Crowninshield, secretary
of the navy, Washington.

List of killed and wounded on board the U.S. frigate Constitution, of 44 guns, (mounting thirty-two 24-pounders, and twenty 32-pound carronades,) on the 20th of February, 1815, in action with H.B.M. ships Cayane and Levant.

Killed, and since dead—4 seamen, 2 marines.
Wounded—9 seamen and marines:—total 15.

Statement of the actual force of H.B.M. ships Levant, Captain the Hon. George Douglass, commander, and Cyane, Captain Gordon Falcon, commander; with the number killed and wounded on board each ship on the 20th February, 1815, as near as could be ascertained, while engaged with the U.S. frigate Constitution.

Levant.

18 thirty-two-pounders, carronades.
1 twelve-pounder, ditto.
2 nine-pounders, long guns.
—
21 guns; 156 officers, seamen, and marines.
Prisoners—133 officers, seamen, and marines.
Killed, 23; *wounded*, 16:—total killed and wounded 39.

Cyane.

22 thirty-two-pounders, carronades.
10 eighteen-pounders, ditto.
2 twelve-pounders, long guns.
—
34 guns; 180 officers, seamen, and marines.
2 brass swivels.

Prisoners—168 officers, seamen, and marines.
Killed, 12; *wounded*, 26; total killed and wounded, 38.

No. 109.

American minutes of the action between the U.S. frigate Constitution, and H.M. ships Cyane and Levant, on the 20th February, 1815.

Commences with light breezes from the east, and cloudy weather. At 1, discovered a sail two points on the larboard-bow; hauled up and made sail in chase. At a quarter past 1, made the sail to be a ship. At three-quarters past 1, discovered another sail a-head; made them out, at 2 P.M. to be both ships, standing close-hauled, with their starboard-tacks on-board. At 4 P.M. the weathermost ship made signals, and bore up for her consort, then about 10 miles to-leeward; we bore up after her, and set lower, top-mast, top-gallant, and royal studding-sails in chase. At half-past 4, carried away our main-royal-mast, took in the sail, and got another prepared. At 5 P.M. commenced firing on the chase from our two larboard bow-guns; our shot falling short, ceased firing. At half-past 5, finding it impossible to prevent their junction, cleared ship for action, then about 4 miles from the two ships. At 40 minutes past 5, they passed within hail of each other, and hauled by the wind on the starboard-tack, hauled up their courses, and prepared to receive us. At 45 minutes past 5, they made all sail, close-hauled by the wind, in hopes of getting to-windward of us. At 55 minutes past 5, finding themselves disappointed in their object, and we were closing with them fast, they shortened sail, and formed on a line of wind, about half a cable's length from each other. At 6 P.M. having them under command of our battery, hoisted our colours, which was answered by both ships hoisting English ensigns. At 5 minutes past 6, ranged up, on the starboard side of the sternmost ship, about 300 yards distant, and commenced the action by broadsides, both ships returning our fire with great spirit for about 15 minutes; then the fire of the enemy beginning to slacken, and the great column of smoke collected under our lee, induced us to cease our fire, to ascertain their positions and conditions. In about three minutes the smoke cleared away, we found ourselves a-breast of the headmost ship, the sternmost ship luffing up for our larboard-quarter; we poured a broadside into the headmost ship, and then braced a-back our main and mizen-top-sails, and backed a-stern, under cover of the smoke, a-breast the sternmost ship, when the action was continued with spirit, and considerable effect, until 35 minutes past 6, when the enemy's fire again slackened, and we discovered the headmost ship bearing up; filled our top-sails, shot a-head, and gave her two stern rakes. We then discovered the sternmost ship wearing also; wore ship immediately after, and gave her a stern rake, she luffing-to on our starboard-bows, and giving us her larboard-broadside; we ranged up on her larboard-quarter, within hail, and was about to give her our starboard-broadside, when she struck her colours, fired a gun, and yielded. At 50 minutes past 6, took possession of H.M.S. Cyane, Captain Gordon Falcon, mounting 34 guns. At 8 P.M. filled away after her consort, which was still in sight to-leeward. At half-past 8, found her standing towards us, with her starboard-tacks, close-hauled, with top-gallant-sails set, and colours flying. At 50 minutes past 8, ranged close alongside to-windward of her, on opposite tacks, and exchanged broadsides; wore immediately under her stern, and raked her with a broadside; she then crouded all sail, and endeavoured to escape by running; hauled on board our tacks, set spanker and flying-jib in chase. At half-past 9, commenced firing on her from our starboard bow-chaser; gave her several shot, which cut her spars and rigging considerably. At 10 P.M. finding they could not escape, fired a gun, struck her colours, and yielded. We immediately took possession of H.M. ship Levant, the Hon. Captain George Douglass, mounting 21 guns. At 1 A.M. the damages of our rigging were repaired, sails shifted, and the ship in fighting condition.

No. 110.

American minutes of the chase of the U.S. frigate Constitution, by an English squadron of three ships, from out the harbour of Port Praya, island of St. Jago.

Commences with fresh breezes and thick foggy weather. At 5 minutes past 12, discovered a large ship through the fog, standing in for Port Praya. At 8 minutes past 12, discovered two other large ships a-stern of her, also standing in for the port. From their general appearance, supposed them to be one of the enemy's squadrons; and, from the little respect hitherto paid by them to neutral waters, I deemed it most prudent to put to sea. The signal was made to the Cyane and Levant to get under weigh. At 12, after meridian, with our top-sails set, we cut our cable, and got under way, (when the Portuguese opened a fire on us from several of their batteries on shore,) the prize-ships following our motions, and stood out of the harbour of Port Praya, close under East Point, passing the enemy's squadron about gun-shot to-windward of them: crossed our top-gallant-yards, and set fore-sail, main-sail, spanker, flying-jib, and top-gallant sails. The enemy, seeing us under way, tacked ship, and made all sail in chase of us. As far as we could judge of their rates, from the thickness of the weather, supposed them two ships of the line, and one frigate. At half-past meridian cut away the boats towing a-stern, first cutter, and gig. At 1 P.M. found our sailing about equal with the ships on our lee-quarter, but the frigate luffing up, gaining our wake, and rather dropping a-stern of us; finding the

Cyane dropping a-stern, and to-leeward, and the frigate gaining on her fast, I found it impossible to save her if she continued on the same course, without having the Constitution brought to action by their whole force. I made the signal, at 10 minutes past 1 P.M. to her to tack ship, which was complied with. This manœuvre, I conceived, would detach one of the enemy's ships in pursuit of her; while, at the same time, from her position, she would be enabled to reach the anchorage at Port Praya, before the detached ships could come up with her; but if they did not tack after her, it would afford her an opportunity to double their rear, and make her escape before the wind. They all continued in full chase of the Levant and this ship, the ship on our lee-quarter firing, by divisions, broadsides, her shot falling short of us. At 3 P.M. by our having dropped the Levant considerably, her situation became (from the position of enemy's frigate) similar to the Cyane. It became necessary to separate also from the Levant, or risk this ship being brought to action to cover her. I made the signal, at 5 minutes past 3, for her to tack, which was complied with. At 12 minutes past 3, the whole of the enemy's squadron tacked in pursuit of the Levant, and gave up the pursuit of this ship. This sacrifice of the Levant became necessary, for the preservation of the Constitution. Sailing-master Hixon, Midshipman Varnum, a boatswain's-mate, and 12 men, were absent on duty in the fifth cutter, to bring the cartel brig under our stern.

No. 111.

Lieutenant M'Donald's official letter.

(Not before published.)

U.S. ship Hornet, off Tristan d'Acunha, W.S.W. three or four miles, April 6, 1815.

Sir,

I have the honor to inform you, that H.M. brig Penguin arrived off the above island on the 17th of March; and, receiving information of an American brig of war having been off the day previous, Captain Dickinson determined, if possible, to intercept her; and succeeded in falling in with her on the 20th, at 9 A.M. At noon, H.M. brig closing fast, enemy shewed his colours, and commenced firing his stern-guns. At 1 P.M. enemy, with a fine breeze, at N.N.W. Penguin becalmed. At 9 P.M. lost sight of him, being thick weather; and, at midnight, hauled up for the island, which we made on the 23d, bearing W.N.W.

At 11. 15 A.M. standing up for the island, a sail was seen N.W. by W.; all sail was immediately made in chase, and the stranger being shortly after made out to be a ship, under easy sail, at 1 P.M. shortened sail, and prepared for action. At 1. 45. fired a shot, to induce him to shew his colours, which he immediately did by hoisting American, and firing a broadside. At 1. 50. the island S.W. three or four miles, rounded-to on the starboard-tack, within pistol-shot, when the action became warm and brisk. At 2. 15. enemy inclined to bear away, orders were given by Captain Dickinson so lay her on board. H.M. brig much cut up in her sails and rigging, several shots through both masts, all the officers at the fore-mast quarters either killed or wounded; and, at this time, I regret much to say, a severe loss was felt generally by Captain Dickinson receiving a mortal wound. I then conceived, as our masts were momently expected to fall, our only chance of success was to board, and, at 2. 25. succeeded in passing our bowsprit through his starboard-quarter. Bowsprit and fore-mast both fell at this instant; the latter on board, directly on the larboard-guns. Vessels separating, every exertion was then made to bring our starboard-broadside to bear, without effect. H.M. brig a perfect wreck, and the larboard after-guns rendered useless by drawing of the breeching-bolts, I deemed it only sacrificing the lives of the remaining crew, making further resistance; I therefore, at 2. 25. hailed, to say we had surrendered. At 3, was taken possession of by the U.S. ship of war Hornet, mounting eighteen 32-pounder carronades, two long 18-pounders, musquetoons, &c. in his tops, and a complement of, at least, 165 men: not a boy amongst them. I regret much the killed and wounded have been severe: 10 killed, and 28 wounded. The enemy's I have not been able to ascertain. Report says, 10 killed, but they acknowledge only 1, and 11 wounded; among them their captain and first lieutenant: the former severely; the latter dangerously. The Hornet is in a leaky state from our shot, which, I trust, will shorten her cruize. I am happy H.M. brig was not destined to bear American colours, or assist the squadron of the enemy. She was destroyed, after taking out a few stores. Two sail hove in sight, shortly after the action, which proved to be the U.S. ship of war Peacock, and a store-brig. The one chased by us, we have since heard, had a similar cargo; and were both intended, by all accounts, for the supplies of a squadron expected for this island, consisting of three frigates and two corvettes, sent out, I conjecture, for the destruction of our East India fleet.

I cannot close this without noticing the exemplary conduct of Lieutenant Elwin, and Mr. Atkinson, the master: the former was most severely wounded, while animating his men; also Mr. Bond, master's-mate, who lost a leg, and has passed nearly two years; also Mr. Hoyes, who has also lost a leg, and nearly served his time. Mr. Elliott, the surgeon, and his assistant, Mr. Joyce, deserve every praise for their attention to the wounded. Thus fell H.M. brig Penguin; and, I trust, the defence made will meet your approbation.

I have the honor to be, &c.

JAMES M'DONALD, senior surviving officer
late of H.M. brig Penguin.

No. 112.

From Captain Biddle to Commodore Decatur.

U.S. sloop Hornet, off Tristan d'Acunha,
March 25, 1815.

SIR,

I have the honor to inform you, that on the morning of the 23d instant, at half-past 10, when about to anchor off the north-end of the island of Tristan d'Acunha, a sail was seen to the southward and eastward, steering to the eastward, the wind fresh from the S.S.W. In a few minutes she had passed on to the westward, so that we could not see her for the land. I immediately made sail to the westward, and shortly after getting sight of her again, perceived her to bear up before the wind. I hove-to for him to come down to us. When she had approached near, I filled the main-top-sail, and continued to yaw the ship while she continued to come down, wearing occasionally, to prevent her passing under our stern. At 1. 40. P.M. being nearly within musket-shot distance, she hauled her wind on the starboard tack, hoisted English colours, and fired a gun. We immediately luffed-to, hoisted our ensign, and gave the enemy a broadside. The action being thus commenced, a quick and well-directed fire was kept up from this ship, the enemy gradually drifting nearer to us; when, at 1. 55. he bore up, apparently to run us on board. As soon as I perceived he would certainly fall on board, I called the boarders, so as to be ready to repel any attempt to board us. At the instant, every officer and man repaired to the quarter-deck, where the two vessels were coming in contact, and eagerly pressed me to permit them to board the enemy; but this I would not permit, as it was evident, from the commencement of the action, that our fire was greatly superior, both in quickness and effect. The enemy's bowsprit came in between our main and mizen-rigging, on our starboard-side, affording him an opportunity to board us, if such was his design, but no attempt was made. There was a considerable swell on, and, as the sea lifted us a-head, the enemy's bowsprit carried away our mizen-shrouds, stern-davits, and spanker-boom, and he hung upon our larboard-quarter. At this moment an officer, who was afterwards recognized to be Mr. M'Donald, the first lieutenant, and the then commanding officer, called out that they had surrendered. I directed the marines and musketry-men to cease firing; and, while on the taffrail, asking if they had surrendered, I received a wound in the neck. The enemy just then got clear of us, and his fore-mast and bowsprit being both gone, and perceiving us wearing to give him a fresh broadside, he again called out that he had surrendered. It was with difficulty I could restrain my crew from firing into him again, as he had certainly fired into us after having surrendered. From the firing of the first gun, to the last time the enemy cried out he had surrendered, was exactly 22 minutes by the watch. She proved to be H.B.M. brig Penguin, mounting sixteen 32-pound carronades, two long 12s, a 12-pound carronade upon the top-gallant-forecastle, with swivels on the capstan, and in the tops. She had a spare port forward, so as to fight both her long guns of aside. She sailed from England in September last. She was shorter upon deck than this ship by two feet, but she had a greater length of keel, greater breadth of beam, thicker sides, and higher bulwarks than this ship, and was, in all respects, a remarkably fine vessel of her class. The enemy acknowledge a complement of 132; 12 of them supernumerary marines, from the Medway, 74, received on board, in consequence of their being ordered to cruize for the American privateer, Young Wasp. They acknowledge a loss, also, of 14 killed, and 28 wounded; but Mr. Mayo, who was in charge of the prize, assures me that the number of killed was certainly greater. Among the killed is Captain Dickenson, who fell at the close of the action, and the boatswain. Among the wounded is the second lieutenant, purser, and two midshipmen. Each of the midshipmen lost a leg. We received on board, in all, 118 prisoners, four of whom have since died of their wounds. Having removed the prisoners, and taken on board such provisions and stores as would be useful to us, I scuttled the Penguin this morning, before day-light, and she went down. As she was completely riddled by our shot, her fore-mast and bowsprit both gone, and her main-mast so crippled as to be incapable of being secured, it seemed unadvisable, at this distance from home, to attempt sending her to the United States.

This ship did not receive a single round shot in her hull, nor any material wound in her spars. The rigging and sails were very much cut; but, having bent a new suit of sails, and knotted and secured our rigging, we are now completely ready, in all respects, for any service. We were eight men short of complement, and had nine men upon the sick-list the morning of the action.

Enclosed is a list of killed and wounded. I lament to state, that Lieutenant Connor is wounded, dangerously. I feel great solicitude on his account, as he is an officer of much promise, and his loss would be a serious loss to the service.

It is a most pleasing part of my duty to acquaint you, that the conduct of Lieutenants Connor and Newton, Mr. Mayo, Acting-lieutenant Brownlow, of the marines, Sailing-master Romney, and the other officers, seamen, and marines, I have the honor to command, was in the highest degree creditable to them, and calls for my warmest recommendation. I cannot, indeed, do justice to their merits. The satisfaction which was diffused throughout the ship, when it was ascertained that the stranger was an enemy's sloop of war, and the alacrity with which every one repaired to quarters, fully assured me, that their conduct in action would be marked with coolness and intrepidity.

I have the honor to be, &c.

J. BIDDLE.

Commodore S. Decatur, &c. &c.

No. 113.

From Lieutenant Boyce to the secretary of the East India company's marine-board.

Sir,

I beg leave to acquaint you, for the information of the board, that the wounds received by me on 30th June last, in a short but smart action with an American sloop of war, off Anjier, in the straits of Sunda, have hitherto prevented my transmitting an official report of the circumstances attending that melancholy affair.

I am happy to state, that my health is now tolerably re-established; and I think myself particularly fortunate, considering the nature of my wounds, that the honor of addressing you on this subject has been reserved for my pen, although, no doubt, public rumour has, ere this, put you in possession of most of the facts which I now do myself the honor to state, and request that you will do me the favor to submit them to the honorable board.

On the 30th June last, being off Anjier, in the straits of Sunda, on my passage to Bengal, in charge of public despatches from the Java government, about 4 P.M. a strange sail hove in sight, standing with a fair wind to the north-eastward; and, as the honorable company's cruiser Nautilus, under my command, was working to the south-westward, the two vessels approached each other rapidly; and, when the stranger was distant about three miles, I observed that she had British colours hoisted, and knowing that universal peace had been restored to Great Britain, I despatched a boat in charge of my master, Mr. Bartlett, to obtain intelligence, which reached the stranger nearly at the same time as the master-attendant's from the shore; and I observed, with my spying-glass, that the officers had no sooner got up the ship's side than the crews were forcibly taken out, and both boats made fast a-stern. I prepared for action, and the stranger at once opened her tier of ports, and bore down towards us. To prevent her crossing our hawse I tacked, then shortened sail, hove to, and soon afterwards hailed the stranger, "What ship is that?" To which I received no reply, until repeated four times, and then merely "Halloo!" About this period the English blue ensign was hauled down, and American colours hoisted. I then asked, "Am I to consider you in the light of a friend or an enemy?" The reply was, "An enemy." I then informed the American captain that peace had been ratified between Great Britain and the United States of America; also, that I had the proclamation on board, and hoped that a due consideration of this would induce him to spare bloodshed. I was then commanded, in a very loud and peremptory manner, to "haul down my colours," which was immediately repeated still louder, and with the addition of "instantly;" to which I replied, "I shall do no such thing." The American then opened his fire on us, by which two men were killed at the gun near me, and I received a grape-shot, in a slanting direction, through the right cheek of my posteriors. A short but brisk action ensued, and observing some casualties, my first lieutenant, Mr. Robert Mayston, and several others, wounded, and being myself disabled by a 32-pound shot, which shattered my right knee-joint, and splintered my thigh-bone; also considering the great disparity of force, I deemed it my duty, although I must confess that it was with no small degree of reluctance, to strike the British colours to the American. Her first lieutenant, about dusk, took possession of us. She proved to be the U.S. sloop of war Peacock, Captain Warrington, carrying twenty 32-pound carronades, and two long 18-pounders. Her crew is said to consist of 220 men.

Both vessels anchored for the night about six miles off Anjier, and in the morning I was permitted to be taken on shore, as well as the rest of the wounded, in compliance with my request to that effect.

About 2 P.M. on the day following the action, the honorable company's cruiser Nautilus was restored, and Captain Warrington addressed a letter to Mr. Macgregor, master-attendant at Anjier, stating, that in consequence of the information received from him, and *the several different sources* from which he had heard that a peace had been concluded between the United States and Great Britain, he felt himself bound to desist from hostilities, and regretted that his *reasonable demand* had not been complied with by the commander of Nautilus brig the preceding afternoon.

On the 4th of July the Nautilus sailed for Batavia, where she arrived the day following, and was sent from thence to Rembang, on the coast of Java, in the temporary charge of acting lieutenant Barnes, (who was ordered on board from the honorable company's cruiser Malabar, by Captain Hepburn,) to receive such repairs as the damages she had sustained required. In the mean time I remained, on account of my wounds, on shore at Anjier, where I was most handsomely received and accommodated by the kindness of Colonel Yule, resident, and attended by Mr. Hervey Thompson, surgeon of the district. On the 14th July it was deemed necessary to amputate my right leg. I submitted to the operation, and it was accordingly taken off above the knee. On the 20th following I was removed to the residence of Colonel Yule, at Ceram, and there I remained, experiencing every mark of hospitality, and the most unlimited attention, until the return of the Nautilus from Rembang; at which period, finding my health intolerably restored, I rejoined her on the 23d instant.

I beg leave to subjoin a list of the killed and wounded on board the honorable company's cruiser Nautilus, on the 30th of last June; and, in having to lament the loss of so many, I regret that a fairer opportunity for their exertions was not afforded them, and myself, with a vessel of more equal force.

[*Here follows a list of 6 killed, and 8 wounded.*]

What loss the American may have sustained I am not able to say. If report is to be relied on, they had four or five men wounded, and their bow-gun dismounted.

The damage the Nautilus received in the action was considerable both to her hull and rigging. The bends on the starboard-side, (the side engaged,) were shivered from aft to the fore-chains, and the bulwark, from the chess-tree aft, much torn. The launch and cutter were both perforated with shot, the lower masts and tiller slightly wounded with grape, and the boom-mail-sail shot through in many places. Two guns were disabled by the enemy's shot, and the sheet-anchor completely so, by the loss of its iron stock, ring, and fluke. Four 32-pound shot, that were found lodged, have been picked out of her: one was under the counter, very nearly level with the water. A great number of small-arms and gunner's stores were thrown overboard by the Americans, on their taking possession, to clear the deck. The packets, I am happy to say, remained on board without being touched, but almost every thing below was ransacked.

It now only remains for me to do that justice to the conduct of the officers and crew of the Nautilus, on the 30th of last June, which they so well deserve, by declaring my admiration of their firmness, and thus publicly expressing my satisfaction with their conduct throughout.

The two seapoys and native servant, with amputated limbs, have, I understand, recovered, and been sent by Captain William Eatwell, of the honorable company's cruiser Benares, to Calcutta, in the honorable company's cruiser Antelope. Lieutenant Maystone's wound was once healed, but has broken out afresh: he is however now, I am happy to say, again on the recovery.* My own cure has been greatly impeded by two unfortunate fistulas, in my stump, which have caused me to suffer much. The rest of the wounded are all well.

I beg to subscribe myself, with the utmost respect,
Sir, your most obedient servant,
CHARLES BOYCE, commander.

H.C. cruiser Nautilus, 24th September, 1815.
John Lowe, Esq. secretary to the
marine-board.

No. 114.

Evidence of Mr. Joseph Bartlett.

The commission appointed by the bench of magistrates, consisting of the magistrate, Mr. Turr, and the magistrate and acting-bailiff, Mr. Cassa, proceeded on Friday morning, the 7th July, 1815, on board of the honorable company's cruiser Nautilus, lying in Batavia roads, and received the following voluntary depositions of the officers and people of that vessel.

Joseph Bartlett, master, acting commanding-officer, who declared, that in the afternoon, about 4 o'clock, of the 30th June, the cruiser Nautilus was working out to proceed on their passage, when a strange sail was seen, and he was ordered by the captain, C. Boyce, to proceed with the boat to see what ship it was. That on his arrival on board, he was instantly ordered by the commander of the vessel to go below, not being allowed to ask any question. That a short time after he heard say, "Strike your colours, or I will sink you;" and then, that orders were given to fire the bow-gun into the cruiser Nautilus, which did not bear: a second gun was fired. That further, two or three broadsides were fired, when he heard that the Nautilus struck her colours; and after this, three heavy guns and some musquetry were fired into the Nautilus.

No. 115.

Evidence of Mr. Mcgregor.

(Extract.)

Interrogated by the before-named F. E. Turr.

Q. Did you communicate to the officers of the enemy's ship, before the action between her and the honorable company's cruiser Nautilus took place, that peace had been concluded between Great Britain and the United States, and ratified by both parties? *A.* I did:

* The wound subsequently mortified, and he died December 3, 1815.

I communicated to the first lieutenant, on his informing me that I was a prisoner of war; but I scarce said it, when the captain came forward and ordered me to be taken below. I communicated the above also to the purser of the ship, in the ward-room.—*Q*. What time had you been on board before the commencement of the said action? *A*. Rather more than a quarter of an hour.—*Q*. Has any reply been made by any of the officers of the American sloop of war on your communication? *A*. Yes.—*Q*. By whom? *A*. The purser.—*Q*. What was the reply? *A*. *I do not know how we can avoid a little brush;*—and the purser ordered me to go out of the way into the side-cabin.

No. 116.

From R. B. Macgregor, master-attendant of Anjier, to Lieutenant-colonel Yule, resident at Bantam.

SIR,

I have the honor to report for your information, that I was this afternoon released, as a prisoner of war, from the U.S. sloop of war Peacock, Captain Warrington, in consequence of the intelligence forward to him by me, which he deemed perfectly satisfactory, that peace had been ratified between the United States and Great Britain at Washington, by Mr. Madison, on the 18th February, 1815.

Enclosed I have the honor to transmit a copy of a letter from Captain Warrington, acquainting me that he would desist from hostilities.

I have the honor to be, Sir,
your most obedient servant,
R. B. MACGREGOR, deputy
master-attendant.

Anjier, July 1, 1815.

No. 117.

(Enclosure.)

From Captain Warrington to Mr. Macgregor, master-attendant at Anjier.

July 1st, 1815.

SIR,

In consequence of the information received from you, and the several different sources from which I have heard that a peace had been concluded between the United States and Great Britain, I feel myself bound to desist from hostilities, and regret that my reasonable demand had not been complied with by the commander of the Nautilus brig yesterday afternoon.

Respectfully your obedient servant,
L. WARRINGTON, captain U. S. navy,
com. the U. S. sloop of war Peacock.

No. 118.

From Captain Warrington to the American secretary of the navy.

(Extract.)

U. S. ship Peacock, Nov. 11, 1815.

As it is probable you will hereafter see or hear some other account of a rencontre which took place between the Peacock and the East India company's brig Nautilus, on the 30th of June last, in the straits of Sunda, I take the liberty of making known to you the particulars.

In the afternoon of that day, when a-breast of Anjier, as we closed with this brig, which appeared evidently to be a vessel of war, and completely prepared for action, her commander hailed, and asked, if I knew there was a peace. I replied in the negative, directing him, at the same time, to haul his colours down, if it were the case, in token of it; adding that, if he did not, I should fire into her. This being refused, one of the forward guns was fired at her, which was immediately returned by a broadside from the brig; our broadside was then discharged, and his colours were struck, after having six lascars killed, and seven or eight wounded. As we had not the most distant idea of peace, and this vessel was but a short distance from the fort of Anjier, I considered his assertion, coupled with his arrangements for action, a finesse on his part, to amuse us, till he could place himself under the protection of the fort. A few minutes before coming in contact with the brig, two boats, containing the master-attendant at Anjier, and an officer of the army, came on board, and as we were in momentary expectation of firing, they were, with their men, passed below. I concluded that they had been misled by the British colours, under which we had passed up the straits. No questions, in consequence, were put to them; and they, very improperly, omitted mentioning that peace existed. The next day, after receiving such intelligence as they had to communicate on the subject, (part of which was official;) I gave up the vessel, first stopping her shot-holes, and putting the rigging in order.

I am aware that I may be blamed for ceasing hostilities without more authentic evidence that peace had been concluded; but, I trust, when our distance from home, with the little chance we had of receiving such evidence, are taken into consideration, I shall not be though to have decided prematurely.

I have the honor to be, & c.

L. WARRINGTON.

No. 119.

A list of British national cruizers, captured or destroyed by the Americans during the late war; excluding, from the former, such as were re-captured in their way into port.

Date.		Ships' names.		Guns.	Comple-ment	Tons.	Captd. or destroyed.	By what force.
1812								
Aug.	13	Alert,		20	86	393	Cap.	Essex frigate.
	19	Guerriere,		49	263	1084	Do.*	Constitution do.
Oct.	25	Macedonian,		49	292	1081	Do.	United States do.
Dec.	29	Java,		47	370	1073	Do.*	Constitution do.
1813								
Feb.	24	Peacock,	B.	19	122	386	Do.*	Hornet 20.
April	26	D. of Glo'ster,	B.†			164	Do.	Com. Chauncey, on L. Ontario.
Aug.	5	Dominica,	Sc.‡	15	77	217	Do	Decatur privateer.
Sept.	5	Boxer,	B.	14	66	179	Do.	Enterprise 16.
	9	Highflyer,	Sc.	5	39	209	Do.	President frigate.
	10	Squad. of 6 vessels on Lake Erie,		63	345	865	Do.	Commodore Perry's squadron.
1814								
Feb.	14	Picton,	Sc.	14	72	211	Do.*	Constitution frigate.
April	29	Epervier,	B.	18	117	382	Do.	Peacock 22.
		Ballahou,	Sc.	4	20	74	Do.	Perry privateer.
June	28	Reindeer,	B.	19	118	385	Do*.	Wasp 22.
Aug.		Nancy,	Sc.	2		54	Dest.	Americans on Lake Huron.
	5	Magnet,	B.	14		144	Do.	Commodore Chauncey.
Sept.	1	Avon,	B.	18	‖	391	Do.	Wasp 23.
	11	Squad. of 4 vessels§ on L. Champlain,		74	420	1303	Cap.	Com. Mcdonough's squadron.
	15	Hermes,		21	¶	512	Dest.	American battery at Mobile.
1815.								
Feb.	20	Cyane,		33	171	539	Cap.	Constitution frigate.
	26	St. Lawrence,	Sc.	13	51	240	Do.	Chasseur privateer.
March	23	Penguin,	B.	19	122	387	Do.*	Hornet 20.
		No. 30.	Total,	530	2751	10273		

† Also a 20-gun ship in frame, burnt.
‡ Re-captured, but not as a cruizer.
§ Including two re-captured American cutters.
* Destroyed immediately after capture.
‖ Saved by the Castilian.
¶ Do. by vessels in company.

No. 120

List of American national cruizers, captured or destroyed by the British during the late war; excluding, as in the last list.

Date.	Ships' names.	Guns.	Complement	Tons.	Captd. or destroyed.	By what force.
1812.						
July 16	Nautilus, B.	14	106	213	Cap.	Shannon & others.
August 3	Com. Barry, R.C.	6		98	Dest.	Spartan frigate.
22	Js. Madison, R.Sc.	10	65	114	Cap.	Barbadoes do.
Oct. 18	Wasp,	18	130	434	Do.	Poictiers 74.
Nov. 22	Vixen, B.	14	130	217	Do.	Southampton frig.
1813.						
Jan. 17	Viper, B.	12	93	148	Do.	Narcissus do.
Feb. 22	Two gun-boats,	4		154	Dest.	Brit. Troops on L. Ontario.
June 1	Chesapeake,	49	391	1135	Cap.	Shannon frigate.
2	Growler, Cut.	11	51	110	Do.	Br. Troops on L. Champlain.
	Eagle, Cut.	11	48	102		
12	Surveyor, R. Sc.	6	25	100	Cap.	Narcissus, frigate.
July 4	Gun-boat,	1		76	Dest.	Brit. Troops on L. Ontario.
14	Asp, Sc.	3		88	Do.	Mohawk & Contest.
27	Gun-boat, No. 121	2	35	78	Cap.	Junon and Martin.
Aug. 10	Growler, Sc.	2	40	94	Do.	On L Ontario, by Sir J. L. Yeo.
	Julia, Sc.	2	40	86		
	Scourge, Sc.	10	118	235	Upset	In carrying sail to avoid Sir James.
	Hamilton, Sc.	9				
14	Argus, B.	20	125	315	Cap.	Pelican brig.
1814.						
March 28	Essex,	46	265	867	Do.	Phœbe and Cherub.
11	Frolic,	22	171	539	Do.	Orpheus and Shelburne.
July 4	Two gun-boats,	2		160	Dest.	Severn and Loire.
11	Rattlesnake, B.	16	131	305	Cap.	Leander frigate.
12	Syren, B.	16	137	350	Do.	Medway 74.
Aug. 12	Somers, Sc.	2	35	94	Do.	Capt. Dobbs, on Lake Erie.
	Ohio, Sc.	1	35	87		
22	Scorpion, Slp.	8		1130	Dest.	Rear-admiral Cockburn, in the Petapsco.
	Fifteen gun-boats,	30				
	One gun-boat,	2		85	Cap.	
24	Essex, (2,)	58		1590	Dest.	At Washington; also the frame of a 74, in pieces, &c. &c.
	New York,	46		954		
	Boston,	42		790		
	Argus,	22		539		
29	Gun-boat,	2		85	Cap.	Seahorse frigate.
Sept. 3	Tigress, Sc.	1	28	96	Do.	Lieut. Worsley, on L. Erie.
	Adams,	26		783	Dest.	Br. At Castine.
6	Scorpion, Sc.	2	34	86	Cap.	Lieut. Worsley, on L. Erie.
Oct. 5	Gun-boat, No. 160.	5	35	86	Do.	Lacedemonian frig.
10	Eagle, R. Cut.	2		75	Dest.	Despatch brig.
Dec. 15	Seahorse, Sc.	1		73	Do.	Captain Lockyer, at Lake Pontchartrain.
	Alligator, Slp.	3	20	76	Cap.	
	Five gun-boats, Nos. 5, 23, 156, 162, and 163.	29	225	443	Do.	
27	Carolina, Sc.	14		225	Dest.	Br. at New Orleans.
1815.						
Jan. 15	President,	58	477	1533	Cap.	Endymion; squad. in sight.
	No.64. Total,	660	2994	14848		

No. 121.

List of British and American national cruizers, captured at sea, which the opposite party succeeded in getting into port.

BRITISH.				AMERICAN.			
Ships' names.	Guns.	Comp.	Tons.	Ships' names.	Guns.	Comp.	Tons.
Macedonian,	49	292	1081	President,	58	477	1533
Cyane,	33	171	539	Chesapeake,	49	391	1135
Alert,	20	86	393	Essex,	46	265	867
Epervier, B.	18	117	382	Frolic,	22	171	539
Dominica, Sc.	15	77	217	Argus, B.	20	125	315
Boxer, B.	14	66	179	Wasp,	18	130*	434
St. Lawrence, Sc.	13	51	240	Rattlesnake, B.	16	131	305
Highflyer, Sc.	5	39	209	Syren, B.	16	137	350
Ballahou, Sc.	4	20	74	Nautilus, B.	14	106	213
				Viper, B.	12	93	148
				Jas. Madison, Sc.	10	65	114
				Gun-boat,	9	45	112
				Surveyor, Sc.	6	25	100
				Nine gun-boats,	34	267	549
No. 9. Total,	171	919	3314	No. 22. Total,	330	2430	6714

* Number of prisoners received.

Index

Numbers in brackets after ship names indicate guns. Abbreviations: Br - British, capt – captain, com – commodore, E.I.C. – East India Company, Fr - France, mas-com – master and commander, mid – midshipman, sch – schooner, sl – sloop, priv - privateer, RN - Royal Navy, USN - United States Navy.